Masterplots

Fourth Edition

Masterplots

Fourth Edition

Volume 12
When We Dead Awaken—Zuleika Dobson
Indexes

Editor

Laurence W. Mazzeno
Alvernia College

12/10

SALEM PRESS
Pasadena, California   Hackensack, New Jersey

Editor in Chief: Dawn P. Dawson

Editorial Director: Christina J. Moose   *Editorial Assistant:* Brett S. Weisberg
Development Editor: Tracy Irons-Georges   *Research Supervisor:* Jeffry Jensen
Project Editor: Desiree Dreeuws   *Research Assistant:* Keli Trousdale
Manuscript Editors: Constance Pollock,   *Production Editor:* Joyce I. Buchea
    Judy Selhorst, Andy Perry   *Design and Graphics:* James Hutson
Acquisitions Editor: Mark Rehn   *Layout:* William Zimmerman

Cover photo: Kurt Vonnegut (Ulf Andersen/Getty Images)

Library of Congress Cataloging-in-Publication Data

Masterplots / editor, Laurence W. Mazzeno. — 4th ed.
    v.   cm.
    Includes bibliographical references and indexes.
    ISBN 978-1-58765-568-5 (set : alk. paper) — ISBN 978-1-58765-580-7 (v. 12 : alk. paper)
    1. Literature—Stories, plots, etc.   2. Literature—History and criticism.   I. Mazzeno, Laurence W.
    PN44.M33 2010
    809—dc22

                                                 2010033931

Fourth Edition
First Printing

Contents

Complete List of Titles

Volume 1

Volume 2

Contents lvii

Complete List of Titles. lxi

Volume 3

Volume 4

Contents cxxxiii
Complete List of Titles cxxxvii

Volume 5

Contents . . . .
Complete List of Titles . . . .

Volume 6

Volume 7

Contents ccxlvii
Complete List of Titles ccli

Volume 8

Contents cclxxxv
Complete List of Titles cclxxxix

Volume 9

Volume 10

Volume 11

Volume 12

Contents . . . . cdxxxvii
Complete List of Titles. . . . . cdxxxix

Masterplots

Fourth Edition

When We Dead Awaken

Author: Henrik Ibsen (1828-1906)
First produced: Naar vi døde vaagner, 1900; first
    published, 1899 (English translation, 1900)
Type of work: Drama
Type of plot: Psychological symbolism
Time of plot: Nineteenth century
Locale: A coastal town of Norway

Principal characters:
ARNOLD RUBEK, a sculptor
MAIA RUBEK, his wife
IRENE VON SATOW, his former model
ULFHEIM, a landed proprietor and hunter

The Story:

Professor Arnold Rubek, a noted sculptor, and his young wife Maia return to their home on the coast of Norway after four years abroad. At the baths and the hotel they admit to being bored, and to break the summer tedium they plan to sail northward around the coast. Rubek becomes world-renowned with the fashioning of his masterpiece, "The Resurrection Day," and success brings him worldly riches. Other visitors at the baths are a sportsman named Ulfheim, called the bear-killer, and a strange pale woman, Madame von Satow, who, with a companion dressed in black, takes the nearby pavilion for the summer. As Rubek and Ulfheim converse, the dark Sister passes from the pavilion to the hotel, and Ulfheim says her passing is a portent of death. Maia accepts his invitation to see his sledge dogs fed, but Rubek remains seated on the lawn. The lady in white emerges from the pavilion. Rubek feels strangely drawn to her. Years before, he wanted to create a sculpture that would represent Woman awakening from the dead on the Resurrection Day after the sleep of death. After he found Irene, he saw in her the perfect model for his composition, and she became his great inspiration. Irene wanted his human love, but he felt that if he touched her his soul would be profaned.

Now Rubek recognizes the strange woman in white as Irene. When he questions her about her life since she left him, she declares that she died then and is not really alive now, though she married a South American diplomat who later committed suicide, and then a Russian who owned gold mines in the Urals. Rubek admits that after she left him he made no marble creations of lasting beauty but instead began doing portrait busts that were, literally, double-faced, because behind the visible face he hid the face of the animal that the artist maliciously considered the subject of the portrait to be. He tells Irene that he and Maia are leaving the next day on a sea voyage. She suggests that he might prefer the mountains where she is going. At that moment Maia returns and announces that she will not make the sea voyage; instead, she wants to go to the mountains with the bear-killer. To her

surprise Rubek does not object. Maia runs out to inform Ulfheim. Meanwhile, unseen near the pavilion door, the Sister of Mercy watches intently.

The next day the bear-killer goes off to hunt with his dog trainer Lars and his dogs, and Maia accompanies them. Before they leave, Rubek tells Maia that he can no longer live a life of indolent enjoyment with her.

Rubek finds Irene near a brook. She says she returned from the dead and made the journey for the sake of the statue, which she calls their child. She loves it and wants to see it. When Rubek implores her not to, saying he altered it since she left, Irene covertly unsheathes a knife but stays her hand as he explains the changes he made and tells how he also is in the altered sculpture, a man eaten by remorse, imprisoned in a hell from which he can never rise. At this she sheathes her knife, rejoicing that he suffers. She bitterly reminds him that when he finally finished the statue he shrugged off their years together.

Together they stand and watch the sun go down. He then asks her to return and live with him in his villa, to help him find his real life again, but Irene says that for the life they led there is no resurrection. Suddenly Irene challenges Rubek to dare the mountain heights and spend a summer night with her. Joyfully he agrees. As he does so a face stares down at Irene, the face of the Sister of Mercy. On the wild mountainside, cut by sheer precipices and overhung with snow-clad peaks, Maia and Ulfheim quarrel but make up as they tell each other of the disappointments of their youth. When the dangerous mountain mist begins to close in, they decide to journey down together, but as they make ready to descend they see Rubek and Irene climbing up. Ulfheim warns them of the impending storm and the dangers ahead and urges them to take shelter in a nearby hut. He says that he will send them help; he himself can assist only one person at a time down the precipice.

After Ulfheim and Maia go, Irene, terrified not by the approaching storm but that she might be taken away, that the woman in black might seize her, shows Rubek her knife ready for such an emergency. She adds that the knife was intended for him the previous evening. Startled, he asks why she did not use it; she tells him she then realized that he is already dead. Rubek passionately assures her that their love is not dead, for he realizes with glaring certainty that she is the woman of his dreams. Irene says that such a love comes too late, that desire for life is dead in her, and that she looks on him, too, as dead.

With his whole soul Rubek calls on her, even if they both seem dead, to awaken and live life to its fullest before they are forever put away in the grave. Exalted, they spurn the safety of the hut and joyously fight their way up to the peaks, through mist and storm, toward the sunrise. Far below the voice of Maia sings out free as a bird. The Sister of Mercy suddenly appears. As Rubek and Irene are carried along and buried in the snow, she makes the sign of the cross and wishes that peace be with them.

Critical Evaluation:

When We Dead Awaken departs from the principles of art to which Henrik Ibsen's earlier social and later psychological dramas conform, and for this reason it is sometimes considered inferior to them. It delves into the realm of pathology, dealing with improbabilities rather than probabilities, with symbolic motive rather than actual motive. Solely as an artistic creation, however, the play has enduring merit. It is Ibsen's last production; the audience may read in it the intention of the dramatist to express some deeply felt final message, one that could be clothed only in poetically suggestive and symbolic language.

When Arnold Rubek, the aged sculptor hero of Ibsen's last work, describes the three stages of his masterpiece "Resurrection Day," he is actually presenting a thinly disguised outline of Ibsen's career as a playwright. After the early apprentice works came the idealized, poetic plays, *Brand* (1866; English translation, 1891) and *Peer Gynt* (1867; English translation, 1892). Then came the great social and psychological plays of his middle period, from *Samfundets støtter* (1877; *The Pillars of Society*, 1880) through *Hedda Gabler* (1890; English translation, 1891). Finally came the late symbolic and highly personal—even autobiographical—dramas, beginning with *Bygmester Solness* (1892; *The Master Builder*, 1893) and ending with *When We Dead Awaken*.

Two kinds of characters dominate the plays of this final phase: the aging but powerful artist, who, having been driven by his obsessive ambition to the top of his profession, finds that he pays too high a spiritual price, and the mysterious female out of his past who, acting as a kind of nemesis figure, forces the hero to recognize and come to terms with his past failings, even though it destroys him. Although *When We Dead Awaken* may lack some of the dramatic intensity of *The Master Builder* or of *John Gabriel Borkman* (1896; English translation, 1897), the play is the most complete and final exploration of this process, and so it stands as Ibsen's final statement on the artist's relation to society and to his or her own soul.

Having achieved great personal success with his masterpiece, yet feeling unaccountably uneasy about it, Rubek attempts to satisfy his needs by taking a young wife and living in moderately luxurious indolence, satisfying his artistic and financial needs by turning out satirical portrait busts. He grows tired of Maia, and the ironical pleasure of making fun of his clients while taking their money wears off. He then attempts to find out what it is that bothers him.

When he meets Irene, she reminds him of their life together many years before when, as an innocent young girl, she modeled for the first version of "Resurrection Day." On the realistic level, Irene simply wants revenge on the man who cast her off and thereby turned her to a life of promiscuity, prostitution, and, finally, insanity. This is not a realistic play, however, and Irene's function is to probe Rubek's soul, not to get some mundane revenge. As he tells her about the evolution of the statue, Irene toys with her knife, but she declines to use it when Rubek confesses his own anguish and sense of failure. "I suddenly realized you are already dead," she tells him, "dead for years."

Rubek's crime in rejecting Irene's love to "create the one great work of my life" is the major reason for his failure not only as a human being but also as an artist. By withholding his emotions from her, he stifles them, and, ironically, dissipates his own talent in the process. Without the knowledge and experience of love, Rubek is unable to respond to humanity's nobler aspects, and so his works can, at best, be inhuman, merely satirical portraits. When Irene understands the reason for his depression and sense of failure, her desire for revenge changes to a feeling of pity and rekindled love. Rubek cannot fully understand what is happening to him, but his feelings for her are awakened; he senses that his own vindication—salvation, perhaps—lies in her.

The Irene-Rubek affair is juxtaposed against that of Rubek's wife, Maia, and the bear hunter, Ulfheim. The young couple represents youth, vigor, and sensual experience of all kinds—eating, drinking, sex, physicality, and a joyous relationship to the immediate, natural environment. Rubek and Irene, on the other hand, stand for age, wisdom, and spiritual realization.

When We Dead Awaken ends on a note of reconciliation. Although he spurns her love in his youth, Rubek is ready to accept it in age. He and Irene go to seek a higher reality in the frozen mountains than Maia and Ulfheim will find in the lush valley. The living dead can awaken only into a spiritual reality beyond death. Ibsen suggests this idea at the play's conclusion, and it is exactly what happens to Irene and Rubek as they are swept up in an avalanche. With Maia's voice echoing "I am free as a bird" in the background, the nun in black, apparently a symbol for Irene's tainted past, emerges and blesses the couple with the sign of the cross and a *pax vobiscum.*

Further Reading

Binding, Paul. *With Vine-Leaves in His Hair: The Role of the Artist in Ibsen's Plays.* Norwich, England: Norvik Press, 2006. Examines the character of the artist-rebel in *When We Dead Awaken* and four other Ibsen plays. Binding demonstrates how this character represents the tensions of contemporary society.

Bloom, Harold, ed. *Henrik Ibsen.* Philadelphia: Chelsea House, 1999. The interpretive essays include analyses of *When We Dead Awaken* and several other plays.

Durbach, Errol. *"Ibsen the Romantic": Analogues of Paradise in the Later Plays.* Athens: University of Georgia Press, 1982. An exploration of the lingering presence of romantic elements in Ibsen's later plays. Provides an interesting discussion of the relationship between man and woman in *When We Dead Awaken.*

Holtan, Orley I. *Mythic Patterns in Ibsen's Last Plays.* Minneapolis: University of Minnesota Press, 1970. A study of the mythic content in Ibsen's last seven plays, the book offers valuable insights to beginners and to more experienced readers. The chapter on *When We Dead Awaken* is focused on the resurrection myth.

Lyons, Charles R. *Henrik Ibsen: The Divided Consciousness.* Carbondale: Southern Illinois University Press, 1972. A study of how many of Ibsen's protagonists are simultaneously drawn to a life of thought and one of sensuous experience. Includes a good chapter on *When We Dead Awaken.*

McFarlane, James, ed. *The Cambridge Companion to Ibsen.* New York: Cambridge University Press, 1994. Collection of essays, including discussions of Ibsen's dramatic apprenticeship, historical drama, comedy, realistic problem drama, and working methods. The references to *When We Dead Awaken* are listed in the index.

Meyer, Michael. *Ibsen: A Biography.* Garden City, N.Y.: Doubleday, 1971. A standard biography of Ibsen. Contains a chapter on *When We Dead Awaken* that is a good introduction to the play and a useful summary of various critical attitudes toward it.

Robinson, Michael, ed. *Turning the Century: Centennial Essays on Ibsen.* Norwich, England: Norvik Press, 2006. Collection of the essays published in the journal *Scandinavica* during the past four decades, including discussions of Ibsen's style, language, and the reception of his plays in England. One of the essays analyzes *When We Dead Awaken.*

Templeton, Joan. *Ibsen's Women.* New York: Cambridge University Press, 1997. Templeton examines the women characters in Ibsen's plays and their relationship to the women in the playwright's life and career. Chapter 12, "The Revolt of the Muse: *When We Dead Awaken*," analyzes this play.

Weigand, Hermann J. *The Modern Ibsen: A Reconsideration.* New York: Henry Holt, 1925. Reprint. Salem, N.H.: Ayer, 1984. Long a standard in Ibsen criticism, this volume covers each of the last twelve plays and presents a careful reading of Ibsen's final drama.

Where Angels Fear to Tread

Author: E. M. Forster (1879-1970)
First published: 1905
Type of work: Novel
Type of plot: Social realism
Time of plot: Early twentieth century
Locale: England and Italy

Principal characters:
LILIA HERRITON, a young English widow
GINO CARELLA, an Italian
PHILIP HERRITON, Lilia's brother-in-law
HARRIET HERRITON, Lilia's sister-in-law
MRS. HERRITON, Lilia's mother-in-law
IRMA HERRITON, Lilia's daughter
CAROLINE ABBOTT, a friend

The Story:

Lilia Herriton, a widow of several years who has been living with her husband's family since his death, cheerfully leaves Sawston, England, with her friend Caroline Abbott for an extended visit in Italy. The Herriton family encouraged such a visit because of their concern over Lilia's growing relationship with a man they consider unsuitable for her and also because they welcome a chance to train her daughter during the mother's absence. The trip, which is Philip's idea, is quickly agreed to by everyone concerned. Fortunately, Caroline, a woman ten years younger but much more level-headed than Lilia, is also planning such a trip and needs a companion.

The winter passes peacefully for everyone, and the tour seems to be a success. Lilia is apparently gaining some degree of culture and taste under Miss Abbott's guidance, and back in England Lilia's daughter Irma is improving through the efforts of Mrs. Herriton. In the spring, however, Mrs. Herriton hears from Lilia's mother that Lilia is engaged to an Italian, supposedly someone she met in a hotel. She immediately wires Caroline for details but is answered only by the terse comment that Lilia is engaged to an Italian nobleman. Instinctively recognizing this to be a lie, she insists that Philip go at once to Italy and stop the marriage.

Caroline meets Philip's train when he arrives at Monteriano, the village in which Lilia and Caroline are staying for a month. Nervously, she agrees to tell him everything. According to her story, Lilia and the man fell in love with each other, so she rather offhandedly suggested marriage. Unfortunately, Signor Carella, who is about twelve years younger than Lilia, is the son of a dentist in that provincial village, and he has no money. His social position, therefore, is little better than that of a peasant. Philip is even more appalled when he sees the man, for everything about him except his physique is extremely vulgar. Philip is, however, too late to stop the marriage, for the couple married as soon as they heard he was coming. He can do nothing but return home, and he takes Caroline with him. The Herriton family refuses to have anything more to do with Lilia, but they keep Irma with them to be brought up as one who bears the Herriton name.

It is some time before Lilia realizes that she does not love her husband and can never be happy with him and that he married her only for her money. She is never able to understand that as an Italian wife she can neither expect nor receive from her husband the things that English wives receive from theirs as a matter of course. By the time she realizes her unhappiness, she is cut off from everything in England and there is nothing she can do. Once, when she is particularly upset, she writes to her daughter, telling of her unhappiness

and the reasons for it, but the letter is intercepted by Mrs. Herriton and nothing ever comes of it.

Lilia often thinks that if she can present her husband with a son they might eventually regain some happiness. His one ambition is to be the father of a man like himself. Lilia does finally have a son, but she dies in childbirth. The Herritons decide they must tell Irma about her mother's death but that it will be best if no one knows about the child, who is, after all, no real relation of theirs.

Irma finds out about the child when she begins receiving postcards sent her by the father. Her childish pride prevents her from keeping such an event a secret, and soon all Sawston knows of it. Much to the chagrin of the Herritons, Caroline, who still considers herself partly responsible for all that happened, begins to insist that something be done for the child, either by them or by herself. Mrs. Herriton, whose pride will not allow anyone else to do something that will in any way reflect on her family, immediately begins negotiations that she hopes will enable her to adopt the boy.

When her letters elicit only polite refusals, she decides that Philip must again go to Monteriano and gain custody of the child at any cost; Harriet is to go along to see that he accomplishes his mission. On their arrival, however, they find that Caroline preceded them and is also intent on seeing that the child be taken back to England. Philip and Caroline soon begin to be affected by the romantic and charming atmosphere. They still mean to carry out their mission, but they quickly lose all feeling of urgency in the matter.

On their second day in the village, they are to meet with Signor Carella. Caroline goes to the house early and alone; she is afraid that Philip will fail. While there, she is completely won over by the father's devotion to the son, and she finds herself on the Italian's side and against the Herritons, although she knows she can do nothing to hinder their plans. Philip sees Signor Carella that day; although he will not openly admit that the Italian is right, he finds that he is completely indifferent to the outcome of his mission, and he becomes friendly with his adversary. Success in the affair is left to Harriet, who, after apparently accepting Philip's failure, prepares to leave the village. Shortly before it is time for them to catch the train, she sends a note to Philip, telling him to pick her up just outside the gate to the village. When he gets there, he finds that she also visited the Carella household and, not finding Signor Carella at home, simply picked up the baby and walked away.

On the way down the mountain to the train, their carriage accidentally overturns, and the baby is killed. Philip has to tell Signor Carella what happened, and the Italian almost kills him. Caroline, whom Signor Carella always revered, is the only person who can calm him and prevent the situation from resulting in yet more pain. By the time the English group recuperates enough to leave Italy, the two men are good friends again.

On the way back to England, Philip receives another disappointment. Because of the romantic atmosphere and their close association, he falls in love with Caroline. He almost proposes to her when they are talking about love and the future, but she, thinking he suspected it long before, tells him of her passion for Signor Carella. Philip for years thought that he understood the world, but he now recognizes that he really understands nothing.

Critical Evaluation:

E. M. Forster does more than mock English society. His comic novels perform the serious task of questioning the assumptions upon which identity is based. At the same time readers laugh at Forster's pompous or pathetic characters, they are being taught to recognize how much damage can result from human beings passing judgment on one another. *Where Angels Fear to Tread*, Forster's first novel, established his reputation as both artist and humanist.

More often than not, Forster's novels are set outside England. The irony of this strategy is that, while abroad, his characters satirize English social custom as acutely as do the homebound characters created by Forster's predecessor, Jane Austen. Forster incorporates many of her satiric impulses into his style. Social snobbery, religious hypocrisy, flighty liberalism, and ill-conceived romanticism are just a few of the aspects of the English character that Forster, like Austen, makes the target for his comic abuse.

In *Where Angels Fear to Tread*, Mrs. Herriton is the emblem of British arrogance. She fiercely guards a code of conduct that she would describe as "decency" but that really represents only a preference for English as opposed to continental customs. The cruelly immoral consequences of Mrs. Herriton's brand of decency become gradually apparent as the plot unfolds. Mrs. Herriton's ferocity works as a baseline in the novel. Even though she is unlikable, the strength of her character is a foil against which the feebleness of the others is revealed.

Lilia, whose low breeding and high spirits make her the kind of ingenue who can be an agent of chaos in both Austen and Forster, threatens Mrs. Herriton's jealously guarded sense of order. Philip and Harriet, Mrs. Herriton's own children, help fill out the satiric register: Harriet, who is warped by an embittered and ineffectual religiosity, and Philip, who is a snobbish worshiper of beauty. Through Philip, Forster car-

ries out his trademark spoof of aesthetics, a school of literary criticism initiated by Walter Pater that dominated English letters in the period of transition between 1870 and 1930.

Perhaps Forster drops these stereotypical English characters into the provincial Italian setting of Monteriano (a fictional town modeled after San Gimignano near Florence) to draw attention to the fact that the novel is, at its core, a discussion of difference. English society, with its sometimes stuffy rules and expectations, becomes the source from which a series of divisions emerge. These divisions, all a form of the difference between the familiar and the strange and between self and other, form the intellectual substance of the novel. Forster thereby identifies and criticizes the often intolerant human instincts by which culture proceeds.

Indeed, the mistrust of cultures for one another, particularly England's low opinion of its European neighbors and colonial subjects, is the first opposition upon which Forster draws in *Where Angels Fear to Tread*. In his later *A Passage to India* (1924), the issue of cultural division finds its fullest expression. However, the tone of resentment—sometimes comic, then again verging upon the tragic—that flavors the relations in that novel between native Indians and Anglo-Indians is already present in the Herritons' concerted attempt to run roughshod over Monteriano.

The arrogantly unyielding manner in which the English respond to other cultures is present throughout the novel. It is most comically concentrated in the theater scene, where Harriet tries to impose her reverential method of listening to music on the Italians, whose good-natured custom it is to respond with lustful exuberance. For a time, Harriet's sense of decorum prevails, but when the Italian audience mobs the heroine of that evening's opera (*Lucia di Lammermoor*), throwing flowers and playbills, Harriet pronounces the whole affair disrespectful and stomps out of the theater. In this comic scene, Forster does not allow the English sensibility to imperialize the Italian, but the tide tragically turns at the end of the novel when Harriet has her grim revenge. Tragedy is too often the result of intolerance. Forster issues this warning while testing his readership's tolerance of differences in class, gender, and even race.

Lilia's marriage to the dentist's son Signor Carella repulses the Herritons because it introduces middle-class stock into their patrician family. Philip somehow understands this violation of class distinction as the death of romance. Always evenhanded in his satire, Forster also uses the Italian Carella as the representative of gender bias. After marrying Signor Carella, Lilia is maddened by the dull, domestic life her new husband expects her to lead. Race is not an overt aspect of *Where Angels Fear to Tread*, but it is an underlying component in the power and menace of the swarthy Mediterranean Carella, who seduces both Lilia and the novel's true heroine, Caroline Abbott. Forster here introduces a hint of the kind of racial "contamination" that outrages the Anglo-Indians in *A Passage to India*.

The uneven ending of *Where Angels Fear to Tread* serves as an object lesson in the complex process of judging human behavior. Philip, Caroline, and Harriet all at various times attempt to persuade or coerce Carella into giving up his child. When Philip and Caroline gradually realize that Carella's right to the child is vindicated by his obvious love for him, they abandon the attempt to get the boy away from him. Forster champions this kind of learning, the gradual acquisition of wisdom, and Philip's and Caroline's spiritual growth earns for them at least partial redemption. Harriet, however, never loses her conviction that all that is English must triumph over all that is Italian. Harriet's inability to reform her prejudices results in the novel's tragic outcome. Forster shocked some of his readers by allowing the baby to die, but in doing so he hoped to nourish the spirit of tolerance not yet suffocated by the human inclination toward pettiness and spite.

"Critical Evaluation" by Nick David Smart

Further Reading

Bradshaw, David, ed. *The Cambridge Companion to E. M. Forster.* New York: Cambridge University Press, 2007.

Collection of essays analyzing various aspects of Forster's life and work, including discussions of Forster and the novel, women, and England, Forsterian sexuality, and postcolonial Forster. The many references to *Where Angels Fear to Tread* are listed in the index.

Furbank, P. N. *E. M. Forster: A Life.* New York: Harcourt Brace Jovanovich, 1978. An exhaustive biography of Forster that also serves as a source of cultural information concerning Forster's settings in England, Italy, and India.

Medalie, David. *E. M. Forster's Modernism.* New York: Palgrave, 2002. Medalie examines the relationship of Forster's writings to modernism, analyzing his works to demonstrate their modernist elements. He places Forster within the context of early twentieth century social, political, and aesthetic developments.

Trilling, Lionel. *E. M. Forster: A Study.* Rev. ed. New York: New Directions, 1969. Appreciative readings of Forster's works that are intended to elevate the novelist to the artistic status he deserves. Forster is seen as a practitioner of what Trilling termed the "liberal imagination."

Wilde, Alan. *Art and Order: A Study of E. M. Forster.* 1964. Reprint. New York: New York University Press, 1979. Focuses on Forster's practice of and contribution to the aesthetic view of life. The value of beauty in human existence and art's role in defining beauty are the motivating issues in Wilde's first chapter, which begins with a discussion of *Where Angels Fear to Tread*.

Where I'm Calling From

Author: Raymond Carver (1938-1988)
First published: 1988
Type of work: Short fiction

With Raymond Carver's death from lung cancer on August 2, 1988 (at the age of fifty), American letters lost a major voice. Carver is credited with beginning the renaissance of realism in the short story, countering the experimental fiction of the 1960's with a carefully observed, clean prose that inspired a generation of writers after him. Though he published his first story, "Pastoral," in 1963, his first short-story collection, *Will You Please Be Quiet, Please?* did not appear until 1976. One year later, the collection was nominated for the National Book Award, and that same year Carver suddenly stopped drinking, after having been hospitalized several times for alcoholism.

Carver's second collection, *What We Talk About When We Talk About Love* (1981; written with the support of a Guggenheim Fellowship), is considered a minimalist masterpiece. Critic Michael Gorra defines minimalism as a kind of writing "in which the intentional poverty, the anorexia, of the writer's style [mirrors] the spiritual poverty of [the] characters' lives." In his essay "On Writing" (1981), Carver sketches his own views by citing the influence of three famous writers: Ezra Pound, from whom he took the quotation that "fundamental accuracy of statement is the one sole morality of writing"; Anton Chekhov, who showed him the importance of sudden awakenings, or epiphanies; and Geoffrey Wolff, from whose exhortation "No cheap tricks" he got his notion of no tricks at all. Carver's writer's creed is "Get in, get out. Don't linger. Go on." Reflecting this fear of wasted language, the stories of Carver's first two collections are lean and spare. Indeed, what is absent often matters as much as—or more than—what is present. With *Cathedral* (1983; nominated for the National Book Critics Circle Award and runner-up for the 1984 Pulitzer Prize), Carver began to move away from the bleak pessimism of his first two collections toward a fuller and warmer vision of human nature.

Where I'm Calling From is Carver's tenth book and includes his selection of the best thirty stories from the earlier collections mentioned above, combined with seven new stories that previously appeared only in *The New Yorker*. Maintaining his dedication to his craft, Carver revised or retitled a number of the stories for what he knew would be his last—and definitive—short-story collection. By organizing them in an essentially chronological sequence, Carver laid out a twenty-five-year writing career.

Carver begins *Where I'm Calling From* with "Nobody Said Anything," a story whose emphasis on fishing recalls the influence of Ernest Hemingway and his Nick Adams stories. In "Nobody Said Anything," a boy whose parents are quarreling bitterly feigns illness and cuts school. Once his parents are gone he heads for the creek, where he and another boy struggle together to catch a fish of near mythic proportions and color. When they catch their fish, they must decide how to apportion the single product of their shared labors and agree to divide the fish in half. The narrator takes the headed half home, where his parents are arguing so vigorously they do not notice the pan smoking on the stove. When he interrupts their quarrel to show them the fish, his mother screams and his father yells at him to get rid of it. The story closes with the narrator looking at the fish and saying, "I held him. I held that half of him." Of course he only has half the fish but, as critics have noted, things are not what they seem in Carver's fiction. Rather, they are much more than they seem. In "Nobody Said Anything" the dividing of the fish implies the imminent division of the family by divorce, while the half of the fish the boy holds suggests the one parent with whom he may soon be living.

"Neighbors" is the first story Carver published in *Esquire* (in 1971), where he published other stories under the guiding eye of the fiction editor, Gordon Lish, who moved Carver's writing from the careful work he did with John Gardner

at California State University, Chico, to the pruned style that marked his most minimalist period. When the Stones go out of town, they ask their neighbors, the Millers, to care for their cat, plants, and apartment. The Millers take turns handling the responsibilities, each visit to the Stones' apartment becoming longer and more interesting as Bill and Arlene Miller, in turn, delve into the Stones' lives and belongings. Bill tries on both Jim and Harriet Stone's clothing, smokes her cigarettes, drinks their Scotch, and returns to his own apartment with heightened desires. The Millers' sex life improves dramatically as a result of their visits across the hall. Finally, they decide to go into the Stones' apartment together, but Arlene discovers that she has locked the key inside. They are denied access to the apartment, to lives more interesting than theirs, and to the possibility of vicarious living.

"Are These Actual Miles?" (originally titled "What Is It?") is the last of twelve stories chosen from *Will You Please Be Quiet, Please?* Leo and Toni fall on hard times and are about to declare bankruptcy. Leo sends Toni out to sell their convertible before a creditor can "slap a lien on the car." The sale has to be that night and it has to be cash. Toni spends two hours on her hair and face, preparing to negotiate. Leo stays home, drinking Scotch. He relives their history while waiting, and the reader comes to know him and Toni: They are a blue-collar couple who, for a time, had more money than they could spend but then "sign up for it all" and get into credit-card debt. Hours pass; Toni should be home by now. Leo "understands he is willing to be dead." His wife comes home the next morning with a check for "six and a quarter." The car dealer pulls into Leo's driveway in the convertible, leaves Toni's makeup bag on the porch, and Leo runs out to say, "Monday." What is absent, but implied, is that Toni was deliberately unfaithful to her husband to punish him for going bankrupt. Leo's enigmatic comment, "Monday," refers to the new beginning he hopes for Monday, but, typical of the stories of Carver's first collection, the ending seems pessimistic rather than hopeful.

Carver selected seven stories from *What We Talk About When We Talk About Love*, the collection that established his reputation as an important writer and a minimalist. In "So Much Water So Close to Home," Stuart Kane goes on a three-day fishing trip with his friends, returning home a day earlier than expected. The next morning, his wife, Claire, discovers that Stuart and his friends found the nude body of a young woman but rather than report their discovery to the police opted to stay on, only stopping their drinking and fishing long enough to secure the dead woman's body by tying a nylon cord around her wrist. Though nothing changes for Stuart and nothing will change in their marriage, Claire perceives her husband differently as she identifies with the victim. Carver said he likes it "when there is some feeling of threat or sense of menace in short stories," and in "So Much Water" the menace is Stuart's possible violence toward his wife. Susan Miller died at a man's hand, a victim of rape. When Claire refuses to have sex with Stuart after his first night home, he tries to force her and does not understand her behavior. He accepts no responsibility for his actions or inaction regarding Miller and seems to feel that all his wife needs to make her happy is sex—the very thing she rejects because she now sees herself, like the dead woman, as an object and victim of men's desires.

Where I'm Calling From includes eight stories from *Cathedral*, among them the story that gives Carver's last collection its title. *Cathedral* manifests the definite shift in Carver's fiction from hopelessness and despair to the possibility of hope and redemption. Tragedies still occur, loss is a daily event, but characters cope better with the disasters of their lives and they do so in fuller narrative settings. In "A Small, Good Thing," for example, Scotty, a seven-year-old only son, dies as a result of being hit by a car on his birthday. When his parents go to the bakery to berate the baker for repeatedly calling them to pick up a cake for their now-dead boy, the baker confesses that his difficult life makes him less humane. He apologizes, and the three adults break bread together in a communion of life's difficulties. In "Cathedral," a blind man comes to visit the narrator's wife, who worked for him years ago and maintains their friendship. Bub, the narrator, belittles the blind man even before meeting him, and the early part of their evening together is awkward. After his wife is asleep, however, Bub finds himself "watching" television with Robert. He attempts to describe the cathedral on the screen but cannot, so he guides Robert's hand to sketch the structure. Robert has Bub close his eyes and complete the drawing. "It's really something," says Bub, whose attitude changes as a result of his sudden understanding.

The last seven stories Carver published differ substantially from his earlier works. They are longer and more detailed; they deal with family relationships rather than domestic situations between a husband and wife; their characters range beyond the blue-collar marginalized characters of earlier stories; and, as Carver commented, they are "somehow more affirmative." The collection closes with "Errand," a story of Chekhov's last days and of his death from tuberculosis. When the end is obvious and immutable, Chekhov's doctor brilliantly orders champagne. Chekhov, his wife, and his physician toast his life. He dies, but the wife waits with his body until morning, when a delivery boy comes to collect the

glasses and bring her some flowers. She asks him quietly to find the best mortician in the city, without raising an alarm about the great writer's death. He nods in agreement, but before leaving on his errand he leans down and picks up the champagne cork that fell under the edge of the bed. The large event of Chekhov's death is paired with the small event of an anonymous errand boy's attention to detail. Carver brought the same attention to all of his stories, those of his minimalist period and those of his rich last days.

Linda Ledford-Miller

Further Reading

Campbell, Ewing. *Raymond Carver: A Study of the Short Fiction.* New York: Twayne, 1992. A good overview of Carver's stories, with an analysis of twenty-seven stories from the four major collections. A section on "The Writer" includes an interview and Carver's own essay, "On Writing." "The Critics" contains essays by three critics. Also includes a chronology and a bibliography.

Kleppe, Sandra Lee, and Robert Miltner, eds. *New Paths to Raymond Carver: Critical Essays on his Life, Fiction, and Poetry.* Columbia: University of South Carolina Press, 2008. Includes essays on the impact of television, McCarthyism, and Alcoholics Anonymous on Carver's fiction and the elements of humor and of voyeuristic empathy in these works.

Lainsbury, G. P. *The Carver Chronotope: Inside the Life-World of Raymond Carver's Fiction.* New York: Routledge, 2004. Examines Carver's significant role in American minimalist fiction. Compares his work to that of Ernest Hemingway and of Franz Kafka and discusses the function of the family in his fiction.

Meyer, Adam. *Raymond Carver.* New York: Twayne, 1995. An excellent overview of Carver's work. Contains a biographical sketch and situates Carver's influence on minimalism, renewed realism, and the renaissance of the short story. Discusses each of his collections and comments briefly on his poetry. Includes an annotated bibliography of selected criticism.

Nisset, Kirk. *The Stories of Raymond Carver.* Athens: Ohio University Press, 1994. The first dissertation on Carver, which has been expanded into a useful introduction to his work.

Saltzman, Arthur M. *Understanding Raymond Carver.* Columbia: University of South Carolina Press, 1988. The first book-length study of Carver's work. Discusses three of the major collections. Does not include commentary on the seven new stories collected in the closing section of

Where I'm Calling From. An empathetic reading that considers Carver a "connoisseur of the commonplace."

Zhou, Jingqiong. *Raymond Carver's Short Fiction in the History of Black Humor.* New York: Peter Lang, 2006. Analyzes Carver's short fiction within the context of

other American writers, such as Mark Twain, John Barth, and Joseph Heller, who use black humor as an element in their fiction. Describes how Carver uses black humor to mitigate the presence of menace and bring some hope to his characters' lives.

Where the Air Is Clear

Author: Carlos Fuentes (1928-   )
First published: La región más transparente, 1958 (English translation, 1960)
Type of work: Novel
Type of plot: Mythic
Time of plot: Early to mid-1950's
Locale: Mexico City

Principal characters:
FEDERICO ROBLES, a banker
NORMA LARAGOITI, his wife
HORTENSIA CHACÓN, Robles's mistress
RODRIGO POLA, Norma's lover
IXCA CIENFUEGOS, shadowy character symbolizing the spirit of Mexico City
MANUEL ZAMACONA, poet and friend of Ixca

The Story:

Rising from his peasant origins, Federico Robles subscribes to the myth of bourgeois stability and eventually makes his way to the top of a powerful financial empire in Mexico City. He creates this empire in the years immediately following the Mexican revolution. In an act of rebellion against his mestizo heritage, Robles marries a green-eyed woman named Norma Laragoiti, a self-absorbed materialist. During his marriage to Norma, Robles takes as his mistress the blind mestizo woman Hortensia Chacón, who abandons her petty functionary husband. With Hortensia, Robles is able to find true love and happiness.

During one of the many intensely emotional battles between Norma and Robles, Norma accidentally burns to death in the Robles mansion. The fire begins when Robles rushes downstairs from his wife's bedroom after she refuses to give him her jewels to sell. He needs the money because his financial empire is crumbling. Robles loses all his money and worldly possessions and returns to his peasant origins. He moves to a farm in the north of Mexico, where he lives with Hortensia and their son.

The writer Rodrigo Pola is on the opposite side of the social spectrum from Robles. Their sharing of Norma (whom Pola loved) underscores their parallel and contrasting movements in the novel. Pola is transformed from an aspiring poet to a successful screenwriter. Artistically, Pola experiences a rise in terms of worldly success that is a fall in terms of artistic accomplishment. Federico, in turn, experiences a financial fall that is a spiritual rise.

Moving among these lives, serving as a kind of adhesive, is Ixca Cienfuegos. Often described as a misty, insubstantial presence, he represents the spirit of the city. His mother, Teódula Moctezuma, is a genuine Aztec sorceress. Teódula keeps dead family members under her floorboards and believes that for her ancestors to remain contented and for her life to continue, Ixca needs to sacrifice a human life for the gods. At dawn, after Norma burns to death, Teódula points to the sun, which she believes rises again because of the rejuvenating sacrifice. Ixca searches for a victim in order to put his mother's beliefs into practice, but near the end of the novel he is exhausted by his attempts to conform to ancient rituals.

A number of briefer portraits surround the central figures of Carlos Fuentes's novel. These minor characters suffer in obscurity throughout the city. Gabriel, a migrant worker, whose brother occasionally serves as a waiter at parties attended by the more affluent characters, returns from the United States with a blender for his mother, only to find that his family's shack has no electricity. They use the blender as a flower vase. Gabriel, one of the novel's many sacrificial victims, is senselessly killed by a local thug in a cheap dive on the poor side of town.

Critical Evaluation:

In *Where the Air Is Clear,* Carlos Fuentes offers a kaleidoscopic presentation, in numerous vignettes, of contemporary life in Mexico City. The title of the novel is a quotation from the work of the Mexican writer Alfonso Reyes and refers to Anahuac, the valley of Mexico, as a region where the air is clear. At least the region was so at one time, before the drying up of Lake Texcoco and modern industrialization brought dust and smog, changing what was once a high tableland with a relatively low population density into an overcrowded metropolis with air pollution.

Fuentes's novel is divided into three sections that are not equal in length or intent. Each section is in turn subdivided into parts, each with a title, generally the name of a character who provides the point of view for the section. Fuentes's great contribution to this modernist technique of fragmentation of point of view is largely the novel's use of setting, both philosophical and psychological. The novel presents a portrait of Mexico City.

In *Where the Air Is Clear*, myth occupies a significant place. Fuentes presents a mythical history of Mexico City and its inhabitants. The characters who represent the historical aspects of the novel are products of the Mexican revolution and, at the same time, are representative of Mexican society during the 1950's. Federico Robles is a revolutionary turned into a conservative banker. His wife Norma Laragoiti is a social climber who marries for money. Manuel Zamacona is a brooding intellectual.

Each one of the main characters is sacrificed for the sake of a myth. It is the myth of bourgeois stability in the case of Robles the banker. It is the myth of success in the case of the poet Rodrigo Pola. It is the myth of narcissism in the case of Norma. It is the myth of the intellectual in the case of Zamacona (who dies by the pistol of a deadly drunk while trying to buy gas to escape from Acapulco). All myths, the author demonstrates, are false; all are deadly; all are projections of human desires.

Ancestral voices and indigenous mythologies are very powerful in the novel. For Fuentes, myth combines past, present, and future. As a creator and perpetuator of myths, Fuentes builds a modern version of ancient patterns, including rituals of sacrifice and battles between male and female principles. In the narrative, these ancestral voices link the reader not only with the past, present, and future but also with the universe. Fuentes works within the universal time of myth and within the limited, linear, and subjective time of individual history. In *Where the Air Is Clear*, the mythic mode predominates.

Ixca Cienfuegos (the name combines the Aztec and the Spanish; the surname means "hundred fires") moves through the novel as a unifying consciousness, a force for the elicitation of truth and a bearer of transcendence. He symbolizes Mexico's past, a mythical Mexico that still believes in ritual

and in sacrifice as the only way to redemption. The Mexican people have been chosen by the gods to keep the sun moving so that humanity may survive. Without sacrifices this would be impossible. Norma and Zamacona are sacrificed.

This revelation of the mythical nature of Mexican history is accomplished by the use of image and of metaphor. The characters, the city, the action, and the plot are all expressed by uniting two worlds, that of the remote past and that of the present. The interactions among the characters representing both cultures become the central technique of mythmaking. History and myth balance each other to give the novel equilibrium.

Cienfuegos listens to the stories of many characters who are incarnations of Mexican history, constituting a landscape of moral, psychological, and social destiny. There are the revolutionary turned tycoon, the aristocratic woman frozen in nostalgia and sexlessness, the ambitious young woman from the provinces, the self-pitying unsuccessful poet, the aged avatar of Mexico's pagan past, and the lower-class youth yearning murderously for some way to feel alive.

All of these characters also function on another level within the novel's narrative. There is tension between their existence as specific examples of Mexican society and the deeper truth that Cienfuegos extracts from them. Interlocked, their destinies unfold in extreme violence. One by one, the shameful and false routes to social standing are blocked. On the other hand, the innocent, the ones who have remained true to themselves, suffer deaths of terrifying meaninglessness.

Fuentes presents many aspects of Mexican life in the novel, all, in one way or another, a reflection of the impact of the revolution on the city and its people. There is nostalgia for prerevolutionary Mexico City, the city of palaces that was orderly and reasonable, and for the times of Porfirio Díaz. There is the betrayal and fear in the death of Gervasio Pola, father of the poet Rodrigo, who leaves his wife and dies facing the firing squad with the three companions he betrayed. There is the somewhat inhuman curiosity of Cienfuegos, who takes a sadistic delight in trying to make people face the truth about themselves. Through it all, there is the brutally frank presentation of a thoroughly tawdry society, mestizo and rootless. Finally, the question, posed by the author himself—What is the origin and identity of Mexico?—is unanswerable, and the reader is left only with questions.

In *Where the Air Is Clear*, an extraordinary and influential first novel, Fuentes attempts a "biography of a city" and a synthesis of Mexico. The novel contains insights into a country whose social revolution soon ceases to be truly revolutionary. Everyone—oppressed and oppressors—is represented in rapid, cinematic scenes. Through this spectrum of characters, the author seeks the essence of the modern Mexican among a collection of people and finds no shared philosophy or sense of purpose, nothing to prevent the strong from preying on the weak.

The novel is an attempt to extricate a living imagination from the entombed, self-devouring Mexican consciousness, forever mourning its divided past, incessantly projecting its possible future, and torn between its ill-defined cultural heritage and the influence of more advanced societies. Fuentes's wish is to understand and to create images of the metamorphoses that the Mexican spirit has undergone, to work his way through old myths in search of a more viable new one, and finally to emerge at some point where form and experience cooperate to raise an adequate philosophical and psychological structure.

Genevieve Slomski

Further Reading

Boldy, Steven. *The Narrative of Carlos Fuentes: Family, Text, Nation.* Durham, England: University of Durham, 2002. Analyzes *Where the Air Is Clear,* describing how this book and Fuentes's other early novels used the genre of the family drama to address broader issues of Mexican identity, history, and intellectual traditions.

Brody, Robert, and Charles Rossman, eds. *Carlos Fuentes: A Critical View.* Austin: University of Texas Press, 1982. Good and varied collection of essays on the stories and the novels.

Duran, Gloria. *The Archetypes of Carlos Fuentes.* Hamden, Conn.: Archon Books, 1980. Discusses female archetypes in Fuentes's major works of fiction.

Faris, Wendy B. *Carlos Fuentes.* New York: Frederick Ungar, 1983. Excellent introduction to Fuentes's works. Focuses upon Fuentes's capacity to absorb, transform, and transmit multiple voices.

Guzman, Daniel de. *Carlos Fuentes.* Boston: Twayne, 1972. Overview of Fuentes's work, placing it in a historical, social, psychological, economic, and cultural context. Includes bibliography.

Gyurko, Lanin A. *Lifting the Obsidian Mask: The Artistic Vision of Carlos Fuentes.* Potomac, Md.: Scripta Humanistica, 2007. Designed as a guidebook for students of Latin American literature, this book provides analysis of all of Fuentes's work.

The White Album

Author: Joan Didion (1934-   )
First published: 1979
Type of work: Essays

Joan Didion's literary reportage from the 1960's and 1970's holds a prominent place in New Journalism, whose advocates generally attempted to write with a more personal, idiosyncratic voice to record the phantasmagoria of life in post-1950's America. New Journalism, however, was neither a school nor a movement.

Insofar as it concerns itself mostly with contemporaneous events, Didion's prose could be called traditional journalism, but the similarity ends here. Her crystalline style and practiced eye for allegorical detail, her ear for dialogue, her delineation of character and fact, and her affinity for irony lend Didion's cinematic narratives a kind of absurdist sheen. *The White Album* is a follow-up to her book of essays *Slouching Towards Bethlehem* (1968) and collects previously published magazine articles. On the whole, the period pieces in

The White Album form a melancholy coda to the selected fragments of a bygone time. In 2006, this book was included in an omnibus edition of her work called *We Tell Ourselves Stories in Order to Live: Collected Nonfiction.*

In the opening title essay (named for the Beatle's record album), Didion offers an anguished glimpse of her life in California from the mid-1960's to the early 1970's to give the reader an intimate framework for the stories and reports that follow. Her physical and psychological problems mirror the social and political disintegration conveyed through local stories and happenings that are juxtaposed with bulletins on political events, war, and mass murder. Underlying this framework is Didion's apprehension that narrative is no longer capable of giving order and meaningful shape ("intelligibility") to personal or collective experience. For Didion, this threatened lapse into aesthetic incoherence has ethical and moral implications. Despite the potential for anomic circumstances to overwhelm her ability to find and convey significance, Didion manages in *The White Album* to decode the edgy signs and symbols from that era.

In the second section of *The White Album*, "California Republic," Didion depicts her native state as a theater of simulacra. A biographical note about a former Roman Catholic bishop of California, James Pike, is evoked by a cathedral on San Francisco's Nob Hill. Pike's weird contradictions and even stranger death in the Jordanian desert serve as a metaphor for the American style of aggressive self-reinvention and abrupt endings. Didion's preoccupation with California's waterworks, in "Holy Water," demonstrates her ability to personalize facts and reveal hidden bureaucratic processes. Here, the essay form is used to localize narrative and create psychic stability from facts. She writes in a similar vein on the management of California's freeway system by the state's transportation department, better known as Caltrans, in which readers learn that certain drivers report using highway congestion to achieve a vigilant, trancelike state of heightened awareness. Architectural semiotics is evident in two articles about old governor's mansions in California and about the J. Paul Getty Museum in Southern California. For Didion these structures are somehow insufficient; they are monuments to private eccentricities or smug vanity. In the concluding two essays in this section, "Good Citizens" and "Notes Toward a Dreampolitik," Didion writes about California people, moods, and sensibilities from the late 1960's. Her tales include a droll aside on outlaw biker films and another on a young woman whose dreams of stardom seem both typical and impossible.

The third section of *The White Album*, "Women," opens with a critical account of second-wave American feminism as a contrived movement that trivializes political agency while sinking into a collective morass of manufactured resentments and self-indulgent posturing. When originally published in *The New York Times* in 1972, this viewpoint sparked controversy. From politics, Didion moves to aesthetics in short essays on novelist Doris Lessing and artist Georgia O'Keefe, respectively. This exercise offers contrasting versions of artistic self-realization. Where Lessing's fiction is viewed as heavily didactic and unpersuasive, O'Keeffe's distinctive paintings are, for Didion, clear evidence of O'Keeffe's lifelong integrity and imaginative vitality. Lessing's receipt of the 2007 Nobel Prize in Literature confirms that taste is personal.

In the fourth section, "Sojourns," Didion maps Hawaii as a personal sanctuary, a stage for social preening, a burial ground for Vietnam War casualties, and as the film set for *From Here to Eternity*. In a related essay, she portrays her involvement with Hollywood culture as if she were an anthropologist, describing a motion-picture industry filled with phoniness and existing chiefly to make money and, occasionally, to make an excellent film. Her travel essay on Bogotá, Colombia, is a collage of finely observed images from that time and place. A description of a hectic book tour and some notes on shopping malls offer rather whimsical displays of her versatility. Oddly, the piece on malls is her most explicit statement in *The White Album* on American consumerism. Another essay, about Hoover Dam (along the Arizona-Nevada border), recalls her preoccupation with water and the reassuring utility of large-scale technical processes. In the next and last section of the book, "On the Morning After the Sixties," Malibu is the scene for a harrowing account of nature's sudden destructive powers. A contrasting essay on orchids is a sensitive meditation on the skilled cultivation of nature as a workshop of fragile beauty.

Didion is a writer of wide interests. She embraces both the ordinary and the strange perturbations that are found in nature and the zeitgeist. That *The White Album* may be criticized on the basis of ideas supplied by Didion herself is in some ways a testament to her honesty and clarity. The key title essay from the fifth section of the book epitomizes her sense of fatalism and pessimism. Except for certain pieces, this mood permeates the entire volume, though a glance at contemporary history indicates that this perspective might be somewhat blinkered. The twentieth century was arguably the most murderous century ever. The enormity of Mao Zedong's "cultural revolution" or the genocide in Cambodia, two conspicuous examples from the 1960's and 1970's, would seem to offer a more substantial basis for despair than the incidents of casual nihilism and criminal mayhem cited by Didion in *The White Album*. Perhaps the undercurrent of anguish in *The White Album* stems from a belief in American exceptionalism or, at minimum, an America of grace and innocence that was somehow betrayed by the excesses of that era.

Furthermore, because of the book's many cultural references to film (with the 1974 film noir classic *Chinatown* a curious omission) or literary fiction, the work seems to privilege metaphor over history. While Didion does not claim to be a reporter of history, this blurring of history (through literary jump cuts and dissolves) into an impressionistic collage has aesthetic consequences, suggesting that her style is a highly conscious form of mimesis.

The fragments of Didion's text, however, cannot prop up the larger philosophical themes she only hints at in *The White*

Album, like those concerning human nature, social chaos, randomness, or the nature of evil. This is odd considering Didion is also a reader of George Orwell. In Orwell's minimalist parables, the storyteller becomes the story. The problem in Didion's case is that the storyteller often resembles a tightrope walker with a bad case of vertigo.

Robert N. Matuozzi

Further Reading

Felton, Sharon, ed. *The Critical Response to Joan Didion.* Westport, Conn.: Greenwood Press, 1994. Reprints of selected secondary literature on Didion's work (including *The White Album*) arranged chronologically from 1963 through 1992. Entries within chapters are listed alphabetically by author. Contains a useful and concise treatment of themes and styles in *The White Album*.

Friedman, Ellen G., ed. *Joan Didion: Essays and Conversations.* Princeton, N.J.: Ontario Review Press, 1984. Essays by various authors on Didion's work, including a short chapter by Irving Malin on *The White Album* that argues that the book is, at its core, an affirming work.

Houston, Lynn Marie, and William V. Lombardi. *Reading Joan Didion.* Santa Barbara, Calif.: Greenwood Press, 2006. A close examination of Didion's works, including her essays in *The White Album*. Also focuses on Didion as a critic and as a founder of New Journalism. A good place to start for readers new to Didion.

Loris, Michelle C. *Innocence, Loss, and Recovery in the Art of Joan Didion.* New York: Peter Lang, 1989. Chapters treat particular books by Didion in chronological order. Declares that the personal quality of the essays in *The White Album* lends the book a prophetic dimension.

Muggli, Mark Z. "The Poetics of Joan Didion's Journalism." *American Literature* 59, no. 3 (October, 1987): 402-421. A critical article that examines Didion's little-studied "imagistic journalistic technique" as well as the narrative strategies in her writings.

Weingarten, Marc. *The Gang That Wouldn't Write Straight: Wolfe, Thompson, Didion, Capote, and the New Journalism Revolution.* New York: Crown, 2005. This accessible study of 1960's New Journalism argues that Didion brought a deeply personal voice to narrative nonfiction.

Winchell, Mark R. *Joan Didion.* Rev. ed. Boston: Twayne, 1989. A synthetic examination of Didion's life and career through 1987. Notes the connection between Henry Adams's 1907 autobiography and Didion's skepticism about meaning and coherence in history.

The White Devil

Author: John Webster (c. 1577/1580-before 1634)
First produced: c. 1609-1612; first published, 1612
Type of work: Drama
Type of plot: Tragedy
Time of plot: Sixteenth century
Locale: Rome and Padua, Italy

Principal characters:
VITTORIA COROMBONA, a Venetian lady
PAULO GIORDANO URSINI, duke of Brachiano
FRANCISCO DE MEDICIS, duke of Florence
CARDINAL MONTICELSO, his brother
CAMILLO, Vittoria's husband
FLAMINEO, Vittoria's brother, secretary to Brachiano
MARCELLO, another brother, attendant on Francisco de Medicis
COUNT LODOVICO, a banished nobleman
ISABELLA, sister of Francisco de Medicis, Brachiano's wife
GIOVANNI, son of Isabella and Brachiano

The Story:

Antonelli and Gasparo, courtiers of Francisco de Medicis, duke of Florence, bring to Count Lodovico in Rome the news that he is banished because of his notorious intrigues and bloody murders. Lodovico cannot understand why he is singled out for punishment when other noblemen, especially the duke of Brachiano, are guilty of crimes just as heinous.

Brachiano is trying to seduce Vittoria Corombona, wife of the aging Camillo. Helping Brachiano in his scheme is Vittoria's unscrupulous brother Flamineo, who convinces

Camillo that the best way to keep Vittoria virtuous is to give her unlimited freedom. This privilege granted, Vittoria keeps an assignation with Brachiano. Through the transparent symbolism of a dream that she fabricates, Vittoria urges her lover to murder Isabella, his wife, and Camillo, her husband. Just as Brachiano declares his love for Vittoria and his understanding of her design, Vittoria's mother, Cornelia, discloses herself to denounce the two and to announce the arrival of Brachiano's wife in Rome.

Isabella's brothers, Francisco and Cardinal Monticelso, summon Brachiano to remonstrate against his philandering. When their appeal to Brachiano's sense of virtue results only in mutual recrimination, the brothers produce Giovanni, Brachiano's son, whose youthful innocence, they hope, will inspire Brachiano with a sense of family duty. Confronted alone by Isabella, Brachiano proves the folly of such a hope by berating his wife and vowing never again to sleep with her. To forestall the war that will surely ensue if Francisco learns of this vow, Isabella pretends that she is unable to forgive her husband and declares that she is abandoning her husband's bed. Her ruse and Brachiano's acquiescence in it fools Francisco so completely that he denounces Isabella for mad jealousy.

Disgusted by their sister's vow but convinced that she will soon retract it, Francisco and Monticelso turn their attention to Camillo and Marcello, another of Vittoria's brothers, whom they decide to appoint joint commissioners in charge of combating the pirates reportedly led by the banished Lodovico. Camillo objects because he fears he will be cuckolded during his absence from home, but Monticelso's promise to keep an eye on Vittoria quiets him. Actually, Monticelso and Francisco are giving Camillo the commission to get him away from Rome so that Brachiano might have free access to Vittoria. By this scheme the two brothers hope to plunge Brachiano into a shameful scandal.

Brachiano, however, makes his own plans, arranging for Flamineo to murder Camillo, and for Julio, a physician, to kill Isabella. Through the magic of a conjurer, Brachiano is able to watch the murders, Isabella dying from kissing a poisoned portrait of her husband, and Camillo, from being pushed off a vaulting horse in a gymnasium.

Monticelso and Francisco immediately bring Vittoria to trial for the murder of her husband, although they know they have no evidence other than her ill repute. At her trial before the ambassadors to Rome, a hearing presided over by Monticelso, Brachiano admits that he stayed at Vittoria's house the night of the murder. This testimony, along with other incriminating but circumstantial evidence of her adultery, is sufficient to convict Vittoria, although she protests her innocence

and denounces the conduct of the trial. Monticelso sentences her to confinement in a house of reformed prostitutes.

Immediately after the pronouncement of this sentence, Giovanni arrives to tell his uncles of his mother's death. Accompanying him is Lodovico, who secretly was in love with Isabella and who, in fact, witnessed her death. Francisco and Monticelso realize that Brachiano was responsible for the murder of their sister but disagree on how to avenge it. Fearing that a war might result from an open attack on Brachiano, yet unwilling to defer vengeance, Francisco, inspired by a vision of Isabella's ghost, devises a trick. He writes a letter to Vittoria, professing his love for her, and instructs his servant to deliver it when some of Brachiano's men are close by.

As Francisco hopes, Flamineo intercepts the letter and gives it to Brachiano, who is, as expected, enraged by Vittoria's apparent infidelity. A violent quarrel ensues between the two, refereed by the pandering Flamineo. It ends in a reconciliation so sweet that Brachiano resolves to have Vittoria stolen away from the home and then to marry her. To trick Brachiano into marrying a woman of ill repute is exactly what Francisco hoped for, but his lust for revenge is not yet satisfied. He engages Lodovico, who was pardoned, to murder Brachiano.

Monticelso, who has just been elected pope, excommunicates Brachiano and his bride; then, learning of the plotted murder, he forbids Lodovico to commit it. Monticelso's command is ignored, however, when Francisco sends Lodovico a thousand crowns in Monticelso's name, a gift that convinces Lodovico that the pope was craftily insincere.

Francisco apparently decides to oversee the murder himself, for he disguises himself as Mulinasser, a Moor, and proceeds to Brachiano's palace in Padua, accompanied by Lodovico and Gasparo, who are disguised as Knights of Malta. Welcomed by Brachiano, the trio plan a horrible death for him.

Before they can carry out their scheme, another murder is committed. A quarrel between Marcello and Flamineo over the latter's amorous attentions paid to Zanche, Vittoria's Moorish maid, results in Flamineo's killing his brother. While Brachiano passes judgment on the murderer, Lodovico sprinkles Brachiano's helmet with poison. The poison drives Brachiano mad. Soon thereafter, Lodovico and Gasparo, dressed as Capuchins, enter the room where the count lies raving; they reveal their true identity and strangle him.

After his lord's death, Flamineo asks Vittoria for a reward in payment of his long, treacherous service. Rebuffed, he produces two pairs of pistols, claiming that he promised Brachiano to kill himself and Vittoria after Brachiano's death. Vittoria persuades Flamineo to die first, but when she and Zanche fire the pistols at him they learn that Flamineo, to test Vittoria, did not load the weapons. Before he can murder the women, however, Lodovico and Gasparo rush in and kill all three. Giovanni and a group of ambassadors discover the murderers standing over the corpses. Wounded, Lodovico confesses and then discloses the part Francisco played in these bloody deeds. Giovanni swears vengeance on the duke of Florence.

Critical Evaluation:

The White Devil is one of John Webster's two exceptional revenge tragedies. The revenge tragedy is a subgenre that flourished during the Elizabethan and Jacobean periods. It is characterized by actions of lust, murder, and vengeance. The dark passions and questionable motives that govern the revengers distinguish these plays from more classically conceived tragedies, in which the hero who falls is noble, if flawed, and the fall arouses pity and awe. The high moral message is noticeably absent from revenge tragedies such as *The White Devil*.

To plot his play, Webster used real events that occurred some twenty-seven years before the play's first production. Conveniently, the scandalous affair between Vittoria Corombona and the duke of Brachiano took place in Italy, a country traditionally associated with corruption for the English. It is an appropriate setting for Vittoria, the white devil of the title. While some critics are unsure to whom the epithet is applied, only Vittoria combines satisfactorily its dual nature. Beautiful, intelligent, articulate, strong, Vittoria is also an unrepentant adulterer who is implicated in the murders of her husband Camillo and Brachiano's duchess Isabella. It is no accident, however, that in this drama of moral ambiguity, the extent of Vittoria's responsibility is left unclear; she may be guilty of no more than a wish, revealed in a dream, that Isabella and Camillo die.

In a world lacking nobility and goodness, Vittoria's stoicism and integrity emerge as admirable. By virtue of Webster's art, they contrast favorably with the pale pieties of her mother, Cornelia, and with the unfortunate Isabella. While one can sympathize with Cornelia's displeasure over her daughter's flagrant infidelity, the violence of her own language reveals her own viciousness. She curses Vittoria, wishing her life shortened if she should betray her husband—a dolt who is scorned by even his own faction. Later, her parading of her own sense of moral rectitude is revealed as a symptom of her madness in act 5, in which she appears onstage to strike Zanche, accusing her of being a whore. That she is, for the most part, correct does not redeem her behav-

ior; rather, it serves to set her up in opposition to Zanche. They are two extremes of the same failing.

Part of the equivocal moral atmosphere of this play is that Vittoria's adultery must demand censure, but it is impossible to imagine a life of contentment or fulfillment with Camillo. Modern readers might remind themselves that divorce is unavailable to Vittoria. Webster forces audiences to confront squarely the experience of joyless virtue. Isabella also faces this problem.

Isabella's situation is more complicated. Scorned by Brachiano, she nevertheless feigns repugnance to him in an effort to preserve his reputation. In this play-acting, she rails against Vittoria in a manner that all critics see as revelatory of her real feelings. She dies kissing a poisoned picture of her unfaithful husband. All of this wifely devotion cries out for more pathos than it gets because Isabella's virtue is a barren thing. It brings her neither pleasure nor power, nor does it inspire or animate her after her death. Even her dying is presented at a remove, in a dumb show, further distancing her from the audiences's compassion. In a better world, she would be a sympathetic figure, but ultimately, she comes across as unrealistic and slightly foolish, someone who knows no better than to cast her pearls before swine.

It is the hardheaded, luxurious Vittoria around whom the action revolves. Isabella expires in a dumb show, but Vittoria announces at her trial that all she can do is have a voice. She puts that voice to good use. The leaden-tongued lawyer bringing charges against her is no match for her poise and wit, forcing the judge, Cardinal Monticelso (Camillo's uncle), to take over for the prosecution. Even the judge is forced to a grudging admiration.

Webster steadily keeps the play's moral compass spinning. Vittoria is guilty of adultery, and perhaps complicity in the deaths of Camillo and Isabella, but her trial is manifestly corrupt, as she is quick to point out. The Cardinal is no better than she, only more powerful. He derives his power from his office, but Vittoria owes hers only to herself, to her own beauty and intelligence. The Cardinal, furthermore, abuses the power of his ecclesiastical office by participating in the mockery of justice that is the trial. Vittoria's is the fight of the underdog; her tragedy is that her aims are so impoverished.

The White Devil is a play in which reality and illusion are constantly shifting. The chaste women, Cornelia and Isabella, are exposed as self-deceived. Flamineo sets up the scene for his own death—with unloaded pistols—only to be actually slain moments later. Isabella dies kissing an image of her husband instead of a real man. The real ecclesiastic, Cardinal Monticelso, presides over a compromised court, while Brachiano's assassins disguise themselves as Capuchins. It is a shimmering world of inconstancy and unreliability, but not an amoral one as some have claimed. In the play, morality and immorality are shifting and relative. What is most chilling in the play's landscape is the inefficacy of virtue. The innocent people such as Isabella and Marcello die just as the bad people do and with rather less attention.

It is not surprising that when Count Lodovico tries to pass off the murders of Vittoria, Zanche, and Flamineo as a kind of pardonable vengeance for the deaths of Isabella and Camillo, he is rightly disabused of this idea. His refusal to confront his culpability is just as misplaced as Isabella's inability to confront the breakdown of her marriage. At the final moral tallying up, Vittoria proves to have been one of the better players. While the value of her successes is dubious, she accomplishes what she sets out to do, and she meets her death unsurprised and stoical. With the clarity of vision that never deserts her, she confesses that her soul is embarked on a journey, but where, she knows not. Her worldly resourcefulness cannot help her in death.

The universe of *The White Devil* is one of moral collapse. In the hectic glamour of Vittoria's career, audiences see the final emptiness of a life defined only by pleasure. Her end is truly final, and her lasting achievement is notoriety.

"Critical Evaluation" by Linda J. Turzynski

Further Reading

Aughterson, Kate. *Webster: The Tragedies.* New York: Palgrave, 2001. A student guide to Webster's tragedies, analyzing their key moments, scenic and dramatic structures, characters, and imagery. Argues that his plays critique a deceased world of patriarchal and aristocratic politics.

Bliss, Lee. *The World's Perspective: John Webster and the Jacobean Drama.* New Brunswick, N.J.: Rutgers University Press, 1983. Discusses Webster in the context of his relation to his contemporaries and predecessors. Seeks to establish the existence of a social commentary of disillusionment in the play.

Braunmuller, A. R., and Michael Hattaway, eds. *The Cambridge Companion to English Renaissance Drama.* 2d ed.

New York: Cambridge University Press, 2003. Although none of the essays in this collection deals specifically with Webster, there are references to *The White Devil* and some of his other plays listed in the index. These references help place his plays within the broader context of English Renaissance drama.

Forker, Charles R. *Skull Beneath the Skin: The Achievement of John Webster.* Carbondale: Southern Illinois University Press, 1986. A comprehensive study of Webster's life and work. Recounts the historical incidents upon which *The White Devil* is based and explores the nuances of the characters' relationships with one another by close reading.

Pearson, Jacqueline. *Tragedy and Tragicomedy in the Plays of John Webster.* New York: Barnes & Noble, 1980. Documents *The White Devil*'s pattern of repetitions—often ironic—that make for a tight, interconnected structure. Less convincing in the attempt to establish these patterns as tragicomic.

Shellist, Elli Abraham. "John Webster." In *A Companion to Renaissance Drama*, edited by Arthur F. Kinney. Malden, Mass.: Blackwell, 2002. In addition to this essay focusing on Webster's plays, this book contains many other essays that describe the Renaissance theater, its actors, and audiences; explain the type of plays presented; and place Renaissance drama in its historical and social context. References to *The White Devil* are listed in the index.

Waage, Frederick O. *"The White Devil" Discover'd: Backgrounds and Foregrounds to Webster's Tragedy.* New York: Peter Lang, 1984. A close reading of the play, with emphasis on how its structure reflects Webster's ethical stance. In the balance of action scenes with scenes of stasis, Waage discovers a calculated attempt to capture more closely the rhythms and "irresolution" of life than traditional five-act divisions do.

Wymer, Rowland. *Webster and Ford.* New York: St. Martin's Press, 1995. Discusses the relevance and appeal of Webster's work to twentieth century audiences. The chapter on *The White Devil* explores the dramatic potential of the play's symbolism of black and white—for example, having black actors take on some of the major roles—to highlight Webster's sense of moral ambiguity.

The White Goddess
A Historical Grammar of Poetic Myth

Author: Robert Graves (1895-1985)
First published: 1948
Type of work: Literary criticism

Begun in 1944, *The White Goddess* was to illuminate the path of Robert Graves's literary career for the next forty years, the larger part of his creative life. Beliefs expressed in this work concerning the obligations of poetry and poets, the rightful relationship of man to woman, and the priority of inspiration would shape all of Graves's novels, essays, and books of poetry that succeeded it. So central would it remain to his work that it is possible to claim that *The White Goddess* represented a way of life, or perhaps a religion, to Robert Graves. The book represents a way of life for scholars of his work as well. Some analyses of his work have stressed the influence of *The White Goddess* not only on the poems written after it but also the poems that preceded it, examining them for the ideas and attitudes that *The White Goddess* crystallized.

The White Goddess is an indispensable tool for gaining fuller understanding of Graves's poetry. One may even suggest that this function is the book's saving grace. Although, as a work of prodigious learning, it leads readers to reevaluate their understanding of the Bronze Age, anthropologists have preferred to ignore *The White Goddess* or to marginalize it as a poetical fancy or an idiosyncratic embellishment on the studies of James George Frazer, author of *The Golden Bough* (1890).

The blunt boldness and heterodoxy of Graves's assertions seem calculated to ward off conventional scholars. Indeed, assessing their anticipated reaction, Graves writes, "They cannot refute it—they dare not accept it!" The richness of reference and the fluid intellectual arguments presented in *The White Goddess*, and the catlike balance it maintains among research, interpretation, and pure imagination, make it one of the most idiosyncratic prose works of the twentieth century.

The White Goddess asserts that poetry embodies fundamental principles, and these may be traced back in time in Europe to a Neolithic faith that celebrated an inspirational figure linked with the moon, known subsequently in a diversity of ancient and modern languages as the white goddess. "In Europe there were at first no male gods contemporary with the Goddess to challenge her prestige or power," Graves declares. For evidence of this faith, Graves extends the anthropological and mythological studies of Jane Ellen Harrison and James George Frazer, weaving together an intricate system of natural, celestial, linguistic, and numerological relationships.

Graves constructs what he terms a historical grammar of poetic myth. The figure at the center of his grammar is the theme, or the story of the birth, life, death, and resurrection of the god of the waxing year and of his combat with his brother, the god of the waning year, for the love of the capricious threefold goddess. The goddess was, in her various incarnations, their mother, lover, and destroyer. "The male role was that of consort-lover, represented by a star-son, the Hercules type with which poets have traditionally identified themselves," Graves explains, "and a wise spotted serpent, Erechtheus, his hated rival. As summer succeeded winter, Star-son and Serpent superseded each other in the Moon-woman's favor."

This fundamental myth of Bronze Age matriarchal society also has served as inspiration for all poems capable of moving readers profoundly, according to Graves. He asserts that every poem succeeds only insofar as it recapitulates a part of the theme. Graves demonstrates the extraordinary precision of this statement in a succession of polarities, contrasting inspirational and classical poetry, poetic and prosaic modes of perception, proleptic and linear thought, intuitive and deductive reasoning, and so on. Graves argues that such dichotomies mirror the ancient struggle between the old matriarchal religion and the patriarchal one that came later to vanquish and replace it.

Graves organizes his anthropological insights within a facile analysis of two Welsh poems preserved in the thirteenth century manuscript *The Red Book of Hergest*. The two poems are "Câd Goddeu," or "The Battle of the Trees," and the *Hanes Taliesin*, or *The Tale of Taliesin*. Speculating that their lack of sustained clarity derives from their having been jumbled in order to conceal (and thus safeguard) heretical secrets they may contain, Graves seeks to decipher the poems by reordering their lines. He discovers that the *Hanes Taliesin* reflects a seasonal progression from winter solstice to winter solstice in which is encoded the story of the year. The story of the year, in turn, is about the theme. The theme is the story of the birth, life, death, and resurrection of the god of the waxing year. "The Battle of the Trees" records a crucial intellectual conflict between rival bardic traditions, or a battle for religious mastery waged between the patriarchal worshipers associated with Dôn and the matriarchal worshipers associated with the gods Arawn and Bran. The patriarchal bards prevail by discovering and revealing the name of their adversaries' secret deity.

A great deal of readers' fascination with *The White Goddess* rests with Graves's wholly unorthodox assertions. Graves is able to argue persuasively that the secret name of the ancient Welsh deity revealed by the patrist bards (but not recorded in "The Battle of the Trees") is none other than Jehovah, the God of the Old Testament. Graves finds corroboration for this surprising conjecture in a number of interesting parallels between the Hebrews and the ancient Britons, which include shared dietary laws that forbid the eating of pigs, rabbits, and certain seafood. Graves ascribes the Jewish suppression of vowels in written texts to reverence for the secret name.

Graves's discovery of Jehovah's origin provides no less of a shock. Noting Plutarch's remark that the God of the Jews was actually Dionysus Sabazius, the barley god of Thrace and Phrygia, Graves documents various cultural similarities, such as comparable ritual celebrations in honor of Jehovah and of Dionysus. Pursuing the identification further, through African and Mediterranean religions, Graves establishes a basis in myth and in linguistics to associate Jehovah or Iahu with the worship of the moon goddess: Iahu, he asserts, stood for "the Moon-goddess as ruler of the whole course of the solar year." Thus, the name of the God uncovered in "The Battle of the Trees" is, in reality, one name of the White Goddess, a name that endowed Bran with authority "to speak oracularly from her kingdom of Dis." Bran had earned this privilege by progressing through the five significant stages of the year, or "by being born to her, initiated by her, becoming her lover, being lulled to sleep by her, and finally killed by her."

The seasonal progression depicted in *Hanes Taliesin* represents an anthropomorphic view of nature; this view is central to matriarchal religion. The patriarchal victory of "The Battle of the Trees" symbolizes the fall of humanity into history and out of affinity with the natural world. Having established the beliefs and practices of the matriarchal age, Graves seeks to compare them with historical beliefs and practices. This comparison yields an understanding of all poetry.

In the matriarchal past, myth and ritual celebrated birth, life, death, and resurrection as indivisible elements of the sacred entirety of nature. This indivisibility was palpable in the seasonal round and in the process of human life. In the succeeding, Olympian, age, myth was turned toward recording "images of man's political will," as patriarchy sought to consolidate its triumph over woman by vanquishing nature. The Olympian age introduced the self-reliant Thunder-child, Axe-child, or Hammer-child, superseding the Star-son and the serpent. This age divided the power of the goddess among a plurality of lesser female deities.

The purely patriarchal age, in which there are no goddesses at all (Mary is not a goddess), followed the transitional Olympian phase. This modern age is unfavorable to poetry. Not only has the theme been displaced from the center of culture, but also, concomitantly, an emphasis has been placed on balance and stability, with an implicit warning to avoid extremes. The poet's quest for inspiration or poetic intoxication is denigrated. For Graves, the graceful classical verses of Horace, Vergil, and John Milton, for all their majesty and metrical beauty, never attain the immediacy of Catullus's verse. Lacking inspiration, or a genesis in love—for Graves the sole surviving feature of the matriarchal world—the verse of patriarchs falls short of being poetry. Rather, it qualifies as Apollonian poetry, which, Graves suggests, is a type of musical prose, a poor substitute for the material it replaced.

Poetry and prose for Graves are not merely literary genres but also radically divergent modes of thought. The difference between them is crucial in Graves's system. Prose, he asserts, originated with the classical Greeks and belongs to the patriarchal world. The prosaic mode of thought finds articulation through words carrying only a single sense at a time. The final effect of the prosaic mode is to produce specialists with stringently limited expertise. Of them Graves writes, "To know only one thing well is to have a barbaric mind."

The poetic mode, however, "resolves speech into its original images and rhythms and re-combines these on several simultaneous levels of thought into a multiple sense." The language of the poetic mode, Graves argues, must seem like nonsense to a mind trained only in comprehending prose. Words in poetry mean more than one thing at a time.

Appraising the modern development of poetic thought, Graves contrasts the ideas of originality held by poets of the Augustan Age and the Victorian era with those of poets he accepts as true poets, such as William Shakespeare, Edmund Spenser, and John Keats. The Augustan Age discouraged originality because of its subversiveness. The mid-Victorian era, in which the monarchy and the social order it represented were unpopular, reevaluated originality. This era's yoking of originality to pedestrian themes, however, meant that originality became trivialized. By contrast, the true poet, addressing his poem to a real woman rather than to posterity, always has to be original, in the simple sense of telling the truth, in his own passionate and peculiar words, about himself and his beloved. Graves's sincere dedication to this romantic vision makes *The White Goddess* one of the most significant poetic treatises by an English poet.

Michael Scott Joseph

Further Reading

Canary, Robert H. *Robert Graves*. Boston: Twayne, 1980. Includes an abstract of *The White Goddess*, a survey of critical perspectives on the work, and a look at the book's relationship to Graves's novels and poems that succeeded it.

Firla, Ian, and Grevel Lindop, eds. *Graves and the Goddess: Essays on Robert Graves's "The White Goddess."* Selinsgrove, Pa.: Susquehanna University Press, 2003. Collection of essays offers a wide range of interpretations, including discussions of the book's sources, context, and meaning; *The White Goddess* as a proselytizing text; how Graves proceeded as a poet after publishing *The White Goddess*; and a comparison of the poetry of Graves, William Butler Yeats, and Seamus Heaney.

Graves, Robert. *Five Pens in Hand*. Garden City, N.Y.: Doubleday, 1958. Contains "The White Goddess," a lecture delivered in New York in 1957, in which Graves tells how he came to write *The White Goddess*. Repeats some of the book's central themes, including Graves's idea of the poetic mode of thought.

Kernowski, Frank L. *The Early Poetry of Robert Graves: The Goddess Beckons*. Austin: University of Texas Press, 2002. Portrait of Graves and his work benefits from the author's own interviews with his subject and from input from Graves's daughter.

Seymour-Smith, Martin. *Robert Graves: His Life and Work*. 1982. Reprint. London: Bloomsbury, 1995. Provides a chronology of the evolution of *The White Goddess*. Seymour-Smith is dismissive of Graves's notion of a prehistoric matriarchy, but he emphasizes the book's indispensability as a tool for understanding Graves's poetry.

Vickery, John B. *Robert Graves and the White Goddess*. Lincoln: University of Nebraska Press, 1972. Biographical work provides one of the most thorough examinations available of Graves's debt to James George Frazer's *The Golden Bough*.

White-Jacket
Or, The World in a Man-of-War

Author: Herman Melville (1819-1891)
First published: 1850
Type of work: Novel
Type of plot: Adventure
Time of plot: 1840's
Locale: Aboard a vessel of the U.S. Navy

Principal characters:
WHITE-JACKET, a sailor on board the USS *Neversink*
JACK CHASE, the captain of the maintop in the ship
CAPTAIN CLARET, the commander of the vessel

The Story:

White-Jacket, as he is later nicknamed, is a common sailor, a member of the crew of the United States frigate *Neversink* on a cruise of the Pacific Ocean during the 1840's. After the ship leaves Callao, Peru, the sailor tries to purchase a heavy jacket that he will need as protection when the *Neversink* passes into the colder climate off Cape Horn. Because a heavy jacket is not available from the ship's purser, the vessel having been at sea for more than three years, the sailor has to make a canvas jacket for himself.

The jacket is full of pockets and quilted with odds and ends of rags and clothing for warmth. When the maker re-quests some paint to make it waterproof and to darken its color, he is told that no paint is available for the purpose.

As the ship moves southward toward the Antarctic, the sailor gradually comes to be called White-Jacket by the crew because of the strange garment he wears. Some of the sailors, superstitious as old wives, dislike him because of the jacket; they say that White-Jacket is too much like a ghost when he goes about his duties high in the rigging of the frigate.

The offensiveness of White-Jacket's strange apparel is revealed only a few days after the ship reaches Callao. White-Jacket is forced to leave the mess group to which he was assigned, because the sailors tell him that anyone who wears such a weird garment is unwelcome. That White-Jacket proved himself a very poor cook during his tour of duty for the group did not help his cause.

White-Jacket is taken into the mess to which belongs the petty officer of the maintop under whom White-Jacket serves. Jack Chase, a gentlemanly Britisher who shares White-Jacket's love of literature and who returned to the *Neversink* after an absence of months, during which he served as an officer on a Peruvian insurrectionist vessel, is admired by the rough sailors and respected by all the officers aboard the ship.

As the *Neversink* sails southward along the western coast of South America the general ship's duties continue. White-Jacket and his fellows set sails and take them in, wash down the decks, stand their watches, and prepare for colder weather. To relieve the tedium of the long voyage, Captain Claret gives out word that the men will be permitted to stage a theatrical entertainment. The captain permits such entertainments in the earlier stages of the cruise but discontinues them because one of the actors behaves in an objectionable manner. White-Jacket notes that before the play, the captain peruses and censors the script. Neither the captain nor the commodore who is aboard the *Neversink* dignifies the men's entertainment by being present.

During the coastal voyage, a man falls overboard and drowns. The incident demonstrates to White-Jacket how risky life aboard a ship is and how quickly a lost man is forgotten. The *Neversink* is becalmed in the waters off Cape Horn. After three days of cold and calm, the captain gives the unusual order for the crew to "skylark." The men give themselves over to all kinds of activity and games of a rougher sort, all in an attempt to keep warm and to prevent frozen hands and feet. Shortly thereafter a wind comes up. The ship rounds the cape and begins to cruise steadily northward.

One day the lookout sights a number of casks floating on the ocean. When they are hauled aboard, it is discovered that they contain very fine port wine. The discovery causes great joy among the crew. In the 1840's, the Navy still serves spirits to the men twice a day, but the *Neversink*'s steward, for some unaccountable reason, neglects to replenish the ship's supply of rum during the stop at Callao.

The most significant events during the run from Cape Horn to Rio de Janeiro, so far as White-Jacket is concerned, are a series of floggings, at that time still a punishment for offenses at sea. White-Jacket hates the cruel whippings, which all crew members and officers are forced to watch. White-Jacket reflects that even in Rome no citizen could be flogged as punishment and that the great naval officers of the nine-

teenth century are opposed to a practice so brutal and unnecessary.

The *Neversink* finally reaches Rio de Janeiro. During many days in port, the men are not to be permitted ashore. At last, the petty officers appoint Chase, the captain of the maintop, to request shore leave for the men. At first, the captain is unwilling to grant leave, but the commodore intercedes and gives his approval. Once again, Chase is the hero of the men aboard the vessel.

One day, the emperor of Brazil is expected to visit the vessel. White-Jacket, amazed at preparations made by men and officers for the royal visit, wonders how men from a democratic nation could so easily fawn upon royalty. He decides the men would make fewer preparations to receive the president of the United States.

On the voyage northward along the eastern coast of South America, one of White-Jacket's shipmates falls ill and dies. White-Jacket watches the preparations for burial, including the traditional final stitch of the shroud through the nose, then stands by during the service. That event is as moving to him as an amputation demonstrated by the ship's doctor while the *Neversink* rested in the harbor at Rio de Janeiro. The operation was performed, White-Jacket believes, because the surgeon wished to show off to colleagues from other vessels anchored there at the same time. Convinced that the operation was unnecessary, White-Jacket is very bitter when the injured man dies of shock.

White-Jacket has a close escape from death when the ship is off the Virginia capes. Sent aloft to reeve a line through some blocks, he loses his balance and falls from the rigging a hundred feet into the sea. He has to cut away his white jacket to keep afloat. He is barely out of his garment when a sailor, mistaking the jacket for a white shark, throws a harpoon into it. White-Jacket, rescued from the sea, is sent aloft ten minutes later to complete his task. White-Jacket is content to close his story of the voyage with the loss of his unlucky garment.

Critical Evaluation:

The fifth of Herman Melville's novels dealing with his travels around the world—on board a merchant ship, a whaler, and finally, a U.S. frigate—*White-Jacket* immediately precedes his greatest work, *Moby Dick* (1851). Critics usually group *Redburn* (1849), *White-Jacket*, and *Moby Dick* together because of their thematic similarities dealing with initiation, isolation, and communal relationships.

Melville was not the first author to use an extended sailing experience as the setting for a novel, but he was the first to publish a poetic, philosophic, maritime novel. Only the later works of Joseph Conrad rival this accomplishment. Several critics believe this work should not be identified as a novel. The many parts of the work—vivid characterizations, harsh depictions of punishment at sea, descriptions of scenes, information about the various divisions of labor, and the account of the daily experience aboard the closed world of a vessel at sea for many years—are insights and information about life at sea rather than incidents in a conventional plot. Although there is a protagonist, the author, by not giving this protagonist a Christian name or surname, seems to warn the reader not to expect conventional character development. Instead, Melville emphasizes his protagonist's symbolic significance by identifying the protagonist with his wearing apparel and calling both him and the work *White-Jacket*.

The title is significant because "white" identifies the fictional persona as a novice on board a man-of-war. It also calls attention to the fact that the protagonist, different in appearance from all the other men on board, who wear navy pea jackets, sees himself as different in character as well, a point he insists on as he relates his maritime experiences. White-Jacket believes he is not like the rough, uneducated, sometimes brutal common seamen who have no other professional alternatives, but he is also unlike the educated, overly genteel officers who seek this profession only because it is appropriate for someone in the upper social class. Out of the hundreds on board the *Neversink*, White-Jacket identifies only with a very select small group: the natural leader, Jack Chase; the poet Lemsford; the reclusive Nord; and his comrades of the maintop—in his estimation, the premier group in this very hierarchical world. Ironically, the narrator's personal bias toward his own superior value seems to compromise his reiterated criticism that a republican frigate should foster greater equality in its treatment of the crew.

The white jacket also underlines the injustice attendant on the protagonist's wearing it. The speaker should have received the same clothing as the other men, but he does not. When he improvises this jacket, he asks for dark paint to obliterate the glaring difference of his uniform but is denied the paint on the basis of its scarcity. This unfair, shortsighted decision becomes emblematic of the incompetent and unjust decisions made by the officers and of the suffering of the crew that results. White-Jacket almost loses his life twice because of the jacket: when the superstitious sailors suddenly lower the halyards and he nearly falls to his death from the main royal yard, and later when the jacket becomes entangled about his head while he is working and causes him to fall from the yardarm into the sea.

The protagonist sheds his white jacket as he approaches the United States, an action emblematic of his departure from a deceptive, artificial life. The action of shedding his jacket provides the only suggestion that some change takes place in the protagonist. Some critics call this change a maturing in a novel of initiation; however, shedding what makes him different and what is a symbol of injustice and superstition is perhaps only an external sign that the fictional persona leaving the frigate no longer has to protect his individuality or fear the injustice experienced on board the frigate.

Melville chiefly uses the perceptions of White-Jacket to filter the extensive amount of information he supplies about every aspect of life on board this man-of-war, from the physical description of the various parts of the ship to the daily activities of the crew and officers. *White-Jacket* not only reports the complicated procedures of daily life but also contains several melodramatic scenes to support the narrator's criticism of the Navy: the use of flogging as a punishment for crimes ranging from the narrator's failure to know his battle station to an older seaman's refusal to shave his beard; the ship's surgeon's needless amputation of a seaman's leg; the illegal smuggling activities practiced by the ship's chief police officer, master-at-arms Bland; and the captain's inept command that almost costs the lives of hundreds of men who know better than the captain how to handle the capricious storms haunting Cape Horn.

Because the chapters are much like informative essays, the philosophical perspective of the narrator is needed to provide unity. The order of the work, with its occasional melodramatic and stormy scenes, parallels the apparent order on a ship that masks the inefficiency, sadism, and brutality of its members. The subtitle, *The World in a Man-of-War*, explicitly identifies the author's theme: Life on board this ship is a microcosm of the real world. The close quarters and enforced confinement highlight and intensify human characteristics of good and evil that are more easily hidden in the constantly changing variables of urban or rural life. Melville's attacks on the inhumane and unjust conditions existing in the Navy also express his criticism of humanity itself.

"Critical Evaluation" by Agnes A. Shields

Further Reading

Arvin, Newton. "*Mardi, Redburn, White-Jacket.*" In *Melville: A Collection of Critical Essays*, edited by Richard Chase. Englewood Cliffs, N.J.: Prentice-Hall, 1962. Unlike many other critics, Arvin believes that *White-Jacket* is inferior to the novel written prior to it, *Redburn*. The title, *White-Jacket*, symbolizes the wearer's isolation from the majority of the crew.

Bloom, Harold, ed. *Herman Melville*. New ed. New York: Bloom's Literary Criticism, 2008. Collection of critical essays analyzing Melville's work, including Peter Bellis's piece "Discipline and the Lash in Melville's *White-Jacket*."

Branch, Watson G., ed. *Melville: The Critical Heritage.* London: Routledge & Kegan Paul, 1974. Eleven rather favorable reviews published when *White-Jacket* was released in 1850 attest to early appreciation of Melville's talent as a writer re-creating life at sea.

Delbanco, Andrew. *Melville: His World and Work.* New York: Knopf, 2005. Delbanco's critically acclaimed biography places Melville in his time, with discussion about the debate over slavery and details of life in 1840's New York. Delbanco also discusses the significance of Melville's works at the time they were published and their reception into the twenty-first century.

Justus, James H. "*Redburn* and *White-Jacket*: Society and Sexuality in the Narrators of 1849." In *Herman Melville: Reassessments*, edited by A. Robert Lee. New York: Barnes & Noble, 1984. Discusses how the unnamed protagonist of *White-Jacket* identifies himself with a highly select group of friends while criticizing both the grog-swigging members of the crew and the silk-stockinged officers on an American man-of-war.

Kelley, Wyn. "'A Regular Story Founded on Striking Incidents': *Mardi*, *Redburn*, and *White-Jacket*." In *Herman Melville: An Introduction.* Malden, Mass.: Blackwell, 2008. Chronicles Melville's development as a writer, providing analyses of his works.

_____, ed. *A Companion to Herman Melville.* Malden, Mass.: Blackwell, 2006. Collection of thirty-five original essays aimed at twenty-first century readers of Melville's works. Includes discussions of Melville's travels; Melville and religion, slavery, and gender; and the Melville revival. Also includes the essay "Artist at Work: *Redburn*, *White-Jacket*, *Moby-Dick*, and *Pierre*" by Cindy Weinstein.

Levine, Robert S., ed. *The Cambridge Companion to Herman Melville.* New York: Cambridge University Press, 1998. An indispensable tool for the student of Melville, this collection of essays includes discussions of Melville and sexuality, his "traveling god," and "'Race' in *Typee* and *White-Jacket*" by Samuel Otter.

Seelye, John. *Melville: The Ironic Diagram.* Evanston, Ill.: Northwestern University Press, 1970. Describes how Melville, using Homeric and domestic similes, contrasts the natural leader, Jack Chase, with the politically appointed, incompetent Captain Claret to exemplify the undemocratic, irrational conditions aboard U.S. naval ships.

White Teeth

Author: Zadie Smith (1975-   )
First published: 2000
Type of work: Novel
Type of plot: Historical
Time of plot: January 1, 1975, to January 31, 1999
Locale: London

Principal characters:
ARCHIBALD JONES, a World War II veteran
CLARA BOWDEN, his wife
IRIE, their daughter
SAMAD IQBAL, a World War II veteran
ALSANA BEGUM, his wife
MAGID and MILLAT, their twin sons
MARCUS CHALFEN, a scientist
JOYCE CHALFEN, a horticulturalist
JOSHUA, a son of Marcus and Joyce
HORTENSE BOWDEN, Clara's mother

The Story:

Archibald "Archie" Jones is trying to commit suicide. He is inhaling carbon monoxide from the exhaust fumes of his running car, which is parked in Willesden Green, a multiracial, multicultural, and mostly immigrant neighborhood of London. Suicide has been Archie's New Year's resolution since the miserable failure of his childless marriage to an insane Italian woman. As with most decisions in his life, he had tossed a coin to determine whether or not he should kill himself. A local butcher saves Archie's life when he sees him in his car, which is parked in the shop's loading area. Archie readily treats this as a good sign that his life has not yet given up on him.

Reinvigorated by his second chance, Archie, a forty-seven-year-old World War II veteran, attends a random New Year's Day party, or rather, whatever is left of the celebration from the night before. At the party he encounters Clara Bowden, a nineteen-year-old Caribbean and a lapsed Jehovah's Witness. Archie and Clara marry just six weeks later.

Born to a highly religious Jamaican mother, Clara immediately sees her marriage to a native-born Englishman as an escape from the old, convoluted ways of her family. Her mother, Hortense Bowden, was born during a 1907 earthquake in her native Kingston, Jamaica. Hortense's mother, Ambrosia, was fourteen years old at the time of Hortense's birth. Ambrosia had become pregnant by a white English captain stationed in Jamaica. Because of the earthquake, Hortense had considered her own birth a miracle, and for the rest of her life she would be a religious zealot. As a Jehovah's Witness, Hortense excitingly continues to anticipate the end of the world because she is firmly convinced that she must be one of the chosen people.

Samad Iqbal, Archie's best friend for nearly thirty years, had encouraged Archie's second marriage to a younger woman, such as Clara. Samad is married, by arrangement, to Alsana Begum, a woman nineteen years younger. Samad and Archie had met long before the Iqbals' immigration from Bangladesh. Having served together at the end of World War II, the two men feel united in that experience, despite neither having done any fighting. They continue to retell their memories of the war at their regular spot, O'Connell's Diner, where they go for drinks, omelets, and discussion.

Clara and Alsana become pregnant nearly at the same time and become close, albeit somewhat slowly and, for Alsana, reluctantly. Clara gives birth to Irie, while the Iqbals welcome twin boys: Magid, the older son by two minutes, and Millat. The three children grow up together and, as the first British-born children of immigrants, go through a process of cultural assimilation much different from that of their parents.

Samad gets obsessively involved with his children's education, attending all parent meetings at their school and promoting all Muslim holidays for the sake of multiculturalism. An affair with his sons' music teacher leads Samad to question English values and his own religion. For his sons' salvation and his own redemption, he decides that the children are better off growing up in his native Bangladesh. However, on his waiter's salary, he can only afford one airline

ticket. After a torturous decision-making process, Samad settles on Magid, the more obedient and seemingly more old-fashioned of the twins. So, unbeknownst to his wife and with assistance from Archie, Samad sends away his older son to the house of Magid's grandparents. Such betrayal is impossible for Alsana to forgive, and she begins to treat Samad with indifference and resignation. Nothing but the return of her firstborn can fix the family's rift, not even Magid's letter about his accomplishments in Bangladesh. Despite his father's original aspirations, however, Magid becomes more interested in science than in religion.

Millat and Irie continue to grow up on English soil. By this point, Irie, an overweight girl of low confidence and with a head full of unruly hair, has developed an enormous crush on the younger son of the Iqbals. After they get caught smoking marijuana on campus, both children join a study group at the home of Joshua Chalfen, an older schoolmate, to avoid further consequences. Joshua's parents—Marcus, a scientist, and Joyce, a horticulturalist—quickly become the children's adopted parents.

The Chalfens are middle class, established, blissfully content, and egotistical. They often speak of themselves in the third person. Irie begins assisting Marcus with his experiments on the genetically manufactured FutureMouse, experiments that become controversial. Joyce, however, dotes on Millat. She supports him financially and defends him sometimes at the expense of her own family's interest. To the children, the Chalfens' middle-class ways are exciting at first, but soon, as in any child-parent relationship, a generational gap arises. Along with the Chalfens' own son, Joshua, the children reject the adults' input, mostly on topics relating to the childrens' future.

In the meantime, a correspondence begins between Marcus and Magid, and it is only through Marcus's investment in a return ticket that the older son of the Iqbals is able to fly back to England. Magid, despite his father's original aspirations for him, returns to England as a more Westernized citizen and immediately becomes an assistant to Marcus. With FutureMouse-related publicity, Marcus is in need of such a companion, while Irie gets shoved off into a role of a filing girl. It seems that she can never escape the Iqbal twins. In a moment of frustration with her unrequited love, she makes love to both of the twins in a single night, first to Millat then to Magid.

In search of a sense of belonging, Millat goes through his own transformation and joins a Muslim fundamentalist group, KEVIN (Keepers of the Eternal and Victorious Islamic Nation). Group members burn writer Salman Rushdie's Satanic Verses and intimidate those whose ways they detest. With his genetic meddling, Marcus becomes an obvious target of KEVIN's retaliation. Chalfen's own son Joshua also has joined a cause: the environmental group FATE. The organization utilizes Joshua as an insider to his father's experiments and plans a violent protest against his work.

It is the last day of the millennium, and Marcus is presenting his FutureMouse to the public and to potential sponsors. The event brings together all of the members of the three families: the Joneses, the Iqbals, and the Chalfens. Clara and Archie are there, but are somewhat disinterested; Irie, who is now secretly pregnant with a child of one of Iqbal twins, is there, too. She will never know the real father of the soon-to-be-born child. Hortense makes her appearance as part of the Jehovah's Witness's next anticipation of the end of the world. It is the end of the millennium, after all, and what other venue can be more perfect? While Millat is at Marcus's side, Magid is at the presentation as part of a religious protest by KEVIN. Joshua attends along with his FATE group in the name of defending animal rights.

Both Samad and Archie have a surprise encounter with a former prisoner of war, a French fascist doctor, who has become a mentor to Marcus. FutureMouse, which represents the future, escapes.

Critical Evaluation:

White Teeth is an immense collision of themes played out in the last decades of the twentieth century. Zadie Smith published her first novel, *White Teeth*, shortly after graduating from Cambridge, making her entrance into England's literary heritage and doing so with unthinkable success. As a writer, she is reminiscent of George Elliot, Charles Dickens, Martin Amis, and Salman Rushdie. However, unlike some of her predecessors, Smith writes about England's contemporary issues, such as immigration and multiculturalism, in the language of those she is writing about. As a true anthropologist, she speaks the dialect of a wide range of people, from a Jamaican Jehovah's Witness to a street-smart Bangladeshi-English teenager. She demonstrates an incredible sense of empathy toward her characters and is fluent in their cultures.

The characters of Smith's London come from various continents, cultures, and religions, which makes the intersection of immigration and race one of the most immediately obvious themes of the novel. Smith describes the immense tragedy of immigration, which includes a loss of stability and status and the struggle to assimilate in a new culture without losing one's native identity. These are daily issues in the household of the Iqbals.

According to critic Mark Rozzo, other immigration/race issues in the novel are the "nationalist fear of miscegena-

tion," or race mixing, and tolerance. Surprisingly, the leading white character, Archie Jones, displays exceptional tolerance of diversity: His wife, Clara, is biracial and his best friend, Samad Iqbal, is Bangladeshi.

Through the Chalfens and their relationship to the children of the immigrant Iqbals, Smith unveils the "counterpart of white racism," what critic Meritt Moseley calls white fascination with the Other. Joyce loves Millat as a fetish, while her husband, Marcus, objectifies the exotic wide hips of Irie. Disguised behind their flashy open-mindedness, the Chalfens continuously comment on the color of the children's skin and on their racial features. To the Chalfens, the children are exotic and fascinating, like Marcus's genetically manufactured FutureMouse and Joyce's plants.

Because the novel spans three generations, themes of heritage and family history are prominent as well. These questions arise in every family's age group. For Samad, it is important to preserve history, as he does with the myth of his great-grandfather, whose heroic contribution to Indian history is questionable. In ways similar to Samad, Archie also is nostalgic about the old ways. His war wound hides a myth of its own: It turns out to be self-inflicted and not the result of some heroic act by a war veteran. Regardless, Archie preserves his memories of the war with self-defensiveness. Samad and Archie continue to retell their wartime woes, most of the time confronting the others' lack of interest toward history. It is essential, however, for them to preserve those memories, even if the memories are based on lies.

Samad belongs to a generation that views history linearly, with every action having a specific consequence. He is a believer in karma and fate. Clara's mother, Hortense, shares his outlook but makes religion the prism through which to see the history of the human race. The youngest generation of the novel is presented with a different world—multifaceted and complicated events that also are chaotic and often inconsequential. The Iqbal twins move in opposite directions. Magid, who spends part of his adolescence in Bangladesh, returns to England more Westernized than the English themselves, while Millat eventually returns to his religion but does so through its fundamentalist branch. The twins cling to extremes. Irie endures her own chaos. She is torn between volunteer work in Africa and a career as a dentist and has many choices for hairdos and weight-loss plans. It is Irie's child who is to inherit the consequences of Irie's choices, however: The new generation, after the information age, will be born to an even smaller world. The demolition of the Berlin Wall marks the death of the metaphor that has divided the world for so long, and children are now confronted with a world with fewer boundaries. A boundless world eliminates the possibility for a pure race. As Alsana states, "You go back and back and back and it's still easier to find the correct Hoover bag than to find one pure person, one pure faith, on the globe."

Smith presents other twentieth century issues. For example, through Marcus's experiments, the novel confronts the question of genetic engineering and its moral and scientific implications. Homosexuality is introduced through the character of Alsana's lesbian niece, Neena, the Niece-of-Shame. The themes of gender equality, sexual freedoms and limitations, and AIDS also appear in the novel.

Because of its ambitious time span, *White Teeth* appears to belong to the genre of historical realism. However, the nearly unbelievable turn of events and the novel's coincidences carry the qualities of Magical Realism. In his review of *White Teeth*, James Wood argues the novel is a kind of "hysterical," not historical, realism. He finds Smith's characters underdeveloped, more like satires, and argues that "information has become the new character." Still, the novel is ambitious and important, taking its own place in the canon of English literature.

Vera Chernysheva

Further Reading

Childs, Peter. "Zadie Smith: Searching for the Inescapable." In *Contemporary Novelists: British Fiction Since 1970*. New York: Palgrave Macmillan, 2005. Childs offers accessible analyses of twelve late twentieth century and early twenty-first century British novelists. Includes a chapter on Smith's *White Teeth*.

Dawson, Ashley. *Mongrel Nation: Diasporic Culture and the Making of Postcolonial Britain*. Ann Arbor: University of Michigan Press, 2007. This study of the beginnings of a postcolonial and multiracial Great Britain includes the chapter "Genetics, Biotechnology, and the Future of 'Race' in Zadie Smith's *White Teeth*."

Head, Dominic. "Zadie Smith's *White Teeth*: Multiculturalism for the Millennium." In *Contemporary British Fiction*, edited by Richard J. Lane, Rod Mengham, and Philip Tew. Malden, Mass.: Blackwell, 2003. Focuses on the multicultural aspects of *White Teeth*. Part of a collection surveying the reception and literary status of contemporary British fiction.

Nasta, Susheila, ed. *Writing Across Worlds: Contemporary Writers Talk*. New York: Routledge, 2004. In an interview conducted by Gretchen Holbrook Gerzina, Smith defends and critiques her own novel and confronts and debates the interviewer.

Rozzo, Mark. "Who's English Now?" *Los Angeles Times Book Review*, May 7, 2000. In this brief review, the author discusses the themes of race, immigration, assimilation, and nationalism. He praises the young writer for her poetry and insight.

Squires, Claire. *Zadie Smith's "White Teeth."* New York: Continuum International, 2002. A reader's guide to the history, plot, and reception of *White Teeth*. Includes a biography of Smith.

Walters, Tracey L., ed. *Zadie Smith: Critical Essays*. New York: Peter Lang, 2008. A comprehensive collection of essays solely devoted to Smith. Section 1 discusses postcolonial and postmodernist readings of Smith. Section 2 discusses racial identity and race mixing in Smith's work.

Wood, James. "Human, All Too Human." *The New Republic*, August 30, 2001. In this often-referenced review of *White Teeth*, Wood coins a new genre for the novel, "hysterical realism." An intense critique of the work.

The Whitsun Weddings

Author: Philip Larkin (1922-1985)
First published: 1964
Type of work: Poetry

Philip Larkin's *The Whitsun Weddings* is his first collection of poems to fully embody his mature style. His early work, collected in *The North Ship* (1945, 1966), shows strongly the influence of Romanticism, especially that of William Butler Yeats and Dylan Thomas. In his second collection, *The Less Deceived* (1955), there is a move toward ironic, measured, occasionally bitter poetry. That shift in tone and in style reflects his involvement with the group of poets known as the

Movement, whose practice generally adhered much more closely to Thomas Hardy than to Dylan Thomas. Indeed, much of the Movement's program centered on a rejection of both the mytho-experimentalism of modernist poetry and the "sloppy excess" of late-phase Romanticism. Instead, these poets—Thom Gunn, Elizabeth Jennings, Donald Davie, John Wain, and Kingsley Amis—sought a more traditional versification and a more accessible message, and they exerted a tremendous influence over poetic practice in the 1950's, 1960's, and beyond. Their irony, skepticism, empiricism, and anti-modernism pushed British poetry in a radically different direction from the freewheeling American poetry of the same period. What the Movement poets shared was an experience of wartime and postwar privation and disappointment. Indeed, Larkin suggested that the severe limitations placed on wartime Oxford University, where he was an undergraduate, did much to shape both his worldview and his poetry.

That sense of limitation is at work from the first page of *The Whitsun Weddings*. In "Here," the opening poem, the speaker describes his northern English city (presumably Hull, where Larkin was for many years head librarian at the University of Hull), in terms of its modern squalor and meanness. The image of contemporary wretchedness recurs throughout the book, notably in "Sunny Prestatyn" (the kind of oxymoron that delights Larkin), in which a travel poster of a bathing beauty is disfigured by obscene graffiti before finally being ripped down and replaced by a Cancer Society poster. In "Here," he contrasts that urban blight first with isolated villages out in the countryside, where life is less demeaned, and finally with the "bluish neutral distance" of the ocean, where existence is "unfenced." The openness contrasts with the hemmed-in quality of city life and the constant reminders of the lack of horizon, yet the openness is ultimately "out of reach." The image anticipates the infinite nothingness of the title poem of *High Windows* (1974) in suggesting the impossibility of attaining freedom and limitless horizons in this life.

The horizon becomes even more delimited in "Mr. Bleaney," where the speaker meditates on the previous occupant of his tiny boardinghouse room. The speaker knows many of the mundane details of Mr. Bleaney's existence: where he summered, that he spent Christmas with his sister in Stoke-on-Trent, even his eating preferences. What he does not know and wonders about is whether Bleaney shared his own sense of loneliness and failure, whether having only this pathetically small room convinced him that it was all he deserved. The room is a kind of coffin, a place that reminds the speaker of his final end, and as such it becomes an instance of death encroaching on life. That sensation is reinforced in the next poem, "Nothing to be Said," which notes that all human activities lead equally to death. It concludes that such information to some people "Means nothing; others it leaves/ nothing to be said." Delineating a divide between people for whom an awareness of mortality is meaningless and those for whom it means everything is characteristic of Larkin, who sees himself as one whose eyes are wide open to harsh reality.

Characteristic, also, is the play on the word "nothing." That such knowledge "means nothing" suggests that it lacks meaning but also that it hints at nothingness. For Larkin, nothing indicates not merely an absence but an entity in its own right. Larkin consistently embraces that paradoxical understanding, so that leaving "Nothing to be said" can be interpreted in the literal sense and also to mean that a knowledge of the void must be explored and articulated. Otherwise, there would be no point in writing poetry in the face of nullity.

Emptiness and disappointment are the hallmarks of the twentieth century for Larkin, who indicates the starting date in "MCMXIV." The great shock to the English nervous system, he contends, was World War I, in which a summer idyll turned into four years of horror. The achievement of "MCMXIV," however, is that the horrors are present without ever being mentioned; the reader is made to see that the Great War ripped out the country's heart by focusing entirely on the idyllic illusion. As if looking at a photograph of the country, the speaker remarks on the long lines at recruiting offices, the men in their now-archaic attire, the outmoded currency, the country still trapped in the previous century, blissfully unaware of the modern warfare to come. Men waited patiently, Larkin recalls, to subdue what they were calling the Hun, and they expected to be home for Christmas, as if they were merely going off for a long weekend. In two mild images he captures the innocence and the lack of understanding that allowed them to leave so blithely. The first image is of the way the men left their gardens neat and orderly, as if they would shortly return to them. The very brevity of the statement points up the error of their thinking, and it recalls, if dimly, the lines in T. S. Eliot's great postwar poem *The Waste Land* (1922) about the corpse planted in the garden. The second image is of "thousands of marriages/ Lasting a little while longer." The couples in these marriages have no idea, of course, that their marriages will last only a little while more; in that naïveté, so soon to be exploded, and in the repeated phrase "Never such innocence," he conjures up all the horrors for which those English men and women of 1914 were so manifestly ill-prepared.

The poem stands as a postlapsarian look at life before the

Fall, in this case a very recent one. Stories of the Fall inevitably deal with being cast out, and the status of the outcast, the outsider, the person peripheral even to his or her own life, runs through the book. In "Afternoons," Larkin looks at young women taking their children to the playground and sees that the demands of marriage and motherhood are "pushing them/ To the side of their own lives." In "Ignorance," he notes that it is "strange" to understand virtually nothing of how the world works, of how people live or why they die. "Ambulances" recognizes the isolating nature of that conveyance, a self-contained room making its way through parted traffic, toward the inevitable (and reminding the reader of the "emptiness" that underlies all human activity). In "The Importance of Elsewhere," he argues that in Ireland his loneliness is reasonable, since the places and rituals are alien to him, while the same loneliness in England, where he is an outsider in his own place, is harder to understand. Throughout the volume, the sense of marginalized existence weighs oppressively on the speaker.

Occasionally, Larkin rises above the bleakness to achieve tenderness toward his fellow humans. The title poem recounts a train ride on Whitsun Saturday (the seventh weekend after Easter), on which he is accompanied by many honeymooning couples. His position remains marginal to their self-involved, unreflective scenes. When the speaker leaves the station, his train is only one quarter full. At first during the sleepy trip, he notices only the countryside, both in its pure and in its adulterated aspects that include farms, hedges, villages, junkyards, and canals filled with industrial waste. All the while, he creates the impression of passivity and displacement that the rail traveler experiences, of sitting in a stationary enclosure and watching through a frame while the world flashes past. The stance as marginalized voyeur leads him to his observation of the wedding parties, which at first do not even register on him but then become a repeating part of the landscape. Indeed, it is the repetition that he emphasizes. It is the generic quality of the experience rather than its uniqueness that catches his attention—the bridesmaids in their "parodies of fashion," the ill-dressed fathers, the foul-mouthed uncles attempting to be clever, the cheap costume jewelry. By the time the train approaches London, newlyweds have filled the carriages and the speaker watches them as they settle into their own watching of the now-suburban landscape of movie houses, power plants, and cricket matches.

The poet himself is cut off from direct understanding of their moment, since he never married, and his speaker seems similarly isolated; he can envision the scene only from the outside. His alienation from the event of these new marriages

shows in his glibly dismissive descriptions. At the same time, however, he recognizes something that eludes the young couples, wrapped up as they are in their private excitement: All their lives, his as well as theirs, will contain this shared experience. That wholly unintended sharing leads him to reflect on the communal necessity of marriage through the image of the cycle of fertility resuming. In an astonishing moment, he envisions the London postal zones resembling fields of wheat, and the sudden braking creating a falling sensation "like an arrow shower/ Sent out of sight, somewhere becoming rain." Although the results, as seen on the rail platforms, are not encouraging, these couples, bringing new life like rain on wheat fields, are the hope for the future, the promise of fertility.

He is brought to a similar consideration in "Dockery and Son" when he discovers that a schoolmate now has a son at university. He decides that "innate assumptions" lead Dockery to have a son, the speaker to have "nothing," while all roads lead to the same end. His brooding on mortality leads him to the ironic notion that all efforts are ultimately futile but that people persist in them anyhow.

The negating quality of death is seen in the final poem, "An Arundel Tomb." The earl and countess have long since ceased to be themselves, having become their effigies. Seasons have swept over them, and, with time, innumerable people have like a tide eroded their identity. The intended message of the tomb, in Latin, is lost on the modern observer, and what remains is the image of a couple joined by the carver's art, nearly proving, the speaker says, what all hope to be true, "What will survive of us is love." While he ironically undercuts that final statement, it nevertheless stands as the gem at the bottom of this Pandora's box of a book: Through all the bleakness and irony, the hope remains that love might be able to provide meaning, to make life worth living, to save humankind.

Thomas C. Foster

Further Reading

Bradford, Richard. *First Boredom, Then Fear: The Life of Philip Larkin*. London: Peter Owen, 2005. Thoroughly researched, generally admiring biography that aims to redress the image of Larkin as a misogynist and a bigot as presented in Andrew Motion's biography (below). Includes analysis of biographical elements in Larkin's poetry.

Hassan, Salem K. *Philip Larkin and His Contemporaries: An Air of Authenticity*. Basingstoke, England: Macmillan, 1988. A survey of Larkin's poetry that focuses on the role of time and attempts to place the poet among his important contemporaries John Wain, Kingsley Amis, Thom Gunn, and D. J. Enright. Contains a separate chapter on *The Whitsun Weddings* and helpful discussions of Larkin's prosody.

Marsh, Nicholas. *Philip Larkin: The Poems.* Basingstoke, England: Palgrave Macmillan, 2007. Critical analysis of Larkin's poems, including a section discussing poems about "weddings and work." Places the poems within a biographical, literary, and historical context and provides a selection of critical views about Larkin's poetry.

Martin, Bruce K. *Philip Larkin.* Boston: Twayne, 1978. A significant early overview of Larkin's poetry and fiction. Makes use of the then-limited biographical information and the social contexts of the poetry.

Motion, Andrew. *Philip Larkin.* London: Methuen, 1982. Places Larkin initially within the tradition of Thomas Hardy and William Butler Yeats, then in that of his Movement contemporaries. Ably captures the poet's wide range of subject matter and treatment and discusses his Symbolist tendencies. Anticipates, in many ways, the author's subsequent biography of the poet.

_____. *Philip Larkin: A Writer's Life.* London: Faber & Faber, 1993. Generally derogatory portrait of Larkin, depicting him as a selfish man who was prejudiced against immigrants, students, unions, and socialists.

Osborne, John. *Larkin, Ideology, and Critical Violence: A Case of Wrongful Conviction.* New York: Palgrave Macmillan, 2008. Osborne maintains that both admirers and detractors have wrongly approached Larkin's work from a biographical perspective. He seeks to "revolutionize" Larkin criticism by focusing on how the poet challenged conventional pieties about the church, Englishness, marriage, gender, and other subjects and helped create the transition to postmodern literature.

Petch, Simon. *The Art of Philip Larkin.* Sydney: University of Sydney Press, 1981. A helpful, brief introduction to Larkin's verse, organized by volume. Emphasizes Larkin's status as a humane poet who closely, if critically, examines important aspects of human experience.

Rossen, Janice. *Philip Larkin: His Life's Work.* New York: Simon & Schuster, 1989. An accessible and intelligent discussion of Larkin's poetry, organized thematically. Particularly useful on the subject of Larkin's "Englishness" and the use of direct and even obscene language in his otherwise conservative and formal poetry.

Stojkovic, Tijana. *"Unnoticed in the Casual Light of Day": Philip Larkin and the Plain Style.* New York: Routledge, 2006. A linguistic and historical study of the plain style in English poetry, including Larkin's work, analyzing the rhetorical strategy and themes of *The Whitsun Weddings* and his other poems.

Who's Afraid of Virginia Woolf?

Author: Edward Albee (1928-   )
First produced: 1962; first published, 1962
Type of work: Drama
Type of plot: Absurdist
Time of plot: Mid-twentieth century
Locale: New Carthage, New England

Principal characters:
MARTHA, a large, boisterous, fifty-two-year-old woman
GEORGE, her thin, graying, forty-six-year-old husband, a history professor
HONEY, a young, rather plain blond woman
NICK, her blond, good-looking husband, a biology professor

The Story:

Returning home at 2 A.M. from a party welcoming faculty, Martha, the college president's daughter, and her husband, George, are squabbling. Martha echoes actor Bette Davis and calls the place a dump but cannot recall from which film the line originated. George suggests *Chicago,* but Martha rejects that title. George has disappointed her, failing to mix at the party. Despite the hour, Martha has invited another couple home. She demands liquor and recalls her delight

when "Who's afraid of Virginia Woolf?" was sung instead of "Who's afraid of the Big Bad Wolf?" George was not amused.

When she asks for a kiss, he demurs, pleading that their guests might surprise them. As the chimes ring, he warns Martha not to mention a certain child, and she curses him. The guests, Honey and Nick, overhear and feel awkward.

After serving brandy to Honey and bourbon to Nick, Martha and George continue skirmishing. The guests agree that "Virginia Woolf" was funny, and they praise the president's party, which served new faculty. George wonders how he grew rich. He regrets having married Martha, who pushes him to become her father's successor. She claims other men would sacrifice an arm to marry a college president's daughter, but George feels more private parts are forfeited.

Responding to Honey's need for the bathroom, Martha shows her the house. While the women are gone, George confesses that he mistrusts biology. Slim-hipped Honey does not appear suited to having children, he observes. On returning, Honey unknowingly retaliates, expressing surprise that he fathered a son. Martha, provocatively dressed, remembers flooring George in a boxing match. Embarrassed, he finds a shotgun, aims, and pulls the trigger. An umbrella pops out. Terrified and stimulated, Martha asks for a kiss, but George refuses, ceding the palm of terror to Nick, since genetic engineers will alter humanity.

George doubts his paternity, Martha says, but he refutes this. When he leaves for more liquor, she confesses that, like Lady Chatterley, she once eloped with a gardener. "Revirginized" by annulment, she graduated from Miss Muff's Academy, returned to her father, and married George, who showed promise. When George returns, she details his failures until he drowns her out with "Virginia Woolf." Honey, nauseated, rushes off, followed by Nick and Martha.

Nick returns, and, though hostile, he exchanges intimate personal details with George such as the fact that Martha spent time in a rest home; that Honey vomits often; and that Nick married her when she "puffed up" and seemed pregnant (the condition passed). George remembers a classmate who accidentally killed his mother. When his prep-school pals visited a speakeasy, he delighted customers by ordering "bergin," and the delighted management treated the boys to champagne. The lad felt lionized, but the following summer, while taking driving lessons, the boy swerved to avoid a porcupine and his father died in the crash. The boy was institutionalized—and remained so, George concluded. As for George's child, he dismisses him as a beanbag. Nick wants an explanation, but Martha returns to announce that she and Honey are drinking coffee.

Alone again, the men talk of marriage. A false pregnancy led to Nick's, but he and Honey, childhood friends, were expected to wed. The money of her preacher father, who built hospitals, churches, and his own wealth, also helped. Martha is wealthy, too, George observes, because her father's second wife is rich.

Nick, coveting power, speaks of wanting to replace colleagues in courses, start his own, and provide sex to impor-

tant wives. George warns him of quicksand, saying that college wives hiss like geese, like South American whores, but Nick dismisses him.

Martha blames Honey's nausea on George, but Honey says she often throws up and that she suffers symptoms of disease without actually having the disease. Martha says George is to blame for their son's vomiting, but he counters that it is the result of her overzealous mothering; she smells of alcohol and was always pawing the boy.

When Honey asks for brandy, George remembers that he loves brandy, but Martha recalls his taste for "bergin." She mentions a novel George wrote but was unable to publish because of her father's objections.

Honey, tipsy, wants to dance and urges Martha to dance with her, but George insists on playing Beethoven. Honey is undeterred, but Martha objects and, rejecting George's suggestion that Igor Stravinsky's *Le Sacre du printemps* (1913) would suit, chooses jazz. George offers to dance with Honey, alluding to her breasts as angelic, and Martha deflects Nick from confronting George by getting Nick to dance with her. When Honey notices their familiarity, George calls it a ritual, this time referring to Honey's breasts as monkeylike.

Martha now launches into the game Humiliate the Host: George's unpublished novel is autobiographical, she claims. As a boy, he accidentally killed his mother and father. When her father vetoed publication of the book, George argued that it was true.

Chagrined, George suggests that the next game involve sex with the host. Martha and Nick seem reluctant, so George substitutes one he calls Get the Guest. When he reveals his knowledge of the hysterical pregnancy, Honey, betrayed, rushes out. Nick follows, promising revenge. Martha upbraids George, but he says that she attacked first. Seething, she claims he married her to be humiliated. George threatens her for mentioning their son.

Nick returns for ice to relieve Honey's headache, and Martha sends George to get it. She turns seductive, and Nick soon proves susceptible. George discreetly sings "Virginia Woolf" before he returns and announces that Honey is asleep. He resolves to read a book. Martha threatens to entertain herself with Nick if George ignores them, but the threat fails. When she and Nick leave together, George reads a few sentences about the decline of the West, then, furious, hurls the book at the chimes.

The noise awakens Honey, who dreamed that her covers were falling away. George deduces that she is pregnant and is intentionally aborting to avoid having children. He confesses that his son, too, is dead; Martha does not know, but he will tell her. Honey responds by getting sick again.

Alone, Martha feels abandoned and, while mixing a drink, invents cordial but improbable exchanges between herself and George. Reminded of "The Poker Night" from Tennessee Williams's *A Streetcar Named Desire* (1947), she confesses to herself that they are miserable.

Nick believes himself the only sane person in the house. As she enters the bathroom with a liquor bottle from which she is peeling the label, Honey winks at him. Madness is refuge from the world's lack of reality, Martha observes, reminding Nick that he failed her sexually. She sees herself as earth mother and men as impotent fools. The only one who satisfies her is George.

The chimes ring, and she orders Nick to the door; failing as a sexual partner, he can play houseboy now. George enters with snapdragons, offering flowers for the dead, another allusion to Williams that delights Martha. George pretends Nick is his son, but Martha prefers houseboys, misidentifying the snapdragons as her wedding bouquet—pansies, rosemary, and "Violence."

George claims the moon lighted his flower gathering. If it went down as Martha asserted, it came up again. It happened to him before, on his family's trip past Majorca after his graduation. Nick reminds George that he killed his parents earlier, but George declares that truth and illusion are intermixed. Even the question whether Nick is lover or houseboy is hard to resolve. George says they are all, like Honey, label peelers, except that they peel skin and muscle. They separate organs and bones to the marrow. Martha, he asserts, tried to bathe their son when he was sixteen, violating him.

When Martha accuses George of bungling, he counters that their son crashed into a tree while trying to avoid a porcupine. Martha denies the death, demanding to see a telegram, but Honey confirms that George ate it. When Nick asserts that the child is fiction, Martha acknowledges that the boy is dead, but she says, weeping, that George should not have killed him. After Nick and Honey leave, George concludes that the death was necessary. He sings "Virginia Woolf" and coaxes Martha into accepting their loss. Tentatively, she resolves to live without the fiction of a son.

Critical Evaluation:

Edward Albee, one of the most distinguished American playwrights, wrote *Who's Afraid of Virginia Woolf?* when he was in his early thirties. The title highlights his concern with fictions and with the way they allay fears and become actual events in people's lives. By substituting a bisexual feminist writer for a more generally threatening enemy, Albee confronts his audience with more pointed fears: Animal death still lurks behind the title, augmented by the bold and frightening challenges represented by Woolf's honesty, experimentation, and suicide.

Albee's great European predecessors, Luigi Pirandello, Samuel Beckett, and Eugène Ionesco, saw the fundamental absurdity of life. They destroyed surface presumptions by presenting as surface the underlying truths that people are characters searching for roles in an unwritten play (Pirandello's *Sei personaggi in cerca d'autore*, 1921; *Six Characters in Search of an Author*, 1922), that they await deliverers who never come (Beckett's *En attendant Godot*, 1952; *Waiting for Godot*, 1954), and that husbands and wives do not know each other (Ionesco's *La Cantatrice chauve*, 1950; *The Bald Soprano*, 1956). Albee's major American predecessors, Eugene O'Neill, Tennessee Williams, and Arthur Miller, were engaged in capturing human experience more realistically, using surreal techniques to help convey the deep psychology of their characters. In *Who's Afraid of Virginia Woolf?* Albee adapts elements from both traditions.

Like his European counterparts, he exposes absurdity with biting comedy in which viewers laugh as much at themselves as at the characters. Like his American counterparts, he deals with problems that can be seen on the surface as "real." He explores the daily absurdity that life imitates art—both the art that declares itself and the fictions by which people guide themselves. People live in a world of allusions, he declares, their actions determined by lines in their heads as well as by unmediated responses to stimuli. Albee regards the composition of his plays as analogous to music, and through his instruments, the actors, sounds sometimes dissonant themes. His characters range temporally through history and spatially across the eclectic spectrum of modern life, creating chords of allusion—to film, literature, and chronicle, as much as to their own pasts—that govern their lives.

Martha and George share a fictional child. They accuse each other of having abused him in ways that became discussed in the twentieth century. Their conversation is a patchwork of quotations, and they fall into prearranged games of assault that differ in specifics but whose results are predictable. Love oddly undergirds the relationship between the would-be adulterous Martha and her inadequate historian husband, who cannot abide the present and takes refuge in the past. Endearing innocence colors the vapid Honey, and touching insecurities drive her seemingly confident husband Nick, who, if George is right, wishes to change the future because he, too, cannot abide the present.

In the end, the frustrating night the audience shares with them may usher in change. Martha goads George into killing their imaginary child, who dies in an imaginary accident that simulates George's unpublished autobiography, which is disguised as a novel. The fictional reality of the play thus mirrors its realized fiction. It replicates the patterning of human lives, forcing the audience to consider what real means in a world interpenetrated by fantasy. When actions and their interpretations are tied to scenarios that enter the mind from outside, only the murder of false offspring can usher in hope.

Albert Wachtel

Further Reading

Bigsby, C. W. E., ed. *Edward Albee: A Collection of Critical Essays*. Englewood Cliffs, N.J.: Prentice-Hall, 1975. Includes five essays in which *Who's Afraid of Virginia Woolf?* is analyzed by Harold Clurman, Diana Trilling, and other critics.

Bottoms, Stephen J. *Albee: "Who's Afraid of Virginia Woolf?"* New York: Cambridge University Press, 2000. A thorough study of Albee's best-known play. Includes an interview with the playwright, a survey of major productions 1962 to 1999, including the film, and examinations of critical responses to the play and of five different performances.

Cohn, Ruby. *Edward Albee*. Minneapolis: University of Minnesota Press, 1969. An invaluable introduction to the playwright. Includes a bibliography.

Kolin, Philip C., ed. *Conversations with Edward Albee*. Jackson: University Press of Mississippi, 1988. In this collection of interviews, Albee assesses the creative process, critics, theater, drama, and life.

Kolin, Philip C., and J. Madison Davis, eds. *Critical Essays on Edward Albee*. Boston: G. K. Hall, 1986. Includes a review of the play by John Gassner and five essays analyzing the work, including "The Mystique of Failure: A Latter-Day Reflection on *Who's Afraid of Virginia Woolf?*" by economist John Kenneth Galbraith and articles by Albee scholars C. W. E. Bigsby and Anne Paolucci.

Konkle, Lincoln. "'Good, Better, Best, Bested': The Failure of American Psychology in *Who's Afraid of Virginia Woolf?*" In *Edward Albee: A Casebook*, edited by Bruce J. Mann. New York: Routledge, 2003. Konkle's analysis of the play is included in a collection of essays examining Albee's innovations in theatrical form and content.

Paolucci, Anne. *From Tension to Tonic: The Plays of Edward Albee*. Carbondale: Southern Illinois University Press, 1972. Reprint. Wilmington, Del.: Griffon House Press, 2000. A thoughtful assessment of Albee's genius and use of language in relation to European absurdist and existentialist traditions.

Roudane, Matthew Charles. *"Who's Afraid of Virginia Woolf?" Necessary Fictions, Terrifying Realities*. Boston: Twayne, 1990. A book-length historical and critical study of the play. Useful and well written.

Zinman, Toby. *"Who's Afraid of Virginia Woolf?"* In *Edward Albee*. Ann Arbor: University of Michigan Press, 2008. Zinman's analysis of the themes and techniques of Albee's theatrical works devotes a chapter to this play.

Wide Sargasso Sea

Author: Jean Rhys (1894-1979)
First published: 1966
Type of work: Novel
Type of plot: Domestic realism
Time of plot: Late 1830's
Locale: Jamaica, Dominica, and England

Principal characters:
ANTOINETTE (BERTHA) COSWAY, a young Creole woman
THE YOUNG ENGLISHMAN, a man who marries Antoinette
CHRISTOPHINE, a servant woman, practitioner of obeah, or voodoo

The Story:

Antoinette's immediate family consists only of her impoverished, widowed mother and her idiot brother; a small number of black servants remain at the dilapidated Coulibri estate. Rejected by blacks and whites because of her mixed heritage and her family's poverty, Antoinette drifts through a troubled and lonely childhood. Her mother ignores her, pushing her away without emotion of any kind, and only Christophine, the servant from Martinique, is kind and nurturing.

Annette Cosway, Antoinette's mother, still young and beautiful, fights for survival by using her beauty, her only resource, marrying Mr. Mason, a wealthy Englishman. This rescue does not last long, however; one night an angry mob of newly freed slaves burns down Coulibri. Antoinette's brother dies. Antoinette is physically attacked. The terror of the night drives Antoinette's mother completely insane.

For six weeks Antoinette lies ill at her Aunt Cora's. After regaining her strength, Antoinette attends convent school. Mount Calvary convent provides a refuge of sorts. Antoinette first prays there for the freedom of death, then stops praying and feels "bolder, happier, more free. But not so safe."

Antoinette's stepfather visits her and finally tells her she will soon be leaving. Just prior to her departure from the convent, she dreams of herself dressed in white following a man with eyes of hatred into the dark of the jungle. She awakens and recalls the dream as one of "Hell," and the hot chocolate she is given to calm her recalls her mother's funeral, one year prior.

The Englishman proceeds on horseback with his new bride, Antoinette, to their honeymoon house, Grandbois. The rain, the colors, the mountains, and even the servants all seem "too much" to him, too bright, too vibrant. All of this world seems uncivilized, including his new wife, and already he regrets this marriage. When Antoinette refused at the last minute to marry, the Englishman persuasively reassured her, most concerned with having to return to England "in the role of the rejected suitor jilted by this Creole girl." After he settles into the house, he writes to his father but leaves out any anxiety regarding his marriage. The Englishman marries for money: Antoinette owns property.

At Grandbois, their differences are inescapable, although initially Antoinette enchants him. He desires the alien nature of the island passionately. He desires Antoinette, yet he is bewildered at the numerous differences between them and is mystified at Antoinette's dependence on him for both her happiness and her very will to live. He "was thirsty for her, but that was not love."

One morning, the Englishman receives a letter from Daniel Cosway that details the wickedness and the history of madness in the slave-owning family into which the Englishman has just married. Antoinette, still unaware of her husband's new knowledge, cries out to him that she does not know who she is, where she belongs, and why she exists. That night, the Englishman wanders into the dark forest and wonders how he can know the truth of anything.

Antoinette soon realizes the truth that her husband does not love her, perhaps even hates her, and, in desperation, she rides to Christophine's in search of obeah, or voodoo. Christophine advises Antoinette to leave him and warns that the obeah can only make him come to Antoinette's bed, not make him love her. Antoinette and the Englishman fight after he tells her that he spoke with Daniel Cosway and learned

about her mother. She tells her husband her side of the story, and he listens reluctantly. She also gives him a potion supplied by Christophine. After their battle, he sleeps with her and awakens to realize he was drugged by his wife. Angered and still influenced by the obeah potion, the Englishman commits adultery with Amélie, a black servant who hates Antoinette, in the room adjacent to his wife's bedroom.

Antoinette, traumatized by this final act of hatred, turns to alcohol. Husband and wife fight again, physically this time. Christophine argues with the Englishman and pleads for him to try again to love Antoinette. Filled with bitterness, the Englishman refuses Christophine's offer to return to England and leave Antoinette behind in Christophine's care. Christophine leaves in anger.

He prepares for the two of them to move to Jamaica and then indulges himself in rum and self-pity, all the while damning the "drunken lying lunatic" to whom he is married. As they begin their departure, the Englishman momentarily wavers in his feelings toward Antoinette only to be finally overcome by his own hatred; the island world is detestable to him, and he hates it most because Antoinette belongs to its "magic and . . . loveliness."

Grace Poole speaks of her acceptance, after careful consideration, of the position as caretaker for Antoinette. Antoinette herself questions the reality of the English prison to which she is brought, amazed that she is captive for so long. She wonders about her lost identity, her name changed from Antoinette to Bertha, and her inability to see her own visage in a mirror. She is smarter than her keeper and easily and frequently steals the keys from the sleeping Grace. Antoinette, renamed Bertha, roams freely through the "cardboard world" of a house that she will not believe is in England.

Antoinette, dwelling on the loss of her dreams and her self, grasps for anything tangible, like her red dress, which she is convinced will reestablish her identity. In a dream state, Antoinette wanders through the halls of the house, searching. She passes a gilt frame mirror, sees her reflection, and is startled by the familiarity and the strangeness of her own image. Her candle, which she drops when startled by the image, causes a fire. She feels a rush of memories descend upon her; the fire returns her to horrible images of burning Coulibri. She knows what she should do. Ultimately, she is successful in burning down the Englishman's house and destroying herself with it.

Critical Evaluation:

Published twenty-five years after Jean Rhys's previous book, *Wide Sargasso Sea* was Rhys's last novel. Different in some respects from the rest of Rhys's work (*Wide Sargasso*

Sea is set in the Caribbean, not in London or Paris, and occurs in the nineteenth rather than the twentieth century), Rhys's last novel continues her passionate explorations into the lives of tragic heroines who are alone, outsiders, and underdogs. Continuing in a long tradition of women's writing, Rhys explores the cultural alienation that results from imperialism and gender roles. *Wide Sargasso Sea* is Rhys's revision of Charlotte Brontë's 1847 novel *Jane Eyre*. The novel's position within the literary canon is thus significant both as a continuation in the tradition of women's writings and as a rebellion to a woman's text within that tradition. Voicing approval and contempt, Rhys creates a dialogue with her literary predecessor.

Rhys grants Antoinette what Brontë denied Bertha, a voice. Rhys does the same for *Jane Eyre*'s Rochester. The two main characters in *Wide Sargasso Sea*, Antoinette Cosway Mason and the unnamed Englishman, tell their versions of the tale in their own voices. *Wide Sargasso Sea* is in three parts: Antoinette's childhood, the newlywed period, and Antoinette's period of imprisonment in the attic of her husband's English home. Of the three parts, the first and third are told in Antoinette's voice. The second is told primarily in the Englishman's voice but is interrupted by a brief section in Antoinette's voice at a point of crisis. This intermingling, modern in technique, symbolizes the attempt at dialogue. The intermixed voices of Antoinette and the Rochester character reveal two sides of the same story, but the characters neither hear nor understand the other person or the other culture.

The dialogue between authors is effected by Rhys's choice not simply to vindicate the West Indian woman who Brontë depicts but also to write that particular woman's story. Writing within the framework of the earlier novel, Rhys responds to the stereotypes informed by Brontë's nineteenth century English culture and social status. Rhys develops sympathetically the complex character of the woman who in *Jane Eyre* is merely a lunatic. Antoinette's story, as told in *Wide Sargasso Sea*, predates the story in *Jane Eyre*. It explains the Englishman's inability to understand or to love his wife, and it shows what lies behind Antoinette's suicide. Rhys speaks back to Brontë but, by placing her story within the narrative of Brontë's work, allows Brontë to have her say. Rhys juxtaposes the English heroine of *Jane Eyre*, who fights for and acquires selfhood, equality, independence, and happiness, with the alienated Antoinette, who not only loses all that the English heroine gains but also loses her freedom and her life.

Still, as obviously as *Wide Sargasso Sea* rejects the optimism of *Jane Eyre*, a kinship exists between the two women characters. Rhys locates her story in five places—Coulibri,

Mount Calvary, Grandbois, Jamaica, and Thornfield—closely paralleling the five physical locations of *Jane Eyre*. Additionally, Rhys's novel shifts smoothly between reality and an otherworldly, dreamlike state, echoing the gothic and romantic elements of the earlier work. Rhys begins and ends *Wide Sargasso Sea* in the voice of Antoinette, the character Brontë leaves utterly voiceless. Rhys also leaves Brontë's main character and narrator not merely voiceless but completely unconsidered. These techniques provide the opportunity to compare the intimacies of both characters and unites them. They are both isolated women struggling for survival in a world dominated by men. Connecting these women and contrasting their fates, Rhys voices the conflict between her theory and that of Brontë on the available opportunities for women, yet ultimately reaffirms Brontë's essential argument in *Jane Eyre*. As Christophine declares: "Women must have spunks to live in this wicked world."

Tiffany Elizabeth Stiffler

Further Reading

Angier, Carole. *Jean Rhys: Life and Work*. Boston: Little, Brown, 1991. Lengthy and thorough discussion of Rhys's early life, schooling, clash of cultural backgrounds, chorus line experience, self-inflicted isolation, and relationships. Angier connects Rhys's life with those of the characters in her books.

Gregg, Veronica Marie. *Jean Rhys's Historical Imagination: Reading and Writing the Creole*. Chapel Hill: University of North Carolina Press, 1995. Examines the relationship between Rhys's Caribbean identity and the structures of her fiction, describing how they are connected to the British colonization of the West Indies. Chapter 2 includes analysis of *Wide Saragasso Sea*.

Hite, Molly. *The Other Side of the Story: Structures and Strategies of Contemporary Feminist Narrative*. Ithaca, N.Y.: Cornell University Press, 1989. Hite maintains Rhys's assertion that the advancement of some groups of women necessitates the deprivation of other women.

Howells, Coral Ann. *Jean Rhys*. New York: St. Martin's Press, 1991. Howells calls *Wide Sargasso Sea* Rhys's "most rebellious text." In discussing Rhys's revolt against, yet ambivalence toward, Charlotte Brontë's *Jane Eyre*, Howells contends Rhys's novel is not easily classified.

James, Louis. *Jean Rhys*. New York: Longman, 1978. A well-detailed account of Rhys's great-grandfather provides insight to Rhys's "fidelity to experience."

Lonsdale, Thorunn. "Literary Allusion in the Fiction of Jean

Rhys." In *Caribbean Women Writers: Fiction in English*, edited by Mary Condé and Thorunn Lonsdale. New York: St. Martin's Press, 1999. Focuses on the many critically neglected, intertextual references to nineteenth and twentieth century European and American literature in Rhys's novels and short stories

Nasta, Susheila, ed. *Black Women's Writing from Africa, the Caribbean, and South Asia*. London: Women's Press, 1991. One chapter explores the "devastating results when the mother-bond is denied" and another establishes Rhys as the literary foremother of following generations of Caribbean women writers.

Plasa, Carl, ed. *Jean Rhys: "Wide Sargasso Sea"—A Reader's Guide to Essential Criticism*. Cambridge, England: Icon Books, 2001. Survey and analysis of some of the critical response to the novel. Describes and compares the initial reactions of British and Caribbean critics; discusses the novel's dialogue with *Jane Eyre*, its racial politics, and its African Caribbean legacy.

Simpson, Anne B. *Territories of the Psyche: The Fiction of Jean Rhys*. New York: Palgrave Macmillan, 2005. Provides a psychoanalytic reading of Rhys's novels and short stories, describing how these works explore the dynamics of the human psyche. Chapter 6 is devoted to an analysis of *Wide Saragasso Sea*.

Thomas, Sue. *The Worlding of Jean Rhys*. Wesport, Conn.: Greenwood Press, 1999. Views Rhys's works as "Dominican autoethnography," emphasizing how Rhys's Creole background is reflected in her writings. Includes analysis of *Wide Saragasso Sea*.

Wieland
Or, The Transformation, an American Tale

Author: Charles Brockden Brown (1771-1810)
First published: 1798
Type of work: Novel
Type of plot: Gothic
Time of plot: Eighteenth century
Locale: Pennsylvania

Principal characters:
THEODORE WIELAND, a madman
CLARA, his sister
CATHARINE PLEYEL, his wife
HENRY PLEYEL, Catharine's brother
CARWIN, a ventriloquist

The Story:

In a long letter to a friend, Clara Wieland tells the story of the tragedy of her family. Her father was something of a religious fanatic, a strange man who feared some dreadful punishment because he did not answer a call to the mission field. He became more and more depressed and withdrawn until his life ended in a horrible fashion. One night, he visited a temple he built for solitary meditation. His wife, fearing the appearance and manner of her husband, followed him and saw his clothing suddenly go up in flames. She found him insensible, muttering incoherently about having been struck down by an unseen hand. Soon afterward, he died. Within a few months, the mother followed her husband to the grave, leaving Clara and her brother orphaned but wealthy. They were happily reared by an aunt who gave them love and comfort and a good education.

One of their companions was Catharine Pleyel, a rich and beautiful girl with whom Theodore Wieland fell in love when he reached young manhood. Catharine returned his love, and when Wieland came of age they were married. Wieland took possession of the family house and half of the fortune, Clara the other half of their inheritance. Since she and Catharine and Wieland were beloved friends as well as relatives, Clara took a house only a short distance from her brother and sister-in-law. The three spent much time together. Clara and Catharine were frank and cheerful, but Wieland was more somber and thoughtful in disposition. He was, however, always considerate of their happiness and nobly devoted his life to it. His melancholy was not morbid, only sober. The temple in which their father met his strange fate was used by the three as a setting for long and delightful conversations, although Wieland's talk dwelt too often on death to suit Clara and Catharine. Their circle was soon augmented by the addition of Catharine's beloved brother Henry, who was for some time in Europe. His boisterous mirth enlivened the little group. Henry and Wieland found one great difference in their beliefs: Wieland built his life on religious necessity, Henry, on intellectual liberty. Their fondness for each other, however, allowed them to differ without altering their mutual affection.

Wieland's family was enlarged during the next six years by four natural children and a foster child whose mother died. About that time, another strange occurrence took place in the Wieland family. One day, Wieland went to the temple to pick up a letter that would settle a minor dispute. Before he reached the temple, he was stopped by his wife's voice, telling him that danger lay in his path. Returning quickly to the house, he found his wife there. Clara and Henry verified her statement that she did not leave the room. Although the others soon dismissed the incident from their minds, it preyed on the already melancholy Wieland to the exclusion of everything else.

Not long after that incident, Henry learned that Wieland inherited some large estates in Europe, and he wanted Wieland to go abroad to claim them. Henry would accompany his friend because he had left his heart with a baroness, now widowed and willing to accept his suit. When Wieland seemed reluctant to make the journey, Henry, in an effort to persuade him, asked him one night to go for a walk. Their walk was interrupted by a voice telling them that the baroness was dead. Again, the voice was Catharine's, but again Catharine was nowhere near the men when the voice was heard. More frightening was the verification of the baroness's death given to Henry a few days later. Some dread supernatural power, Wieland believed, spoke to them.

Shortly after these mysterious occurrences, a stranger appeared in the neighborhood. He was dressed like a clown or a pathetically humorous beggar, but his voice had the musical ring of an actor. Clara, who saw him before the others knew of his existence, was strangely drawn to him. She forgot him, however, because of another frightening incident. One night, alone in her room, she heard two voices in the closet planning her murder. One voice advised shooting, the other, choking. She fled to her brother's house and fell at his door in a faint. Wieland and Henry came to her rescue in answer to a summons from an unknown source, a voice calling that a loved one lay dying at the door.

Henry insisted upon occupying a vacant apartment in Clara's home to protect her from her unknown enemies. Clara was beset with nightmares, the mystifying voice warning her of danger from her brother. Soon after the affair of the voices in the closet, she met the stranger she had seen and to whom she was unaccountably drawn. His name was Carwin, and he had known Henry in Spain. His intelligent conversation and his wide travels made him welcome in the little group, and he joined them frequently. When they discussed the supernatural voices they all heard, Carwin dismissed the voices as fancy or pranks.

Clara, beginning to feel herself in love with Henry, believed that he returned her love but feared to tell her of it because he did not know her feelings. Then he confronted her with the accusation that she was a wanton. He said that he heard her and a lover, Carwin, talking and that her words made her a sinner and a fallen woman. Henry also learned that Carwin was wanted for murder, and he heaped abuses on the innocent Clara for consorting with such a man. All of her pleas of innocence went unheeded, and she was thrown into despair. Thinking that Carwin set out to ruin her, she was enraged when she received a note in which he asked for an interview. Reluctantly, she agreed to meet him and hear his story. He was to come to her home, but when she arrived there she found only a note warning her of a horrible sight awaiting her. In her room, she found Catharine on the bed, murdered.

Wieland entered her room, his manner strange and exulted, and begged that this sacrifice not be demanded of him. Before he reached Clara, however, others came into the house. From them she learned that her brother's children were also dead, killed by the same hand that murdered their mother.

Clara was taken by friends to the city. There, after a time, she learned the tragic story. The murderer was Wieland, his hand guided, he said, by a voice from heaven demanding that he sacrifice his loved ones to God. He felt no guilt, only glory at having been the instrument through whom God worked. Twice Wieland broke out of prison, his belief being that he must also kill Clara and Henry. Clara suspected that Carwin somehow influenced Wieland to kill.

Carwin went to Clara and protested his innocence. He admitted that his was the other voices heard. He was a ventriloquist who used his tricks either to play some prank or to escape detection while prying into other people's affairs. Clara refused to believe him. While they talked, Wieland entered the apartment. Prepared to kill Clara, he again broke out of prison to fulfill his bloody destiny. This time Carwin, using his skill to save Clara, called out to Wieland that no voice told him to kill, that only his own lunatic brain guided him. At his words, Wieland regained his sanity and seemed to understand for the first time what he did. Picking up a knife, he plunged it into his throat.

Three years passed before Clara knew peace. Her uncle cared for her and arranged a meeting between Carwin and Henry so that Carwin might confess his part in the defamation of Clara's character. Carwin was jealous and thus tried to destroy Henry's affection for her. Henry also learned that his baroness was not dead; the report was another of Carwin's tricks. Henry married the baroness and settled down near Boston. Carwin, not a murderer but the victim of a plot, escaped to the country and became a farmer. Henry's wife died soon after their marriage, and he and Clara renewed their love. Their later happiness was marred only by sad and tragic memories.

Critical Evaluation:

Wieland was the first gothic novel written and published in America. Gothic fiction, a genre popular in Europe (especially England and Germany), had its inception in Horace Walpole's *The Castle of Otranto* (1765). In the tradition of the romance, the gothic novel offers an outlet for its readers' emotions—particularly fear. Characterized by ghosts, goblins, and supernatural occurrences, gothic tales take place in such places as ruined cathedrals and crumbling mansions. Their usual theme is the restoration of a usurped inheritance to its rightful heir. Although the earlier gothic authors presented supernatural phenomena as objective realities, later writers tended to present the supernatural as perhaps the result of imagination or of sensory delusion.

In *Wieland*, Charles Brown develops and Americanizes the gothic novel by adapting its theme, setting, and purpose. Unlike its predecessors, the work does not center on acquiring a European patrimony. Although Theodore Wieland, Jr., falls heir to lands in Lusatia, he has no desire to claim his holdings in the old country. He prefers to stay in America, where life is stable and familiar.

Rather than setting his novel in an archaic building, Brown has the story take place in a rural region in eastern Pennsylvania. Clara's house is situated on a rugged river bank; the temple sits atop a cliff; and the summer house rests in a rocky crevice near a waterfall. These places are beautiful, and their wild isolation lends them an eeriness suggesting the presence of sprites. In selecting a natural site, Brown began a trend for other American writers, such as Washington Irving and William Cullen Bryant, who emphasized the appeal of nature.

Earlier gothic writers supplied rational explanations for mysterious phenomena, but Brown went a step further in *Wieland* by suggesting that the degree of one's belief in the supernatural derives from one's psychological makeup. That is, some people are predisposed toward the paranormal as a result of childhood memories, their innate psychic status, and their religion. When the elder Wieland undergoes his horrendous experience in the temple, Clara is six. Clara later admits that her father's tragedy left an indelible impression, causing her to ponder the existence of divine intervention. Consequently, she is open to the possibility of supernatural machination when she hears the mysterious voices.

In addition to early experience, one's inherent mental and emotional balance may account for one's receptivity to the supernatural. Clara describes her brother as a brilliant but somber man who never laughs. This signals the reader that he is imbalanced and on the verge of disaster. Since Wieland's temperament is so dark and attuned to gloom, it is not surprising that he should hear a voice telling him to destroy his family, the source of his joy. Clara, on the other hand, is more carefree. It seems significant that although both brother and sister hear voices, Clara's injunctions ("Hold, hold!") are protective while Wieland's voice is destructive.

Brown begins his story with Clara's account of her father's fanaticism. The author thus foreshadows Wieland's insanity. It is possible that the younger Wieland's madness is augmented by religion as well as heredity. Although he and Clara are raised without religion, they seem not to have escaped the traces of Puritanism and Calvinism permeating their culture. The emphasis that these faiths place on the sinfulness of earthly happiness may have convinced Wieland—already predisposed to gloom and tragedy—that his family afforded him too much joy and must therefore be annihilated.

As well as presenting the issue of psychological predisposition, Brown treats the issue of moral responsibility. In *Wieland*, responsibility for the most part is assigned to the individual level. For example, Carwin uses his ventriloquism only to remove himself from embarrassing situations. Nevertheless, he is indirectly and partially responsible for Wieland's tragic act. Had Wieland not been accustomed to hearing inexplicable voices, he might not have heard the command to sacrifice his family.

Brown also uses his novel to portray eccentricities of human nature. Unlike earlier gothic characters—simplistic figures representing shades of vice and virtue—Clara and Carwin are complex and real. Although Clara is a learned and independent woman, she seems to have no life of her own. She centers her activities entirely on her brother and his wife. Her fascination with Carwin appears to be her first attraction to the opposite sex. Despite her outward contentment, it seems possible that inwardly she aches for a love of her own and easily mistakes Henry's friendship for romantic attachment. Her lonely life removed her from reality.

Carwin exemplifies those persons who set out to test and to undo one whose integrity they envy. In counterfeiting a dialogue between two murderers, for example, he intends to test Clara's alleged courage, to see whether she will run or stay to protect her servant. Carwin also simulates Clara's voice to delude Henry regarding her virtue. Confounding Henry, in Carwin's words, is the "sweetest triumph" over this man of "cold reserves and exquisite sagacity."

Brown's style is erudite and his dialogue stilted. Nevertheless, his story sustains readers' curiosity. Creating a gothic thriller, however, does not seem to have been Brown's sole purpose. In addition to presenting the intrigue of the voices, he subtly introduces themes of psychology, morality, and society.

"Critical Evaluation" by Rebecca Stingley Hinton

Further Reading

Barnard, Philip, Stephen Shapiro, and Mark L. Kamrath, eds. *Revising Charles Brockden Brown: Culture, Politics, and Sexuality in the Early Republic*. Knoxville: University of Tennessee Press, 2004. A collection of thirteen essays on various aspects of Brown's works, placing them within the context of the political and ideological issues of his time, questions of gender and sexuality, and the culture of the Enlightenment.

Christopherson, Bill. *The Apparition in the Glass: Charles Brockden Brown's American Gothic*. Athens: University of Georgia Press, 1993. Chapter 2 provides a good discussion of the American romance, while a separate chapter is devoted to *Wieland*.

Jones, Howard Mumford. *Belief and Disbelief in American Literature*. Chicago: University of Chicago Press, 1967. Discusses the religious ideologies characterizing American thought from the colonial era to the twentieth century. Cites specific writers, including Brown. Explains eighteenth century rationalism and its coexistence with Calvinistic guilt.

Kafer, Peter. *Charles Brockden Brown's Revolution and the Birth of American Gothic*. Philadelphia: University of Pennsylvania Press, 2004. Focusing on *Wieland*, Kafer explains how Brown adapted the European gothic novel into a purely American genre. Describes the social and political influences on Brown's work.

MacAndrew, Elizabeth. *The Gothic Tradition in Fiction*. New York: Columbia University Press, 1979. Maintains that from the inception of the gothic novel, authors consciously employed symbolic elements and sought to educate their readers in the workings of the mind. Claims that the infusion of psychology into literature derived from the interest generated by the studies of eighteenth century thinker John Locke.

Punter, David. *The Literature of Terror*. New York: Longman, 1980. Treats the relationship between the eighteenth century novel and the philosophy of rationalism. The chapter on early American gothic fiction discusses Brown's contribution regarding the effects of heredity and Puritanism on one's psychological composition.

Ringe, Donald A. *American Gothic: Imagination and Reason in Nineteenth Century Fiction*. Lexington: University Press of Kentucky, 1982. Recounts the characteristics of gothic fiction, and discusses the psychological and moral insight Brown brings to his writing.

Thompson, G. R., ed. *The Gothic Imagination: Essays in Dark Romanticism*. Pullman: Washington State University Press, 1974. Argues that gothic literature is directly descended from the Gothic architecture of the Middle Ages. A chapter on religious terror in the gothic novel describes *Wieland*'s perception of grace.

The Wild Ass's Skin

Author: Honoré de Balzac (1799-1850)
First published: La Peau de chagrin, 1831 (English translation, 1896)
Type of work: Novel
Type of plot: Allegory
Time of plot: Early nineteenth century
Locale: Paris

Principal characters:
RAPHAEL DE VALENTIN, the hero
PAULINE, his wife
FOEDORA, a countess loved by Raphael
RASTIGNAC and ÉMILE, Raphael's friends

The Story:

In a poor quarter of Paris, Raphael de Valentin walks hesitantly into a gaming room. Inside are the usual raffish hoodlums. To them, the young man appears marked for mischance. Raphael plays his last coin on a turn of the wheel and loses.

Resolved to commit suicide, he wanders to the Seine. For a time, he leans over the parapet of the Pont Royal and looks at the cold water below. Only the thought of the paid rescuers keeps him from jumping. He finally seeks shelter in an antique shop, where he poses as a customer. The proprietor, a wizened old man, takes him upstairs and shows him a piece of shagreen, or untanned animal skin, on which are engraved words in Sanskrit telling the power of the skin. The possessor of the skin will get anything he or she wishes for, but, in return, the wisher's life will belong to the talisman, and he or she will die when the skin, shrinking with each wish, dwindles to nothingness.

Despite the antique dealer's warning, Raphael recklessly takes the piece of skin and wishes for a great banquet furnished with much wine, carousing companions, and ladies of light virtue. As he leaves the shop, he meets his friends Rastignac and Émile, two penniless adventurers. They have a great scheme in mind for him—he is to be the editor of a new periodical backed by a rich banker. To celebrate the appointment, the banker is giving a banquet in Raphael's honor that very evening. Disquieted only a little by the prompt and complete granting of his wish, Raphael goes willingly enough to the banquet.

A rich table is laid in the banker's apartment. After eating and drinking far too much, the company of men withdraw to another room, where a group of joyous ladies are waiting for them. In his somewhat drunken state, Raphael thinks that the women all look pure and beautiful. Settling himself with two complaisant entertainers and Émile, Raphael decides to tell them the story of how he has come to be where he is.

After his mother's death, his rather stern father did his best to train his son for a scholarly career. The boy was destined to be a lawyer, and to that end he read law diligently. Shortly before he was to take a law degree, however, his father died. Instead of leaving the son financially secure, the estate amounted to only a few francs. Thinking to achieve a fortune, Raphael decided to shut himself up in a garret and produce literary works of genius. He found that by living strictly on cold meat, bread, and milk, he would have enough money for a while.

He found a cheap room under the eaves of a modest house and settled into his laborious routine of writing. Soon, he had begun his projects. He spent half of his time writing a comedy, and the rest of his efforts went into the composition of a discourse on the human will. The family from whom he rented his room consisted of a mother, Madame Gaudin, and her young daughter, Pauline. The father, an army captain, had been lost in Siberia; only his wife believed him still alive. Pauline was an attractive child. Raphael gave her piano lessons, and Pauline performed small household chores for him in return.

For a long time, Raphael stuck to his spartan schedule, but at last the poor diet and the effort of intense concentration proved too much for him to endure. He went out for a short walk one day and ran into Rastignac, who teased him about the way he lived. Rastignac had no money and many bills, yet he lived a life of luxury. Resourceful at finding jobs, he secured a hack writing commission for Raphael. The advance payment was enough to settle Raphael's debts and to leave a little extra money.

After faithfully paying his account with Pauline's mother, Raphael took his remaining capital to Rastignac, who was to gamble with it. Fortunately, Rastignac won a large sum. Raphael bought new clothes before Rastignac took him to see the Countess Foedora, who entertained lavishly. Since he was a well-educated man, Raphael was soon a favorite at Foedora's salons, and by hook or crook he managed to keep up appearances so as to stay in her circle of close friends. He even took Foedora driving when he had the money. Pauline, ever the faithful friend, occasionally gave him small sums to see him through the times when he had little money.

Foedora was a woman of mystery. She was a young widow, wealthy and surrounded by admirers. Some dark secret in her past, however, kept her from marrying again or even taking a lover. Although she had many male friends, she had no inclination for a serious affair. She finally explained her attitude very clearly to Raphael, who was very disappointed.

Determined to win his lady, he hid behind her bed one evening and waited while Foedora prepared herself for sleep. From this close observation, Raphael romantically expected to learn how to break down her reserve. The effort, however, was in vain. Convinced at last that he could not win Foedora, Raphael gave up his social life; not even Pauline could console him. Without funds and with no prospects, he began to think of suicide.

As he finishes telling this story, Raphael notices that Émile and the women are not seriously interested; Émile even jokes about his trials and discomfiture. Soon everyone in the company falls into drunken sleep. When they all awake, Raphael is disgusted at the tawdry appearance of his fellow rioters. Going back to the banquet table, he tells of his piece of skin and, in a spirit of bravado, wishes for six million francs. Before he leaves the table, a messenger arrives to announce the death of Raphael's mother's brother; the dead man has bequeathed his nephew six million francs. Even though he is elated by his good fortune, Raphael is disturbed to see that the magic skin is growing smaller.

Riches bring no peace to Raphael. Although he now lives in greatest luxury, he also lives in fear. He constantly has to guard against any desires, as even inadvertent wishes shrink the magic skin.

One night at the opera, he sees Foedora again. Leaning aside so that she will not see him, he brushes against his neighbor. As he turns to apologize, he discovers that the woman beside him is Pauline Gaudin. She is now wealthy, for her father has returned with a fortune. Raphael and Pauline are soon married, and for a few weeks Raphael knows a little happiness.

Because the skin continues to shrink steadily, Raphael decides to take stern measures. He shows the skin to a zoologist, who informs him that it is a piece of skin from a rare, wild Persian ass. Then he visits a mechanic and has him try to stretch the skin in a press, but to no avail. Even in a white hot forge, the skin remains cool and pliable. A chemist tries immersing the wild ass's skin in hydrofluoric acid, but the skin will still not stretch.

With his health failing fast, Raphael leaves his bride to seek safety in the mountains. The change of air does him no good, however, and his condition grows steadily worse. One day a braggart challenges him to a duel. Raphael accepts, knowing bitterly that his unspoken wish will make him the victor. After shooting his opponent in the heart, he flees back to Paris with his magic skin, which is now no larger than an oak leaf.

Although Raphael consults the best doctors available, they give him no comfort or help. They can scarcely believe his story of the skin, yet they can find no cause for his grave illness. At last he lies dying. Wanting to have Pauline near him but knowing that his desire will consume the last shred of the magic skin, he asks her to leave him. As he calls her name, she sees the skin growing smaller. In despair, she rushes into the next room and tries to kill herself by knotting a scarf around her neck. The dying man totters after her, and as he tears away the scarf, he tries vainly to utter a final wish, but no words will come. He dies while holding her in that last, desperate embrace.

Critical Evaluation:

The Wild Ass's Skin is the first volume of the sprawling sequence of novels known as *La Comédie humaine*, or *The Human Comedy*, which occupied Honoré de Balzac between 1829 and 1848. The French title, *La Peau de chagrin*, embodies an untranslatable pun, in that the name of the material of which the magical object is made (equivalent to the English shagreen) also carries the meaning that crosses directly into English in the word "chagrin": a kind of vexation that grates continually and tortuously on the mind. When Raphael has acquired his talisman, he invites his friend Émile to bear witness to "how my chagrin will shrink"—and so it does, in both senses of the word. Unfortunately for Raphael, the shrinkage

of the skin quickly reaches the point at which his own state of mind acquires a new and much sharper desperation; the temporary banishment of his chagrin merely serves to clear the way for a more profound and inescapable regret.

Balzac is famous as one of the boldest pioneers of narrative realism, and there are descriptive passages in *The Wild Ass's Skin* that are closely observed studies of life in contemporary Paris, foreshadowing the naturalistic triumphs to come in literature. Before this, however, Balzac had written a number of pseudonymous thrillers heavily influenced by gothic tales of terror, and he understood well enough the imaginative power exerted by such motifs as the diabolical bargain. In bringing such a motif out of the quasi-medieval settings favored by the gothic novelists and planting it firmly in contemporary Paris, he was helping to pave the way for a distinctly modern kind of horror story as well as recruiting a useful allegorical device.

Like any modern hero would, Raphael looks to science for assistance when the power of his magic is exhausted, but science cannot help him; he has surrendered his soul to the judgment of superstition and must accept its cruel verdict. This is the fear that haunts all modern tales of unease: that knowing the truth might not be enough if there is some deeper and darker region of the mind that cannot and will not admit it. The juxtaposition of the gothic and the realistic in Balzac's allegory thus anticipates later ideas regarding the uneasy relationship between the conscious and the unconscious minds, the one being unsafely held by reason and the other, unconquerably, by desire.

The final section of the book is called "The Agony" not so much because of the depth of Raphael's anguish—*agonie* in French signifies a struggle against death rather than excruciating pain—as because of the way in which he is fatally divided against himself. No matter how anxious he becomes to preserve the skin by conserving his demands, he is helpless to prevent it from wasting away; he is not the master of his own desires, and his uncontrollable appetites destroy him by degrees. Such, Balzac implies, is the fate of anyone who cannot control his or her lusts. Pauline's attempts to help Raphael serve only to prove to him that had he adopted a realistic view of his own potential and made a life with her much sooner, instead of chasing after the deceptive Foedora, he would have done far better in the long run.

To some extent, this message must be construed as an attack on the bourgeois materialism that Balzac affected to hate and despise (in himself as well as in others), but the allegory is not simply political. It cuts much deeper than that, to the root causes of human envy and human unhappiness. When Balzac wrote it, he had only just begun to accumulate the debts that were to burden him for the rest of his life, and he had only recently introduced into his name the fanciful "de" that laid false claim to an aristocratic heritage; even so, he clearly had an anxious understanding of where such pretentious follies might eventually lead him.

The motif of wish fulfillment in *The Wild Ass's Skin* is obvious. Raphael is an ambitious writer who divides his time between a comedy and a study of the will; his tempter, Rastignac, initially bribes him away from these endeavors with commissions for vulgar hackwork, then seduces him into reckless gambling. Had he been left to his own devices, Raphael might still have been inclined to make a Faustian bargain with the devil, offering his soul for an enlightenment that might have made his work brilliant, but under Rastignac's influence the treasures he claims are far more transitory. In real life, Balzac had it both ways; he obtained the transitory delights and a reputation as a man of considerable insight and ability, one of the great chroniclers of his age. Raphael de Valentin would doubtless have envied him, but the author of *The Wild Ass's Skin* might well have felt fully entitled to say to his later self, "I told you so."

"Critical Evaluation" by Brian Stableford

Further Reading

Bloom, Harold, ed. *Honoré de Balzac.* Philadelphia: Chelsea House, 2003. Collection of essays on some of Balzac's individual novels includes "Epigrams and Ministerial Eloquence: The War of Words in Balzac's *La Peau de chagrin*," by David F. Bell. Other essays discuss topics such as Balzac's creation of a fictional universe and his use of narrative doubling.

Garval, Michael D. "Honoré de Balzac: Writing the Monument." In *"A Dream of Stone": Fame, Vision, and Monumentality in Nineteenth-Century French Literary Culture.* Newark: University of Delaware Press, 2004. Chapter on Balzac is part of a volume that describes how France in the nineteenth century developed an ideal image of "great" writers, viewing these authors' work as immortal and portraying their literary successes in monumental terms. The work as a whole traces the rise and fall of this literary development by focusing on Balzac, George Sand, and Victor Hugo.

Madden, James. *Weaving Balzac's Web: Spinning Tales and Creating the Whole of "La Comédie humaine."* Birmingham, Ala.: Summa, 2003. Explores how Balzac structured his vast series of novels to create continuity both within and between the individual books. Describes how internal narration, in which characters tell each other stories about other characters, enables the recurring characters to provide layers of meaning that are evident throughout the series.

Pritchett, V. S. *Balzac.* 1973. Reprint. London: Vintage Books, 2002. Beautifully illustrated book by an eminent writer and literary critic enables readers to understand the milieu in which Balzac wrote. Presents an interpretation of *The Wild Ass's Skin* that is especially thought-provoking.

Robb, Graham. *Balzac: A Life.* New York: W. W. Norton, 1994. Detailed biographical account of the life and work of Balzac focuses on his philosophical perspectives as well as on his fiction and speculates on the psychological motivations underlying his work. *The Wild Ass's Skin* is discussed in chapter 8, "Absolute Power."

Testa, Carlo. *Desire and the Devil: Demonic Contracts in French and European Literature.* New York: Peter Lang, 1991. Section titled "Balzac's Laicized Demonism" presents a detailed analysis of *The Wild Ass's Skin.*

Weber, Samuel. *Unwrapping Balzac: A Reading of "La Peau de chagrin."* Toronto, Ont.: University of Toronto Press, 1979. Provides a close examination of the novel from a psychoanalytic viewpoint.

The Wild Duck

Author: Henrik Ibsen (1828-1906)
First produced: *Vildanden*, 1884; first published, 1885
   (English translation, 1891)
Type of work: Drama
Type of plot: Social realism
Time of plot: Nineteenth century
Locale: Norway

Principal characters:
WERLE, a wealthy industrialist
GREGERS WERLE, his son
OLD EKDAL, Werle's former partner
HJALMAR EKDAL, his son
GINA EKDAL, Hjalmar's wife
HEDVIG, their daughter
RELLING, a doctor

The Story:

Gregers Werle, the son of a rich industrialist and a sensitive, high-minded mother, early in life develops a loathing for the unscrupulous means his father uses to amass his fortune. After his mother's death, young Gregers leaves his father's house for a time, but he eventually returns. His father, hoping to persuade his son to accept a partnership in the business, gives a large dinner party to which Gregers invites a thirteenth guest, his old school friend, Hjalmar Ekdal. This act displeases his father very much because Hjalmar does not belong in the Werles' social set and because he is the son of a former business partner old Werle wronged. The older Ekdal now holds a menial position in Werle's employ, to which he was reduced after a term in prison broke his mind and spirit.

Gregers is aware that his father's machinations sent Ekdal to prison after a scandal in which both were involved, and he hated his father for this injury to his friend's father. He discovers also that the older Werle arranged a marriage between Hjalmar and Gina Hansen, a former maid in the Werle household and, Gregers suspected, his father's mistress. Gregers is therefore displeased both at his father's offer of a partnership and at his father's forthcoming marriage to Mrs. Sorby, his housekeeper. Gregers announces that his future mission in life is to open Hjalmar's eyes to the lie he has been living for the past fifteen years.

The Ekdal home is shabby. Werle set Hjalmar up as a photographer after marrying him to Gina, but it is really Gina who runs the business while her husband works on an invention he hopes will enable his aged father to recoup some of his fortune. Old Ekdal himself, now practically out of his mind, spends most of his time in a garret where he keeps a curious assortment of animals. Ekdal believes that the garret is a forest like the one in which he hunted as a young man. He occasionally shoots a rabbit up there, and on holidays and special occasions he appears before the family dressed in his old military uniform.

Although based almost entirely on self-deception and illusion, the Ekdal home is a happy one. Gina takes good care of her husband, Hedvig, their fourteen-year-old daughter, and Hjalmar's father. Hedvig is very dear to both Hjalmar and Gina, who keep from her the fact that she is rapidly losing her eyesight. Gregers is shocked when he sees the Ekdals' home. Old Ekdal shows him Hedvig's prize possession, a wild duck that Werle's father once shot and wounded; the duck dived to the bottom of the water, but Werle's dog retrieved it. Gregers sees himself as the clever dog destined to bring the Ekdal family out of their straitened circumstances.

To accomplish his end, he rents a room from the Ekdals, though Gina is unwilling to let him have it. She is not the only one to resent his presence in the house. Dr. Relling, another roomer, knows Gregers and is aware of his reputation for meddling in the affairs of others. He agrees that Gregers is the victim of a morbid conscience, probably derived from his hysterical mother. Hjalmar, in his innocence, sees nothing amiss in his friend's behavior and allows him to stay.

Gregers sets about the task of rehabilitating his friend in a systematic way. He discovers that the family is supported by the older Werle and not, as Hjalmar supposed, by the photographic studio. More important, the coincidence of Hedvig's progressive blindness and Werle's father's weak eyesight makes Werle suspect that Hjalmar is not the child's natural father. During a long walk he takes with Hjalmar, Gregers tries to open his friend's eyes to his true position in his own house; he tells him everything he discovers except his suspicion of Hedvig's illegitimacy.

Having no real integrity or resources within himself, Hjalmar falls into all the clichés of stories he read about the behavior of wronged husbands. He demands an accounting from Gina of all the money Werle paid into the household, and he asserts that every cent should be paid back out of the proceeds from his hypothetical invention. His outburst does nothing but disturb Gina and frighten Hedvig. Hjalmar's pride might have been placated and the whole matter straight-ened out had not a letter arrived from old Werle, who is giving Hedvig a small annuity. Hjalmar announces that Hedvig is no child of his and that he wants nothing more to do with her. Hedvig is heartbroken at her father's behavior, and Gregers, beginning to realize the consequences of his meddling, persuades the girl that her one hope of winning back her father's love is to sacrifice for his sake the thing she loves most. He urges her to have her grandfather kill the wild duck.

Gina succeeds in convincing Hjalmar that he is quite helpless without her. They are discussing their plans for the future when they hear a shot. At first they think old Ekdal is firing at his rabbits, but it is Hedvig, who, in her despair, puts a bullet through her breast.

Critical Evaluation:

The Wild Duck is one of Henrik Ibsen's most important problem plays. From the time of its first appearance, it captured audiences and readers with its vitality and universality. Ibsen, known as the founder of modern drama, achieved this recognition over tremendous obstacles, not the least of which was that he wrote in a little-known language. Born into a provincial milieu in Norway, Ibsen suffered early poverty and hardships, including poor education. In 1851, he became the assistant manager of the Bergen Theater, studied stage production abroad, and in the next six years gained invaluable practical theatrical experience by putting into production 145 plays. By the time he started writing his own plays, he had a knowledge of the theater and its literature matched by very few playwrights.

In *Et dukkehjem* (1879; *A Doll's House*, 1880), *Gengangere* (1881; *Ghosts*, 1885), *En folkefiende* (1882; *An Enemy of the People*, 1890), *The Wild Duck*, and *Hedda Gabler* (1890; English translation, 1891), Ibsen introduced realism to the stage and established it so overwhelmingly that it became the dominant approach to the stage throughout the twentieth and twenty-first centuries. Ibsen substituted middle-class protagonists for kings and queens and wrote prose dialogue rather than poetry, stating that "My plays . . . are not tragedies in the old meaning of the word; what I have wanted to portray is human beings and that is just why I did not want them to speak the language of the gods." He introduced detailed stage directions to authenticate the background scene, and he approached his characterizations with a desire to reveal them to the audience almost scientifically, thus incorporating his age's new discoveries of the importance of instincts, biology, heredity, and environment. In his plot innovation, he dispensed with the intrigue and trickery of then popular "well-made plays." While maintaining his skillful manipulation of plot, he ended each act with strong, theatrical curtain scenes.

Some of his innovations—as in his extensive use of light-dark imagery; his pervasive irony; his elimination of all events antecedent to the critical situation; and his use of the unities of time, place, and action—reveal his study of Greek tragedy.

The Wild Duck marked Ibsen's turning away from realistic problem plays. From that time on his plays were complex, enigmatic studies of the human condition, and they employed expressionistic and symbolic techniques. *The Wild Duck* reflects some of his most important preoccupations. These include the presentness of the past; man's search for his true identity and place in life; the effects of idealism as a social force; the conflict of reality and illusion; and the problem of man's ultimate freedom. Ibsen himself said that the critics would "find plenty to quarrel about, plenty to interpret" in this play.

The key to the universality of the play lies in the complexity of the strong, well-rounded characters. A lesser playwright would have settled, for example, for making old Werle the villain of a melodrama. Ibsen, instead, presents his human complexity. Gregers, the son, sees the elder Werle as an unredeemable villain who ruined old Ekdal, made his housemaid pregnant, and then foisted her off on the unsuspecting son of Ekdal. Hjalmar Ekdal, however, describing what old Werle did for him and his family, sees him as a fairy godfather. The truth in Ibsen, as in life, lies somewhere in between—perhaps in old Werle's espousal of "the attainable ideal." Gina Ekdal, too, moves far beyond the stereotype of the fallen woman redeemed by marriage. It is Gina's work on the photographs and her sewing, her concern for practicalities and the welfare of Hedvig and her husband, that keep the family going and enable Hjalmar to indulge in his dreams.

The two major characters, Gregers and Hjalmar, are even more complex. Both men see themselves as intellectually and morally superior to all around them; both are judged by the audience as self-indulgent, egocentric men with no true sympathy or love for others, not even their own family. Both wish to attain truth, but both harbor illusions about the nobility and goodness of their actions. Gregers admires Hjalmar as the most gifted and intelligent of his schoolmates, yet Ibsen characterizes his intelligence as that of a photographer and speech writer, not of an artistic creator. Gregers lacks the moral strength to stop his father from trapping Ekdal; Hjalmar lacks the courage to commit suicide as he claims to wish to do; both men fail to face their responsibility in the death of Hedvig. However, Ibsen does not dismiss the quest for truth out of hand but shows instead the ambiguity and complexity of the undertaking.

Dramatic irony is an important device throughout the

play. Gregers, who ends up destroying a home and contributes to the suicide of a young girl, earlier accuses his father of leaving things like "a battlefield strewn with broken lives." Hjalmar remarks that happiness is home, just as Gregers knocks on his door to bring the information that will help destroy that happiness and that home. Many of the ironic reverberations are connected with the sense of sight. Those who are blind—old Werle and Hedvig—often see more clearly than those who have good physical vision. Like Oedipus, Gregers and Hjalmar are metaphorically blind to the real truth of their human condition. Unlike Oedipus, however, they never face the truth and thus remain in darkness at the end of the play. Ibsen also employs light and dark imagery in the set and the dialogue: Act 1 begins in brightness and candle glow, but the other acts grow ever darker and act 5 ends cold and gray.

The title of the play carries the complexity of meanings with it. The duck, wounded by old Werle, is saved and trapped. Relling sees it as a symbol of all people who are wounded while attempting to live in this world. Hedvig associates the duck with herself, wounded and unable to fly yet happy to stay at home in that created world. Old Werle connects the duck with old Ekdal, who is unable to live in reality. Gregers at one time sees himself as the dog who rescues the duck from drowning in the sea of lies and illusions; later he identifies with the duck; still later, he suggests the identification of Hedvig with the duck. The duck's world is a surrogate for the real forest in which, with its clipped wings, it can no longer live. The family questions whether the duck can adapt; they decide that as long as it cannot see the real sky, it can survive unconscious of its trapped condition. The sky, associated with light and freedom and the natural state of bird and man, is thus juxtaposed with the darkness of Ekdal's attic, the unnatural state that humans create for themselves. Old and young Ekdal are capable only of hunting tamed or disabled animals in their artificial forest and are as unable as the duck to survive in the real world.

"Critical Evaluation" by Ann E. Reynolds

Further Reading

Caputi, Anthony, ed. *Eight Modern Plays*. 2d ed. New York: W. W. Norton, 1991. Dounia B. Christiani's translation of *The Wild Duck* is supplemented with excerpts from Ibsen's letters and speeches and two chapters from books by M. C. Bradbrook and Dorothea Krook. Bradbook's contribution explains how the play works on different levels simultaneously, and Krook remarks on the subtlety of Ibsen's theme of self-deception. Caputi's foreword provides an excellent introduction to Ibsen and twentieth century drama.

Clurman, Harold. *Ibsen*. New York: Macmillan, 1977. An introductory study that provides the general reader with a good starting place for reading about Ibsen. Clurman, a renowned stage director, comments with sensitivity on the plays as both theater and literature. Includes an instructive discussion of *The Wild Duck*, which concludes that Gregers's zealotry leads him to misjudge Hjalmar's essentially mundane nature.

Fjelde, Rolf, ed. *Ibsen: A Collection of Critical Essays*. Englewood Cliffs, N.J.: Prentice-Hall, 1965. Sixteen essays cover, among other topics, Ibsen's conception of truth, realism, and stage craftsmanship. Robert Raphael discusses the theme of self-deception in *The Wild Duck* and two other Ibsen plays.

Goldman, Michael. *Ibsen: The Dramaturgy of Fear*. New York: Columbia University Press, 1999. Analyzes dialogue, plot, and other elements of Ibsen's plays to demonstrate how he challenges his audience's opinions and expectations. Includes a discussion of *The Wild Duck*.

Lyons, Charles R., ed. *Critical Essays on Henrik Ibsen*. Boston: G. K. Hall, 1987. A thorough and useful volume of essays that address the ideology, realism, and dramatic form of Ibsen's plays. The remarks on *The Wild Duck* explore the play's structure, language, and exposition.

McFarlane, James, ed. *The Cambridge Companion to Ibsen*. New York: Cambridge University Press, 1994. A collection of sixteen newly written essays on Ibsen's life and work, which include discussions of Ibsen's working methods and the stage history of the plays. A helpful source.

Moi, Toril. "Losing Touch with the Everyday: Love and Language in *The Wild Duck*." In *Henrik Ibsen and the Birth of Modernism: Art, Theater, Philosophy*. New York: Oxford University Press, 2006. A reevaluation of Ibsen, in which Moi refutes the traditional definition of Ibsen as a realistic and naturalistic playwright and describes him as an early modernist.

Robinson, Michael, ed. *Turning the Century: Centennial Essays on Ibsen*. Norwich, England: Norvik Press, 2006. Collection of the essays published in the journal *Scandinavica* during the past four decades, including discussions of Ibsen's style, language, and the reception of his plays in England.

Templeton, Joan. *Ibsen's Women*. New York: Cambridge University Press, 1997. Templeton examines the women characters in Ibsen's plays and their relationship to the women in the playwright's life and career. Chapter 7 includes an analysis of *The Wild Duck*.

The Wild Geese

Author: Mori Ōgai (1862-1922)

First published: Gan, 1911-1913 (English translation, 1959)

Type of work: Novel

Type of plot: Psychological realism

Time of plot: 1880

Locale: Tokyo

Principal characters:

OKADA, a medical student

OTAMA, a beautiful and innocent girl

OTAMA'S FATHER

SUEZO, a moneylender

OTSUNE, Suezo's wife

The Story:

Okada, a medical student at Tokyo University, is viewed by his fellow students as an exceptionally balanced young man. A good student, an athlete, and a man who knows how to relax in his free time, he lives a well-ordered life free from any kind of obsession. When he is not studying, he likes to go for walks, and he often stops to browse in the local bookshops, looking for the historical romances that are his preferred reading.

Once, during his evening walk, Okada notices an attractive young woman entering a small house that seems to be an oasis of calm in a generally noisy neighborhood. He thinks little about it at the time, but when he passes the house two days later, he sees the woman in the window, and she smiles at him. After that, he always looks for her when he passes by and begins to feel that in some way he and she are friends. One evening, he spontaneously takes off his cap and bows to the woman, who smiles warmly in return. From then on, Okada bows to the woman whenever he passes her house.

The woman's name is Otama, and she is the daughter of a candy dealer who sells his wares from a stall. Otama's mother died giving birth to Otama, and the girl is being reared by her father, who adores her. She grows to be a beautiful, charming, and obedient young woman in whom it is difficult to find fault. Otama's father refuses various proposed matches for Otama because he does not want to lose his daughter, but ultimately he permits her to marry a police officer. The police officer forces the issue because he desires Otama, and the father is afraid to refuse the somewhat frightening prospective son-in-law. As it turns out, the police officer already has a wife and children, and Otama's marriage breaks up when that information comes to light. Although it is obvious to everyone that Otama did nothing wrong, the incident makes it almost a certainty that she will never receive a decent proposal of marriage.

A local man named Suezo learns of the disaster that befell Otama and her father. Suezo began his career as a servant working for medical students at Tokyo University. Most of his time was spent running errands for the students. Suezo, however, had no intention of remaining a servant all of his life, and he began to lend small amounts of money to students who were in need, making a small profit on each transaction. Over a long period of time, he becomes wealthy. He dresses in fine clothes and dreams of living in even greater comfort. As his financial status improves, Suezo becomes dissatisfied with his wife. Although she does a good job of caring for the children, Otsune is undeniably ugly and argumentative. Suezo begins to believe that he deserves the companionship of a better kind of woman. He tells himself that, since he never frequents geisha houses or wastes his money gambling, he has every right to indulge himself by having a mistress.

Remembering how beautiful Otama is and her skill in playing the samisen, Suezo decides that he will use a go-between to propose that Otama become his mistress. He knows that her prospects are limited, but he decides to improve his chances of success by concealing the fact that he is a usurer, since that means of livelihood is despised in Japan. He courts Otama and finally wins her by offering to provide generously for her father. The girl accepts his proposal primarily because she believes that it is her duty to see that her father will be cared for.

Suezo installs Otama, along with a maid, in the small house in which she lives when Okada first sees her. He also rents a house nearby for her father. All goes fairly well until Otama learns from a fish seller that Suezo is a usurer. She is upset that he tricked her, and she decides that she will never again be so trusting and naïve.

After Otama first sees Okada, she begins to fantasize about him, viewing him as a romantic savior. She tries to think of ways in which she can meet him. As she thinks more and more about Okada, Otama begins to be less attentive to Suezo, and even her father notices that she has changed. One day, Okada walks toward Otama's house and finds the place in an uproar. A snake crawled up the eaves of the house and into a cage that held two linnets that Suezo gave Otama. The snake kills one of the birds. A crowd of women and children gathers, and one of the women asks Okada to help. With the help of a young boy, Okada kills the snake before it can kill the other bird. Otama helps Okada wash the snake's blood from his hands, but, in spite of her desire to do so, she cannot bring herself to speak to him at length. After that, however, she begins to think about Okada even more.

Otama finally decides that she will speak to Okada when he passes by. For the occasion, she has her hair done and wears makeup, which is something she usually does not do. That evening, however, Okada is walking with a friend (the novel's narrator), and Otama is unable to speak to Okada. The friend notices that Okada is visibly disturbed at the sight of Otama, who looks even more beautiful than usual. Later, Okada and the narrator meet a friend, Ishihara, who points out some wild geese at the far end of a pond. Ishihara urges Okada to try to hit one of the geese with a stone, but Okada is reluctant to hurt the geese. Okada finally agrees to throw a stone because he knows that if he does not, Ishihara will attempt to kill one of the geese. Okada intends only to make the geese fly away, but his stone strikes and kills one of the birds. Ishihara later retrieves the goose, intending to cook and to eat it. The three students walk back to their boardinghouse, and Okada carries the dead goose under his cloak. When the trio come near Otama's house, they see her there waiting for Okada, but because Okada is with his friends, Otama is again unable to speak to him. She never has another opportunity to meet Okada. The next day, he travels to Germany, where he goes to work translating Chinese medical texts into German.

Critical Evaluation:

Mori Ōgai, one of Japan's most highly respected writers, was a member of the samurai class who studied Dutch and German and went to Germany to study medicine. In Germany, he was deeply influenced by the concern for the individual that is so much a part of Western culture. He became a lifelong advocate of logic and the scientific method, as well as a champion of Westernization in those areas—particularly those of scholarship and science—in which he believed the West to be superior to the East. At the same time, however, he believed that Japan had to retain what was unique and valuable in its own culture. He never proposed breaking with tradition unless he was convinced that tradition could be improved in some way.

Mori became known for the quality of his prose. He was thoroughly versed in literary Chinese as well as in Dutch and German, and his writing is that of the quintessential classicist. His work is clear, precise, and graceful, and it reflects the various traditions with which he was familiar. Although Mori never hesitated to deal with emotions, passions, and

controversial subjects (his novel *Vita Sexualis*, 1909, was banned because of its frank treatment of sexuality), he always believed that logic was more important than emotion. He was an Apollonian, rather than a Dionysian, artist.

One of the primary characteristics of Mori's work is its examination of the problems that arise in people's lives when their desires conflict with the demands made upon them by society. This is certainly true of Otama in *The Wild Geese*, who, as a woman in Meiji-era Japan, has little freedom to make choices in her life. She understands all too well that she is being badly treated through no fault of her own, but she continues to be bound by duty. She accedes to Suezo's wishes out of filial piety, so that her father can live out his remaining years in comfort. When she finally decides to rebel by making contact with Okada, she is thwarted because she is unable to overcome her fear of speaking to him when he is not alone. Societal constraints win out against the desires of the individual.

In the same way that Otama is hemmed in by society, so are Okada, Suezo, Otsune, and Otama's father. Okada makes no real move to meet Otama; instead, he simply bows to her so that he can continue to indulge in his own fantasies while keeping his distance. Perhaps he is afraid of the consequences of becoming involved with her; perhaps he is simply afraid of intimacy. It is certainly easier to deal with idealized female characters in Chinese romantic novels than it is to relate to a real woman with real desires and problems. Suezo, who is perhaps the most realistic character in the novel—he is certainly the most effective manipulator—is also bound by convention. His relatively uncomplicated life becomes problematic when he tries to keep a mistress while keeping his wife in the dark. His wife, Otsune, knows on some level that he is unfaithful, although he is able to confuse her with clever explanations whenever her accusations become too strident. She finally retreats into sullenness and passive aggression, which Suezo finds difficult to control. Otama's father is probably the weakest character in the novel. He turns down various marriage proposals in an attempt to keep his daughter to himself, only to have a strong, threatening man force himself upon Otama, thereby ruining her chances of having a good, socially acceptable marriage. (In fact, the only character in the novel who gets what he wants, if only temporarily, is the police officer, although there is no question that the author disapproves of his behavior.) Otama is finally destroyed by her situation and her powerlessness, just as the innocent goose is destroyed by Okada's unintentional act of violence.

It is clear that no one in the novel is free from the shackles of social demands and expectations, and Mori shows no way out for anyone. In fact, the author believed that people have to resign themselves to their positions in society. He himself gave in to societal pressure when he rejected the lover whom he had met in Germany. She followed him to Japan when he returned home, but he sent her away when his family and peers insisted that he marry within his class. Mori believed that society should be changed from within to accommodate more effectively the needs and desires of individuals, but he was unwilling to flout conventions that were still firmly in place.

In spite of its brevity and outward simplicity, *The Wild Geese* is a rich and complex work. Although it is a novel, it has the flavor of a fairy tale. Its symbolism is powerful and evocative, and it does not lend itself to clear-cut interpretation. There is, for example, no consensus regarding the symbolism of the linnets and the snake. Many widely divergent interpretations have been put forward. Ultimately, the power of the novel lies in its use of believable and sympathetic characters to portray the inherent sadness of the human condition.

Shawn Woodyard

Further Reading

Johnson, Eric W. "Ōgai's *The Wild Goose*." In *Approaches to the Modern Japanese Novel*, edited by Kinya Tsuruta and Thomas E. Swann. Tokyo: Sophia University Press, 1976. An excellent examination of the novel. Particularly good regarding the problem of the narrator and the difficulties of interpreting the novel's symbolism.

Kato, Shuichi. "The Age of Meiji." In *The Modern Years*, translated by Don Sanderson. Vol. 3 in *A History of Japanese Literature*. Tokyo: Kodansha International, 1979-1983. Contains a section that examines Mori's life and works. Provides interesting historical background.

Keene, Donald. "Mori Ōgai." In *Fiction*. Vol. 2 in *Dawn to the West: Japanese Literature in the Modern Era*. New York: Holt, Rinehart and Winston, 1984. A fine study of Mori by a foremost American expert on Japan. Includes a brief examination of *The Wild Geese*.

McDonald, Keiko I. "*The Wild Geese* Revisited: Mori Ōgai's Mix of Old and New." In *Inexorable Modernity: Japan's Grappling with Modernity in the Arts*, edited by Hiroshi Nara. Lanham, Md.: Lexington Books, 2007. Describes how the novel reflects the intermingling of Japanese tradition and Western concepts of modernity that occurred in the Meiji period. Analyzes the novel's depiction of Otama as reflecting the conflict between feudal ideas about women and the struggle for freedom in the "new" Japan.

Powell, Irena. "In Search of Logic and Social Harmony." In *Writers and Society in Modern Japan*. Tokyo: Kodansha International, 1983. Contains a brief but informative section on Mori and his work. Especially useful for placing the author and his work in a societal perspective.

Rimer, J. Thomas. *Mori Ōgai*. New York: Twayne, 1975. A thorough study of Mori's life and work that includes much information about *The Wild Geese*.

The Wild Palms

Author: William Faulkner (1897-1962)
First published: 1939
Type of work: Novel
Type of plot: Tragicomedy
Time of plot: 1927 and 1937
Locale: United States

Principal characters:
HARRY WILBOURNE, a twenty-seven-year-old medical intern
CHARLOTTE RITTENMEYER, a young married woman
FRANCIS "RAT" RITTENMEYER, her husband
THE TALL CONVICT, a man serving a ten-year term for train robbery
THE PALE CONVICT, his work partner in the flood
THE WOMAN, pregnant and stranded in the flood

The Story:

Old Man. There are two convicts. One is tall, lean, about twenty-five, with long Indian-black hair, who is serving prison time for a botched train robbery. The second convict is short, plump, and almost hairless, like something exposed when one turns over a rock or a log. The second convict is serving 139 years for his participation in a gas station robbery in which the attendant was killed, although probably not by the second convict. Both convicts are doing time at the

Mississippi State penal farm, which runs along the Mississippi. The river is flooding over its banks, forcing the evacuation of the prisoners.

The convicts are moved by truck, train, and boat, and everywhere they are surrounded by National Guard troops and by the muddy water of the rising river. The two convicts are provided with a skiff and told to pick up stranded farmers and their families. The short convict returns to the staging area alone and reports to the authorities that the boat overturned and that the tall convict disappeared beneath the water. The warden decides to list the tall convict as missing and presumed dead while trying to save lives; the tall convict served his time.

The tall convict in fact resurfaces. He manages to scramble back into the skiff but is unable to control it. He drifts for some time before he encounters a pregnant woman sitting in a tree. He tries to paddle upstream with her but at night they are swept downstream. They meet others who are stranded by the flood; the others refuse to give food and shelter to the convict and the woman. The convict also encounters some National Guard troops and tries to surrender, but they misunderstand and shoot at him. He flees. Finally, the two find higher ground and struggle ashore. The convict passes out.

By the time he revives, the woman has delivered her baby. They get back on the water and are picked up by a riverboat and taken farther south. They are left beside a levee. Taking to the water again, they are befriended by a Cajun, and the convict helps him hunt for alligators. The convict flees again, however, unable to tell the Cajun and the woman that the area is about to be flooded. All three are rescued again and evacuated to safety with other refugees. The convict surrenders himself, dressed in his cleaned prison uniform, to a sheriff's deputy.

A state official and the warden discuss the prisoner's case. Officially he is dead and therefore free; the young state official is afraid that the administrative mistake will be discovered. The warden points out that the prisoner turned himself in and that he even returned the skiff. To avoid declaring a mistake was made, the prisoner is nevertheless declared to have attempted escape and is given ten additional years to his sentence. The tall prisoner reunites with the short one, and the novel concludes with them talking about women and prison life, especially the tall one's extra ten years.

The Wild Palms. A young man calls on a local doctor to help an ailing woman. The doctor and his wife live next door, and they are intrigued by the couple but know nothing about them. The doctor has been speculating for days about the woman's condition, which he diagnoses in various ways. Before he is admitted to see her, he overhears the delirious rav-

ings of the woman; during these ravings, she calls the young man a "bloody bungling bastard."

The young man and the woman are Harry Wilbourne and Charlotte Rittenmeyer. Harry is an intern at New Orleans Hospital. He is an orphan who struggled through medical school on a two-thousand-dollar legacy left him by his doctor father. On the day he meets Charlotte, he turns twenty-seven, and his roommate lends him a suit and drags him to a party in the artist's quarter. Charlotte is a little older; she is married to Francis "Rat" Rittenmeyer and has two daughters. She immediately adopts Harry at the party and insists that he see her home. Harry and Charlotte begin to have lunch together; eventually, they seek out a hotel—but nothing happens. Soon they talk of escaping New Orleans together; the lack of money, however, prevents them from doing so. Then Harry finds a wallet containing more than a thousand dollars. He debates whether to turn it in, but, instead, they use the money to run away to Chicago. In a strange scene at the train station, Rat gives Harry a Pullman check for three hundred dollars to cover the costs of Charlotte's return ticket if she decides to come back to him. He also exacts a promise from Charlotte to write on the tenth of every month to let him know that she is all right; otherwise, he will send a detective after her. Finally, in a drawing room on the train, they consummate their love.

In Chicago, Charlotte finds an inexpensive apartment with a skylight; she can work at her art while Harry works. At first, Harry has difficulty finding a job, since he did not complete his internship, but he is eventually hired to do syphilis testing at a charity hospital in the Negro tenement district. Charlotte makes figurines which, initially, sell well in local department stores. Harry is fired, however, because Charlotte forgets to write Francis one month, and the detective contacts the hospital. Soon, Charlotte cannot sell her creations; to save money, the couple retreat to a cabin overlooking the lake in Wisconsin.

Here they live an idyllic life, swimming, sketching, and making love, until winter arrives, and their food runs out. They move back to the city; they live in a dreary, one-room efficiency apartment; and Charlotte takes a temporary holiday job dressing windows for a local store. When the job becomes permanent, Harry decides that they are becoming too much like a conventional, married couple, the very condition they once escaped. He takes a job as company doctor for a mining operation in the mountains of Utah; in February they leave Chicago.

In Utah, it is midwinter, and they are unprepared for the bitter cold and the isolation of the mountains. They meet the mine foreman and his wife, Buck and Billie Buckner, and learn that the operation is about to collapse, that the men have not been paid for months, and that they will not be paid.

Forced to live with the foreman and his wife, even sleeping in the same room with them to keep warm, Charlotte and Harry cease having sex. Buck confides to Harry that Billie is pregnant; Buck asks him to abort the fetus. At first, Harry refuses, but he finally does perform the operation. Soon after, the Buckners leave, and Harry assumes the role of overseer of the mine. He then realizes that the situation is futile, and he informs the miners, sending them off with the contents of the company store. Charlotte and Harry take the mining train out of the mountains; they go to San Antonio, Texas. Charlotte confides in Harry that she is pregnant, too, the result of a period of passion following the weeks of abstinence. At first, Harry tries to find medicine to induce the abortion, but when that proves ineffective, he reluctantly performs it himself. Charlotte is rejected by her daughters during an attempted meeting with them back in New Orleans. Charlotte, who knows that she is ill from the abortion, makes Francis promise not to prosecute Harry if she should die.

Back on the Mississippi Gulf coast, Charlotte is dying of a botched abortion. The doctor agrees to call an ambulance to take Charlotte to the hospital, but he admits that she is going to die. He also insists on calling the police to arrest Harry, and they take Harry to the hospital where Charlotte dies. Harry is then taken to jail to await the legal proceedings. He is tried and convicted of manslaughter and sentenced to fifty years at hard labor. True to his promise, Rat tries to help Harry, but the judge refuses to be lenient. Rat makes one last attempt to help Harry by smuggling him a cyanide capsule to save himself the fifty years at hard labor. Harry refuses.

The end of the novel focuses on Harry's musings about his life as he gazes out his cell window. He notices a woman hanging out her washing on the deck of an abandoned ship in the harbor. That domestic scene reminds him of the time he and Charlotte spent together. A palm tree rustling in the wind makes a dry, wild sound that fills Harry's cell. Harry decides to remain alive to keep the memory of Charlotte and their time together alive; this thought gives him the courage to face his long hard time. Between grief and nothing, Harry muses, I will take grief.

"The Story" by Charles L. P. Silet

Critical Evaluation:

The Wild Palms has a curious history, for it has often been reprinted as two short novels, *The Wild Palms* and *Old Man* (which is part of *The Wild Palms*), sometimes in the same volume and more often as two separate books. That it was so casually treated is unfortunate, because structurally it is perhaps the subtlest and most demanding of William Faulkner's

novels, and it is also his best approach to the comically absurd world of male-female relationships.

Most of the misunderstanding of the novel grows from its unique structure. The two short novels, either of which appears to be able to stand alone, are presented in alternating chapters. Their plots never cross or relate directly to each other; but they are so deeply involved in theme and symbolic and imagistic texture that apart each seems almost a thematic contradiction of the other. Together, however, they form an organic unit in which contrasts form parallels and contradiction becomes paradox. The novel demands of its readers an imaginative commitment beyond that of a more conventionally constructed novel, for its paradox, of both meaning and structure, must be solved by readers willing to read the book with the attention to rhythm and to form that they would normally give to a piece of music and the attention to images and words that they would normally give to a poem.

The pattern of events of the two parts of the novel are relatively simple. "The Wild Palms" takes place in 1937, in the heart of the Depression, and is the love story of Harry Wilbourne and Charlotte Rittenmeyer. Charlotte leaves her husband for Harry, who, not having finished his internship, is incapable of gaining any steady work. They wander from New Orleans to Chicago to Wisconsin and even to a remote mining camp in Utah until Charlotte accidentally becomes pregnant; their journeys, too, carry them deeper into squalor and their love from romance into the physically sordid. Urged by Charlotte, Harry performs an unsuccessful abortion that results in her death. In prison for her death, he refuses suicide, choosing grief over nothing.

The events in "Old Man" take place ten years earlier, during the great Mississippi River flood of 1927. They are the chronicle of a comic hero in a physical world gone quite as mad as the social world of the Depression has in "The Wild Palms." A young convict is sent out onto the flooded Mississippi in a skiff with another convict to rescue a woman stranded in a tree and a man on a cotton house. He loses the other convict, rescues the woman, who proves to be very pregnant, and is carried downstream by the flood. Battered by gigantic waves, he is offered three temptations for escape. After a time killing alligators with a group of Cajuns, he returns the boat and the woman with her safely born child and is given an additional ten-year sentence for attempted escape.

Neither of these brief descriptions approaches the complexities of the two stories, separately or as a unit, for theirs is an artistic value of reflection and texture in which event is a matter of form, and form a vehicle for imaginative idea. "The Wild Palms" is a tragicomedy, a parody of Ernest Hemingway's romantically anti-Romantic ideas (particularly those in *A Farewell to Arms*, 1929), a parable of a fallen world. "Old Man" is also a bitter comedy, but one in which the comic hero, God's fool, bears the burdens of the world and finds his victory in seeming defeat, his reward in the last ironic slap of "risible nature." "The Wild Palms" resolves itself in onanistic frustration, and "Old Man" discovers the spiritual rewards of struggle. The novel's comic sense makes it more than an existential lament for a meaningless world. The novel transforms the world's madness and ugliness into a Christian comedy of human folly that shows people at their worst, only to remind readers of the necessity of striving toward their best. The novel is not simply a moral allegory, although "Old Man" often verges on Christian parable. It is a compendium on the vanity of human wishes and on the follies of this earth.

The primary themes of both parts of the novel are those of human folly: the tragic consequences of romantic but earthly ideals and the failure of sex as the essential element of human fulfillment. Harry and the convict are victims of romantic ideals: The convict is sent to prison for an attempted train robbery inspired by reading dime novels and intended to impress a young woman; Harry is led into his affair with Charlotte by an impulse away from his ascetic student's life and his belief (fostered by Charlotte) in physical love and the value of the physical in a spiritless world.

The heroes of both stories are innocents in a confusing world, and women offer them little aid or solace. The women in the novel represent the two emasculating extremes of the female character. Charlotte is the defeminized female artist of masculine mind and manner, the aggressor in the sexual act and in life. The woman in "Old Man" is simple nearly to mindlessness; she is the mother, the primitive force of life to be borne by man as the weight of his duty. Charlotte is destroyed by the sex that she attempts to use as a man would. She cannot do so, however, because she is what she wishes to deny—a woman, a vessel, and bearer of man's seed and progeny. The woman in "Old Man" realizes and fulfills her role as mother but in this comic world fails as a romantic sexual figure. She lives on but without her man, the convict who complains that she, of all the women in the world, is the one with whom he is thrown by chance.

The men are innocents; the women are failures with them. "Old Man" ends with the convict's brief, violent summation of his feelings about the world of sex and women. "The Wild Palms" ends with Harry's refusal to kill himself only because in his grief he can find the onanistic solace of the memory of Charlotte's flesh. Both stories end in hollowness and ugliness. Each, taken by itself, presents a vision of frustration and despair, yet the novel itself has no such effect.

The two stories present opposing accounts of the nature of failure and success. The novel's dualistic, contradictory vision causes readers to apply their own norms to the events and to see the exact nature of the folly of both extremes, of sex and sexlessness, of romantic and antiromantic ideals. The world of *The Wild Palms* is a mad world, but its madness resembles this world, mad in its own right but held in the balance of equal and opposing forces.

Faulkner does not explicitly offer his reader the moral of his novel, but it is there to be drawn. That readers find it by an imaginative and creative act of synthesis is the true power of the novel. When one can laugh for joy even as one weeps in sorrow, one can survive and prevail. Such is the message of this novel, which, for all of its difficulty, is an extraordinary example of Faulkner's artistic genius.

Further Reading

McHaney, Thomas L. *William Faulkner's "The Wild Palms": A Study.* Jackson: University Press of Mississippi, 1975. Traces the origins of *The Wild Palms* and provides analyses of its themes and its characters. Includes a chronology of the story.

Marius, Richard. *Reading Faulkner: Introduction to the First Thirteen Novels.* Compiled and edited by Nancy Grisham Anderson. Knoxville: University of Tennessee Press, 2006. A collection of the lectures that Marius, a novelist, biographer, and Faulkner scholar, presented during an undergraduate course. Provides a friendly and approachable introduction to Faulkner. Includes a chapter on *The Wild Palms*.

Mortimer, Gail L. "The Ironies of Transcendent Love in Faulkner's *The Wild Palms.*" *Faulkner Journal* 1, no. 2 (Spring, 1986): 30-42. Despite the fact that this novel contains a love story, Mortimer argues that Faulkner's use of language and imagery denies transcendent love as being anything but illusory.

Towner, Theresa M. *The Cambridge Introduction to William Faulkner.* New York: Cambridge University Press, 2008. An accessible book aimed at students and general readers. Focusing on Faulkner's work, the book provides detailed analyses of his nineteen novels, discussion of his other works, and information about the critical reception for his fiction.

Zender, Karl F. "Money and Matter in *Pylon* and *The Wild Palms.*" *Faulkner Journal* 1, no. 2 (Spring, 1986): 17-29. Projects Faulkner's Hollywood experience onto *The Wild Palms* as a meditation on the theme of money. Zender reads the novel as a reflection on the plight of the artist in the world of wage labor and commercial art.

Wilhelm Meister's Apprenticeship

Author: Johann Wolfgang von Goethe (1749-1832)
First published: Wilhelm Meisters Lehrjahre, 1795-
1796 (English translation, 1824)
Type of work: Novel
Type of plot: Bildungsroman
Time of plot: Late eighteenth century
Locale: Germany

Principal characters:
WILHELM, a young poet and actor
MARIANNE, an actor and Wilhelm's lover
OLD BARBARA, Marianne's maid
WERNER, Wilhelm's best friend
PHILINE, an actor
LAERTES, an actor and Philine's companion
MIGNON, Wilhelm's adopted daughter
LOTHARIO, a nobleman
NATALIE, Wilhelm's wife
FELIX, Wilhelm's son
JARNO, an actor and teacher

The Story:

A naïve young man from a prosperous family, Wilhelm Meister is allowed to choose between a bourgeois, middle-class life in business and a bohemian, independent life as an artist. Rejecting his father's advice that he settle down and study business, Wilhelm decides to pursue a career in the theater as both an actor and a playwright. Wilhelm is distracted, though, by his love for Marianne, an actor, who, with her maid Old Barbara, conspires to keep Wilhelm in addition to a rich, older lover. One evening, Wilhelm observes his rival leaving Marianne's room. Heartbroken, Wilhelm finally takes his father's advice and begins a business trip that his father and Wilhelm's best friend, Werner, hope will teach him about the world.

Before leaving, Wilhelm breaks down weeping in front of Werner. He declares that he has no artistic talent and, parting with his Muses, he throws the bundles of his poetry into a fire. He then sets off on his journey to collect the debts his father holds on account. In his heart, however, Wilhelm remains "a restless, disorganized youth who wanted to live apart from the humdrum circumstances of middle-class life." In a small town not far from his father's estate, Wilhelm finds himself drawn to an amateur theater production. Observing the director beat a young girl for refusing to play her part, Wilhelm rescues her, ousts the director, and begins his association with the troupe. As the company's new director, Wilhelm takes on the girl, Mignon, as his adopted daughter, and together they travel the countryside staging plays and amusements for the local nobility.

Laertes and Philine, two of the best actors in the troupe, take Wilhelm and Mignon on sunny picnics where they flirt and joke. One afternoon, they are attacked by bandits in the forest. Wilhelm fights valiantly, drawing a pistol and shoot-

ing a bandit from his horse. Laertes joins him in the battle, but the other actors flee, and Wilhelm is badly wounded. Near death, he is saved by Mignon, who gathers up her long hair and uses it to stanch the flow of blood from a bullet wound in his chest.

Taken to recuperate at the house of a nobleman, Wilhelm slowly regains his health. During his convalescence he engages in many debates on the nature of art and poetry, especially on the topic of William Shakespeare. In the company of educated people, Wilhelm realizes that the actors took advantage of him, that they spent his money freely and failed to thank him, and that worst of all they abandoned him and left him for dead.

Forced to see that his own talent is mediocre, Wilhelm again feels compelled to choose a life in business. His new friend, the nobleman Lothario, encourages him to develop all of his talents, without focusing on any one in particular. To inform himself further, Wilhelm reads the diary of a saintly woman and concludes that there are two sources of truth, internal and external. He has just come to this realization when Mignon, who long endured poor health, suffers a heart attack and dies in his arms. Wilhelm then encounters Old Barbara, who tells him that his former lover Marianne died, swearing her love for him.

At his host's castle, Wilhelm is surprised to meet his old friend Werner, who traveled into the countryside on business. Each quickly sees that the other has changed. Werner has become rich, but also sickly, stoop-shouldered, and bald, whereas Wilhelm, who is relatively poor, has grown into a handsome, fine figure of a man.

Parting from Werner, Wilhelm continues his journey and discovers that he has a son by Marianne. The boy, Felix, comes into Wilhelm's care and changes his father's outlook on life. Wilhelm realizes that he lacks the talent to succeed in the theater. When he faces the truth about himself he discards his illusions and ends his apprenticeship, realizing that "art is long, life is short." Having matured, he proposes to Natalie, a young woman his friends select as the perfect mate. She refuses to give him an answer, but Wilhelm is distracted from his hopes and fears when Felix accidentally drinks opium. Fearing for the child's life, Wilhelm summons a doctor. Natalie swears that if Felix survives, she will accept Wilhelm's hand in marriage. Felix recovers, and Wilhelm joyfully accepts his new responsibilities as father and husband. Renouncing the artistic life, he takes his friend Jarno's advice and begins a happy domestic life, while Jarno sets sail for the New World in America.

Critical Evaluation:

Considered the prototype of the bildungsroman, a novel focusing on a character's coming of age, *Wilhelm Meister's Apprenticeship* is both a chronicle of the German theater and a sort of handbook for innocents. Wilhelm's many adventures and mishaps create the obstacles that force him to learn about the world around him. Johann Wolfgang von Goethe shows the reader that, even in the face of temptation and greed, and despite his naïveté, Wilhelm remains true to his principles and morals. When he is surrounded by scoundrels and abused and taken advantage of, Wilhelm never repays these injustices in kind. Instead, he simply accepts the foolishness and the selfishness of others and moves on, hoping steadfastly to encounter not only his one true love but also a friend to whom he can entrust his heart.

The plot of the novel is episodic, without being tightly connected. Characters often engage in long philosophical debates, acting more as mouthpieces for the author than as independent personalities. The narrative is therefore uneven, especially during breaks in the action when characters function primarily as pawns or ciphers. Nevertheless, Goethe executes one rhetorical flourish after another and creates a lyrical prose that is symphonic in its scope and fluidity. Nor is this musicality lacking in content. The author sows the dialogue with so many epigrammatic seeds and nuggets of wisdom that he creates the impression that he might yet create a dazzling whole from the revealing bits of a cosmic puzzle. Instead, however, it becomes clear that the author considers it his task to deepen the mystery of life, not to explain it. Wilhelm learns that "the sum of our existence divided by reason never comes out exactly and there is always a wondrous remainder."

Goethe celebrates the end of Wilhelm's apprenticeship with an epiphany, a sudden burst of inner knowledge, for having passed through the gates of initiation Wilhelm witnesses the death of his adolescent self and the birth of his adult identity. In embracing his son Felix, Wilhelm continues the cycle of life. The irony is that in the acceptance of responsibility and parenthood Wilhelm finds freedom. Goethe's thesis is that people must accept the natural evolution of the self, and that they must not seek to retard their growth by indulging in nostalgia or by clinging to youthful dreams and illusions. On the contrary, individuals must embrace their lost innocence in order to grasp something new, in a process of accepting and letting go at the same time. Change must be cultivated, as it is the agent that propels the individual through a happy and productive life.

Goethe considers the movement forward more important than the success of the venture. The author thus poses a moral question, whether it is better to exist in a state of being or in one of becoming. Existence in a state of being may imply inertia and stagnation, whereas existence in a state of becoming may degenerate into counterproductive restlessness. The central theme of *Wilhelm Meister's Apprenticeship* lies in the search for a compromise not only between being and becoming but also between thought and action and, with regard to the influences that cause an individual to act, between the external—which is the world—and the internal, which is the heart. Life is thus seen as a series of judgment calls. However, it is precisely this free will that Goethe celebrates, for the human ability to raise and improve its own consciousness reveals its connection to the divine. The ability to imagine God, and to reveal that conception with good works—that is to say through loyalty, devotion, and steadfastness—is to confirm God's existence. Particularly in the section entitled "Confessions of a Beautiful Soul," Goethe illustrates the distance between the mind of God and the human mind, while also suggesting that this gap may be bridged by faith and courage. Again, however, Goethe implies that the source of this faith must not come from outside the individual but must be the product of that individual's heart. The alternative is to accept "the monster that grows and feeds in every human breast, if some higher power does not preserve us."

Despite the strength of this section, it might be critically faulted for its form. The transition from a third-person, omniscient point of view, centered in Wilhelm, to the first-person confession is abrupt and jarring. This threatens the book's unity and raises the question whether the novel is about theatrical life or about a young man finding himself. As it happens, the author composed the novel during two different time periods separated by eight years—1786 and 1794—which may account for the shift in focus and for the feeling that the work comprises two halves that do not necessarily make a whole.

Wilhelm Meister's Apprenticeship remains an important novel about initiation. When Wilhelm accepts Felix as his son, he reaches the end of his quest for identity. He acknowledges what he has created and claims it for his own, rejecting the illusions foisted on him by his society and by his own idealism. Intellectually he learns to separate the wheat from the chaff. He sees what he can and cannot do, and he accepts the difference. The ultimately pragmatic philosophy that emerges from the novel is that people should play to their strengths and avoid their weaknesses. Such intellectual honesty, however, can only be achieved through a brutal though not despairing candor with the self and with trusted friends. *Wilhelm Meister's Apprenticeship* is about the ongoing discovery of self and the continuing process of maturation and development—universal themes that secure Goethe's place and that of this novel.

David Johansson

Further Reading

Armstrong, John. *Love, Life, Goethe: Lessons of the Imagination from the Great German Poet*. New York: Farrar, Straus and Giroux, 2007. Goethe's works are analyzed and his life examined in this comprehensive volume. Armstrong discusses a wide range of Goethe's writings, including his lesser known works, and gives a close study of his personal life. Knowing German and English, Armstrong provides translations of several key passages, while keeping his writing style plain and clear. This volume offers readers a better understanding of Goethe's writing, and the circumstances that inspired it.

Brown, Jane K. *Goethe's Cyclical Narratives: "Die Unterhaltungen deutscher Ausgewanderten" and "Wilhelm Meisters Wanderjahre."* Chapel Hill: University of North Carolina Press, 1975. Examines Goethe's use of episodic technique and cyclical narrative. Presents a methodology that allows the reader to appreciate the contradictions and parody in Goethe's work.

Curran, Jane V. *Goethe's "Wilhelm Meister's Apprenticeship": A Reader's Commentary*. Rochester, N.Y.: Camden House, 2002. Curran provides an in-depth, accessible analysis of the novel, including discussion of its narrative techniques, character development, use of symbols and irony, and the parallels between Wilhelm Meister's experiences and Goethe's life.

Hutchinson, Peter, ed. *Landmarks in the German Novel*. Part 1. New York: Peter Lang, 2007. This study traces the development of the German novel from the eighteenth century until 1959 by analyzing thirteen milestone works, including separate essays discussing Goethe's *Wilhelm Meister's Apprenticeship*, *Elective Affinities*, and *The Sorrows of Young Werther*.

Maugham, W. Somerset. "The Three Novels of a Poet." In *Points of View*. London: Heinemann, 1958. Maugham argues that Goethe was a better poet than novelist. Maugham, who brings a creative as well as a critical faculty to bear on Goethe's work, examines poetic technique, including imagery and meter.

Pascal, Roy. "The Bildungsroman: Johann Wolfgang von Goethe." In *The German Novel: Studies*. New York: Manchester University Press, 1956. Considers the formal and stylistic features of *Wilhelm Meister's Apprenticeship*. Briefly discusses Goethe's career as a theater director in Weimar and its influence on his novels.

Reiss, Hans. *Goethe's Novels*. New York: St. Martin's Press, 1969. Critical discussion of *Wilhelm Meister's Apprenticeship*, *The Sorrows of Young Werther*, and *Elective Affinities*. Examines Goethe's natural philosophy, the sociological aspects of his writings, and his influence on German theater.

Sharpe, Lesley, ed. *The Cambridge Companion to Goethe*. New York: Cambridge University Press, 2002. Collection of newly commissioned essays analyzing Goethe's prose fiction, drama, and poetry; Goethe and gender, philosophy, and religion; and Goethe's critical reception, among other topics. Includes bibliography and index.

Swales, Martin, and Erika Swales. *Reading Goethe: A Critical Introduction to the Literary Work*. Rochester, N.Y.: Camden House, 2002. A comprehensive critical analysis of Goethe's literary output, which argues that the writer is an essential figure in German modernity. Chapter 3, "Narrative Fiction," focuses on Goethe's novels. Includes bibliography and index.

Wilhelm Meister's Travels

Author: Johann Wolfgang von Goethe (1749-1832)
First published: Wilhelm Meisters Wanderjahre: Oder,
 Die Entsagenden, 1821; revised, 1829 (English
 translation, 1827)
Type of work: Novel
Type of plot: Philosophical
Time of plot: Early nineteenth century
Locale: Germany

Principal characters:
WILHELM MEISTER, a Renunciant
FELIX, his son
HERSILIA, a girl admired by Felix
HILARIA, a young girl
LENARDO, Wilhelm's friend

The Story:

Wilhelm Meister is traveling on foot with his young son, Felix. As a consequence of his liberation from ordinary desire through the noble Lothario and the abbot, the once-troubled Wilhelm becomes a Renunciant. Under the terms of his pledge, he is to wander for years, never stopping in one place more than three days. His travels are intended to give him a final philosophical polish. Gone are the countinghouse and the stage; he is now undertaking a last purifying sacrifice.

While Felix plays merrily on the mountainside, Wilhelm muses beside a steep path. Hearing voices, he turns to see his son with a group of children running downhill before a donkey driven by a holy-looking man. The beast carries a sweet-faced woman with a small baby. The adults smile at Wilhelm, but the path is too steep for them to stop. When Wilhelm catches up with the party, the man invites him to visit his household, and his wife amiably seconds the invitation. It is decided that Felix should go on ahead with the family and Wilhelm will follow the next day, after he retrieves his wallet, left high on the mountain.

When he arrives, Wilhelm is charmed to find the family living in a restored chapel. He is struck by the fact that the man's name is Joseph and his wife's is Mary; they do indeed seem a holy family. When he learns their story, Wilhelm is reverent.

Joseph's father was a rent collector for an absentee landlord. Joseph was promised that if he grew to be a steady man and a competent craftsman, he would succeed his father, but instead he decided to be a woodworker. When he was sufficiently skilled, he began to restore the paneling in the old chapel. His best work was the reworking of an elaborate wood panel depicting the flight of the Holy Family into Egypt.

One day, as Joseph was wandering on the trail, he found a beautiful woman weeping beside the path. Her husband was killed by robbers. Joseph, alarmed by the woman's distress and condition, took her to his home and summoned his mother. Soon the widow delivered a child. After a patient courtship, Joseph married the widow, Mary, and took her to live in the old chapel. Now he is the rent collector in his father's place and possesses a loving family.

While playing, Felix comes upon a box of stones that was given to Joseph by a scientist searching for minerals in that region. He learns that the geologist's name is Montan, a name frequently used by his old friend Jarno. Wilhelm hopes to overtake the scientist in the course of his own wanderings. He and Felix start out, led by Fitz, a beggar boy who was a playmate for Felix during the stay with the collector and his wife. On the way, they come to a barrier of fallen trees. While their guide is looking for another path, Felix wanders into a nearby cave and there finds a small box, no larger than an octavo volume, rich-looking and decorated with gold. Wilhelm and his son decide to conceal the box among their belongings and to tell no one of its discovery for the time being.

A short time later, Fitz leads them to the place where Montan is prospecting. As Wilhelm expected, the scientist is Jarno, whom Wilhelm knew in his acting days, now a Renunciant geologist. They stay with Jarno for three days, while the scientist tries to satisfy Felix's great curiosity about minerals and their properties.

The party leaves Jarno and starts off to survey a natural phenomenon known as the Giant's Castle. Sending the pack animals around by road, the travelers follow a rugged path until they come in sight of a beautiful garden, separated from them by a yawning chasm. Fitz leads them into an aqueduct that gives entrance to the garden. Suddenly they hear a shot. At the same time, two iron-grated doors begin to close behind them. Fitz springs back and escapes, but Wilhelm and his son are trapped. Several armed men with torches appear, and to them Wilhelm surrenders his only weapon, a knife. He tells his son to have no fear, for there are pious mottoes carved on the walls leading to the castle to which their captors conduct them.

After spending the night in a well-appointed room, father and son breakfast with the lively Hersilia and her older, more sedate sister Julietta. Felix is charmed with Hersilia, as is his father. Hersilia gives Wilhelm a romantic manuscript to read. The next day the eccentric uncle of the girls appears and takes them to lunch in a shooting lodge.

Finding himself in such agreeable and learned company, Wilhelm exerts himself to please. Hersilia accepts him as one of the family; to show her trust, she gives him a packet of letters to read, which tell of her cousin Lenardo. Some years ago Lenardo determined to set out on his travels. To get the necessary funds, his uncle collected all outstanding debts. While arranging his affairs, he dispossessed a tenant farmer with a beautiful daughter called the Nut-Brown Maid. Although the girl pleaded with Lenardo for mercy, she and her father were evicted. Now Lenardo writes his aunt that he will not come home until he learns what happened to the girl.

After reading the letters, Wilhelm takes his son to visit the aunt, a wise woman called Makaria. In her castle Wilhelm meets an astronomer who reveals to him many of the secrets of the stars. Advised by the savant, Wilhelm deposits the box Felix found with an antiquarian until the key can be located.

At a distant castle, a major comes to visit his sister. His intention is to consolidate the family fortunes by marrying his son Flavio to his sister's daughter Hilaria. To his surprise, Hilaria claims to love him. Then the major, after getting a valet to make him look younger, goes to tell Flavio the news. He is heartened to learn that Flavio is in love with a widow.

One night, Flavio bursts hysterically into his aunt's castle. The widow repulsed him when he became too eager in his lovemaking. Flavio soon finds solace in Hilaria's company. When the major returns, the atmosphere grows tense. The gloom lifts only after Hilaria's mother writes for advice to Makaria, who advises the widow to tell the major that young Flavio and Hilaria fell in love. Then Hilaria and the pretty widow set out to travel to Italy.

In his wanderings, Wilhelm comes upon Lenardo, who begs his aid in learning what became of the Nut-Brown Maid. When Wilhelm agrees to the quest, Felix is put in a school run by wise men who teach the dignity of labor and the beauty of art. Shortly after Wilhelm leaves the school, he is able to send Lenardo word that the girl is now well-off and happy. The wandering nephew then returns to Makaria.

With an artist friend, Wilhelm travels among the beautiful Italian lakes. This neighborhood is especially dear to him, for it was the home of his beloved Mignon, his foster daughter. The two men are lucky enough to meet Hilaria and the widow, but the ladies disappear before any serious interests can develop.

Hersilia writes to Wilhelm that she is keeping Felix's box, as the antiquarian went away, and that she also has a key to the chest. Returning to Germany, Wilhelm goes to the school to get Felix. He is pleased to find him a well-grown young man with considerable artistic ability. Father and son, once more together after their long separation, begin to visit their old friends.

They discover that Hilaria and Flavio married and that Flavio became a prosperous merchant. Felix is greatly attracted to Hersilia. When he learns that she has both key and box, he persuades her to let him try to open it. The key, however, is magnetic, and the halves come apart when he tries to turn the lock.

Felix tries to embrace Hersilia, and the girl pushes him away much harder than she intends. Fearing she does not love him, Felix impetuously dashes away and is injured when he falls on the shore beside a stream. There Wilhelm finds him unconscious. His old training in medicine proves valuable, however, and Wilhelm is able to bleed his son and restore him to consciousness.

Critical Evaluation:

Johann Wolfgang von Goethe was considered by many critics to be the greatest writer of his time. His output included works of poetry and plays, as well as works in the novel form. An innovator in each of the genres he mastered, Goethe experimented freely and dynamically with the novel. Indeed, in *Wilhelm Meister's Travels*—also known as *The Renunciants*—Goethe expanded the novel form to reach beyond the story of the individual to the story of society itself. At the onset of *Wilhelm Meister's Travels*, in a continuation of the story in *Wilhelm Meisters Lehrjahre* (1795-1796; *Wilhelm Meister's Apprenticeship*, 1824), a letter written by the protagonist sets the stage for the rest of the work. Wilhelm Meister writes, "My life is to become a restless wandering. Strange duties of the wanderer have I to fulfill, and peculiar trials to undergo." The novel concerns the main character's continuing pilgrimage toward an understanding of himself and of the world.

Goethe was a master of the mosaic. Throughout *Wilhelm Meister's Travels*, Goethe successfully weaves several different narrative strands and thereby expanded the structure of the novel as it was then known. The early part of the nineteenth century was generally a time of growth and of experimentation in the novel form, but Goethe reached far beyond anything then being done to create a highly complex narrative structure.

Throughout the work, Goethe interweaves soliloquies and dialogue, letters and observations, all of which demonstrate varying points of view on the nature of reality and knowledge, geology and art, and the practice of learning one's place in the world. Within this complex structure a narrator describes Wilhelm's travels. The letters inserted into the narrative structure—letters from Wilhelm to Natalia; from Lenardo to his aunt, from his aunt to Julietta; and from Julietta back to the aunt—show different temperaments and responses to stated events. Each letter works without a narrator or the interpretation the narrator provides. Through these shifting points of view on the same event it may be said that Goethe questions the validity of a singular point of view. In addition, the letters demonstrate the intimate connection among human lives.

Some of the letters in the narrative contain stories that could stand on their own as separate tales. Such is the case in one letter sent to Wilhelm, in which Hersilia, an admirer of Felix, relates a story that explores the context of Wilhelm's travels and thus weaves the story of Wilhelm Meister the individual into a larger social and cultural framework.

Interestingly, Hersilia orders Wilhelm to deduce whether the story she relates to him in her letter is true or fictitious. By doing so, she sets the whole act of storytelling on its head. Not only must Wilhelm decide for himself the veracity of what he is told, but the reader, too, must question the validity of the plot. In this sense, Goethe transforms the reader into a pilgrim as well, who must sort through the available evidence of the journey to determine fact from fiction and perhaps eventually understand the present and the past.

To further complicate matters, the reader is also addressed by an "Editor," who comments on the difficulty of selecting and arranging the anecdotes, "more complex narratives," and poems that make up *Wilhelm Meister's Travels.* In his comment on the arduous process of selection, the Editor laments: "We still find ourselves in more than one way impeded, at this or that place threatened with one obstruction or another." Goethe constructs *Wilhelm Meister's Travels* so that the reader experiences the sense of obstruction and diversion created by the complex narrative. The reader's reaction may parallel that of Wilhelm when he encounters obstacles and diversions on his spiritual, moral, and psychological journey toward wisdom and understanding. Among other things, the protagonist journeys through castles, jostles with armed men, weaves his way through the lakes region, and wrestles with locked boxes to which he cannot find the key. Goethe sets up his novel in such a way that the reader takes a parallel journey of questions and of discovery.

Beyond the experiment with form, *Wilhelm Meister's Travels* also provides a glimpse into the interrelation between human beings and their environment. The obstacles that Wilhelm confronts during his pilgrimage have a profound effect on him, yet it is Goethe's belief that individuals, too, shape the society in which they live. Speculations on mathematics, astronomy, and geology are interspersed throughout the story, reflecting the importance of constantly questioning one's world. It can be said that part of the purpose behind the pilgrimage carried out by Goethe's protagonist is to determine his relationship to his age.

Wilhelm Meister's Travels was created during a time of great social, economic, and religious flux in Europe. Napoleon had instigated great political strife, which was followed by the restoration of the monarchy. Goethe, grown older, used *Wilhelm Meister's Travels* to look back at the ways in which the individual moves through society and at the eternal reshaping and changing of society itself.

Further Reading

Armstrong, John. *Love, Life, Goethe: Lessons of the Imagination from the Great German Poet.* New York: Farrar, Straus and Giroux, 2007. Goethe's works are analyzed and his life examined in this comprehensive volume. Armstrong discusses a wide range of Goethe's writings, including his lesser known works, and gives a close study of his personal life. Knowing German and English, he provides translations of several key passages, while keeping his writing style plain and clear. This volume offers readers a better understanding of Goethe's writing and the circumstances that inspired it.

Bahr, Ehrhard. *The Novel as Archive: The Genesis, Reception, and Criticism of Goethe's "Wilhelm Meisters Wanderjahre."* Columbia, S.C.: Camden House, 1998. Concise examination in which Bahr describes the novel's genesis and structure, context in which it was written, reception at the time it appeared, and twentieth century scholarship about the book. He points out how Goethe used several literary devices to distance himself from the role of author-narrator.

Boyle, Nicholas. *Goethe, the Poet and the Age.* New York: Oxford University Press, 1991. An exceptionally detailed study of Goethe's development as an artist. Discusses Goethe's novels and includes an extended analysis of the culture and times in which he lived and worked.

Dieckmann, Liselotte. *Johann Wolfgang von Goethe.* New York: Twayne, 1974. A lucid overview of Goethe's novels, plays, and poetry. An excellent introductory source. Contains interesting chapters on biography and autobiography and chapters focused on the novels, including *Wilhelm Meister's Travels.*

Goethe, Johann Wolfgang von. *Goethe's Literary Essays.* Arranged by J. E. Spingarn. 1921. Reprint. New York: Frederick Ungar, 1964. Several essays place *Wilhelm Meister's Travels* in the context of Goethe's theories on the art of world literature. Contains Goethe's own thoughts on the development of fiction and art.

Kerry, Paul E. *Enlightenment Thought in the Writings of Goethe: A Contribution to the History of Ideas.* Rochester, N.Y.: Camden House, 2001. Kerry analyzes Goethe's novels and other works to demonstrate how he was influenced by Voltaire, David Hume, and other Enlightenment philosophers and writers. Chapter 9 analyzes "Religious Freedom in *Wilhelm Meisters Wanderjahre.*"

Lange, Victor, ed. *Goethe: A Collection of Critical Essays.* Englewood Cliffs, N.J.: Prentice-Hall, 1968. A representative selection of essays. Important pieces on Goethe's craft of fiction shed light on the construction of *Wilhelm Meister's Travels* for the beginning reader. Includes a selected bibliography.

Sharpe, Lesley, ed. *The Cambridge Companion to Goethe.* New York: Cambridge University Press, 2002. Collection of newly commissioned essays analyzing Goethe's prose fiction, drama, and poetry; Goethe and gender, philosophy, and religion; and Goethe's critical reception, among other topics. Includes bibliography and index.

Swales, Martin, and Erika Swales. *Reading Goethe: A Critical Introduction to the Literary Work.* Rochester, N.Y.: Camden House, 2002. A comprehensive critical analysis of Goethe's literary output, which argues that the writer is an essential figure in German modernity. Chapter 3, "Narrative Fiction," focuses on Goethe's novels. Includes bibliography and index.

Wright, Joan. *The Novel Poetics of Goethe's "Wilhelm Meisters Wanderjahre": Eine Zarte Empirie.* Lewiston, N.Y.: Edwin Mellen Press, 2002. Wright maintains that the novel reflects the diversity and infinity of life in a society that was becoming more complex for both individuals and the community as a whole.

The Will to Believe, and Other Essays in Popular Philosophy

Author: William James (1842-1910)
First published: 1897
Type of work: Philosophy

Of the ten essays in William James's *The Will to Believe, and Other Essays in Popular Philosophy*, three have had lasting philosophical importance: "The Will to Believe" and the two that augment or clarify this piece, "Is Living Worth Living?" and "The Sentiment of Rationality." The general subjects of these three essays are the nature of faith and the concept of self-verifying belief. The other seven essays have mostly historical or topical themes in philosophy, psychology, and physiology.

James opens the essay "The Will to Believe" by characterizing any hypothesis as one of three kinds of dilemma: living or dead, forced or unforced, momentous or trivial. For James, if the dilemma concerns a live issue, if it is one in which a decision must be made, and if it is one whose expected consequences are momentous, then the option is genuine. Otherwise, the option is of little or no import. Any option, whether genuine or not, may be thus reduced to a strict exclusive disjunction in which just two possibilities exhaust all cases. The question need only be stated properly, according to the logic of its own practicality—that is, consistent with James's standard radical empiricist or pragmatic approach to philosophical issues: What works and what does not?

James argues in favor of the rationality and practical value of any kind of faith, not necessarily Christian or even religious. His ultimate aim, however, seems to be to bolster the Christian faith. He establishes his position between those of philosopher-mathematicians Blaise Pascal and William Kingdon Clifford. He criticizes both positions severely, but remains closer to Pascal's theism.

In *Pensées* (1670; English translation, 1688), Pascal places religious faith into four exclusive categories: (1) God is real, and we (humans) so believe; (2) God is real, yet we do not so believe; (3) God is fictitious, yet we believe that God is real; and (4) God is fictitious, and we so believe. The decision the faithful make among the four has become known in both philosophy and theology as Pascal's wager. If we choose (1), then we go to Heaven; but if we choose (2), then we go to Hell. If we choose either (3) or (4), then we probably just pass into gentle nonexistence upon death. It would then turn out that if we had chosen (3), we would have been wrong, and if we would have chosen (4), we would have been right. However, because there would be neither Heaven nor Hell, this difference would not matter. If humans choose to believe in God, humans have everything to gain and nothing to lose; if humans choose not to believe, then humans have nothing to gain and everything to lose. The decision between theistic belief and atheistic nonbelief is forced. Agnosticism—or refusing to decide—are not options, insofar as they are tantamount to the atheistic nonbelief of either (2) or (4). For Pascal and James, any faith short of full faith is not faith.

James declares that faith according to Pascal's wager is merely expedient, and he jokes that God would take special delight in condemning to Hell any Christians who had acquired their faith in such a shallow way. James further asserts that Pascal himself, who was known as a deep and abiding Roman Catholic, could not possibly have developed such faith by gambling on the reality of God, but only by spiritual experience and devout immersion in Church doctrine.

Clifford takes the skeptical attitude of philosopher David Hume to an extreme of distrust, and he couches this new skepticism in social morality. Clifford proclaims that to believe without reason is unethical, given that humans have a natural duty to try their best to learn the truth and to ensure that humans, insofar as possible, act in accord with accurate information. In his campaign against founding society upon false premises, Clifford specifically excludes Christianity from his domain of justifiable belief, as there is no hard evidence for its truth, only its faith. For Clifford, faith is belief against evidence and can never be part of any practical strategy for developing civilization or any sensible plan for individual life. Only beliefs and actions based on either strong inductive evidence—such as that of the hard sciences—or incontrovertible deductive reasoning—such as that of mathematics—can serve the worthiest goals of humanity.

James caricatures Clifford's claim that to believe nothing at all would be better than to believe anything that might someday be proved false. James agrees with Pascal's dictum that the heart has its own reasons that reason cannot know, and he thinks that Clifford is too intellectual for his own good. Human nature exists in two facets, passional and intellectual. Pascal is too much a champion of the passional and tends to deny the intellectual, though not consistently. Clifford is a stout and consistent champion of a strictly conceived intellectuality and actively denies the usefulness of the passions. In criticizing both Pascal and Clifford, James asserts that to prefer either facet to the other is to suffer from a psychological imbalance, which is respectively personified in Pascal and Clifford. He occupies a middle position that acknowledges the validity and practicality of both facets and sees them both as necessary for human wholeness, life, health, and success.

Thus, James comes to the central thesis of "The Will to Believe," namely, that tangible benefits accrue to humans who can arrange for cooperation between the passional and the intellectual, especially when the passional supports the intellectual or takes over from the intellectual when the intellectual would otherwise fail. Even the scientific quest for empirical or inductive truth, and the rationalistic or philosophical quest for absolute, universal, or deductive truth, can be analyzed in terms of faith, because to be able to do any scientific or philosophical investigations at all, a person must have faith that some truth exists to be discovered. James therefore claims that any viable system, however much it may pretend to be objective, must include elements of human subjectivity. Whenever humans determine that their minds cannot cope, they must trust their instincts. Learned opinion comes as much from the heart as from the mind, but from neither one alone.

James denies that faith is belief against evidence. Rather, he claims that faith can work in harmony with both empirical evidence and rational knowledge to add pragmatic value to this evidence and knowledge. The practical value of faith is that its presence or absence, strength or weakness, and sincerity or artificiality can materially affect the outcome of an existential situation. Moreover, faith has specific creative power.

In "Is Living Worth Living?" James introduces the metaphor of the alpine climber. A skillful mountaineer finds his path blocked by a deep crevasse that may or may not be narrow enough to jump over. The climber cannot judge the crevasse's width accurately; that is, he cannot know whether he will live or die. Return is impossible, so his only chance of survival is to try the leap.

James's point is that faith, boldness, self-confidence, resoluteness, and similarly optimistic emotions enhance the climber's probability of surviving the leap; whereas defeatist attitudes like despair, hesitation, or disbelief are likely to kill him. Fear is always present, but faith conquers fear, while uncertainty increases it.

In "The Sentiment of Rationality," James repeats the mountaineer metaphor and emphasizes that faith is self-verifying, and therefore self-justifying, when it creates its own truth. If people in such dilemmas believe that they will succeed and survive, then they are likely to get advantageous results; but if they believe that they will fail and die, then they are certain to do so.

Eric v.d. Luft

Further Reading

Carmody, Denise Lardner, et al. *The Republic of Many Mansions: Foundations of American Religious Thought.* St. Paul, Minn.: Paragon House, 1998. A study of American religious thought from the eighteenth to the twentieth centuries. Centers on the ideas of William James as a philosophical pragmatist, Jonathan Edwards as a Puritan thinker, and Thomas Jefferson as an Enlightenment secularist.

Gale, Richard M. *The Philosophy of William James: An Introduction.* New York: Cambridge University Press, 2005. Considers James's theory of belief in the context of his ethics, metaphysics, logic, and pragmatism, and as his theory of belief relates to mysticism, selfhood, and wider issues of religious experience and philosophical inquiry.

O'Connell, Robert J. *William James on the Courage to Believe.* New York: Fordham University Press, 1984. A detailed and multifaceted analysis of James's philosophy of self-verifying belief, with sections on the logic of the argument, alternatives to the argument, Blaise Pascal's influence on James, and James's influence on later thinkers.

Pawelski, James O. *The Dynamic Individualism of William James.* Albany: State University of New York Press, 2007. Examines how one's mind could be changed through the exercise of faith or will, how the social role of faith helps with making decisions, and how perception affects volition.

Perry, Ralph Barton. *The Thought and Character of William James as Revealed in Unpublished Correspondence and Notes, Together with His Published Writings.* Boston: Little, Brown, 1935. Still the essential resource for James studies. A massive two-volume work that relies mostly on primary material to create an authoritative intellectual biography. Chapter 63 includes seven letters pertaining to *The Will to Believe.*

Taylor, Charles. *Varieties of Religion Today: William James Revisited.* Cambridge, Mass.: Harvard University Press, 2002. Transcript of lectures by scholar Taylor in Vienna in 2000. Taylor assesses the religious thought of James as he considers the place of religion in the present secular age.

Wernham, James C. S. *James's Will-to-Believe Doctrine: A Heretical View.* Montreal: McGill-Queen's University Press, 1987. Argues that both James and Pascal reduce religious faith to gambling, that James's version of this theory is basically secular, and that what James really advocates is not a genuine faith but a "foolish-not-to-believe" doctrine.

William Tell

Author: Friedrich Schiller (1759-1805)
First produced: Wilhelm Tell, 1804; first published, 1804 (English translation, 1841)
Type of work: Drama
Type of plot: Historical
Time of plot: Fifteenth century
Locale: Switzerland

Principal characters:
WILLIAM TELL, an Alpine hunter
WALTER TELL, his son
WALTER FÜRST, his father-in-law
HERMANN GESSLER, the Austrian governor of the Swiss Forest Cantons
JOHN PARRICIDA, a Habsburg nobleman and an assassin
WERNER, THE BARON OF ATTINGHAUSEN, a Swiss nobleman
ULRICH VON RUDENZ, his nephew
BERTHA VON BRUNECK, a wealthy heir
CONRAD BAUMGARTEN, a villager accused of murder

The Story:

A storm is rising on Lake Lucerne. The ferryman makes his boat fast to the shore as villager Conrad Baumgarten rushes up, pursued by the soldiers of the tyrannous governor, Hermann Gessler. He implores the ferryman to take him across the lake to safety. The crowd asks why he is being pursued. Baumgarten tells them that the seneschal of the castle had entered his house, demanded a bath, and started taking liberties with Baumgarten's wife. She escaped and ran to her husband in the forest, whereupon Baumgarten returned home and, while the seneschal was in the bath, split his skull with his ax. Baumgarten must now flee the country.

The sympathies of the common people are with Baumgarten, and they beg the ferryman to take him across the now stormy lake. The ferryman, afraid, refuses to do so. The hunter William Tell hears Baumgarten's story. Tell, the only person in the crowd with the courage to steer the boat in a tempest, makes preparations to take the fugitive across the lake. As they cast off, soldiers thunder up. When the soldiers see their prey escaping, they take revenge on the peasants, killing their sheep and burning their cottages.

The Swiss are greatly troubled because the emperor of Austria has sent Gessler to rule as viceroy over the three cantons around Lake Lucerne. Gessler, a second-born noble son without land or fortune, is envious of the prosperity and the independent bearing of the people. The Swiss hold their lands in direct fief to the emperor, and the rights and duties of the viceroy are strictly limited. Hoping to break the proud spirit of the people, Gessler places a cap on a pole in a public place and requires that each man bow to the cap.

Gessler's soldiers come to the farm of an upright farmer and attempt to take from him his best team of oxen. Only when Arnold, the farmer's son, springs on the men and strikes them with his staff do they release the oxen and leave. Arnold thinks it best to go into hiding. While he is away, the soldiers return to torture his old father and put out his eyes. Arnold joins the outraged Swiss against Gessler. Walter Fürst becomes their leader, and it is agreed that ten men from the three cantons will meet and plan the overthrow of the viceroy.

At the mansion of the nobleman Werner, the baron of Attinghausen, the common people and their lord gather for a morning cup of friendship. Old Werner is happy to drink with his men, but his nephew, Ulrich von Rudenz, refuses, for he is drawn to the Austrian rulers and feels no bond to free Switzerland. Werner upbraids Ulrich for being a turncoat and accuses him of turning to Austria because he is in love with the wealthy heir Bertha von Bruneck.

The representatives of the people of the three cantons meet secretly at night in a forest clearing. Tell is not among them. Some of the more fiery members are in favor of an immediate uprising, but the cooler heads follow Fürst and vote to wait until Christmas, when by tradition all the peasants will be present in the castle.

Ulrich at last declares his love for Bertha. She, a true Swiss at heart, spurns him for his loyalty to Austria.

Tell and his sons happen to pass by the hated cap. When Tell pays no attention to the authority symbol, he is arrested by two guards who try to bind him and lead him to prison. Although Fürst arrives and offers bail for his son-in-law, the law-abiding Tell submits to his captors. He is being led away when Gessler rides by.

Gessler orders an apple placed on the head of Tell's son, Walter, and commands Tell to shoot the apple from his son's head. Tell protests in vain. Ulrich courageously defies Gessler and hotly opposes the tyrant's order, but Gessler is unmoved. In the uproar, Tell takes out two arrows, fits one to his crossbow, and neatly pierces the apple.

While the crowd rejoices, Gessler asks Tell why he has taken out two arrows. Tell refuses to answer until Gessler promises not to punish him no matter what the reply might be. Tell then boldly declares that if he had missed the apple and hurt his son, he would have killed Gessler with the second arrow. Infuriated, Gessler orders Tell led away to life imprisonment in a dungeon.

Tell is chained and put on a boat for Gessler's castle. Gessler goes along to gloat over his victim. Again a terrifying storm arises. Fearing for his life, Gessler has Tell unbound and made helmsman. Tell watches for his chance and steers the boat close to shore, springing to safety on a rocky ledge.

In the evening, Tell positions himself on an outcropping in a pass he knows Gessler must pass through if he is to escape the fury of the storm. Beneath Tell's hiding place, a poor woman and her children wait for Gessler. Her husband is in prison for a minor offense, and she intends to appeal to Gessler for clemency. At last, Gessler approaches with his entourage. The woman blocks his way and appeals in vain for mercy. Tell waits long enough to hear her plea denied and to hear that Gessler plans to ride the woman down; he then pierces the breast of the tyrant with an arrow from his crossbow. Tell announces to the gathered people that he is Gessler's killer, then disappears into the forest.

The people had hoped that Werner would lead them in their revolt, but he is on his deathbed. He dies before he can pass the leadership to Ulrich, but when his nephew arrives, the assembled peasants acknowledge him as their leader, finding him to be a loyal Swiss after all—the more so as the Austrians have abducted Bertha. At last, the three cantons rise up against the harsh Austrian rule, and Ulrich rescues Bertha.

At the height of the revolt, news comes that the emperor has been assassinated. Duke John Parricida of Austria, his nephew, has struck down the emperor for being robbed of his estates. John seeks refuge with Tell, but the forester refuses, considering himself a soldier for freedom, not a murderer. His natural humanity, however, keeps him from exposing John, and the duke leaves for Italy.

Tell puts away his crossbow for good when the announcement comes that the count of Luxembourg had been elected emperor. The cantons look forward to peaceful days. Bertha gives her hand freely to Ulrich, and both pledge to be proud and determined Swiss husband and wife.

Critical Evaluation:

William Tell was Schiller's last complete play before his death in 1805. Ten years earlier, he had succeeded in entering into a close intellectual association with Johann Wolfgang von Goethe, the leading figure in German literature at the time. At one of their meetings, Goethe gave Schiller a detailed account of his travels to and his particular fascination with Switzerland.

Schiller subsequently suggested that Goethe compose either an epic poem or a play on the William Tell legend. Instead, Goethe presented Schiller with his complete Swiss materials, which stimulated the noted historian Schiller to immerse himself in Swiss history and the work recently published by his contemporary Johann Müller. Schiller learned that the legend, possibly myth, of William Tell did not appear in documents until well after the historical period of the play.

A historical play is, of course, not a historical document. In *William Tell*, Schiller is able to unite the many disparate historical and personal threads into the signal aesthetic achievement of his play, one that stimulates readers today as it did when published more than two centuries ago.

William Tell brilliantly synthesizes classical and Romantic elements in his play. The setting and the idyll intoned by the rustic voices in iambic quatrameter at the opening of *William Tell* are archly Romantic. This is immediately followed by one of Schiller's strongest traits: dramatic, Shakespearean blank verse. Schiller gives masterfully convincing voice both to the large assembly scenes and to the intimate ones in his play.

Although Schiller, unlike the well-traveled Goethe, was never outside Germany, he succeeded in providing Switzerland with its national play. He gives compelling life to Swiss archetypes and convincingly depicts their attainment of national independence.

The natural backdrops required by the play make it difficult to present on stage. It is read more often than it is performed. It has, however, proven apt for outdoor productions. It is performed every summer in Switzerland, and at Swiss American festivals around the United States, particularly in Wisconsin.

In a classical play, violence is not shown on stage but is reported by a messenger as having taken place. At first, Schiller conforms to the classical tradition, but from act 1 he begins to prepare the representation of violent actions, first in Tell's partially hidden shooting of the apple from his son's head in act 3, then presenting a fully visual act of violence in act 4—Tell's killing of Gessler. With this, *William Tell* as-

sumes a characteristic of many of William Shakespeare's plays: *William Tell* becomes a problem play, for how can an assassin be presented as a hero?

This question comes to the fore in the final act, which opens with a classical recitation of the brutal murder of the Habsburg emperor. Contrary to history, Schiller has his Swiss assume that the murder of the emperor and Tell's murder of Gessler have allowed the populace to revolt and allowed Switzerland to become free.

On Tell's return home from the murder, he finds Duke John, the assassin of the emperor, in his hut, awaiting refuge. An interesting dialect between Tell and John about their respective killings takes place—John's killing, in Tell's judgment, had been for personal gain, and Tell's killing had been to rid Switzerland of a tyrant bent on personal vindictiveness against an innocent citizenry. Tell then notes to John the alpine passes he should take to get to Italy, then to Rome to acquire the Roman Catholic pope's absolution for his deed.

The reader is left to wonder: Should not Tell, likewise, have to atone for taking a life? By not giving Tell any more lines in the play, Schiller silences him and has the now-assembled Swiss hail him as their deliverer, making him into Switzerland's national hero and leaving the reader to ponder a Hamlet-like question.

Revised by Robert B. Youngblood

Further Reading

Graham, Ilse. *Schiller's Drama: Talent and Integrity*. New York: Barnes & Noble, 1974. A serious study of Schiller that gives a reading and explanation of *William Tell*; many quotations are in German. Concentrates on symbolism and the character of William Tell as archetypal hero.

Kerry, Paul E., ed. *Friedrich Schiller: Playwright, Poet, Philosopher, Historian*. New York: Peter Lang, 2007. A collection of essays examining Schiller's various vocations, including historian and prose writer. Examines the status of his work two centuries after his death.

Martinson, Steven D., ed. *A Companion to the Works of Friedrich Schiller*. Rochester, N.Y.: Camden House, 2005. Essays include discussions of Schiller's philosophical aesthetics, lyric poetry, reception in the twentieth century, and relevance to the twenty-first century. One chapter analyzes *William Tell*.

Richards, David B. "Tell in the Dock: Forensic Rhetoric in the Monologue and Parricida-Scene in *Wilhelm Tell*." *German Quarterly* 48 (1975): 472-486. A compelling critical exegesis of the final act of *William Tell*. Calls Tell to account for his assassination.

Ryder, Frank G. "Schiller's *Tell* and the Cause of Freedom." *German Quarterly* 48 (1975): 487-504. A good article outlining the cause of freedom for Switzerland and the role of Schiller's play in the maintenance of the freedoms it expresses.

Sharpe, Lesley. *Friedrich Schiller: Drama, Thought, and Politics.* New York: Cambridge University Press, 1991. Studies the story from which Schiller borrowed and reinvented the dialogue for *William Tell.* Compares Schiller with Goethe. Extensive chronology, bibliography, notes, and index to Schiller's works.

_____. *A National Repertoire: Schiller, Iffland, and the German Stage.* New York: Peter Lang, 2007. Examines Schiller's influence on the German theater of his time. Places his theatrical career in parallel with that of August Wilhelm Iffland, an actor and playwright who eventually produced Schiller's plays at the Berlin National Theatre. Describes the relationship between Schiller and Goethe as playwrights.

Simons, John D. *Friedrich Schiller.* Boston: Twayne, 1981. Includes a discussion of Schiller's aesthetics and examinations of his poetry and dramatic works. Notes Schiller's research into the Swiss legend of William Tell and analyzes elements of his subsequent drama and its success as a monomyth.

Thomas, Calvin. *The Life and Works of Friedrich Schiller.* 1901. Reprint. New York: AMS Press, 1970. Discusses Schiller's works in chronological order and in detail. Explains Schiller's attention to local color and describes the public reception of *William Tell.* Analyzes the plot and several scenes and characters.

Youngblood, Robert B. "John Parricida: Swabian Prince and Assassin." In *Great Lives from History: Notorious Lives*, vol. 1, edited by Carl L. Bankston III. Pasadena, Calif.: Salem Press, 2007. Furnishes the historical information on Duke John Parricida, his life before he assassinated the Habsburg emperor, a description of the act, and the duke's end.

The Wind in the Willows

Author: Kenneth Grahame (1859-1932)
First published: 1908
Type of work: Novel
Type of plot: Allegory
Time of plot: Early twentieth century
Locale: England

Principal characters:
MOLE, an introvert
WATER RAT, an extrovert
TOAD, a playboy
BADGER, a philosophical recluse

The Story:

Mole has spring fever, for he has been busy with his cleaning and his repairing for too long. Because the new spring smells and the sight of budding green are everywhere about him, he cannot resist them. Throwing aside his tools and his mops, together with his ambition for cleaning, he leaves his little home under the ground and travels up to a lovely meadow. There he wanders through the grass and along the river. He never saw a river before, and he is bewitched by its chuckling and its glimmering in the sunlight.

As he watches, Mole sees a dark hole in the bank. From it protrudes the bewhiskered face of Water Rat, who promptly invites Mole to visit him. Mole, of course, cannot swim, and so Rat takes his little boat and rows across to get him. Such enchantment is almost too much for quiet Mole. As they glide across the gurgling water, he thinks this is the best day

of his entire life. After a little accident, they reach Rat's house. There they pack a picnic basket and set out on a real excursion. They stay carefully away from the Wild Wood, for fierce animals live there. Badger keeps his home there, but nobody will dare bother Badger.

As they float down the river, Rat tells Mole about other animals and about the Wide World. Rat never saw the Wide World and never wanted to see it, and he warns Mole against it. It is no place for respectable animals. When they stop for their picnic lunch, they are joined by Otter. Badger looks in on them but will not join them. Badger hates society. He likes people all right, but he hates society. Rat promises that they will meet Badger later, for Mole can learn much valuable knowledge from Badger.

After another accident, which is Mole's fault, the two new

friends go to Rat's home and eat supper. Following the meal, Rat entertains Mole with many wonderful tales. It is a sleepy but happy Mole who is helped into bed by the kind Rat that night. From then on, the two remain friends. Rat teaches Mole to swim and to row, to listen to the music of the running water, and to catch a little of the meaning of the song the wind sings as it whispers in the willows.

One day, the two go to visit Toad at Toad Hall. It is the most beautiful residence in animal land, for Toad is wealthy. He is also a playboy. Every new fad that comes along attracts him. When Rat and Mole arrive, Toad is busy getting together a gypsy caravan. He persuades the others to join him on the open road. Although the venture is against Rat's better judgment, poor Mole is so desirous of joining Toad that Rat finally submits.

Their adventure is short-lived. When the wagon is upset by a racing motorcar, Rat is so furious that he wants to prosecute the owners of the car to the limit. Toad has other ideas; he must have the biggest, fastest, gaudiest car that money can buy.

Spring, summer, and fall pass—days filled with pleasure for Mole and Rat. Then, one cold winter day, Mole goes out alone and gets lost. He finds himself in the Wild Wood and is terrified by the strange noises and evil faces he sees around him. Rat finally finds him, but before they can reach Rat's home, snow begins to fall. By luck, they stumble upon Badger's home, where the old philosopher welcomes them, although he hates being disturbed from his winter's sleep. Badger asks for news of the other animals, particularly of Toad. He is not surprised to learn that Toad is in trouble constantly because of his motorcars. There were seven crashes and seven new cars. He was hospitalized three times, and he paid innumerable fines. Badger promises that when the proper time comes, he will attend to Toad.

When their visit is over, Badger leads Rat and Mole through a labyrinth of tunnels and underground passages until they reach the far edge of the Wild Wood. There he says good-bye, and the two animals scamper for home. Not long afterward, in December, Mole feels a great desire to return to his own house that he left on that spring day so long ago. Rat understands the feeling and gladly goes with Mole to find his old home. It is a shabby place, not at all as fine as Toad Hall or Rat's house, but Rat is polite about it and praises it to Mole. On their first night there, they give a party for the field mice; Mole then rolls into bed and sleeps the sleep of weary travelers.

Early the next summer, Badger turns up and says that now he is ready to deal with Toad. Taking Mole and Rat with him, he goes to Toad Hall and tries to persuade Toad to give up his cars and his reckless ways. Since only force can accomplish that end, they lock Toad in his room until he should come to his senses. Toad, however, slips out of the window and steals a car. He is arrested, tried, and sentenced to prison for twenty years. There Toad has ample time to think about his foolish ways, but he could not be restrained for long. Bribing the jailer's daughter, he escapes in the disguise of a washerwoman.

Finally, Mole learns the true meaning of the wind's song in the trees. One evening, when birds and insects are still, Mole suddenly feels the awe that brings peace and contentment. He feels himself in the presence of he who brings life and death. There is not terror, only peace. Then Mole and Rat really see him, his horns gleaming and his eyes smiling. The mood is over soon, and with its passing comes complete forgetfulness. While the wind sings gently on through the willows, Mole and Rat feel only as if they had an unremembered dream.

That fall Rat, while out walking, meets Sea Rat, a seafarer who tells wonderful tales of adventure throughout the Wide World. Rat gets a dreamy look in his eyes as Sea Rat paints his word pictures. It is all Mole can do to remind Rat of the fearsome things he said about the Wide World. The spell, however, is broken at last, and Rat settles down again, content with his narrow world.

Meanwhile, Toad's escape is almost ruined by his conceit and his carelessness. As he is about to be caught again, Rat rescues him and takes him home. There Rat tells Toad that the weasels and stoats took over Toad Hall while Toad was in prison. Badger has a plan to recover Toad Hall. Through a tunnel known only to Badger, the four friends sneak up on the intruders and capture Toad Hall again for its rightful owner. Toad, of course, takes all the credit.

The four continue to live in joy and contentment. Unafraid, they walk in the Wild Wood, for the weasels have learned their lesson, and they hear the wind whispering its gentle song.

Critical Evaluation:

Kenneth Grahame wrote his fantasy-allegories, including *The Wind in the Willows*, while employed as Secretary of the Bank of England. His animal characters belong to the same world in which human beings live; the same foibles and excesses and the same motives and loyalties possess them. Nevertheless, it is an optimist's world as well, where hope exists and where the visionary experience reveals "The Friend and the Helper."

Whether or not *The Wind in the Willows* is a children's book is a moot question. Mole's discoveries parallel a child's explorations in the world. The story, however, has wider appeal, for Mole learns, as all human beings must, to live in the larger world outside his home. When he returns to the familiar scents and the simple welcome of his home, Mole realizes that, although it is an important part of his life, home is no longer his entire life. He returns to the world of sunlight and further discoveries. Together with his friends—Rat, Badger, and Toad—he learns to live in the world they call the "Wild Wood."

The theme of escape, therefore, is quite important in the novel. Mole desires to escape from the boredom of maintaining his home and his everyday existence; Badger's escape is from society. Although he does not succumb, Rat is strongly intrigued by the stories of the Wide World told by Sea Rat, and Toad desires to elude every trace of responsibility to the rest of the world. Children's story or not, Grahame's book contains a certain amount of didacticism. Animals in the story, especially Rat, live according to a codified standard of existence. In this standard, the reader finds an implied but not explicit correspondence between the codes of conduct in the story and those normally taught to children. The reader is encouraged to reach for one's potential but not to exceed it—a difficult concept to explain to adults, let alone children. Nevertheless, maturity emerges here as the ability to recognize oneself realistically.

Grahame combines gentle satire with a keen understanding of the psychological realities that lie behind his characters' actions. Rat is the cautious judgmental teacher; Badger is the philosopher who hates society but likes people; and Toad is the incorrigible playboy, conceited, careless, and always in trouble. Along with Mole, the four represent an example of true friendship. By banding together, they retake Toad Hall from the weasels and restore the place to order with clean bed linens and fresh bars of soap.

The meaning of the song of the wind in the willows is revealed only to Rat and Mole. Badger survives through his philosophical stance, Toad with his indomitable will to have fun. Rat and Mole, however, need a vision. Like modern-day Everymen, Rat and Mole are allowed to see the pantheistic "Friend and the Helper," the horned, hook-nosed creature who plays panpipes at dawn and smiles benevolently through his beard. The vision is a moment when Rat and Mole fear neither death nor life, and, as they drop into the sleep of forgetfulness, their faces keep a blissful smile of peace.

Further Reading

Carpenter, Humphrey. "The Wind in the Willows." In *Secret Gardens: A Study of the Golden Age of Children's Litera-ture*. Boston: Houghton Mifflin, 1985. Carpenter, coauthor of *The Oxford Companion to Children's Literature*, concludes that, of all the subjects in his study, only Grahame managed to create a utopian world. Carpenter argues that the level at which *The Wind in the Willows* explores the artistic imagination gives the book its coherence.

Chalmers, Patrick R. *Kenneth Grahame: Life, Letters, and Unpublished Work*. London: Methuen, 1933. This biography, appearing a year after Grahame's death, sentimentalizes the genesis of *The Wind in the Willows*. Valuable in its extracts from Grahame's letters to his son documenting the development of the story and for the correspondence between Grahame and his readers and publishers.

Green, Peter. *Kenneth Grahame 1859-1932: A Study of His Life, Work, and Times*. London: John Murray, 1959. Considered a groundbreaking study. Presents an in-depth analysis of the psychological undercurrents, social context, literary sources, and creative method that produced *The Wind in the Willows*.

Hunt, Peter. *"The Wind in the Willows": A Fragmented Arcadia*. New York: Twayne, 1994. A student's guide to the book. Discusses Grahame's life, the significance and critical reception of the book, and its narrative structure, characters, symbolism, political and universal themes, and use of language. Also provides advice for teaching the book.

Kuznets, Lois R. *Kenneth Grahame*. Boston: Twayne, 1987. Cogently discusses the work's thematic and formal complexity, from its mock-epic structure and density of style to its archetypal associations. Surveys modern evaluations and adaptations.

Prince, Alison. *Kenneth Grahame: An Innocent in the Wild Wood*. London: Allison & Busby, 1994. Biography, tracing Grahame's unhappy childhood, marriage, and the birth of his only child, Alastair, for whom he wrote *The Wind in the Willows*.

Sale, Roger. "Kenneth Grahame." In *Fairy Tales and After: From Snow White to E. B. White*. Cambridge, Mass.: Harvard University Press, 1978. Examines *The Wind in the Willows* as a classic of children's literature. Sale argues that the book, reflecting Grahame's own anxieties, offers reassurance in the face of the demands of adult life.

Scholbin, Roger C. "Danger and Compulsion in *The Wind and the Willows*, or Toad and Hyde Together at Last." In *The Haunted Mind: The Supernatural in Victorian Literature*, edited by Elton E. Smith and Robert Haas. Lanham, Md.: Scarecrow Press, 1999. Focuses on the supernatural elements in the book, describing how these elements are an interior force expressed through the characters' behavior.

Wullschläger, Jackie. "Kenneth Grahame: Et in Arcadia Ego." In *Inventing Wonderland: The Lives and Fantasies of Lewis Carroll, Edward Lear, J. M. Barrie, Kenneth Grahame, and A. A. Milne*. New York: Free Press, 1995. Analyzes *The Wind in the Willows* and other children's literature written between 1865 and 1930. Describes how the five childlike authors, living in a society that idolized childhood, expressed their personal longings and frustrations in their literature.

Wind, Sand, and Stars

Author: Antoine de Saint-Exupéry (1900-1944)
First published: Terre des hommes, 1939 (English translation, 1939)
Type of work: Memoir

Principal personages:
ANTOINE DE SAINT-EXUPÉRY, a writer and an airline pilot
HENRI GUILLAUMET, his friend, also a pilot
EL MAMMOUN, a Moorish chieftain

In 1926, Antoine de Saint-Exupéry embarked on a career as an airline pilot for the aviation company that eventually became Air France. His memories of adventurous and fulfilling years as a pilot and, to a lesser degree, his experiences as a newspaper reporter at the front during the Spanish Civil War constitute the raw material for the varied and isolated episodes of this work. It is a memoir in the form of a novel, although it lacks continuity of action and does not disguise its autobiographical orientation. However, the brilliance of the imagery, the epic proportions of the narration, and above all, the unity of meaning that fuses together the episodes, transform the work beyond pure autobiography or memoir.

Despite the legendary aspect of the pilot's exploits, the tone of the work is one of sobriety and modesty. For Saint-Exupéry, courage in its highest conception comes from a sense of responsibility. When courage becomes temerity, tempting death for the sake of vanity and excitement, it serves no moral purpose and therefore should be condemned. For this reason, toreadors do not elicit the admiration of the narrator of *Wind, Sand, and Stars*, a memoir in novel form. Toreadors seek primarily the glory of one Sunday afternoon, whereas the sacrifices of the pilots who carry the mail are performed out of a feeling of chosen and accepted duty. Those who carry out a dangerous mission conscientiously, quietly, and to its final conclusion discover a kind of spiritual truth; they free themselves of earthly and selfish concerns and discover that what really animates them are the bonds that connect them to other human beings.

Lucid gravity in the face of imminent death and a profound sense of duty are vividly illustrated by the harrowing experience of Henri Guillaumet, the narrator's close friend

and fellow pilot. When he crashed in the Chilean Andes in midwinter of 1930, he took shelter from a blinding snowstorm and remained under his cockpit for two days and two nights. On the third day, he set out in temperatures far below zero. He had to hack out steps in steep ice walls with his boots, and his feet soon became swollen and bleeding from frostbite. On the third day, he fell from exhaustion many times. At last, he no longer tried to get up. Then he remembered that when a pilot disappears without a trace, his death is not declared legal for four years and his wife cannot receive the pension. He decided to prop his body up against a rock so that it would be found when the snows melted. Once on his feet again, however, he continued on for three more days, and was eventually rescued by a peasant woman. For Saint-Exupéry, Guillaumet's grandeur resided in his refusal to discuss his act in terms of courage; his determination was born of the realization that he held in his hands the fate of his wife and comrades and that he was still responsible for the mail that had gone down in the plane. His greatness was in his disinterestedness.

Through the act of flying, Saint-Exupéry was able to perceive another basic verity that he illustrates concretely in his work: The obstacles that natural elements place in the way of human beings offer them the means to discover themselves. In measuring himself against the forces of nature—the mountains, the snowstorm, the cyclone, the desert—Saint-Exupéry the pilot finds himself face-to-face with the fundamental problems of his relationship to the earth and to death. Like farmers who use their plows to struggle against the soil, aviators have a tool—their airplanes—that put them in contact with the natural elements.

In 1936, the author had flying adventures that led to certain self-discoveries. He recounts these adventures vividly in *Wind, Sand, and Stars*. On a flight from Paris to Saigon, he and his navigator crashed in the Egyptian desert. They made a march of three days in the torrid heat, covering about 125 miles, and had only a little more than one pint of liquid between them. Yet the sterility of the desert and the proximity of death were spiritually rewarding. The smallest signs of life—the tracks of a desert fox, for example—prompted feelings of appreciation and gratitude for the pleasures that existence offers. The imminence of death led not to panic but to a detached sense of self-fulfillment. Because of his tool, the plane, and his combat with nature, the pilot felt himself rich with treasures that cannot be judged by material standards.

The plane becomes for this "poet of the air" a way of annihilating time and space to link human beings of all nations and races. Pilots themselves profit enormously from the opportunity to deepen their knowledge of humanness. Writing at a time when people were obsessed with the performance of machines, Saint-Exupéry stressed above all the plane's capacity for surmounting the natural barriers that separate human beings. At the beginning of his career, the author spent a great deal of time among the refractory Moorish tribes in the western Sahara. In charge of a refueling station in this almost uninhabited part of the world, he succeeded in gaining the esteem of these nomads and was eventually regarded by them as a kind of sage. They were struggling to preserve their freedom, and in this book, Saint-Exupéry evokes the memory of one of his friends, El Mammoun, who could not bear the degradation of being a vassal of another people. Honored and trusted by white officers, El Mammoun revolted against them one day during an excursion into the desert, massacred them, and fled into free territory. This Moor had suddenly realized that he was betraying his tribe, his religion, and his past as a famous warrior by submitting to Christians who had encroached on his people. Contact with this desert chieftain permitted Saint-Exupéry to develop one of the most important tenets of his code of ethics: All people seek a climate and terrain favorable to their self-fulfillment, and each individual must acquire tolerance and sympathy for each other individual's particular truth.

In Argentina, the narrator's plane took him for a brief moment into the mysterious domain of the human soul. After landing in a field near Concordia, the pilot was taken into a strange house that, like a massive citadel, seemed to want to keep all of its secrets. The two girls who lived there assessed the stranger to determine whether he merited acceptance into their intimate world. At dinner, the aviator heard a noise under the table and was informed that snakes had made a nest there. The girls awaited his reaction. He smiled, and was admitted. As he notes, these two young girls seemed to possess a universal quality. The plane opens new horizons to the pilots and raises the veil of mystery that surrounds people who differ from them.

The first step on the road to this humanism is the willingness to give of the self. In the closing pages of *Wind, Sand, and Stars*, a Spanish soldier who is about to take part in a suicidal attack is presented as another living incarnation of the quintessence of Saint-Exupéry's thought. This soldier who smiles on the eve of battle has consented to sacrifice his life for a goal situated completely outside his own selfish interests. He has given up a comfortable existence in Barcelona because he sensed intuitively that a struggle accepted in common with others—the esprit de corps that motivated the pilots of the airmail service—is a condition of inner liberation. The ideologies in conflict in the Spanish Civil War hold no interest for this soldier; selfless action and duty inspire in him a love infinitely more elevated and satisfying than he had ever known before.

Further Reading

Cate, Curtis. *Antoine de Saint-Exupéry*. 1970. New ed. New York: Paragon House, 1990. Contains many informative details and is well written. Portrays Saint-Exupéry as an eccentric figure.

DeRamus, Barnett. *From Juby to Arras: Engagement in Saint-Exupéry*. Lanham, Md.: University Press of America, 1990. Examines four of Saint-Exupéry's works, including *Wind, Sand, and Stars*, focusing on his views of engagement, or commitment, to the major themes of nature, the desert, flight, and the enemy. Discusses the influence of World War I on Saint-Exupéry's postwar writing, and analyzes the role of airplanes and flight in the literature of the 1920's and 1930's.

Des Vallieres, Nathalie. *Saint-Exupéry: Art, Writing, and Musings*. New York: Rizzoli International, 2004. Des Vallieres, Saint-Exupéry's great-niece, compiled this collection of her great-uncle's photographs, letters, drawings, and private notebooks, which recount the writer's life in both words and images.

Migeo, Marcel. *Saint-Exupéry*. Translated by Herma Briffault. 1960. New ed. Paris: Flammarion, 1966. An interesting, reliable account of Saint-Exupéry's life. Migeo, who knew the pilot-writer, is mainly concerned in this book with Saint-Exupéry's personal life, but he also examines the role played by his experiences as a pilot in the French military in forming his theories of art.

Robinson, Joy D. Marie. *Antoine de Saint-Exupéry*. Boston: Twayne, 1984. Explores the philosophies and themes that underlie all Saint-Exupéry's works. The study is enriched by the extensive use of biographical material. Includes a chronology and a selected bibliography of English and French sources. Essential for any literary discussion of Saint-Exupéry.

Schiff, Stacy. *Saint-Exupéry*. New York: Alfred A. Knopf, 1995. Contains previously unavailable material on Saint-Exupéry's life and career, especially his experience as a war pilot. Draws on extensive interviews in considering the relationship between Saint-Exupéry the aviator and Saint-Exupéry the writer. Includes detailed notes and a bibliography.

The Wind-up Bird Chronicle

Author: Haruki Murakami (1949-   )
First published: Nejimaki-dori kuronikuru, 1994-1995,
    3 volumes (English translation, 1997)
Type of work: Novel
Type of plot: Surrealist
Time of plot: 1984-1985
Locale: Tokyo

Principal characters:
TORU OKADA, the narrator
KUMIKO OKADA, his wife
NOBORU WATAYA, Kumiko's brother
MALTA KANO, a clairvoyant
CRETA KANO, her sister
NUTMEG, a psychic healer
CINNAMON, her son
MAY KASAHARA, the Okada's neighbor

The Story:

Toru Okada is thirty years old and has just resigned from his job as a lawyer's assistant. His wife, Kumiko, works for the publisher of a health food magazine. While cooking spaghetti one evening, Okada gets strange phone calls from a woman who seems to know details about his life; she solicits phone sex from him. Okada ignores the woman and goes out to look for his and his wife's missing cat, Noboru Wataya, named for Okada's brother-in-law. While searching for the cat, he meets May Kasahara, a sixteen-year-old girl on sick leave from school, who promises to keep an eye out for the cat while out of her house.

Meanwhile, the Okada's marriage has become increasingly strained, as Kumiko returns home from work later and later. A woman named Malta Kano calls Okada and asks to meet him. She turns out to be a clairvoyant who researches the mystic elements of water. She tells Okada that her sister, Creta Kano, had been raped by Okada's brother-in-law, Wataya, and claims that the disappearance of the cat marks the beginning of a series of life-changing events in Okada's life. Okada remembers how another medium, Mr. Honda—whom Kumiko's father had demanded Okada and Kumiko see—had warned him to be careful of water.

While again searching for the cat, Okada runs into May at

the vacant house in their neighborhood. She calls him Mr. Wind-up Bird for the bird with a creaking call that Okada hears every morning. May reveals that she has been working for a wig company in Tokyo and asks him to join her on the job. She also shows him the dried-up well near the house, and Okada notes how he is attracted by the darkness inside the well.

Okada reflects on what Kumiko tells him about her difficult childhood, during which her sister, the favorite of the family, had died. Okada, in turn, reveals his hatred for his brother-in-law, a pompous academic with no real conviction and an increasingly prominent presence in the media.

Soon after Okada and Malta meet, Malta's sister, Creta, goes to the Okada house to take a water sample from the tap. After Okada urges her to give him more information about his missing cat, she tells him that she does not know how everything will add up, but that she must tell him about her past. She recounts how, when she was young, she had suffered from physical pain so terrible that she decided to commit suicide at the age of twenty. She crashed her brother's car into a wall but survived to discover that the pain had gone away. To pay for the damage to the car and the wall, she became a prostitute. Creta then reveals that Okada's brother-in-law had been a client of hers. Surprised, Okada asks her why her sister Malta said she had been raped by Wataya. Creta leaves Okada's house as he is fetching her more coffee.

Okada goes with May to work, and as part of their jobs, they survey men in Tokyo and label them according to their degree of baldness. They end up discussing how balding is so frightening because it is as if life itself is being worn away.

Okada hears from an uncle about the history of the vacant house, nicknamed The Hanging House, in Okada's neighborhood. A former military officer and his wife had lived there. After fearing trial for war atrocities he had committed in China, the two committed suicide. Another former owner, an actor who had been going blind, killed herself, too, by drowning herself in the tub.

Okada receives a letter from a man named Tokutaro Mamiya, who had served in the army with Mr. Honda. After Honda's death, he says, he had been put in charge of distributing Mr. Honda's keepsakes. Mamiya tells Okada a story about the time when he and Mr. Honda had been sent on a reconnaissance mission. Mongolian officers had discovered them, and the civilian investigator in charge of the mission, Yamamoto, was flayed alive. Mamiya was given the choice of being shot or jumping into a deep well. Mamiya chose the well, and Mr. Honda, who had escaped, came back to save him. Mamiya tells Okada that the time that he spent in the well had been life-changing, that the experience had taken away his sense of what it means to be alive.

One evening, Kumiko does not return home from work. Wataya calls to say that she has run off with another man. He claims that Okada has ruined her life and refuses to allow him to communicate with her. Meanwhile, Okada dreams about having sex with Creta. He later finds out that they have been having shared dreams, and that the sex occurs in a realm between dreaming and reality. In an attempt to get his wife back, Okada turns inward and goes down the well in the lot of the vacant house to think. He reflects deeply on the time when he and Kumiko first met. He remembers her abortion, the deterioration of their marriage, and her affair. After spending the night in the well, he discovers that the ladder has disappeared; he cannot climb out. May reveals that she has taken the ladder. Okada stays in the well until Creta finds him.

After returning home, Okada receives a letter from Kumiko that graphically recounts her affair and asks him to agree to a divorce. He also discovers that after being in the well, a strange mark that emits heat had appeared on his cheek. Okada starts spending a lot of time at the Shinjuku station in Tokyo, watching the crowds. During these trips in the city, he meets Nutmeg and her mute son, Cinnamon, psychic

healers who employ Okada to use his mark to heal others. The mark, they say, has mystical powers.

Meanwhile, the cat returns, and Okada renames him Mackerel. Okada, also, decides to rent the vacant house. Nutmeg later tells Okada a story of what her father, a veterinarian, had witnessed during the Japanese occupation of Manchukuo, on the Chinese mainland. Because there was no food to feed the animals at the zoo, the army slaughtered all the animals.

Okada and Kumiko finally communicate, messaging each other through computers, and she tells him that he should forget about her. Okada tells her that he has been trying to find her by looking into the darkness and searching for something he calls More of everything. Kumiko says she does not understand, and they say good-bye.

Prompted by Nutmeg's story, Okada reads about Manchukuo. One morning, he discovers on the computer a document, "The Wind-up Bird Chronicle," which further recounts Nutmeg's father's experiences in China. Okada learns that, not wanting to waste ammunition, Japanese soldiers had used bayonets to kill Chinese prisoners. One lieutenant had asked a young soldier to beat a prisoner to death with a baseball bat. Okada wonders if Cinnamon had made up the story, and how he and Nutmeg came up with the term "wind-up bird," May's nickname for Okada.

Okada goes down the well again and has a vision that he beats someone up with a baseball bat. When he awakes from the vision, he realizes that water is flooding the well. He remembers Mr. Honda's warning to him to be careful of water. Nutmeg saves him from the flooding well.

After returning home, Okada finds out that Wataya has been hospitalized after being beaten with a bat by someone resembling Okada. He also discovers a new "Wind-up Bird Chronicle" document on the computer from Kumiko, a document that tells him that she will go to the hospital to kill her brother. She claims that Wataya has spiritually defiled both her and her sister, who had committed suicide years ago.

Critical Evaluation:

Haruki Murakami's fiction is best known for its cosmopolitan integration of both Japanese and American cultures into the narrative. In his short stories and novels, Murakami frequently alludes to rock and roll, jazz, and classic European literature and music. The son of teachers of Japanese literature, he also grew up with an extensive knowledge of traditional Japanese culture. *The Wind-up Bird Chronicle* shows how, for Murakami, both Japanese history and Western art, music, and commodities, inseparable from contemporary Japanese culture, are essential to a relevant representation of Japanese society.

The Wind-up Bird Chronicle is regarded as Murakami's most important novel. The ideas for the book originally came from Murakami's short stories "The Wind-up Bird" and "Tuesday's Women," and the novel was first serialized in the Japanese magazine *Shincho* (1994-1995). Murakami says that he had developed his stoic, deadpan writing style by first writing in his limited English and then translating that writing into Japanese.

Although *The Wind-up Bird Chronicle* recounts Okada's experiences in the first-person *boku*, the Japanese informal pronoun for boys and men (and rarely girls and women), Okada is largely reticent about his emotions, even when his wife disappears. Instead, the narrative reveals Okada's thoughts and emotions through dreams and mystic events. Prominent in the novel are psychic healing and communal dreaming, in which two characters share the same subconscious vision. After his wife leaves, Okada descends the well near the vacant house to search within the darkness for what caused her to disappear. Also appearing in the novel are clairvoyants, such as Malta Kano, Creta Kano, and Nutmeg, who are there to help Okada and to tell him their own stories.

The novel blurs the boundaries between dreams and reality, as Okada frequently has visions in the well that echo the stories of the clairvoyants and have tangible ties to reality. For instance, after Okada hears Nutmeg's story about how a Japanese soldier had been forced to beat a prisoner to death with a baseball bat, Okada, too, has a vision in the well about beating someone up with a bat. After emerging from the well, he learns that he might have beaten his brother-in-law Noboru Wataya to near death with a bat. The novel implies that there is an inseparable connection between history, vision, and reality.

Despite the disappearances of Okada's wife and the cat, events that hold the narrative together, the novel is largely characterized by a series of stories told by the strangers whom Okada meets. The connections between each story and the next appear ambiguous, but many of the stories deal with the violence in Japan's past. Mamiya tells Okada about his experiences in the army in Outer Mongolia, and Nutmeg recounts the Japanese massacre of prisoners and of zoo animals in China. These stories suggest that to understand himself and the events in his life, Okada must reflect on Japan's violent history in the twentieth century.

Wataya, Okada's brother-in-law, embodies the kind of senseless violence that recurs in the characters' stories. He is the figure of patriarchal control as he dominates his sister Kumiko and seeks to protect their family's reputation. Wataya considers Okada unworthy of the family and attempts to control Kumiko's communication with Okada. Creta accuses Wataya of having raped her, and the novel ends with Kumiko's determination to kill him for spiritually raping her and her sister.

Alice Chuang

Further Reading

Fisher, Susan. "An Allegory of Return: Murakami Haruki's *The Wind-up Bird Chronicle*." *Comparative Literature Studies* 37, no. 2 (2000): 155-170. Argues that *The Wind-up Bird Chronicle* is the most Japanese of Murakami's novels through 1999. Provides a useful overview of Murakami's life, his fascination with Western culture, and the historical events that shaped the novel.

Japan Foundation, comp. and trans. *A Wilde Haruki Chase: Reading Murakami Around the World.* Berkeley, Calif.: Stone Bridge Press, 2008. A compilation of essays by Murakami's translators as well as by writers and critics who reflect on his global appeal. Accessible to students and general readers.

Rubin, Jay. *Haruki Murakami and the Music of Words.* London: Harvill Press, 2002. Written by Murakami's official translator, this book looks at Murakami's use of music in his novels as well as the untranslatable nuances to his use of language. Useful for students interested in the gap between the original work and the translation. Includes a chapter on *The Wind-up Bird Chronicle*.

Seats, Michael. *Murakami Haruki: The Simulacrum in Contemporary Japanese Culture.* Plymouth, England: Lexington Books, 2006. Focuses on idea of the simulacrum (a representation of reality) as a mode of critique of Japanese culture in Murakami's novels. Provides a useful overview of contexts for and critical reception of *The Wind-up Bird Chronicle*.

Suter, Rebecca. *The Japanization of Modernity: Murakami Haruki Between Japan and the United States.* Cambridge, Mass.: Asia Center, Harvard University, 2008. Examines Murakami's novels in terms of how American readers and critics sense Japan as a new center of modernity and cosmopolitanism. A useful metacritical look at Western assumptions about Japanese culture.

The Winds of War *and* War and Remembrance

Author: Herman Wouk (1915-　　)
First published: The Winds of War, 1971; *War and
　Remembrance*, 1978
Type of work: Novels
Type of plot: Historical realism
Time of plot: 1939-1945
Locale: Washington, D.C.; Berlin; New York; Siena,
　Italy; Warsaw; London; Moscow; Rome; Pearl
　Harbor, Hawaii; Singapore

Principal characters:
VICTOR "PUG" HENRY, a U.S. Navy officer
RHODA HENRY, his wife
WARREN HENRY, his son, a naval aviator
BYRON HENRY, his son, a U.S. submariner
AARON JASTROW, a novelist
NATALIE JASTROW HENRY, Byron's wife and Aaron's niece
LOUIS HENRY, Natalie and Byron's son
JANICE LACOUTURE HENRY, Warren's wife
MADELINE HENRY, Pug's daughter
BEREL JASTROW, Aaron's cousin
ALISTAIR "TALKIE" TUDSBURY, a British war
　correspondent
PAMELA TUDSBURY HENRY, his daughter, and Pug's
　second wife
PALMER KIRBY, an American industrialist
LESLIE SLOTE, a U.S. foreign service officer
HUGH CLEVELAND, a New York radio personality
HARRISON PETERS, a U.S. Army officer, and Rhoda's
　second husband

The Story:

Victor "Pug" Henry, a U.S. naval officer, is sent to Berlin as a naval attaché. On the boat to Berlin, he and his wife meet British war correspondent Alistair "Talkie" Tudsbury and his daughter, Pamela. In Berlin, Pug plays a significant role in the interaction between the German and U.S. governments. He and Rhoda become socially involved with Nazi officials as well.

As the war intensifies, Rhoda returns to the United States. U.S. president Franklin D. Roosevelt calls Pug to the White House and involves him in nonofficial diplomatic missions to the English, leading Pug to play an important role in the Lend-Lease program with the British government. Rhoda has an affair with Palmer Kirby, an industrialist. Pug goes to England, observes the British work, with radar, and goes on a bombing raid to Germany as an observer. Upon his return, Pamela is waiting for him and suggests that they begin an extramarital affair. Pug is tempted but his strict moral code prevents him from pursuing such an arrangement. Pug goes to Moscow during the German invasion of Russia. While there, he is once again in Pamela's company, as she has accompanied her father, Talkie, to Moscow. Pug continues his work for Roosevelt, tours the battlefields, and becomes more involved with Pamela. He is then reassigned to the Pacific as a battleship captain, the assignment he has always wanted.

During this time, Warren Henry, Pug's son, becomes a naval aviator; marries Janice Lacouture, a U.S. senator's daughter; and is assigned to duty in the Pacific. Pug's daughter, Madeline, goes to New York and takes a job in radio with Hugh Cleveland. While Pug is very pleased with Warren's choice of a naval career, he is highly upset by Madeline's choice of work. In contrast to Warren, son Byron has not opted for a naval career and has gone to Italy as a research assistant to Aaron Jastrow, a renowned Jewish scholar and author of *A Jew's Jesus*. He falls in love with Jastrow's niece, Natalie, and goes to Poland with her; she wants to visit her relatives there, especially Berel Jastrow and his family, and Leslie Slote, her fiancé, who is working at the American embassy in Warsaw.

Natalie and Byron are caught in the bombing of Warsaw. They are finally able to leave German-occupied Poland with the American embassy staff and other Americans. As the staffs of the various embassies depart under German supervision, only the Americans refuse to identify Jews among them and to leave them behind. Byron returns to Berlin, and Natalie returns to Siena, Italy. They are then reunited in Siena, and Natalie realizes that she loves Byron, not Slote.

Encouraged by his father, Byron returns to the United States and enters submarine school. Natalie's father dies, which brings her back to the United States as well. She and Byron plan to marry, but Natalie feels she must return to Siena and convince Aaron to return to the United States with her. Aaron's stubbornness as well as his passport problems and questions of his citizenship trap Natalie in Italy. Byron's submarine arrives in Lisbon, Portugal, and Natalie meets him there. They marry. She stays in Siena with Aaron.

Natalie is pregnant and soon gives birth to a boy; they name him Louis. Eventually, Natalie and Aaron decide to embark to Palestine because of the passport problems. Then, Jastrow's former student, Werner Beck, who is charged with transporting Jews from Italy to Germany, arrives and flatters Aaron into staying in Italy.

Pug arrives in Pearl Harbor after the bombing and finds the ship *California* destroyed. He also finds a letter from Rhoda, asking for a divorce. Shortly thereafter, Pug receives command of the cruiser *Northampton* and a letter from Rhoda withdrawing her request for a divorce.

Pug, Warren, and Byron, now in Europe, are all involved in the battles that liberate the Jews in the concentration camps. Janice begins an affair with Aster, Byron's fellow submariner, but he is soon killed; Warren and Talkie die as well in separate military campaigns. Pug continues to play an important role as adviser in the war under both Roosevelt and U.S. president Harry S. Truman.

Berel Jastrow, Natalie, and Aaron are sent to concentration camps. As a captured Russian soldier, Berel, Aaron's cousin, is sent to Auschwitz with a work detail. He eventually escapes and is instrumental in rescuing children from the camps. Natalie and Aaron are interred in Theresienstadt, a camp specially created to convince the Danish Red Cross that life is idyllic in the camps. Active in a Zionist group, Natalie will soon be transported to Auschwitz; Aaron risks his life to speak to the camp commander to save her. Risking all, he refuses to play his role for the Danish if Natalie is transported. Natalie is spared, but is subjected to a tortuous encounter with the commander in which her son Louis's life is threatened. Berel arranges Louis's escape. After the Danish visit, Natalie and Aaron are no longer useful and are transported to Auschwitz, where Aaron dies. Natalie is sent to Ravensbruck and then put on a train for Buchenwald. She is found hiding under the train and says she is an American; she is identified by Avram Rabinovitz, who had tried to help her escape from Italy. He notifies Byron, who then locates Louis and is reunited with Natalie.

As the war concludes, Rhoda and Pug have divorced. She has married Harrison Peters, an Army officer; Pug has married Pamela, Talkie's daughter; and Madeline has left Hugh and remarried. Berel lies buried in an unmarked grave.

Critical Evaluation:

In *The Winds of War* and *War and Remembrance*, Herman Wouk weaves together three major story lines: a historical account of the events leading up to World War II, and an account of the war itself; a detailed account of the devastating Nazi campaign to eradicate the Jews in Europe; and the personal story of Victor "Pug" Henry and his family. Wouk adds to the complexity of the novels' structures by including Pug's translation and commentaries of *World Empire Lost* and *World Holocaust*, books adapted from an account of the war written by the German general Armin von Roon.

Although the war is primarily portrayed through experiences and opinions of Americans, and although Pug's commentaries often point out von Roon's errors of judgment, the inclusion of this fictitious account by the fictional von Roon gives the novels a certain balance of viewpoint, which adds to their realism and gives the reader a sense of actually being privy to the German conduct of the war. Wouk also manages to depict the interaction of the historical characters in the novels with the fictional characters in such a way that the fictional characters appear as real as the historical characters. The novels become real accounts of the war only on a deeper, more personal level than is found in a work of history.

Wouk's portrayal of the battles in the Pacific and the conflict with the Japanese is more technically oriented than the account of the European conflict. His depiction of the submarines, battleships, and aircraft in battle, and the interaction among the various commanders and officers, shows his meticulous research and attention to detail.

It is in his portrayal of the concentration camps and the transport of the Jews that Wouk's talent is most notable. From Aaron Jastrow's and Natalie Jastrow Henry's first attempts and failures to leave Italy, he creates a sense of foreboding and inevitable disaster, yet he always maintains a sense of hope. Slowly, Aaron and Natalie become more and more entangled in the plight of being Jewish in World War II Europe. For some time, they tend to see themselves as privileged and surrounded by a certain security that the common, nameless Jews do not have. Aaron is a famous scholar and author; Natalie has a U.S. passport. Then, little by little, they come to realize that they are just like the others, vulnerable and unable to control their destinies. Wouk's detailed portrayal of the procedures and the depiction of the dead little girl still clutching the sprig of apple blossoms at Auschwitz poignantly portray the horror and absurdity of the camps.

While most of Wouk's characters are static and undergo little development, Aaron, Natalie, and Leslie Slote change considerably through the two novels. Slote once evaluated all of his actions in terms of his foreign service career. As he becomes more convinced of the reality of the atrocities committed by the Germans and of the impossibility of any action from the U.S. government, his values change. He becomes a paratrooper and loses his life in France. Natalie, self-confident and defiant, is reduced to groveling and begging when her son Louis's life is threatened. Once she knows he is safe, she stoically endures suffering, determined to survive and find him. However, it is Aaron who develops most. From the dilettante, academic snob, he metamorphoses into someone willing to risk a gruesome death to save Natalie, and he dies fully realizing the importance of his Jewish heritage.

Wouk uses repetition to give his novels a sense of the ever-flowing sameness of human life in spite of catastrophe. Warren Henry and Janice Lacouture's marriage appears to be a reenactment of the marriage of Pug and Rhoda. Both Rhoda and Janice come from families more affluent than those of their husbands. Both Rhoda and Janice are bored and dissatisfied with the everyday, mundane life of a U.S. Navy wife. Both Pug and Warren are totally devoted to the Navy and their careers, giving them a self-centeredness that eclipses anyone around them. Left alone in Washington, D.C., Rhoda has an affair with a businessman, Palmer Kirby; Janice, left alone in Pearl Harbor, becomes involved with submariner "Lady" Aster. This repetitive theme is further enhanced by references to the dissatisfaction of Navy wives and to the frequent divorces.

It is interesting to note from a feminist viewpoint that Wouk's female characters, regardless of their education or social status, tend to subordinate themselves to a man's career. Rhoda and Janice accept lives based on their husbands' careers; Natalie devotes herself to Aaron's writing and almost sacrifices her son and herself to his stubborn vanity; and Pamela follows her father into all kinds of danger and discomfort because he no longer sees well and needs her help to continue his career. At the end of the novel, Rhoda hands Pug's belongings to Pamela and tells her how to play the role of his wife. Thus, Wouk anchors his novels in the sameness that pervades everyday life.

Shawncey Webb

Further Reading

Beichman, Arnold. *Herman Wouk: The Novelist as Social Historian*. New Brunswick, N.J.: Transaction, 2004. Treats both the historical and literary aspects of the novels. This book is carefully researched, and is based on interviews with Wouk and on his personal papers.

Bolton, Richard R. "*The Winds of War* and Wouk's Wish for the World." *Midwest Quarterly* 16 (1975): 389-408. A good discussion of Wouk's views on peace, tolerance, and brotherhood.

Guttmann, Allen. *The Jewish Writer in America: Assimilation and the Crisis of Identity*. New York: Oxford University Press, 1971. This study examines Wouk's importance and place in the tradition of the American Jewish novel.

Klingenstein, Susanne. "Sweet Natalie: Herman Wouk's Messenger to the Gentiles." In *Talking Back: Images of Jewish Women in American Popular Culture*, edited by Joyce Antler. Hanover, N.H.: University Press of New England, 1998. Klingenstein examines the character of Natalie Jastrow. Describes how Wouk uses his character to personalize the Holocaust for non-Jewish readers.

Paulson, Barbara A., ed. *The Historical Novel: A Celebration of the Achievements of Herman Wouk*. Washington, D.C.: Library of Congress, 1999. This work helps place Wouk in the context of American literature.

Raphael, Marc. "From Marjorie to Tevya: The Image of Jews in American Popular Literature, Theater, and Comedy." *American Jewish History* 74 (1984): 66-72. This journal article is especially valuable for those wishing to understand Wouk's portrayal of Aaron Jastrow and Berel Jastrow.

Shapiro, Edward S. "The Jew as Patriot: Herman Wouk and American Jewish Identity." In *We Are Many: Reflections on American Jewish History and Identity*. Syracuse, N.Y.: Syracuse University Press, 2005. This collection includes a retrospective review of Wouk's career. Shapiro argues persuasively that Wouk is concerned principally with defining American Jewish identity.

Winesburg, Ohio
A Group of Tales of Ohio Small Town Life

Author: Sherwood Anderson (1876-1941)
First published: 1919
Type of work: Novel
Type of plot: Psychological realism
Time of plot: Late nineteenth century
Locale: Winesburg, Ohio

Principal characters:
GEORGE WILLARD, a young reporter
ELIZABETH WILLARD, his mother
DR. REEFY, Elizabeth's confidant
HELEN WHITE, George's friend
KATE SWIFT, George's former teacher
THE REVEREND CURTIS HARTMAN, Kate's unknown
　admirer
WING BIDDLEBAUM, a berry picker

The Story:

Young George Willard is the only child of Elizabeth and Tom Willard. His father, a dull, conventional, insensitive man, owns the local hotel. His mother, who was once a popular young belle, has never loved Tom Willard; she married him in the hope that marriage would somehow change her life for the better, because it seemed to her that the young married women of the town were happy and satisfied. Soon after her marriage, however, she realized that she was now caught in the dull life of Winesburg, her dreams turned to drab realities by her life with Tom Willard.

The only person who has ever understood her is Dr. Reefy. Only in his small, untidy office does she feel free; only there does she achieve some measure of self-expression. Their relationship, doomed from the start, is nevertheless beautiful, a meeting of two lonely and sensitive people. Dr. Reefy, too, has his sorrows. Once, years ago, a young woman, pregnant and unmarried, had come to his office, and shortly afterward he married her. The following spring she died, and from that time on, Dr. Reefy has gone around making little paper pills and stuffing his pockets with them. On the pieces of paper that become the pills, he scribbles his thoughts about the beauty and strangeness of life.

Through her son George, Elizabeth Willard hopes to express herself; she sees in him the fulfillment of her own hopes and desires. More than anything, she fears that George will settle down in Winesburg. When she learns that he wants to be a writer, she is glad. Unknown to her husband, she has put away money enough to give her son a start in life, but before she can realize her ambition, she dies. Lying on her bed, she does not seem dead to either George or Dr. Reefy. To both, she is extremely beautiful. To George, she does not seem like his mother at all. To Dr. Reefy, she is the woman he has loved, now the symbol of another lost illusion.

Many people of the town seek out George Willard, who works as a reporter for the local newspaper; they tell him of their lives, their compulsions, and their failures. Old Wing Biddlebaum, the berry picker, had been a schoolteacher years before in another town. He had loved the boys who were in his charge, and he was, in fact, one of those few teachers who understand young people. One of his pupils, however, having conceived a strong affection for his teacher, had accused him of homosexuality, and Wing, although innocent, had been driven out of town. In Winesburg, he has become the best berry picker in the region, but always the same hands that earn his livelihood are a source of wonder and fear to him. When George Willard encounters him in the berry field, Wing raises his hands as if to caress the young man, but a wave of horror sweeps over him, and he hurriedly thrusts them into his pockets. To George, also, Wing's hands seem odd, mysterious.

Kate Swift, once George's teacher, had seen in him a future writer. She had tried to tell him what writing is, what it means. George had not understood exactly, but he had understood that Kate was speaking not as his teacher but as a woman. One night, in her house, she embraces him, for George is now a young man with whom she has fallen in love. On another night, when it seems that all of Winesburg is asleep, she goes to his room, but just as she is on the point of yielding to him, she strikes him and runs away, leaving George lonely and frustrated.

Kate lives across the street from the Presbyterian church, and the church's pastor, the Reverend Curtis Hartman, has learned accidentally that he can see into Kate's room from his study in the bell tower of the church. Night after night, he looks through the window at Kate in her bed. He wants at first to prove his faith, but his flesh is weak. One night, the same night Kate has fled from George Willard, the pastor sees her enter her room. He watches her as, naked, she throws herself on the bed and furiously pounds the pillows. Then she arises, kneels, and begins to pray. With a cry, he gets up from his chair, sweeps his Bible to the floor, smashes the glass in the window, and dashes out into the darkness. Running to the newspaper office, he bursts in on George. Wild-eyed, his fist dripping blood, he tells the astonished young man that God has appeared to him in the person of a naked woman, that Kate Swift is the instrument of the Almighty, and that he is saved.

In addition to Kate Swift, there are other women in George's life. One is Helen White, the banker's daughter. One night, George and Helen go out together. At first, they laugh and kiss, but then a strange new maturity overcomes them and keeps them apart. Louise Trunnion, a farm girl, writes to George, saying that she is his if he wants her. After dark, he goes out to the farm, and he and Louise go for a walk. There, in a berry field, George Willard enjoys the love that Helen White has refused him.

Like Louise Trunnion, Louise Bentley also wants love. Before coming to live in Winesburg, Louise had lived on a farm, forgotten and unloved by a greedy, fanatical father who had desired a son instead of a daughter. In Winesburg, she lives with the Hardy family while she goes to school. She is a good student, praised by her teachers, but she is resented by the two Hardy girls, who believe that Louise is always showing off. More than anything, she wants someone to love. One day, she sends young John Hardy a note, and a few weeks later, she gives herself to him. When it becomes clear that she is pregnant, Louise and John are married.

After their son, David, is born, John reproaches Louise for her cruelty toward the boy. She will not nurse the child, and she ignores him for long periods of time. As she has never really loved her husband, nor has he loved her, the marriage is not a happy one. At last, Louise and John separate; shortly afterward, Louise's father, Jesse Bentley, takes young David to live with him on the farm.

Old Jesse Bentley is convinced that God has manifested himself in his grandchild, that the young David, like the biblical hero, will be a savior, the conqueror of the philistines who own the land Jesse wants for himself. One day the old man takes the boy into the fields with him. Young David has brought along a little lamb, and the grandfather prepares to offer the animal as a sacrifice to the Almighty. The youngster, terrified, strikes his grandfather and runs away, never to return to Winesburg.

The time comes when George Willard has to choose between staying in Winesburg and starting out on his career as a writer. Shortly after his mother's death, George gets up early one morning and walks to the railroad station. There, with the postmistress's expression of good luck in his ears, he boards the train and leaves Winesburg behind.

Critical Evaluation:

Winesburg, Ohio has the stature of a modern classic. It is at once beautiful and tragic, realistic and poetic. Without constituting a novel in the usual sense of the word, the connected stories that make up the work have the full range and emotional impact of a novel. In simple though highly skillful and powerful language, Sherwood Anderson tells the story of a small town and the lonely, frustrated people who live there. Although regional in its setting and characters, the book is also intensely American. No one since Anderson has succeeded in interpreting the inner compulsions and loneliness of the national psyche with the same degree of accuracy and emotional impact.

Using young George Willard as protagonist and observer, Anderson creates his probing psychological portrait of small-town America. Although his characters outwardly seem dull and commonplace, Anderson is acutely tuned to the tensions between their psychological and emotional needs and the restrictions placed on their lives by the small-town atmosphere of Winesburg. Although not methodically psychoanalytical, Anderson's work probes deeply into the psychological lives of the characters to discover the emotional wounds that have been inflicted by the puritanical attitudes of the midwestern village. Anderson may not have been directly influenced by Sigmund Freud or Carl Jung, but his interests clearly parallel the interest in psychology among American intellectuals during the first quarter of the twentieth century. In this respect, Anderson can legitimately be called America's first psychological novelist.

Anderson believed that the traditional forms of the novel were too restrictive and formal to adapt well to his American subject matter, so *Winesburg, Ohio* represents in part an experiment in form. Rather than unifying his work through a plot in the usual sense, Anderson uses patterns of imagery, tone, character, and theme to achieve a sense of wholeness. It is, however, George Willard's narrative voice—and his presence as either observer or protagonist—in the stories that ultimately unifies them. As a small-town reporter, Willard can credibly serve as a confidant for his townspeople. Also, he is a kind of professional observer recording the surface lives of his people for the newspaper. At the same time, readers see him as a budding artist who is interested in discovering the deeper and more meaningful truths of individuals' lives than those seen at the surface. Eventually, George must make his choice as to which of these roles he will elect, and his function as the central consciousness of the book is vital to its aesthetic success.

Winesburg, Ohio also follows the classic pattern of the bildungsroman, or novel about reaching maturity, as it traces George Willard's growth from adolescence to maturity. Central to this aspect of the novel is George's relationship with his mother, whose death eventually frees him to escape from Winesburg. Mrs. Willard is the first person to see, in George's ambition to write, a potential release for her own inarticulate suffering, so she encourages his ambition partly to fill her own needs. As George comes into contact with other characters in the novel, they too see in him a way to make their voices heard, and they tell him their stories so he might write them down.

Part of George's growing maturity results from the understanding he finds as a result of his willingness to listen, but this passive development is paralleled by more overt experience. In particular, sexual initiation is an essential part of George's learning and growth, as is his coming to understand something of the nature of love in its various aspects. Through this combination of active and passive experiences, George eventually comes to understand that isolation is an essential part of the human condition. He realizes, in the sketch titled "Sophistication," that people must learn to live with the limited relationships possible in a world that isolates them, and they must develop the strength not to be destroyed by loneliness. This knowledge gives George the maturity he needs to break with Winesburg and face the future as an adult and an artist. In "Departure," the final sketch, he goes toward that responsibility.

"The Book of the Grotesque," Anderson's introduction to *Winesburg, Ohio*, suggests yet another way in which this work is unified. Conceived as a whole within which the sketches and stories are pulled together by the idea of the grotesque, the work can be seen as a group of stories connected by a central thematic concern. Anderson defines grotesques as people who have seized upon some aspect of the truth that so dominates their lives as to distort their entire beings. This definition, however, only loosely fits the characters actually encountered in the novel. Rather, the failure in some way of emotional life seems to account for the twists of character that lead Winesburg's citizens to their universal sense of failure and isolation. In spite of apparent differences, virtually all of Anderson's figures suffer from a deep sense of failure—frequently material failure as well as emotional—and from a frustrating inability to express their pain and rage in meaningful ways. Essentially, they are emotional cripples who must turn to George Willard in search of a voice to articulate their suffering.

Paralleling the level of *Winesburg, Ohio* that is concerned with individual psychology is a general reaction against the American small town and its atmosphere of puritanical repression. Although Anderson is not without some nostalgia for the village life that was already passing from the American scene when *Winesburg, Ohio* was published in 1919, he does not allow his sentiment to stand in the way of a powerful condemnation of the cultural and spiritual sterility characteristic of American village life. While other writers were mourning the passing of the nation's innocent youth by sentimentalizing the small agrarian community, Anderson revealed its dark underside of destroyed lives, thwarted ambitions, and crippled souls—all of which resulted in part from the repressive atmosphere of towns like Winesburg. Thus, while *Winesburg, Ohio* marks the end of an era of agrarian order in the United States, it raises the possibility that an innocent past was less of a paradise than the sentimentalist would have one believe.

Studies of the modern American novel tradition often begin with *Winesburg, Ohio*, which, with its pioneering of new techniques, introduction of new subject matter, and development of new attitudes and ideas as well as a new frankness, changed the course of American literary history. In addition, Anderson's generous help to such younger writers as Ernest Hemingway and William Faulkner, who would continue to shape the course of the American novel, justifies his position as the father of the modern American novel.

"Critical Evaluation" by William E. Grant

Further Reading

Anderson, Sherwood. *Winesburg, Ohio: Authoritative Text, Backgrounds and Contexts, Criticism.* Edited by Charles E. Modlin and Ray Lewis White. New York: W. W. Norton, 1996. In addition to the text of the novel, this edition contains some of Anderson's letters and a portion of his memoirs in which he discusses the book. Also reprints reviews that appeared at the time of the novel's publication and features later essays that explore various aspects of the book, including its representation of the feminine, simplicity, and godliness.

Bassett, John Earl. *Sherwood Anderson: An American Career.* Selinsgrove, Pa.: Susquehanna University Press, 2006. Provides a thorough critical overview of Anderson's work. Includes discussion of *Winesburg, Ohio*, particularly in the chapter titled "Literary Success."

Crowley, John W., ed. *New Essays on "Winesburg, Ohio."* New York: Cambridge University Press, 1990. Presents a variety of critical points of view on the work in essays by scholars who employ a number of different interpretive methods.

Dunne, Robert. *A New Book of the Grotesques: Contemporary Approaches to Sherwood Anderson's Early Fiction.* Kent, Ohio: Kent State University Press, 2005. Offers a new interpretation of Anderson's early fiction by looking at it from a postmodern theoretical perspective, especially from poststructuralist approaches. Describes how the early novels laid the groundwork for *Winesburg, Ohio* before examining that work.

Rideout, Walter B. *Sherwood Anderson: A Writer in America.* 2 vols. Madison: University of Wisconsin Press, 2006-2007. Comprehensive biography recounts the details of Anderson's life and discusses *Winesburg, Ohio* and his other writings.

Whalan, Mark. *Race, Manhood, and Modernism in America: The Short Story Cycles of Sherwood Anderson and Jean Toomer.* Knoxville: University of Tennessee Press, 2007. Compares *Winesburg, Ohio* and Toomer's *Cane* (1923). Includes discussions of narrative, gender, and history in *Winesburg, Ohio* and of this work as an example of Anderson's primitivism.

White, Ray Lewis. *"Winesburg, Ohio": An Exploration.* Boston: Twayne, 1990. Presents a close reading of the text as well as discussion of the work's historical context, its general importance, and its critical reception.

The Wings of the Dove

Author: Henry James (1843-1916)
First published: 1902
Type of work: Novel
Type of plot: Psychological realism
Time of plot: c. 1900
Locale: London and Venice

Principal characters:
MILLY THEALE, a wealthy American girl
MRS. SUSAN SHEPHERD STRINGHAM, an American friend of Milly Theale
MRS. MAUD LOWDER, an English friend of Mrs. Stringham
KATE CROY, Mrs. Lowder's niece
MERTON DENSHER, Kate Croy's fiancé
LORD MARK, another suitor for Kate Croy's hand
SIR LUKE STRETT, an eminent British doctor

The Story:

Kate Croy is dependent on her aunt, Mrs. Lowder, because Kate's own father is a ne'er-do-well. Mrs. Lowder has great plans for her niece and encourages Lord Mark as a suitor for Kate's hand. Kate's own mind is set on a young reporter, Merton Densher, who works for one of the London papers. Mrs. Lowder likes Densher and even invites him to her home, but she does not want him to marry her niece, for he has no apparent prospects of money or a place in society. Mrs. Lowder breathes more easily when she learns that the young man is being sent by his newspaper to the United States to write a series of articles on life there.

While he is in New York, Densher makes the acquaintance of a pretty young American, Milly Theale, who recently inherited a large fortune through the death of her parents. A few weeks later, Milly asks a Boston friend, Mrs. Susan Stringham, a widow and a writer, to go with her to Europe. They take passage on a liner and arrive in Italy, from where they traveled up the Italian peninsula and into Switzerland. Milly is restless, though, and soon decides that she would like to go to London.

Once they arrive in England, Mrs. Stringham sends word to Mrs. Lowder, the only acquaintance she has in that country from her school days many years before. Mrs. Stringham and Milly immediately become familiar callers at Mrs. Lowder's home. Because of her beauty, money, and attractive personality, Milly is a great success in London society. Lord Mark becomes infatuated with her, and Milly and Kate become fast friends.

Aware that she is ill, Milly goes to see Sir Luke Strett, an eminent surgeon, who informs her that there is nothing surgery or medicine can do to save her; he advises her to make the best of the time she has left. Although Kate, Mrs. Lowder, and Mrs. Stringham know that she has only a few months to live, Milly requests them not to mention it to others. She intends to enjoy herself as much as possible.

Great friends as Kate and Milly are, they never discuss

their mutual acquaintance, Densher. One day, while walking in the National Art Galleries, Milly sees him and Kate together. Kate and Densher enlist the aid of Mrs. Stringham and Milly to further their courtship. Milly, herself a little in love with Densher, is only too glad to help.

Eventually Kate devises a way to bring her affair with Densher to a happy conclusion. Noticing that Milly is falling in love with Densher, Kate suggests that Densher marry Milly and make her happy for the few remaining months of her life. After her death, Milly's fortune will go to Densher, who will then be free to marry Kate and be in a financial position to allay any objections Mrs. Lowder might have to the match. Kate is sure that neither Mrs. Lowder nor Mrs. Stringham will try to prevent a marriage between Milly and Densher, for both of them love Milly and will go to any lengths to make her final days happy.

On the advice of Sir Luke Strett, the three women and Densher accompany Milly to Venice for the winter months. Densher makes little effort to bring about Kate's plan and marry Milly until after Mrs. Lowder and Kate return to England for a few weeks. Before they leave, Kate makes Densher promise to follow her plan. Densher's conscience rebels at the duplicity of the scheme, however, and he is not sure that when the plan works out to its finish Kate will still want him. As a sign that there is mutual trust between them, he asks Kate to come to his rooms with him. She does so the day before she leaves Venice.

One day, as Densher approaches the house Milly takes for the winter, he sees Lord Mark leaving. He soon finds out from Mrs. Stringham that Lord Mark proposed to Milly and was rejected because the girl detects unwanted sympathy in his proposal and suspects that he is after her money rather than her love. Densher believes, rightly, that Lord Mark's rejection gives him some reason to be hopeful. He informs Milly that she is the only reason he is neglecting his work. She is pleased and hopes that he will propose.

Lord Mark disappears from Venice for almost a month. Then, shortly after he is refused admittance to Milly's house, Densher sees Lord Mark in a café. Densher knows immediately that Lord Mark somehow discovered and told Milly about the engagement between Densher and Kate. Densher tries to think of a way to right the situation. Three days later, Mrs. Stringham comes to him and tells him that it is as he guessed. What he did not guess, however, is that Milly no longer takes any interest in living and is refusing to eat or to talk to anyone. Mrs. Stringham is in despair and sends for Sir Luke.

Densher returns to London but does not, at first, go to see Kate. He cannot face her after the turn that their plans take, and he cannot bear the idea of having hurt Milly as he did. Finally, on Christmas Day, he has a premonition. He hurries to Sir Luke's residence. There he finds Mrs. Lowder, who tells him that she received a telegram the previous day with news of Milly's death. A few days later, a letter arrives from Venice. Without opening it, Densher knows what the message is, for it is addressed in Milly's handwriting. He immediately goes to see Kate, who also guesses that it is a letter to tell Densher that Milly left him part of her fortune so that he and Kate might marry. Neither of them dare open the letter because they are ashamed of their conduct, and they burn the letter in the fireplace.

Ten days later, a letter comes from a New York law firm. Densher sends it to Kate unopened, whereupon she comes to his rooms, wanting to know why he sent it to her. He replies that it is up to her whether he should take the money that is offered, but that he can never marry her with the money Milly left him.

Kate refuses to answer him or to open the letter, lest the large amount of the fortune tempts either of them into accepting it. Finally Densher says he wants to marry her, but only as they were before the arrival of Milly. Kate leaves, after reminding him that they can never be the same.

Critical Evaluation:

Henry James came from a family whose members considered themselves observers of, rather than participants in, society. James and his father both suffered from physical disabilities that to some degree enforced this detachment, which was emotional as well as physical. The family traveled continually during the author's youth. As an adult, James lived chiefly in Europe, and though he maintained close relations with his parents and siblings, he considered himself a citizen of the world. He regarded the life of his countrymen with the same objective, albeit curious and sympathetic view he accorded society in general. Coming as he did of parents whose chief business in life was the cultivation of their own and their children's sensibilities, and sharing the family's strong if eccentric religious bent, he took it as his artistic mission to examine the condition of human society at large as that condition manifested itself in the most subdued and civilized of human milieus.

The outline of the plot of *The Wings of the Dove* was suggested to the author by the premature death of his cousin Mary Temple, called Minny. The girl had charm, beauty, money, and love. She had, as it is said, everything for which to live and she resisted her fate to the end. After her death from tuberculosis in 1870, James was, as he later wrote, "haunted" by the tragedy of her situation. Two of his most appealing heroines take their essential lines from her, Isabel Archer of *The Portrait of a Lady* (1880-1881), and Milly Theale.

James wrote three of his best novels in quick succession shortly after 1900. As the new century began, he produced *The Wings of the Dove* (1902), *The Ambassadors* (1903), and *The Golden Bowl* (1904). According to one critic, the three themes that impel these novels, as well as most of James's previous works, are "the contrast of American sincerity and crudity with European deceit and culture, the conflicting realities of life and art, and the substitution of psychological for ethical measurements of good and evil."

The first is most neatly illustrated by the characters Mrs. Lowder and Mrs. Stringham. Mrs. Lowder's wardship of Kate has a monetary quality to it that is made explicit in her remark to Merton Densher: "I've been saving [Kate's presence] up and letting it, as you say of investments, appreciate, and you may judge whether, now it has begun to pay so, I'm likely to consent to treat for it with any but a high bidder." Mrs. Stringham's attachment to Milly, on the other hand, has the quality of a holy mission to shepherd through the hazards of the world a being so exalted that the heroines of literature pale beside her. Her view of Milly is essentially romantic; she calls her "an angel," "a princess in a palace," and, ironically, "the real thing." The differences between Kate and Milly enlarge on this theme; Kate accepts her aunt's definition of herself and uses it but succumbs to its corrupting influence, thus losing both love and honor. Milly, resisting the dehumanizing effects both of hero worship and of pity, works her own salvation as well as Densher's.

The life that Milly makes for herself, knowing her days are numbered, comprehends abysses both sublime and terrible. She recognizes from the first the effects of her money on the company into which she is betrayed by her shepherd, so graphically if unintentionally particularized for her by kind, corrupt Lord Mark, who takes her to see the Bronzino portrait, which is so like her but, most poignantly to Milly's sense, "dead, dead, dead." She has, even before she hears her sentence pronounced by Sir Luke Strett, a trick of deferring judgment, of not permitting the baseness of others to circumscribe or to debase her experience. Afterward, this tendency flowers into a kind of divine duplicity, a double reverse, which consists of her keeping from everyone but Mrs. Stringham the fact that she is dying. After a certain point, she inevitably sees everyone else acting in the knowledge of her limited future, yet she makes no move to defend herself but simply, profoundly, trusts. In short, she offers herself as a dove for sacrifice, a gesture that parallels the willingness of others to sacrifice her to their own designs. All her putative

friends deceive themselves in regard to her, acting in the name of her happiness but actually for their own good. Milly does not deceive herself. Her surrender is deliberate. In this she is a supreme artist; she makes of her life an instrument for Mrs. Stringham's gratification, for Kate's enlightenment, and for Densher's redemption, a creative act of the highest kind.

James captures these characters, as well as diverse strokes of their wickedness, in a few murmured words, a nod or a look, an invitation accepted or declined, gestures always within the bounds of propriety. Such an exposition of the instincts of the jungle expressed in the manners of the salon generates, in the end, more force than many a less-subdued narrative. For the reader is treated not only to the powerful spectacle of Kate Croy prowling within her situation with the disciplined rage of a caged tiger but also to the vision of Milly triumphant over betrayal and death and fulfilling her extraordinary nature.

"Critical Evaluation" by Jan Kennedy Foster

Further Reading

Cargill, Oscar. *The Novels of Henry James*. New York: Macmillan, 1961. In a substantial chapter on *The Wings of the Dove*, Cargill analyzes the novel's plot, central characters, and main themes. He also reviews and critiques previous scholarship.

Coulson, Victoria. *Henry James, Women, and Realism*. New York: Cambridge University Press, 2007. Examines James's important friendships with three women: his sister Alice James and the novelists Constance Fenimore Woolson and Edith Wharton. These three women writers and James shared what Coulson describes as an "ambivalent realism," or a cultural ambivalence about gender identity, and she examines how this idea is manifest in James's works, including *The Wings of the Dove*.

Flannery, Denis. *Henry James: A Certain Illusion*. Brookfield, Vt.: Ashgate, 2000. An analysis of the concept of illusion in James's works, including *The Wings of the Dove*.

Fowler, Virginia. "The Later Fiction." In *A Companion to Henry James Studies*, edited by Daniel Mark Fogel. Westport, Conn.: Greenwood Press, 1993. Discusses the structure, international theme, possible redemption motif, and psychodynamics of the main characters in *The Wings of the Dove*. Emphasizes the constraints placed by society on the female characters, especially Kate Croy and Milly Theale, and analyzes Merton Densher's threatened masculinity.

Freedman, Jonathan, ed. *The Cambridge Companion to Henry James.* New York: Cambridge University Press, 1998. A collection of essays that provide extensive information on James's life and literary influences and describe his works and the characters in them. William Stowe's essay, "James's Elusive *Wings*," analyzes *The Wings of the Dove.*

Gale, Robert L. *A Henry James Encyclopedia.* Westport, Conn.: Greenwood Press, 1989. Contains a critical summary of the plot of *The Wings of the Dove* and descriptive identifications of its twenty-five characters. Discusses James's preface to the novel and entries in James's *Notebooks* that are relevant to the book.

Kventsel, Anna. *Decadence in the Late Novels of Henry James.* New York: Palgrave Macmillan, 2007. Kventsel interprets *The Wings of the Dove* and two other novels from the perspective of fin-de-siècle decadence. Includes bibliography and index.

Stevens, Hugh. *Henry James and Sexuality.* New York: Cambridge University Press, 1998. A study of sexuality as it presents itself in James's work, including discussions of homosexuality and gender roles. Chapter 2 examines gender and representation in *The Wings of the Dove.*

Tanimoto, Yasuko. *A New Reading of "The Wings of the Dove."* Dallas, Tex.: University Press of America, 2004. Focuses on the psychology of the three main characters—Milly, Kate, and Densher—and discusses the novel's irregular structure. A useful text for students and general readers.

Wagenknecht, Edward. *The Novels of Henry James.* New York: Frederick Ungar, 1983. Includes a conservative discussion of *The Wings of the Dove* that touches on composition and publication data, the inspiration that led to the work, an analysis of the plot that refers to the two-part structure and stresses the closure, and an evaluation of the central characters.

The Winter of Our Discontent

Author: John Steinbeck (1902-1968)
First published: 1961
Type of work: Novel
Type of plot: Social realism
Time of plot: 1960
Locale: New Baytown, Long Island

Principal characters:
ETHAN ALLEN HAWLEY, a storekeeper
MARY HAWLEY, his wife
JOE MORPHY, a bank teller
MARULLO, a store owner and Ethan's boss
MARGIE YOUNG-HUNT, a divorced woman
MR. BAKER, the town banker
DANNY TAYLOR, the town drunk

The Story:

Ethan Allen Hawley awakens on a Good Friday morning in April, 1960, and greets his wife, Mary, in his usual manner by making funny faces at her. Mary is amused but a bit unnerved; she disapproves of his constant teasing and flippancy, especially on "serious" holidays. At breakfast she asks him if he is going to close the store early for Good Friday. Ethan works as a grocery clerk in Marullo's store, a position he resents when he remembers that his Puritan forebears were once influential in the village. His grandfather, in fact, owned a ship, which was mysteriously burned, and his father failed in business.

On his way to work, Ethan chats with Joe Morphy, the teller at Mr. Baker's bank. "The Morph," as he is called, is the village "newspaper" and knows the local gossip and every-

one in town. This morning, he tells Ethan, purely as small talk between friends, his "philosophy" on how to rob a bank. At the store, Ethan plunges into his daily routine, beginning with his ritual of addressing the shelves of canned goods. It is a ritual he performs half in celebration of life, half in self-deprecation, sensing how far he, a Harvard graduate and veteran of World War II, fell. As he is sweeping, Ethan is greeted by Mr. Baker, president of the bank. A leading citizen of New Baytown and respectable, moneyed, and secure, Mr. Baker reminds Ethan of the money Mary inherited and urges him to invest it wisely. He assures Ethan that in spite of the Hawleys' setback, he wants to see Ethan and his family succeed for the sake of the Hawley "tradition."

Later that day Margie Young-Hunt enters the store. An attractive divorcé, flirtatious and sexually predatory, she has on occasion slept with Joe and shared her evenings with other men such as Biggers, the traveling salesman. She is attracted to Ethan. On this morning, she announces to him that she is going to read her cards for Mary that night, and she predicts good fortune for Ethan.

After Margie leaves, Marullo comes in. Half bully, half father figure, Marullo offers Ethan, whom he calls Kid, advice on how to run the store better by thinking more of making money than of friends. At Marullo's departure, Ethan is approached by an agent for a grocery distributor who offers Ethan a bribe to stock his product; Ethan refuses.

At home, Ethan learns that his children are entering the I Love America essay contest. Disappointed at his son's attempt to find an easy way to write the essay, Ethan tells him to read the books in the attic, books of the great American orators and statesmen. That night, before going to bed, Ethan walks to his place by the water, where he meditates on the day's events and gives Danny Taylor, his boyhood friend and now the town drunk, a dollar so that Danny can buy a "skull buster" and sink into drunken oblivion.

On Saturday, Margie holds a card reading and predicts that Ethan's fortunes will turn. Ethan himself is cynical, but he begins to feel the pressure of Margie's prediction, Mr. Baker's advice, Marullo's admonitions, and Joe's playful remarks on how to rob a bank. He begins to formulate his own plan for making money. His meditations that night are filled with images of Danny, whose personal failure is to be connected with Ethan's success.

Easter Sunday sees the Hawleys invited to tea at the Bakers'. Ethan is suspicious and resentful, convinced that Baker will try somehow to further his own ends under the pretext of helping Ethan, The conversation between them that afternoon centers on Baker's conviction that New Baytown is the perfect place for an airport and that with the right money buying the right land fortunes will be made. That night Ethan goes to Danny's shack by the edge of the meadow. Danny is drunk, as usual, and Ethan learns that Baker gave Danny the bottle and tried to get him to sign over the property, but Danny refused. Ethan pleads with Danny never to sell the land, telling him that his meadow is coveted by Baker and others for an airport. Danny accepts Ethan's offer of a thousand dollars for a "cure," though Danny cynically—and rightly—accuses Ethan of harboring his own designs on Taylor Meadow.

The next day, when Ethan and Joe talk about Marullo, Joe suggests that the old man probably came to America illegally after the immigration laws changed. Back at the store, Ethan begins to plot the bank robbery. After learning that Danny made him a beneficiary in his will, Ethan at first feels bad, realizing that he tricked Danny into trusting him. Later, when Marullo offers Ethan fatherly advice, Ethan calls the Department of Immigration and turns him in.

Now deeply involved in treachery, Ethan once again contemplates his actions, judging personal success as a form of immorality. Baker tells him of a scandal that is about to break—the town leaders are involved in bribery and payola. Meanwhile, Marullo ostensibly leaves the country and, as a father would do, leaves Ethan the store. Danny is found dead, which puts Ethan in possession of Taylor Meadow and gives him an advantage over Mr. Baker, who now has to deal with Ethan in his airport plans.

Ethan's own scheme to rob the bank is almost concluded, but he is frustrated at the last minute by the arrival of the Immigration official inquiring about Marullo. Ethan drops the plan. On returning home he learns that his son won honorable mention in the national essay contest but that he cheated, plagiarizing whole passages from the great orators to whose works Ethan directed him.

Ethan now has Taylor Meadow, Marullo's store, and, given the town scandal, a favored position to become town mayor. His personal life, however, is in ruin: His son is a cheat, he himself is as dishonest as those earlier "pirates" who brought down his family, and he becomes a stranger even to his wife.

In a final confrontation with Baker, Ethan demands a controlling interest in the corporation formed to build the airport in exchange for his turning over Taylor Meadow. Later, sensing Ethan's essential loneliness, Margie tries to seduce him, but Ethan declines. That night, he goes back to his private place by the sea and attempts to kill himself. At the last minute, however, he resists, preferring instead to go on, hoping for self-renewal.

Critical Evaluation:

John Steinbeck's last novel, *The Winter of Our Discontent*, had its origins in a short story Steinbeck first published in *The Atlantic Monthly* in 1956, entitled "How Mr. Hogan Robbed a Bank." More than one critic has noted the story's clarity and narrative drive. The basic plot is meshed, though somewhat awkwardly, with the broader events surrounding Ethan Allen Hawley's "temptation" and "fall." The novel centers on Ethan as a basically honest man whose fall into corruption is paradigmatic of the moral disease of society as a whole. The time of the novel, 1960, was a time of public scandals in America, including a quiz show fraud and cases of payola and other forms of venality. Steinbeck obviously believed that the materialism of American society had weak-ened the moral fiber of even basically good men such as Ethan. During the late 1950's, in fact, Steinbeck wrote letters to Adlai Stevenson, then a senator and presidential candidate, and United Nations Secretary General Dag Hammarskjold, among others, in which he lamented America's pursuit of "Things." He was fearful, he wrote, that his sons would not understand the ways of virtue and courage in an age of treachery and deceit.

Such basic pessimism, first notable in Steinbeck's work after 1945, is the formative principle of the novel. The corruption is so pervasive as even to reach Ethan's son Allen, who seeks the easy way to success because "everybody does it." Characters such as Mr. Baker talk of nothing but money; decent people such as Joe Morphy are discontented with their present but uncertain of their future; Margie is unable to keep a husband and is dependent on alimony to survive; Marullo is hardened by the ethos of making money and continually preaches his ethic to Ethan; Danny Taylor keeps the pressure of life at bay with alcohol.

The time of the main action corresponds with the mystery of Easter. The "passion" of Ethan begins on Good Friday, and the first stages of his lapse into corruption as a kind of moral death occur ironically on Easter Sunday at Baker's tea and later in Danny's shack. Ethan's total collapse occurs over the Fourth of July holiday, America's birthday. The connection between the holiest of Christian holidays and the most patriotic of American holidays is clear—moral corruption is all-pervasive. The novel is thus a kind of domestic allegory. The characters, as if in a medieval play, appear in procession, approach Ethan, tell their "story" of greed or disaffection, and then recede, forcing Ethan to contemplate his role and make his next decision.

Steinbeck's last novel is, in some ways, a disappointment. The plot involves incidents of domestic life hardly distinguishable from those portrayed on television sitcoms of the period, and the action is static, lacking the force and clarity of Steinbeck's best work. Much of the action is stalled by Ethan's "philosophizing" and his wry observations, and the story's direction is further slowed by the rather awkward, if interesting, narrative structure. The first two chapters of each of the two parts use the conventional third-person narrator, but the remaining chapters in each section are told from Ethan's first-person point of view.

Steinbeck used a similar method in earlier works. *The Grapes of Wrath* (1939), for example, unfolds the action by a series of intercalary chapters that shift the point of view from the Joads and their personal experiences to that of the country at large. Such a technique had the effect of universalizing the Joads' experience, as one world and one chapter commented on the other. In *The Winter of Our Discontent*, however, the third-person narration neither comments on nor illuminates Ethan's thoughts and actions.

The characters, too, lack the sense of commitment or mystical brotherhood of many of Steinbeck's people. Ethan is vaguely reminiscent of Doc in *Cannery Row* (1945). Like Doc, Ethan often ponders great questions of ethics and laments the loss of honesty and courage in himself and in others. Doc's philosophy was largely based on a kind of biological determinism, but it was infused with a deeper belief in the ultimate triumph of the group, in humankind as a force in itself. Doc had a zest for living. Ethan's philosophy, on the other hand, is more cynical and hopeless. His near suicide at the end is testament to his personal pessimism and despair.

It is this aspect of the book, finally, that separates *The Winter of Our Discontent* from Steinbeck's previous work. Though Ethan pulls back from the brink of suicide and decides to try living the honorable life, his act is almost like an afterthought. Though he may be saved from a physical death, his spiritual death has already come to pass, a death brought on by disillusionment, failure, and discontent.

Edward Fiorelli

Further Reading

Fontenrose, Joseph. *John Steinbeck: An Introduction and Interpretation.* New York: Barnes & Noble, 1963. A very readable study that discusses Steinbeck's use of myths and legendary material as structural elements in his plots. An influential work.

French, Warren. *John Steinbeck.* Boston: Twayne, 1961. One of the best general treatments of Steinbeck's work, and an example of the approach called New Criticism, which was prevalent in the 1960's. Each major work is closely analyzed, with discussions centered on the meaning of the text.

George, Stephen K., and Barbara A. Heavilin, eds. *John Steinbeck and His Contemporaries.* Lanham, Md.: Scarecrow Press, 2007. A collection of papers from a 2006 conference about Steinbeck and the writers who influenced or informed his work. Some of the essays discuss his European forebears, particularly Henry Fielding and Sir Thomas Malory, and his American forebears, such as Walt Whitman and Sarah Orne Jewett, while other essays compare his work to Ernest Hemingway, William Faulkner, and other twentieth century American writers

Heavilin, Barbara A., ed. *"The Winter of Our Discontent."* Lewiston, N.Y.: Edwin Mellen Press, 2000. A collection of critical essays about the novel, including discussions of the psychological journey of Ethan Allen Hawley, Ethan as Lancelot, the depiction of the 1950's quiz show scandals, and the novel's reception in Thailand.

Hughes, R. S. *Beyond "The Red Pony": A Reader's Companion to Steinbeck's Complete Short Stories.* Metuchen, N.J.: Scarecrow Press, 1987. Deals exclusively with Steinbeck's more than fifty works of short fiction. Provides particularly interesting discussions of Steinbeck's uncollected works, stories he published in magazines during the 1940's and the 1950's. Discusses the source of *The Winter of Our Discontent*.

Levant, Howard. *The Novels of John Steinbeck: A Critical Study.* Columbia: University of Missouri Press, 1974. A constructionist approach, this study discusses the structural patterns of the novels. Suggests that Steinbeck's intentions, his "blueprints," were often at odds with the finished products and that his works reveal his inability to effectively fuse material with structure and theme with pattern. Interesting discussion of the similarities between Steinbeck's first novel, *Cup of Gold* (1929), and his last, *The Winter of Our Discontent*.

Meyer, Michael J., ed. *The Betrayal of Brotherhood in the Work of John Steinbeck.* Lewiston, N.Y.: Edwin Mellen Press, 2000. Describes how Steinbeck adapted the biblical story of Cain and Abel in many of his works. Includes two essays focusing on *The Winter of Our Discontent*.

Simmonds, Roy S. *A Biographical and Critical Introduction of John Steinbeck.* Lewiston, N.Y.: E. Mellen Press, 2000. Charts Steinbeck's evolution as a writer from 1929 through 1968, discussing the themes of his works and the concepts and philosophies that influenced his depictions of human nature and the psyche. Interweaves details about his writings with accounts of his personal life.

The Winter's Tale

Author: William Shakespeare (1564-1616)
First produced: c. 1610-1611; first published, 1623
Type of work: Drama
Type of plot: Tragicomedy
Time of plot: The legendary past
Locale: Sicilia and Bohemia

Principal characters:
LEONTES, the king of Sicilia
HERMIONE, his queen
POLIXENES, the king of Bohemia
CAMILLO, Leontes' counselor
MAMILLIUS, Leontes' son
PERDITA, Leontes' daughter
FLORIZEL, Polixenes' son
PAULINA, Hermione's maid
AUTOLYCUS, a rogue

The Story:

Polixenes, the king of Bohemia, is the guest of Leontes, the king of Sicilia. The two men were friends since boyhood, and there is much celebrating and joyousness during the visit. At last Polixenes decides that he must return to his home country. Leontes urges him to extend his visit, but Polixenes refuses, saying that he has not seen his young son for a long time. Then Leontes asks Hermione, his wife, to try to persuade Polixenes to remain. When Polixenes finally yields to her pleas, Leontes becomes suspicious and concludes that Hermione and Polixenes must be lovers and that he is cuckolded.

Leontes is generally of a jealous disposition, and he seeks constant reassurance that his son, Mamillius, is his own offspring. Having now, out of jealousy, misjudged his wife and his old friend, Leontes becomes so angry that he orders Camillo, his chief counselor, to poison Polixenes. All Camillo's attempts to dissuade Leontes from his scheme only strengthen the jealous man's feelings of hate. Nothing can persuade the king that Hermione is true to him. Eventually Camillo agrees to poison Polixenes, but only on condition that Leontes return to Hermione with no more distrust.

Polixenes notices a change in Leontes' attitude toward him. When he questions Camillo, the sympathetic lord reveals the plot to poison him. Together, they hastily embark for Bohemia.

Upon learning that Polixenes and Camillo fled, Leontes is more than ever convinced that his guest and his wife are guilty of carrying on an affair. He conjectures that Polixenes and Camillo were plotting together all the while and planning his murder. Moreover, he decides that Hermione, who is pregnant, is in all likelihood bearing Polixenes' child and not his. Publicly he accuses Hermione of adultery and commands that her son be taken from her. She herself is imprisoned. Although his servants protest the order, Leontes is adamant.

In prison, Hermione gives birth to a baby girl. Paulina, her attendant, thinks that the sight of the baby girl might cause Leontes to relent, so she carries the child to the palace. Instead of forgiving his wife, Leontes becomes more incensed and demands that the child be put to death. He instructs Antigonus, Paulina's husband, to take the baby to a far-off desert shore and there abandon it. Although the lord pleads to be released from this cruel command, he is forced to put out to sea for the purpose of leaving the child to perish on some lonely coast.

Leontes sends two messengers to consult the Oracle of Delphi to determine Hermione's guilt. When the men return, Leontes summons his wife and the whole court to hear the verdict. The messengers read a scroll that states that Hermione is innocent, as are Polixenes and Camillo, that Leontes is a tyrant, and that he will live without an heir until that which is lost is found.

The king, refusing to believe the oracle, declares its findings false and again accuses Hermione of infidelity. In the middle of his tirade, a servant rushes in to say that young Mamillius died because of sorrow and anxiety over his mother's plight. On hearing this, Hermione falls into a swoon and is carried to her chambers. Soon afterward, Paulina returns to announce that her mistress is dead. At this news Leontes, who begins to believe the oracle after news of his son's death, beats his breast with rage at himself. He reproaches himself bitterly for the insane jealousy that led to these unhappy events. In repentance, the king swears that he will have the legend of the deaths of his son and wife engraved on their tombstones and that he himself will do penance thereafter.

Meanwhile, Antigonus takes the baby girl to a desert country near the sea. Heartsick at having to abandon her, the old courtier lays a bag of gold and jewels by her with instructions that she should be called Perdita, a name revealed to him in a dream. After he does this, he is attacked and killed by a bear. Later, his ship is wrecked in a storm and all hands are lost. Although no news of the expedition reaches Sicilia, the kind shepherd who finds Perdita also sees the deaths of Antigonus and his men.

Sixteen years pass, bringing with them many changes. Leontes is a broken man, grieving alone in his palace. Perdita grows into a beautiful and a charming young woman under the care of the shepherd. She is so lovely that Prince Florizel, the son of Polixenes and heir to the throne of Bohemia, falls madly in love with her.

Unaware of the girl's background, and knowing only that his son is in love with a young shepherdess, Polixenes and Camillo, now his most trusted servant, disguise themselves and visit a sheep-shearing festival, where they see Florizel, dressed as a shepherd, dancing with a lovely young woman. Although he realizes that the shepherdess is of noble bearing, Polixenes in great rage forbids his son to marry her. Florizel thereupon makes secret plans to elope with Perdita to a foreign country. Camillo, pitying the young couple, advises Florizel to embark for Sicilia and to pretend that he is a messenger of goodwill from the king of Bohemia. Camillo supplies the young man with letters of introduction to Leontes. It is part of Camillo's plan to inform Polixenes of the lovers' escape and to travel to Sicilia to find them, thus taking advantage of the situation to return home once more.

The poor shepherd, frightened by the king's wrath, decides to tell Polixenes how, years before, he found the baby and a bag of gold and jewels by her side. Fate intervenes, however, and the shepherd is intercepted by the rogue Autolycus and put aboard the ship sailing to Sicilia.

Soon Florizel and Perdita arrive in Sicilia, followed by Polixenes and Camillo. When the old shepherd hears how Leontes lost a daughter, he describes the finding of Perdita. Leontes, convinced that Perdita is his own abandoned infant, is joyfully reunited with his daughter. When he hears this, Polixenes immediately gives his consent to the marriage of Florizel and Perdita. The only sorrowful circumstance to mar the happiness of all concerned is the earlier tragic death of Hermione.

One day, Paulina asks Leontes to visit a newly erected statue of the dead woman in Hermione's chapel. Leontes, ever faithful to the memory of his dead wife—even to the point of promising Paulina never to marry again—gathers his guests and takes them to view the statue. Standing in the chapel, amazed at the wonderful lifelike quality of the work, they hear strains of soft music. Suddenly the statue descends from its pedestal and is revealed as the living Hermione. She spent the sixteen years in seclusion while awaiting some word of her daughter. The happy family is reunited, and Hermione completely forgives her repentant husband. He and Polixenes are again the best of friends, rejoicing in the happiness of Perdita and Florizel.

Critical Evaluation:

Written after *Cymbeline* (pr. c. 1609-1610, pb. 1623) and before *The Tempest* (pr. 1611, pb. 1623), *The Winter's Tale* is as hard to classify generically as is the fully mature dramatic genius of its author. Partaking of the elements of tragedy, the play yet ends in sheer comedy, just as it mingles elements of realism and romance. William Shakespeare took his usual freedom with his source, Robert Greene's euphuistic romance *Pandosto: The Triumph of Time* (1588). Time remains the most crucial element in the play's structure, its clearest break with the pseudo-Aristotelian unities. The effect of time on Hermione, moreover, when the statue is revealed to be wrinkled and aged, heightens the pathos and credibility of the triumphant discovery and recognition scene. To allow that final scene its full effect, Shakespeare wisely has Perdita's discovery and recognition reported to the audience secondhand in act 5, scene 2. In keeping with the maturity of Shakespeare's dramatic talent, the poetic style of this play is clear, unrhetorical, sparse in its imagery as well as metaphorically sharp. Verse alternates with prose as court characters alternate with country personages.

Mamillius tells his mother, who asks him for a story, that "a sad tale's best for winter." Ironically the little boy's story is never told; the entrance of Leontes interrupts it, and Hermione's son, his role as storyteller once defined, strangely disappears. In his place, the play itself takes over, invigorated by Mamillius's uncanny innocent wisdom, which reflects a Platonic view of childhood. The story that unfolds winds a multitude of themes without losing sight of any of them. It presents two views of honor, a wholesome one represented by Hermione and a demented one represented by Leontes. Like many of Shakespeare's plays, the narrative concerns the unholy power of kings who can be mistaken but whose power, however mistaken, is final. However, the finality, here, is spared, the tragic ending avoided. The absolute goodness of Hermione, Paulina, Camillo, the shepherd, and Florizel proves to be enough to overcome the evil of Leontes. Moving from the older generation's inability to love to the reflowering of love in the younger, the play spins out into a truly comic ending, with the reestablishment of community, royal authority, and general happiness in a triple *gamos*. The balance of tension between youth and age, guilt and innocence, death and rebirth is decided in favor of life, and the play escapes the clutches of remorseless tragedy in a kind of ultimate mystical vision of human life made ideal through suffering.

Leontes is a most puzzling character. His antifeminism, as expressed in his cynical speech on cuckoldry, seems more fashionable than felt. In his determined jealousy, he resembles Othello, and in his self-inflicted insanity, Lear. In fact, the words of Lear to Cordelia resound in Leontes' great speech, beginning, "Is whispering nothing?" and conclud-

ing, "My wife is nothing; nor nothing have these nothings,/ If this be nothing." It is almost impossible to sympathize with him further when he condemns even his helpless child in the face of Paulina's gentle pleas; and it is not surprising that he at first even denies the oracle itself. However, his sudden recognition of culpability is no more convincing than his earlier, unmotivated jealousy. It is as if he changes too quickly for belief; perhaps this is the reason for Hermione's decision to test his penitence with time, until it ripens into sincerity. Certainly his reaction to his wife's swoon shows only a superficial emotion. Leontes is still self-centered, still regally assured that all can be put right with the proper words. Only after the years have passed in loneliness does he realize it takes more than orderly words to undo the damage wrought by disorderly royal commands. His admission to Paulina that his words killed Hermione paves the way for the happy ending.

Even the minor characters are drawn well and vividly. Camillo is the ideal courtier who chooses virtue over favor. Paulina, like the nurse Anna in Euripides' *Hippolytos* (428 B.C.E.; *Hippolytus*, 1781), is the staunch helpmate of her mistress, especially in adversity, aided by magical powers that seem to spring from her own determined character. Her philosophy is also that of the classical Greeks: "What's gone and what's past help/ Should be past grief." This play does not have the tragic Greek ending, because Paulina preserves her mistress rather than assisting her to destroy herself. Even the rogue Autolycus is beguiling, with his verbal witticisms, his frank pursuit of self-betterment, and his lusty and delightful songs. His sign is Mercury, the thief of the gods, and he follows his sign like the best rascals in Renaissance tradition: Boccaccio's Friar Onion, Rabelais's Panurge, and Shakespeare's own Falstaff.

In Hermione and Perdita, Shakespeare achieves two of his greatest portraits of women. Hermione's speech reflects her personality, straightforward, without embroidery, as pure as virtue itself. Her reaction to Leontes' suspicion and condemnation is brief but telling. "Adieu, my lord," she says, "I never wish'd to see you sorry; now/ I trust I shall." She combines the hardness of Portia with the gentleness of Desdemona; in fact, Antigonus's oath in her defense recalls the character of Othello's wife. Like Geoffrey Chaucer's patient Griselda, Hermione loses everything, but she strikes back with the most devastating weapon of all: time. However, in the final scene of the play, it is clear that her punishment of Leontes makes Hermione suffer no less. Perdita personifies, though never in a stereotyped way, gentle innocence: "Nothing she does or seems/ But smacks of something greater than herself/ Too noble for this place." Indeed, when Polixenes' wrath, paralleling Leontes' previous folly, threatens Perdita's life for a second time, the audience holds its breath because she is too good to be safe. When Shakespeare saves her, the play, sensing the audience's joy, abruptly ends on its highest note.

In its theme and structure, *The Winter's Tale* bears a striking resemblance to Euripides' *Alkēstis* (438 B.C.E.; *Alcestis*, 1781). In both plays, the "death" of the queen threatens the stability and happiness of society and, in both, her restoration, which is miraculous and ambiguous, restores order to the world of the court. Shakespeare, however, widens the comic theme by adding the love of the younger generation. *The Winter's Tale* defies the forces of death and hatred romantically as well as realistically. The sad tale becomes happy, as winter becomes spring.

"Critical Evaluation" by Kenneth John Atchity

Further Reading

Hall, Joan Lord. *"The Winter's Tale": A Guide to the Play.* Westport, Conn.: Greenwood Press, 2005. Introductory overview, describing the play's textual history, contexts, sources, dramatic form, use of language, presentation of character, and themes. Discusses critical approaches to the play and the play in performance.

Lloyd Evans, Gareth. *The Upstart Crow: An Introduction to Shakespeare's Plays.* London: J. M. Dent and Sons, 1982. A comprehensive treatment of the dramatic works of Shakespeare, with major emphasis on critical reviews of the plays. Discusses the sources from which Shakespeare drew and the circumstances surrounding the writing of his plays.

Lucas, John. *Student Guide to Shakespeare's "The Winter's Tale."* London: Greenwich Exchange, 2005. Considers the significance of Shakespeare's decision to defy the expectations of Jacobean drama in *The Winter's Tale.* Analyzes the play's depictions of sexual jealousy, the contrasting worlds of court and country, and how women successfully oppose male power. Relates *The Winter's Tale* to some of Shakespeare's other plays.

Lyne, Raphael. *Shakespeare's Late Work.* New York: Oxford University Press, 2007. Provides a detailed reading of *The Winter's Tale* and other plays written at the end of Shakespeare's career, placing them within the context of his oeuvre. Argues that the late works have a distinct identity, defined as an ironic combination of belief and skepticism regarding faith in God, love of family, reverence for monarchs, and the theatrical depiction of truth.

Muir, Kenneth, ed. *Shakespeare—The Comedies: A Collection of Critical Essays.* Englewood Cliffs, N.J.: Prentice-Hall, 1965. An anthology of essays by a variety of authors, discussing Shakespeare's comedies from various points of view. Derek Traversi's treatment of *The Winter's Tale* is mainly concerned with the later scenes of the play and includes an intensive discussion of the characters' motivations.

Overton, Bill. *The Winter's Tale.* Atlantic Highlands, N.J.: Humanities Press International, 1989. A critical evaluation of Shakespeare's play from a wide variety of perspectives, including Marxism, feminism, and psychoanalysis. Discusses previous critical studies of the play.

Partee, Morriss Henry. *Childhood in Shakespeare's Plays.* New York: Peter Lang, 2006. Examines the depiction of the child characters in *The Winter's Tale* and some of Shakespeare's other plays. Challenges the idea that Shakespeare regarded children as small adults; demonstrates that he did not portray children as either unnaturally precocious or sentimentally innocent.

Sanders, Wilbur. *The Winter's Tale.* Boston: Twayne, 1987. A thorough critical evaluation of the play. Includes information on the work's stage history and original reception by critics. Discusses the psychological factors in the play and its use of language.

Shakespeare, William. *The Winter's Tale.* Edited by J. H. P. Pafford. Cambridge, Mass.: Harvard University Press, 1963. This edition of the play contains more than eighty pages of introductory notes and twenty pages of appendixes. Discusses the sources, the text itself, and the music and songs in the production. Includes an extensive critical evaluation of the play.

Winterset

Author: Maxwell Anderson (1888-1959)
First produced: 1935; first published, 1935
Type of work: Drama
Type of plot: Tragedy
Time of plot: Twentieth century
Locale: New York

Principal characters:
ESDRAS, an old man
GARTH, his son
MIRIAMNE, his daughter
TROCK, a murderer
SHADOW, his henchman
JUDGE GAUNT
MIO, Romagna's son

The Story:

Trock and Shadow walk warily under the bridge by the tenement where Garth lives with his old father, Esdras, and his fifteen-year-old sister, Miriamne. Trock is just released from prison, where he served a sentence for his part in a murder for which Romagna was electrocuted. Judge Gaunt, who presided over the trial when Romagna was convicted, is said to be mad and to be roaming the country telling people that the trial was unfair. A college professor also begins an investigation of the old murder trial. Trock comes to the tenement district to see Garth, who witnessed the murder that Trock really committed. Garth did not testify at the trial, and Trock wants to warn him never to tell what he saw.

Trock threatens to kill Garth if he talks. Miriamne knows nothing about her brother's part in this crime, but after she hears Trock threaten her brother, she questions him and learns a little about the killing. Miriamne loves Garth, but she knows that his silence about the murder is wrong. Old Esdras watches and comforts his two children.

To the same tenement district comes Mio and his friend, Carr. Mio is seventeen, and he learns that somewhere in the tenements lives a man who knows that Romagna is innocent. Mio and Miriamne see each other on the street and fall in love. Knowing that he has to speak to Miriamne, Mio sends Carr away. When Miriamne hears Mio's full name, Bartolemeo Romagna, she tells him that he must go away and never see her again, for Miriamne knows then that Mio is the son of the man who died for the murder Trock committed. Mio tells Miriamne that he was four years old when his father was electrocuted and that he lives only to prove his father's innocence.

While the lovers are talking, Shadow and Trock appear on the street, and Miriamne hides Mio in the shadow so that the two men cannot see him. The gangsters are looking for Judge Gaunt in order to silence him. The judge also comes to the tenement, and Garth, meeting him, makes the crazed man go

to Esdras's apartment for safety. Shadow, however, wants no part in killing the judge. As he leaves, Trock sends two henchmen after Shadow to kill him. Mio sees the shooting. Feeling that he came to the right place to learn the truth of the old killing, he waits.

In Esdras's room the judge awakens, refreshed and normal once more. Realizing where he is and what he did, the judge asks Garth and Esdras to say nothing of his mad claims that Romagna's trial was unfair. The judge does not want the case to be reopened any more than does Trock. Esdras offers to guide Judge Gaunt partway back to his home.

After the two old men leave, Mio knocks on the door. He was directed to Garth's home by neighbors. He is bewildered at the sight of Miriamne until she explains that Garth is her brother. She asks Mio to leave, but first she wants him to tell her that he loves her. Garth angrily interrupts the lovers and orders Mio to leave. As Mio prepares to go, Judge Gaunt and Esdras return, forced to turn back by driving sleet. Mio recognizes the judge and begins questioning him and Garth about the trial. Garth's story is that he did not witness the murder for which Mio's father died. Judge Gaunt insists that Romagna was guilty. Mio points out that evidence at the trial was biased because his father was an anarchist. The judge says that if he thought the trial unjust, he would have allowed a retrial.

The steady denials of Garth and Judge Gaunt nearly break Mio's spirit. Suddenly Trock enters the apartment. Mio grows more suspicious. Then Shadow comes to the door. The sight of the henchman he thought dead terrifies Trock. Shadow was shot, but he lives long enough to accuse Trock of his murder. After Shadow dies, Judge Gaunt again becomes deranged. He thinks he is in court, and Mio tricks him into admitting that Romagna was an anarchist and as such should have been put to death. When Trock threatens to kill them all, Mio knows that he is near the end of his search.

In the middle of Mio's discoveries, the police come looking for Judge Gaunt, who has been missing from his home for many days. Mio accuses Trock of murdering Shadow, but when he sends the police into an inner room where Garth dragged the body, the corpse is not there. When Miriamne also denies his charges, Mio admits that he must have been dreaming, for he saw a pleading message in Miriamne's eyes that directed his decision.

As the police take Judge Gaunt away, Trock goes also, leaving Garth to face Mio's accusations. Mio is helpless, however, because he loves Miriamne. Free at last to vindicate his father's name, he is tied by Miriamne's love for her brother. In spite of Miriamne's fears that his life is in danger, Mio leaves Esdras's home.

Mio feels that there is nothing left for him but to die, for he cannot live and remain silent about his father's death. While he hesitates outside the tenement, Miriamne comes to join him, and they see Garth carrying the body of Shadow from the alley. Esdras joins Mio outside. The boy's search for justice and his courage make the old man see that Garth's silence is wrong. Esdras tells Mio that he is going to the police to report Shadow's murder. Mio cautions Esdras that he will not try to save Garth by remaining silent about the Romagna case, but Esdras says that Mio owes them nothing. He goes to inform the police.

Alone with Mio, Miriamne tries to find hope of happiness for him. At last she reminds him that his father would forgive his killers, and Mio realizes that she is right. Still, he is determined to reveal the truth. Then Esdras returns and tells him that Trock's henchmen are guarding the streets and that there is no way of escape.

As Mio dashes down a passage toward the river, Miriamne hears the sound of shooting. She runs to her lover and finds him dying. Then she runs toward the same passage, into the fire of Trock's machine gun. Dying, she crawls back to Mio. Esdras and Garth, still alive, carry the dead lovers out of the cold, wet winter night.

Critical Evaluation:

Throughout his career, Maxwell Anderson boldly attempted to bring poetic drama to the American commercial theater. Always convinced that drama should provide a spiritual experience for the audience and committed to tragedy, Anderson also believed that poetry was the most appropriate medium for the expression of the emotions inherent in humanity's tragic condition. He revered the Greek and Roman tragedies and was devoted to William Shakespeare. He followed these models in most of his commercial successes, choosing historical plots and characters to speak to ageless human concerns. Plays such as *Elizabeth the Queen* (1930) and *Anne of the Thousand Days* (1948) found receptive audiences who appreciated the Shakespearean echoes and accepted the poetic lines with enthusiasm. In *Winterset*, however, Anderson rejected the tragic stories of the distant past when he decided to write a poetic tragedy about contemporary events. That the play, in spite of unevenness, was a popular success and continues to be Anderson's best-known effort suggests the skill of the author and his creative ability at draping contemporary events with an aura of timelessness.

The notorious case of Nicola Sacco and Bartolomeo Vanzetti provides the background for *Winterset*. Anderson, like many other artists and intellectuals of the time, believed that the two radical Italian aliens were wrongly accused and convicted of murder. Several years after their executions, a friend of Anderson told him that the judge in the case was now nearly out of his mind and was continuously attempting to justify his decisions during the trial to any who would listen. From this kernel, Anderson built the drama.

The surface structure of the play parallels Renaissance revenge tragedy with Mio, the son of the wronged father, setting out to avenge the injustice of the court system to his father by finding the real murderer and punishing him. In its revenge pattern and in the characterization of Mio, the Anderson play seems consciously patterned on William Shakespeare's *Hamlet, Prince of Denmark* (pr. c. 1600-1601, pb. 1603). Mio, like Hamlet, is the wronged son in search of vengeance. Like Hamlet, Mio was recently a student, is given to cynicism, and seems indecisive and inconsistent in his speeches and actions.

It is not only *Hamlet* that the play parallels. There are similarities to *Macbeth* (pr. 1606, pb. 1623) in the characterization of Trock, a murderer who blames others for his act and who wants to destroy those who know the reality of his guilt. His sidekick, Shadow, seems equivalent to Banquo, when he mysteriously reappears after his "death." The character of Judge Gaunt mirrors the central figure of *King Lear* (pr. c. 1605-1606, pb. 1608). Lear and Gaunt both misjudge on emotional, not rational, grounds; both go mad; both abdicate official positions, but want to hold on to the trappings of their offices; both become insanely eloquent in the middle of storms; both neglect their clothes; and both have a fool (in Gaunt's case, the hobo).

Unlike the typical revenge tragedy, however, *Winterset* does not end with the punishment of the villains. Anderson was convinced that the best tragedies involved recognition scenes. In *Winterset*, Anderson attempts to show that revenge is evil and that love and forgiveness are good. Rather, therefore, than have Mio be successful in his punishment of the murderer, Anderson instead has Mio transformed by love for Miriamne. In its love plot, *Winterset* is imitative of yet another Shakespeare play: *Romeo and Juliet* (pr. c. 1595-1596, pb. 1597). Like the two famous Shakespearian star-crossed lovers, Mio and Miriamne are from alienated families, they fall in love at first sight, and they are transformed by their love. When Mio finds out the truth about his father's innocence in act 2, his love outweighs his desire for vengeance, and he refuses to take action because he does not want to place Miriamne's brother in jeopardy. In act 3, Miriamne convinces Mio that his father also would forgive, had he been alive. This recognition of the importance of love and forgiveness prepares the way for the Romeo-and-Juliet-like deaths of the two lovers, in each other's arms, as the play ends. *Winterset*, like *Romeo and Juliet*, includes an abundance of light and dark imagery. Mio's final speech links light to love and forgiveness: "I came here seeking/ light in darkness, running from the dawn,/ and stumbled on a morning."

The stage setting underscores the starkly contemporary events traced in the drama. The backdrop—a huge representation of a bridge—emphasizes the mechanistic elements of twentieth century life as well as the contrast between wealth and poverty, a particularly important statement for the Depression-era audience who first viewed the production. Huddled at the foot of the bridge are the lower-class masses, at least as isolated as they are connected by the bridge.

As noble as Anderson's attempt was in linking contemporary events to poetic tragedy, most critics have recognized some of the weaknesses of the effort. The play has been criticized as being a disunified mishmash of Shakespeare and as being overly melodramatic and implausible. The reliance on love and forgiveness has been thought to be unduly simplistic as a means of dealing with the dilemma of twentieth century social injustice. Similarly, critics have harshly judged the poetry in the play. Anderson's irregular blank verse has seemed inadequate to the task, both in its occasional inclusion of overly purple passages as well as in its long sections of relatively mundane language. In spite of such criticism, however, the play remains among the most successful and challenging American commercial artistic attempts at verse tragedy in the twentieth century.

"Critical Evaluation" by Delmer Davis

Further Reading

Abernathy, Frances E. "*Winterset:* A Modern Revenge Tragedy." *Modern Drama* 7 (September, 1964): 185-189. Provides a careful comparison of the play to Renaissance revenge tragedies, with special emphasis on *Hamlet*. Contrasts the Hebraic code of an eye for an eye in *Hamlet* with the Christian gospel of love and forgiveness in *Winterset*.

DiNapoli, Russell. "Fragile Currency of the Last Anarchist: The Plays of Maxwell Anderson." *New Theatre Quarterly* 18, no. 3 (August, 2002): 276. A reconsideration of Anderson's plays. DiNapoli maintains that the plays were both influenced by their times and atypical of their times, and this conflict has affected Anderson's posthumous reputation.

Hazelton, Nancy J. Doran, and Kenneth Krauss, eds. *Maxwell Anderson and the New York Stage*. Monroe, N.Y.: Library Research Association, 1991. A collection of essays in honor of Anderson's centennial in 1988. Contains an insightful interview with George Schaefer regarding a production of *Winterset*.

Horn, Barbara Lee. *Maxwell Anderson: A Research and Production Sourcebook*. Westport, Conn.: Greenwood Press, 1996. A guide to Anderson's plays. Includes an introductory essay about his life and work and individual chapters devoted to synopses and critical overviews of each play, including *Winterset*. Contains bibliographies of critical reviews of the plays and of secondary sources of information about Anderson.

Shivers, Alfred S. *The Life of Maxwell Anderson*. Briarcliff Manor, N.Y.: Stein & Day, 1983. Provides numerous details about the writing and the staging of *Winterset*.

_____. *Maxwell Anderson*. Boston: Twayne, 1976. One of the best brief critical introductions to Anderson and his works. Shivers sees *Winterset* as a continuation of Anderson's compulsion to portray an idealistic central character "marked for some kind of self-willed defeat for the sake, usually, of a worthwhile cause."

_____. *Maxwell Anderson: An Annotated Bibliography of Primary and Secondary Works*. Metuchen, N.J.: Scarecrow Press, 1985. A very complete listing, often with annotations, of works by and about Anderson, including numerous citations about *Winterset*.

Wise Blood

Author: Flannery O'Connor (1925-1964)
First published: 1952
Type of work: Novel
Type of plot: Psychological realism
Time of plot: Early twentieth century
Locale: Taulkinham, a city in the American South

Principal characters:
HAZEL MOTES, a preacher despite himself
ENOCH EMERY, Hazel's disciple
ASA HAWKS, charlatan preacher, rival to Hazel
SABBATH LILY, Hawks's daughter
HOOVER SHOATS, Hazel Motes's rival
MRS. FLOOD, Hazel's landlady

The Story:

When Hazel Motes is released from the army, he finds his old home place deserted. Eastrod is the home of his grandfather, a backwoods preacher who assured Hazel that Jesus is hungry for his soul. Hazel packs up his mother's Bible and reading glasses and catches the train for Taulkinham. He rides uneasily in his $11.98 suit, startling one middle-class lady by suddenly telling her, "If you've been redeemed . . . I wouldn't want to be."

In the army, Hazel decides that his grandfather's preaching was false, that sin does not exist. In Taulkinham, Hazel intends to prove this to himself, but even the cabdriver who takes him to his first room identifies him as a preacher.

On his second night in the city, Hazel meets Enoch Emery as they watch a sidewalk potato-peeler salesman. Enoch comes to Taulkinham from the country and finds a job working for the city zoo. He is desperately lonely, and despite Hazel's surliness, Enoch immediately attaches himself to Hazel as a potential friend. Hazel's attention, however, is focused on a blind man whose face is scarred. The blind man's daughter, Sabbath Lily, accompanies him, handing out religious pamphlets. Hazel and Enoch follow the pair until the blind man, Asa Hawks, insists that he can smell sin on Hazel and that he was marked by some past preacher. Hazel denies it, saying that the only thing that matters to him is that Jesus does not exist.

The next day Hazel buys a car. Even at forty dollars it is no bargain, an ancient Essex that barely runs, but it pleases Hazel. Later that day he meets Enoch Emery at the zoo so that Enoch can show Hazel something at the museum. Enoch leads Hazel to a case that contains a tiny mummified man. Enoch finds the mummy very compelling and believes that he received a sign to show it to Hazel, whose only response is to demand Hawks's address.

That evening Hazel begins his career as a street preacher; he calls his church "the Church Without Christ" and denies the existence of sin, judgment, and redemption. Later that evening he rents a room in the rooming house where Hawks

and his daughter live, planning to seduce Sabbath Lily and thus to make the blind preacher take his denial of Christ seriously. Hazel has no idea that Hawks's blindness is fake; he believes a news clipping Hawks shows him that described Hawks's promise to blind himself by way of dramatizing his conviction that Jesus' death redeemed him. Hawks did not show Hazel the second clipping: "Evangelist's Nerve Fails." At the moment when he planned to rub lime into his eyes, Hawks believed that he saw Jesus expel the devils that drew him to this testing of God, and the sight made him flee.

The next afternoon, Sabbath Lily tricks Hazel into taking her for a ride in the country. As they lie in a field, Hazel is beginning to formulate his plan for seducing her without realizing that she already planned the same thing. When she looks into his eyes and playfully says "I see you" to Hazel, however, he suddenly bolts.

Meanwhile, Enoch is going through an elaborate cleansing ritual in preparation for his theft of the mummy from the museum. He calls it the "new jesus" and feels that Hazel needs it for his church. At the same time, Hazel is coping with unwanted help from a volunteer preacher, Onnie Jay Holy, who confides to Hazel that they can make a lot of money from his church with the right promotion. Outraged, Hazel refuses. The same night, Hazel learns that Hawks is not blind. His deception revealed, Hawks skips town, leaving Sabbath Lily behind.

When Enoch delivers the "new jesus" to Hazel, he is obliged to leave the mummy with Sabbath Lily instead. When Hazel finds her holding the mummy like an infant, he becomes furious and slams the thing against a wall, releasing its sawdust stuffing. Then he goes out to preach, only to find that Onnie (his real name is Hoover Shoats) hired a double, Solace Layfield, to preach a distorted version of Hazel's "Church Without Christ." Furious, Hazel lures the man into the country and kills him by running over him with the Essex. Enoch also disappears into the country, wearing a gorilla suit stolen from a movie promotion.

After he kills his rival preacher, Hazel returns to town and blinds himself in just the way Hawks failed to. The last months of Hazel's life are marked by his increasing need to scourge himself until at last, blind and wearing barbed wire under his clothes, Hazel is dead in a ditch in a wintry rain.

Critical Evaluation:

Wise Blood was the first of Flannery O'Connor's novels to be published. It bears some marks of the writer's learning her way, but it also contains many of the elements that mark O'Connor's mature fiction—her strong sense of character and voice, her comic vision, and her concern with religious themes.

It is in the novel's structure that some scholars have seen *Wise Blood* as suffering from O'Connor's apprenticeship. Although the early scenes of Hazel Motes on the train, his confrontations with the passengers, and his first day in Taulkinham begin to establish Hazel's character, they seem not to be tied securely to the novel's main narrative. The same might be said for O'Connor's disposal of Enoch Emery and his retreat into the world of beasts. It may be an appropriate conclusion for a character like Enoch, but it seems detached from the novel's central concerns. Concerns about minor failures of structure seem insignificant, however, in the light of the novel's successes, particularly in its characters and their language. Hazel is one of many of O'Connor's Christ-haunted characters. Inarticulate, uneducated, unsophisticated, and distrustful of sophistication (and rightly so, O'Connor implies), he nevertheless is able to focus on one of life's most important concerns—the gospel's message of salvation. Hazel's attempt to reject that message is the central action of the novel, and the fact that it cannot be rejected is O'Connor's chief theme. Even after he tries to create an antichurch, after he distracts himself with the world in the form of his car and Sabbath Lily, Hazel is still left with his sense that Jesus is hunting him down. Hazel's murder of the person he calls the false prophet, Solace Layfield, is in some ways the crisis of the novel. Layfield is hired to mimic Hazel's preaching; he even dresses like Hazel. In killing him, Hazel seems to be killing himself. Only after the murder does Hazel take on the penances he acts out at the end of his life.

The voices of O'Connor's characters often reveal their author's skill at re-creating southern speech. Hazel says, for example, "Nobody with a good car needs to be justified." Enoch relates how he escaped the head teacher at Rodemill Boys Bible Academy when he "giver a heart attack." Sabbath Lily describes a woman whose allergies made her break out in "welps." The inflections of the rural South become a point of entry to O'Connor's comic vision of the world.

O'Connor's is a dark world and her humor is often satiric, portraying a secular society in which God is essentially irrelevant. Sabbath Lily, for example, once writes to an advice columnist, Mary Brittle, in an attempt to reconcile her belief that her illegitimacy condemns her with her interest in men. The heart of the columnist's answer lies in her last sentence: "A religious experience can be a beautiful addition to living if you put it in the proper perspective and do not let it warf you." Toward the end of the novel, when the blind Hazel moves into Mrs. Flood's house, she questions him about the barbed wire he wears under his shirt. When he says it is natural, she retorts: "Well, it's not normal . . . it's something that people have quit doing—like boiling in oil or being a saint or walling up cats."

O'Connor prods the reader to recognize and to laugh at the ugly and vulgar in her characters' worlds. Enoch's rented room contains a picture of a moose whose gaze intimidates him. He loses his front teeth to the spring in a can of gag gift candy. The movies Enoch attends are either violent or sentimental.

The sense that the world is fraudulent is tied directly to O'Connor's central theme: In a world of falsities, the only reality is the grace that leads to salvation. This is the reality that Hazel tries to deny throughout the novel. At the end, however, his ruined eyes looking like the star at Bethlehem, he seems to have submitted to the inexorable call of the Jesus who haunts him. As a character, Hazel is so inarticulate that by the end of his tortured life he is quite incapable of talking to anyone about his spiritual state. Readers draw their conclusions about the significance of the ending through the viewpoint of Mrs. Flood, a woman who is little given to insights about others. It is she who thinks of Bethlehem when she looks at Hazel's eyes. At the very end of the novel, she believes that in Hazel's empty eye sockets she sees him retreating away from her into tiny pinpoints of light, and she suspects that somehow she was cheated of something. O'Connor implies that she loses what she refuses to be found by—the Christ who insists on finding Hazel.

Ann D. Garbett

Further Reading

Baumgaertner, Jill P. *Flannery O'Connor: A Proper Scaring.* Wheaton, Ill.: Shaw, 1988. Analyzes O'Connor's work as religious fiction, including essays on her most frequently collected short stories and her novels. Baumgaertner treats *Wise Blood* as a semiallegory about a "Christian in spite of himself." Includes a bibliography.

Brinkmeyer, Robert H., Jr. *The Art and Vision of Flannery*

O'Connor. Baton Rouge: Louisiana State University Press, 1989. The "Narrator and Narrative" chapter includes a lengthy discussion of *Wise Blood*, concentrating on the texture of the novel's world and on the relationship of point of view to theme.

Cash, Jean W. *Flannery O'Connor: A Life*. University of Tennessee, 2002. A painstakingly researched portrait of O'Connor. Includes a bibliography and an index.

Darretta, John. *Before the Sun Has Set: Retribution in the Fiction of Flannery O'Connor*. New York: Peter Lang, 2006. Focuses on the biblical ideas of retribution, salvation, and grace in O'Connor's fiction, including *Wise Blood*.

Giannone, Richard. *Flannery O'Connor and the Mystery of Love*. Urbana: University of Illinois Press, 1989. Giannone devotes a thirty-five-page chapter to *Wise Blood*, arguing that the novel articulates the disparity between "inept human bungling" and the power of God. Includes a bibliography.

Gooch, Brad. *Flannery: A Life of Flannery O'Connor*. New York: Little, Brown, 2008. Gooch's biography provides much critical analysis of O'Connor's fiction, both the individual works and the scope of her career. He concludes that despite writing two novels, including *Wise Blood*, she was not really a novelist but was perhaps the greatest twentieth century American short-story writer.

Kirk, Connie Ann. *Critical Companion to Flannery O'Connor*. New York: Facts On File, 2008. A good introduction to O'Connor. Contains a concise biography, entries on O'Connor's two novels and other works, with subentries on her characters as well as entries about her friends, literary influences, and the places and themes of her fiction. Includes a chronology and bibliographies of works by and about O'Connor.

Kreyling, Michael. *New Essays on "Wise Blood."* New York: Cambridge University Press, 1995. Five essays, including an introduction to the novel and discussions of its depiction of consumer culture, wounding and "sacramental aesthetics," and "anti-angel aggression."

Stephens, Martha. *The Question of Flannery O'Connor*. Baton Rouge: Louisiana State University Press, 1973. Stephens devotes a fifty-two-page chapter to *Wise Blood*, concentrating particularly on the novel's structural problems.

Walters, Dorothy. *Flannery O'Connor*. New York: Twayne, 1973. Good general introduction to O'Connor's work. The twenty-page chapter on *Wise Blood* discusses its early critical reception, summarizes the action, and analyzes its religious themes.

The Witches of Eastwick

Author: John Updike (1932-2009)
First published: 1984
Type of work: Novel
Type of plot: Satire and fantasy
Time of plot: Late 1960's
Locale: Eastwick, Rhode Island

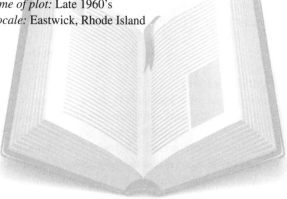

Principal characters:

JANE SMART, one of three witches who are friends and coven-mates, a cellist

SUZANNE "SUKIE" ROUGEMONT, another of the witches, a newspaper reporter

ALEXANDRA "LEXA" SPOFFORD, the third witch, a sculptor

JOE MARINO, a plumber, Alexandra's married lover

OZZIE SPOFFORD, Alexandra's former husband

MARCY,

BEN, and

ERIC, Alexandra's children

RAYMOND NEFF, a high school music teacher, Jane's sometime lover

GRETA NEFF, his wife

DARRYL VAN HORNE, an eccentric, supposedly wealthy inventor who has just moved to Eastwick; possibly the devil

Principal characters (continued):

ED PARSLEY, the Unitarian minister, Sukie's sometime lover

BRENDA PARSLEY, the minister's wife, who assumes his duties after he runs off with his lover

MONTY ROUGEMONT, Sukie's former husband

CLYDE GABRIEL, newspaper editor, Sukie's employer and sometime lover

FELICIA GABRIEL, Clyde's wife, a social activist

FIDEL, Darryl's manservant

DAWN POLANSKI, the young woman Ed Parsley leaves his wife and job for, a political radical

JENNIFER "JENNY" GABRIEL, Clyde's daughter, a medical technician, who returns upon her parents' death and marries Darryl

CHRISTOPHER "CHRIS" GABRIEL, Clyde's son, who returns upon his parents' death and leaves town with Darryl after his sister's death

The Story:

Jane Smart, Alexandra Spofford, and Sukie Rougemont are divorced single mothers in a small town in Rhode Island. They are also witches. One day in September, Jane tells Alexandra that a new man has moved to town, a New Yorker. Alexandra begins to reflect on her past as she returns to putting away the jars of spaghetti sauce she has made from her summer tomato crop. She continues these reflections as she walks her dog Coal on the beach.

Alexandra is an artist; she sculpts small clay figurines of women and sells them locally. Jane is a cellist and teaches piano. Sukie writes a gossip column for the local newspaper. They meet every Thursday for drinks and talk. At their next meeting, they discuss Greta, the awful wife of Raymond Neff, with whom Jane plays music. They also talk about Darryl Van Horne, the town's newest resident.

On Sunday night, Jane and Neff play in a concert at the Unitarian church. Van Horne attends. He talks to Alexandra about her sculptures, and she decides that she hates him. Jane meets him, and he critiques her performance and makes suggestions about her playing. Ed Parsley, the minister, joins them, as does Sukie. Van Horne reveals that he is attempting to invent some sort of protective coating that generates electricity.

Sukie is the first to visit Van Horne, and she publishes a newspaper story about him. She tells Alexandra that Van Horne wants to get to know all of them. Alexandra reflects on her life and her struggles with depression. She is waiting for something to happen. Sukie is attracted to her editor, Clyde; she talks about his wife Felicia's obsession with causes. Jane is practicing pieces by Johann Sebastian Bach at Van Horne's suggestion. The women think about visiting the newcomer.

Alexandra takes Coal for a walk on the beach near the Lenox mansion, the house Van Horne has bought. He happens upon her and persuades her to come into his house. When she notices the smells of sulfur, he explains that there is a laboratory in the house. Van Horne encourages Alexandra to try sculpting larger pieces, and he tells her that he knows of a gallery where she might be able to sell them.

The three witches visit Van Horne together, and soon a tennis match on his new court is in progress. Sukie and Van Horne play against Jane and Alexandra. Afterward, Sukie leaves, but the two remaining women bathe with Van Horne in a huge teak tub he has had custom built for a room with a skylight. This will be the first of many such baths. They smoke a joint and discuss men and women and the history of withchcraft. Sukie returns and joins them, having checked on her children. The women caress one another, listen to Janis Joplin, and, when they all leave the bath, bring the naked Van Horne to orgasm. They will become a subject of town gossip that winter.

Ed Parsley runs off with a local teenager named Dawn. Alexandra and Jane talk on the phone about the minister and about Sukie's attraction to Clyde. They think that Felicia is awful. Meanwhile, Clyde and Felicia are also discussing Ed's defection. As she speaks, Felicia begins to find small bits of various things, such as feathers, in her mouth. Removing the items, she admits to Clyde that this has been happening to her lately. Clyde has been unhappy with his wife for a long time.

Sukie receives letters from Ed describing his and Dawn's escape to the underground, where they are learning to make bombs. She is with Van Horne and resists telling him that she and Jane are responsible for Felicia's torment, having cast a spell on her. Sukie and Van Horne have lunch and talk about her attraction to Clyde and Van Horne's scientific projects. Sukie and Clyde finally make love, after which Clyde and Felicia have a confrontation: She continues to spit out garbage, and he kills her with the fireplace poker. Clyde then hangs himself.

Sukie talks to Jane and Alexandra, revealing that she feels some responsibility for Clyde's death. The Gabriel children come to town to arrange their parents' funeral and dispose of their estate. Sukie invites the oldest child, Jennifer, a laboratory technician from Chicago, to Van Horne's mansion. The others are upset at the invitation; they see Jennifer's presence as an intrusion. Soon, however, the women feel an instinct to mother Jennifer, enjoying her innocence and pristine beauty as she joins them in their rites of the tub. When Jennifer moves in with Van Horne to become his lab assistant, their maternal instincts turn to jealousy.

Ed is blown up by a bomb he was constructing. There is no evidence of Dawn's body at the site of the explosion, and it is unknown whether she was also killed or whether she escaped. Jennifer and Van Horne get married. The witches decide to dispense with the young new wife. They conjure a spell which results in her contracting cancer. Jennifer deals bravely with her slow and agonizing death: She bears her condition with strength and good humor, and she innocently fails to blame the witches for her disease.

Jennifer and Van Horne begin attending church, where Ed Parsley's wife, Brenda, has become a growing force by preaching in his stead. The town admires both Jennifer and Brenda, much to the witches' chagrin. They exhibit some signs of remorse. Alexandra and Sukie seek out the wax figure upon which they cast the spell in the bog where Alexandra tossed it. Ultimately, the witches lose Van Horne despite their efforts. After delivering a eulogy for his wife, he escapes his creditors and Eastwick with Jennifer's brother Christopher, who turns out to be his lover.

The witches attempt to deal with their role in Jennifer's death. Sukie wonders if they were not fulfilling Van Horne's will by killing his wife, clearing the way for him to run off with her brother. Sukie claims that Jennifer was not so sorry to die because she knew about the relationship between her husband and brother.

It is fall again, the seasons have come full circle, and the witches must get on with their lives. Alexandra builds her ideal husband and enrolls part-time in the Rhode Island School of Design, where she meets him, a ceramicist from Taos. The two eventually marry, and Jim takes Alexandra and her children out West. Jane, still teaching piano, likewise creates a husband from the remains of her precious, smashed cello; he is a small man in a tuxedo who is quite well-to-do. Sukie, who has become editor of the town newspaper, also conjures up a husband, a sandy-haired man from Connecticut. At the end of the novel, the witches are all gone.

Critical Evaluation:

John Updike is known mostly as a novelist whose fictional territory is white, Protestant, middle-class suburbia—especially small-town New England. He is generally a realist, celebrated for a writing style that is sometimes described as lyric, even baroque, in its detail. *The Witches of Eastwick*—published after the second of Updike's critically acclaimed Rabbit Angstrom novels, *Rabbit Is Rich* (1981)—

represented a departure for the author, in that its protagonists were women and it incorporated supernatural elements. Nevertheless, Updike addresses some of his favorite topics in the novel, including nature, religion, the difficulties of marriage, adultery and its fallout, and the meaning of human struggles within the inanity of suburbia.

Before he wrote *The Witches of Eastwick*, Updike was repeatedly criticized for creating women characters who occupied the margins of his stories, as sex objects and wives and mothers, but who were rarely developed in their full humanity. The novel was thus partly an attempt to answer this criticism. Updike was also motivated by an interest in witchcraft and, as he said repeatedly, in what it must be like to be a woman. Just as he returned in later novels to Rabbit Angstrom, sometimes after decades of that character's life had passed, he returned to the witches in his last novel, *The Widows of Eastwick* (2008).

Given the background of the novel, which is set against the women's movement and the Vietnam War, Updike's witches might have found dignity and strength in their own nature as women, worshiped mother nature, and practiced a benign, healing sort of magic. Instead, the author chose to portray bad witches, who cast dangerous spells, alter the weather, fly, and even commit murder. Their supernatural abilities are ascribed to two conditions: Divorce has liberated them as women, and they are empowered by the very atmosphere of Eastwick and Rhode Island. The famously insubordinate Anne Hutchinson, who was exiled to Rhode Island, is mentioned more than once in the novel.

In the wake of their divorces, the witches' freedom has allowed them to "find themselves" through artistic endeavor. Alexandra makes small clay figurines of women called "bubbies," Sukie writes as a gossip columnist for the local paper, and Jane is a cellist. Updike makes it clear that none is as serious or gifted an artist as she might be. Like Hester Prynne in Nathaniel Hawthorne's *The Scarlet Letter* (1850), they are marked, watched with some hostility, and gossiped about, because they are sexually liberated, sleeping with many of the husbands of their small town. If they are not quite indifferent mothers, they could hardly be described as maternal.

The narrator of the novel is one of the townspeople, who uses "we" and sometimes the more general "you." As is typical of Updike's novels, the plot of *The Witches of Eastwick* is fairly simple and straightforward, incorporating long passages in which the protagonists reflect on their lives and surroundings. Although the narrator is omniscient, the narration is usually filtered through Alexandra's point of view. Also typical of Updike's work, the setting, especially the natural world, is richly described. The novel begins and ends in the fall, and the cycle of seasons figures significantly within the trajectory of the narrative: Easter and Christmas, equinox and solstice, focus the sequence of events. The witches learn of Jennifer's marriage to Van Horne, for example, at Easter, and, ironically, they soon determine she must be "sacrificed" and concoct their spell.

Nature is beautiful but not benign in Eastwick. Alexandra describes it as "hungry," and Van Horne in his sermon at the Unitarian Church after Jennifer's death describes it as "cruel" and "terrible." While nature is powerful, it is a comment on the church that its former pastor is named Ed Parsley and that Van Horne, who may be the devil himself, is giving the sermon. Parsley's wife, who assumes his role as pastor, has no theological training whatsoever. To her credit, she is the only one who names the evil at work in their town, but, in implicating the witches, she provokes them to bewitch her as well.

Marriages in *The Witches of Eastwick* are generally unhappy, in part because of the witches' sexual dalliances with so many of the town's husbands. The witches themselves have hidden away the remains of their former husbands; Sukie's former mate is laminated in a place mat, for example. Clyde Gabriel, after becoming Sukie's lover, is so incensed with his constantly talking, angry wife that he kills her and then hangs himself. Even when Van Horne marries Jennifer, it is implied that the marriage is a trick to get at her money and her younger brother, with whom he is actually in love.

The novel and its characters often speak about or meditate on the differences between the sexes. Updike said more than once that this novel and *S.* (1988), with their women protagonists, were his way of exploring what it might be like to be a woman. Van Horne says outright that he wants to be one. The witches, very hard on the wives of the town, are often tender as they contemplate their lovers' bodies and fragile hold on their own masculinity. One scene in Van Horne's bath, in which the women bring him to orgasm, could be described as phallic worship. Flat statements about who men and women are and what they want abound. For example, one passage says that women need to give up serving everyone so that they can also let go of feeling angry about it. Another says that women deal better with pain than men do, another that men are "squeamish" about the kinds of things women take in stride.

In the end, the witches all remarry, conjuring husbands they hope will be to their liking, and leave Eastwick. Only their afterimages remain, as well as their stories, which lend some lingering excitement, however beyond common understanding, to life in the town. The novel represents life in suburbia as complex and even dangerous, as divorcees may turn out to be witches. Portraying a time during the women's movement when women were gaining power, the question of what they would do with that power was important. Updike's women create, but, bored and sometimes angry, they also destroy.

Susie Paul

Further Reading

Atwood, Margaret. "Wondering What It's Like to Be a Woman: *The Witches of Eastwick*, by John Updike." In *Moving Targets: Writing with Intent, 1982-2004*. Toronto, Ont.: Anansi, 2005. This lengthy and positive review of the novel is often cited and includes detailed analysis as well as summary. It is especially useful in its discussion of Updike, of his portrayal of women, and of the relationship between women and power in the novel.

Bloom, Harold. Introduction to *John Updike*, edited by Bloom. New York: Chelsea House, 1987. Refers to Updike as "a minor novelist with a major style"; discusses *The Witches of Eastwick*, arguing that it is Updike's most successful novel.

Loudermilk, Kim A. *Fictional Feminism: How American Bestsellers Affect the Movement for Women's Equality*. New York: Routledge, 2004. This study of representations of feminism in mainstream fiction includes a chapter on *The Witches of Eastwick*.

Plath, James. "Giving the Devil His Due: Leeching and Edification of Spirit in *The Scarlet Letter* and *The Witches of Eastwick*." In *John Updike and Religion: The Sense of the Sacred and the Motions of Grace*, edited by James Yerkes. Grand Rapids, Mich.: William B. Eerdmans, 1999. Contends that a comparison of these two novels is productive though the novels might seem dissimilar initially. Topics include: comparison of Hester Prynne and the three witches in relation to adultery, sexual freedom, and guilt; Chillingworth and Van Horne; the "election sermons" of both novels; and women and nature.

Wives and Daughters
An Every-Day Story

Author: Elizabeth Gaskell (1810-1865)
First published: serial, 1864-1866; book, 1866
Type of work: Novel
Type of plot: Domestic realism
Time of plot: Mid-nineteenth century
Locale: Hollingford, England

Principal characters:
MOLLY GIBSON, the only child of a widower
MR. GIBSON, the town physician, Molly's father
CLARE HYACINTH KIRKPATRICK, Gibson's second wife
CYNTHIA KIRKPATRICK, Molly's stepsister
OSBORNE and ROGER, the sons of Squire and Mrs. Hamley

The Story:

When Molly Gibson's widower father, the town doctor, marries the widow Clare Hyacinth Kirkpatrick, Molly loses her preeminent position in her father's household and acquires a frivolous, silly stepmother as well as a stepsister with whom she has little in common. The marriage is undertaken for practical reasons on both sides; the father thinks that his motherless young daughter needs the protection and tutelage of a mature woman, and the widow is grateful for a rise in social status and material comfort in place of the struggle to make a living as a governess. The marriage is not a happy one because of differences in temperament and intellect.

Molly and Cynthia, the two young girls, do become fast friends, however, although they are very different in character and personality. Each girl admires the other for qualities she herself lacks. Cynthia captivates Roger Hamley, the younger son of Squire Hamley, and they become unofficially engaged just before Roger leaves England to do two years of scientific research in Africa. Molly never speaks of her own love for Roger.

While Roger is gone, Cynthia writes to him to break off the relationship because she realizes that she does not love the young scientist; moreover, she receives a more advantageous proposal from Walter Henderson, a young lawyer whom she met while visiting relatives in London.

Squire Hamley counts on his son Osborne, Roger's older brother and the heir to the Hamley estate, to save the family's declining fortunes by marrying into a wealthy family. Osborne is, however, secretly married to a penniless Frenchwoman whom he met in France. When he develops a heart ailment, Osborne returns home ill and depressed. He dies before he reveals to his father that a son was born, but his wife, Aimée, comes to Hollingford when she hears of Osborne's illness.

The squire immediately dotes upon his young heir, but he is unable to accept Aimée. Molly tries hard to reconcile the two; when Roger returns to England upon learning of his

brother's death, the squire acknowledges his daughter-in-law and agrees that she should live nearby where she can care for her son.

Roger hopes to persuade Cynthia to marry him, but when he sees her with Henderson, he himself realizes that he was merely infatuated with her and that he really loves Molly, who loved him steadfastly so long. They reach an understanding before Roger leaves to complete his contractual obligation to his research sponsors. They look forward confidently to the future, when they plan to marry, leave Hollingford, and live in London.

Critical Evaluation:

Although *Cranford* (1851-1853), Elizabeth Gaskell's idyll of village life, was probably her most popular work, scholars and critics as well as many serious readers of fiction consider *Wives and Daughters* her greatest novel. This work, too, concerns provincial life in the first half of nineteenth century England, but it is more complex in scope and deals with broader social and moral issues. It was Gaskell's last novel, and it was not quite complete at the time of her death. The romantic, satisfying conclusion toward which she was working, however, was clear.

Born on September 29, 1810, in London, Gaskell was the daughter of a Unitarian minister, and she grew up in her aunt's household after the death of her mother in 1811. She was educated in a school for young ladies and was well read in literature and in philosophy. She married a Unitarian minister and was active in working with the poor and the sick, but after her only son died, she fell into a depression. With the encouragement of her husband, she became a professional writer and eventually attained an international reputation, a distinction earned by only a handful of other female writers of her time. She was the author of five novels, a biography of Charlotte Brontë, and numerous short stories.

The title *Wives and Daughters* indicates the only two recognized roles for women in the society that Gaskell describes. She presents a cross section of provincial society, in which Lord and Lady Cumnor and their family represent the aristocracy; Squire Hamley, his wife, and their two sons represent the landed but not wealthy gentry; and the physician, known as Mr. Gibson, and his young daughter, Molly, represent the professional middle class. Many other characters—including servants, townspeople, and laborers—round out the picture of this society. Gaskell depicts the changes that take place in the lives of the main family groups as well as the changes in their relations with each other. The principle upon which all the members of these groups base their lives is the sanctity of the family, and the novel focuses on the duties and obligations of family members. All the action and the shortcomings, as well as the successes, of the characters are related to the overriding importance of the basic social unit, the family.

The story is told primarily through the thoughts and actions of the main character, Molly Gibson. Most of the characters reach an understanding of the truth about themselves during the course of the novel, but it is primarily Molly who facilitates this, though without intending to do so. She exercises influence over others because, although she is a simple, uneducated country girl, she is able to see things as they are and has a strong sense of how they ought to be. She represents the moral conscience of her world and acts as a mediator and source of moral strength, especially for her father, her stepmother, her stepsister Cynthia, and her friend, Osborne Hamley.

The author of *Wives and Daughters* makes very few authorial comments; instead, she allows her characters to reveal themselves in their conversations, their inner reflections, and their behavior toward each other. With gentle, good-humored satire, Gaskell creates a picture of rural society that can easily be seen to represent the larger human condition, regardless of time or setting. One of the many critics who have lauded the author's works commented that Gaskell's vision and tone provided a link between the Romantics of the nineteenth century and the psychological realists of its waning years.

Natalie Harper

Further Reading

Foster, Shirley. *Elizabeth Gaskell: A Literary Life.* New York: Palgrave, 2002. This accessible introduction to the author relies on the best available biographies. It offers interesting comparisons of Gaskell's novels with others of the period and emphasizes women's issues as addressed by Gaskell.

Gérin, Winifred. *Elizabeth Gaskell: A Biography.* New York: Oxford University Press, 1976. A highly personal rather than scholarly discussion of Gaskell's work. Includes a chapter on *Wives and Daughters.*

Horsman, Alan. *The Victorian Novel.* New York: Oxford University Press, 1990. Includes a chapter on Gaskell, in which Horsman analyzes the way she discussed the problems of a changing society in her work. The analysis of *Wives and Daughters* emphasizes the effect of outsiders in a self-contained society.

Hughes, Linda K., and Michael Lund. *Victorian Publishing and Mrs. Gaskell's Work.* Charlottesville: University Press of Virginia, 1999. Places Gaskell's writing in the context of the Victorian era, describing how she negotiated her way through the publishing world by producing work that defied the conventions of her times but was also commercially successful. *Wives and Daughters* is discussed in chapter 1.

Lansbury, Coral. *Elizabeth Gaskell.* Boston: Twayne, 1984. Introductory overview of Gaskell's life and work. One of the chapters considers *Wives and Daughters* in detail.

_____. *Elizabeth Gaskell: The Novel of Social Crisis.* London: Elek, 1975. An evaluation of Gaskell's work. Emphasizes the economic and social aspects of *Wives and Daughters.*

Rathburn, Robert C., and Martin Steinmann, eds. *From Jane Austen to Joseph Conrad.* Minneapolis: University of Minnesota Press, 1958. This collection includes an essay by Yvonne French, who presents an overview of Gaskell's life and work and gives a balanced analysis of *Wives and Daughters.*

Rubenius, Aina. *The Woman Question in Mrs. Gaskell's Life and Works.* 1950. Reprint. New York: Russell & Russell, 1973. Discusses women's issues and focuses on the treatment of these matters in *Wives and Daughters.*

Wizard of the Crow

Author: Ngugi wa Thiong'o (James Ngugi, 1938-   )
First published: Mŭrogi wa Kagogo, 2004 (English
    translation, 2006)
Type of work: Novel
Type of plot: Magical Realism
Time of plot: Early twenty-first century
Locale: Aburĩria, Africa

Principal characters:
NYAWĨRA, the leader of an underground political group
KAMĨTĨ, a homeless man
THE RULER, the dictator of Aburĩria
TAJIRIKA, the owner of Eldares Construction, Nyawĩra's
    boss

The Story:

The Ruler of the fictional Kingdom of Aburĩria has been in power for so long that no one can remember how long he has been governing. Now, the country is in such devastation that most average people are starving. In the midst of this poverty, The Ruler decides to build a testimony to his legacy—a massive skyscraper called Marching to Heaven that will be high enough to reach space. Having run out of the people's Buri notes (the national currency, whose name means "worthless" in Gikuyu), he resolves to approach the Global Bank and ask for a loan to pay for the building.

Meanwhile, when a rumor circulates that the Eldares Construction Company is hiring, a queue of applicants builds that wraps around the entire city. Kamĩtĩ decides to try his luck and is the first to inquire about a position. He makes an unsuccessful bid for the job, failing to convince Tajirika that his Indian postgraduate degrees are of any value. Tajirika even humiliates him, and Kamĩtĩ leaves feeling angered and frustrated. Nyawĩra has witnessed the humiliating scene and is strangely drawn to Kamĩtĩ. They meet again the same night. Both of them are dressed in beggar's clothing, and they are run out of Paradise, an exclusive restaurant. Two policemen follow them to Nyawĩra's apartment, and Kamĩtĩ creates a sign for the door to ward them off: "enter at your own risk." Tying chicken bones and string to the sign, he hurriedly signs it with a wizard's moniker. To protect himself, Kamĩtĩ is forced to adopt the new identity he created for the sign: The police are frightened away, but they return soon after, seeking advice from the one who calls himself the Wizard of the Crow.

When the police leave, Kamĩtĩ and Nyawĩra begin talking. Nyawĩra shocks Kamĩtĩ when she throws a plastic snake at him, the same kind that had created the disturbance at Paradise earlier that evening. The night ends with each of them increasingly interested in the other but afraid to know more. Nyawĩra returns the next day to Eldares, and Kamĩtĩ stays behind and waits for her. While he is waiting, one of the policemen returns; remembering his moniker, Kamĩtĩ does his best to conjure the spirits by consulting a mirror. The policeman leaves, satisfied by Kamĩtĩ's wizardly powers and confident that his own path to success has been assured. It is not long before others hear about the Wizard of the Crow.

At work, Nyawĩra notices that her boss has been bringing in Buri notes by the sackful. After a meeting with The Ruler, Tajirika has been put in charge of organizing the construction for Marching to Heaven. Afraid that a thief will steal his money, he soon starts carrying a gun. His paranoia builds, and he begins acting very strangely; his wife and children suspect that he has changed into an ogre, the African creature of greed. Tajirika even refuses to wash the hand that shook The Ruler's hand, and he covers it with a protective glove. Eventually, Tajirika goes mad, and his wife takes him to see a diviner whose name has been gaining in popularity—the Wizard of the Crow.

Kamĩtĩ consults his mirror again and explains that Tajirika has been struck with the need to be white. Embarrassed, Tajirika leaves Kamĩtĩ with three sacks of Buri notes as payment. Kamĩtĩ finds that the money has a foul smell, and he decides to bury it in a field. The money begins to sprout trees that produce American dollars.

Meanwhile, Nyawĩra plots a demonstration during a visit by the Global Bank. Her female political dissent group, the Movement for the Voice of the People, stages a protest against the building of Marching to Heaven. On camera, the women expose their buttocks—the ultimate show of disgust. They also hurl trademark snakes at the politicians. Infuriated at the display, The Ruler sends Machokali and Sikiokuu, his "eyes and ears," to find and arrest the leader of the dissidents.

As the Wizard of the Crow, Kamĩtĩ is soon busy with visits from all over Eldares. He eventually starts believing in his conjuring skills as he gains repeat customers. Because Kamĩtĩ tells his customers only that their enemies will be struck down, without naming them, he leaves the door open for the person's true enemy to emerge. Often these enemies turn out to be the people themselves.

The Ruler becomes tired of his sycophant Sikiokuu after he fails to gain the loan from the Global Bank. Resolved to see Marching to Heaven made a reality, The Ruler decides to seek monetary help from the United States. While there, he is struck with a sudden and mysterious illness that causes him to blow up like a balloon and float on the ceiling. The Wizard of the Crow is kidnapped from Aburīria and flown to New York to cure The Ruler.

Kamītī's diagnosis for The Ruler is simple: He is pregnant. Everyone, including The Ruler, is shocked. Kamītī escapes New York and attends a meeting of the People's Assembly. The hunt is on to capture the Wizard of the Crow and Nyawīra. Kamītī leads a prodemocracy demonstration and, claiming that Nyawīra is merely a lover of freedom, encourages anyone who loves freedom to announce that they, too, are Nyawīra. One by one, everyone at the assembly stands, claiming to be Nyawīra. Suddenly, an explosion erupts within the State House; Kamītī is shot, but the real Nyawīra finds him and leads him to safety.

The blast in the State House is actually The Ruler, who has become so overblown with inner corruption that he explodes. Afterward, he is left with a forked, snakelike tongue. He announces on television that he was indeed pregnant because he is the same as the nation, and what they have both given birth to is multiparty democracy. The arrival of democracy, however, is accomplished in name only.

Finally, Tajirika, who has acquired a white arm and leg from a genetics clinic, convinces an angry mob that he is a deity and that The Ruler has ceded all power to him. In fact, Tajirika has killed The Ruler, and a new era arrives in Aburīrian history: the Empire of Tajirika. Focusing on building the country into a new Rome, Tajirika fails to deliver on simple tasks such as garbage collection. As a result, the country is in an even worse state than before. Together, Kamītī and Nyawīra vow to keep fighting until true democracy becomes a reality for Aburīria.

Critical Evaluation:

At nearly one thousand pages, *Wizard of the Crow* is a massive work. Writing since the 1960's, Ngugi wa Thiong'o has always been concerned with the politics of his native Kenya. It would be impossible to discuss the relevance and structure of the novel without understanding first the background of its author. Imprisoned for a year in 1977 for his involvement in the Gikuyu-language play *Ngaahika Ndeenda* (pr. 1977, pb. 1980; with Ngugi wa Mirii; *I Will Marry When I Want*, 1982), Ngugi was able to escape further persecution, and perhaps even execution by the Moi government, only by choosing exile in the West. This exile has proven to be a hindrance to him as a Kenyan trying to affect Kenyan politics, yet it has also given him visibility as an African writer in the West. Ngugi's interest in issues of dominant and dominated languages has its roots in the postcolonial histories of Kenya and other African nations. Ngugi has contributed much to the writing on colonialism and language.

Unlike Ngugi's other novels, *Wizard of the Crow* portrays not Kenya but a fictional African country. In the vein of oral literature, *Wizard of the Crow* weaves together several different stories and characters that may seem unrelated but in the end create a much larger and more vibrant picture. The main plot is often interrupted by stories-within-the-story, tales, and rumors passed between villagers, all of which serve to mimic the feel of African orality. In addition, Ngugi provides allusions to his own work, including direct references to his novel *Caitaani Mūtharaba-Inī* (1980; *Devil on the Cross*, 1982). It can be conjectured that the story he begins in *Devil on the Cross*, of a Kenya mired in the desire for capitalist trappings, is one he finishes with *Wizard of the Crow*, which features a country indistinguishable from any other postcolonial country in Africa—complete with incessant corruption leading to starvation and one leader just as irresponsible as the next.

The characters of Kamītī and Nyawīra are two representations of the "native intellectual" described in Frantz Fanon's *Les Damnés de la terre* (1961; *The Damned*, 1963; better known as *The Wretched of the Earth*, 1965). Ngugi, who has been influenced by Fanon's writing, has crafted characters that embody the Marxist fundamentals necessary to overthrow a stalwart regime. Educated and culturally proud, Kamītī and Nyawīra are also young enough to be optimistic but experienced enough to know that their struggle is one that has been fought for generations. Also important is Ngugi's choice of a woman as the main hero. Nyawīra shares the role of sorcerer with Kamītī; it is her home that he uses as his shrine, and it is she who leads the Movement for the Voice of the People by organizing demonstrations. Ngugi's usage of a woman as the leader of a freedom movement underscores the important role women have always played as revolutionaries, especially in Mau Mau-era Kenya.

Ngugi utilizes emotional imagery to depict another theme common in African postcolonial literature, a theme he refers to as "white-ache." Ngugi has coined this term to designate the desire not merely to possess what a rich white person possesses but actually to be white—to become the symbol of the power and dignity that white colonizers long denied to Africans. The Ruler experiences white-ache to such a degree that he physically blows up like a balloon, in a satirical nod to the innumerable African postcolonial dictators (such as Robert

Mugabe, Daniel Arap Moi, and Charles Taylor) who no doubt provided Ngugi with his inspiration. Tajirika, who has the benefit of being aware of his own white-ache, could choose to take the road of Kamĩtĩ and Nyawĩra and become a freedom fighter. Instead, at the last minute he reverts to his white-ache and becomes a mutant. Self-mutilated to the point of grotesquerie, Tajirika betrays himself and his country. The further symbolism of the tree that grows dollars that are eaten by white grubs shows Ngugi's belief in the ephemeral nature of capitalism, which ingests what is produced and still remains unsated.

Wizard of the Crow appropriates a phrase from Ngugi's earlier *Devil on the Cross*. The latter work's "The nation is pregnant; what it will give birth to, no one knows" becomes the former's "The Ruler is pregnant; what he will give birth to, no one knows." The country hopes to rid itself of its leader, only to find that the new leader is equally incompetent and greedy. The unfortunate truth, as Ngugi knows, is that neocolonialism is one stage in the long and arduous process of moving from colonialism to modernity. In the end, the characters maintain their resolve, as do ordinary citizens all over Africa, that one day freedom and democracy will take root.

Shannon Oxley

Further Reading

Cantalupo, Charles, ed. *Ngugi wa Thiong'o: Texts and Contexts*. Trenton, N.J.: African World Press, 1995. A collection of critical essays written by Kenyan scholars. Provides a fresh look at Ngugi's life from those within the country Ngugi left behind; discusses why his work is still important in his homeland.

_____. *The World of Ngugi wa Thiong'o*. Trenton, N.J.: African World Press, 1995. A second collection of essays on Ngugi's work, covering even the minor texts, including his children's book. The criticism also covers Ngugi's language arguments and historical research.

Gikandi, Simon. *Ngugi wa Thiong'o*. New York: Cambridge University Press, 2009. Juxtaposes Ngugi's life with a social history of Kenya, providing a level of detail that only a native Kenyan could offer.

Ngugi wa Thiong'o. *Decolonising the Mind: The Politics of Language in African Literature*. London: James Currey, 1986. An important contribution to the theory and criticism of African, postcolonial, and Marxist literature. Although some of the material may be dated, the argument that language can be used as a tool in colonial domination is still a valid one.

Ogunde, James. *Ngugi's Novels and African History: Narrating the Nation*. London: Pluto Press, 1999. Ogunde provides a critical examination of Ngugi's earlier novels, while discussing Ngugi's positioning of female characters and his value to Kenyan history.

Simatei, Triop Peter. *The Novel and the Politics of Nation Building in East Africa*. Edited by Eckhard Breitinger. Bayreuth African Studies Series 55. Bayreuth, Germany: Bayreuth University Press, 2001. Simatei examines Ngugi's place among other writers from East Africa and ways in which his literary contributions have shaped nationalistic agendas in Kenya.

The Woman in the Dunes

Author: Kōbō Abe (1924-1993)
First published: Suna no onna, 1962 (English translation, 1964)
Type of work: Novel
Type of plot: Allegory
Time of plot: 1962
Locale: A Japanese seaside village

Principal characters:
NIKI JUMPEI, a teacher
THE WOMAN, a widow living in a small seaside village

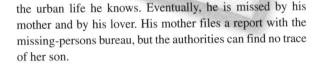

The Story:

A teacher and an amateur entomologist, Niki Jumpei decides to take a vacation to gather specimens for his collection of insects. He takes a train to a small town near the ocean and, carrying a canteen and a large wooden box, disappears from the urban life he knows. Eventually, he is missed by his mother and by his lover. His mother files a report with the missing-persons bureau, but the authorities can find no trace of her son.

Jumpei's story is as follows: After arriving in a small beach town, he walks from the railroad station to an area of dunes near the ocean. He comes upon a strange village, where many of the houses are located in pits created by huge sand dunes. As night approaches, he begins to look for a place to sleep; villagers direct him to a building that is little more than a shack, located in one of the depressions in the dunes. It turns out to be the home of a young woman, who offers to accommodate Jumpei. Unenthusiastically, Jumpei accepts the woman's hospitality.

Jumpei is horrified by the woman's story. He learns, soon after his stay begins, that she is a widow whose husband and young daughter were both victims of the ever-encroaching sand. Her life now is a constant struggle against the sand, shoveling it to a place from which it can be hauled up for shipment to shoddy contractors for use in making cheap concrete. This industry is the sole economic support of the entire village. The woman makes it clear that Jumpei is expected to help with the work of shoveling sand in exchange for his room and board. Their shoveling is essential; without constant efforts to remove sand and send it to the top, the little house would be overwhelmed by sand slides.

Jumpei soon discovers that he cannot escape from the depression in the dunes in which the house is placed. He attempts to evade the fate to which he has been condemned. He tries to bully and threaten the woman to force her to help him leave, but he fails. He tries to bargain with and to threaten the only other villagers he sees, the men who arrive at the top of the dune, lowering buckets to the pit below to be filled with sand, and raising the buckets on ropes; they do not respond to his overtures. Finally and reluctantly, he gives in and helps the woman with her unceasing labor, but he cannot get used to the constant presence of sand. It is in his clothes, in his eyes, on his skin, and in his mouth; when he sleeps, it coats his entire body.

When he is not shoveling sand, sleeping, or eating his meals, Jumpei continues to spend his time plotting ways of escaping from his prison. He tries to climb out, only to be half-buried by a slide. He threatens the villagers with criminal prosecution if they fail to provide him with a ladder, but they have no reason to fear him; the police do not interfere with the villagers. Even if someone were to report his absence, an investigation would unlikely reach the village, and, if it does, the villagers will simply deny knowledge of Jumpei's existence.

Jumpei and the woman form a strange kind of relationship. As the days pass, she becomes more attractive to him, and they finally become sexual partners, although their other interactions remain tense and intermittent. She nurses him when he is sick and begins to treat him with some tenderness. She points out that her life is easier, now that he is helping her shovel the sand, and Jumpei shows at least some affection in helping her with the chores. Still, there is no escaping the relentless sand.

Finally, Jumpei finds a way out. Using a rope ladder that catches onto something on the surface, he hoists himself out of the pit. He is free for a while, passing through the village and finding his way to the sea, but this freedom is an illusion. During this attempt at escape, he carries on internal dialogues with the woman, with a friend from his earlier life, and with himself. He is chased by dogs and loses his way several times, and he never finds his way out of the village area. He finds the ocean, but he strays into quicksand and survives only because the villagers, who are aware of his attempts to escape, follow him. They save him from the quicksand and return him to the woman's care.

Jumpei makes one final attempt to flee. When the workers come to take away the accumulated sand, he pleads with them to help him leave. They laugh at him, but finally an old man offers him escape if he and the woman agree to have sexual intercourse in front of a crowd. Jumpei tries to persuade the woman and, when she refuses, he tries to force her, finally pleading with her to pretend to submit, since he is unable to perform anyway. She beats him, hurting his stomach and bloodying his nose, and the watching villagers lose interest. Finally, Jumpei realizes that they had no intention of letting him go.

In the end, Jumpei accepts the struggle against the sand as a way of life. He does not give up planning to escape, but it becomes an abstraction for him, with no real effect on the way he lives. The woman becomes pregnant, but this seems to affect him very little. When she suffers great pain and a villager (who is related to a veterinarian) diagnoses her condition as an extrauterine pregnancy, Jumpei hardly pays any attention when she is taken away to a hospital in the city. The rope ladder that was used to lift her from the pit remains in place, and Jumpei climbs it, getting a view of the sea. He is tempted to try to escape once again, since the attention of the villagers is on the woman. Rather than try to leave, however, he returns to continue an experiment he had begun. Escape can wait for another day.

Critical Evaluation:

The Woman in the Dunes is the best known of Kōbō Abe's works, at least in the Western world, perhaps in part because it was made into a memorable motion picture. More important, however, is that this grim, almost allegorical picture of the state of humanity echoes a Greek myth that resonates in the twenty-first century: the myth of Sisyphus, who was condemned to spend his days pushing a heavy rock up a steep slope, only to have the rock slide back down every time. Albert Camus, one of the major writers influenced by French existentialism—a philosophy that dominated much of Western thought and literature after World War II—used Sisyphus as a symbol of human fate in one of his major essays. Very simply stated, the existentialists held that life was similar to the experience of Sisyphus: Human hopes and dreams (particularly that of the Christian afterlife) were doomed never to be realized, but human nobility was nevertheless confirmed in accepting this fact and carrying on with the struggle.

The Woman in the Dunes has a distinctly Japanese style. The setting for almost all the action is an isolated village whose inhabitants have no interest in and little connection with the larger world outside their immediate area. They are primitives who accept their harsh fate, condemned to an eternal struggle with the encroaching sand, because they can conceive of no other way of life. Their sense of humor is crude and cruel, and their imaginations are limited. The simple experiment with water that Jumpei conducts at the end of the novel would never occur to any of them, and yet it could lead to a major easing of one of the harsh conditions of their existence. Still, even should the experiment turn out to be a success, there is no reason to believe that the villagers will use Jumpei's results to their benefit.

The allegorical nature of *The Woman in the Dunes* is underlined by the relatively small amount of interest Abe shows in making his characters into individuals; the fact that the second of the novel's two major characters, the woman in the dunes herself, is never given a name is evidence of this. Even Jumpei is almost always referred to as "he" or "him" in the narrative. He is a most ordinary man, with the single unusual character trait of an interest in collecting insects. The reader knows only that he has a mother and a lover, as well as a single friend, and that he is a teacher. Otherwise, he is simply Everyman, and he is lost.

The central symbol in this allegory is the sand. Its presence in the novel is relentless, representing not only the dreariness and inevitability of everyday life but also the material out of which people make their living and the capriciousness of the natural world in which they are fated to try to survive. It is sand that kills the woman's husband and daughter and that almost kills Jumpei in his attempt to escape. More than anything, however, the sand is the symbol of a reality that is so continuously present, forming a kind of film over everything in the lives of these characters, that it becomes an integral part of every moment of their lives. They

nearly come to a point at which they are no longer aware of the unpleasantness of its continual presence.

Abe, with Yukio Mishima and Nobel Prize winner Kenzaburō Ōe, was a leader of a post-World War II generation of Japanese writers who took a major interest in politics, a subject not traditionally important in Japanese literature. There is evidence of this interest in *The Woman in the Dunes*: The villagers are exploited to haul sand that is then sold by a corrupt business society to make shoddy concrete. A political dimension exists in the helplessness of the characters, who continue providing this sand for corrupt businesses without questioning or attempting to change the situation.

More important, however, is that many critics see in *The Woman in the Dunes* a distinct similarity to Czech writer Franz Kafka's works, especially *Der Prozess* (1925; *The Trial*, 1937) and *Das Schloss* (1926; *The Castle*, 1930). Both writers use the same kind of nearly anonymous characters, both place their characters in hopeless situations they did little or nothing to create, and both depict people at the mercy of forces they have no means of understanding. Abe once said that he intended to provide hope for his characters, and perhaps Jumpei's experiment can be seen as a small ray of light, but the tone of *The Woman in the Dunes* and the fate of its characters leave little room for this possibility. Abe, like Kafka, creates in his works situations that mirror humanity's helplessness in the face of incomprehensible and overwhelming forces.

John M. Muste

Further Reading

Abe, Kōbō. "Interview with Kōbō Abe." Interview by Nancy Hardin. *Contemporary Literature* 15, no. 4 (Autumn, 1974): 439-456. A major published interview with Abe that includes important critical comment about his life and his literary influences.

Dissanyake, Wimal. "Kōbō Abe: Self, Place, and Body in *Woman in the Dunes*—A Comparative Study of the Novel and the Film." In *Literary Relations East and West*, edited by Jean Toyama and Nobuko Ochner. Honolulu: University of Hawaii Press, 1990. Pays special attention to the themes of alienation and identity and to the importance of sense of place in *The Woman in the Dunes*.

Keene, Donald. *Five Modern Japanese Novelists*. New York: Columbia University Press, 2003. Abe is one of the novelists whom Keene discusses. The chapter devoted to Abe features biographical material and discussions of *Woman in the Dunes* and his other novels.

Leithauser, Brad. "Severed Futures." *The New Yorker*, May 9, 1988. This essay discusses the recurrent theme of the uncertainty of human life in Abe's fiction.

Pollack, David. "Kōbō Abe: The Ideology of Science in *Woman in the Dunes*." In *Reading Against Culture: Ideology and Narrative in the Japanese Novel*. Ithaca, N.Y.: Cornell University Press, 1992. Pollack investigates Abe's novel and works by other Japanese novelists in terms of their ideology, use of narrative, and treatment of the self and of Japanese culture.

Van Wert, William F. "Levels of Sexuality in the Novels of Kōbō Abe." *International Fiction Review* 6, no. 2 (Summer, 1979): 129-132. Discusses Abe's affinities with Fyodor Dostoevski, Franz Kafka, and Alain Robbe-Grillet.

The Woman in White

Author: Wilkie Collins (1824-1889)
First published: 1860
Type of work: Novel
Type of plot: Detective and mystery
Time of plot: 1850's
Locale: England

Principal characters:
WALTER HARTRIGHT, a young artist
FREDERICK FAIRLIE, the owner of Limmeridge House
LAURA FAIRLIE, his niece and ward
MARIAN HALCOMBE, her half sister
SIR PERCIVAL GLYDE, Laura Fairlie's suitor
COUNT FOSCO, a scheming nobleman
ANNE CATHERICK, the woman in white

The Story:

Through the help of his Italian friend Professor Pesca, Walter Hartright is engaged as drawing master to the nieces of Frederick Fairlie, of Limmeridge House in Cumberland. On the day before he leaves to take up his new position, he meets a young woman dressed in white wandering about the outskirts of London. Walter discovers that she knows Limmeridge and once went to school there with Laura Fairlie. The young woman leaves him very suddenly, and soon after a coach comes by whose passenger leans from the window to ask a police officer if he saw a girl in white. The police officer did not, and Walter hesitates to intrude. As the coach leaves, he hears the man say the girl escaped from an asylum.

Upon his arrival at Limmeridge, Walter meets the first of his two pupils, Marian Halcombe. Marian is homely but intelligent and charming in manner. Her half sister, Laura, is the beauty of the family and heir of Limmeridge House. The two girls are living under the protection of Laura's uncle, Fairlie, a selfish and fastidious hypochondriac. Walter falls in love with Laura almost at once. After hearing his story about the mysterious woman in white, Marian searches her mother's letters and discovers that she must be Anne Catherick, a young woman in whom Mrs. Fairlie took great interest because she so greatly resembled Laura.

After several months, Marian realizes that Walter is deeply in love with Laura. She advises him to leave, as Laura's father asked her on his deathbed to marry Sir Percival Glyde. One day, Walter meets the woman in white again. She is in the graveyard cleaning the stone that bears Mrs. Fairlie's name, and she admits that she hopes to thwart Laura's coming marriage to Sir Percival. Told of this incident, Marian promises to ask Sir Percival for a full explanation.

Walter leaves Limmeridge. When Sir Percival arrives, he explains to Marian that Anne is the daughter of a woman who was in his family's service in the past and that she is in need of hospital treatment. He says he kept her in an asylum at her mother's request, and he proves the statement with a letter from Mrs. Catherick. His explanation is accepted, and his marriage to Laura takes place. Walter, heartbroken, goes to Central America as a painter for an archaeological expedition.

When Sir Percival and Laura come home from their wedding trip some months later, Marian finds them much changed. Laura is extremely unhappy, and Sir Percival shows his displeasure at having Marian living with them in his house at Blackwater Park. Count Fosco, a huge and self-assured Italian, arrives with his wife, Laura's aunt, for a visit. Marian soon learns that the count is involved in money matters with Sir Percival. When Laura is asked to sign a document without looking at it, both she and Marian know Sir Percival and Count Fosco are trying to obtain money from her by fraudulent means. Over Sir Percival's loud protests, Laura refuses to sign the paper unless he will let her read it. The count interferes and makes Sir Percival give up the matter for a time. Marian overhears a conversation between the two men, in which they decide to get loans and wait three months before trying again to persuade Laura to sign away her money. The household becomes one of suspicion and fear.

By chance one day, Laura meets the woman in white and learns that there is a secret in Sir Percival's life involving both Anne and her mother. Before Anne can tell her the secret, Count Fosco appears and frightens the woman away. Sir Percival becomes alarmed when he learns that Anne is in the neighborhood. He locks both Marian and Laura in their rooms, but Marian spies on the two men by climbing to the roof during a pouring rain and overhears a plot to get Laura's money by killing her. Before she can act on this information, however, Marian catches a fever from the chill of her rain-soaked clothing. She is put to bed, and Laura, too, becomes mysteriously ill.

When Laura is better, she is told that Marian went to London. She cannot believe her sister left without saying good-bye and insists on going to London herself. Actually, Marian is moved to another room in the house. When Laura arrives in London, she is met by Count Fosco. She is given drugs, falsely declared insane, dressed in Anne's old clothes, and taken to the asylum from which Anne escaped. Sir Percival finds Anne in the meantime. Because of her resemblance to Laura, he plans to kill her and bury her as Laura. Anne is already very ill, and when she dies suddenly in London of natural causes, Sir Percival announces that Laura, Lady Glyde, died.

After Marian recovers, she is told that her sister is dead. She refuses to believe either the count or Sir Percival. Determined to find Anne, she discovers that the woman in the asylum is really Laura. She arranges Laura's escape and takes her back to Limmeridge. At Limmeridge, however, Fairlie refuses to recognize the sickly Laura as anyone but Anne. Laura's memory is so impaired by the experience that she cannot prove her identity. Marian and Laura go to look at the false tomb bearing the name of Lady Glyde. There they meet Walter, recently returned from Central America. He came to pay his respects at Laura's grave.

There is no possibility of returning Laura to her rightful estate as long as her mind is impaired by her terrible experience. While she is recovering, Walter attempts to learn Sir Percival's secret. He finally discovers that Sir Percival's father and mother were never legally married. Hoping to destroy the evidence of his birth, Sir Percival attempts to burn an old church record that Walter needs. In the fire he sets, Sir Percival burns up the church and himself as well. After his death, Mrs. Catherick hints that Laura's father was the father

of illegitimate Anne as well. After searching, Walter finds that this must be true.

Walter returns to London. Together, the three plan to clear Laura by forcing the count to confess. Walter's old friend Pesca reveals that Count Fosco is a traitor to the secret society to which both Pesca and the count belong. Through Pesca's help, Walter is able to frighten the count into giving him a confession and written proof in Sir Percival's handwriting that Laura was still alive when Anne was buried under the name of Lady Glyde. The count flees England and is killed soon afterward by the secret society he betrayed.

Walter, Marian, and a much-improved Laura are happy to have proof of the substitution that was made. Walter and Laura marry and go to Limmeridge to confront Fairlie with the evidence. He is forced to admit Laura's identity. The friends then leave and do not return until after Fairlie's death, when the son of Laura and Walter takes over the estate. Marian lives with the family until she dies.

Critical Evaluation:

Throughout his career, Wilkie Collins, like many other writers, was torn between a need to satisfy the demands of the popular reading public and a personal desire to create works of lasting artistic merit. He achieved the desired synthesis only twice, initially with *The Woman in White* and, a few years later, with *The Moonstone* (1868). *The Woman in White* was both his most popular work and his most important serious book.

Although the plot of *The Woman in White* is fantastic, it is based, as were many of Collins's crime stories, on an actual case history he discovered in Maurice Méjan's *Recueil des causes célèbres* (1808). In 1787, Madame de Douhault was cheated out of a portion of her father's estate by a brother. On her way to Paris to launch proceedings against her brother, she stopped at a relative's home, where she was drugged, confined to a mental hospital, and declared dead. The unscrupulous relatives collected all that remained of the father's estate. Like her fictional counterpart, Madame de Douhault—wearing a white dress—finally escaped, but, unlike Laura Fairlie, she was never able legally to reestablish her identity, despite positive identifications from friends and associates. She died a pauper in 1817.

The crime becomes more elaborate and complicated in Collins's hands. Not only is the heroine drugged and secreted in an asylum, but a deceased double is buried in her place. "The first part of the story," Collins commented in a newspaper interview, "will deal with the destruction of the victim's identity. The second with its recovery." Collins added a number of secondary lines to this basic plot movement: the question of Laura's marriage to Percival Glyde; the identity and story of Anne Catherick, the mysterious "woman in white"; the love affair between Laura and Walter Hartright; Laura's supposed death and the events surrounding it; Percival's relationship with Anne's mother, Mrs. Catherick, and his mysterious secret; and, finally, Count Fosco's mysterious background.

Complex as the plot is, Collins handles the threads of the narrative in such a way that they support and complement one another without obscuring the central thrust of the book. While answering one question, Collins uses that answer to introduce new, more provocative questions. As the puzzles are gradually unraveled, the pressures on the hero and the heroines become more extreme. Throughout much of the book, the victims seem nearly helpless before the villains' power. The reversal does not come until late in the novel and, when it does, the shift is sudden. Nevertheless, even in the last important scene, Walter's confrontation with Fosco, when the initiative is clearly the hero's, the sense of danger remains intense. Nowhere does Collins demonstrate his mastery of intricate plotting more effectively than in *The Woman in White*, and it remains, with the possible exception of *The Moonstone*, the most perfectly structured example of the sensation novel.

The gradual revelation of the intricate conspiracy is made doubly effective by Collins's narrative method. The story is told in bits and pieces by a number of characters who reveal only as much as they know. Some of the narrators, among them Walter, Marian Halcombe, and Fosco, are major participants who explain and interpret events as they occur or after the fact. Others, such as Laura's uncle, Frederick Fairlie, Glyde's housekeeper, and Eliza Michelson (and even Laura's tombstone), can provide only fragments of information that reflect their brief connections to the story. This technique, in which he reveals only so much information at any one time as convenient, gives Collins a great deal of flexibility and control over the suspense; ensures variety in the narrative style, mood, and tone; and sharpens the characterizations. As the speakers offer their information, they characterize themselves through their diction, prose style, habits, and attitudes. Collins's narrative method offers readers a gigantic prose jigsaw puzzle. A few years later, Collins uses this same method in writing what many have called the first English detective novel, *The Moonstone*.

The object of the conspiracy, Laura, is a passive creature with little color or character. The real conflict is between Marian and Walter on the one hand and Percival and Fosco on the other. In the first half of the book, leading up to Laura's falsified death, Marian acts as a foil to the villains. After Laura's escape, Walter becomes the principal hero. Percival

enters the novel before Fosco but quickly retreats in the reader's mind to a subordinate position. Fosco, the most impressive character, dominates all the other characters.

As Walter describes her, Marian is a physically unattractive woman: "the lady's complexion was almost swarthy, and the dark down on her upper lip was almost a mustache. She had a large, firm, masculine mouth and jaw; prominent piercing resolute brown eyes and thick coal-black hair, growing unusually low on her forehead." Morally and intellectually, she is nevertheless a very strong character. Her qualities, when summed up—loyalty, steadfastness, courage, propriety, intelligence, sensitivity—sound like a list of stock Victorian virtues, but as Collins presents her she seems real.

It is Marian who first senses a conspiracy. It has gone too far to stop, but she manages to hamper the villains for a time. The irony of her situation is that when, having courageously risked her life and gained the information she needs to expose the plot, she catches pneumonia in the act—thus exposing herself and becoming helpless at the critical point. Her illness gives Fosco an opportunity to read her journal and learn everything about her counterstrategy. Having read Marian's comments, however, Fosco is so impressed by her character and resourcefulness that, for the first time, he allows sentiment to mitigate his treatment of an adversary. This slight moral hesitation is ultimately a significant factor in his downfall.

Fosco is one of the most memorable literary criminals of all time. By contrast, Percival, in Collins's own words, is "a weak shabby villain." Percival is clearly dominated by Fosco and does very badly when he operates alone. He reacts to situations emotionally and physically, with little planning and crude execution; the most obvious example is the vicarage fire that costs him his life. Because Collins thought "the crime too ingenious for an English villain," he felt it necessary to create Isidor Ottavio Baldassare Fosco.

Collins wisely never introduces or describes Fosco directly but allows his presence to grow by means of the reactions and the impressions experienced by the other characters. The count's most obvious physical feature is his size; he is the first of the great fat criminals, a common type in later crime fiction but still unusual in Collins's time. "I had begun my story when it struck me that my villain would be commonplace, and I made him fat in opposition to the recognized type of villain." Fosco's physical size is matched by his appetites for food, culture, money, and intrigue: he is, in short, a demonic Falstaff.

Fosco's intellectual powers are likewise impressive. His conspiracy has style as well as intelligence, and he is witty, extremely articulate, and suavely ironical. Furthermore, he is no ordinary criminal; he justifies his amoral actions philosophically. "Crime," he tells Marian, "is a good friend to man and to those about him as often as it is an enemy."

Despite the evil he does, Fosco is an attractive man. In addition to his intelligence, style, courage, and strong, if distorted, sense of honor, he also possesses a number of vivid humanizing traits: his fondness for animals, especially his birds and mice; his feelings for his wife; and his honest admiration, even devotion, toward Marian. Perhaps Collins assigns Fosco's punishment to a mysterious Italian political group rather than to Walter because he realized that his readers' ambiguous feelings about Fosco will place some onus on the man who brings him to justice.

Although critics have long lauded the characterizations of Marian and Fosco, they have tended to ignore Walter, though he is too important to the novel to be so easily dismissed. He lacks some of the color and sympathy of Marian but is, nevertheless, her equal in courage and intelligence. More important, looking at the novel from the standpoint of a nineteenth century reader, it is Walter with whom one would most likely identify, and it is he who upholds the English national character and middle-class morality in the face of Fosco's threat.

Walter, the hardworking son of a thrifty drawing-master, confronts a nobleman, a baronet, and a decadent member of the gentry (Fairlie), all vestiges of aristocracy. Walter takes his work seriously; he is industrious, loyal, rational, courageous, and tenacious—in short, he possesses all the Victorian middle-class virtues. In contrast to the amoral Fosco, Walter believes that virtue, truth, and justice must ultimately triumph, and he is given the job of demonstrating that assumption in the action. Because he does it so efficiently, the novel answers the intellectual and moral expectations of the Victorian reading public. Despite Fosco's style and charm, even twenty-first century readers find Walter's final victory satisfying.

"Critical Evaluation" by Keith Neilson

Further Reading

Bachman, Maria K., and Don Richard Cox, eds. *Reality's Dark Light: The Sensational Wilkie Collins.* Knoxville: University of Tennessee Press, 2003. Collection of fourteen essays analyzing Collins's novels, focusing on the themes and the techniques that he introduced to these works. Interpretations of *The Woman in White* are provided in two essays: "Marian's Moustache: Bearded Ladies, Hermaphrodites, and Intersexual Collage in *The Woman in White*" by Richard Collins and "The Crystal Palace, Imperialism, and the 'Struggle for Existence': Victorian Evolutionary Discourse in Collins's *The Woman in White*" by Gabrielle Ceraldi.

Collins, Wilkie. *The Woman in White.* Edited by Harvey Peter Sucksmith. New York: Oxford University Press, 1980. A most accessible edition with a valuable bibliography and notes explaining vocabulary and the legal statutes of the era. Sucksmith's introduction contains a good discussion of the Dauhault case that served as the probable source of inspiration for Collins.

Gasson, Andrew. *Wilkie Collins: An Illustrated Guide.* New York: Oxford University Press, 1998. A well-illustrated, alphabetical guide to the characters, titles, and terms in Collins's works. Includes a chronology, the Collins family tree, maps, and a bibliography.

Nayder, Lillian. *Wilkie Collins.* New York: Twayne, 1997. An introductory overview of Collins's life and work. *The Woman in White* is discussed in chapter 4, "Sensation Fiction and Marriage Law Reform: Wives and Property in *The Woman in White, No Name,* and *Man and Wife.*"

Peters, Catherine. *The King of Inventors: A Life of Wilkie Collins.* Princeton, N.J.: Princeton University Press, 1993. Contains an extensive bibliography especially pertaining to the Collins family's personal documents. Also provides an interesting discussion of the theme of identity in *The Woman in White.*

Pykett, Lyn. *Wilkie Collins.* New York: Oxford University Press, 2005. Pykett traces the various debates that have arisen since 1980, when literary critics began seriously reevaluating Collins's work. Her analysis of Collins's work focuses on his preoccupation with the themes of social and psychological identity, class, gender, and power.

_____, ed. *Wilkie Collins.* New York: St. Martin's Press, 1998. An excellent introduction to Collins for the beginning student. In addition to essays that discuss Collins's place within Victorian detective fiction and the "sensation novel," there are four essays analyzing *The Woman in White.* Includes bibliographical references and an index.

Symons, Julian. *Mortal Consequences: A History from the Detective Story to the Crime Novel.* New York: Harper & Row, 1972. Analyzes *The Woman in White* and discusses Collins's role as one of the earliest masters of the suspense novel.

_____, ed. *The Cambridge Companion to Wilkie Collins.* New York: Cambridge University Press, 2006. All aspects of Collins's writing are discussed in this collection of thirteen essays. His common themes of sexuality, marriage, and religion are examined, as well as his experiences with publishing companies and the process of adapting his works for film. This book does a superb job of chronicling Collins's writing career and includes a thorough bibliography and index.

A Woman Killed with Kindness

Author: Thomas Heywood (c. 1573-1641)
First produced: 1603; first published, 1607
Type of work: Drama
Type of plot: Tragedy
Time of plot: Early seventeenth century
Locale: Yorkshire, England

Principal characters:
JOHN FRANKFORD, a provincial gentleman
ANNE, his wife
WENDOLL, her paramour
SIR FRANCIS ACTON, her brother
SIR CHARLES MOUNTFORD, a provincial nobleman
SUSAN, his sister
NICHOLAS, servant of the Frankfords
SHAFTON, a schemer

The Story:

John and Anne Frankford celebrate their marriage feast in the company of a group of relatives and friends. Everyone joins in complimenting the bride on her beauty and on her charming submission to her husband. As the group joins the crowd dancing in the great hall of the house, Sir Francis Acton and Sir Charles Mountford arrange a wager on hawking for the next day. Out in the courtyard, tenants of the Frankford estate celebrate their master's wedding.

Early the next morning Acton and Mountford and their companions go into the field to match their falcons. Acton loses the wager but declares that Mountford's falcon broke the rules of the hunt. Following an exchange of hot words, the hunting party divides into two sides. In the fighting Mountford kills two of Acton's men. Susan, Mountford's sister, goes to him in the field and advises him to flee, but he declares that he can never leave her. The sheriff arrives and apprehends Mountford.

Frankford, at his home, feels himself supremely happy; he is affluent, well-educated, and blessed with a lovely and virtuous wife. As he reflects upon his felicity, Wendoll, who was in the hunting party, excitedly arrives to report the details of the fatal fight. Frankford, already impressed by Wendoll's manner, invites the young gentleman to live in his house and to be his companion. Nicholas, Frankford's faithful servant, observes to himself that there is something about Wendoll that he does not like; he and the other servants express distaste that Wendoll should become a guest in the house.

Mountford, meanwhile, is forced to spend almost his entire patrimony to gain his liberty. As he leaves the jail, he encounters Shafton, an unprincipled man who forces a large sum of money upon him. It is Shafton's purpose eventually to cheat Mountford out of a small ancestral house he possesses and somehow to win the hand of Mountford's sister Susan.

Wendoll falls passionately in love with Anne. Conscience-stricken, he is distracted by the dreadful thoughts that go through his mind. When Frankford rides away on business, Anne innocently tells Wendoll that Frankford wishes him to take his place in the household during his absence. Torn between reason and passion, Wendoll succumbs to passion and discloses to Anne his great love for her. Anne at first resists his blandishments, but she is soon overcome by his insistence that his love for her in no way reduces his great affection for and obligation to Frankford. Nicholas, undetected, overhears the conversation and vows to bring the affair to light.

The term of Mountford's debt to Shafton comes due, and the lender offers to buy Mountford's house, his last worldly possession. When Mountford refuses to sell at any price, Shafton orders a sergeant to handcuff Mountford and clap him in jail for debt. Hearing what happened, Acton, filled with hatred for Mountford because of the violent dispute over the hawks, declares that he will seduce Susan. When Acton actually sees Susan, he immediately falls in love with her.

On his return Frankford learns from Nicholas that Anne and Wendoll are unfaithful, she to her marriage vows, Wendoll to the bonds of friendship. When Frankford, Anne, Wendoll, and a guest, Cranwell, play cards after dinner, it seems all too clear from the irony revealed in the conversation that Nicholas indeed told the truth. Frankford plans to make certain that Anne is untrue to him.

Susan, meanwhile, asks her uncle, Old Mountford, to help her brother. The old man refuses, as do other men to whom Mountford was generous in former days. When Acton offers Susan a bag of gold, she spurns help from her brother's enemy. Acton clears Mountford's debts anonymously. Mountford, released again from jail and from all of his debts, encounters Susan and, to her bewilderment, thanks her for her good work. When the jailer informs the pair that it is Acton who aided them, Mountford, unable to accept the generosity of an enemy, proposes to return to jail. The jailer, already paid, refuses to admit him. At last Susan confesses that Acton paid the debts because of his love for her. Knowing that fact, and shamed by his debt to Acton, Mountford feels that there is only one thing to do.

During supper at the Frankfords, Nicholas, by prearrangement, brings a letter to his master at the table. Frankford announces that he is called away immediately on legal business. After he goes, Wendoll thanks fortune that matters work out so well for him and Anne. Anne, however, is not happy in her affair with Wendoll; her conscience tells her that she is lost in sin. Although she succumbed to Wendoll because of his clever rhetoric, she suffers remorse. After dining with Wendoll in her chamber, she directs the servants to lock up the house and to bring her the keys.

Frankford, meanwhile, ties his horse to a tree near the house and with keys that he made for the purpose he and Nicholas creep into the darkened house at midnight. Discovering Wendoll and his wife asleep in each other's arms, Frankford expresses a desire to turn back the clock so that the shame to his honor might be prevented. Awaking the couple, he chases Wendoll with drawn sword, but a housemaid catches his arm and keeps him from taking Wendoll's life. Anne, conscience-stricken, asks Frankford to end her life. He decides, however, that death is too good for her; he condemns her to live the rest of her life comfortably but in seclusion in a house on the estate. She is never to set eyes on him again.

In the meantime Mountford suggests to Susan that she give herself to Acton in return for his deed. When Susan objects on grounds of honor, Mountford declares that his soul will not rest until Acton is repaid, and Susan finally agrees to this proposal. When Acton goes to their house, Mountford bitterly offers his sister as payment. Acton is overcome by the magnanimous gesture. At one time he could not dream of marrying poverty-stricken Susan; now he declares that he will proudly take her as his wife.

As Anne, accompanied by her servants, prepares to start on her exile, Nicholas rides up and hands her a lute, the only one of her possessions she left behind her. Tearfully, she declares that the lute, untuned as it is, is a symbol of her marriage. Wendoll, now repentant, meets Anne on the road. When he begins to express his remorse, she, fearful lest he tempt her again before she dies, commands the coachman to drive on to the house where she will end her days.

Later, learning that Anne is near death from a broken heart, Frankford goes to her and forgives her sins. After her death Frankford declares that her epitaph will recall her as a woman killed by her husband's kindness.

Critical Evaluation:

A Woman Killed with Kindness is commonly regarded as the best of the domestic tragedies of its time. Domestic tragedies are so called because of their treatment of the lives of ordinary people rather than of royalty. The conflicts in a domestic tragedy may bring down the head of a household but never a head of state. The family struggle in *King Lear* (pr. c. 1605-1606, pb. 1608), with its ensuing horrors, may suggest some great breach in nature, but the ordinariness of life in the domestic tragedies works against grand, cosmic interpretations. The simple, direct language of the domestic tragedy contrasts with the grandiloquent rhetoric of Renaissance tragedies involving royalty or other larger-than-life figures.

Thomas Heywood did not invent the plots of *A Woman Killed with Kindness*. The subplot featuring Sir Francis Acton and Sir Charles Mountford has been traced to an Italian source that evolved through several versions and appeared in William Painter's popular collection of stories *The Palace of Pleasure*, the first edition of which appeared in 1566. Painter summarized the story this way: "A gentleman of Siena, called Anselmo Salimbene, curteously and gently delivereth his enemy from death. The condemned party seeing the kinde parte of Salimbene, rendreth into his hands his sister Angelica, with whom he was in love, which gratitude and curtesie, Salimbene well markinge, moved in conscience, would not abuse her, but for recompence tooke her to his Wife." As for the main plot, several sources have been suggested, especially several other stories from Painter's collection.

Critical judgments on *A Woman Killed with Kindness* vary widely. Some critics charge that the two plots fail to come together in any unity and that both plots are improbable and sentimental. Frankford, moreover, is a despicable man among a cast of unconvincing characters. These are major criticisms, but the play's supporters argue passionately for it as a tragic masterpiece. They assert that both plots are set in motion in the first scene and run parallel, and that Wendoll joins the two plots by playing a crucial role in each.

Furthermore, structural parallels appear in the scenes that counterpoint masters and servants. The servants' dancing party in the second scene follows the opening wedding feast, and the two lighthearted celebrations set a mood that contrasts with the events that follow, serving as an emotional foil to the tragedy. The masters debate intensely the virtues of their hawks and hounds and the country people quarrel amiably over the dances they will perform. Supporters of Heywood's dramatic techniques cite more instances of contrasts and parallels. In the seventeenth and final scene, for instance,

Frankford and Anne's reunion parallels the reunion scene of the subplot and differs from it in being a reunion only in death. In this final scene, only one figure from the wedding party is absent: Wendoll, the villain. Only one person, Susan, appears who was not at the wedding, and she represents the virtue that the weak Anne lacked. Admirers of the play point also to the contrasts between paired characters as a unifying device: Susan and Anne, Frankford and Acton, and Acton and Wendoll. All of these patterns provide evidence of Heywood's careful craftsmanship.

Sentimentality is the most difficult charge against which to defend *A Woman Killed with Kindness*. Even the play's admirers generally concede the weaknesses of the subplot, in which the characters lack the complexity that would generate the audience's sympathy for their plights. Attacks on the main plot center on Anne. Her qualities as the perfect wife are never demonstrated, only stated; she never earns, in the audience's eyes, the virtue attributed to her that makes her fall into sin pathetic. Her death is sentimental rather than tragic.

Domestic tragedies such as *A Woman Killed with Kindness* avoid affairs of court and focus on the lives of ordinary people. Heywood stresses this feature when he opens his prologue with the remark, "Look for no glorious state, our Muse is bent/ Upon a barren subject, a bare scene." This strain in domestic tragedy reflects the influence of fifteenth century morality plays, which introduced ordinary people as suitable subjects for serious theater. The best-known morality play, *Everyman*, an anonymous play whose earliest extant version dates from 1508, is no more than a parade of allegorical figures. *Everyman*, however, represents all humanity rather than a courtly elite, and the gritty realism that pervades his story agrees with the settings in domestic tragedy.

The strong didactic strain of the morality plays also appears in the domestic dramas. In both types of plays, there are lessons for all to learn about good and evil. *A Woman Killed with Kindness* dramatizes Christian teachings about sin, repentance, and forgiveness, and Frankford alludes several times to the biblical story of Judas. For instance, Frankford's reference to "that Judas that hath borne my purse,/ And sold me for a sin . . ." refers to John 13:29 and to Matthew 27:3-4. Later, when Frankford discovers the sinners, he says, "Go, to thy friend/ A Judas; pray, pray, lest I live to see/ Thee Judas-like, hang'd on an elder tree," a passage alluding to Matthew 27:5.

Other biblical references include Frankford's remark about the book of life (the record of those who shall live eternally) with sources in Philippians 4:3 and Revelation 20:12. Sir Charles also refers to "a huge beam/ In the world's eye," which is drawn from the Sermon on the Mount in Matthew 7:3. These biblical references, along with the many proverbial expressions (the title, for example) all contribute to making the play a text of moral instruction.

"Critical Evaluation" by Frank Day

Further Reading

Baines, Barbara J. *Thomas Heywood*. Boston: Twayne, 1984. An excellent overview of Heywood's life and works, with a list of primary sources and an annotated secondary bibliography. Analyzes in detail the themes and structure of *A Woman Killed with Kindness* and responds to criticisms of the play's characterizations and moral vision.

Clark, Arthur Melville. *Thomas Heywood: Playwright and Miscellanist*. New York: Russell & Russell, 1967. A detailed account of Heywood's life and career. A chapter praises *A Woman Killed with Kindness* as preeminent among domestic tragedies and says it "anticipates the bloodless tragedies of Ibsen."

Dessen, Alan C. "'The Difference Betwixt Reporting and Representing': Thomas Heywood and the Playgoer's Imagination." In *Acts of Criticism: Performance Matters in Shakespeare and His Contemporaries—Essays in Honor of James P. Lusardi*, edited by Paul Nelsen and June Schlueter. Madison, N.J.: Fairleigh Dickinson University Press, 2006. Examines the function of stage direction and scripted allusion in Heywood's plays.

Heywood, Thomas. *A Woman Killed with Kindness*. Edited by R. W. Van Fossen. Cambridge, Mass.: Harvard University Press, 1961. A superb modern edition with full notes, an appendix on the source of the subplot, and analyses of sources, theme, structure, characters, style, stage history, and the text.

Huebert, Ronald. "One Wench Between Them: Thomas Heywood, Francis Beaumont, and John Fletcher." In *The Performance of Pleasure in English Renaissance Drama*. New York: Palgrave Macmillan, 2003. An analysis of *A Woman Killed with Kindness*, which Huebert describes as "a fantasy of male omnipotence."

Johnson, Nora. *The Actor as Playwright in Early Modern Drama*. New York: Cambridge University Press, 2003. Johnson devotes a chapter to Heywood in her examination of English Renaissance actor-playwrights.

McClintock, Michael. "Grief, Theater, and Society in Thomas Heywood's *A Woman Killed with Kindness*." In *Speaking Grief in English Literary Culture: Shakespeare to Milton*, edited by Margo Swiss and David A. Kent. Pittsburgh, Pa.: Duquesne University Press, 2002. Focuses on Heywood's depiction of loss and bereavement in the play.

McLuskie, Kathleen. *Dekker and Heywood: Professional Dramatists.* New York: St. Martin's Press, 1994. Focuses on the performances of the two playwrights' works, examining the relationship between their plays and the cultural moment when these plays were produced

Velte, Mowbray. *The Bourgeois Elements in the Dramas of Thomas Heywood.* New York: Haskell House, 1966. Finds the main plot much superior to the subplot and discusses their parallels to their sources. Praises *A Woman Killed with Kindness* for its realism and points out that the play does not resort to a depiction of a murder or of a sensational local event.

The Woman of Rome

Author: Alberto Moravia (1907-1990)
First published: La romana, 1947 (English translation, 1949)
Type of work: Novel
Type of plot: Naturalism
Time of plot: 1930's
Locale: Rome

Principal characters:
ADRIANA, a prostitute
HER MOTHER
GINO, a chauffeur
MINO, a student
SONZOGNO, a thug
ASTARITA, a police official
GISELLA, Adriana's friend

The Story:

Sixteen-year-old Adriana is beautiful. Her lips are red and full, her breasts high and firm. Her mother, a poor sewing woman, thinks of Adriana as her only capital; the family has been poverty-stricken since the illness and death of the father. Adriana's mother does not conceal her opinion that their poverty can be traced to her marriage and to Adriana's unwanted birth.

Thinking her daughter mature enough, the mother takes her to an artist to arrange for her career as a model. Adriana is not embarrassed by undressing before a strange man, nor is she much embarrassed when her mother punches and pats her naked body as she stresses her good points. Nevertheless, her mother's shrill arguing about the pay is quite rude. She is especially violent with polite people, such as the artist, because they usually give in before her displays of temper.

The artist agrees to pay a higher fee with good grace. As he talks with Adriana afterward, he tries to tell her that her mother loves money above all else. Adriana is unconvinced. The artist is about forty years old and always correct in his behavior. When his pictures do not sell, he has no more work for Adriana. She has little difficulty in obtaining other jobs, because her figure is so fine, even heroic in proportions.

When modeling does not pay well enough, her mother tries to get Adriana a job as a dancer, and she secures an interview with a vaudeville manager. Adriana does her best, but she is miserably conscious of her clumsy feet. Even her mother's shrewish scolding cannot win Adriana a job on the stage.

Adriana dutifully takes as many modeling jobs as she can, builds up a reputation for virtue among the artists, and sews shirts in the afternoons and the evenings. A turning point comes when she meets Gino.

Gino is soft-spoken and gentle despite his rough workman's hands. He is a chauffeur for a wealthy family, and when he can, he takes Adriana for long rides. Her mother objects to the friendship, for she thinks Adriana's beauty can win her a gentleman.

Adriana does not object when Gino invites her to his employer's villa while the family is away. She willingly goes to his room, and afterward they sleep until past midnight. Adriana was never out so late before, and her suspicious mother is furious. She sets on her daughter with her fists and beats her as long as she has strength. Then she takes Adriana to an all-night clinic and has her examined by a doctor. When the doctor confirms her fears, she is glum but calm.

It is understood that Gino and Adriana will marry, but Gino finds excuses for delaying the wedding. The mother is pessimistic about the marriage. Gisella, Adriana's friend, is also doubtful of Gino's intentions and urges her to accept a rich lover while she can. She finally induces Adriana to go out to dinner with Astarita, a rich police official who is anxious to meet her. At the dinner in a hotel Gisella almost forces Adriana to go into a bedroom with Astarita. On the way home Astarita gives Adriana money.

So Adriana is launched on a new career. She does not dissolve her relationship with Gino, for she still thinks that perhaps they will be married. That hope vanishes, however, when Astarita produces evidence that Gino is married and has a daughter. For revenge, Adriana lets Gino take her to the villa again, but she insists on making love in the mistress's bed. After she tells Gino that she knows the truth about his wife, she steals a compact from the dresser.

Adriana becomes a prostitute. She usually brings her clients home, and her mother accepts the state of affairs with good grace because there is more money in the house. Adriana usually sleeps late and leads an indolent, satisfied existence. She really likes men. Her mother becomes fat and much less attractive.

One night she meets Gino again. He wonders about the compact. On their return home, the wealthy family misses it, and Gino suspects Adriana. Gino arranges to have suspicion fall on a maid, who is arrested and sent to jail. After getting the compact from Adriana, Gino plans to sell it to a fence. When he says he will divide the money with her, Adriana, filled with pity for the falsely arrested maid, refuses.

She finds Gino one night in company with Sonzogno, a strong man and a thug. When Gino and Adriana leave a café together, she feels repelled by her former fiancé and on an impulse calls to Sonzogno for help. He promptly knocks Gino down and goes home with Adriana. Adriana is both attracted to Sonzogno and in terror of him. He has the stolen compact in his possession. Gino gave it to Sonzogno to sell, and Sonzogno murders an old jeweler to whom he took it for that purpose. After listening to callous boasts of his crime, Adriana succeeds in getting the compact away from him. She experiences a horrible evening, for Sonzogno beats her. Later she has her confessor give the compact to the police, and the maid is released.

Gisella and Adriana go out for the evening and are picked up by two men. The four go to Adriana's house. Soon afterward, Gisella becomes the mistress of her pickup and is promptly installed in her own apartment. Adriana's pickup is Mino, a nineteen-year-old student. Thin and withdrawn, he is not much interested in lovemaking. His attitude attracts Adriana and thereafter she pursues him, even to his respectable rooming house.

Adriana's affairs become more complicated. The friendly clinic doctor confirms her fears; she is pregnant. As she thinks back, she knows that Sonzogno is the father. She is rather pleased to have a child, but her baby will be born of a murderer and a prostitute. When Mino comes to live at her house, she tells him that he is the father of her expected baby.

Mino is an anti-Fascist engaged in subversive work. When he is arrested, he promptly betrays his fellow conspirators under the sympathetic questioning of Astarita. As soon as he learns that Astarita is an admirer of Adriana, he proposes that she invite him to her house, and there Mino will shoot him.

Sonzogno, sure that Adriana betrayed him to the police, arrives just before Astarita is expected. When Astarita appears, he slaps the submissive Sonzogno's face and sends him away. Then he tells Adriana that Mino's confession was not written down and the police took no action against his friends.

Adriana is nevertheless apprehensive. It is not like Sonzogno to be meek. When she goes to the ministry, her fears are justified. Astarita is dead in the courtyard; Sonzogno followed him to his office and threw him off a balcony. Adriana goes home to find Mino gone. He left a note saying that his parents will look after her and his son; he is going to kill himself. His body is found in a hotel near the station.

Critical Evaluation:

Alberto Moravia self-published his first novel, *Gli indifferenti* (1929; *The Indifferent Ones*, 1932; also known as *The Time of Indifference*, 1953), at the age of twenty-two, and it became an overnight scandal in Italy. Controversy swirled about Moravia, who was called immoral by some, while others pointed out that he was simply the messenger bringing the bad news about the collapse of Italian society. Six more novels consolidated his reputation in Italy, but it was not until *The Woman of Rome* was published in English in 1949 that he achieved an international reputation.

Moravia was a thinker who wrote novels to embody his ideas, which often concerned the present and the ways in which it differed from the past in European civilization. People were losing touch with their humanity, he said, and they were becoming caught up in a life of action rather than in a life of contemplation. Humanity was no longer its own goal; human beings were being turned into a means to another end. Moravia believed that the mindless, uncontemplative activity of modern people, whether acquiring money or squandering it, amounts to nothing, and that, he added, is what modern art embodies: nothingness.

The bustle of Euro-American civilization in the twentieth century was inauthentic, he declared, and he went so far as to maintain that, given that state of affairs, authenticity existed solely in thought and fantasy. *The Woman of Rome* can be read as part demonstration and part embodiment of Moravia's beliefs. Adriana's first step on the road to prostitution is taken when she allows herself to be date-raped by Giacinta, a man she does not desire, because he threatens to tell her fiancé, Gino, that he, Giacinta, has already had sex with her. Adriana, instead of holding firm to her feelings, is betrayed by the end she has in mind: her forthcoming happy marriage with Gino. She permits herself to be blackmailed into having sex with an unappealing stranger because she doesn't want to risk losing her marriage. For that afternoon, Adriana turns herself into the means to an end, instead of preserving her authentic being as an end in itself.

Under the circumstances, it would not have been easy to have behaved in an authentic manner. Moravia's skill as a novelist enables him to show just how compromised Adriana finds herself on this day in Viterbo, pressured not only by Giacinta but also by her best friend, Gisella, and her boyfriend, Riccardo, as well as by the wine she has drunk. Her naïveté and inexperience are also handicaps. Then, after the deed is done, the unexpected thrill she feels when Giacinta pays her with a large sum of money virtually seals her fate. Given the poverty of her background, given her considerable physical charms, given her mother's constant sermonizing on the need for Adriana to marry a rich man in order to get the proper cash value for her beauty, Adriana has already had a lot of pressure pushing her in this direction.

Although sex becomes her job, refreshingly, Adriana continues to enjoy the act, and, although for some months she takes care not to fall in love, she appreciates—and can be stirred by—the physical qualities of her clients as well as by their personalities. She takes society's judgment of her as a criminal, however, seriously enough to think, "Might as well be hung for [stealing] a sheep as a lamb," and to become a thief in the bargain. Her confusions seem similar to those of anyone living in such a society: Do people work for pleasure, or for survival, and do people resent or relish their work?

Moravia, in other books as well, suggests that in a society as empty of meaning as the one he writes about and for, even sex without love can provide a good, kindling feeling between creatures otherwise empty and numb. Some critics assert that Moravia is imposing a male-centered view upon his female mouthpiece, just as he is accused of giving her powers of intellectual reflection that would not belong to a woman of her class. The first charge remains controversial: Might there not be a woman, and more than one, whose self is substan-

tially composed of male-introjected elements? The second charge is more telling: Adriana's powers of intellectual reflection—indeed, her very vocabulary—are those of Moravia rather than of a poor woman from the slums of Rome. Although this discrepancy violates the realism of the novel, it also paints a marvelous psychological portrait—it is as if Moravia is an analyst providing commentary behind her every move.

The strongest passages of the novel are those in which Adriana learns something new about herself and about life. She is forever saying that she knows how and who she is, and then she discovers through some new experience that, in fact, she is not that way or not only that way. The plot is second-rate, and its climax is a near-farcical concatenation of coincidence, but the novel is always readable, because readers want to learn about love and sex—and the entire life of the feelings—along with the young heroine.

"Critical Evaluation" by David Bromige

Further Reading

Heiney, Donald. *Three Italian Novelists.* Ann Arbor: University of Michigan Press, 1968. Discusses Moravia's change in technique in *The Woman of Rome* to a first-person, female, lower-class narrator. Examines Moravia's impatience with omniscient narration.

Lewis, R. W. B. "Eros and Existence." In *The Picaresque Saint.* New York: Lippincott, 1959. Worth looking at for Lewis's analysis of Moravia's use of sexual encounters as proving grounds of the existential.

Moravia, Alberto. *Man as End.* New York: Farrar, Straus & Giroux, 1966. Eighteen essays that provide invaluable information about the author's philosophy and his approach to the novel as a literary form.

Moravia, Alberto, and Alain Elkann. *Life of Moravia.* Translated by William Weaver. South Royalton, Vt.: Steerforth Italia, 2000. A biography written in the form of an extended interview of Moravia by his friend, Elkann. Moravia discusses his life, his work, and the events that shaped his imagination, shedding light on the way his writings were built upon his experiences. Weaver, who knew Moravia, provides an introduction in which he discusses the writer.

Peterson, Thomas Erling. *Alberto Moravia.* New York: Twayne, 1996. Comprehensive coverage of Moravia's life and works. Includes critical analysis of major works as well as information on personal and public activities. Describes the political climate in Italy and its relevance to Moravia's life.

Ross, Joan, and Donald Freed. *The Existentialism of Alberto Moravia.* Carbondale: Southern Illinois University Press, 1972. Places Moravia's writings in relation to existential philosophy.

Stella, M. John. *Self and Self-Compromise in the Narratives of Pirandello and Moravia.* New York: Peter Lang, 2000. Analyzes works by Moravia and Luigi Pirandello to examine how they treat issues of identity, focusing on how the two writers' concepts of individual identity were influenced by Buddhist doctrines.

The Woman Warrior
Memoirs of a Girlhood Among Ghosts

Author: Maxine Hong Kingston (1940-   )
First published: 1976
Type of work: Memoir

Maxine Hong Kingston's *The Woman Warrior: Memoirs of a Girlhood Among Ghosts* focuses on Chinese and American female identities by blending mythology, history, and poetry. She explores these identities by reconstructing her mother's (Brave Orchid's) life for fifteen years in China during the 1920's and 1930's and through her own experiences growing up in Stockton, California, in the 1940's and 1950's. A second book, *China Men* (1980), a companion piece to *The Woman Warrior,* tells the story of the Chinese men in Kingston's family. Both books span continents and generations, the first focusing on the women, the second on the men, although *China Men* has a female storyteller.

Kingston, a writer of both fiction and nonfiction, received her first great acclaim after the publication of *The Woman Warrior.* Although her work continues to be well received, her later books moved in other directions. Kingston published *Hawai'i One Summer* in 1987, exploring the Chinese American history of Hawaii. The novel *Tripmaster Monkey: His Fake Book* (1989) tells the story of twenty-three-year-old Berkeley graduate Wittman Ah Sing. In the early 1990's, Kingston's only copy of a recent novel was destroyed by fire, and she had to start over from scratch. (The story was later published in 2003 in a memoir-novel hybrid titled *The Fifth Book of Peace.*)

The Woman Warrior is divided into five sections, each of which can be easily anthologized. "No Name Woman" and "Tongue-Tied," for example, may be read alone. Despite the stories' ability to be separate and remain powerful, they tie together into a coherent whole. The second and fifth sections focus on Kingston, who identifies herself as a "legendary warrior woman." The other three sections focus on Kingston's mother's stories and Kingston's retelling of them. The complex narrative patterns of *The Woman Warrior* are intertwined; the first three stories are about the mother, and the final two stories are about the daughter.

"No Name Woman," the first and shortest section, begins with the voice of Kingston's mother warning the young Kingston, "You must not tell anyone . . . what I am about to tell you." In telling the story of her father's nameless sister, Kingston, as narrator, breaks the taboos and the silence of tradition. The breaking of the silence begins Kingston's war on traditions that have destroyed people, women in particular. Once Kingston breaks the silence by repeating her mother's story, she tries to fill in the gaps.

Her mother tells her what Kingston calls only a "story to grow up on," the parts necessary to guide a growing adolescent, so that she will not humiliate her parents. The nameless aunt has a child two years after her husband's departure for America. The villagers, to punish the family for their daughter's impropriety, come to the home when the child is due. Disguised, they kill livestock, stone the house, and destroy everything inside the home. The disgraced family stands together in the middle of the room and looks straight ahead. They neither lock their doors against the attack nor resist it. During the night, the aunt gives birth, unattended, in the pigsty. Kingston's mother concludes, "The next morning when I went for the water, I found her and the baby plugging up the family well." The story is meant to introduce Kingston to the dangers that accompany the beginning of menstruation. Kingston, however, hungers for the details of the aunt's story, details that she cannot get from her mother because the details are not necessary to make her point: "Adultery is extravagance."

Kingston fills in the gaps in the story through various retellings of it. In these retellings, she explores gender inequality in her speculations about the lives of the men who leave their wives behind and the life of the man who fathered her aunt's child. Kingston acknowledges her guilt for participating in the punishment of the aunt for twenty years. She says that she still does not know her aunt's name, but at least she breaks the silence, an act that ends her participation.

"White Tigers," the second section, retells Kingston's mother's story of Fa Mu Lan, the woman warrior who takes her father's place in battle. Kingston becomes the woman warrior, doing battle against the devaluation of girl children, especially in Chinese culture. Fa Mu Lan is led away from her family by a white crane who teaches her boxing and then delivers her to an "old brown man" and an "old gray woman." They give her a choice of returning home to the life of a traditional girl—a wife and slave—or staying with them for fifteen years of hard training to become a woman warrior. She chooses the hardships of the rigorous training over the devaluation of tradition.

In the seventh year of her training, at age fourteen, she is taken blindfolded to the mountains of the white tigers, where she must learn to survive on her own. In the mountains, she learns many lessons about survival, both physical and spiritual. For example, she realizes that hunger "changes the world—when eating can't be a habit, then neither can seeing," and she learns to make her "mind large, as the universe is large, so that there is room for paradoxes." Fa Mu Lan, when she eventually returns home, is valued like a son by her family.

Kingston deals squarely with gender issues in this section. As Fa Mu Lan, she liberates a group of abandoned women, who become a mercenary army that takes in unwanted girls and that kills men and boys. When she returns to her modern narrative, she explores her devaluation as a Chinese American girl, one who earns high grades in school but must listen to Chinese sayings about the worthlessness of girl children. "Even now," Kingston says, "China wraps double binds around my feet." She realizes that, unlike Fa Mu Lan, she dislikes armies and she cannot save her relatives from the horrors they experience in China. She can, nonetheless, use words—both Chinese and English—to fight the devaluation of females.

"Shaman," the third section, begins as Brave Orchid shows Kingston the metal tube that holds the medical diploma from China. Through the mother's recollections and Kingston's imagination, Brave Orchid's years in China as a married woman are reconstructed. Her two children die; her husband is in the United States. When Brave Orchid finds herself alone, she decides to attend medical school. Among Brave Orchid's stories from these times are accounts of facing ghosts, of buying a slave girl, and of trying to stop people from stoning a crazy woman. Six months after the stoning, in the winter of 1939, Brave Orchid leaves China and arrives, almost a year later, in New York Harbor.

As Brave Orchid ages, she laments the loss of her medical practice in China, her inability to return to her homeland, and finally, her powerlessness in keeping her six children and their families close to her. The section ends with her urging Kingston, a mature woman, to remain with her. Ultimately, however, Brave Orchid realizes that her daughter must go out into the world.

"At the Western Palace," the fourth section, begins as Brave Orchid awaits the arrival of her sister, Moon Orchid, from China. After her arrival, Moon Orchid, clearly disoriented, stays for several weeks with Brave Orchid's family and with her own daughter, who is visiting from Los Angeles. The suspense builds throughout the story as the sisters debate if, how, and when Moon Orchid will reunite with the husband who left her behind in China thirty years earlier. When Moon Orchid's daughter announces that it is time for her to return to her husband and children, Brave Orchid's oldest son drives her and the two elderly sisters to Los Angeles, where Moon Orchid's husband also lives with his younger wife. When the sisters go to the husband's place of business, he becomes angry and distraught. He sends them away and agrees that he will continue to send money to Moon Orchid. She never sees him again and ends up in a California state mental asylum, where she dies.

Moon Orchid's unhappy fate greatly alters Brave Orchid's family. Brave Orchid fears that her elderly husband may take a younger wife—although he promises he will not. Her daughters decide "fiercely" that they will "never let men be unfaithful to them." All of Brave Orchid's children decide to "major in science or mathematics." The family's faith in family and tradition is shaken.

"A Song for a Barbarian Reed Pipe," the final section, relates several events from Kingston's childhood. Among the most jarring of these stories is that of her attack on a schoolmate, a Chinese American girl a year older than Kingston. Kingston corners the odd schoolmate after school and tries to force her to speak. Kingston realizes, even as she repeatedly hurts the girl, that this is "the worst thing [she] had yet done to another person." When the girl refuses to make any sound, Kingston becomes unnerved and cries. Immediately following this event, Kingston becomes ill and spends the next eighteen months "sick in bed with a mysterious illness." Upon her return to school, she learns that the odd classmate will not need to speak, that she comes from a well-to-do family that can take care of her. Through these experiences, Kingston explores the ideas of justice and necessity in women's lives. As Kingston contemplates variations of oddness and insanity in Chinese women, she worries that she, too, may be destined for insanity.

Ultimately, she and her mother end up in a noisy scene in which both are talking, refuting each others' misunderstandings. The scene shows both the separation and the unity of Kingston and her mother. Kingston, the adult, wants to go to China to learn the truth about her relatives and about communism. She needs to distinguish between what is fiction and what is true, yet she recognizes the irony of her need. The final story of the section is a synthesis, a story begun by Kingston's mother and finished by Kingston. It is the story of Ts'ai Yen, a poet born in 175 C.E. During Ts'ai Yen's twelve years as a captive of the barbarians, she composes "Eighteen Stanzas for a Barbarian Reed Pipe." When Ts'ai Yen returns from her captivity, she brings the music with her. Kingston concludes, "It translated well."

The Woman Warrior earned its place in literary studies. In 1976, it won the National Book Critics Circle Award for nonfiction. In 1979, it was named one of the top ten nonfiction works of the decade by *Time* magazine. It is a staple in classrooms in American colleges and has been translated into other languages. It is a book with international appeal. Through *The Woman Warrior*, Kingston explores not only gender identity and national identity but also human identity. The five narrative sections of her memoir become the vehicle for this exploration. The locations, China and the United States, are as much psychological states for Kingston, for her parents, and for her readers as they are places on a map. The human and global qualities of *The Woman Warrior* no doubt account for its continuing success.

Carol Franks

Further Reading

Cheung, King-Kok. *Articulate Silences: Hisaye Yamamoto, Maxine Hong Kingston, Joy Kogawa.* Ithaca, N.Y.: Cornell University Press, 1993. In her chapter on Kingston, Cheung notes the way in which historical and parental silence provokes the author to use her imagination to create possible versions of stories that her taciturn parents refuse to convey.

Grice, Helena. *Maxine Hong Kingston.* New York: Manches-

ter University Press, 2006. Analyzes *The Woman Warrior* and Kingston's other novels to trace her development as a writer and a cultural activist.

Huntley, E. D. *Maxine Hong Kingston: A Critical Companion.* Westport, Conn.: Greenwood Press, 2001. Provides information about Kingston's life, assesses her place within the Asian American literary tradition, and devotes a chapter to an analysis of *The Woman Warrior*.

Johnson, Diane. *Terrorists and Novelists.* New York: Alfred A. Knopf, 1982. Comparing Kingston to Carobeth Laird and N. Scott Momaday, Johnson writes that *The Woman Warrior* is an "antiautobiography," a work that blurs the boundaries between fiction and autobiography. Johnson argues that Kingston, in challenging the "female condition," resists her culture to triumph over it.

Lim, Shirley Geok-lin, ed. *Approaches to Teaching Kingston's "The Woman Warrior."* New York: Modern Language Association, 1991. This collection of essays is an excellent source for cultural background and close readings of the text. Includes a helpful bibliographic essay, a personal statement from Kingston on *The Woman Warrior*, a section providing sociohistorical information to help readers better understand references to the Chinese American culture contained in the work, and close analyses of the text. Also highlights different approaches to the text, including feminist, postmodernist, and thematic perspectives.

Ling, Amy. *Between Worlds: Women Writers of Chinese Ancestry.* New York: Pergamon Press, 1990. Ling locates Kingston's work within a historical tradition of Chinese American writers. She highlights Kingston's need for "writing wrongs" by "writing about the wrongs."

Perry, Donna, ed. *Backtalk: Women Writers Speak Out.* New Brunswick, N.J.: Rutgers University Press, 1993. Perry's collection of interviews contains a brief introduction, photographs of the writers, and an interview with Kingston on her work, including *The Woman Warrior*.

Sabine, Maureen. *Maxine Hong Kingston's Broken Book of Life: An Intertextual Study of "The Woman Warrior" and "China Men."* Honolulu: University of Hawaii Press, 2004. Kingston originally wrote *China Men* as part of *The Woman Warrior*, but she decided to publish it as a separate work focusing on the Hong family men. Sabine analyzes both books as a whole, describing their combined depiction of male and female family members.

Smith, Sidonie. *A Poetics of Women's Autobiography: Marginality and the Fictions of Self-Representation.* Bloomington: Indiana University Press, 1987. Smith notes the ways in which Kingston uses autobiography as a means of creating identity and breaking out of the silence that her culture imposes on her. She also states that *The Woman Warrior* is "an autobiography about women's autobiographical storytelling," emphasizing the relationship between genre and gender.

Wong, Sau-ling Cynthia, ed. *Maxine Hong Kingston's "The*

Woman Warrior": A Casebook. New York: Oxford University Press, 1999. Collection of essays providing various interpretations of the novel, including a Chinese woman's response to the book, the novel's depiction of gender, and the tradition of Chinese American women's writing prior to Kingston's work.

A Woman's Life

Author: Guy de Maupassant (1850-1893)
First published: Une Vie, 1883 (English translation, 1888)
Type of work: Novel
Type of plot: Naturalism
Time of plot: Early nineteenth century
Locale: Normandy, France; island of Corsica

Principal characters:
JEANNE DE LAMARE
JULIEN DE LAMARE, her husband
PAUL DE LAMARE, her son
BARON SIMON-JACQUES LE PERTHUIS DES VAUDS, her father
ROSALIE, her foster sister

The Story:

In the spring of 1819, Jeanne Le Perthuis des Vauds and her parents go to live in an old chateau, The Poplars, on the Normandy coast. Baron Simon-Jacques Le Perthuis des Vauds was left a large inheritance, but he so reduces it by his freehandedness that he is eventually forced to reconcile himself for the remainder of his days to a simple country life.

Jeanne, who spent the preceding five years in a convent, looks forward happily to her new life and dreams of the day when she will find the man who loves her. All her expectations are fulfilled. She finds a beautiful countryside to wander over and the sea to bathe in and to sail on. She meets a neighbor, the handsome young Viscount Julien de Lamare, who comes to call, and they quickly become good friends. When the baron presents his daughter with a boat, he invites the village priest and his acolytes to christen it. To Jeanne, the ceremony seems like a wedding, and under the spell of her illusion, she accepts his proposal when Julien asks her to marry him. The wedding takes place that summer, six weeks after they became engaged.

At Jeanne's wish, the couple journeys to Corsica on their honeymoon. She was romantically in love with her husband before her marriage, but during the two months she is away from home with him her emotion grows into a passion. Thus she is amazed, when they stop in Paris on their way home, to find that Julien is not perfect. She gives him her filled purse, her mother's present, to look after, and when she requests it

back to buy some gifts for her family, he gruffly refuses to dole out more than a hundred francs. Jeanne is afraid to ask for more.

When Jeanne and Julien return to The Poplars, Julien takes over the management of the estate. During the long, monotonous days of winter, he begins to wear old clothes and he no longer bothers to shave. He pays little attention to his wife. Having sold the carriage horses to save the cost of their feed, he uses the tenants' nags and becomes furious when Jeanne and her parents laugh at the ugly team.

In January, Jeanne's parents go to Rouen and leave the young couple alone. It is then that Jeanne becomes completely disillusioned with her husband. One day, the maid, her foster sister Rosalie, has a child. Julien insists that the mother and her illegitimate infant should be sent off immediately, but Jeanne, who is fond of Rosalie, opposes him. A few weeks later, she finds the pair in bed together.

The shock is so great that Jeanne can only think of getting away from her husband. Still in her nightclothes, she runs out of the house to the edge of the cliffs that hang over the sea. There Julien finds her and brings her back to the house before she can jump. For several weeks, the young wife is ill as the result of her exposure. When she begins to recover and has an opportunity to convince her parents of her discovery, Rosalie confesses that Julien seduced her on the first day he came to call at the house.

The maid and her baby are sent away. Jeanne prefers separation from her husband, but the knowledge that she is pregnant and the priest's intercession on Julien's behalf cause her to agree to a reconciliation.

Jeanne's baby is born in July, nearly a year after her marriage. She lavishes all the love that Julien does not accept on the infant Paul. After the baby's birth, the de Lamares become friendly with their neighbors, the Count and Countess de Fourville. The count is passionately in love with his wife, Gilberte de Fourville, but she rides alone with Julien almost every day. One morning, as Jeanne is walking her horse through the woods where Julien proposed, she finds her husband's and Gilberte's horses tied together.

Shortly afterward, the baroness dies after an illness that kept her partly crippled for many years. To Jeanne, who was deeply attached to her mother, it comes as a great shock to find that she, too, was not above an affair, documented in the letters she saved.

Jeanne keeps the secret of Julien's latest affair to herself, fearful of the steps the count might take if he ever discovers his wife's unfaithfulness. The old village priest, Abbé Picot, also holds his peace. Unfortunately, Abbé Picot is called elsewhere. His successor is not so liberal in his views. Abbé Tolbiac is conscious of his parishioners' morals and is determined to guard them. By chance he discovers the affair between Julien and Gilberte. He has no hesitation about discussing the subject with Jeanne, and when she refuses to desert her husband or to inform the count, he takes the story to Gilberte's husband. One day, while the couple is in a shepherd's hut, the count, a powerful giant, pushes the building down an incline and into a ravine. He then dashes home without being seen. Under the wreckage of the hut lie the two mangled bodies.

That night, after Julien's body is carried home, Jeanne has her second child, a stillborn girl. Although she suspects that Julien's death was not an accident, she remains silent. The memories of her husband's infidelities fade quickly, leaving her at peace with her recollections of their early life together, as it was on Corsica. Soon even these memories begin to dim, and she turns all of her attention to her son. Paul does not go to school until he is fifteen years old. At home, he is petted and indulged by his mother, grandfather, and a maiden aunt who comes to live at The Poplars after the death of the baroness. When he is finally sent off to Le Havre to school, Jeanne visits him so frequently that the principal begs her to restrict her visits.

In Paul's third year away from home, he stops spending his Sundays with his mother. When a usurer calls on her to collect money for the young man's debts, Jeanne visits his school and learns that he has not been there for a month. He is living with a mistress and he signs his mother's name to letters stating that he is ill.

After this escapade, Paul is taken home to The Poplars and closely watched. He manages to escape, however, and two days later Jeanne receives a letter from him from London. It is the first of many begging notes he sends her. In addition to asking for money, he announces that the woman he knew in Le Havre is living with him.

For more than a year, Paul sends a series of requests for financial help that are never ignored, even though they mean the mortgaging of The Poplars and the two farms that go with the estate. Anxiety over his grandson and his property causes the baron's death from apoplexy.

Soon after the baron's death, Jeanne's aunt follows him to the grave. Jeanne would be alone if Rosalie, who was married and widowed, did not return to look after her. Her foster sister insists on working without pay and on putting a much-needed check on Jeanne's expenditures. It is necessary to sell The Poplars, however, and the two women settle down in a small farmhouse.

Although Jeanne is forced to limit the sums she sends Paul, her affection for him does not decrease. When he has been away for seven years, she writes, begging him to come home. Paul's reply is that before he will return he wants her consent to marry his mistress, with whom he is living in Paris. Jeanne, who is not without a strain of jealousy, decides that she will persuade him to come without the woman. As quickly as possible she sets out for Paris. Although she writes to announce her visit, Paul does not meet her. To avoid his creditors, he moves without leaving a forwarding address. His disconsolate mother returns to Normandy.

Some months later, Jeanne hears from her son once more. His wife, whom he married without his mother's blessing, is dying, and he entreats Jeanne to come for their little daughter. This time, it is Rosalie who goes to Paris. When she returns, she has the infant with her, and she brings the news that Paul will follow her the next day.

Critical Evaluation:

The first of Guy de Maupassant's six novels, *A Woman's Life* was published in 1883, three years after the death of his teacher, Gustave Flaubert. Maupassant tried and mostly failed to please Flaubert by aspiring to the highest distinction as an artist in poetry and in the theater. With the publication of "Madame Tellier's Excursion" in 1881, he found a ready market for short stories that were admirably crafted but—judged by Flaubert's exacting standards—needlessly cynical, inelegant, and often mechanically contrived. Nevertheless, their pungency, realism, and shrewd observation of character attracted many readers who had ignored *Des Vers* (1880; *Romance in Rhyme*, 1903), Maupassant's only volume of poetry. Many of the qualities of the stories also appear in *A Woman's Life*, a sustained, psychologically honest study of Jeanne de Lamare from the time she completes her idealistic education at a Rouen convent in 1819 until about 1855, when she is middle-aged, disillusioned, and worn with many sorrows.

Maupassant's novel has frequently been compared, usually to its disadvantage, with two other novels that examine the fate of disappointed women, Flaubert's *Madame Bovary* (1857) and Arnold Bennett's *The Old Wives' Tale* (1908). For subtlety, richness of characterization, and harmonious prose style, *Madame Bovary* is assuredly a more profound work of art. Bennett's novel, which was inspired by *A Woman's Life*, is more detailed than its model and has a surer grasp of social history and of specific place and a deeper sense of the poignancy of time passing. Nevertheless, Maupassant's short novel—half as long as *Madame Bovary* and less than a third the length of *The Old Wives' Tale*—is remarkable in its own right. Compact, unsentimental, and stark, this work is a disturbing but affectionate study taken from human experience. The portrayal of Jeanne is thought to have been drawn, emotionally if not exactly, from Maupassant's memories of his mother, and his description of The Poplars recalls the setting of the Chateau de Miromesnil in Normandy, where the author spent his early childhood. The book, which was Maupassant's favorite among his novels, is memorable for its tender appreciation for the sufferings of women who are dominated by insensitive men.

Indeed, although Jeanne's story is central to the narrative, she is not the only woman whose life is one of disillusionment and quiet despair. Her mother, the Baroness Adelaide, lives a protected yet narrow life; she dissembles her knowledge of her husband's philandering with house servants and secretly takes revenge on the baron with her own infidelity. Rosalie, Jeanne's foster sister, is seduced and betrayed by her brother-in-law. Aunt Lison, neglected and pathetic, voices the lonely agony of a woman who has never been attractive to men. When Julien, courting pretty Jeanne early in the novel, solicitously asks whether her "darling little feet" are cold, Lison exclaims, "No one has ever asked me a question like that . . . never . . . never." Even when women give themselves to their lovers out of passion, Maupassant sees them as frail, unequal partners in romance. Rosalie confesses to Jeanne that she submitted to Julien's lust, despite knowing the consequences and her delicate position in the household, because he pleased her sexually. The Countess de Fourville imprudently hazards a liaison with Julien out of a similar weakness. Paul's mistress submits to her lover, excusing his spendthrift ways and casual neglect of her, because she is without resources of her own. While *A Woman's Life* focuses on the history of Jeanne, her experiences are shown to represent those of her sex.

It is important to note that the story begins during the spring of 1819 and concludes about thirty-five years later. Hence Maupassant's view is retrospective, looking backward to a time of relative calm and a settled, conservative society. Most of his short stories, however, concern his own time, the Third Republic, from 1870 to 1890. Reviewing the sources of his own turbulent age, Maupassant shows that the calm of Jeanne's provincial society is illusionary, fixed in complacency rather than in real tranquillity. It is founded on hypocrisy and outworn traditions. The Abbé Picot, Jeanne's casuistic parish priest, is more a diplomat than a religious man, who smooths over problems of moral turpitude for the sake of expediency. His successor, the Abbé Tolbiac, is a fanatic, inflexible in his doctrine of sin. In the narrow society in which she moves, Jeanne has not the freedom to change or to reconstruct her life, guided as she is by the dead hand of tradition.

In spite of her limited opportunities, Jeanne never surrenders to self-pity. Instead, she develops strength of character. Although she does not master her fate, she learns to endure its vicissitudes. She is brutally mistreated (if not, indeed, raped) on her bridal night; denied the affection and even attention of her husband; humiliated, almost maddened, by his infidelities; and finally neglected by her wastrel son Paul. However, she maintains a sense of personal dignity and courage in the face of defeat. Like Rosalie, who also suffers much and matures in worldly competence, she sustains life. At the end of the book, Jeanne accepts the infant daughter of Paul and his dead wife, probably only to repeat with this child the pattern of indulgence that began with her worthless son. Although she is life's victim, she is willing to take further risks for the sake of advancing life. Rosalie's final words, which express Maupassant's stoic philosophy, allow the reader to understand the ambiguities of her choice: "You see, life is never as good or as bad as one thinks."

"Critical Evaluation" by Leslie B. Mittleman

Further Reading

Bloom, Harold, ed. *Guy de Maupassant*. Philadelphia: Chelsea House, 2004. Although most of the essays in this collection focus on Maupassant's short stories, some of the essays also pertain to his novels, including a discussion of the influence of Maupassant's realism and critiques by Anatole France and by Joseph Conrad.

Donaldson-Evans, Mary. *A Woman's Revenge: The Chronology of Dispossession in Maupassant's Fiction.* Lexington: French Forum, 1986. A structural analysis of the chronological development in Maupassant's depiction of male-female relationships.

Gregorio, Laurence A. *Maupassant's Fiction and the Darwinian View of Life.* New York: Peter Lang, 2005. Maupassant, like other naturalist writers, believed in Charles Darwin's theory of evolution. Gregorio describes how evolutionary theory and social Darwinism figure significantly in Maupassant's fiction, demonstrating how these writings reflect the concepts of natural selection, heredity, and materialism.

Harris, Trevor A. Le V. *Maupassant in the Hall of Mirrors.* New York: St. Martin's Press, 1990. Posits that Maupassant's use of irony is an attempt to separate himself from and to criticize the excesses of French society. Examines Maupassant's narratives and journalism and focuses on his narrative technique, syntax, characterization, structure, and imagery.

Lerner, Michael G. *Maupassant.* New York: George Braziller, 1975. Reviews Maupassant's early life, his tutelage under Gustave Flaubert, the influence of Émile Zola, and the use of naturalistic techniques in his work. Includes photographs.

Sullivan, Edward D. *Maupassant the Novelist.* Princeton, N.J.: Princeton University Press, 1954. Reviews aesthetics and theme in Maupassant's novels. Addresses the function of a critic, the opposition between realism and idealism, style, and Maupassant's objective point of view. Sullivan traces a subtle but growing element of the psychological in Maupassant's last three novels. Presents *A Woman's Life* as a collection of short stories about a central, passive character.

Wallace, A. H. *Guy de Maupassant.* New York: Twayne, 1973. Depicts Maupassant's fiction as reflections of the life of a "doer" rather than an observer. Offers analysis of specific themes in Maupassant's work, including infidelity, female servitude in marriage, and naturalism.

Women Beware Women

Author: Thomas Middleton (1580-1627)
First produced: c. 1621-1627; first published, 1657
Type of work: Drama
Type of plot: Tragedy
Time of plot: Early seventeenth century
Locale: Florence, Italy

Principal characters:
LEANTIO, a Florentine clerk
BIANCA, his wife
FABRICIO, a Florentine gentleman
ISABELLA, his daughter
LIVIA, Fabricio's sister
HIPPOLITO, brother of Livia and Fabricio
THE DUKE OF FLORENCE
A CARDINAL, the duke's brother
THE WARD
GUARDIANO, his uncle and guardian

The Story:

Leantio, a Florentine merchant's clerk, marries Bianca, a beautiful and well-born Venetian, and brings her to his mother's house. On her arrival there, she responds graciously to his mother's words of welcome and speaks of her love for Leantio. He, in turn, informs his mother of Bianca's luxurious background and of his inability to equal it. He explains also that Bianca is a great prize who must be kept hidden from other men's eyes. His mother fears that Bianca will be discontented with her new and poorer home.

In a richer house, Livia entertains her brother Fabricio, the father of Isabella, and Guardiano, the uncle of a rich and foolish boy called the Ward. They discuss the proposed marriage between the Ward and Isabella. Livia, protesting against loveless marriages, lectures Fabricio on man's unfaithfulness and woman's obedience and declares that she will never remarry. When Isabella is sent for, Fabricio declares that her uncle Hippolito will surely follow her in her married state because they are as inseparable as links in a chain. Isabella's ideals, especially her ideas on marriage, are in marked contrast to the Ward's foolishness and vulgarity. She dreads marriage to him and regards it as slavery. This is her explanation to Livia, who sends Hippolito to comfort her. At that time, Isabella's conscious feelings toward her uncle are those of deep friendship. Unaware at the time of any sexual attraction toward him, she is horrified and sadly leaves him when he tells her he loves her as a man loves his wife.

When Leantio finally leaves Bianca at his mother's house and returns to his work, Bianca weeps bitterly. She is distracted from her grief by the noise and excitement of the annual religious procession to the cathedral. Deeply impressed by the noble bearing of the duke of Florence, Bianca is sure that he notices her as she watches him passing by.

Meanwhile, Hippolito tells Livia of his love for Isabella and of her reaction, and Livia promises to procure Isabella as his mistress. When Isabella confides her unhappiness to Livia, her aunt takes the opportunity to tell her that Hippolito is not her uncle, that she is in fact the child of Fabricio's wife by a Spanish nobleman. She insists, however, that Isabella keep this matter a secret, because Fabricio and Hippolito are ignorant of it. Thus Isabella welcomes Hippolito with a kiss when he returns and he marvels at Livia's skill. Isabella decides that she will still marry the Ward to conceal her love affair with Hippolito.

Guardiano tells Livia that the duke of Florence is enamored of a girl he saw on the balcony of Leantio's mother's house. Livia undertakes to win her for the duke and summons Leantio's mother for a game of chess. Under pressure, the mother admits that she has a daughter-in-law in her home, and Bianca is sent for. She is taken on a tour of the house by Guardiano, who thus leads her to the duke.

While the duke speaks of his passion for her, Bianca pleads for her honor, virtue, and safety. The duke, continuing his token pleading, intimates to Bianca that she does not have the power to refuse him. When she returns to the two chess players, Bianca is half pleased by the duke but also eager to have revenge on Livia.

At home, Bianca's ensuing frustration and discontent infuriate her mother-in-law, who is glad that Leantio will soon return. On his arrival, Leantio anticipates an ecstatic reunion with his wife, but he is greeted coldly by Bianca and angrily repulsed. Before long, Bianca is sent for by the duke and goes to the palace with Leantio's mother. Left alone, Leantio abandons himself to jealousy, but he fails to realize the extent of his betrayal until he, too, is summoned to dine with the duke.

When offered the command of a distant city, Leantio is as powerless to refuse as he is to disrupt the affair between his wife and her noble lover, and he is forced to stand by when Bianca, bored by the banquet, leaves with the duke.

Livia, who fell in love at first sight with Leantio, is determined to woo him from his grief. When she indirectly offers herself as his mistress, he accepts because of the wealth and luxury she promises. Some weeks later, Leantio visits Bianca in her apartment at the court, and they jeer at each other's finery and new place in the world. Bianca tells the duke of her husband's visit and discloses that he became Livia's lover. Jealous of Leantio, the duke informs Hippolito, who, as the ruler expects, threatens to kill his sister's lover to preserve publicly Livia's honor.

The duke's pleasure at the idea of Leantio's death increases when his brother, the cardinal, threatens him with the fires of hell if he continues to live adulterously. Vowing that he will reform, he decides that with Leantio dead he can lawfully marry Bianca, so Leantio is murdered. Livia, finding Hippolito with her lover's body is driven almost to madness by grief, fury, and malice. She betrays him and Isabella and admits that she lied to Isabella about her parentage to make her Hippolito's mistress. Isabella, who transgressed, unlike the others, through ignorance, resolves to leave Hippolito and avenge herself by destroying Livia.

The separate revenges plotted by these people result in their own deaths. At a masque held ostensibly in honor of the duke's marriage to Bianca, poisoned incense kills Isabella and Livia. Hippolito stabs himself, and Bianca has the duke poisoned and then drinks also from the poisoned cup.

Critical Evaluation:

This Jacobean drama is set in Italy, the background that, in tragedies of the period, implies luxury, vice, and violence. Within this framework, Thomas Middleton dispassionately and ironically records human—especially feminine—motivation and passion. As she dies from drinking a poisoned cup, Bianca exclaims: "Oh the deadly snares/ That women set for women . . ./ Like our own sex, we have no enemy, no enemy!" However, her judgment, like that expressed in the title of the tragedy, is false. The action of Middleton's play proves quite the opposite: that women should beware men, who set the snares of money and power that destroy women. Livia schemes in behalf of her brothers Fabricio and Hippolito; her motives have nothing to do with selfish exploitation. When she takes a lover of her own choosing, Leantio, she is abused as sinful, and her lover is murdered so that the family "honor" may be restored. Set in the corrupt and libertine atmosphere of Renaissance Florence, the play shows, with cool detachment, the terrible effects of passions mingled with greed.

Middleton skillfully combines two separate stories that conclude with one explosive catastrophe. The Bianca plot was based upon the notorious true history of Bianca Capello, born in approximately 1548 to a family of Venetian nobility. In 1563, she eloped with a Florentine, Pietro Buonaventuri, who was not of the noble class; later she married him and gave birth to a daughter. The powerful Francesco de' Medici soon favored her; she became his mistress, and her husband—doubtless on Francesco's orders—was assassinated in 1569. Francesco and Bianca, in turn, died suddenly of a fever in 1587, under circumstances that, in the popular imagination, appeared suspicious; Francesco's brother, the cardinal, succeeded him as grand duke of Tuscany. This story of lust and betrayal is combined with the Isabella-Hippolito plot. In its theme of adultery and deceit, the second plot corresponds to the first, emphasizing the moral object of the drama: to expose the ruinous effects of amorous plots and counterplots conceived through guile or greed.

In his moral vision, Middleton is different from the other great Jacobean tragedians. Unlike John Webster and Cyril Tourneur, in whose poetic drama horror is heaped upon horror, Middleton avoids melodramatic scenes of sheer terror until the final moments of the play, when the complications of the plot are resolved in a compressed action of mass slaughter. Unlike John Ford, who is masterful in pathetic scenes of sexual aberration, Middleton is a realist who avoids "abnormal" psychosexual behavior. Although Isabella willingly submits to the embraces of Hippolito—and thus commits incest—she is deceived by Livia into believing that her uncle's bloodline is different from hers. As soon as she learns the truth about the relationship, she plots revenge on her betrayers. However, her passion for Hippolito, so long as she can deny to herself the incest inhibition, is as fierce as the man's.

Middleton is interested in the ruthlessness of men, who are dominating, even sadistic, lovers, and in women as men's victims, who often masochistically acquiesce in their own destruction. Bianca, like Beatrice-Joanna in Middleton and Samuel Rowley's *The Changeling* (1622), is a sensual woman who fixes her love on one man and then, driven by sexual urges, on another. Just as Beatrice-Joanna comes to love—or at least lust for—her seducer, the abhorrent De Flores, so Bianca comes to champion the duke over her husband Leantio. It is not riches alone that tempts her to cancel her marriage vows; it is lust for the more powerful man. Because of her sexual weakness she is without moral resources; and the man, through his sexual power, uses her as property—as a mere physical possession to be bought and sold. Middleton objectively records the actions, without senti-mentality or preaching, and allows the audience a chance to judge whether women should indeed beware women.

The moral ending of *Women Beware Women* is conventional. The dramatic structure of the play is unbalanced, and the slow entanglement of destructive passions is abruptly changed to the final, almost farcical, holocaust. The lasting impression left by the play is one of the movement of characters from deliberate scheming to uncontrollable involvement and destruction. The tragedy is memorable not for its moral ending but for the nightmare quality of human passions revealed by the force of richly dramatic verse.

Further Reading

Chakravorty, Swapan. *Society and Politics in the Plays of Thomas Middleton*. New York: Oxford University Press, 1996. Reassesses the cultural significance of Middleton's plays, arguing that he was a pioneer of politically self-conscious theater. Chapter 6 is devoted to an analysis of *Women Beware Women*.

Dawson, Anthony B. "*Women Beware Women* and the Economy of Rape." *Studies in English Literature 1500-1900* 27, no. 2 (Spring, 1987): 303-320. Argues that Middleton presents female characters as trapped in an economic hierarchy that reduces them to commodities for male use. This presentation is complicated by a need to maintain a conventional Elizabethan perception of women as naturally corrupt.

Holmes, David M. "*Women Beware Women* and *The Changeling*." In *The Art of Thomas Middleton*. Oxford, England: Clarendon Press, 1970. Places the play within the context of Middleton's late work. Asserts that Bianca is vulnerable to seduction because of a repressive upbringing that does not prepare her for a morally corrupt world.

Huebert, Ronald. "An Art That Has No Name: Thomas Middleton." In *The Performance of Pleasure in English Renaissance Drama*. New York: Palgrave Macmillan, 2003. Examines how English Renaissance dramatists, including Middleton, pursue and create pleasure, both the erotic pleasure presented onstage and the aesthetic pleasure experienced by readers and theatergoers.

Kistner, A. L., and M. K. Kistner. "*Women Beware Women*: Will, Authority, and Fortune." In *Middleton's Tragic Themes*. New York: Peter Lang, 1984. Asserts that Middleton insists upon the individual moral responsibility of his characters. Characters ignore their awareness of sin to satisfy their overriding will, thus bringing on catastrophe.

Taylor, Gary, and John Lavagnino, eds. *Thomas Middleton*

and Early Modern Textual Culture: A Companion to the Collected Works. New York: Oxford University Press, 2007. This companion to a complete collection of Middleton's works contains numerous essays that place the writer in his literary and cultural context. Also provides introductory essays and textual notes for all of his writings.

Wigler, Stephen. "Parent and Child: The Pattern of Love in *Women Beware Women*." In *"Accompaninge the Players": Essays Celebrating Thomas Middleton, 1580-1980*, edited by Kenneth Friedenreich. New York: AMS Press, 1983. Examines three dominant love relationships of the play, which demonstrate a similar parent-child incest pattern and explain the stylistic shift in the final act. Suggests that a possible source of the play lies in Middleton's biography.

Women in Love

Author: D. H. Lawrence (1885-1930)
First published: 1920
Type of work: Novel
Type of plot: Psychological realism
Time of plot: Early twentieth century
Locale: England and Austria

Principal characters:
RUPERT BIRKIN, a school inspector
GERALD CRICH, a coal mine operator
URSULA BRANGWEN, a teacher
GUDRUN BRANGWEN, her sister, an artist
HERMIONE RODDICE, a wealthy intellectual
LOERKE, a sculptor

The Story:

Ursula Brangwen and her sister Gudrun first notice Rupert Birkin and Gerald Crich as the sisters are watching a wedding party arrive at a church. Ursula explains that Rupert, the best man, is trying to terminate his prolonged affair with Hermione Roddice, one of the bridesmaids. Some days later, Rupert comes to inspect Ursula's classroom with Hermione in tow. Hermione, after arguing fiercely with Rupert, invites Ursula and Gudrun to visit her home. Once alone, Ursula inexplicably weeps. Gudrun is drawn to Gerald, the bride's older brother; when the sisters catch sight of him swimming, Ursula tells Gudrun that when he was a boy, Gerald accidentally killed his brother.

When Rupert and Gerald meet on a train to London, they discuss whether love is the "center of life"; Rupert expresses his pessimism about humanity. That evening, Gerald joins Rupert and some bohemian friends at a café and sleeps with a young model after they all retire to her former lover's flat. In the morning, Gerald joins Rupert and his friends as they chat, naked, around the fireplace.

The Brangwen sisters become better acquainted with Rupert and Gerald when they visit Breadalby, Hermione's home. Gerald finds Gudrun arousing when the women, in silk robes, improvise a modern ballet. After Rupert and Hermione again quarrel, Hermione tries to break his skull with a paperweight.

Some days afterward, Gerald appalls the sisters when he brutally forces his horse to stand as a train passes. Gerald and Hermione later find Gudrun sketching by the lake. Gudrun clumsily drops her sketchbook into the water. Gudrun, though blaming Gerald, establishes a silent intimacy with him. Meanwhile, Ursula finds Rupert repairing a punt, and, on an overgrown island, they discuss true happiness. Ursula finds Rupert's misanthropic vision of a world rid of humans strangely pleasing. Afterward, having tea with Gerald and Hermione at Rupert's new lodgings, Ursula objects when Rupert compares a horse's will to submit to its master to a woman's will to submit to a man. When she meets Rupert alone, however, he avows that while he does not "love" her, he seeks a relationship deeper than love, a "pure balance." They watch as a cat playfully cuffs a female stray, and Rupert suggests that the cat wants the same equilibrium, like a star in orbit. Ursula still believes he wants a mere satellite.

When Gerald's father gives the annual "water party" for the townspeople, the Brangwen sisters take a canoe to a clearing on the far shore. There, Gudrun dances as Ursula sings, and when some cattle appear, Gudrun brazenly dances before their horns until suddenly Gerald intrudes and, alarmed, shoos them off. Gudrun, repudiating his protection, strikes his face. As night falls, the couples row by lantern light, and Ursula reaches an understanding, a shared pessimism, with Rupert. They hear screams; Gerald's sister fell into the water, and her fiancé dived in after her. In vain Gerald tries desperately to find the pair in the darkness. Rupert assures him that death is better for them. Toward dawn, they find the bodies, the girl's arms clasped round her lover's neck.

Rupert later drops in on Ursula at home. The profound sympathy between the young pair becomes evident as compared with her parents' conventionality. After Rupert leaves, however, Ursula feels a strange hatred for him, even as she feels his possession of her. Still unable to reconcile himself to any marriage, Rupert begins to envision some new, freer relationship with women. When Gerald visits, the tenderness between them induces Rupert to invite him to swear blood-brotherhood, but Gerald demurs.

Gudrun is invited to tutor Gerald's young sister in drawing, and when they agree to sketch the girl's pet rabbit, it scratches Gudrun as she takes it from its cage. When it also scratches Gerald, he subdues it with a blow, and they share an appreciation of the fierce energy in the rabbit's "madness."

Near the lake by moonlight, Ursula discovers Rupert talking to himself. Rupert again tries to explain what he wants: not Ursula's love exactly, but her spirit. They kiss, despite her misgivings. The next evening, Rupert comes to her home to propose but, instead, quarrels with her father and angrily leaves. He finds Gerald, and the two men agree to wrestle naked. They fight to complete exhaustion, then they clasp hands as Gerald confesses his love for his friend.

Later, while waiting for Rupert in his lodgings, Hermione advises Ursula not to marry him. Ursula decides that all of Hermione's ideas are merely abstractions, but after Rupert arrives, Ursula is mortified by the easy familiarity between Rupert and Hermione. She leaves abruptly as they plan Hermione's departure for Italy. Soon afterward, Rupert drives Ursula into the countryside to give her three gemstone rings, but when she learns that he intends to join Hermione for dinner, she angrily throws them away and walks off. She immediately relents, and after reconciling, they spend the night in the car in Sherwood Forest.

As Gerald holds vigil over his father's demise, Gudrun brings needed comfort, and as he walks her home, they kiss passionately under a bridge. At last his father dies, and Gerald hurries to the Brangwen home and steals into Gudrun's bedroom where he silently makes love to her.

When Gerald suggests a double wedding, Rupert argues against conventional marriage, insisting that love between man and man is marriage's necessary complement. Again, Gerald resists. When Ursula tells her family that she plans to marry Rupert the next day, her outraged father strikes her,

and Ursula moves in with Rupert that evening. Gerald suggests the four of them go away together.

The couples travel separately to the Continent, met in Innsbruck, and proceed to a hostel high in the Alps. In this brilliant, snow-bound, silent world, Gudrun and Gerald immediately began to drift apart.

Among the guests is a German sculptor, Loerke, who, with his aesthetic theory and scorn for opinion and "life," exercises a perverse fascination over Gudrun. Ursula becomes repelled, and she leaves with Rupert for Italy.

Alone in this otherworldly realm, the hostility between Gudrun and Gerald intensifies. To Gerald's disgust, Gudrun falls further under Loerke's spell. She decides to leave Gerald, but while she is tobogganing with Loerke, Gerald appears and begins to strangle her. He then wanders off into the snow until he falls, exhausted. After Rupert returns with Ursula, he gazes grief-stricken at Gerald's icy corpse. He tells Ursula that things would be different if Gerald accepted his love.

Critical Evaluation:

Although at first poorly received, *Women in Love* has come to be considered D. H. Lawrence's most important novel, and it is one of the most remarkable novels of its time, both for its innovative narrative technique and for its psychological depth. Although the novel employs a narrative strategy familiar from nineteenth century novels, in developing the relationships among four distinct personalities, Lawrence revolutionizes narrative technique, replacing the traditional concept of character. He includes more basic dimensions of human existence: blood and flesh. His characters are motivated not primarily by conscious, ego-driven wills but by drives that originate at a deeper, more physical level. Lawrence, who knew the work of Sigmund Freud long before it became widely known in England, believed that "blood" possessed its own consciousness and had its own ways of knowing.

The novel's plot results from the characters' discovery of and attempts to satisfy their most basic demands. These struggles frequently entail reversals and paradoxes that are difficult to account for in strictly rational terms, since their motivation is at a deeper level than the rational mind. Rupert Birkin is the chief exponent of this point of view, but while he possesses some of Lawrence's personal traits and often voices the author's views, he does not function simply as a mouthpiece. Lawrence is careful to show Rupert's flaws and to make him occasionally ridiculous. All the central characters somehow "represent" Lawrence as reflections of the self and antiself. At the same time, all four central characters, in trying to understand themselves and to make themselves understood to others, articulate a philosophy that, while it is persistently challenged and problematized within the novel, also possesses enough cogency to stand as a powerful statement against the hypocrisies and the complacencies of Lawrence's era.

Women in Love had its beginnings around 1913 in a work called *The Sisters*, which Lawrence eventually divided into two independent novels, publishing the first as *The Rainbow* in 1915. After *The Rainbow* was suppressed on grounds of obscenity in 1915, Lawrence found it impossible to publish his writing and had to endure poverty as he completed *Women in Love* during 1916-1917. Although the war never enters the novel, the pessimistic atmosphere reflects not only Lawrence's personal crisis but also his sense that Europe was committing suicide. The older generation are fools, and the futureless, godless young contemplate humanity's annihilation. This hopelessness, however, does not prevent Rupert and his friends from seeking authentic interpersonal relationships and radical solutions to questions of marriage and friendship. They stand disdainfully apart from the world, yet seem to grow larger than life in the icy crucible of the Alps.

Lawrence treats aspects of human experience that few novelists of his time dared to touch. He treats sexuality not only in the narrow sense but also forbidden passions and thoughts. Lawrence offers no simple answers; in the end the tragedy of Gerald Crich's suicide marks the failure of Gerald's relationship with Rupert as much as his relationship with Gudrun. Rupert's unsatisfied need for a deep connection with a man as a complement to marriage has a physical dimension that stops just short of homosexuality. Lawrence explicated its significance for Rupert in a prologue that he ultimately decided to omit from the published version.

Gudrun's spiritual death is almost as final as Gerald's physical death. Always inclined toward aestheticism, her friendship with the sculptor Loerke draws her into decadence and depravity. Loerke's sculpture of Lady Godiva embodies Loerke's philosophy of art as a self-enclosed, autonomous realm without reference to morality or to life. Gudrun succumbs to Loerke's sterile influence and finally becomes reduced to a cheap artist's model.

Ursula and Rupert, on the other hand, ultimately reach an understanding that makes their marriage possible. Their relationship is based on polarity; each partner preserves a distinct identity within a balance of opposites. The disastrous opposite to this balance is symbolized by the entwined corpses of Gerald's sister and her fiancé. Ursula's independence and assertiveness make such an end impossible. Her relationship with Rupert is based on more than mere affection; she finds with him a profound bond based on a mutual understanding and a shared outlook on the world.

Matthew Parfitt

Further Reading

Burack, Charles Michael. *D. H. Lawrence's Language of Sacred Experience: The Transfiguration of the Reader.* New York: Palgrave Macmillan, 2005. Burack maintains that Lawrence structured *Women in Love, Lady Chatterley's Lover, The Rainbow,* and *The Plumed Serpent* as if they were religious initiation rites intended to evoke new spiritual experiences for their readers.

Cushman, Keith, and Earl G. Ingersoll, eds. *D. H. Lawrence: New Worlds.* Madison, N.J.: Fairleigh Dickinson University Press, 2003. Collection of essays that seek to reinterpret Lawrence's work. Includes discussions of his influence on British fiction, debates over Lawrence's English identity, and the chapter "Metaphor in *Women in Love*" by Kyoko Kay Kondo.

Day, Gary, and Libby Di Niro, eds. *"The Rainbow" and "Women in Love": D. H. Lawrence.* New York: Palgrave Macmillan, 2004. Features ten essays interpreting the two novels, including discussions of the politics of sexual liberation in both books, Lawrence and feminist psychoanalytic theory in *The Rainbow,* and historical change in *Women in Love.*

Draper, R. P. *D. H. Lawrence.* New York: Twayne, 1964. An accessible introduction to Lawrence's chief works, including useful biographical background and extensive commentary on *Women in Love.*

Fernihough, Anne, ed. *The Cambridge Companion to D. H. Lawrence.* New York: Cambridge University Press, 2001. Collection of essays interpreting Lawrence's work from various perspectives, including discussions of Lawrence and modernism, Lawrence in the 1920's, and "Sex and the Nation: 'The Prussian Officer' and *Women in Love*" by Hugh Stevens.

Kermode, Frank. *D. H. Lawrence.* New York: Viking Press, 1973. Sheds light on the novel's philosophical concerns.

Leavis, F. R. *D. H. Lawrence: Novelist.* New York: Alfred A. Knopf, 1968. Includes a lengthy chapter on *Women in Love* that draws attention to overlooked themes. Reassesses the novel's importance.

Oates, Joyce Carol. "Lawrence's Götterdämmerung: The Apocalyptic Vision of *Women in Love*." In *Critical Essays on D. H. Lawrence,* edited by Dennis Jackson and Fleda Brown Jackson. Boston: G. K. Hall, 1988. A brilliant discussion of symbolism and eschatology in *Women in Love*, informed by Oates's own experience as a novelist.

Ryu, Doo-Sun. *D. H. Lawrence's "The Rainbow" and "Women in Love": A Critical Study*. New York: Peter Lang, 2005. Focuses on Lawrence's concept of "essential criticism" to analyze how he presents his ideas in both novels.

Wright, T. R. *D. H. Lawrence and the Bible*. New York: Cambridge University Press, 2000. Wright maintains that the Bible played a significant role in almost all of Lawrence's works, and he analyzes Lawrence's use of biblical allusions and themes. *Women in Love* is discussed in chapter 8.

The Women of Brewster Place
A Novel in Seven Stories

Author: Gloria Naylor (1950-   )
First published: 1982
Type of work: Novel
Type of plot: Social realism
Time of plot: 1930's-1960's
Locale: A northern urban neighborhood

Principal characters:
MATTIE MICHAEL, the stable "mother" figure
ETTA MAE JOHNSON, Mattie's longtime friend
LUCIELIA (CIEL) TURNER, Mattie's young friend
KISWANA BROWNE, a young would-be revolutionary
CORA LEE, a young unwed mother
LORRAINE, a lesbian schoolteacher
THERESA, her lover
BEN, the tenement janitor

The Story:

At twenty-three, Mattie Michael is seduced by Butcher Fuller, a handsome ne'er-do-well. When she becomes pregnant, her father beats her to get her to reveal her unborn child's father. Mattie, disgraced in her father's eyes, moves from home in Rock Vale, Tennessee, to North Carolina, where her friend Etta Mae Johnson takes her in. After Mattie's son is born and Etta Mae moves on, Mattie starts boarding with Miss Eva and her granddaughter Ciel. After several years, Miss Eva dies, Ciel's parents come for her, and Mattie is left with the responsibility for paying the mortgage and for raising her son Basil.

Miss Eva always said that Mattie is too indulgent and protective of Basil, but Mattie will not listen. When Basil, now grown, gets into a barroom fight and accidentally kills a man, his lack of moral fiber is apparent. He allows his mother to put up her now mortgage-free home as bond for his bail. He will not face the slim possibility of going to prison, though conviction is unlikely. He skips town and disappears. Mattie, homeless again, finds a home through Etta Mae in Brewster Place.

Etta Mae Johnson is in Brewster Place after many years of roaming from place to place, making and breaking off liaisons with men who temporarily support her. When she

reaches the age where, as she says to Mattie, "each year there's a new line [on her face] to cover" and her body "cries for just a little more rest," she decides it is time to find a good man, marry, and settle down. She thinks she finds that man in a dynamic preacher, Moreland Woods. Woods knows, however, that Etta Mae is a "worldly" woman whom he can use and discard with no fear of entanglement, which he does, leaving Etta Mae resigned to relying for "love and comfort" on her friend Mattie.

Brewster Place is also home to younger women. Kiswana Browne is a twenty-three-year-old college dropout who leaves her middle-class life in Linden Hills for Brewster Place to be close to "her people." Her mother, a proud, genteel woman, visits Kiswana in Brewster Place to try to persuade the young woman that living in poverty is not the only way Kiswana can show her solidarity with the black masses. Kiswana's rebellion, however, requires that she remove all traces of her middle-class background, including changing her name from "Melanie," her grandmother's name, to one she finds in "an African dictionary."

Ciel, Mattie's young friend dating back to their days in North Carolina, marries Eugene and has a baby girl, Serena. When Ciel gets pregnant a second time, Eugene feels trapped. He loses his job and blames Ciel for all his troubles. Ciel, out of love for him, gets an abortion, which depresses her and causes her to be unhealthily focused on Serena. The day Eugene decides to leave, ostensibly to take an out-of-town job, Serena is accidentally and fatally electrocuted when she sticks a fork into an electrical outlet. Ciel nearly dies of despair, but Mattie helps pull her out of her painful despondency.

Cora Lee as a child was fixated on baby dolls. By the time she was thirteen, her parents realized there was something not quite normal in the way Cora Lee demanded and expected a brand-new baby doll each Christmas. Thirteen was also when she found out about sex and making real babies on her own. Very soon thereafter, she was having babies by "shadow" men identified, even in her own mind, only as the fathers of her various children. Living on welfare in Brewster Place with seven children, one an infant, Cora Lee spends most of her days watching television and caring for her baby while giving the older children little attention.

Kiswana befriends Cora Lee when Kiswana tries to organize a tenants' association among the Brewster Place community. She persuades Cora Lee to take her children to a production of a modern version of "A Midsummer Night's Dream." When Cora Lee sees how her older children are enthralled with the play, she realizes she neglected them once they stopped being infants, and she vows to do better by them.

Lorraine and Theresa move to Brewster Place when their lesbianism is suspected at their former residence. Lorraine, a first-grade teacher, is afraid she will lose her job if her sexual orientation becomes known. The people of Brewster Place, especially a self-righteous busybody named Sophie, begin to suspect that the two women are "that way," and some of them begin to ostracize them. Lorraine has a run-in with one of the area's thugs, C. C. Baker, who calls her a freak. Lorraine, more needy of acceptance than her partner Theresa, befriends Ben, the janitor, who sees in her the same qualities as were in his long-lost daughter.

One night, Baker and his gang trap Lorraine in an alley and rape her. Brutalized, she lies in the alley, unseen and unheard, all night. The next morning, Ben, nearly drunk, takes his usual early-morning seat on a garbage can in the alley. Lorraine, deranged from her brutalization, attacks him with a brick and kills him. She never knows what she did.

After Ben's death, Kiswana's attempts to organize the Brewster Place residents culminate in a block party to raise money for a lawyer to fight the landlord. Mattie dreams that the block party manages a miracle: The Brewster Place residents tear down the ugly wall that cuts Brewster Place off from the rest of the city. Mattie awakens believing that maybe the block party will bring improvements to the lives of the people of Brewster Place.

Critical Evaluation:

The women of the title are the main characters, and Brewster Place is the setting in which they act on, and react to, the circumstances of their lives. Those circumstances are usually disheartening and usually caused by men, who are seen generally as malign forces. Throughout the book, males are shown as causing the adverse condition of women.

Mattie Michael is a pleasant, God-fearing, churchgoing woman with moral strength, who, without the support of other women, might not have survived. Butch Fuller, when he impregnates her, not only destroys her relationship with her father but also changes the course of her life, possibly for the worse. Her father, in his angry frustration, nearly destroys her life when he beats her. Her son Basil breaks her heart by deserting her without a backward glance. Each time, a woman helps Mattie survive. Her mother rescues her from her father's savage beating by firing a shotgun close enough to his head to get his attention. Etta Mae gives her sanctuary so Mattie can have her child. Miss Eva gives her a home when the one she has becomes unlivable because of rats. The men in her life give little or nothing.

Etta Mae uses men all her life and apparently asks no more from them than she wants. She is a kind of floating concubine for most of her adult life, learning at an early age in Tennessee that her sexual charms attract men who are willing to pay for them. As she grows older and her looks and energy diminish, she wants to settle down, preferably with a kind man who will take care of her. She thinks the Reverend Mr. Moreland Woods is right for her. He seems "well-off," with his "manicured hands and a diamond pinkie ring," but he turns out to be a hypocritical opportunist, viewing Etta Mae as someone who can satisfy his "temporary weakness of the flesh." Forewarned about him by Mattie, who recognizes that Woods is interested only in a "quick good time" with her, Etta Mae finally accepts that her friendship with Mattie might be the only abiding relationship left to her.

While the women are fully drawn characters whose stories explain why they are what and where they are, the only rounded male characters are Basil, Ben, and Eugene Turner, Ciel's husband. He is shown to be a whiner and an emotional abuser who takes flight whenever the going gets tough. Ciel ultimately realizes that he is worthless when he complains that her love for him just "ain't good enough" to compensate for the life he is being forced to live as husband, father, and provider. Ciel then sees him at last as a "tall, skinny black man with arrogance and selfishness" whom she knows she will soon grow to hate.

Ben is the kindest male figure, and he is emotionally crippled and morally bankrupt (as revealed in the story of his spineless passivity regarding his daughter's adversity). He is kind and supportive to Lorraine, and for his trouble, he is killed by her—a woman with whom he has a close, almost father-daughter relationship. The only relationships that work out consistently in the novel are those between women.

This novel portrays women as survivors who must deal with the damage done to them by men. Usually the men are those with whom the women have a close relationship. The one episode in which a woman encounters males with whom she has no prior connection is the rape of Lorraine by C. C. Baker and his gang. These young men inspire a condemnation unlike any other in the book. They are described as always "moving in a pack," needing one another "continually near to verify their existence." They have fifty-word vocabularies, ninth-grade educations, and strive to emulate the "blaxploitative" Shaft and Superfly. They are "the most dangerous species in existence—human males with an erection to validate." They are the most mindlessly brutal characters in the book, evidence of the need for women to band together in support of one another.

Episodic in organization, with flashbacks providing background on the major characters, *The Women of Brewster Place* portrays seven very different African American women. The familiar stereotypes are there: the motherly, religious woman who accepts things and goes on, the hussy with the heart of gold, the welfare mother who has one baby after another by different men, the gossip (Sophie), the middle-class matron. They fall into the two stereotypical categories: the good woman (Mattie, Ciel, Miss Eva, Lorraine) and the bad woman (Etta Mae, Ben's wife Elvira, Cora Lee). The circumstances of their lives individualize them into believable human beings.

In their characterization, the dialogue rings true without resorting to excessive dialect, slang, profanity, or obscenity. Capturing the sound of African Americans in their familiar surroundings, it communicates the moment and the milieu of the story.

The Women of Brewster Place defines the black experience and illustrates the strength of friendship among women, never once suggesting that often-accepted view that women cannot be friends to other women. Men are shown as base. Perhaps Gloria Naylor is trying to balance the literary scales that so often show men as heroic and steadfast.

Jane L. Ball

Further Reading

Christian, Barbara. "Gloria Naylor's Geography: Community, Class, and Patriarchy in *The Women of Brewster Place* and *Linden Hills*." In *The New Black Feminist Criticism, 1985-2000*, edited by Gloria Bowles, M. Giulia Fabi, and Arlene R. Keizer. Urbana: University of Illinois Press, 2007. Contrasts the two worlds of Brewster Place and Linden Hills, regards Kiswana as the link between the novels, and places Naylor in literary context.

Felton, Sharon, and Michelle C. Loris, eds. *The Critical Response to Gloria Naylor*. Westport, Conn.: Greenwood Press, 1997. A collection of essays analyzing four of Naylor's novels, including *The Women of Brewster Place*, from a variety of perspectives.

Fowler, Virginia C. *Gloria Naylor: In Search of Sanctuary*. New York: Twayne, 1996. Fowler analyzes Naylor's first four novels; she also explains how the Jehovah's Witnesses religion, of which Naylor was a member until she was twenty-five, and Naylor's commitment to feminism have influenced her fiction. Includes an interview that Fowler conducted with Naylor, a bibliography, and a chronology of Naylor's life.

Gates, Henry Louis, Jr., and K. A. Appiah, eds. *Gloria Naylor: Critical Perspectives Past and Present*. New York: Amistad, 1993. Focuses on Naylor's first four novels, with reviews of each book and essays analyzing her work. Two of the essays examine the role of William Shakespeare and of black sisterhood in Naylor's novels.

Matus, Jill L. "Dream, Deferral, and Closure in *The Women of Brewster Place*." *Black American Literature Forum* 24 (Spring, 1990): 49-64. Discusses the women's variety of "dreams" and explores Naylor's intent in communicating their postponement.

Montgomery, Maxine L. "The Fathomless Dream: Gloria Naylor's Use of the Descent Motif in *The Women of Brewster Place*." *CLA Journal* 36 (September, 1992): 1-11. Discusses Naylor's use of the descent motif to explore her characters' search for self-knowledge and their nontraditional lifestyles.

Naylor, Gloria. *Conversations with Gloria Naylor*. Edited by Maxine Lavon Montgomery. Jackson: University Press of Mississippi, 2004. A compilation of previously conducted interviews and conversations with Naylor, in which she addresses a wide range of topics. Includes Naylor's conversations with writers Toni Morrison and Nikki Giovanni.

Wells, Linda, Sandra E. Bowen, and Suzanne Stutman. "'What Shall I Give My Children?' The Role of Mentor in Gloria Naylor's *The Women of Brewster Place* and Paule

Marshall's *Praisesong for the Widow.*" *Explorations in Ethnic Studies* 13 (July, 1990): 41-60. Asserts that Naylor uses a series of mentors who are linked to other mentors by healing communal experiences. Sees Mattie Michael as the central consciousness and the moral agent in the novel. The negative image of men is seen as a product of their selfishness.

Whitt, Margaret Earley. *Understanding Gloria Naylor.* Columbia: University of South Carolina Press, 1998. A thoughtful examination of Naylor's novels, through *The Men of Brewster Place*, which discusses major themes, symbolism, character development, Naylor's critical reputation, and her literary influences.

Wilson, Charles E., Jr. *Gloria Naylor: A Critical Companion.* Westport, Conn.: Greenwood Press, 2001. An analysis of Naylor's first five novels, with a separate chapter devoted to an examination of each book through *The Men of Brewster Place*. The first chapter chronicles the events of Naylor's life, including information obtained in an interview conducted for this book, while another chapter establishes Naylor's place within African American literature.

The Women of Trachis

Author: Sophocles (c. 496-406 B.C.E.)

First produced: Trachinai, c. 435-429 B.C.E.; first published, c. 435-429 B.C.E. (English translation, 1729)

Type of work: Drama

Type of plot: Tragedy

Time of plot: Antiquity

Locale: Trachis

Principal characters:
HERAKLES
DEIANIRA, his wife
HYLLUS, their son
LICHAS, herald of Herakles
IOLE, captive of Herakles
CHORUS OF TRACHINIAN MAIDENS

The Story:

Fifteen long months pass since Deianira has received word from Herakles, her husband, who, when he left on his last journey, gave her a tablet setting forth the disposition of his estate and stating that it was decreed that after a year and three moons pass he will either die or live happily thereafter in untroubled peace. The fated day arrives, and Deianira is filled with foreboding.

Before she can send her son Hyllus to get accurate news of her husband, a messenger, outstripping the herald Lichas, arrives to announce that Herakles is living and will soon appear. Lichas himself follows shortly with a group of captive maidens and, answering Deianira's question, assures her that her husband, alive and sound of limb, is at that time sacrificing the fruits of his victories to great Zeus in fulfillment of a vow made when he took from towered Oechalia the captive women. Deianira is touched by the plight of the captives. Lichas tells her they are from the city ruled by Eurytus, selected by Herakles as chosen possessions for himself and for the gods. He adds, however, that it is not the taking of the city that delays the hero this long time. He is detained in Lydia. Sold into bondage, he passed a year as servant to Omphale, the barbaric queen. Before this bondage, Eurytus, an old friend, so taunted and incensed him that Herakles, encountering Iphitus, one of Eurytus's four sons, without warning hurled him from a cliff. This act roused the ire of Olympian Zeus who, because Herakles slew a foe by treachery and not in fair fight, drove him out to be sold as a slave to Omphale. Those who reviled Herakles are conquered, however, and now Lichas brings the virgins by Herakles' order to Deianira.

A strange pity comes over Deianira as she gazes at the captives. One in particular, Iole, holds her attention. Lichas pretends not to know Iole; Iole herself speaks no word, bearing in silence her grief and suffering. The messenger, however, informs Deianira that Lichas did not tell the truth, which is that Herakles for love of Iole destroyed Eurytus, the maiden's father; that it was not his adventures in Lydia, his serfdom with Omphale, or the death of Iphitus that held him these many moons, but love for this maid. Failing to persuade her father to give up his daughter, Herakles attacked Oechalia, sacked the city, slew Eurytus, and took Iole for his concubine. Deianira, cruelly hurt, calls upon Lichas to tell her everything. He confirms the news. Sorrowfully she asks the herald to wait while she has suitable gifts prepared for Herakles in return for those he sent.

Deianira cannot bear the thought of having another share her husband's affections. Judging it unwise to give way to anger, she thinks of another course. In an old urn she long hid a keepsake of Nessus, the centaur whose work it is to ferry wayfarers across the river Evenus, carrying them in his arms. When Deianira, as a bride, was on her way to Herakles, she, too, was carried across by the centaur, but in midstream he lewdly sought to take her. Her screams brought from the waiting son of Zeus an arrow that pierced the centaur's lungs. Dying, he told Deianira that as the last to be ferried across the river she should profit by receiving from him a love philter made by taking the curdled gore from his wound. This would act as a charm so that Herakles would never find any other woman fairer than she. Now, recalling these words, Deianira selects a festal robe and smears it with the magic ointment. Then she presents the robe to Lichas, telling him he is to instruct Herakles to put it on immediately, before sun or light strikes it, and stand before the people with it on as he makes his sacrifices to the gods.

No sooner does Lichas depart, however, than Deianira feels uneasy because she resorts to magic to win back her husband's love. Quickly her fears are realized. She faithfully follows the instructions of the centaur by preserving the drug unexposed to light or fire or sun until the moment of application. Secretly, indoors, she spread the unguent on the robe with some wool and, folding the gift, placed it securely in a chest. Now, by chance, she throws the tuft of wool on the flagstones in the blazing sun, whereupon there boils up from it clots of foam as it consumes itself and disappears into nothingness. In consternation Deianira realizes that the black-venomed gore, instead of winning anew her husband's love, is dying Nessus's trick to cause his death, and she will be his murderer. Overwhelmed, she determines to end her own life.

Hyllus returns. He sees Herakles receive from Lichas the robe and put it on. Then, when the fierce rays of the sun melt the venom with which the deadly garment is coated, it clings to his body, the sweat bursting out, and, before the assembled company, he writhes in dreadful pain. Herakles in his agony calls out to Lichas, who tells him the robe is Deianira's gift, whereupon the unhappy man seizes the messenger by the foot and dashes out his brains against a rock. When, shouting and shrieking, Herakles calls on Hyllus to carry him away to die where no one might see him, they place him on a ship and bring him to his home.

Hyllus now accuses his mother of her vile deed and calls down on her the vengeance of the Erinyes. Silently Deianira goes indoors and in the bedchamber of Herakles bids fare-

well to her bridal bed. Then with a sword she pierces her heart and dies. Hyllus, told by others that his mother's gift of the robe to Herakles was instigated by the centaur, realizes too late her innocence, and he grieves to lose in one day both mother and father.

Hyllus, still lamenting, leaves, but returns with attendants bearing his father on a litter. Herakles, fighting off the deadly spasms that shake him, entreats his son to end his miserable life. He recalls his great labors and the fact that he never met defeat. Now death comes by a woman's wile. Hyllus tells him that Deianira was innocent of murderous intent in her act, that she wished only to win back his love, that it was the centaur's venom that brought about his undoing, and that Deianira, not wishing to live without him, now lies cold and dead.

Herakles admits that it was foretold that he would perish not by any living being but by a dweller in the realms of the Dead. The prophecy also promised him release from his toils, but he misinterpreted it as meaning a happy life; instead, it portended death, for with death comes the end of toil.

Knowing thus that his death is the will of the gods, Herakles faces it nobly. He bids Hyllus bear him to the peak of Oeta, place him on a great funeral pyre of oak and olive, and ignite it. Hyllus consents to carry his father to his destination and prepare the pyre, but he refuses to light it. Herakles, not pressing him, asks as one other boon that Hyllus take Iole to wife and care for her. Unwillingly, but moved by filial obedience, Hyllus assents. In these dread matters he sees the will of immortal Zeus.

Critical Evaluation:

The Women of Trachis, recounting the last crisis in the life of Herakles, is the only surviving tragedy of Sophocles that ends in death for both of the chief characters. The tragedy also presents the devotion and love of ideal womanhood in Deianira and the heroic endurance and strength of ideal manhood in Herakles. *The Women of Trachis* has as its tragic protagonist not one person but a family of three. For this reason critics sometimes claim that the play lacks unity, since half is devoted to Deianira and half to Herakles, with neither appearing onstage at the same time. To consider this drama properly, however, one must regard the tragedies of Deianira, Herakles, and Hyllus as one large event instigated by the gods, carried out by human will, and transcended in the end by strength of character.

Although the play lacks the smoothness and facility of *Oidipous Tyrannos* (c. 429 B.C.E.; *Oedipus Tyrannus*, 1715), it is significant, and it treats the major problem of Sophocles' dramatic career, that of human freedom. The problem is this:

When events are determined by the will of the gods, as revealed in oracles and prophecies, and by the passionate compulsions of the human animal, freedom lies in learning the truth and accepting it—not passively but with all the force of one's being. For one to be free one must knowingly seek to accomplish one's destiny in harmony with divine law. In Sophocles that destiny is always hard and terrible, which makes the acceptance of it truly ennobling. This problem and its solution are at the heart of *The Women of Trachis*, which was probably written when the dramatist was in his sixties, an age when he looked at life fully and accurately. The play is a mature statement of Sophocles' deepest convictions.

The action moves from ignorance to truth, and from misconceptions to a revelation of the total pattern imposed by divine will. Each of the three tragic characters acts from a lack of understanding and then must confront the awful truth. The audience sees this first in Deianira. Her greatest apprehension in the beginning is that her husband, Herakles, will not live much longer. Then she learns that he is both alive and returning home in triumph. She sympathizes with the most miserable of the captive women, Iole, only to learn that Herakles took Iole as his concubine. Deianira does not find fault with either Iole or Herakles, but determines to win her husband's love by black magic. The potion is made from the poisoned gore of Nessus, the centaur that Herakles killed. After sending the deadly robe to Herakles, she realizes how dangerous it is. When her son Hyllus reviles and curses her for murdering Herakles by slow agony, she knows that she herself accomplished her worst fear. Her knowledge is subject to reversal upon reversal until the original prophecy and dread are fulfilled.

Deianira's character is as much a part of this sequence as fate. She is a fearful, devoted, and rather gullible wife. Her only reason for resorting to magic is to regain Herakles' love, and it wins for her his undying hatred, not to mention Hyllus's condemnation. She does not excuse herself but accepts full responsibility for the deed she commits in ignorance, and she atones for it by suicide, choosing the noble method of stabbing herself. In that acceptance of her guilt and in that atonement, she achieves true freedom. Deianira's tragic courage lifts her above the fate to which the weakness of her character brings her.

Herakles, in an ironic twist, is dying not from a foe but at the hands of a rather pathetic woman, which humiliates him tremendously. He bawls and rages in pain, wishing to murder his wife. As he cites his triumphs in killing beasts and monsters, the audience realizes that the beasts take their revenge through Nessus's poisoned blood. The centaur, the most lustful of creatures, repays Herakles his lust; it is Herakles' bes-tial lust for Iole that precipitates his doom. Ironically, the beast-slayer is possessed of the same violence and lechery as the beasts he killed, and his body is mortally infected with the centaur's gore.

Once again the process of revelation begins. As Herakles learns that his death is being caused by Nessus's cunning, it dawns on him that the prophecy of his death is being completed and that Deianira is an innocent agent of the gods. When this is driven home by Hyllus's penitent and intrepid honesty, Herakles addresses himself to the fact of his death in earnest. He chooses the manner of his death freely, just as his wife does. He determines to be burned alive rather than suffer death by poison passively. In that resolve he shows the same tragic courage as Deianira. He seizes the terrible will of Zeus and makes it his own. The audience is aware that Herakles will be transfigured as a god on his funeral pyre, but the important thing for Sophocles is the heroic determination of Herakles to make his death his own, in which he, too, transcends fate.

The third tragic figure is Hyllus, the son of Herakles and Deianira. Like his parents, he acts in ignorance, must suffer the truth, and make an atonement. Hyllus lays a dreadful curse on his mother, thinking she murdered Herakles out of jealousy and spite. By the time he learns what actually happened, Deianira kills herself, and he bears some of the guilt for her death. He loves both of his parents. Thus, he finds himself in an unbearable situation. He atones in part by braving Herakles' rage to justify his mother's intentions, which in turn leads to Herakles' recognition of the truth. Herakles, the audience recalls, recently dashed out the brains of a hapless messenger. Hyllus's father makes two very hard demands on him and binds him to them by oath. The first is that he build the funeral pyre on which Herakles is to perish, thus taking a hand in the death of his father as well as his mother. The second is that Hyllus marry the woman he loathes—Iole, the "cause" of all the trouble. It seems likely that this forthcoming marriage will put an end to the blood-and-lust syndrome that destroys Hyllus's parents. Hyllus shows his manliness in the fortitude with which he accepts both conditions.

The final statement of the play, "there is nothing here which is not Zeus," expresses Sophocles' faith that while the gods lay down the tragic circumstances of human life and that people fulfill these tragedies through inner compulsion, people can triumph over necessity by strength of character. The divine pattern imposes hopeless suffering, which gives people the opportunity to show their nobility. This is a stern faith, but a stern faith is essential in a hard world.

"Critical Evaluation" by James Weigel, Jr.

Further Reading

Beer, Josh. *Sophocles and the Tragedy of Athenian Democracy*. Westport, Conn.: Praeger, 2004. Analyzes Sophocles' plays within the context of Athenian democracy in the fifth century B.C.E., focusing on the political issues in the dramas. Examines Sophocles' dramatic techniques and how they "revolutionized the concept of dramatic space." Chapter 6 discusses *The Women of Trachis*.

Bowra, C. M. *Sophoclean Tragedy*. Oxford, England: Clarendon Press, 1967. Includes a chapter on each of the seven plays by Sophocles. Discusses the motives and the conflicts of the characters in *The Women of Trachis* and its themes. Explains the plot and gives several lines in the original Greek; includes many lines in English translation.

Garvie, A. F. *The Plays of Sophocles*. Bristol, England: Bristol Classical, 2005. Concise analysis of Sophocles' plays, with a chapter devoted to *The Women of Trachis*. Focuses on Sophocles' tragic thinking, the concept of the Sophoclean hero, and the structure of his plays.

Kirkwood, Gordon MacDonald. *A Study of Sophoclean Drama*. Ithaca, N.Y.: Cornell University Press, 1958. Reprint. 1994. Analysis of Sophocles' structures and methods of dramatic composition. Considers *The Women of Trachis* in context with the other plays of Sophocles for characterization, irony, illustrative forms, and the use of diction and oracles.

Levett, Brad. *Sophocles: Women of Trachis*. London: Duckworth, 2004. A companion to the play, discussing its context, plot, characters, theme, reception, and performance.

Morwood, James. *The Tragedies of Sophocles*. Exeter, England: Bristol Phoenix Press, 2008. Analyzes each of Sophocles' seven extant plays, with chapter 3 devoted to *The Women of Trachis*. Discusses several modern productions and adaptations of the tragedies.

Ringer, Mark. *"Electra" and the Empty Urn: Metatheater and Role Playing in Sophocles*. Chapel Hill: University of North Carolina Press, 1998. Focuses on elements of metatheater, or "theater within theater," and the ironic self-awareness in Sophocles' plays. Analyzes plays-within-plays, characters who are in rivalry with the playwright, and characters who assume roles in order to deceive one another. *The Women of Trachis* is discussed in chapter 4.

Scodel, Ruth. *Sophocles*. Boston: Twayne, 1984. Provides a synopsis of *The Women of Trachis*; discusses the play's structure and the mythological gods and oracles. Considers other works that may have influenced Sophocles. Includes information on the seven plays by Sophocles, a chronology of Sophocles' life, a bibliography, and an index.

Seale, David. *Vision and Stagecraft in Sophocles*. Chicago: University of Chicago Press, 1982. Distinguishes Sophocles from other playwrights of his time and demonstrates his influence on later ones. Considers the theatrical technicalities in the Sophoclean plays. Contains an extended section on *The Women of Trachis* and a long section of notes following it.

Segal, Charles. *Tragedy and Civilization: An Interpretation of Sophocles*. Cambridge, Mass.: Harvard University Press, 1981. Treats all of Sophocles' plays. Considers the Odyssean themes in *The Women of Trachis*; elaborates on the plot and possible meanings.

Wonderland

Author: Joyce Carol Oates (1938-   )
First published: 1971
Type of work: Novel
Type of plot: Psychological realism
Time of plot: 1939-1971
Locale: Upstate New York; Ann Arbor, Michigan; Chicago; Wisconsin; New York City; Toronto, Ontario, Canada

Principal characters:
JESSE HARTE, an orphan, later Jesse Vogel
DR. KARL PEDERSEN, his adoptive father
MARY PEDERSEN, Dr. Pedersen's wife
BENJAMIN CADY, Jesse's college professor
RODERICK PERRAULT, Jesse's supervising surgeon
HELENE CADY, Cady's daughter, later Jesse's wife
T. W. MONK, a student and poet
SHELLEY VOGEL, Jesse and Helene's daughter
REVA DENK, Jesse's lover

The Story:

One December day, fourteen-year-old Jesse Harte comes home to find his family brutally murdered and his crazed, chronically unemployed, and spiritually desolate father coming after him with a shotgun. Jesse barely escapes through a window; his father's subsequent suicide leaves him to make his way alone as a traumatized orphan. He first goes to live with his silent, bitter grandfather, where he takes the surname Vogel for a time. That proves to be unacceptable, so he moves on to his uncomprehending cousins, and then to an orphanage.

Eventually, he encounters and comes to live with the Pedersen family. The father, Karl, is a dogmatic morphine-addicted doctor/mystic; the mother, Mary, is an obsequious alcoholic; the son, Frederich, is a blithering piano virtuoso; and the daughter, Hilda, is an angry mathematical genius. The Pedersens are all grotesquely obese, and, with them, Jesse swells accordingly. He takes their surname and their ways and strives to become one of them. He never gives himself completely, however, to the doctor's maniacal and philosophical egoism. In the end, after helping Mrs. Pedersen in an aborted attempt to escape, Jesse is disowned, dislocated, and, again, left homeless and nameless.

He once again becomes Jesse Vogel. He attends college at the University of Michigan, studying medicine. An excellent student, he comes under the tutelage and influence of Dr. Benjamin Cady, Dr. Roderick Perrault, and an errant scientist-poet named T. W. Monk. Each of these men espouses a distinct and limited worldview—empiricism, behaviorism, and nihilism, respectively. Cady takes a mechanistic view of human life; Perrault believes in the interchangeability of personalities and in the ethical merits of brain transplants; and Monk challenges the premise of Jesse's career with Monk's desire for death, disdain for creativity, and adulation of chaos. While Jesse partially adopts each philosophical outlook in turn, he ultimately proves unable to fully possess or embody any of them.

Nevertheless, he becomes a brilliant surgeon, marries Cady's daughter Helene and fathers two daughters, Shelley and Jeanne. In time, the marriage grows unfulfilling, and Jesse becomes inexplicably obsessed with Reva Denk, a woman he encounters at a chance moment in the emergency room, where they both witness a man's self-castration. Obsessed with Reva, Jesse decides impulsively to begin a new life with her. Once she agrees, however, he equally impulsively reverses his determination and, in a measured frenzy, decides to return at once to his wife and his home in Chicago.

Years later, Jesse and Helene's older daughter Shelley runs away with her boyfriend Noel. Shelley taunts Jesse with long letters from various locales across the country, where she and Noel live and travel, lost in poverty, illness, aimlessness, and drug addiction. The letters are filled with probing questions, detailed reminiscences, sharp accusations, and enigmatic expressions of love. Jesse sets out in search of Shelley and finally catches up with her in Toronto, Canada, among a community of draft dodgers, where he confronts her in an effort to rescue her from her self-inflicted oblivion and bring her home. In an alternate ending published in the hardcover edition of the novel, Jesse and Shelley are floating out in a rowboat on a Toronto lake, and Shelley's death seems imminent.

Critical Evaluation:

Wonderland is divided into three sections. Book 1, entitled "Variations on an American Hymn," follows Jesse's journey from family tragedy through life with the Pedersens; book 2, "The Finite Passing of an Infinite Passion" (a phrase drawn from the Danish philosopher Søren Kierkegaard), depicts his academic career, marriage, and relationships with Monk and Reva; and book 3, "Dreaming America," is an account, through letters and prose, of Jesse's search for Shelley. As the titles imply, Joyce Carol Oates is concerned with the nature of American passion and dreams.

Oates uses Lewis Carroll's *Alice's Adventures in Wonderland* (1865) and *Through the Looking-Glass and What Alice Found There* (1871) as thematic sources for her novel. The Alice novels were important influences in Oates's literary development, and she has thoroughly investigated their psychological and dramatic structures. Thus, like Alice, Jesse bursts into new worlds and must deal with characters that verge on caricatures. The Pedersens, Monk, and others in *Wonderland* parallel Alice's Mad Hatter, Red Queen, Cheshire Cat, and other Carroll creations. Oates takes Carroll's thematic framework and applies it sharply and imaginatively to the American scene.

That scene is Oates's "Wonderland." It is the name of the new shopping mall where the dissatisfied Helene meets her lover. "Wonderland" is the name of a poem by T. W. Monk that describes a dizzying, visceral, primal emergence and that is set as a prologue to the novel. In a larger sense, "Wonderland" is an Oatesian world of unnatural proportions where, like the Pedersens' obesity and the doctors' fanaticism, ideas, emotions, and aspirations are often ridiculously reduced or horrendously magnified. The portraits Oates creates are exaggerated, narcissistic, and often very comical.

The game of proportions contributes to the novel's schizophrenic character. At times it is recognizable naturalism, detailing life-sized actions, thoughts, and events; at other times it is nearly psychedelic surrealism, full of swirling movements and syncopated rhythms, more evocative of a dream or of a nightmare than of documentary reality. Throughout *Wonderland*, Oates's language and imagery are palpable and graphic. Certain scenes are striking and link the physical manifestations of excess to the emotional phenomena of obsession. Hilda Pedersen gluttonously devours chocolates during a mathematical competition. Helene's obsession with her own reproductive capacities turns to panic during a gynecological examination. A man, who turns out to be Reva Denk's lover, arrives at Jesse's hospital self-mutilated. Later Jesse, tracking Reva to a small town in Wisconsin and agreeing to marry her and to father her child, symbolically lacerates himself with a rusty razor before abandoning her altogether.

Wonderland's more graphic scenes reinforce the thematic presence of science and medicine as means of knowing and experiencing life. There are recurrent perceptions of living organisms as reduced to their simplest form, protoplasm, and as beings that emerge from and consume other beings. The concept of "homeostasis" (the natural tendency toward balance), which Dr. Pedersen asks Jesse to explain one evening at the dinner table, provides a standard for the desirable pattern of functioning that Jesse, not to mention the characters who surround him, cannot achieve. Psychological balance is rare in *Wonderland*, for the Oatesian universe is subject to constant and sudden flux and revolution.

Amid this whirlwind, Jesse is virtually lost, for he lacks an inherent personality. Before his character is definitively established—in the novel or in his life—his father's atrocities thrust him into the world, scrambling to pick up the shattered pieces of his identity. Jesse embarks on a lifelong search for a father figure, a permanent home, true love, and a viable belief system. In the process, he goes through a series of impressive but ultimately vacant surrogates and unwittingly becomes a reflection or an embodiment of the people and ideas around him. Thus, the other characters take on the dimensions of allegory. They become emotional or philosophical options for him to review and try, but his movement through and experience of them, like his movement from name to name and home to home, leaves him at the novel's end only barely less innocent and passive than he was at its start. Ultimately, his search for identity and his longing for a sense of solidity in his existence are the only reliable facts of his life.

Ironically, however, what Jesse learns from those who absorb or torment him is how to absorb others as well. The entire third book, "Dreaming America," focuses on an impulse

that is opposite to the aspirations prevalent throughout the first two books: Shelley's desire to disappear, to become smaller, to simplify, to be left alone, to refuse to commit to love or family or place or belief. In pursuing that desire, she robs Jesse of the only power—illusory at best—that he gains in his life.

Wonderland bears certain characteristic markings of the Oatesian novel. Like *A Garden of Earthly Delights* (1967), it follows several generations of a family through stages of rage, searching, and emptiness. Like *The Assassins: A Book of Hours* (1975), it offers critical comment on the lust for knowledge and for power. It spans a particular period of American political and economic history and is set against a backdrop of that history, including such events as the technological revolution, the assassination of John F. Kennedy, and the Vietnam conflict. It moves irregularly, with sudden shifts and changes; rather than a unified story, it is built on numerous episodes, shifting viewpoints, and quick juxtapositions.

Wonderland also stakes its own ground on the Oatesian landscape. It is stylistically unnaturalistic, its commentary verges on the broadly satirical, and its concern for the issues of dislocation and identity are fully focused on a single central character. Oates has also been criticized for the novel's unsatisfactory conclusion; in both versions it has been deemed unequal to the novel's overall sharpness and color. Oates herself noted that *Wonderland* "is the first novel I have written that doesn't end in violence, that doesn't liberate the hero through violence, and therefore there is still a sickish, despairing, confusing atmosphere about it." There is certainly plenty of violence in the novel, and, given the amount of criticism Oates has received for being such a violent writer (criticism she considers blatantly sexist), it is not certain that Jesse's violent liberation would have assuaged all critics. Nevertheless, in *Wonderland*, Oates meditates vividly and passionately on the American Dream, on the way people navigate the narrow channel between the psychological and material worlds, and on how the individual identity is forged.

Barry Mann

Further Reading

Cologne-Brookes, Gavin. *Dark Eyes on America: The Novels of Joyce Carol Oates*. Baton Rouge: Louisiana State University Press, 2005. Traces the evolution of Oates's novels, demonstrating how she moved from abstract introspection to a more pragmatic concern with understanding personal and social problems and possibilities.

Creighton, Joanne V. *Joyce Carol Oates*. Boston: G. K. Hall, 1979. Creighton discusses *Wonderland* in the context of

Oates's earlier novels and in tandem with *Do with Me What You Will* (1973). She explores the series of father figures that the novel offers and rejects, as well as its parallels to *Alice's Adventures in Wonderland*.

Daly, Brenda. *Lavish Self-Divisions: The Novels of Joyce Carol Oates*. Jackson: University Press of Mississippi, 1996. Traces the development of Oates's female characters from father-identified daughters in the 1960's to self-identified women in the 1980's. Chapter 3 is devoted to a discussion of *Wonderland*.

Friedman, Ellen G. *Joyce Carol Oates*. New York: Ungar, 1980. An exploration of alienation through Oates's first nine novels. In the chapter entitled "Journey from the 'I' to the Eye: *Wonderland*," Friedman looks at the novel's links with *Alice's Adventures in Wonderland* and its treatment of the individual's relationship to the external world.

Grant, Mary Kathryn. *The Tragic Vision of Joyce Carol Oates*. Durham, N.C.: Duke University Press, 1978. Grant's long essay interweaves discussion of several Oates novels and other writings into a meditation on the elements of violence and of tragedy in modern America. Her references to *Wonderland* bring out themes of self-mutilation, spiritual homelessness, and the alienation of urban life.

Johnson, Greg. *Invisible Writer: A Biography of Joyce Carol Oates*. New York: Dutton, 1998. Johnson recounts the events of Oates's life and describes how she transforms them in her fiction.

Oates, Joyce Carol. *The Faith of a Writer: Life, Craft, Art*. New York: Ecco, 2003. Reprints twelve essays and an interview in which Oates discusses the writing life.

_____. *Joyce Carol Oates: Conversations, 1970-2006*. Edited by Greg Johnson. New York: W. W. Norton, 2006. In this collection of reprinted interviews, Oates discusses literature, her work, and her life.

Wagner, Linda, ed. *Critical Essays on Joyce Carol Oates*. Boston: G. K. Hall, 1979. A diverse anthology of seventeen reviews and eleven essays spanning the Oates oeuvre. In addition to excerpts from the other entries in this bibliography, discussions of *Wonderland* are found in a skeptical *Newsweek* review, in an essay by Robert H. Fossum exploring the themes of control and salvation, and in Joanne V. Creighton's piece examining Oates's women.

Waller, G. F. *Dreaming America: Obsession and Transcendence in the Fiction of Joyce Carol Oates*. Baton Rouge: Louisiana State University Press, 1979. Waller's chapter on *Wonderland* discusses the novel as social commentary on some of the more manifest obsessions of modern American life—materialism, sex, and violence—treated with a unique mixture of surrealism and satire.

Woodcutters

Author: Thomas Bernhard (1931-1989)
First published: Holzfällen: Eine Erregung, 1984
   (English translation, 1987)
Type of work: Novel
Type of plot: Social realism
Time of plot: 1980's
Locale: Vienna

Principal characters:
THE NARRATOR, a writer
AUERSBERGER, a composer
HIS WIFE, a wealthy heir
JOANA, a deceased actor and dancer
JEANNIE BILLROTH, a writer
ANNA SCHREKER, another writer
AN ACTOR, appearing at the Burgtheater

The Story:

One evening the Auersbergers give a so-called artistic dinner at their home in the Gentzgasse to honor the Actor who is playing the role of Ekdal in a performance of Henrik Ibsen's *Vildanden* (1884; *The Wild Duck*, 1891) at the Burgtheater in Vienna. The nameless narrator observes the guests in the music room from his vantage point in a wing chair (in German, an *Ohrensessel*, literally an easy chair with ears) situated in a dimly lighted anteroom.

The narrator's invitation to this gathering is the result of a fortuitous meeting with his hosts several days earlier in Vienna's inner city. The Auersbergers assumed the role of the city's patrons of "high culture" during the past two decades, a position that gives them high status in Viennese society. The narrator was a member of their circle twenty-five years earlier, but he fled to London when he realized that his fellow artists merely continued to live off their early reputations rather than develop their artistry.

Sitting in his wing chair and speaking only to himself, the narrator directs his greatest malevolence toward Auersberger, who was once described as a "composer in the Anton von Webern tradition." In all the intervening years he never progressed musically beyond being a poor imitator of that composer. At the time of the dinner he is known for such works as his four-minute chorus, twelve-minute opera, three-minute cantata, and even a one-second opera. On the evening of the dinner Auersberger contributes nothing of artistic value to the conversation. Indeed, the narrator observes that he just becomes more and more inebriated, to the point of falling asleep in the presence of his guests, who are also all "well-known" and "celebrated" artists. His wife is described as a light-minded but charming host who bubbles about the "distinguished" Actor while serving more champagne every fifteen minutes.

The narrator expresses great passion for Joana, a dancer and actor whose funeral he attended earlier that day. Joana showed great talent thirty years earlier when she first established herself in Vienna. Rather than pursuing her own career, however, she assisted in making her husband a world-renowned artist. Once his position was secure, he left Joana, a trauma from which she never recovered. She succumbed to alcoholism, which eventually drove her to suicide. In reflecting on her life, on the funeral earlier that day, and on Ravel's *Bolero*, which the Auersbergers were playing a recording of that evening, the narrator decides that the evening's gathering is a requiem for Joana.

The guests wait several hours before the Actor finally arrives after midnight. At that point, the narrator's vantage point shifts from the anteroom to the dining room table. Rather than expose himself to the Actor's pompousness and to hearing pretentious nonsense about the Burgtheater tradition, the narrator employs Jeannie Billroth as his pettifogger.

Jeannie is the spokesperson for and representative of the Viennese literary establishment that evening. For many years she has fancied herself to be the brilliant Virginia Woolf of Vienna. She successfully maneuvers the cultural and political powers of the city to award her literary prizes for her few novels, which are of questionable merit, and for her service as editor of a minor literary journal. That evening she is supported by her longtime friend and even less-competent writer, the high school teacher Anna Schreker, who assumes

for herself the pose of being the local Gertrude Stein and Marianne Moore.

At dinner, Jeannie attempts to draw the Actor into one of her "intellectual conversations," but to no avail. Finally she confronts the tired and aging Actor with the question: "Do you think now at the end of your life that you've found fulfillment in your art?" The Actor is outraged and refuses to speak to her any longer, but the narrator is delighted that Jeannie is finally berated for the repulsive insolence she has exhibited her entire life.

The Actor, reflecting on Jeannie's attack and wondering why he has to contend with the never-ending artificiality of life in the theater, becomes meditative. His ideal, he philosophizes, was not to be on the stage speaking the words others wrote but to be at home in nature, to enter deep into and yield himself to the forest: "The forest, the virgin forest, the life of a woodcutter—that has always been my ideal." The narrator finds that the Actor's pronouncement has great insight, and as he leaves the gathering, he resolves to write about this "artistic dinner" at once.

Critical Evaluation:

Thomas Bernhard, one of the most prolific and provocative writers of German literature, published about fifty volumes, representing all the major genres of literature. He is best known for his ten novels, fourteen plays, and seven volumes of memoirs, and most of his prose and dramatic works were translated into English and the other world languages. In his work and in his life, Bernhard publicly castigated the values, institutions, and cultural and political personalities in post-World War II Austria.

The publication of a Bernhard novel or the premiere of one of his plays was always a noteworthy event in Austria. Indeed, *Woodcutters*, a *roman à clef*, unleashed a tumultuous scandal in Austria because the major characters were so thinly disguised. The Austrian writer Jeannie Ebner was Jeannie Billroth, Maja Lampersberg was Auersberger's wife, the choreographer Joana Thul was Joana, and Bernhard himself was clearly the narrator. Gerhard Lampersberg, the composer portrayed in the character of Auersberger, sued for defamation of character, to which Bernhard responded by prohibiting the sale of all his books in Austria for the next fifty years. Newspaper editors and literary critics entered the fracas with debates on the freedom of expression in the arts and for the press. By the time the entire affair was concluded three months later, even more copies of the novel had been sold than anticipated by the publisher.

It is, however, ultimately less important to know about the historical figures being portrayed or the specific Austrian institutions being criticized than it is to experience the novel as a work of art and as a philosophical statement. Bernhard is intent on exposing the manner in which artists can become famous through institutions that award literary prizes, whereupon the artists use that commendation, rather than honest attempts at creative work, to promote themselves. In criticizing the institution of the Burgtheater, Bernhard wants to expose the unjustified dictatorship that cultural institutions can bring about merely by virtue of their long and well-entrenched position in society. Bernhard believes that neither artists nor artistic institutions should automatically be granted the right to speak and that they should continually be subjected to scrutiny and critical evaluation. Bernhard includes himself as one of those artists whose work must constantly be validated, because he witnessed too many artists who fell prey to dangerous institutions and ideologies.

Woodcutters exposes a dilemma. The true and honest artist is here represented most forcefully by the character of Joana. The reader is told that there is absolutely no question that she has extraordinary artistic talent, but it is also clear that she is too sensitive to survive in her society. After living a marginal and precarious life in the artistic world, she is finally forced to live in her mountain retreat—among ignorant woodcutters—with whom she is unable to communicate her art. This environment brings about her eventual destruction through suicide. Thus the Actor—who, after all, must remain a public figure in society—could not survive if he were to pursue his ideal of "The forest, the virgin forest, the life of a woodcutter."

At the conclusion of the novel, the reader is momentarily led to believe that the narrator experiences euphoria and insight, for he seems to discard his long-standing detestation for all whom he revisits in his thoughts that evening at the "artistic dinner." In his jubilation, however, he fails to provide a convincing statement of purpose. The question remains open whether it is the pessimist Thomas Bernhard who wants to write "something at once, no matter what . . . before it's too late?" That might be the novel that—like Ibsen's drama—would remove the veil of illusion and destroy the private fantasies that every human being needs to make life bearable.

Thomas H. Falk

Further Reading

Demetz, Peter. "Thomas Bernhard: The Dark Side of Life." In *After the Fires: Recent Writing in the Germanies, Austria, and Switzerland*. San Diego, Calif.: Harcourt Brace Jovanovich, 1986. This comprehensive survey of German literature since 1945 includes a chapter on the important role that Bernhard has played in defining new directions in literature.

Dowden, Stephen D. *Understanding Thomas Bernhard*. Columbia: University of South Carolina Press, 1991. An excellent and complete introduction to the life and works of Bernhard. Dowden correctly places *Woodcutters*, along with the five-volume memoirs, in the chapter on the autobiographical works.

Fetz, Gerald. "Thomas Bernhard and the 'Modern Novel.'" In *The Modern German Novel*, edited by Keith Bullivant. New York: Berg, 1987. A critical analysis of the eight major prose works published between 1963 and 1985, concentrating on the uniqueness of Bernhard's contribution to the genre of the modern novel.

Honegger, Gitta. *Thomas Bernhard: The Making of an Austrian*. New Haven, Conn.: Yale University Press, 2001. The first comprehensive biography of Bernhard in English, it examines the complex connections of Bernhard's work with the geographical, political, and cultural landscape of twentieth century Austria.

Konzett, Matthias. *The Rhetoric of National Dissent in Thomas Bernhard, Peter Handke, and Elfriede Jelinek*. New York: Camden House, 2000. Konzett analyzes how the three Austrian writers have created new literary strategies in order to expose and to dismantle conventional ideas that impede the development of multicultural awareness and identity.

_____, ed. *A Companion to the Works of Thomas Bernhard*. Rochester, N.Y.: Camden House, 2002. Collection of essays examining numerous aspects of Bernhard's work, including his aesthetic sensibility, his impact on Austrian literature, his relation to the legacy of Austrian Jewish culture, and his cosmopolitanism.

Long, Jonathan James. *The Novels of Thomas Bernhard: Form and Its Function*. Rochester, N.Y.: Camden House, 2001. Long's study aims to be an accessible introduction to Bernhard's novels for an English-speaking audience. He devotes chapter 6 to an analysis of *Woodcutters*.

Ryan, Simon. "New Directions in the Austrian Novel." In *The Modern German Novel*, edited by Keith Bullivant. New York: Berg, 1987. An excellent survey of the experimentation in language and in writing that has become the hallmark of Austrian literature since the 1960's. This article should be read in conjunction with Fetz's study of Bernhard's novels.

The Woodlanders

Author: Thomas Hardy (1840-1928)
First published: serial, 1886-1887; book, 1887
Type of work: Novel
Type of plot: Social realism
Time of plot: Nineteenth century
Locale: Rural England

Principal characters:
GEORGE MELBURY, a timber merchant
GRACE MELBURY, his daughter
GILES WINTERBORNE, a traveling farmer
FELICE CHARMOND, a lady of the manor
EDGAR FITZPIERS, a doctor

The Story:

The timber merchant George Melbury spares no expense in educating his only daughter, Grace. She was away from home for one year, and he is eagerly awaiting her return. Giles Winterborne, a traveling farmer and apple grower, also looks forward to Grace's homecoming. Mr. Melbury wronged Giles's father many years before; to atone for this, he half promises Giles that he should have Grace for his wife.

When Grace returns, it is immediately evident that she is much too cultured and refined for the ways of a simple farmer. However, Grace knows that her father promised her to Giles, and she means to go through with it even though she shrinks a little from his plainness. Mr. Melbury is the most concerned. He is an honorable man and likes Giles, but he loves his only child above everything else. He cannot bear to see her throw herself away when she can marry better.

Giles agrees that he is not worthy of Grace, and so the three vacillate, no one wanting to make a decision. Then through a series of unfortunate and unforeseen circumstances, Giles loses the houses that ensured his livelihood. His loss decides the matter. Although Mr. Melbury can easily support them both, it is unthinkable that such a lady as Grace should be tied to a man without a steady income. However, when her father tells her that she must forget Giles, Grace finds herself for the first time thinking of her would-be lover with real affection.

The local doctor, Edgar Fitzpiers, is the descendant of a formerly fine family and in his own right a brilliant and charming man. The local folk thinks he consorts with the devil, for he performs many unusual experiments. From the first time that Edgar sees Grace, he is enchanted with her beauty and her bearing. At first, he thinks she must be the lady of the manor, Mrs. Charmond, for he cannot believe that the daughter of a merchant can be so well-educated and charming. Before long, the two young people meet, and Edgar asks Grace's father for her hand. Mr. Melbury gladly gives his permission, for Edgar is far above Grace in position. Despite his sorrow at disappointing Giles and at failing to keep his pledge, Mr. Melbury encourages Grace to accept Edgar. She always obeys her father in all things, so she accepts Edgar even as she realizes that she is growing fonder of Giles by the day.

When the young couple return from a long honeymoon, they settle in a newly decorated wing of her father's house. Edgar continues his practice. It grows alarmingly smaller, however, for the country folk who once looked up to him now consider him one of their own. He decides that perhaps he should accept a practice in a neighboring town.

Before he can make a final decision on this question, Mrs. Felice Charmond enters the picture. The lady of the manor is well known for her many love affairs and for her questionable reputation. When she has a slight accident and sends for Edgar, he is attracted to her immediately. The few scratches she suffers are enough to take him to her house day after day, until even the servants and farmers are talking about them. At last, Mr. Melbury decides he cannot stand idly by and see his daughter suffer; he appeals in person to Mrs. Charmond to leave Edgar alone. Grace herself is rather immune to the whole affair, for she does not care enough for her husband to suffer great jealousy.

The climax to the situation comes when Mr. Melbury finds Edgar after he is thrown from a horse near Mrs. Charmond's home. Mr. Melbury picks him up and places him on his own mount, but Edgar is drunk and unaware that he is riding with his father-in-law. He berates Mr. Melbury and Grace as ignorant peasants and curses his ill luck in having married beneath himself. His drunken ravings are too much for the kindhearted merchant, who throws Edgar off the horse and rides away. When he comes to, Edgar, who was injured in the first fall, makes his way to Mrs. Charmond and begs her to hide him until he can travel. He must now leave the district; there can be no forgiveness for his many sins.

Mrs. Charmond leaves her home to travel on the Continent. Before long, there are rumors that Edgar is with her. Grace remains stoic. Unknown to her husband, she is aware that he had an affair with a peasant girl in the neighborhood before his marriage. She would let things stand, but an unscrupulous lawyer persuades her father that a new law will permit her to divorce Edgar. While he is making arrangements for the divorce, Mr. Melbury encourages both Giles and Grace to renew their old plans to marry. By that time, they are both sure that they love each other, but they are more cautious than Grace's father. Thus when the word comes that she cannot be free of her husband, they are resigned to their unhappiness.

Grace and Giles do resume the friendship they knew since childhood, but decorously in all respects, for neither wishes a hint of scandal to touch the other. Many months later, Grace hears from her husband that he wants her to live with him again. Mrs. Charmond is dead, killed by a thwarted lover who afterward commits suicide. Edgar does not mention this fact, but a newspaper article informs them of the whole story. Grace and her father decide she should not meet Edgar as he asked, so he comes to their home.

When Grace hears Edgar approaching, she slips out of the house and runs into the woods. Stumbling and afraid, she comes at last to the hut occupied by Giles. Learning that she does not wish to see her husband, Giles installs her in his hut and goes out into the rain to sleep. What Grace does not know is that Giles is very ill of a fever, and a few days and nights in the cold rain make him desperately ill. When she finds her faithful friend so ill, she runs for Edgar, forgetting her desire not to see him in her anxiety for Giles. Edgar returns with her, but there is nothing to be done. Grace holds her love in her arms as he dies, seeming unaware that her husband is present.

For a long time, Grace will not listen to her husband's pleas to return to him. She wants to hurt him as she was hurt, and she tells him that she and Giles lived together those last few days. Even before he learns that her self-accusation is not true, Edgar realizes that he truly loves her. When a man trap, set for Edgar by the husband of the peasant girl he once wronged, almost catches Grace in its steel jaws, Edgar helps his wife to safety. After he tells her that he bought a practice at a great distance from her old home and that he will be a faithful husband, devoting himself to her happiness, she goes away with him. She intends to be a good wife, but part of her remains with Giles in the country churchyard grave.

Critical Evaluation:

Written between *The Mayor of Casterbridge* (1886) and *Tess of the D'Urbervilles* (1891), this novel, with its plot full of melodramatic excess, is neither strict tragedy nor comedy, nor does it have the depth or majesty of Thomas Hardy's later works. Rather, in its efforts to combine realism and sensationalism, it exhibits affinities with such earlier novels as *Desperate Remedies* (1871).

The oppressively enclosed society of Hintock, where the woodlanders dwell, is one of contrasting sets of individuals, both rural and urban. Giles Winterborne, Marty South, George Melbury, and the workers are opposed to the exotic Felice Charmond of Hintock Manor and Edgar Fitzpiers, the new doctor. Grace Melbury vacillates between the two groups, finally committing herself, after the death of Giles, presumably to life with Fitzpiers in another area; Hardy leaves the end of the novel rather ambiguous.

The story revolves not only around Grace's decisions and indecisions but also around those of Fitzpiers, who is trapped in marriage with Grace at the same time he is having an affair with Felice; around those of Mr. Melbury, who cannot make up his mind whether to marry his daughter to the apple grower or to the doctor; and around those of Felice, who cannot settle on one lover.

Most events in the novel take place in dense woods, on forest paths, or in remote huts almost hidden by foliage. Trees and undergrowth are so omnipresent as to appear stifling. Hintock dwellers plant, trim, and tend trees, fell them at maturity, and strip the bark to sell. The woods have utilitarian as well as symbolic significance. They are real, and so are Giles and Marty, who accept with stolid, earthlike quality their fate of endless hard work. The woodland here lacks the gentleness and beauty of that in *Under the Greenwood Tree* (1872); it demands a high price from those who make it their living. The characters are compared implicitly to trees and plants: Giles and Marty are the indigenous trees, Felice and Fitzpiers the imported ones that finally uproot themselves and seek climates more favorable to their growth.

After an almost unbelievable network of promises made and broken, infidelities, romantic seductions, and accidental deaths, Grace and the repentant Fitzpiers are left to repair their ill-starred marriage. The last chapter, however, points to no satisfactory or simple solution. Hardy does not extol their renewed love; instead, he focuses on Marty's devoted soliloquy as she places flowers on Giles's grave. She, too, loved him faithfully. In contrast to other women in the novel, she is the epitome of self-sacrifice, and it is Marty whom Hardy leaves with the reader, perhaps embodying in her the residual human values when he comments, "she touched sublimity at points, and looked almost like a being who had rejected . . . the attribute of sex for the loftier quality of abstract humanism." Marty, however, is more a figure of stoic resignation than of sublimity; and even Giles, despite his loyalty and sacrifice for Grace, does not attain tragic stature.

Further Reading

Boumelha, Penny. *Thomas Hardy and Women: Sexual Ideology and Narrative Form*. Totowa, N.J.: Barnes & Noble, 1982. Comparison of contemporary notions of women with Hardy's view. Includes a chapter on *The Woodlanders*, which notes elements of disparate genres and treats the novel's self-consciousness and its echoes of pastoral elegy. Also points out the realistic treatment of sex and marriage.

Brooks, Jean R. *Thomas Hardy: The Poetic Structure*. Ithaca, N.Y.: Cornell University Press, 1971. Includes a chapter on *The Woodlanders*, which emphasizes the organic connection between plot and place. Stresses social hierarchies in comparison with natural environment. Lucid explication of characters and themes and of the interconnections of natural, human, and cosmic themes.

Daleski, H. M. *Thomas Hardy and Paradoxes of Love*. Columbia: University of Missouri Press, 1997. Daleski reevaluates the treatment of gender in Hardy's novels, defending the author from charges of sexism and maintaining that some of Hardy's female characters are depicted sympathetically. Daleski argues that Hardy is the premodern precursor of sexual failures and catastrophic ends.

Kramer, Dale, ed. *The Cambridge Companion to Thomas Hardy*. New York: Cambridge University Press, 1999. An essential introduction and general overview of all Hardy's work and specific demonstrations of Hardy's ideas and literary skills. Individual essays explore Hardy's biography, aesthetics, and the impact on his work of developments in science, religion, and philosophy in the late nineteenth century. The volume also contains a detailed chronology of Hardy's life and Penny Boumelha's essay "The Patriarchy of Class: *Under the Greenwood Tree, Far from the Madding Crowd, The Woodlanders*."

Kramer, Dale, and Nancy Marck, eds. *Critical Essays on Thomas Hardy: The Novels*. Boston: G. K. Hall, 1990. Helpful overview. Includes a chapter on *The Woodlanders* that synthesizes earlier criticism and analyzes divisions in characters that reflect Hardy's conflicts. Stresses a strand of "secret humor" that keeps the novel realistic.

Mallett, Phillip, ed. *The Achievement of Thomas Hardy*. New York: St. Martin's Press, 2000. A collection of essays that analyze some of the novels and other works and discuss Hardy and nature, the architecture of Hardy, and the presence of the poet in his novels, among other topics. Includes bibliography and index.

Moore, Kevin Z. *The Descent of the Imagination: Postromantic Culture in the Later Novels of Thomas Hardy*. New York: New York University Press, 1990. Approaches Hardy's relationship to and departure from Romanticism. Concludes that *The Woodlanders* represents William Wordsworth's crossroads of British culture, where choices are forced between the culturally antithetical railway and the woodland.

Page, Norman, ed. *Oxford Reader's Companion to Hardy*. New York: Oxford University Press, 2000. An encyclopedia containing three hundred alphabetically arranged entries examining Hardy's work and discussing his family and friends, important places in his life and work, his influences, critical approaches to his writings, and a history of his works' publication. Also includes a chronology of his life, lists of places and characters in his fiction, a glossary, and a bibliography.

Sumner, Rosemary. *Thomas Hardy: Psychological Novelist*. New York: St. Martin's Press, 1981. Analyzes the character of Grace Melbury as a divided woman, an educated woman in a static village. Points out that Hardy drew Grace with clinical precision. Also treats the "modern" elements of *The Woodlanders* and notes that surface conflicts reflect deeper divisions.

Tomalin, Claire. *Thomas Hardy*. New York: Penguin Books, 2007. This thorough and finely written biography by a respected Hardy scholar illuminates the novelist's efforts to indict the malice, neglect, and ignorance of his fellow human beings. Tomalin also discusses aspects of his life that are apparent in his literary works.

Works and Days

Author: Hesiod (fl. c. 700 B.C.E.)
First transcribed: Erga kai Emerai, c. 700 B.C.E.
   (English translation, 1618)
Type of work: Poetry

The details of Hesiod's biography at times overshadow his contributions to the literary tradition. Whether he was a contemporary of Homer (proven unlikely by careful linguistic analysis); whether he ever bested the author of the *Iliad* (c. 750 B.C.E.; English translation, 1611) and *Odyssey* (c. 725 B.C.E.; English translation, 1614) in a poetry contest (equally unlikely); even whether the brother to whom *Works and Days* is addressed actually lived (a fact questioned skillfully by twentieth century scholar Gilbert Murray)—all are of little importance in comparison to his works, especially his long didactic poem on the joys and vicissitudes of the agricultural life. In *Works and Days*, Hesiod explains how the people of his day fit into a cosmos peopled by gods who interact frequently, if indirectly, with them and with the creatures of the natural world. His advice, sometimes philosophical, sometimes extremely practical, shows how one can live a life that can be at some times happy, at all times virtuous.

Perhaps the best way to appreciate the significance of Hesiod's accomplishment is to compare his work to that of Homer. The latter fills his stories with heroes and gods engaged in political and military struggles; personal bravery, cunning, and might serve as measures of greatness. By contrast, Hesiod focuses on the commonplace, on life outside the limelight of national issues and international conflict. Hesiod is the first in the history of Western civilization to think earnestly about problems of conduct and to embody these thoughts in literary form. Hesiod is the first writer in Greek history to judge deeds by their rightness and not their strength, brilliance, or cleverness. In fact, Hesiod consciously set out to oppose the Homeric ideal in his works, becoming in the process the champion of the commoner and the proponent of righteous living. Numerous scholars have noted the similarities between Hesiod's moralizing and the works of the Hebrew prophets and teachers whose admonitions and prescriptions fill the pages of the Old Testament.

The Western literary tradition has come to venerate the Homeric writings, but the significance of Hesiod's investigation of the moral dimensions of human nature should not be overlooked. The immediate source for Vergil's *Georgics* (36-29 B.C.E.), *Works and Days* is also the first work of a tradition that finds exponents in every century: The pastoral poems of the Greeks and Romans and their European inheritors and moralistic poems owe much to this Greek ancestor, who believed that people should be judged by the strength of their character rather than by their might in deeds.

Facts about the existence of a writer who flourished more than two thousand years ago are hard to find. Herodotus, liking to exaggerate the antiquity of people, wrote that Hesiod lived "not more than four hundred years before my time," putting him about 850 B.C.E. Most scholars, however, are inclined to place him about a century later.

At any rate, Homer and Hesiod left the only Greek writing of the epic age. It is clear from Homeric influences in Hesiod that Homer came first. In *Works and Days*, the gods are contemporary, directly influencing life in Boeotia. Hesiod speaks about his own environment. From internal evidence (lines 636-640), it is assumed that the author's father migrated across the Aegean from Cyme in Aeolia on account of poverty. He settled at Ascra, a village of Boeotia, at the foot of Mount Helicon. Ovid, in referring to Hesiod, uses the adjective "ascraeus." The poet himself, heir to the traditions of minstrelsy in this colony of Hellas, says that he once sailed to Chalcis in Euboea, where he competed in a poetry contest held by Amphidamas, and won the prize, a tripod with handles, which he gave to the Muses of Helicon.

The poem also contains details of a lawsuit brought against Hesiod by his brother Perses. Apparently by bribery of the judges, Perses was awarded Hesiod's sheep, but the diligent Hesiod accumulated another fortune, whereas Perses lost all he had and was forced to beg further help from the poet. Without hard feelings, Hesiod gave him assistance, with the warning not to ask again, and put his admonitions in a poem of 828 lines, of which the title well sums up its content: Rules for work and days on which luck is favorable.

Works and Days is neither a scientific treatise on farming nor a lesson on economic recovery through diligence, but rather a combination of moral precepts and an agricultural almanac. Under the symbols of Prometheus and Epimetheus (Forethought and Afterthought), Hesiod epitomizes himself and his brother.

In epic style, Hesiod begins *Works and Days* with an appeal to the Muses of Pieria, to sing of their father Zeus, who determines one's fame or dishonor, provides the good and the bad, destroys the mighty, and rewards the humble. The poet adds that there are two kinds of Strife on earth, one good and one bad. The good Strife, the elder daughter of Dark Night and of Zeus the Son of Chronos, makes people industrious so that they strive to imitate and surpass their neighbors.

Then, addressing himself to his brother Perses, Hesiod begs him not to follow the other Strife, in marketplace or in courthouse. First, lay up food for a year, he advises, and then, if necessary, enter disputes of law. This section contains references to Perses' unbrotherly lawsuit to get more than his rightful share of their father's possessions.

Prometheus by craft recovered the fire that Zeus took from men, and in revenge Zeus created a woman of water and earth. Pandora ("The All-Endowed") received all the lures provided by the gods to deceive men. She was eagerly accepted by Epimetheus, who had forgotten his brother's warning against gifts from the gods. Before her advent, men lived on earth free from wearying toil and death-bringing diseases. Pandora removed the great lid from the jar, and all the evils flew out and scattered over the earth.

Hesiod then tells another tale about the way gods and humanity came from the same seed. In the time of Chronos there existed a golden race of mortals, living like gods and ignorant of sorrow and of old age. Everything good belonged to them: abundant flocks, fruits, the blessings of the gods. After the earth covered them, the gods created an inferior race of silver. After a hundred years of idiotic childhood, they came of age, only to kill off one another in warfare. A third race followed whose delight was war; they died and went to chill Hades. Then came the demigods, the heroes of Thebes and Troy, preceding the present race of iron, whose daily lot is weariness and woe. To them, might is right. They have no reverence for justice and for oaths.

At this point in the poem Hesiod tells the first animal fable in Greek literature, the tale of a hawk who flies high into the sky with a nightingale, lecturing her against the folly of trying to compete with stronger people. To Perses, he adds a warning that violence is a bad quality in a poor man. For him, justice is better.

A city that provides honest judgments, says Hesiod, is blessed by Zeus, who protects it from war and famine. Its citizens never have to make sea voyages (which Hesiod hated); their earth provides their living. An insolent city, even one with a single insolent citizen, is plagued by the gods because Justice, the daughter of Zeus, is quick with rewards or punishment. Then follows a series of homilies as encouragement to the lazy and improvident Perses: "Work is no disgrace; it is idleness that is disgraceful." "The idle envy the wealth of the hard worker and try to seize it violently. God-given wealth is better."

After these homilies the poet rhymes a sort of farmers' almanac: Plow when the Pleiades set (in November). After forty days they come back. Then sharpen your sickle. When the autumn rains come, cut your wood. Choose oak for ploughbeams, and bring home two, in case one breaks. Get two nine-year-old oxen to plow. A forty-year-old slave is most reliable in the fields. Have everything ready to start plowing when the cry of the crane is heard. If the cuckoo sings, plant quickly, for it will rain in three days. When winter comes, your slaves will need twice as much food, your oxen half their regular ration. Prune your grapes before the return of the swallow, sixty days after the sun turns. When Orion is overhead, it is time to harvest your grapes. Sun them for ten days, cover them for five, and then press out the wine.

His theories on husbandry extend into domestic life. The ideal time for a man to marry, he says, is at the age of thirty; for a woman, the fifth year after puberty. Marry a neighbor, but be sure the others will not laugh at your choice. Finally, the poet records holy days and the lucky days for different tasks. He concludes that the wise man is the one who works blamelessly before the deathless gods, for he knows the propitious omens and avoids sin.

Revised by Laurence W. Mazzeno

Further Reading

Athanassakis, Apostolos, trans. *Hesiod: Theogony, Works and Days, Shield.* Baltimore: Johns Hopkins University Press, 1983. A superior translation of three major works. Includes a concise introduction to Hesiod and his historical period as well as useful notes to the text.

Clay, Jenny Strauss. *Hesiod's Cosmos.* New York: Cambridge University Press, 2003. An analysis of two of Hesiod's poems: *Works and Days* and *Theogony*. Clay argues that each poem represents one-half of Hesiod's total conception of the cosmos, with *Works and Days* depicting the human dimension, and *Theogony* portraying the divine. She describes how these two works, which present the earliest accounts of Greek religion and the nature of human life, laid the foundation of future Greek literature and philosophy.

Fränkel, Hermann. *Early Greek Poetry and Philosophy.* Translated by Moses Hadas and James Willis. New York: Harcourt Brace Jovanovich, 1975. Fränkel's work provides an exhaustive scholarly study of the major contributions to literature in ancient Greek society. His third chapter is an interesting exploration of Hesiod's role in the dialogue between the literary genres.

Gotshalk, Richard. *Homer and Hesiod: Myth and Philosophy.* Lanham, Md.: University Press of America, 2000. Examination of the nature and function of the two poets' work, including *Works and Days.* Focuses on the poets' attempts to transcend religion and myth to express the truth, and how this aspiration established the basis for Greek philosophy.

Lamberton, Robert. *Hesiod.* New Haven, Conn.: Yale University Press, 1988. Brief, excellent introduction to Hesiod. Provides line-by-line interpretation of Hesiod's poems and focuses on the meaning of his imagery. Chap-

ter 3 focuses exclusively on *Works and Days.* Includes extensive bibliography, notes on translations, and index.

Marsilio, Maria S. *Farming and Poetry in Hesiod's "Works and Days."* Lanham, Md.: University Press of America, 2000. Focuses on the relationship between Hesiod's poetry and his discussion of farming, describing how *Works and Days* connects a "farmers' almanac" with moral themes.

West, M. L. *Hesiod: Works and Days.* New York: Oxford University Press, 1978. The standard scholarly commentary on Hesiod's poem. Includes Greek text and copious notes. A rewarding introduction to the poet and his society, as well as to issues surrounding the poem's composition.

The World According to Garp

Author: John Irving (1942-   )
First published: 1978
Type of work: Novel
Type of plot: Tragicomedy
Time of plot: Mid-twentieth century
Locale: New Hampshire and Massachusetts

Principal characters:
T. S. GARP, a wrestling coach and an aspiring writer
JENNY FIELDS, his mother
HELEN HOLM GARP, his wife, an English professor
DUNCAN,
WALT, and
JENNY, their children
CUSHMAN PERCY, Garp's childhood friend
BAINBRIDGE PERCY, her sister
MICHAEL MILTON, Helen's lover
ELLEN JAMES, a young woman, raped and maimed as a child

The Story:

Jenny Fields is the only daughter of a New England shoe manufacturer and lives in her family's enormous house in Dog's Head Harbor, New Hampshire. After a few years, Jenny leaves the expensive private school her parents had selected for her and instead enrolls in nursing school. Attractive and self-assured, she has definite opinions about lust and sex; she is opposed to lust and abstains from sex. She is young, attractive, and self-assured, so friends and family assume she is sexually active.

Jenny had never had sex until one night at work at a hospital during World War II. She had decided to have sex for the sole purpose of procreation; she wanted a child. In the hospital where she works, many badly wounded soldiers are in recovery, or dying. Jenny sorts the soldiers into categories, including The Goners, those who are most severely injured.

One night, Jenny sexually arouses one of the Goners, a soldier identified only as Technical Sergeant, or T. S., Garp, who had been horribly wounded while serving as a gunner on a warplane.

As planned, Jenny became pregnant with the soldier's child—Garp, however, died. The baby was given the last name Garp, but because the boy had to have a first name as well, he was given the initials *T* and *S*, which officially stood for nothing; only Jenny knew the initials stood for "technical sergeant." She never knew the soldier's first name.

Jenny loved being a nurse. To simplify her life and solidify her identity, she wore her nurse's uniform at all times. She took a job at Steering School, an all-boy's preparatory school near her parents' home. She could work as a nurse every day and provide for her young son a quality education. A lover of books, she remained committed to the rejection of lust and sex and became a curious but respected member of the Steering School community.

The Steering family, who resides in the nicest, biggest house on campus, is represented by Midge Steering Percy; her fat husband, Stewart; their three sons and two daughters; and a large, mean Newfoundland dog named Bonkers. As young Garp grows up at Steering School, he plays with the Percy children. One fateful day, Garp is viciously attacked by Bonkers, who bites off Garp's left earlobe. The Percy sons do not play much of a role in Garp's life, but the daughters, Cushman, or Cushie, and Bainbridge, or Pooh, are important to him. With Cushie, Garp has his first sexual experience, in the infirmary annex at Steering School.

Jenny decides that Garp should participate in a sport. After some investigation, she decides on wrestling. The wrestling coach, an Iowa native named Ernie Holm, has a bespectacled bookworm of a daughter named Helen. Helen loves to read, perhaps even more so than Jenny. Garp falls in love with both wrestling and the wrestling coach's daughter. Garp's other passions are running and writing. He writes poetry and stories and dreams of someday being a successful author. He believes that most successful authors had either lived in or traveled extensively in Europe. His English teacher, Mr. Tinch, who stutters, had once spent time in Vienna. He recommends the city to Jenny and her aspiring writer son.

It is in Vienna that Jenny is bitten by the writing bug, and she begins penning her autobiography, to be called *A Sexual Suspect*. This work, which had been envisioned as a true account of Jenny's views and opinions on gender and sex, is mistakenly received as a feminist masterpiece, a life-transforming book for a generation of women. Jenny becomes rich and famous overnight.

Garp's first work of literary merit, a story, is inspired by Vienna as well. Titled "The Pension Grillparzer," the story concerns an odd circus family, their unicycle-riding bear, and the narrator's family, whose job is to rate guest accommodations in Austria. The story wins the heart of Helen Holm, the wrestling coach's daughter, and she and Garp are soon married. Helen becomes an English professor while Garp continues to write, clean house, cook, and run or wrestle every day. In no time, he is also caring for two sons, Duncan and Walt.

An attractive young couple, Garp and Helen are not without their faults. Garp has sex with the occasional babysitter, and both Helen and Garp enjoy the physical company of Harrison and Alice Fletcher. Helen and Harrison, colleagues at the university, have an affair, and Alice, who has an affair with Garp, is an aspiring writer with a strong lisp. The foursome eventually dissolves, as the Fletchers move away. Garp

writes two novels and gains a reputation as a minor but serious writer. He and his mother share the same New York editor, John Wolf, who is tolerant of both Jenny and Garp and encourages Garp through his many cases of writer's block.

Helen has a love affair with a graduate student named Michael Milton, who had pursued Helen. Not finding an attentive lover in Garp, Helen had turned to Michael for love; in some important ways, Michael reminded her of Garp. Over the years, Garp had become overprotective of his family, a protectiveness that bordered on an obsession with safety. He would chase down speeding cars in his neighborhood and lecture their drivers.

One rainy night, a car crash kills young Walt, partially blinds Duncan, and causes Helen to accidentally bite off three-fourths of Michael's penis. Garp, Helen, and Duncan recuperate after being nursed back to health by Jenny. The family then decides to get away from it all; they visit Vienna to help them forget their awful past. Helen becomes pregnant and has another child, a girl; she is named Jenny for her grandmother.

Meanwhile, Garp's mother, Jenny, is in the middle of a controversy at home: She is the subject of hatred because she is assumed to be lesbian and because of her apparent disdain for men. While attending a political rally, she is gunned down, assassinated by a man with a deer-hunting rifle. Garp's family rushes home, just as Garp's newest novel is being published. The book is a best seller but is critically panned. The novel deals with the rape of a woman and the effect of her rape on her family. Garp is viewed by some as a traitor to his mother's image, but as the executor of her will, he must carry on her work, whether he likes her past work or not.

Jenny's political involvement had included forming a movement in response to the rape and assault of Ellen James, a child, whose attacker also had cut out her tongue. In sympathy, a group of women in her community volunteered to have their own tongues cut out. They called themselves the Ellen Jamesians. Jenny had taken them in at her home in Dog's Head Harbor over the years. Garp despises them for their cheap victimization and their stupidity in maiming themselves to make a political statement. He cannot contain his outrage, especially after meeting Ellen James—she tells him that she hates the Ellen Jamesians.

Like his mother, Garp becomes a target of extremists. After one failed attempt at his life, Garp is approached in the gymnasium at Steering School during wresting practice by a woman wearing a nurse's uniform. The woman is Pooh Percy, his childhood friend and a recent convert to the Ellen Jamesians. Pooh guns Garp down, and Helen holds him in her arms as he dies.

Critical Evaluation:

John Irving novels, written before *The World According to Garp*, including *Setting Free the Bears* (1969), *The Water-Method Man* (1972), and *The 158-Pound Marriage* (1974), led to his modest reputation as a writer of some promise. However, *The World According to Garp* launched Irving into the mainstream of American literature.

In reading an Irving novel, one comes to expect and depend on the appearance of, especially, bears, the sport of wrestling, and lovable dysfunctional families who seem to invent and then subsist on their own definitions of morality and fairness. A repeated theme in *The World According to Garp* is the injured character, the character who has lost part of him- or herself but who carries on boldly with life. Irving's injured character may have lost a limb, an eye, part of an ear, or the ability to speak plainly, yet this character does not shrink from life.

Injured, "incomplete" people are everywhere in this novel: T. S. Garp loses part of his left ear to a dog; Technical Sergeant Garp dies from wounds suffered in battle; Mr. Tinch and Alice Fletcher have speech disorders; the circus performer in Garp's short story walks on his hands because he cannot use his legs; Michael Milton loses most of his penis in a freak car accident that takes the life of Garp's son, Walt; Duncan Garp loses an eye and later an arm in this same accident; Ellen James loses her tongue, cut out by her rapist; and Jenny Fields is murdered by a man with a deer-hunting rifle.

What could all this disability signify? One possibility is that perfection is not possible; another possibility is that no person is created perfect. Even the characters in this novel who do not lose a body part or suffer injury either miss something or perceive an imperfection: Roberta Muldoon, a transsexual, had been the epitome of masculinity as Robert Muldoon, a tight end for the Philadelphia Eagles football team. Jenny Fields, who lacked desire for physical intimacy, was a nurse who could care for others.

Lack of perfection is also evident in Garp's obsession with safety. More than just a doting father, Garp goes to extreme measures to discourage speeding drivers from his neighborhood, chasing them down by foot and lecturing them, even lying to them about the presence of his children. His fear overcomes him one night when Duncan stays over at a friend's house; Garp finds himself prowling about that friend's house at 3 A.M., hoping to protect his son from dangers real and imagined.

It is not the imagined dangers, or the obvious threats, that finally bring tragedy. Tragedy comes through human frailty: for example, Helen's affair with a graduate student and Garp's stubbornness and unwillingness to compromise; both bring disaster on their children and on themselves. The least likely suspects, the mother and father, turn out to be the destroyers.

Garp does learn, however. He learns that life, like wrestling, is a total contact sport that can leave permanent damage, scars both physical and mental. Life is dangerous, and there is no guarantee of protection, only of extinction. It is this realization that fuels Garp's anger toward the Ellen Jamesians. With so many dangers in the world, he asks, how could a person voluntarily maim him- or herself and then look to the world for understanding and sympathy? As Garp calls out these impostors, he brings about the means of his own destruction.

Randy L. Abbott

Further Reading

Bloom, Harold, ed. *John Irving*. Philadelphia: Chelsea House, 2001. Examines Irving's works critically. Also includes an introduction by Bloom, a brief biography of Irving, and a chronology of his life and career.

Campbell, Josie P. *John Irving: A Critical Companion*. Westport, Conn.: Greenwood Press, 1998. Provides a bibliography of Irving's works from 1968 to 1998 and discusses each of the novels published in this thirty-year period.

Davis, Todd F., and Kenneth Womack. *The Critical Response to John Irving*. Westport, Conn.: Greenwood Press, 2004. Presents a detailed discussion of the critical reception of all of Irving's novels through *The Fourth Hand*. Includes a chronology, a bibliography, and an index.

McKay, Kim. "Double Discourses in John Irving's *The World According to Garp*." *Twentieth Century Literature* 38, no. 4 (Winter, 1992): 457-475. This journal article discusses the use of narration in *The World According to Garp*, presenting Garp the character as both writer and narrator.

Shostak, Debra. "Plot as Repetition: John Irving's Narrative Experiments." *Critique* 37, no. 1 (Fall, 1995): 51-69. This journal article examines the narrative theme of repetition in Irving's works, including *The World According to Garp*.

Wilson, Raymond J., III. "The Postmodern Novel: The Example of John Irving's *The World According to Garp*." *Critique* 34, no. 1 (Fall, 1992): 49-62. This journal article presents a theoretical overview of the postmodern novel, including its characteristics, arguing that *The World According to Garp* is a postmodern novel.

The World as Will and Idea

Author: Arthur Schopenhauer (1788-1860)
First published: Die Welt als Wille und Vorstellung,
    1819 (English translation, 1883-1886)
Type of work: Philosophy

The three volumes of *The World as Will and Idea* constitute Arthur Schopenhauer's major contribution to the literature of philosophy. At the time of the book's writing, the philosophy of Georg Wilhelm Friedrich Hegel, with its vision of the dialectic process underlying the tensions and currents of human history, held sway over the thinking of many.

The European rationalists, led by the formidable figure of René Descartes, had previously promoted an optimistic view of the almost limitless possibilities of penetrating the nature of reality by means of human reason. Contrary to the Hegelian vision and to rationalist hopefulness, Schopenhauer maintained a fierce pessimism about the limitations of human knowledge and certainty. Even though *The World as Will and Idea* sold poorly and aroused little interest at the time of its first publication, the thought behind the book, carried forward as it is by Schopenhauer's strongly individualistic and wide-ranging literary style, remains a weighty counterbalance to Enlightenment-era optimism and assurance.

Schopenhauer's philosophy has at times been considered by critics to be an elaborate metaphysical justification for a profoundly pessimistic and gloomy temperament brought about by several factors. While Schopenhauer was still in his teens, his father died, apparently by suicide, and a serious disagreement with his mother continued throughout his adult life. He also experienced early frustrations in both the business and academic worlds; these continued throughout his publishing and lecturing career until late in life, when his two-volume collection of essays, *Parerga und Paralipomena* (1851; English translation, 1974), 1974) brought him a following and a measure of fame that increased steadily for the remainder of his life. Even though gratified by his late success, Schopenhauer considered his earlier work, especially *The World as Will and Idea*, his primary philosophical statement, despite its poor reception, and never entertained doubts as to its worth: "Subject to the limitation of human knowledge," he wrote, "my philosophy is the real solution of the enigma of the world."

Volume 1 of *The World as Will and Idea* is divided into four books, two dealing with "The World as Idea" (books 1 and 3) and two with "The World as Will" (books 2 and 4). Volume 2 consists of supplements to books 1 and 2, while volume 3 presents supplements to books 2 through 4. In addition, volume 2 contains an extensive criticism of certain points of the philosophy of Immanuel Kant, who remained, however, the philosopher whom Schopenhauer admired most and was influenced by to the greatest degree. In his original preface, Schopenhauer said of Kant's works that "the effect these writings produce in the mind to which they truly speak is very like that of the operation for cataracts on a blind man." In his preface to the revised version of the book, Schopenhauer repeated his praise: "Kant's teaching produces in the mind of every one who has comprehended it a fundamental change that is so great that it may be regarded as an intellectual new birth."

Two other major influences on Schopenhauer's philosophy were the metaphysical idealism of Plato and, somewhat surprisingly, the Eastern philosophy in the Upanishads, a portion of the Hindu scriptures. To Schopenhauer, the "greatest advantage" the nineteenth century held over previous centuries was the new availability in European languages of the "sacred, primitive Indian wisdom" contained in Sanskrit literature. In volume 2, he confesses that

> next to the impression of the world of perception, I owe what is best in my own system to the impression made on me by the works of Kant, by the sacred writings of the Hindus, and by Plato.

What all three of these influences have in common is a rather pessimistic view of the possibilities of human knowledge of reality. In particular, Kant's conception of the *Ding an sich*, the "thing in itself," is crucial to an understanding of Schopenhauer's work. The *Ding an sich* is that aspect of existence that lies beyond all human perception, since according to Kant people only know their own perceptions and understandings of objects in the world; they can never know the thing in itself, the object as it actually is. This insight, Kant's "Copernican revolution" of philosophy, shifts the locus of reality from the external world typically thought of as real to the consciousness of the subject perceiving this world. The perceiver is forever cut off from the thing perceived, for immediate experience is only that of the perceiver's perception of the thing. Consequently, people know no other world than that subjective world that is placed before their own perception and understanding; as the Upanishads maintain, the world thought of as real is actually mere appearance. In fact, the word *Vorstellung* in Schopenhauer's title is sometimes translated as "representation" rather than "idea," for that which is present in the consciousness of the perceiving subject is a mere representation of the object itself.

Accepting this line of thought led Schopenhauer to the startling assertion with which he opens his book: "The world is my idea." He goes on to explain,

> This is a truth which holds good for everything that lives and knows, though man alone can bring it into reflective and abstract consciousness. If he really does this, he has attained to philosophical wisdom. It then becomes clear and certain to him that what he knows is not a sun and an earth, but only an eye that sees a sun, a hand that feels an earth; that the world which surrounds him is there only as an idea, i.e., only in relation to something else, the consciousness, which is himself.

The intellect, according to Schopenhauer, organizes the body's perceptions into the world in which it lives, and thus "the whole world of objects is and remains idea, and therefore wholly and forever determined by the subject." This does not mean that the universe of experience does not objectively exist or that it is not somehow created by the perceiving subject. Schopenhauer follows Kant in distinguishing between mere sensory impressions and the intellectual understanding that converts these impressions into ideas. The external world must actually exist, for the intellect would lie dormant were it not stimulated into activity by the body's perception of itself and its place in the external universe.

All of this is equally true of every consciousness, including animal consciousness. What sets humans apart from animals is the capacity for "reflective and abstract consciousness," that is, reason, which enables humans to transcend the universe of things and to achieve inner quiet and calm as they contemplate the world of suffering.

In book 2, Schopenhauer carries his argument beyond the philosophy of Kant, who, holding that the "inner nature" of things is forever sealed to human understanding, never identifies the *Ding an sich*. According to Schopenhauer, however, this can only be identified with the will, for the awareness that people possess of themselves as will is quite distinct from the awareness that they possess of themselves as body or thing. People know themselves in two primary ways: as bodily objects, no different in any respect from the world of objects with which they interact, and as self-directing beings whose actions are the embodiment of the will's direction. The operation of the will and the operation of the body thus appear to be one and the same, although they can be contemplated separately for the purpose of analysis; the body is the objectified will. In knowing themselves as such unified beings, such objectifications of the autonomous will, people know themselves to be irreducible, the *Ding an sich*, which thereby stands revealed as the will in their own consciousness.

If this principle is applied not merely to humanity but to all phenomena (Schopenhauer's "great extension"), the universe becomes a much different place from that described by more traditional metaphysics. From its least significant aspect to its greatest, the universe as a macrocosm takes on the character of will ascribed to the microcosmic human. The reality behind the phenomenal universe becomes not rational, not orderly or designed, but nonrational, nondesigned, purposeless, and meaningless, the endless striving and conflict of wills. If this is indeed the state of affairs—if the thing in itself behind reality is in fact the will—then all philosophies that purport to find meaning, purpose, or design behind natural and human history (such as the philosophy of Schopenhauer's archrival Hegel) are delusory, and the real purpose of philosophy is to reveal the grim and stark nature of the universe and of the human condition. Thus, Schopenhauer's profound pessimism would have a metaphysical justification.

In book 3, Schopenhauer uses this doctrine of the will to help explain his theories of art. Schopenhauer places a higher importance on art and the artist than any other modern philosopher, for he believes that it is by means of art that humanity is enabled to separate itself from and transcend the world of will and conflict. In contemplating a work of art, observers enter a disinterested state of will-less perception that is quite different from the ordinary perception of sensory impressions; they escape for a time from the ordinary struggles and desires of life and disappear into or become one with the "permanent essential forms of the world and all its phenomena." In thus adapting Plato's Ideal Forms, Schopenhauer considers artistic knowledge more valuable than scientific knowledge, for that concerns itself with the shifting and imperfect appearance of reality conveyed by sensory impression, while artistic knowledge penetrates to the archetypal reality behind the appearance. In particular, the artistic expression known as music dispenses with all forms of surface appearance and grants immediate access to its subject, the will itself.

Finally, in book 4, Schopenhauer explores the implications of this will-less perception, this disappearance from the world of strife, particularly as presented in the Hindu formula *Tat tvam asi* ("That art thou"). When the world of sensory impressions is rejected as mere appearance, the recognition of the illusory nature of surface phenomena enables a person to perceive the deeper underlying unity among all things. Desire and the individual will are renounced, even to the extent of renouncing the will to live.

This renunciation does not lead to suicide, for suicide would also imply desire or will (the desire or will for death). Rather, this renunciation leads to a peaceful state of freedom from the will's demands, in which the subject "draws less distinction between" him- or herself and others "than is usually done" and is enabled to rise above the meaningless universe in a state of mystical insight. According to Schopenhauer, to accept this philosophy would lead to humanity's ultimate triumph.

Craig Payne

Further Reading

Atwell, John E. *Schopenhauer on the Character of the World: The Metaphysics of Will*. Berkeley: University of California Press, 1995. Atwell's extended analysis of *The World as Will and Idea* attempts, against the views of others, to establish that Schopenhauer has a metaphysics, though a severely limited one. Discusses the concepts of time, space, and causality, as well as Schopenhauer's ideas about ethics and epistemology. Like other explorations of will, this one gives primacy to intellect and thus unearths numerous inconsistencies.

_____. *Schopenhauer: The Human Character*. Philadelphia: Temple University Press, 1990. A topical, highly readable approach to an exploration of Schopenhauer's ethics. Presses Schopenhauer's examples logically to the point that they break down and reveal contradictions; major divisions concern the self, ethics, virtue, and salvation. Recognizing Schopenhauer's inclination toward hyperbole and paradox, Atwell offers a clear interpretation of the philosopher's concepts of virtue and ethical action.

Gardiner, Patrick L. *Schopenhauer*. Dulles, Va.: Thoemmes Press, 1997. A piercing analysis of Schopenhauer's life and philosophy, his philosophy's historical significance, and the affect of his work on modern philosophies. Part of the Key Texts series.

Hamlyn, D. W. *Schopenhauer*. Boston: Routledge & Kegan Paul, 1980. A general survey of Schopenhauer's philosophy. Clarifies his terms, explains his epistemology, and offers extensive analysis of his philosophical debt to Immanuel Kant.

Hannan, Barbara. *The Riddle of the World: A Reconsideration of Schopenhauer's Philosophy*. New York: Oxford University Press, 2009. Provides an overview of Schopenhauer's main ideas, including the major themes of transcendental idealism, panpsychism, and determinism. Describes inconsistencies in his thought, including the tension between denial and affirmation of the individual will.

Jacquette, Dale, ed. *Schopenhauer, Philosophy, and the Arts*. 1996. Reprint. New York: Cambridge University Press, 2007. A penetrating look at Schopenhauer's philosophy and aesthetics. Examines the aesthetic theory Schopenhauer developed to explain the life and work of artists.

Magee, Bryan. *The Philosophy of Schopenhauer*. 1983. Rev. ed. New York: Oxford University Press, 1997. A scholarly introduction to Schopenhauer's philosophical system. Explores the effects of his early life on his thought and places his ideas in their philosophical tradition. Numerous appendixes trace his influence on others.

Safranski, Rüdiger. *Schopenhauer and the Wild Years of Philosophy*. Cambridge, Mass.: Harvard University Press, 1990. Essentially a biography, this book recounts the life and works of Schopenhauer. Safranski suggests that events in Schopenhauer's life contributed to his outlook and the formation of his pessimistic system. In addition, he places the philosophy within the aesthetic and intellectual currents of Schopenhauer's time.

Tanner, Michael. *Schopenhauer*. New York: Routledge, 1999. An excellent biographical introduction to the thoughts of the philosopher, clearly presented and requiring no special background. Includes a bibliography.

Wicks, Robert. *Schopenhauer*. Malden, Mass.: Blackwell, 2008. An introductory overview of Schopenhauer's life and theoretical and practical philosophy. Examines the influence of Asian philosophy on his thinking; defends his position that absolute truth can be known and described as the universal will. Chapter 6 examines critical interpretations of *The World as Will and Idea*.

World Enough and Time
A Romantic Novel

Author: Robert Penn Warren (1905-1989)
First published: 1950
Type of work: Novel
Type of plot: Philosophical realism
Time of plot: 1801-1826
Locale: Kentucky

Principal characters:
JEREMIAH BEAUMONT, an idealist
COLONEL CASSIUS FORT, a frontier politician and
    Jeremiah's benefactor
RACHAEL JORDAN, a woman betrayed by Fort and, later,
    Jeremiah's wife
WILKIE BARRON, an opportunist
DR. LEICESTER BURNHAM, Jeremiah's teacher
LA GRAND' BOSSE, a river pirate

The Story:

Jeremiah Beaumont is born in Kentucky in 1801. His father is Jasper Beaumont, one of the first settlers in Glasgow County, and his mother is the disinherited daughter of a wealthy planter. Jasper never prospers as he hoped, and his unfulfilled ambitions breed in him a strain of awkward moodiness that is reflected in his son.

Jasper dies, debt-ridden, when Jeremiah is thirteen. Before that time, the boy is in school with Leicester Burnham. Hoping for a better life than his father's, Jeremiah is diligent in his studies. He is also stubbornly independent, for he refuses to become his grandfather's heir because the old man insists that he take his mother's maiden name, Marcher. When he is seventeen, Dr. Burnham introduces him to Colonel Cassius Fort, a famous frontier lawyer and politician who is looking for a young man to train in his law office at Bowling Green. Jeremiah is eager to accept Fort's offer but cannot do so because of his ailing mother. Fort says that he is willing to wait for anyone Dr. Burnham recommends so highly.

The next spring, Mrs. Beaumont dies, and Jeremiah goes to Bowling Green to study law, not in Fort's office, however, for the lawyer returned to Congress. Jeremiah's only friend in the town is Wilkie Barron, another law student, from whose mother Jeremiah rents a room. Fort returns from Washington in 1820 and takes the young man under his patronage. From him, Jeremiah learns to look on the law not as a collection of dry statutes but as humanity's agent of truth and justice. Times are hard in Kentucky following the Panic of 1819, and the legislature passes a law allowing a twelve-month stay of sale for debt. Fort is on the side of the Relief Party, as those who support the measure are called.

Wilkie first tells Jeremiah of a scandal linking Fort's name with that of Rachael Jordan, daughter of a planter who died heavily in debt. Called in to help settle the estate, Fort is supposed to have seduced the girl and fathered her stillborn child. Grieved by that story of innocence betrayed, Jeremiah decides to have nothing more to do with his benefactor. In a letter he informs Fort, who is away at the time, of his decision. Fort writes in reply, but before his letter reaches Bowling Green, Jeremiah goes to visit Wilkie's uncle, old Thomas Barron, in Saul County. The Jordan place is only a few miles away from his host's. There he meets Rachael, wins her confidence, and, after hearing from her own lips the story of her shame, marries her. She accepts him on the condition that he kill Fort.

In the meantime, Jeremiah becomes involved in local politics. Percival Scrogg, fanatic liberal editor of a Frankfort newspaper, and Wilkie arrive to take part in a disputed election. After a riot at the polls, in which he and Wilkie fought side by side, Jeremiah is dismayed to learn that his friend is working for Fort. Wilkie advises him to put aside personal grudges for the public good.

Jeremiah and Rachael are married in 1822. At the time, Fort is away on private business. Taking over the Jordan plantation, the young husband devotes all his energies to making the place productive. Sometimes he feels that he has his father's score to settle as well as his wife's, that his hard work will vindicate his bankrupt father against men such as Fort, to whom wealth and fame come easily. Ambitious for the future and foreseeing expansion of the settlements, he forms a partnership with Josh Parham, a rich landowner, and, with Parham's son Felix, surveys town sites in the unclaimed western lands. The venture in land speculation falls through, however, when Desha, the Relief candidate, is elected governor in 1824. Parham, an anti-Relief man, swears that he will never spend money opening up land in Kentucky while the Relief Party is in office.

Rachael and Jeremiah are expecting their first child when Fort returns from the East. Rachael, begging her husband to give up his intention of killing Fort, persuades him that his first duty is to her and the unborn child. A week later, Wilkie arrives at the plantation with a handbill in which Fort, announcing his candidacy for the legislature, disavows membership in the Relief Party. Urged by Wilkie, Jeremiah also becomes a candidate for office. The campaign is a bitter one. Unknown to Jeremiah, the Relief Party prints a broadside in which the scandal involving Fort and Rachael is revived. Jeremiah is defeated by Sellars, the candidate he opposes.

Two months later, Rachael has a miscarriage. On the same day, a handbill is mysteriously delivered to the house. Signed by Fort, it refutes the campaign slanders against him and accuses Rachael of having her first child by a mulatto slave. That night Jeremiah reaches his decision to kill Fort. As soon as he can leave his wife in a neighbor's care, he rides to Frankfort. Disguised, he goes at night to the house in which Fort is staying, calls him to the door, and stabs him to death. He then rides home and tells Rachael what he did.

Four days later, officers appear and summon him to Frankfort for examination in connection with the murder. Believing that there is no evidence against him, he goes willingly. His enemies, however, are already busy manufacturing false clues, and, to his surprise, he is bound over for trial. By the time of his trial, bribery and perjury do their work. In spite of the efforts of Dr. Burnham and other loyal friends, his case is lost when Wilkie appears to testify against him. Although many believe him innocent, Jeremiah is sentenced to be hanged on August 20, 1826. Meanwhile, Rachael is arrested and brought to Frankfort, where she and her husband share the same cell. Jeremiah's lawyers appeal the sentence. When they fail to produce one of the handbills defaming Rachael, the appeal is denied.

Two days before the execution date, Wilkie and several men break into the jail and free the prisoners, who are taken secretly to a refuge ruled by La Grand' Bosse, a river pirate. There, from one of Wilkie's former henchmen, Jeremiah learns that Scrogg and Wilkie forged the handbill responsible for Fort's death. In despair, Rachael kills herself. Realizing how he was duped, Jeremiah tries to return to Frankfort and reveal the truth. Wilkie's man overtakes him and cuts off his head.

Wilkie goes into partnership with the Parhams and becomes rich. Still politically ambitious, he is elected senator. One night in Washington, he shoots himself. Among his effects, to be uncovered in an old trunk years later, are some letters and a manuscript in which Jeremiah, during his months in prison and in the outlaw camp, wrote his story of deceit and betrayal. No one will ever know why Wilkie kept those incriminating papers. Unable to destroy the truth, he tried to conceal it. Perhaps at the end, like Jeremiah, he wondered whether the striving, pride, violence, agony, and expiation were all for nothing.

Critical Evaluation:

Colonel Solomon P. Sharp, Solicitor General of Kentucky, was killed by a masked assassin in 1825. Shortly afterward, Jeroboam Beauchamp, a young lawyer and a member of the political party opposing Sharp, was arrested and charged with the crime. During the trial, it was revealed that Beauchamp had married a planter's daughter whom Sharp had seduced. Found guilty and awaiting execution, Beauchamp was visited in his cell by his wife. The husband and wife stabbed themselves after a dose of laudanum failed to kill them. The wife died in her husband's cell. Beauchamp was hanged. The Kentucky Tragedy, as this story of intrigue and revenge was called, became a popular subject during the nineteenth century, among writers as dissimilar as Edgar Allan Poe, Charlotte Barnes, Thomas H. Chivers, Charles F. Hoffman, and William Gilmore Simms. Robert Penn Warren, reworking the old tale, has filled it with philosophical speculation and symbolic moral overtones. His Jeremiah Beaumont is an idealist confronted by the realities and compromises of the world, a man betrayed not only by an acquisitive and self-seeking society but also by the very idealism that sustains him in loneliness and in doubt. The plot, centering on a theme of community guilt and expiation, illustrates the complex moral issues of the era.

Given his lifelong preoccupation with southern history, it is not surprising that Warren was attracted to the Kentucky Tragedy as a vehicle for the expression of his thoughts and feelings about idealism, fanaticism, politics, love, sex, and violence. In adapting this historical event—almost a folk legend—Warren begins with a story of innocence violated, villainy rewarded, revenge, political corruption, and backwoods violence. The raw material is, therefore, highly dramatic. Warren's first problem is how to tell the story without descending to sentimental romance or lurid melodrama.

First, he mutes the obvious sensationalism of the events through his handling of point of view. An unnamed historian, piecing together the story from Jeremiah's "confession" and other data, narrates the events with scholarly objectivity and frequent moralizing in an ornate prose style. This elaborate, indirect approach, with the highly charged dramatic scenes, gives the book both historical distance and dramatic intensity.

Second, Warren shifts the usual focus of the tale from the sentimental, revenge-seeking woman, Rachael Jordan, to her idealistic but confused husband, Jeremiah. Therefore, the novel takes on a shape not unlike Warren's earlier masterpiece *All the King's Men* (1946). As in the previous book, the novel revolves around the relationship between a young man (Jeremiah), a powerful father figure (Cassius Fort), who combines idealistic good with pragmatic evil and who inspires worship as well as revulsion, and a woman (Rachael), who is the victim both of the older man's attractiveness and of his ruthlessness. Again, the father figure is murdered by the young man to avenge the honor of the woman.

Warren's analysis of the political context of the act further differentiates his handling of the Kentucky Tragedy from previous ones. The results of Jeremiah's act demonstrate the potential dangers of fanatical idealism in conflict with corrupt pragmatic politics. He is finally convicted not because he committed the crime but because his guilt serves the selfish needs of those in power.

Warren's biggest deviation from the original events, however, lies in the novel's resolution. The historical couple attempted mutual suicide; the woman died, and the man was hanged. In Warren's version, an escape is arranged. In the course of their flight, Jeremiah and Rachael learn the truth of their situation, which drives Rachael to suicide and Jeremiah to an attempt at public confession. The important thing to Warren is not Jeremiah's legal punishment but the growth of his personal awareness. Jeremiah, like other Warren protagonists, must finally accept responsibility not only for his own deed but also for the sequence of turbulent events provoked by that first act of violence.

Further Reading

Burt, John. "The Self-Subversion of Value: *World Enough and Time*." In *Robert Penn Warren and American Idealism*. New Haven, Conn.: Yale University Press, 1988. Discussion of the novel as romance and of Beaumont as unaware of the world's complexity. Argues that the novel's major images reinforce the idea that humankind's best instincts lead to self-destruction.

Grimshaw, James A., Jr. *Understanding Robert Penn Warren*. Columbia: University of South Carolina Press, 2001. Comprehensive introduction to Warren's work, analyzing his fiction, poetry, and drama. Discusses the nature of his protagonists and common themes, such as history, time, truth, responsibility, and love. The references to *World Enough and Time* are listed in the index.

Guttenberg, Barnett. "*World Enough and Time*." In *Web of Being: The Novels of Robert Penn Warren*. Nashville, Tenn.: Vanderbilt University Press, 1975. Existential interpretation of Beaumont as an absolutist whose reliance upon the "idea" has not prepared him for the "reintegration of self" that is necessary when he perceives reality. Argues that the novel develops the conflict between humankind's need for order and the world's incoherence.

Hendricks, Randy. *Lonelier than God: Robert Penn Warren and the Southern Exile*. Athens: University of Georgia Press, 2000. Focuses on the theme of exile in Warren's work and how that theme relates to his ideas about regionalism, race, and language.

Justus, James H. "Dream and Drama: *World Enough and Time*." In *The Achievement of Robert Penn Warren*. Baton Rouge: Louisiana State University Press, 1981. Discussion of Warren's double point of view, as the narrator at various times supports, undercuts, and simply relates Beaumont's account. Another of Warren's egoist idealists, Beaumont struggles but fails to remake the world to conform to his nebulous ideals.

Kallsen, Loren J. *The Kentucky Tragedy: A Problem in Romantic Attitudes*. Indianapolis, Ind.: Bobbs-Merrill, 1963. Collects nineteenth century publications that have served as the sources for literary treatments of this historical incident. Supposedly, these documents are Jeroboam Beauchamp's confession, Ann Cook Beauchamp's letters to a friend in Maryland, the transcript of the couple's trial, and a brother's vindication of Solomon Sharp's character. Also includes a bibliography and discussion questions.

McDowell, Frederick P. W. "The Romantic Tragedy of Self in *World Enough and Time*." In *Robert Penn Warren: A Collection of Critical Essays*, edited by John Lewis Longley, Jr. New York: New York University Press, 1965. Discussion of the novel's theme as typical of Warren's emphasis upon the self-induced alienation of the individual who cannot distinguish between romance and reality. Beaumont journeys west in search of Edenic innocence; instead, he finds a savage wilderness.

Madden, David, ed. *The Legacy of Robert Penn Warren*. Baton Rouge: Louisiana State University Press, 2000. Collection of essays interpreting Warren's work, including discussions of Warren as a mentor and a moral philosopher, Warren and Thomas Jefferson, and the function of geography as fate in his writings.

The World of the Thibaults

Author: Roger Martin du Gard (1881-1958)
First published: Les Thibault, 1922-1940; includes *Le Cahier gris,* 1922; *Le Pénitencier,* 1922; *La Belle Saison,* 1923; *La Consultation,* 1928; *La Sorellina,* 1928; *La Mort dupère,* 1929; *L'Été 1914,* 1936; *Épilogue,* 1940 (English translation, 1939-1941)
Type of work: Novels
Type of plot: Social realism
Time of plot: Early twentieth century
Locale: France

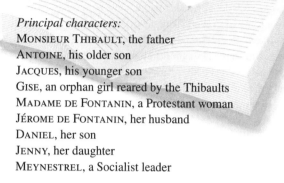

Principal characters:
MONSIEUR THIBAULT, the father
ANTOINE, his older son
JACQUES, his younger son
GISE, an orphan girl reared by the Thibaults
MADAME DE FONTANIN, a Protestant woman
JÉROME DE FONTANIN, her husband
DANIEL, her son
JENNY, her daughter
MEYNESTREL, a Socialist leader

The Story:

Monsieur Thibault is furious when he learns that Jacques lied to him and had run away with young Daniel de Fontanin. The Abbé Binot, Jacques's teacher, has even more disquieting news. From a copybook that fell into the abbé's hands, it is apparent that Jacques, not yet fourteen years old, formed an unnatural friendship with Daniel. What is worse, the de Fontanins are Protestants.

Antoine Thibault, already a doctor, goes to see Madame de Fontanin to learn what he can about Daniel and his friendship with Jacques. Antoine finds her a very attractive, sensible woman, who rejects Antoine's hints of an improper relationship between the boys. They question Jenny, Daniel's younger sister, who has a fever. To Antoine's practiced eye, Jenny is suffering from meningitis. When neither Antoine nor the other doctors can help Jenny, Madame de Fontanin calls in her minister, Pastor Gregory. He effects a miraculous cure of the girl by faith healing.

Jacques and Daniel get as far as Marseilles. Although Jacques is the younger of the two boys, he is the moving spirit in the escapade. He is rebelling against the smug respectability of his father and the dull Thibault household. Monsieur Thibault is such an eminent social worker that he has no time to try to understand his own family. The suspicions of the Thibaults, however, are unfounded; Jacques's feelings for Daniel are no more than a schoolboy crush.

When the runaways are returned by the police, Daniel is scolded and forgiven by his mother. Jacques, on the other hand, is put in a reformatory founded by his father. There, the boy's spirit is nearly broken by brutal guards and solitary confinement. Only by devious means is Antoine able to get his brother away from his father's stern discipline. He takes a separate flat and has Jacques live with him, assuming responsibility for his younger brother's upbringing.

When Jérome de Fontanin, Daniel's father, runs away with Noémie, a cousin, Noémie's daughter, Nicole, comes to live with the de Fontanins. Nicole is very attractive, and Daniel tries to seduce her. Nicole, however, has before her the unhappy example of her mother, and she resists him.

Under Antoine's care, Jacques slowly recovers his mental health. During the summer vacation he is greatly attracted to Jenny. Just as Jenny is beginning to care for him and to overcome her aversion to physical contact, Jacques disappears.

For three years the Thibaults think Jacques is dead. Only Gise, an orphan girl reared by the Thibaults, hopes that he is still alive. One day, she receives from England a box of rosebuds like those she sprinkled on Jacques just before his disappearance. Convinced that Jacques is alive, Gise goes to school in England, where she hopes to find him.

Antoine follows a different course. By chance, he discovers a Swiss magazine with a story entitled *Sorellina* or *Little Sister.* Antoine thinks he recognizes both the Thibault and the de Fontanin families thinly disguised in the story. Disquieted, Antoine hires a detective agency in Geneva to trace the author.

Antoine's own life is quite unhappy. On an emergency case one night, he meets Rachel, an adventuress, and they become lovers. Little by little, Rachel tells him the story of her sordid past, a story that strangely endears her to Antoine.

She was once the mistress of the ferocious Hirst, a fifty-year-old man who having incestuous relations with his daughter, Clara. Rachel's brother married Clara, and they went to Italy on their honeymoon. A few days later, Clara wrote to her father, asking him to join them. After his arrival, the young husband learned the true relationship between father and daughter. To avoid a scandal, Hirst strangled Clara and her husband and threw their bodies into a lake.

Rachel says she is through with Hirst. One day, she says she has to make a trip to the Congo to see about some investments. When Antoine does not believe her, she admits that she is going back to Hirst, who sent for her. Antoine sadly accompanies Rachel to Le Havre and helps her embark.

According to a report from the detective agency, Jacques is an international socialist and an influential writer in Geneva. Monsieur Thibault develops a serious illness. Fearing that his father will die, Antoine goes to Geneva and asks Jacques to return, but Monsieur Thibault dies without recognizing his errant son. At the funeral, Gise sees Jacques again and realizes that she still loves him. Jacques, however, loses all his affection for her. Jenny is still afraid of Jacques, and in her frigidity she even comes to hate him. Daniel is busy as a successful artist.

Jacques feels no ties in Paris and returns to Geneva. He works there during the fateful summer of 1914. Under the leadership of Meynestrel, a group of socialists are involved in trying to unite the workers of England, France, and Germany in an effort to stop the impending war with paralyzing strikes. Jacques is frequently sent on secret missions. One such trip is to Paris just before general mobilization is decreed. By chance, Jacques sees Jenny again. The new Jacques, mature and valuable to the pacifist movement, soon converts Jenny to his views. They fall in love.

Madame de Fontanin's husband dies in Vienna, where he is suspected of embezzlement. In an attempt to clear his name, she goes to Austria despite the imminence of war. While she is gone, Jacques becomes a frequent visitor to the de Fontanin flat. When Madame de Fontanin returns early one morning, she is shocked to find Jacques and Jenny sleeping together.

Jenny plans to leave for Geneva with Jacques. At the last moment, however, she decides to remain at home. Jacques is free to leave on his humanitarian mission. He and Meynestrel have their own plan for ending the war. Jacques takes off from Switzerland in a light plane piloted by Meynestrel. He has with him several million pamphlets that call on both Germans and French to lay down their arms. The plane crashes near the French lines, and Meynestrel burns to death. Jacques, severely wounded, is captured by the French as a spy. While he is being carried to headquarters on a stretcher, one of the orderlies shoots him in the temple.

Gassed severely during the war, Antoine realizes that his recovery is impossible. On leave, he visits his old country home near Paris, where he finds Madame de Fontanin a competent hospital administrator and Nicole a good nurse. Jenny is happy, rearing her and Jacques's son, Jean-Paul. Daniel comes back from the front a changed man, for a shell splinter unsexed him. Now he spends his time looking after Jean-Paul and helping the nurses.

Back at the hospital in southern France, Antoine receives a necklace from Rachel, who died of yellow fever in Africa. He tries to keep notes on the deteriorating condition of his lungs. He lives until November 18, 1918, but he never knows that the Armistice was signed before his death.

Critical Evaluation:

Roger Martin du Gard, a dramatist as well as a novelist, was born into a professional middle-class family in 1881. He studied to be an archivist and paleographer, served with a motor-transport unit during World War I, and, for a brief period, worked in the theater. Most of his life, however, was spent in seclusion, wholly dedicated to his writing. Literature was Martin du Gard's entire life. His closest friend was André Gide, about whom he eventually wrote a book. His last novel was never finished and remains unpublished, but Martin du Gard's achievement and his influence on French fiction were formidable.

The eight-part novel cycle *The World of the Thibaults* was inspired by the author's desire to emulate for his own time the accomplishment of Leo Tolstoy's *Voyna i mir* (1865-1869; *War and Peace*, 1886). In fact, the work's style and pessimism is closer to Martin du Gard's countryman Gustave Flaubert than to the Russian author. Although the historical background of the action in the novel is of interest, it is the powerful depiction of human relationships that constitutes the book's chief merit.

In many respects, the most influential character in the vast novel is old Monsieur Thibault, the patriarch of the Thibault family. A complete hypocrite, he announces to the world that his conscience is clear, yet he is concerned only with his own convenience and peace. Cloaking his craving for power and authority under a guise of fervent religiosity and philanthropy, he actually has no sense of either religion or generosity. He possesses no love for his sons, demanding only that they be completely docile. Any contradiction or sign of individuality throws him into a rage. For all of his big gestures, he is a petty man. Everyone automatically hides feelings from him, for one never can tell what his reaction might be. He forces his family into hypocrisy. By avoiding all introspection, Monsieur Thibault unknowingly condemns himself to a life of petty pride and cruelty, a life so alone that he must find his only consolation in public honors and the "knowledge" that he is a "good man." As he grows older, however, the fact of approaching death terrifies him increasingly, and he desperately seeks some kind of immortality, as if he subconsciously realizes how futile his busy life is.

The volumes of the series are crowded with fascinating, well-drawn secondary characters. These include Monsieur

Chasle, the middle-aged secretary of Monsieur Thibault, who is suddenly revealed to have his own life, his own preoccupations, fears, and miseries. The reader becomes aware of many other lives lurking in the background, and beyond them still others. In the volume entitled *The Springtime of Life*, the adult Daniel de Fontanin and Jacques Thibault experience the bohemian life of Paris, encountering characters such as Mother JuJu, the retired prostitute, and many colorful girls of the streets, as well as the rich Jew Ludwigson, who sells Daniel's pictures. Earlier, in a powerful scene at young Jenny's sickbed, the Rasputin-like pastor Gregory chants and prays and condemns with equal fury and somehow saves the girl's life.

The growth of the relationship between Jacques and Daniel is shown in many different ways, as the author explores the various paths the boys take in their lives. At first, when they run away together at the beginning of the book, the homely little redheaded Jacques dominates the older, more restrained Daniel. After his first sexual experience, however, Daniel becomes less easily ruled by his friend. When Jacques is sent to the reformatory, their relationship nearly dies, but later it is restored on a quite different level. Martin du Gard skillfully captures the changing attitudes and the emotions of young men in the process of maturing.

The strained relationship between Jacques and Antoine is portrayed with particular subtlety. The family reticence, the legacy of the tyrannical father, prevents an early comradeship between the brothers, but gradually, after Jacques returns from the reformatory, the brothers build a new and solid relationship.

A subplot of complexity and great interest is woven into the tale of the young men: It is the story of Madame de Fontanin and her unfaithful husband. She is a most unusual figure in fiction, a good person who is neither boring nor cloying. Although imperfect, she is admirable in most of her thoughts and acts. She possesses no malice, although she suffers and occasionally reacts with anger. The touching scenes of her reunion in Holland with her husband and his dying mistress, whose daughter Madame de Fontanin cares for, are unforgettable. The complex relationships reveal the subtle and ever changing realities of human emotions. It is as difficult to hate, Martin du Gard seems to be implying, as it is to love.

The death that waits for everyone, as it does for the two brothers in the war, is anticipated when Jacques and Jenny see Daniel and Jenny's dog crushed by an old car. The accident prompts Jacques and Jenny to discuss death, but neither realizes how soon World War I will cause the deaths of millions of young people such as themselves, including Jacques and his brother. The irony is compelling yet not overdone.

Rachel, another of the fascinating secondary characters, tells Antoine that she is afraid of being lonely, a fear shared by most of the characters in the book. There is a gripping horror in Rachel's monologue as she shows Antoine her photographs and tells him about her past life and her lover, the infamous Hirst. The Africa described by Rachel becomes a mythological place of fulfilled desires and strange passions, and Hirst a fabulous man-monster. Nevertheless, the reader is hardly surprised when Rachel leaves Antoine and returns to Hirst. Rachel and Antoine never could find permanent happiness together.

The graphic realism of the sickbed and death scenes, and, in the seventh volume, *Summer 1914*, the dramatic buildup of the war, as the European nations are swept relentlessly to destruction, are impressive achievements. Even more impressive, however, is the fact that as the focus of the novel expands, the author never loses sight of the individuals who make up the world. For this vast, panoramic survey of society and the meaning of life, as well as for his earlier novel of the Dreyfus affair and atheism *Jean Barois* (1913; English translation, 1949), Martin du Gard was awarded the Nobel Prize in Literature in 1937.

"Critical Evaluation" by Bruce D. Reeves

Further Reading

Boak, Denis. *Roger Martin du Gard*. Oxford, England: Clarendon Press, 1963. Discusses Martin du Gard's cyclical novel within the context of humanist philosophy. Boak compares Martin du Gard to existentialist writers and sees this work as symphonic with tragic overtones. Reinforces the connection to Pierre Corneille on the basis of related transcendental qualities.

Brosman, Catharine Savage. *Roger Martin du Gard*. Boston: Twayne, 1968. Analyzes Martin du Gard's artistic vision and places him squarely in the nineteenth century tradition because of his use of omniscient narration and authorial interjections, by which he produces a literature of ideas. Calls attention to Martin du Gard's style for its naturalness, simplicity, and spontaneity.

Gilbert, John. "Symbols of Continuity and the Unity of *Les Thibault*." In *Image and Theme: Studies in Modern French Fiction*, edited by W. M. Frohock. Cambridge, Mass.: Harvard University Press, 1969. Gilbert discusses the structural unity of *The World of the Thibaults* and makes a compelling case for the coherence of the cyclical novel, which has elsewhere been judged to be formless.

O'Nan, Martha, ed. *Roger Martin du Gard Centennial, 1881-1981.* Brockport: State University of New York Press, 1981. This special edition of nine essays is wideranging and comprehensive. Almost all articles refer extensively to *The World of the Thibaults.* The themes discussed include the writer as phoenix, the ethics of ambiguity, the psychology of revolution, and fiction as testimony.

Ru, Yi-Ling. *The Family Novel: Toward a Generic Definition.* New York: Peter Lang, 1992. Ru argues that the family novel is a distinct literary genre, proving her contention by analyzing *The World of the Thibaults*, *The Forsyte Saga* by John Galsworthy, and *The Turbulent Trilogy* by Chinese author Pa Chin.

Schalk, David. *Roger Martin du Gard: The Novelist and History.* Ithaca, N.Y.: Cornell University Press, 1967. Schalk investigates the sudden change in Martin du Gard's literary objectives that led him to incorporate contemporary history into fiction. Includes an impressive collection of critical comments from other scholars.

The Would-Be Gentleman

Author: Molière (1622-1673)
First produced: Le Bourgeois Gentilhomme, 1670; first published, 1671 (English translation, 1675)
Type of work: Drama
Type of plot: Comedy of manners
Time of plot: Seventeenth century
Locale: Paris

Principal characters:
MONSIEUR JOURDAIN, a tradesman
MADAME JOURDAIN, his wife
LUCILE, their daughter
NICOLE, a servant
CLÉONTE, in love with Lucile
COVIELLE, his valet
DORANTE, a count
DORIMÈNE, a marchioness

The Story:

Monsieur Jourdain is a tradesman who aspires to be a gentleman. Thinking, like many of his kind, that superficial manners, accomplishments, and speech are the marks of a gentleman, he engages a dancing master, a music master, a fencing master, a philosophy teacher, and other assorted tutors who are as vain and ignorant as he. They constantly quarrel among themselves as to which art is the most important, and each tries to persuade Jourdain to favor him above the others.

From the dancing master he learns to approach a lady: to bow, to step backward, and to walk toward her bowing three times and ending at her knees. From the philosopher he learns that all speech is either poetry or prose. Jourdain is delighted to learn that he was speaking prose all his life. He also learns that he speaks with vowels and consonants. He believes that this knowledge sets him apart from ordinary citizens and makes him a gentleman.

The primary reason for his great desire to be a gentleman is his regard for Dorimène, a marchioness. He has himself fitted out in costumes so ridiculous that they appear to be masquerades, six tailors being required to dress him in his fantastic costumes. Monsieur Jourdain's wife retains her common sense in spite of her husband's wealth, and she constantly chides him about his foolishness. He considers her a bumpkin, however, and reviles her for her ignorance.

In addition to criticizing his dress and speech, his wife rebukes him for being taken in by Count Dorante, a nobleman who flatters Jourdain's affected gentlemanly customs and at the same time borrows large sums of money from him. Jourdain begs Dorante to accept the money because he thinks it the mark of a gentleman to lend money to a nobleman. Jourdain, engaging Dorante to plead his case with Dorimène, provides money for serenades and ballets and a large diamond ring. Dorante promises to bring Dorimène to Jourdain's house for dinner one evening when Jourdain makes arrangements to send his wife and his daughter away. Madame Jourdain, who suspects that her husband is up to some knavery, sends the maid, Nicole, to listen to the conversation between the two men. Nicole cannot hear all of it before being discovered by Jourdain, but she hears enough to convince Madame Jourdain that her husband needs watching.

Jourdain's daughter Lucile loves and is loved by Cléonte, and the Jourdain servant, Nicole, loves Cléonte's servant, Covielle. When Lucile and Nicole pass the two men on the street without nodding, the men swear to forget the faithless ladies and turn to new conquests. After learning, however, that Lucile's aunt is the cause of their coldness—the old lady thinking it unseemly to speak to men—the four lovers are reconciled. Lucile and Cléonte need only Jourdain's permission to marry, for Madame Jourdain approves of Cléonte and promises to intercede with her husband. Jourdain refuses to accept Cléonte as a son-in-law, however, because the young man is not a gentleman. Cléonte is honorable, and he possesses both wealth and a noble career, but he shuns hypocrisy and false living, conduct he considers unbecoming a gentleman. The lovers plead in vain. At last, Covielle suggests a deception to play on the foolish old man, and Cléonte agrees to the plan.

Dorante, meanwhile, uses Jourdain's money in his own suit for Dorimène's favors. Even the diamond ring is presented as a gift from himself. Dorante secretly thinks Jourdain a fool and enjoys making him a real one.

At the dinner in Jourdain's home, Dorimène is somewhat confused by Jourdain's ardent speeches to her, for she thinks it known that she is Dorante's mistress. She is even more disturbed when Madame Jourdain bursts in and accuses her husband of infidelity. Convinced that she is being insulted by a madwoman, Dorimène leaves in tears.

Covielle, disguised, calls on Jourdain and informs him that he was a friend of Jourdain's father, who was indeed a gentleman. He was not a tradesman but had merely bought fabrics and then gave them to his friends for money. Jourdain, delighted with the news, feels justified in his belief that he is a gentleman. Then Covielle tells Jourdain that the son of the Grand Turk desires to marry Lucile. Jourdain is flattered and promises to give the girl to the Grand Turk's son, even though she vows she will marry no one but Cléonte. Jourdain, duped into accepting initiation into the Grand Turk's religion, a ceremony performed with much silly gibberish, believes he is being honored above all men.

When Cléonte appears, disguised as the son of the Grand Turk, Lucile recognizes him and agrees to be his wife. Madame Jourdain chides her for infidelity to Cléonte until Covielle whispers to her that the Grand Turk's son and Cléonte are one and the same; then she, too, gives her consent to the marriage. Jourdain sends for a notary. After convincing Jourdain that their plan is only in jest, Dorante and Dorimène say that they will be married at the same time. In great joy at his exalted position Jourdain blesses them all and in addition gives Nicole to Covielle, whom he thinks to be the interpreter

of the Grand Turk's son's. Thinking that Dorimène loves him, Jourdain offers his wife to whoever wants her. She, knowing the whole plot, thanks him and proclaims him the greatest fool of all.

Critical Evaluation:

The Would-Be Gentleman was first presented at court in 1670 in the Grand Gallery of Chambord, a royal castle on the Loire, which, like all the royal residences, was large and luxurious. The play, by command of Louis XIV, was to be a "turquerie." In 1699, an ambassador from Turkey had visited the king, and enthusiasm was still high for the exotic. Jean-Baptiste Lully wrote the music and Molière added his comedy to it. The expenditures indicate that the initial production was elaborate. It was a great success, and the play has remained one of Molière's most popular.

Twenty-first century productions of the play often cut the ballet scenes. The play is, however, actually a combination of comedy and ballet, in which the ballet is an integral, if separable, part. Dance has a literary or symbolic function as the extension of Monsieur Jourdain's obsession with display; the more preposterous the ballet, the better Jourdain is shown to like it.

Although in some way no more than light entertainment, *The Would-Be Gentleman* has become one of the best-known French plays and Monsieur Jourdain one of Molière's most celebrated characters. He is something of an archetype in French tradition of the bourgeois who tries to conform to aristocratic manners and circles.

The English translation of the play's title is somewhat misleading, as *gentilhomme* means "nobleman" and the juxtaposition of *Le Bourgeois* and *Gentilhomme* should be understood as a contradiction. It is an idea, according to Molière and the court for which he wrote, worthy only of ridicule. The satire, however, is relatively mild; Monsieur Jourdain is more a buffoon, and the comedy is essentially farce, rather than a profound critique of vicious social traits.

Of the inner circle into which Monsieur Jourdain is trying to gain admittance, the audience never sees more than the marchioness, Dorimène, and the count, Dorante. The marchioness has a minor role and is not only the object of Monsieur Jourdain's absurd affection but also remains relatively untainted by his foolish intrigues. Dorante, too, is of noble birth, but if he associates more or less intimately with the bourgeois, it is clearly to exploit the latter's gullible ambitions and to get the marchioness for himself. His duplicity is charming, however, and he cannot be accused of much more than shallowness, since Monsieur Jourdain appears sufficiently wealthy and remains blissfully deceived to the end.

All of the other characters within the family circle are notable for their relatively good sense. In large measure, this good sense means knowing one's place in the social hierarchy.

The principal counterpoint, or foil, for Monsieur Jourdain is Madame Jourdain. Her loyalty to her class and her proud insistence that both her father and Monsieur Jourdain's were merchants, is presented as solid, if contentious, good sense. When she argues that their daughter Lucile would do better to marry a man proper to her sphere in life, an honest, nice-looking, and rich bourgeois, the absurd response of Monsieur Jourdain is that he himself is rich enough for his daughter to require only "honor," so that she can become a marchioness. When she interrupts the banquet Monsieur Jourdain and Dorante are having for Dorimène, Madame Jourdain is told by Dorante that she needs better eyeglasses. The irony here is that she needs them not at all, and that of the others present, only Dorante has an inkling of what is going on, for it is his private scheme to gull Monsieur Jourdain by courting Dorimène with Jourdain's money and lavish gifts. The deceptions and self-deceptions of the play, chiefly of Monsieur Jourdain, are the main source of the humor in *The Would-Be Gentleman*.

From the series of educational vignettes at the opening to the finale, Monsieur Jourdain is a victim of "stage irony." The audience is aware of something of which he himself is unaware, for not only the examples of his self-deception but also the various tricks played on him are quite evident. A critic has theorized that comic characters are essential types more or less constantly at risk of being revealed, as opposed to the process of self-discovery in tragedy: Monsieur Jourdain's wealth permits him the freedom to reveal himself very liberally. He pursues every foolish symbol that the parvenu par excellence feels he must have. What he constantly reveals is that the symbols, worn by him, are empty of meaning. The main action of the play displays that Monsieur Jourdain cannot see beyond display and thus is easily duped.

An extreme example of his obsession with external symbols of status, as well as his foolish single-mindedness in their pursuit, is when the tailor's assistant addresses him by titles of honor. The boy gets a larger tip for each higher title. If he had gone so far as to say "your highness," Jourdain was going to give him the whole purse. However, if the symbol of status is more profound, as when the philosophy teacher instructs him on moderating the passions, Monsieur Jourdain is unimpressed and completely uninterested.

"Critical Evaluation" by James Marc Hovde

Further Reading

Abraham, Claude. *On the Structure of Molière's Comédies-Ballets*. Paris: Papers on French Seventeenth Century Literature, 1984. An original study, which explores the relationship between Molière's text and the music composed by the court composer Jean-Baptiste Lully for the intermezzos in *The Would-Be Gentleman*. Argues persuasively that Lully's music forms an integral part of this ballet comedy.

Howarth, W. D. *Molière: A Playwright and His Audience*. New York: Cambridge University Press, 1982. Examines Molière's creative use of theatrical conventions both in his spoken comedies and in his ballet comedies. Provides an excellent description of the comic richness of Monsieur Jourdain, a role first played by Molière himself.

Hubert, Judd D. *Molière and the Comedy of Intellect*. Berkeley: University of California Press, 1962. Examines social satire, comic uses of language, and the importance of the intermezzos in *The Would-Be Gentleman*. Stresses the importance of theatricality in Molière's plays.

Koppisch, Michael S. *Rivalry and the Disruption of Order in Molière's Theater*. Madison, N.J.: Fairleigh Dickinson University Press, 2004. Argues that the characters in Molière's plays desperately want something they cannot have, such as Monsieur Jourdain's desire to be a gentleman.

McCarthy, Gerry. *The Theatres of Molière*. New York: Routledge, 2002. Places Molière's life and work within the context of the French theater of his time. Discusses the productions of some of his plays, including their actors, scenes, and costumes.

Polsky, Zachary. *The Comic Machine, the Narrative Machine, and the Political Machine in the Works of Molière*. Lewiston, N.Y.: E. Mellen Press, 2003. Examines the nature of seventeenth century French comedy by analyzing the works of Molière. Discusses the moralism and the political context of Molière's plays and describes the use of speech, voice, and body in their performance. Includes a detailed analysis of *The Would-Be Gentleman*.

Scott, Virginia. *Molière: A Theatrical Life*. New York: Cambridge University Press, 2000. Chronicles Molière's life and provides an overview of his plays, placing them within the context of seventeenth century French theater.

Walker, Hallam. *Molière*. 1971. Rev. ed. Boston: Twayne, 1990. An excellent general introduction to Molière's plays including an annotated bibliography of important critical studies on Molière. Describes the connection between artificiality and self-deception in *The Would-Be Gentleman*.

Woyzeck

Author: Georg Büchner (1813-1837)
First published: 1879; first produced, 1913 (English
   translation, 1927)
Type of work: Drama
Type of plot: Psychological realism
Time of plot: Early nineteenth century
Locale: Germany

Principal characters:
FRIEDRICH JOHANN FRANZ WOYZECK, a military conscript
MARIE, his sweetheart
A DRUM MAJOR, Marie's other lover
ANDRES, another soldier and Woyzeck's friend
A CAPTAIN
A DOCTOR

The Story:

Franz Woyzeck is a conscript fusilier, a poor, simple soldier with a peasant's slow mind and a peasant's superstitions. The only happiness he has in his wretched existence comes from his relationship with his sweetheart Marie and their small son. Because his army pay does not suffice for the support of his household, he is forced to earn additional money by performing menial tasks about the camp and in the garrison town where his regiment is stationed.

Serving as a barber's apprentice in his youth, he is often called in to shave his Captain. The officer, a man of speculative, ironic temperament, likes to talk about such topics as time and eternity, matters often beyond Woyzeck's comprehension. Sometimes the Captain jokingly reproves the poor fellow for his lack of morals, since he fathered a child without benefit of a wedding ceremony. Woyzeck always declares that if he were a gentleman with a laced coat and a cocked hat he, too, could be virtuous. He considers virtue to be a privilege of the educated and great, and not intended for miserable creatures such as himself.

An eccentric Doctor also pays Woyzeck a few coins to act as the subject of fantastic medical experiments. The soldier is supposed to live on a diet of peas and to hold his water for stated periods of time. When Woyzeck tries blunderingly to explain his views on nature and life, the Doctor is delighted. He thinks Woyzeck's halting remarks show an interesting aberration, and he predicts that the man will end in a madhouse.

One day, Woyzeck and his friend Andres go into the country to cut wood for the Captain. Woyzeck begins to talk wildly about the freemasons, claiming that they burrowed under the ground and that the earth they hollowed out is rocking under his feet. Their secret signs were revealed to him in dreams, and he is fearful of their vengeance. Andres, usually a matter-of-fact fellow, becomes rather alarmed when Woyzeck pictures the Last Judgment in the glowing colors of the sunset. Returning home, Woyzeck tries to explain to Marie the vision he saw in the sky. She is hurt because in his excitement he fails to notice his son. That afternoon, a hand-

some, bearded Drum Major ogled Marie while she stood at her window and talked to a friend outside. She wonders about Woyzeck and his strange thoughts. Marie is hearty and earthy. It is easier for her to understand people's emotions than their ideas.

Woyzeck and Marie go to a fair. As they enter one of the exhibits, the Drum Major and a Sergeant come by and follow them into the booth, where the barker is showing a horse that can count and identify objects. When the showman calls for a watch, the Sergeant holds up his timepiece. To see what is going on, Marie climbs on a bench and stands next to the Drum Major. That is the beginning of their affair. A short time later, Woyzeck finds Marie with a new pair of earrings that she claims to have found. The simple-minded soldier remarks that he was never lucky enough to find anything in pairs. While Woyzeck is on duty or doing extra work, the Drum Major visits Marie in her room. Full-blooded and passionate, she yields to him.

Woyzeck has no suspicions of her infidelity. One day, as he bustles down the street, he meets the Captain and the Doctor. The Captain begins to talk slyly about beards and hints that if Woyzeck were to hurry home he will be in time to find hairs from a bearded lover on Marie's lips. Woyzeck becomes pale and nervous, whereupon the Doctor shows great clinical interest in his reactions. The Captain assures Woyzeck that he means well by the soldier and Woyzeck goes loping home. When he peers steadily into Marie's face, however, he can see no outward signs of guilt. His scrutiny disturbs and then angers her. She defies him, practically admitting that she has another lover, but she dares Woyzeck to lay a hand on her. Unable to understand how anyone so unkind could look so beautiful and innocent, he leaves the house. Not knowing what else to do, he goes to the Doctor's courtyard. There the physician makes him appear ridiculous in front of a group of medical students.

The next Sunday, Woyzeck and Andres are together in the barracks, Woyzeck is restless and unhappy because there is a dance at an inn near the town and he knows that Marie and the Drum Major will be there. Andres tries to stop his friend, but Woyzeck says that he has to see them for himself. He goes to the inn and through an open window watches Marie and her lover dancing. Andres, fearing a disturbance, finally persuades him to go back to town. Karl, a fool, is among some loafers near the inn door; he says that he smells blood.

That night, Woyzeck, unable to sleep, tells Andres that he still hears music and sees the dancing. He also mumbles about his vision of a knife in a store window. The next day, when he encounters the Drum Major at the inn, the two men fight and Woyzeck is badly beaten by his swaggering rival. Mad with jealousy, he goes to a pawn shop and buys a knife like the one he saw in his dream. At the barracks, he gives away most of his possessions. Resisting Andres's attempt to get him to the infirmary, Woyzeck goes to Marie and asks her to go walking with him. On a lonely path near the pond he takes out his new knife and stabs her to death.

Then he goes back to the inn and dances madly. When a girl named Käthe notices bloodstains on his hand, he says that he cut himself. Questioned further, he screams that he is no murderer and runs from the inn. Wanting to get rid of the incriminating knife that he had left beside Marie's body, he throws it into the pond. His first throw falls short. Desperate, he wades out to hurl the knife into deeper water, gets in over his depth, and drowns.

A group of playing children hear adults talking about the murder. They run to Woyzeck's son and tell him that his mother is dead.

Critical Evaluation:

Georg Büchner's untimely death in 1837 was fortunate in one respect: His play *Woyzeck* remained unfinished. Had he lived to polish the play's structure and bring it, as most scholars agree was his intent, to its logical conclusion with Woyzeck's trial, conviction, and execution, the result may have been an interesting, perhaps even pioneering work, but it would not have been the completely unprecedented, startling piece that it is in its unfinished state. Indeed, the unordered succession of scenes and fragments seems out of place in the early nineteenth century, seeming to belong much more comfortably with the tortured expressionism of the early twentieth century.

Because the style and the structure of the *Woyzeck* fragments are so perfectly wedded to the work's characterization and theme, the play has, in whatever order it is presented or read, the inevitability of a finished product. One version ends with the court clerk describing the crime with relish as a "beautiful murder," and another ends with the children excit-

edly rushing off to view Marie's body before the authorities move it. The other obvious aspect of the play's being incomplete is the fact that it breaks off shortly after Woyzeck murders Maria, but this very lack of resolution is ideally suited to reflect not only the uncertainties of the twentieth century worldview but, more important, those of Woyzeck's world. The play offers no consoling gesture, just as Büchner offers Woyzeck none. All of society's institutions fail Woyzeck, who is tragic not because he is a great man brought low but because he started low and never had a chance.

Büchner was caught up in the radical protest politics of his day and his primary thematic intent in *Woyzeck* was no doubt political. Woyzeck's troubles can be traced most directly to his low economic class. His pay is so meager that he is forced to hire himself out for scientific experiments that play havoc with his health. Even with supplemental pay, he cannot afford to marry Marie, whose affection, as long as he thinks he has it, is the one redeeming feature of his life. Since they cannot afford to marry, their child is illegitimate and cannot be baptized. Marie is as much a victim of poverty as is Woyzeck. She worries about her bastard child and is so pathetically eager for something to take her away from her drab surroundings and circumstances that she takes up with a vulgar drum major who can afford to buy her a few trinkets.

Poverty, though, is just one aspect of Woyzeck's world that makes his life so hopeless. No age is free of poverty, but most ages offer consolations to the poor, the most obvious being religion, with its promises of the hereafter. Actually, *Woyzeck* is filled with religious imagery and direct quotations from the Bible, but these, rather than healing and consoling, tend toward the apocalyptic and anticipate violence to come. At moments, Marie is acutely aware of her "fallen" state, feels painful remorse, and calls on God for mercy. It is Woyzeck who summons up the apocalyptic imagery, and his wrath most closely resembles the biblical prophets impatient of evil. Had his moral vision been less rigid, Woyzeck might have accommodated himself to the world's imperfections and not been driven to violence; had Marie not come equipped with moral sense, she might at least have enjoyed her dalliance and not been afflicted with remorse. These two not only do not profit from their religious beliefs but are plagued by them.

It is in Büchner's century that there was, at least among many intellectuals, a movement away from religion as a guiding principle and source of truth. What replaced religion for many of these apostates was science. Here, too, however, Büchner was ahead of his time, for *Woyzeck* manifests modern cynicism about the wisdom and worth of scientists and science. Woyzeck's being forced to hire himself out as a guinea pig for the doctor's experiments, who wants to observe the effects of a diet of peas, underscores both the evils of poverty and the inhuman arrogance of science. Indeed, Woyzeck's depression and psychosis were certainly exacerbated by a diet lacking in vitamins and other nutrients. Like the god of religion, the god of science fails Woyzeck.

Referring to Woyzeck as a guinea pig is in keeping with the play's animal motif. Horses, monkeys, and lizards are all present or at least referred to, always with a direct or implied comparison to human beings. The horse can count as well as a person; the monkey sports a uniform and sword just like a soldier; and the death of a lizard, the doctor maintains, would be a greater loss to his experiment than the death of Woyzeck. This underscores the pessimism of the play and also prefigures Charles Darwin, who not long after Büchner's death was to rock the world with the theory that human beings were not higher beings close to a god of creation but animals that, like all animals, evolved according to laws of nature.

Although Woyzeck is a brilliantly conceived character, the play is not a character study so much as the dramatization of the spirit of an age about to be born. Woyzeck is an Everyman suffering through an age when the old certainties eroded and the new ones are suspect. Driven to desperation like so many of his fellow human beings, Woyzeck can only lash out and destroy, but that, too, brings only pain.

"Critical Evaluation" by Dennis Vannatta

Further Reading

Crighton, James. *Büchner and Madness: Schizophrenia in Georg Büchner's "Lenz" and "Woyzeck."* Lewiston, N.Y.: Edwin Mellen Press, 1998. This study of Büchner's depiction of schizophrenia examines his sources of information about the disease and discusses the social and personal circumstances that resulted in the creation of both *Woyzeck* and *Lenz*. Crighton intersperses his analyses of the plays with information about Büchner's life, relationships, and medical education, as well as nineteenth century literature about mental illness.

James, Dorothy. "The 'Interesting Case' of Büchner's *Woyzeck*." In *Patterns of Change: German Drama and the European Tradition*, edited by Dorothy James and Silvia Ranawake. New York: Peter Lang, 1990. Provides a fine introduction to understanding the place of *Woyzeck* in German drama. James also places Büchner in a context of developing European thought.

Kaufmann, Friedrich Wilhelm. *German Dramatists of the Nineteenth Century*. New York: Russell & Russell, 1972. Kaufmann notes that in plays such as *Woyzeck*, Büchner is dramatizing the collapse of old European values and the process of coming to grips with new realities. Woyzeck himself is an Everyman, condemned by his poverty to a life of misery.

Reddick, John. *Georg Büchner: The Shattered Whole*. New York: Oxford University Press, 1994. Seeks to offer new interpretations of *Woyzeck* and Büchner's other works and discusses the playwright's values, ideas, and politics. Reddick argues that Buchner was aesthetically way ahead of his time primarily because his idealistic assumptions and aspirations were far behind the times.

Richards, David G. *Georg Büchner's "Woyzeck": A History of Its Criticism*. Rochester, N.Y.: Camden House, 2001. Compilation of nineteenth and twentieth century criticism of the play, demonstrating the ongoing debate about the authority of its text and the sharply divided opinion about the drama.

Ritchie, J. M. *German Expressionist Drama*. Boston: Twayne, 1976. Notes the influence of *Woyzeck* on twentieth century German expressionist drama and provides compelling evidence that the play was ahead of its time.

Stodder, Joseph H. "The Influences of *Othello* on Büchner's *Woyzeck*." *Modern Language Review* 69 (January, 1974): 115-120. An interesting comparison that points to the plot similarities between William Shakespeare's *Othello, the Moor of Venice* (pr. 1604) and Büchner's *Woyzeck*, which both concern men driven by jealousy to murder women they love and are then tortured by remorse. Leads the author to conclude that Shakespeare's work was a direct influence on Büchner.

The Wreck of the Deutschland

Author: Gerard Manley Hopkins (1844-1889)
First published: 1918, in *Poems of Gerard Manley Hopkins, Now First Published, with Notes by Robert Bridges*
Type of work: Poetry

In a letter written to R. W. Dixon, Gerard Manley Hopkins explains the background of the poem "The Wreck of the *Deutschland.*" In 1875, during cold weather, the German ship *Deutschland* set sail for New York but was shipwrecked on the sands of the Kentish Knock at the mouth of the Thames River in England. Although Hopkins resolved not to compose any more poetry after his ordination as a Jesuit priest, his superior expressed the wish that someone write a poem in the wake of this tragedy. "I was affected by the account," Hopkins wrote in his letter.

Hopkins was moved by the loss of 168 passengers and crew, including five nuns from a convent in Westphalia who were exiled from Germany. Although 138 people were rescued by a Liverpool tugboat, many boats passed by and ignored the distress signals because sailors feared risking their lives in the freezing weather. Stranded off the English coast near Harwich for nearly thirty hours, the *Deutschland* eventually sank. With great descriptive power and depth of emotion, Hopkins depicts the scene of tragedy and the anguish of the drowning victims. The blasts of wind ("For the infinite air is unkind"), the blinding snowstorm ("whirlwind-swivelled snow"), the shock of the ship hitting, not a rock or a reef, but "a smother of sand" all bring the passengers and crew into the jaws of death. After twelve hours of desperate waiting, with no help in sight, "Hope had grown gray hairs," and "lives at last were washing away." The heroic efforts of a man to save a woman from drowning are spent in vain before the awesome power of death: "What could he do/ With the burl of the fountains of air, buck and the flood of the wave?" The piercing sounds of women wailing and children crying echo the roaring of the storm and parallel the blinding of the snow, the wildness of the gales, and the swirling of the sea. In the middle of this tempest, roar, and deluge, a tall nun (a "lioness") speaks above the din of terrifying destruction, crying "O Christ, Christ, come quickly" (stanza 24). In asking "what did she mean?" Hopkins recalls Jesus calming the waters when his disciples, terrified on the lake of Gennesareth, cried "we are perishing" (Matthew 8:23-27). Rebuking the winds and the sea, Jesus calmed the storm and saved the disciples, demonstrating God's mastery of nature. Hopkins empha-

sizes the striking resemblances between the sinking of the *Deutschland* and the tempest on the lake that frightened the disciples. Christ is present in the hour of danger and of death to all who believe. While the disciples on the lake were reproached for their lack of faith, the tall nun in the hour of darkness entrusts all to God's providence: "Christ, King, Head:/ He was to cure the extremity where he had cast her" (stanza 28). While the naked eye observes human victims powerless against nature's forces and drowning in perilous seas, the eyes of faith see God's hand in all events. "There was single eye!" observes Hopkins of the nun who sees in death not only suffering but also consolation.

The Christian faith of the nun does not leave her "comfortless" or "unconfessed," for the eyes of faith see in shipwreck also a harvest and view the tempest as an agent of "grain for thee" (stanza 31). That is, as the Catholic Church always teaches, the blood of the martyrs is the seed of the Church. The heroic death of Christians who embrace their cross and remain steadfast in their faith in the hour of trial wins souls for Christ. The eyes of faith also "Grasp God, throned behind/ Death with a sovereignty that heeds but hides, bodes but abides" (stanza 32). Just as Christ the master commands the winds and the waves, Christ as sovereign rules over death. He comes to claim his own. The five Franciscan nuns accept their crosses with courage and conviction in the knowledge of God's mercy. "The Christ of the Father compassionate, fetched in the storm of his strides" (stanza 33) will not drown them but seal them "in wild waters,/ To bathe in his fall-gold mercies, to breathe in his all-fire glances" (stanza 24).

"The Wreck of the *Deutschland*," then, comes to describe not only the deaths of the passengers and the tragedy of a shipwreck but also the shipwreck of a world devastated by Original Sin. Hopkins alludes in stanza 1 to this greater shipwreck in his reference to fallen man ruining God's original Creation: "And after it almost unmade, what with dread,/ Thy doing." The storm without, on the sea, magnifies the storm within, in the soul. In stanzas 2 and 3, Hopkins examines the destructive effects of Original Sin in the human soul and in the world, and he describes the fear of God's punishment for sin, his "lightning and lashed rod" and Christ's "terror" that evoke the dread of "the hurtle of hell." Stanza 4 describes the constant decay and impermanence of one's mortal life, which is symbolized by the image of the hourglass marking one's progression from life to death. God is as real and present, however, in a fallen world and in sinful human life as he is to the tall nun in the fury of the disaster at sea. Stanza 5 describes the glory of God in the splendor of the star-filled heavens ("lovely-asunder starlight") and in the beautiful sunset ("the dappled-with-damson west").

Creation in all its beauty declares the mystery of God's presence in a fallen world stained with sin. History also gives witness to God's presence as the Word becomes Flesh and dwells among people. Stanza 7 refers to the Incarnation in its references to "manger, maiden's knee." Just as God manifests himself in the beauty of nature and in the miracles of history, God is present in the moment of death.

Christ conquers both sin and death with his "driven Passion and frightful sweat" (stanza 7). He comes as both "lightning and love" and as "a winter and warm" (stanza 9). That is, the wreck of a fallen world or the destruction of passengers at sea do not signify a world devoid of God's grace and love. God is present in the darkness and storm of tragedy. He comes in the wreck of sin and death to call souls to him. Just as he called Saul of Tarsus on the road to Damascus "at once, as once a crash" (stanza 10) or summoned Augustine to repentance and conversion "With an anvil-ding," in a burst of force or energy that erupts like the fire in the forge or the ebullience of spring, God appears in a flash to the drowning victims on the *Deutschland*—not in a "dooms-day dazzle" but "royally reclaiming his own" (stanza 34) in a surge of love and mercy. This divine energy of God's infinite love and goodness overflows on Calvary, where Christ's body bursts with his outpouring blood for man's redemption. Like a ripe fruit whose juices gush upon being tasted—"How a lush-kept plush-capped sloe/ Will, mouthed to flesh-burst,/ Gush!"—God proffers his everlasting mercy throughout the ages to the sinful who are struggling in the wreck of a fallen world. This divine energy Hopkins calls "inscape" or "instress," a dynamic creative power that radiates God's glory in flashes, bursts, explosions, and eruptions in unique, unpredictable, and astonishing ways. The manifold expressions of God's power in the world in wind, lightning, fire, and sea; the myriad forms of beauty in all its colorful variety that infuse nature; and the multiple manifestations of God's mystery and reality all reflect the boundless, kinetic energy of God's being. The passion and sweat of Christ, that burst with the blood of sacrifice, the discharge of the flash of lightning, the day-spring of Easter that swells with life and rebirth all

emanate from the divine energy of God's being that overflows in "God's three numbered form" and hurls itself throughout all of Creation in "The heaven-flung, heart-fleshed, maiden furled/ Miracle-in-Mary-of-flame" (stanza 34). To capture the fullness of God's being that is constantly spilling, flinging, hurling, flashing, and erupting with spontaneous energy and generating life, Hopkins writes in a style called sprung rhythm, which imitates the dynamic surges and bold movements of God's art in the world. Hopkins's verbal power breaks loose in the poem with the same explosive force as God's creative energy. However, sprung rhythm, while not a tame or a rigidly controlled movement, is not a wild, undisciplined, or random force. Rather it is as intricate, designed, and harmonious as God's beauty—a complex pattern of words and rhythms that echoes the music of sound and follows the expansion of the heart in the ecstasy of love. Sprung rhythm, in other words, resembles the vibrations, movements, and passions of a heart in love with God and in awe at His beauty, love, and grace. The lifting of the heart ascends in rapture and ecstasy with breathless wonder: "Our heart's charity's hearth's fire, our thoughts's chivalry's throng's Lord." Hopkins's originality in the use of sprung rhythm, his notions of inscape and instress that inform his poetry, and his use of authentic but unusual diction and syntax with a strong emphasis on alliteration ("lovely-felicitous Providence/ Finger of a tender of, O of a feathery delicacy") all distinguish Hopkins as one of the great pioneers of modern poetry.

Mitchell Kalpakgian

Further Reading

Boyle, Robert. *Metaphor in Hopkins*. Chapel Hill: University of North Carolina Press, 1960. Chapter 1, "The Heroic Breast," discusses the theme of heroic sacrifice in "The Wreck of the *Deutschland*." This chapter provides a careful, close reading of the many religious allusions in the poem.

Brown, Daniel. *Gerard Manley Hopkins*. Tavistock, England: Northcote House/British Council, 2004. An introduction to Hopkins's poetry and prose. Brown argues that Hopkins's poetry was the "complete expression" of his life's work, and its ideas about nature, language, philosophy, theology, and other subjects becomes accessible when read alongside his prose writings.

Downes, David Anthony. *Gerard Manley Hopkins: A Study of His Ignatian Spirit*. Boston: Twayne, 1959. Discusses Hopkins's poetry in the light of his training and background as a Jesuit priest. Chapter 2 applies many of the moral precepts of St. Ignatius to the poem, comparing individual stanzas to specific exercises in St. Ignatius's spiritual classic.

Jenkins, Alice, ed. *The Poems of Gerard Manley Hopkins: A Sourcebook*. New York: Routledge, 2006. A collection of materials about Hopkins's poetry. Contains primary documents, including excerpts from Hopkins's essays on poetic diction and the language of verse and *The Times* report of the wreck of the *Deutschland*. Traces the early and modern critical receptions of Hopkins's work, including discussions of his depiction of gender, use of language, "inscape," and "instress," and three essays from the 1990's that analyze "The Wreck of the *Deutschland*."

MacKenzie, Norman H. *Excursions in Hopkins*. Edited by Catherine Phillips. Philadelphia: Saint Joseph's University Press, 2008. MacKenzie, a Hopkins scholar and Oxford University professor, analyzes the contexts within which Hopkins wrote his poems. Two chapters are devoted to an examination of "The Wreck of the *Deutschland*."

Mariani, Paul L. *Gerard Manley Hopkins: A Life*. New York: Viking Press, 2008. A spiritual biography, focused on Hopkins's inner life, written by a poet and Hopkins scholar. Includes analyses of Hopkins's major poetic works.

O'Brien, Kevin J. *Saying Yes at Lightning: Threat and the Provisional Image in Post-Romantic Poetry*. New York: Peter Lang, 2002. An examination of poems about cataclysmic events in which poets have "said yes to that lightning by writing of it." Chapter 2 is devoted to an explication of "The Wreck of the *Deutschland*."

Peters, Wilhelmus A. M. *Gerard Manley Hopkins: A Critical Essay Towards the Understanding of His Poetry*. New York: Oxford University Press, 1948. This book renders a close, careful reading of Hopkins's poetry, analyzing many of the techniques and devices of Hopkins's verse. Chapter 1, "The Meaning of Inscape and Instress," offers an especially valuable discussion of two major concepts that inform all of Hopkins's poetry.

Wimsatt, James I. *Hopkins' Poetics of Speech Sound: Sprung Rhythm, Lettering, Inscape*. Toronto, Ont.: University of Toronto Press, 2006. Examines Hopkins's theories about the sound of poetic language, analyzing the use of sprung rhythm, lettering, and inscape in his work. The numerous references to "The Wreck of the *Deutschland*" are listed in the index.

The Wretched of the Earth

Author: Frantz Fanon (1925-1961)
First published: Les Damnés de la terre, 1961 (*The Damned*, 1963; as *The Wretched of the Earth*, 1965)
Type of work: Politics

Frantz Fanon's *The Wretched of the Earth* treats many of the central ideas concerning the struggle for liberation against colonialism. Fanon, who was a psychiatrist, worked in a hospital in Algeria during the war for independence from France, and many of the essay's ideas are based on his observations and experiences in Algeria. He wrote during the era that would ultimately lead to the collapse of most colonialism in Africa; his ideas, however, are about liberation in general. Fanon sets forth the idea that Marxist notions of history and of the progression toward freedom need to be adapted to the struggle for independence. Analyzing the movement from colonization to independence, he modifies Marxist ideas. For example, Fanon notes that workers, far from being revolutionary, sometimes have an interest in colonialism and in the maintenance of a colonial economy. In sum, in *The Wretched of the Earth*, Fanon offers ideas that are central to literature on colonialism and on revolution.

The chapter titled "Concerning Violence" lays the groundwork for many of the ideas to come in the rest of the book. Essential in this chapter is Fanon's assertion that decolonization is always a violent process. Decolonization is also the process of creating a "new person." The struggle for independence necessarily entails the destruction of the image of the oppressed that the colonizers have set forth in an attempt to define the colonized. There is no reform of colonialism in the struggle for independence, Fanon argues further; the destruction of colonialism must be total.

Central to Fanon's ideas throughout the work is the role of violence in the struggle for liberation. Fanon's ideas on violence are complex. First, he notes that only force can meet force: Colonialism is held in place by soldiers and police officers. In addition, the takeover of nations by European countries was a violent phenomenon that tried to obliterate the ways of life of the indigenous peoples and to kill their spirits and their cultures. Hence, from its inception and in its maintenance, colonialism is violent. Moreover, as Fanon knew, the colonialist powers could not be expected to leave colonized areas peacefully. Therefore, violent struggle is a necessary agent for colonized peoples to gain independence.

While Fanon's discussion of the need for armed struggle might seem obvious, his discussion of violence is complex and thoughtful. He also describes the psychological violence against the colonized that has been perpetuated by the settlers. For example, colonialism hinges in part on the acceptance by the colonized of their inferior status. This inferiority is economic and social. In fact, the one imposed condition of inferiority hinges on the other. Yet, Fanon asserts, the inequality of colonialism sparks in the indigenous people the desire to overthrow the settler. The indigenous people naturally desire to throw off their inferior status. Hence, while psychological violence against the people (which results in their physical and psychological degradation) helps keep colonialism in its place, Fanon suggests that this very degradation makes clear one of the foremost reasons for the need for violent overthrow of the colonizers. He stresses the need for a revolutionary re-creation of the psychological and economic status of the people. A revolution must entail, according to Fanon, violent thought and deeds. Violence for Fanon seems to be both psychological catharsis and historical process, both of which are necessary for the overthrow of oppressors.

In "Concerning Violence" and in "Spontaneity: Its Strength and Weakness," Fanon discusses some of the problems confronting liberation movements. He clearly has faith in the need for liberation, but he makes evident that liberation is a process, not one quick war that establishes independence. He stresses that in the historical process of attaining liberation, those among the colonized who are part of the struggle must realize the roles they have to play, and this entails a transformation of the consciousness of many people—many received ideas have to go. Central in this process are political activists who can bridge the gap between themselves and the common people. Fanon notes that many political activists and intellectuals are unfamiliar with the people who live in villages and thus have limited their political connections to people who live in towns, and this, he asserts, is a major mistake. Among rural peoples, Fanon believes, one will find those whose cultures have been the least affected by colonialism, and hence those least brainwashed into feeling inferior to the colonizers.

Moreover, people in rural areas cling to their cultures, unlike members of the middle classes and intellectuals who may feel they prosper either from the way things are under colonialism or from immersing themselves in European ideas and values. Thus the common people, Fanon writes, never having lost the value of their own cultures, will actively support those who want to reclaim their lands, their customs, and themselves from European domination. The roles that political activists can play in working with rural people are to keep them involved in the struggle and to illuminate for them the ideas of liberation that motivate the struggle. Fanon is concerned with a major problem of any revolution: the continuance of revolutionary acts. Revolution is a historical process, he points out, and it hinges on the continuance of acts of liberation. Again, a war alone does not a revolution make; the nation's mind must also be freed. Fanon places primary importance on the need for those concerned with the liberation of a nation to value and work with the nation's peasants.

Fanon's ideas about the importance of peasants as revolutionaries is one of the most essential and innovative aspects of *The Wretched of the Earth*. Traditionally, peasants are often discounted as having no significant role to play in their societies. After the Russian Revolution, particularly during the Stalinist era, peasants were killed by the millions, mainly starved to death, because of the belief that they were antirevolutionary. Fanon refutes the idea that farmers and the rural poor are antirevolutionary; he uses Marxist thought to give a central role to the peasants in the march toward liberation.

Other essential ideas are found in Fanon's chapters titled "The Pitfalls of National Consciousness" and "On National Culture." In both chapters, Fanon is concerned with overcoming disunity among colonized peoples. In particular, he writes about how culture and consciousness can be used to fuel liberation. Fanon's comments on intellectuals' concerns with reclaiming their indigenous culture show how oppressed people wage a psychological fight to assert their value—a value denied by the colonizers. Fanon asserts that intellectuals' need to affirm their culture is a response to the way colonialism attempts to destroy the image of the past of an oppressed people. Colonialism asserts that the colonized people's past is worthless. Nigerian writer Chinua Achebe has described the colonizer's version of the colonized's past as "one long night of savagery." This version of history implies that without European constraints and controls, the colonized people would merely be savages. Indigenous people's learning of their own value, independent of the colonialists, is an important ingredient in their valuing themselves enough to reclaim their traditions, their culture, and their country.

Fanon points out a barrier that must be crossed before the value of national culture can be transformed into a part of the process of revolution. He states that it is essential that the intellectuals, writers, and artists who assert the value of national culture not merely focus on the glory of the past as if all one needs to do is look to the past and be proud of it—this is not enough. Intellectuals and artists must use the past to reformulate the present and the future. One example Fanon offers is the use of the oral tradition during Algeria's struggle for independence. Instead of merely prefacing a story by saying, "This happened long ago," many storytellers emphasized that the story might well be happening in the present. The authorities became so concerned, states Fanon, that they started to arrest storytellers. Fanon thus makes clear his argument that the culture of the country needs to be reclaimed and used as a revolutionary agent in struggles for liberation.

Many of Fanon's comments on culture and revolution were later incorporated into African Americans' ideas of the black aesthetic. A product of the 1960's, the black aesthetic movement emphasized that cultural productions by African Americans, such as art and literature, need to be socially committed to improving the condition of African Americans in order to hasten liberation from oppression. In addition, some theoreticians of the black aesthetic pointed out that cultural productions need to inspire the people to become committed to the struggle against racism. Hence, as in Fanon's theories in *The Wretched of the Earth*, an aspect of the black aesthetic was that art can be useful in illuminating concepts for the people and inspiring them to try to change their place in society.

The penultimate chapter of the book, "Colonial War and Mental Disorders," is one of the most powerful. In this chapter, Fanon gives several case studies from his work in a hospital in Algeria during the war for independence to show the psychological scars left by the violent oppression of the people. He offers many striking cases, including one concerning a political activist whose wife was raped by French authorities who were trying to find him. He also relates the story of a man suffering from the psychological aftermath of surviving the mass murder of his village by the French. Another story describes how two Algerian boys, both teenagers, killed a European boy who was a friend of theirs. One reason Fanon offers these examples is to illustrate that the process of recovering from colonialism and establishing independence needs to take into account the psychological scars of the period of colonialism. Fanon also tells of cases of European authorities affected by their torturing of Algerians. In this chapter, one clearly sees the emotional tragedies that have resulted from colonialism. One of the most striking and unique parts of *The Wretched of the Earth* is this section in which Fanon uses his experience as a psychiatrist to make vivid the horrors of colonialism.

In his concluding chapter, Fanon comes back to the beginning point of the book: the creation of new people through the struggle for liberation. Fanon presents a devastating critique of Europe for its oppression of colonized peoples and for failing to live up to the alleged European ideals of liberty and equality. Another point of this critique is that Fanon wants to make it clear that newly independent countries should not try to imitate Europe. In refashioning their economies and their cultures, they must strive to remain true to the ideals of liberation. The book ends with Fanon's challenge to oppressed peoples to create themselves anew in the spirit of freedom.

The Wretched of the Earth is striking in the importance and the complexity of Fanon's ideas. Fanon was able to bring unique insights into his analysis of colonialism as a result of his experiences as a psychiatrist. Furthermore, the book offers many creative ideas, leading readers to rethink the role of the peasant class in revolutions, the importance for political leaders to connect with the masses, the controversial role of violence in liberation struggles, and the need for art and culture to function as tools of liberation. Whether one agrees or disagrees with Fanon's analysis of these important issues, one cannot deny the imaginative and intricate nature of the arguments he presents. For these reasons, *The Wretched of the Earth* is a classic work on oppression, colonialism, and liberation.

Jane Davis

Further Reading

Bulhan, Hussein Abdilahi. *Frantz Fanon and the Psychology of Oppression*. New York: Plenum Press, 1985. Biography, written from a psychiatric perspective, treats Fanon essentially as a contributor to the field of psychiatry. Places his revolutionary activity in the context of his interest in the psychology of oppression.

Cherki, Alice. *Frantz Fanon: A Portrait*. Translated by Nadia Benabid. Ithaca, N.Y.: Cornell University Press, 2006. Biography by a woman who worked closely with Fanon at a psychiatric hospital in Blida, Algeria, and in Tunisia during the Algerian war for independence. Recounts the events of his life, describes his complex personality, and analyzes his work. Devotes a chapter to *The Wretched of the Earth*.

Geismar, Peter. *Fanon*. New York: Dial Press, 1971. Authoritative and sympathetic biography is based on interviews with members of Fanon's family and his friends. Provides a good introduction to Fanon's work.

Gendzier, Irene L. *Frantz Fanon: A Critical Study*. Rev. ed. New York: Grove Press, 1985. Excellent biography should be standard reading for anyone with a serious interest in Fanon's life and writings.

Gibson, Nigel C. *Fanon: The Postcolonial Imagination*. Malden, Mass.: Blackwell, 2003. Examines Fanon's ideas and his legacy; asserts that Fanon devised his theories as a practical way to change the world. Includes discussion of *The Wretched of the Earth*.

Gordon, Lewis R., T. Denean Sharpley-Whiting, and Renée T. White, eds. *Fanon: A Critical Reader*. Malden, Mass.: Blackwell, 1996. Collection of essays is divided into sections covering the following themes: oppression, questions regarding the human sciences, identity and the dialectics of recognition, the emancipation of women of color, the postcolonial dream, neocolonial realities, resistance, and revolutionary violence.

Jean-Marie, Vivaldi. *Fanon: Collective Ethics and Humanism*. New York: Peter Lang, 2007. Provides an interpretation of *The Wretched of the Earth* designed for first-time readers. Discusses Fanon's ideas and his influence on subsequent twentieth century writers.

Sharpley-Whiting, T. Denean. *Frantz Fanon: Conflicts and Feminism*. New York: Rowman & Littlefield, 1998. Evaluates Fanon's commitment, or noncommitment, to feminism through an examination of his commitment to antiracism and revisits many of the previous interpretations of Fanon's work in relation to feminism. Asserts that Fanon was profeminist, contrary to the majority of feminist critiques of Fanon and his work.

Wyrick, Deborah. *Fanon for Beginners*. New York: Writers and Readers, 1998. Combines a detailed account of Fanon's life with a critical view of his major works. Includes illustrations to help make the author's points clearer as well as a glossary.

Writing and Difference

Author: Jacques Derrida (1930-2004)
First published: L'Écriture et la différence, 1967
    (English translation, 1978)
Type of work: Philosophy and literary criticism

Jacques Derrida initiated a seismic wave throughout the field of literary criticism with the essays collected in *Writing and Difference*, in particular with the essay "Structure, Sign, and Play in the Discourse of the Human Sciences," which was first presented at a conference at Johns Hopkins University in October, 1966. Through his challenges to structuralism, Derrida helped give rise to the movement in literary theory known as poststructuralism.

The book presents a series of loosely affiliated essays from earlier presentations and publications, and it ends with a new essay titled "Ellipsis." Taken together, the essays explore the key strategies of what came to be called deconstruction, despite Derrida's own insistence that he created no system or school of thought. The essays in the collection reflect an ongoing effort to avoid closure by introducing and then changing the vocabulary through which Derrida interprets a variety of writers, from philosophers to poets. The essays

both discuss and demonstrate in various ways the role that writing plays in creating difference.

This crucial term, "difference," gives rise to the Derridean alternative, "differance." The change from difference to differance can be read but not heard—that is, while they appear differently on the page, the two words have the same pronunciation, so the neologism can be specified orally only by reference to written language (by uttering a phrase such as "differance with an *a*"). The French verb *différer* means "to differ" (as a thing differs from another thing), "to disagree" (as in the phrase "I beg to differ"), and "to defer." The noun form, *différence*, creates a substantive noun from only the first of those meanings. Thus, in the transition from verb to noun, meanings fall out of the language. Derrida invents the French word *différance* for two reasons: to create a noun that bears those lost meanings (disagreement and deferral, as well as difference) and to demonstrate the importance of writing over speaking as a way to destabilize fixed meanings and to create spaces in apparently closed structures.

Each of the essays in *Writing and Difference* works with specific texts and examples to find the spaces of differance that are covered up by the surface coherence of writing. Derrida breaks with the philosophical tradition of privileging the spoken word as the marker of absolute metaphysical presence when he turns to writing as the field that initiates human history.

The first essay, "Force and Signification," reads literary critic Jean Rousset's *Forme et signification: Essais sur les structures littéraires de Corneille à Claudel* (1962; form and meaning: essays on literary structures from Corneille to Claudel) in order to destabilize the binary opposition between form and meaning. Derrida's own title evokes the idea of force, which he identifies as the element absent from Rousset's structuralist ordering of the authors whom he discusses. Derrida takes pains to reproduce portions of Rousset's arguments before making his own claim that those arguments rely on external, pseudoscientific systems that constrain rather than interpret the works.

This specific critique of Rousset entails a general critique of structuralist approaches to literature, which privilege the synchrony of form and meaning over the historical force that constantly opens up new readings. Derrida admits that his desire to avoid binary opposition is utopian, but he nonetheless insists that the attempt is necessary. He closes the essay by evoking Friedrich Wilhelm Nietzsche's writing on the union of the Apollonian with the Dionysian, comparing Nietzsche's use of "Dionysian" to his own use of the term "force."

In "Cogito and the History of Madness," Derrida takes on another giant of twentieth century cultural theory, Michel Foucault. This essay works to open up and critique the understanding of Descartes proposed by Foucault in *Folie et déraison: Histoire de la folie à l'âge classique* (1961; *Madness and Civilization: A History of Insanity in the Age of Reason*, 1965). Derrida introduces the idea of excess, or extravagance, another key term for evading closure.

"Edmond Jabès and the Question of the Book" reads the work of poet Edmond Jabès, taking specific examples from *Le Livre des questions* (1963; *The Book of Questions*, 1976). Derrida approaches the connection between the Jewish heritage Jabès draws on in his poems and the significance of writing as the mark of human entry into history. For Derrida, the entry into history marks the entry into difference. In this essay, Derrida plays with the term "fold," or "wrinkle," to suggest the multiple layers of meaning that accompany humans' existence within history.

The longest essay in the collection, "Violence and Metaphysics: Essay on the Thought of Emmanuel Levinas," takes on the arguments of French philosopher Emmanuel Levinas on metaphysics and ethics. Derrida traces a distinguished lineage of philosophers for Levinas, and implicitly for himself, from Plato through Georg Wilhelm Friedrich Hegel, Edmund Husserl, and Martin Heidegger. Derrida suggests that the project Levinas undertakes—to reintroduce ethics into the discourse of metaphysics—can be seen as the conjunction of messianic and Hellenistic traditions. Derrida argues that Levinas, in his drive to acknowledge otherness, constricts the nature of language and misreads his own relationship to phenomenology and ontology. Derrida closes with a quotation from James Joyce, which he glosses as saying that humans live in the difference between Greeks and Jews, a difference that Derrida names "history," returning to the dialogue between the messianic and the Hellenistic that he reads in Levinas.

The fifth essay, "'Genesis and Structure' and Phenomenology," offers a reading of the use of these two terms by philosopher Edmund Husserl. Though they appear to function as a binary opposition, Derrida argues that they are fluid terms which do not succumb to a form of structuralist totalitarian reading such as the one he found in Jean Rousset.

In "The Whispered Word," Derrida elucidates the dialogue between psychoanalytic and literary critical discourses, citing Maurice Blanchot's literary exegesis of Friedrich Hölderlin as a mad poet and closing with a discussion of Antonin Artaud's theory of theater. The essay's title plays on the French term *souffleur*, which literally means "whisperer" but which is also the word for a prompter on the stage. Artaud, as another mad poet, seeks to evade all such prompting, and for Derrida this constitutes the evasion of the spoken word and the absolute presence of that word. Theater can therefore be seen as a form of writing.

An extended discussion of the Derridean term "writing" appears in "Freud and the Scene of Writing." Derrida finds his main point in Sigmund Freud's "Notiz Über Den 'Wunderblock'" (1925; "A Note upon the 'Mystic Writing-Pad,'" 1940). The mystic writing-pad can be written upon and then reused after the top plastic sheet is lifted, but traces of the original writing will always remain in the substrate. Freud uses this device as a metaphor for the production of new neural pathways that create memories, and Derrida sees in it a useful metaphor for writing itself, which is path-breaking and which leaves traces. The substrate represents the original writing, *archi-écriture*, which sets difference and history into motion.

Derrida deepens his reading of Artaud in "The Theater of

Cruelty and the Closure of Representation." Derrida emphasizes that Artaud's *Le Théâtre et son double* (1938; *The Theatre and Its Double*, 1958) projects a drama that takes gesture as primary and spoken word as secondary. Derrida sees this projection as a useful illustration of his own interpretation of writing as the site of the supplement and the marker of the absence of an origin. Artaud stresses the unscripted, unrepeatable performance in the moment, which provides a powerful illustration of the limits of representation. Derrida sees in Artaud's notion of the "theater of cruelty" a corollary to Nietzsche's description of the Dionysian force in Greek tragedy. Though this theater can only exist as a future possibility, Derrida claims for it the power of making possible a mode of thought about the history of theater that will open up new spaces.

Derrida turns his project of reading for differences to the work of French critic Georges Bataille in "From the Economy of Restraint to the General Economy: A Hegelianism Without Reservation." He interrogates the ways in which Bataille displaces Hegel's seminal theory of the master-slave dialectic, a displacement that figures as difference in the Derridean sense. The key term is this essay is sovereignty, which must be distinguished from mastery. Bataille claims this sovereignty for poetry, which is willing to exceed the realm of sense and accept nonsense. Mastery, in contrast, requires the making of meaning. Derrida makes his move by suggesting that, in reading Hegel, Bataille reaches an understanding that is less than Hegelian.

"Structure, Sign, and Play in the Discourse of the Human Sciences" is perhaps the most widely disseminated of the essays in *Writing and Difference*. In it, Derrida returns to a critique of structuralism similar to the one offered in the opening essay, but he articulates the need to decenter all structures while acknowledging the need to write as if structural centers exist. In this sense, Derrida sees all philosophical discourse as enmeshed in history.

For Derrida, the illusion of a stable center allows humans to control their deep-seated anguish and to extrapolate a comforting origin of being in absolute presence. He deems the history of philosophy a history of metaphoric and metonymic substitutions of centers. Derrida's ideas here provide powerful means for critiquing the dominance of Western traditions in philosophy and literature by offering a critical reading of concepts that were previously assumed to be true.

Derrida demonstrates this process of critique in the work of French structuralist anthropologist Claude Levi-Strauss. Levi-Strauss himself broke down the binary opposition between nature and culture by identifying the incest taboo as belonging to both categories, and he openly acknowledged his own work as a form of myth-making. Levi-Strauss coined the term *bricoleur*, or "tinkerer," to explain the way in which he took whatever tool, part, or device came to hand to achieve his goal. Derrida links this activity to his own attempt to locate and reveal differences.

In Derrida's analysis, Levi-Strauss remains bound by empiricism in his work, and his abandonment of the search for a center may simply be the result of an empiricist's frustration in the face of infinite diversity. Derrida proposes as an alternative that the search for a center should yield to the infinite process of free play, which escapes all totalizing discourse. He again invokes the ideas of excess and the supplement to figure this realm of play. At the time he published the essay, Derrida saw human history as occupying the contested ground between frustration and play.

The book closes with "Ellipsis," a title that can itself be seen as part of the Derridean vocabulary of differance, suggesting omission, circumlocution, the distortion of the circle, and the orbital path of a planet. In this gesture of opening rather than ending, Derrida returns to the last two volumes of *The Book of Questions* by Edmond Jabès, *Le Livre de Yukel* (1964; *The Book of Yukel*, 1977) and *Le Retour au livre* (1965; *Return to the Book*, 1977). Through readings of various poems, Derrida reemphasizes the role of writing in opening up spaces and once again stresses the absence of a center as an affirmation of play, an infinite deferral of a totalitarian closure.

Amee Carmines

Further Reading

Culler, Jonathan. *On Deconstruction: Theory and Criticism After Structuralism*. 25th anniversary ed. Ithaca, N.Y.: Cornell University Press, 2007. Culler is one of the primary American interpreters of Derrida's thinking for American students and critics of literature.

Norris, Christopher. *Derrida*. Cambridge, Mass.: Harvard University Press, 1987. Philosopher Norris has been a major British figure in the translation of Derridean ideas into English. Norris would become increasingly critical of deconstructionist thought in the twenty-first century.

Norris, Christopher, and David Roden, eds. *Jacques Derrida*. 4 vols. Thousand Oaks, Calif.: Sage, 2003. This massive compendium of secondary sources on Derrida's work aims to be the most comprehensive collection of commentary on Derrida's ideas, writing, and significance published in English.

Rorty, Richard. *Contingency, Irony, and Solidarity*. New

York: Cambridge University Press, 1989. Like Derrida, Rorty engages the intersections between philosophy and literature, though he maintains a more explicit form of social engagement in his writings on literature. This book contains a chapter on Derrida that both explicates and repositions some of the major concepts associated with deconstruction.

_____. *Essays on Heidegger and Others: Philosophical Papers.* Vol. 2. New York: Cambridge University Press, 1991. This collection contains an essay on deconstruction, an essay in dialogue with Christopher Norris on deconstruction, and an essay on Derrida as philosopher.

Wood, David, ed. *Derrida and Difference.* Evanston, Ill.: Northwestern University Press, 1988. This collection of essays offers a range of perspectives on Derrida and this key term used in *Writing and Difference.*

Wuthering Heights

Author: Emily Brontë (1818-1848)
First published: 1847
Type of work: Novel
Type of plot: Love
Time of plot: 1757-1803
Locale: Moors of northern England

Principal characters:
MR. EARNSHAW, the owner of Wuthering Heights
CATHERINE, his daughter
HINDLEY, his son
HEATHCLIFF, an orphan
MR. LINTON, the proprietor of Thrushcross Grange
MRS. LINTON, his wife
ISABELLA, their daughter
EDGAR, their son
FRANCES EARNSHAW, Hindley's wife
HARETON EARNSHAW, Frances and Hindley's son
CATHERINE LINTON, Catherine Earnshaw and Edgar Linton's daughter
LINTON HEATHCLIFF, Isabella Linton and Heathcliff's son
ELLEN "NELLY" DEAN, the housekeeper at Thrushcross Grange
MR. LOCKWOOD, a tenant at Thrushcross Grange and narrator of the story

The Story:

In 1801, Mr. Lockwood becomes a tenant at Thrushcross Grange, an old farm owned by a Mr. Heathcliff of Wuthering Heights. In the early days of his tenancy, he makes two calls on his landlord. On his first visit, he meets Heathcliff, an abrupt, unsocial man who is surrounded by a pack of snarling, barking dogs. When he goes to Wuthering Heights a second time, he meets the other members of the strange household: a rude, unkempt but handsome young man named Hareton Earnshaw and a pretty young woman who is the widow of Heathcliff's son.

During his visit, snow begins to fall. It covers the moor paths and makes travel impossible for a stranger in that bleak countryside. Heathcliff refuses to let one of the servants go with him as a guide but says that if he stays the night he can share Hareton's bed or that of Joseph, a sour, canting old ser-

vant. When Mr. Lockwood tries to borrow Joseph's lantern for the homeward journey, the old fellow sets the dogs on him, to the amusement of Hareton and Heathcliff. The visitor is finally rescued by Zillah, the cook, who hides him in an unused chamber of the house.

That night, Mr. Lockwood has a strange dream. Thinking that a branch is rattling against the window, he breaks the glass in his attempt to unhook the casement. As he reaches out to break off the fir branch outside, his fingers close on a small ice-cold hand, and a weeping voice begs to be let in. The unseen presence says that her name is Catherine Linton, and she tries to force a way through the broken casement; Mr. Lockwood screams.

Heathcliff appears in a state of great excitement and savagely orders Mr. Lockwood out of the room. Then he throws himself upon the bed by the shattered pane and begs the spirit to come in out of the dark and the storm. The voice is, however, heard no more—only the hiss of swirling snow and the wailing of a cold wind that blows out the smoking candle.

The housekeeper at Thrushcross Grange, Ellen Dean, is able to satisfy part of Mr. Lockwood's curiosity about the happenings of that night and the strange household at Wuthering Heights, for she lived at Wuthering Heights as a child. Her story of the Earnshaws, Lintons, and Heathcliffs begins years before, when old Mr. Earnshaw was living at Wuthering Heights with his wife and two children, Hindley and Catherine. Once, on a trip to Liverpool, Mr. Earnshaw found a starving and homeless orphan, a ragged, dirty, urchin, dark as a Gypsy, whom he brought back with him to Wuthering Heights and christened Heathcliff—a name that was to serve the fourteen-year-old boy as both a given and a surname. Gradually, the orphan began to usurp the affections of Mr. Earnshaw, whose health was failing. Wuthering Heights became riddled with petty jealousies; old Joseph, the servant, augmented the bickering, and Catherine was much too fond of Heathcliff. At last, Hindley was sent away to school. A short time later, Mr. Earnshaw died.

When Hindley returned home for his father's funeral, he brought a wife with him. As the new master of Wuthering Heights, he revenged himself on Heathcliff by treating him like a servant. Catherine became a wild and undisciplined hoyden who continued to be fond of Heathcliff.

One night, Catherine and Heathcliff tramped through the moors to Thrushcross Grange, where they spied on their neighbors, the Lintons. Attacked by a watchdog, Catherine was taken into the house and stayed there as a guest for five weeks until she was able to walk again. During that time, she became intimate with the pleasant family of Thrushcross Grange, Mr. and Mrs. Linton and their two children, Edgar and Isabella. Afterward, the Lintons visited frequently at Wuthering Heights. As a result of Hindley's ill-treatment and the arrogance of Edgar and Isabella, Heathcliff became jealous and morose. He vowed revenge on Hindley, whom he hated with all of his savage nature.

The next summer, Hindley's consumptive wife, Frances, gave birth to a son, Hareton Earnshaw, and shortly thereafter she died. In his grief, Hindley became desperate, ferocious, and degenerate. In the meantime, Catherine and Edgar became sweethearts. The girl confided to Ellen that she really loved Heathcliff, but she felt it would be degrading for her to marry the penniless orphan. Heathcliff, who overheard this conversation, disappeared the same night and did not return for many years. Edgar and Catherine married and lived at Thrushcross Grange with Ellen as their housekeeper. There

the pair lived happily until the return of Heathcliff, who was greatly improved in manners and in appearance. He accepted Hindley's invitation to live at Wuthering Heights, an invitation extended because Hindley found in Heathcliff a companion for card-playing and drinking, and because he hoped to recoup his own dwindling fortune from Heathcliff's pockets.

Isabella began to show a strong attraction to Heathcliff, much to the dismay of Edgar and Catherine. One night, Edgar and Heathcliff had a quarrel. Soon afterward, Heathcliff eloped with Isabella, obviously marrying her only to avenge himself and provoke Edgar. Catherine, an expectant mother, underwent a serious illness. When Isabella and Heathcliff returned to Wuthering Heights, Edgar refused to recognize his sister and forbade Heathcliff to enter his house. Despite this restriction, Heathcliff managed to have a meeting with Catherine. Partly as a result of this meeting, she gave birth to a girl, named Catherine Linton, prematurely; a few hours later, mother Catherine died.

Isabella found life with Heathcliff unbearable and she left him, going to London, where a few months later her child, Linton, was born. After Hindley's death, Heathcliff the guest became the master of Wuthering Heights, for Hindley mortgaged his estate to him. Hareton, the natural heir, was reduced to dependency on his father's enemy.

When Isabella died, twelve years after leaving Heathcliff, her brother took her sickly child to live at Thrushcross Grange. Heathcliff soon heard of the child's arrival and demanded that Linton be sent to Wuthering Heights to live with his father. Young Catherine once visited Wuthering Heights and met her cousin Linton. Her father tried to keep her in ignorance about the tenants of the place, but Heathcliff let it be known that he wished the two children to be married. About the time that Edgar Linton became seriously ill, Heathcliff persuaded Cathy to visit her little cousin, who was also in extremely bad health. Upon her arrival, Cathy was imprisoned for five days at Wuthering Heights and forced to marry her sickly cousin Linton before she was allowed to go home to see her father. Although she was able to return to Thrushcross Grange before her father's death, there was not enough time for Edgar Linton to alter his will. Thus his land and fortune went indirectly to Heathcliff. Weak, sickly Linton Heathcliff died soon after, leaving Cathy a widow and dependent on Heathcliff.

Mr. Lockwood went back to London in the spring without seeing Wuthering Heights or its people again. Traveling in the region the next autumn, he had a fancy to revisit Wuthering Heights. There, he found Catherine and Hareton in possession. From Ellen, he heard that Heathcliff died three months earlier, after deliberately starving himself for four days. He was a broken man, still disturbed by memories of the beautiful young Catherine Earnshaw. His death freed Catherine Heathcliff and Hareton from his tyranny, and Catherine was now teaching the ignorant boy to read and improving his rude manners.

Mr. Lockwood went to see Heathcliff's grave. It was next to Catherine Earnshaw's, on whose other side lay her husband. They lay under their three headstones: Catherine's in the middle, weather-discolored and half-buried, Edgar's partly moss-grown, Heathcliff's still bare. In the surrounding countryside, there was a legend that they slept unquietly after their stormy, passionate lives. Shepherds and travelers at night claimed that they saw Catherine and Heathcliff roaming the dark moors as they did so often many years earlier.

Critical Evaluation:

Not only is *Wuthering Heights* a powerful love story and a compelling tale of the supernatural, it also offers readers insightful commentary on issues relating to class and morality. Emily Brontë's novel is a complicated exploration of what happens when the established order of a community is thrown off balance. In the case of the Linton and the Earnshaw families, it is the appearance of Heathcliff, the dark, mysterious orphan, that sets a chain of events in motion that destroys or threatens to destroy the lives of many of the characters. Although it is never clearly articulated, there is some reason to suspect that Heathcliff could be the illegitimate offspring of Mr. Earnshaw, who brings him into his home claiming to have found the child in Liverpool. Heathcliff poses a threat to the Earnshaw family because he is dark-skinned (therefore different), wild, and possibly a half-sibling to the Earnshaw children, Catherine and Hindley. This complication adds a more frightening aspect to the physical, spiritual, and emotional attraction that develops between Catherine and Heathcliff. Added to the possibility of breaking the incest taboo is the problem of social class: Because of his suspect origins, Heathcliff could never fit into the life of the Earnshaw and Linton families.

Brontë employs great skill in making the landscape, the weather, the houses, and even the dogs reflect the opposing emotional climates of the Linton and Earnshaw homes. The Earnshaw residence, Wuthering Heights, is, as its name implies, subject to extremes in weather; winds, snow, and cold buffet the house and grounds. By contrast, Thrushcross Grange, the home of the Lintons and later of Cathy and Edgar, is refined and filled with light, comfort, and opulence. Even the weather seems less severe there. The Grange stands in splendid contrast to the home shared by young Cathy,

Hindley, and Heathcliff, a disjuncture made clear in the scene in which Catherine and Heathcliff spy on the Linton children from outside a window at the Grange. The show of temper between Isabella and Linton as they fight over their delicate dog pales in contrast to the vehemence with which those at Wuthering Heights express their emotions. While Heathcliff is disdainful of these soft children, Catherine is captivated—metaphorically and literally. Significantly, from this chance encounter spring all of the troubles that Heathcliff and the Earnshaw and Linton children will endure. Whereas Catherine grows entranced with the soft life at the Grange and with Linton, Heathcliff falls victim to the destructive envy that will finally drive him to destroy everyone with whom he comes in contact. In his mind, the Lintons represent all that he can never be or have.

However, it is above all the love and passionate attraction between Catherine and Heathcliff that destroys the two families. It is Heathcliff's misunderstanding of the overheard conversation between Catherine and her nurse, Nelly Dean, that causes him to run away and eventually gives him the economic means to effect his revenge against the Earnshaws and the Lintons.

When Heathcliff returns to Wuthering Heights after many years' absence, he finds Catherine and Edgar married. Heathcliff's anger damages everything it touches, from the ignorant child of Hindley and Frances Earnshaw, the wild Hareton, to Edgar Linton's delicate sister, Isabella. Heathcliff's first overt act of revenge against Catherine and Edgar is to pursue and marry Isabella. From this point until he dies years later, Heathcliff's anger at losing Catherine destroys everyone with whom he comes in contact, including Isabella, his own son, Linton, Catherine's daughter, young Cathy, and her cousin, Hareton.

Even though both he and Catherine are married, Heathcliff does not leave her in peace. Not content simply to torture his own wife, Isabella, Heathcliff attacks Catherine verbally, and his violence causes her to fall ill and die soon after, while giving birth to young Cathy. Heathcliff never recovers from the loss of Catherine, which remains the reason for his brutal treatment of everyone whom he associates with her. His anger also directly causes his own death. Yet, for all of his violence, hatred, and vindictiveness, Heathcliff does not attain peace of mind or release from grief. He only succeeds in bringing Hindley to financial ruin; capturing Edgar's fortune; and creating in young Hareton an untutored, violent beast.

As Heathcliff nears his own death, Brontë again uses the weather to mirror a character's interior turmoil. Heathcliff dies alone while a storm rages around the Heights. He is later found, a window open, the implication being that Catherine finally came to claim him for her own. While this scene is a climax, it does not constitute the resolution of *Wuthering Heights*, for Brontë provides an ending that offers a ray of hope in the promised union of young Cathy with Hareton. Not only does Cathy "tame" Hareton and teach him to read, she also learns to love and to value him. The union of these two people represents a transformed version of the passions of Catherine and Heathcliff. The first Catherine could not have Heathcliff in this life, but her daughter can hope to build a satisfying life with Hareton. Although Heathcliff and Catherine's passion cannot survive in this life, Brontë implies that the two lovers are finally united beyond the grave.

"Critical Evaluation" by Peter A. Brier

Further Reading

Barnard, Robert. *Emily Brontë*. New York: Oxford University Press, 2000. Concise, illustrated biography, describing Brontë's isolated childhood, her poetry, and the sources and inspirations for *Wuthering Heights*.

Bloom, Harold, ed. *Emily Brontë's "Wuthering Heights."* Updated ed. New York: Bloom's Literary Criticism, 2007. Collection of essays, including Virginia Woolf's comparison of *Wuthering Heights* with Charlotte Brontë's *Jane Eyre* and discussions of sex and the feminine, reverse imperialism, and the myth of rebirth in the novel.

Brontë, Emily. *Wuthering Heights: Complete, Authoritative Text with Biographical, Historical, and Cultural Contexts, Critical History, and Essays from Contemporary Critical Perspectives*. Edited by Linda H. Peterson. Boston: Bedford/St. Martin's, 2003. In addition to the text of the novel, this edition includes essays placing the book in its historical, regional, political, and legal contexts. Other essays interpret the book from feminist, Marxist, postcolonial, and cultural critical perspectives.

Davies, Stevie. *Emily Brontë: The Artist as a Free Woman*. Manchester, England: Carcanet Press, 1983. Discusses not only the novel but also Brontë's personal life and tragedies, the fantasy worlds created by her and her siblings, and her poetry. Provides an incisive look at the novel's structure and an in-depth study of the personalities and motivations of the main characters.

Everitt, Alastair, ed. *Wuthering Heights: An Anthology of Criticism*. London: Frank Cass, 1967. A collection of introductory critical explorations of the novel that examine such fundamental issues as structure, narrative strategies, origins, the supernatural, madness, and sadomasochism.

Fegan, Melissa. *Wuthering Heights: Character Studies*. London: Continuum, 2008. In addition to analyzing the characters of Heathcliff and Catherine, Fegan examines other characters who play a significant role in the novel and demonstrates how the novel reflects nineteenth century concepts of character and psychology.

Glen, Heather, ed. *The Cambridge Companion to the Brontës*. New York: Cambridge University Press, 2002. Several essays in this collection analyze common characteristics in the work of the Brontë sisters. Another essay, "Three Distinct and Unconnected Tales: *The Professor*, *Agnes Grey*, and *Wuthering Heights*" by Stevie Davies, discusses novels by, respectively, Charlotte, Anne, and Emily.

Ingham, Patricia, ed. *The Brontës*. London: Longman, 2003. Three of the essays in this collection focus on the novel: "*Wuthering Heights*" by Terry Eagleton, "Gender and Layered Narrative in *Wuthering Heights* and *The Tenant of Wildfell Hall*" by N. M. Jacobs, and "Diaries and Displacement in *Wuthering Heights*" by Rebecca Steinitz.

Kavanaugh, James H. *Emily Brontë*. New York: Blackwell, 1985. Offers a late twentieth century critical interpretation of the novel, including a deconstructionist reading. Useful also for its survey of critical approaches to this novel.

Lonoff, Sue, and Terri A. Hasseler, eds. *Approaches to Teaching Emily Brontë's "Wuthering Heights."* New York: Modern Language Association of America, 2006. A guide for teachers. Includes essays discussing the depiction of race, class, gender, domestic violence, and the female gothic in the novel, as well as advice for teaching the novel in an English department course, a class on literary theory and interpretation, and a first-year composition course.

Miles, Peter. *Wuthering Heights*. Basingstoke, England: Macmillan, 1990. Provides various readings of Brontë's novel as well as an introduction that traces the history of the most popular interpretations of and reactions to the book. Includes a helpful bibliography, primarily covering the more traditional critical approaches.

Winnifrith, Thomas John, ed. *Critical Essays on Emily Brontë*. New York: G. K. Hall, 1997. Includes essays discussing Brontë's religion, reading, and education, as well as a variety of pieces interpreting *Wuthering Heights*.

X

Xala

Author: Ousmane Sembène (1923-2007)
First published: 1973 (English translation, 1976)
Type of work: Novel
Type of plot: Social realism
Time of plot: Early 1970's
Locale: Dakar, Senegal

Principal characters:
EL HADJI ABDOU KADER BEYÈ, a businessman
ADJA AWA ASTOU, his first wife
OUMI N'DOYE, his second wife
N'GONE, his third wife
RAMA, his daughter
MODU, his chauffeur
YAY BINETA, N'Gone's aunt
SEREEN MADA, a marabout, or holy man
THE BEGGAR

The Story:

An African has been appointed president of the Chamber of Commerce and Industry, and El Hadji Abdou Kader Beyè and his fellow businessmen are celebrating, as they believe they will acquire greater economic control in Senegal now that the last vestige of foreign rule has been removed. Seated at the right of the newly appointed president, El Hadji rises amid the jubilation inspired by this propitious moment and reminds his colleagues that while they have been celebrating, his third marriage has been "sealed" at the mosque. He has become a captain according to traditional standards of nobility. Together, they all leave the chamber to accompany El Hadji to the home of N'Gone, his third wife, where the wedding festivities are in progress.

Yay Bineta, N'Gone's aunt, officiates proudly over the bustling crowd of guests who have already gathered for her niece's postnuptial celebration. She watches as the women examine enviously the numerous wedding gifts El Hadji has presented to his new young wife as tokens of love. El Hadji has not disappointed her expectations. Adja Awa Astou and Oumi N'Doye sadly observe this grand reception held in honor of their new "co-wife." Adja, El Hadji's first wife, departs after she has made a sufficient show of acceptance of his third marriage. Back at her villa, she reflects on her own unhappiness provoked by renewed feelings of abandonment. Her daughter, Rama, who is vehemently opposed to the marriage and to polygamy in general, tries in vain to console her mother.

At N'Gone's villa, El Hadji's arrival with his entourage of businessmen causes a stir of excitement among the guests. In the middle of the peals of laughter, loud music, and dancing, the lights go out, and the newly wedded couple slip away to their bedroom, where El Hadji prepares himself to deflower his bride.

The next morning, Yay Bineta returns to N'Gone's villa in the company of an old woman. She enters the couple's room and finds El Hadji seated on the edge of the bed, while N'Gone sits gazing blankly at nothing. El Hadji reveals that nothing happened during the night. Struck with dismay at the announcement of this unwanted turn of events in her social victory, Yay Bineta blames El Hadji, who had refused, beforehand, to take traditional precautions to ensure his sexual potency with his new wife. Yay Bineta insists that El Hadji go see a marabout—a healer—to help rid himself of *xala*, the spell of impotence.

El Hadji cannot believe that he has been afflicted with *xala*. He thinks about his other wives, Adja and Oumi, and wonders if one of them could be the author of his malady. Desirous to become potent again, El Hadji confides in the president of the chamber and, later, in his father-in-law, Baboucar. On their advice, El Hadji seeks out a number of reputed marabouts, all of whom provide him with ineffective cures and useless clues for discovering the author of his *xala*.

While in pursuit of a cure, El Hadji increasingly neglects his business affairs, especially avoiding contact with the other businessmen. Burdened with the expense of three villas and the financial demands of his wives and children, he continues to spend extravagantly, paying no attention to the declining state of his finances. He suffers immensely, convinced that his colleagues talk secretly about his *xala*. Previously overcome by his desire to possess the young N'Gone, El Hadji now sees her as a bitter reminder of his own seduction into the third marriage and his present miserable condition. His driver, Modu, also knows about El Hadji's *xala*. Moved by his employer's profound look of sadness, the chauffeur finally tells him about Sereen Mada, a renowned marabout.

Sereen Mada lives in a small village outside the bustling capital of Dakar. Accustomed to the amenities of life in the capital, El Hadji resigns himself to making the difficult journey. Sereen Mada does not disappoint his guest. As the holy man murmurs prayerful incantations over his body, El Hadji feels the return of those pleasurable sensations that had lately deserted him. He pays the marabout by check, and, happy that he is no longer impotent, returns to Dakar.

With his virility restored, El Hadji feels he can now consummate his new marriage. He arrives at N'Gone's villa and is greeted by Yay Bineta, who announces that N'Gone is having her menstrual period and is, therefore, unavailable. Filled with a sense of defeat, El Hadji dismisses the idea of wasting his passion on Adja, who fulfills her conjugal duty with indifference. To her supreme delight, Oumi enjoys a passionate night with El Hadji.

El Hadji returns to work and discovers that his financial affairs are in great jeopardy. Distraught over the disintegration of his life, El Hadji fails to recognize Sereen Mada when he comes to return the worthless check El Hadji had given him. Angered by this display of disrespect, Sereen Mada quickly restores the *xala*.

El Hadji suffers the loss of his business, expulsion from the chamber, and the breakup of his marriages to N'Gone and Oumi. In the depths of his despair, he seeks refuge with Adja. Days later, a beggar, followed by a throng of blind persons and others afflicted with all sorts of disabilities and maladies, approaches Adja's villa. In the presence of everyone, the beggar recounts how El Hadji used fraudulent means to take the land that had belonged to the beggar's clan. The beggar, the real author of El Hadji's *xala*, declares that he can restore his potency. At the mercy of the beggar, El Hadji submits to the scourge of humiliation inflicted on him by the beggar's followers, who take turns spitting on his naked body.

Critical Evaluation:

An internationally acclaimed writer and filmmaker, Ousmane Sembène was a self-taught man. In search of em-

ployment, Sembène traveled from his native Senegal to France, where he wrote and published his first novel, *Le Docker noir* (1956; *Black Docker*, 1987), which launched his literary career. Over the next thirty years, he wrote several novellas and novels, published short stories, and directed and produced a number of films based on his own literary works. Often referred to as a modern-day griot, a term designating the traditional African storyteller, Sembène dramatized the sociopolitical issues affecting the African people and their society.

Apart from his first work, Sembène's novels are set primarily in Senegal. Placing less emphasis on his former preoccupation with the effects of French influence on African society, he concentrated in his subsequent works largely on issues such as corruption, poverty, illiteracy, and other social ills perpetuated by the African elite at the expense of the poorer classes. *Xala* focuses, in particular, on the leadership of postindependence Senegal.

In this novel the forcefulness of Sembène's criticism is intensely conveyed through the symbolic connection established between *xala* and the impotence of the Senegalese leadership. A profoundly powerful work, *Xala* uses traditional elements to create a unique narrative style. The sense of a parable is effectively developed through the unanticipated decline of El Hadji's business affairs. The introductory scene displays the false sense of optimism among the new African masters. By moving from the national context to El Hadji's personal situation, the novel confronts the hero with the true reality of life in Senegal.

The majority of the story focuses on El Hadji's unhappy married life. Through occasional flashbacks interspersed throughout the story, Sembène uses the historical past as a means to illuminate events of the present. The symbolic representation of the three wives underscores the relevance of the past to the present. Adja abandons Catholicism and converts to Islam to marry El Hadji. Her return to the old ways and her aspirations to be a model Muslim wife represent, in part, a retrogressive Africa that refuses to confront the changes of modern times. Oumi's exaggerated imitation of French values exposes the excessive materialism adopted by members of the middle class. Representative of the younger generation, N'Gone becomes a pawn in the hands of her elders and, consequently, forfeits the opportunity to act as a progressive agent of change within society.

Through the depiction of El Hadji's distant relationships with his three wives, Sembène focuses special attention on the problem of polygamy. Adja and Oumi feel emotionally and physically abandoned. Rama, El Hadji's oldest child, attempts to express her dissatisfaction openly, but her small protest is squelched with a slap in the face from her father, who states that she "can be a revolutionary at the university or in the street but not in [his] house." Rama realizes, eventually, that she is powerless to improve her mother's moral plight.

Sembène proceeds to expose the fact that El Hadji and the other businessmen are only middlemen dependent on foreign enterprises to survive. The religious leadership is subject to similar criticism in the guise of Sereen Mada, who "only worked for bosses." The assistance that the marabout provides El Hadji serves only to promote the limited self-interest of the latter. Sembène thereby reveals how the state of impotence permeates Senegal society.

The inconspicuous presence of the beggar is skillfully intertwined in the web of intrigue. He first appears in the story on the day when El Hadji's *xala* is revealed, but it is only in the final pages of the story that he comes to the forefront as a major character, revealing himself as the author of the *xala*. The novel's main theme is expressed through the beggar's personal indictment of El Hadji: "You and your colleagues build on the misfortunes of honest, ordinary people." Typically, it is the common people who rise up as a potential force of change and vindicate their dignity and rightful place in society.

Cherie Maiden

Further Reading

Bayo, Ogunjimi. "Ritual Archetypes: Ousmane's Aesthetic Medium in *Xala*." *Ufahamu: Journal of the African Activist Association* 14, no. 3 (1985): 128-138. Presents a complex analysis of the symbolic images in the novel derived from African traditions and discusses the work's characterization and thematic content. Highlights the significant cultural features that contribute to Sembène's narrative style in order to reveal the subtler dimensions of his social criticism.

Busch, Annett, and Max Annas, eds. *Ousmane Sembène: Interviews*. Jackson: University of Mississippi, 2008. Collection of interviews focuses primarily on Sembène's work as a filmmaker, but his commentary provides insight into his aesthetics, political activism, ideas about gender, and other issues central to his literary work as well.

Cham, Mbye B. "Islam in Senegalese Literature and Film." In *Faces of Islam in African Literature*, edited by Kenneth W. Harrow. Portsmouth, N.H.: Heinemann, 1991. Examines the presence of Islamic influences in the Senegalese literary tradition, devoting a section to discussion of the impact of such influences on Sembène's works, including *Xala*.

Condé, Maryse. "Sembène Ousmane *Xala*." *African Literature Today* 9 (1979): 97-98. Brief essay provides a beneficial introduction to the novel, presenting a succinct but comprehensive overview of its dominant themes and the issues commonly mentioned in discussions of the work.

Hawkins, Peter. "Marxist Intertext, Islamic Reinscription? Some Common Themes in the Novels of Sembène Ousmane and Aminata Sow Fall." In *African Francophone Writing: A Critical Introduction*, edited by Laïla Ibnlfassi and Nicki Hitchcott. Oxford, England: Berg, 1996. Compares two of Sembène's novels with two novels by Aminata Sow Fall, another Senegalese writer. Finds similarities between *Xala* and Sow Fall's *La Grève des bàttu* (1979), describing the books as "short, satirical novellas about the excessive pretensions and Western-style materialism of a corrupt African bourgeois figure."

Iyam, David Uru. "The Silent Revolutionaries: Ousmane Sembène's *Emitai*, *Xala*, and *Ceddo*." *African Studies Review* 29, no. 4 (1986): 79-87. Presents a detailed examination of the major characteristics prevalent in Sembène's literary and cinematic work. Offers insights into *Xala* regarding issues and stylistic techniques present in both media as well as some background on the social and political importance of particular issues in the development of the author's creative expression.

Makward, Edris. "Women, Tradition, and Religion in Sembène Ousmane's Work." In *Faces of Islam in African Literature*, edited by Kenneth W. Harrow. Portsmouth, N.H.: Heinemann, 1991. Asserts that Sembène is one of the few writers of his generation to focus on the African woman as a credible and powerful agent of social change. Offers limited but very insightful commentary on *Xala* within the larger context of Sembène's literary vision.

Murphy, David. "The Indiscreet Charm of the African Bourgeoisie? Consumerism, Fetishism, and Socialism in *Xala*." In *Sembène: Imagining Alternatives in Film and Fiction*. Trenton, N.J.: Africa World Press, 2000. Compares the themes of the novel and the literary techniques used to convey them with the themes and techniques seen in Sembène's 1975 film adaptation of the work.

Tsabedze, Clara. *African Independence from Francophone and Anglophone Voices: A Comparative Study of the Post-independence Novels by Ngugi and Sembène*. New York: Peter Lang, 1994. Comparative study of the fiction of Sembène and Kenyan author Ngugi wa Thiong'o focuses on the two writers' representations of African independence and of neocolonial exploitation.

Y

Year of Wonders

Author: Geraldine Brooks (1955-   )
First published: 2001
Type of work: Novel
Type of plot: Historical
Time of plot: 1665-1666
Locale: Eyam, Derbyshire, England

Principal characters:
ANNA FIRTH, a young woman
MICHAEL MOMPELLION, the village rector
ELINOR MOMPELLION, his wife
MEM GOWDIE, an herbal healer
ANYS GOWDIE, her niece
JOSIAH BONT, Anna's father
APHRA BONT, his wife
THE BRADFORDS, a wealthy family
GEORGE VICCARS, a journeyman tailor

The Story:

It is autumn, 1666, and in the lead-mining village of Eyam in Derbyshire, England, Anna Firth is reflecting on the past year, in which two-thirds of the village's population had died from the effects of the bubonic plague. Anna is keeping house for Michael Mompellion, the village rector, who has been sitting in his room and refusing food and company since his wife, Elinor, had died. Elizabeth Bradford, the daughter of a wealthy family who had fled the village and the plague, returns and demands assistance from the rector, who rouses from his room only long enough to angrily turn her away.

It is spring, 1665. A journeyman tailor, George Viccars, seeks lodging with Anna. Newly widowed and the mother of two young boys, she welcomes the income, Viccars's attention to the boys, and his companionship. However, their budding romance ends as soon as it is declared. A bolt of damp cloth, ordered from London, has carried the bubonic plague into Eyam. Soon, Viccars dies; from his deathbed he had encouraged Anna to burn the fabric. The townspeople, however, still insist on claiming their prepaid clothes-in-progress, on which Viccars had been working, thus spreading the infection.

After a late summer respite, the plague reappears. Anna's sons and the boys of her neighbor Mary Hadfield are among the first to die. The villagers first respond with self-interest. The Bradfords had already asserted, in a dinner-party discussion, that flight from the village was the only sensible response to the plague. Other villagers respond violently, as

the Hadfields and other villagers murder Mem and Anys Gowdie, the town's herbal healers, accusing them of witchcraft. The killers suffer no punishment because no officials will come to the village, and more than half the murderers die of plague within a week.

The Sunday after the murders, Rector Mompellion addresses the village. Supported by his predecessor, Thomas Stanley, a dissenting Puritan minister, Mompellion calls upon the villagers to take an oath to remain in the village and avoid spreading the plague. He presents the plague as an ordeal, a trial that will refine the souls of the village people just as they themselves refine ore into lead. He promises that no one will die alone, and he has obtained a pledge from a nearby earl that the village will receive support and provisions while the plague runs its course. The Bradfords are the only villagers who do not take the oath; they flee immediately, following an angry confrontation with Mompellion.

Anna has been working in the rectory and, after taking the plague oath, she and Elinor Mompellion grow closer. As the deaths spread, the two are pressed into service—first as midwives and then to provide the cures that the Gowdies, the herbal healers, would have offered had they not been killed. While working, Elinor confesses her past to Anna—that she had had a lover before marrying Michael and that she had conceived the lover's child and aborted it with a poker, leaving her unable to have more children. Together, Anna and Elinor study the Gowdies' herbs and the rector's medical texts.

As she and Elinor comfort the sick, Anna finds signs of trouble in the village. Some villagers are obtaining charms, at great cost, allegedly from the ghost of Anys Gowdie. Josiah Bont, Anna's dissolute and abusive father, begins working as a gravedigger, extorting high payments from his clients. One afflicted man insists his wife burn out his bubo, or swollen lymph node, with a hot poker, and another takes up self-flagellation. Townspeople who had stubbornly held Puritan beliefs engage in wild sexual activity.

At the same time, some events are cheering, as villagers come closer together and take on new roles. A newly orphaned girl, Merry Wickford, faces the loss of her family's lead mine because of local tradition, which states that mines could be held only by those who could make them produce. To protect Merry's claim, Anna and Elinor use the fragments of knowledge Anna had from her deceased husband, Sam, to draw a dish of lead from Merry's mine. They are welcomed in the Miner's Tavern, which serves as the village's gathering place and unofficial court, as new miners.

The congregation abandons the church building in favor of gathering in a meadow, in hope of avoiding the plague. The dissenting Mr. Stanley speaks in firm support of Rector Mompellion, and the village's recalcitrant Puritans begin rejoining services.

The plague remains into the spring, and the village's trials grow worse. Josiah continues as a gravedigger, taking advantage of those in need and spending his ill-gotten earnings on alcohol rather than on his family. The rector's attempt at intervention leads to a nearly violent argument, as Bont begins digging an unrequested grave for Christopher Unwin, who has the plague. When Unwin recovers, however, he faces Bont, who attempts to murder, rob, and bury him. Bont is brought before the Miner's Court for justice and sentenced to have his hand nailed to the entrance of a mine. He dies of exposure when no one rescues him. Aphra, Bont's wife, blames Anna for his death.

It is now summertime, and Elinor becomes ill. She begs Anna to take care of Michael and calls out to her former lover in her delirium. Her illness proves to be a simple fever, and she recovers within days. A woman who had lost all of her possessions to her husband's asceticism dies of the plague after receiving bedding and clothes from well-intentioned neighbors, leading Rector Mompellion to conclude that the villagers should burn their surplus possessions. They clean their houses and then gather for this meager bonfire, an act of purification and sacrifice.

During the bonfire, the supposed ghost of Anys Gowdie is caught. The ghost turns out to be Aphra, who has been disguising herself and selling charms to the desperate.

Mompellion protects her from the angry crowd by announcing he will address the charges against her the next day, ordering the young men who had captured her to detain her overnight. The men hold her in a manure pit, reducing her to near-insanity by morning. Mompellion offers sympathy and a light penance, then sends her home. Anna leaves food for Aphra and her daughter but is driven away with shouts and curses, as are other neighbors. After several days the daughter disappears, and Anna peeks in to find the child's body suspended in Aphra's cottage. After that, Aphra is left completely alone.

After the burning, the plague cases decline, until a week goes by with no new deaths. The Mompellions cautiously plan to recognize the end of the plague with a thanksgiving service in mid-August. The villagers gather for one last service in the meadow and are ready to celebrate, but Aphra appears as the service begins. She is carrying her daughter's body and hysterically waving a knife. A scuffle ensues, and Aphra kills Elinor. Rector Mompellion holds Elinor's body until he is forced away at nightfall. The next morning, he sends messages of the end of the plague and of Elinor's death, then retreats to the rectory.

Anna is desperate to help Mompellion and grieves for Elinor, trying to hold on to her friend's life through her work at the rectory. She takes Mompellion's horse, Anteros, on a wild ride through the countryside, celebrating her survival. Mompellion's discovery of this pulls him out of his room, and he and Anna engage in a brief affair. Once after lovemaking, Mompellion confesses to Anna that he and Elinor had never had sexual relations, that he withheld his affections to force her to atone for her sins with her lover.

Anna retreats to the still-closed church to grapple with her feelings, where she encounters Elizabeth Bradford, who is praying for her mother. Mrs. Bradford is in labor with a lover's child and is likely to die, an outcome seemingly desired by her husband. Anna offers assistance and safely delivers the baby girl. She discovers Elizabeth attempting to drown the baby to hide the pregnancy and to protect her mother. Anna offers to take the baby and raise her someplace else, and Elizabeth agrees.

As Anna prepares to leave, Mompellion appears in her cottage, recovered from his madness. He warns Anna that the Bradfords are likely to kill her to hide the baby's birth, and he encourages her to flee. He offers her Anteros, and a letter of introduction to Elinor's family. Rather than go to Elinor's home, however, Anna decides to go her own way and heads to a port city. Pursued by the Bradfords, she takes the first available ship and leaves the port.

Anna arrives in the city of Oran. She becomes an assistant

and wife to a respected Arab physician, finally using the healing knowledge she had struggled to gain with Elinor. She is raising Mrs. Bradford's daughter, Aisha, as her own, and in the harem gives birth to Michael Mompellion's child; she names her Elinor.

Critical Evaluation:

Year of Wonders was Geraldine Brooks's first novel. The Australian-born Brooks had been a correspondent for the *Wall Street Journal*, covering conflicts in the Middle East and in Central Europe. Her first book, *Nine Parts of Desire* (1994), is a collection of firsthand accounts of the lives of women in the modern Middle East. Brooks says that these women, many of whom lived circumscribed lives and were forced into new leadership roles by various crises, were the inspiration for the character of Anna Firth.

Brooks had left journalism after being briefly jailed in Nigeria and turned her efforts to the Eyam story, which had caught her attention on a visit to England some years earlier. She had consulted with Derbyshire historians for this novel, but in her work, generally, she approaches historical fiction as a way of filling in the blanks in the records. The title of the novel, *Year of Wonders*, is drawn from John Dryden's poem, "Annus Mirabilis" (1667; year of wonders or year of miracles), an account of London's Great Plague (1665-1666) and Great Fire (1666). Anna's wonders are on a smaller scale: her village.

Brooks uses historical records to address more timeless themes, such as strong women in a hostile community, friendship, and personal growth in crises. The least believable parts of the story are the true ones; the villagers really did agree to quarantine themselves, at the encouragement of their rector and his predecessor. In a similar but contrasting and wholly fictional story, Albert Camus's *La Peste* (1947; *The Plague*, 1948), the quarantine is forced upon the residents of Oran (the same city where Anna's journey ends).

While Camus shows people giving in to their worst impulses—a more common historical response to the plague—Brooks portrays a population at its best, too good to be true.

Anna is not a person but a perfect character who sees all and understands all with her servant's job and her intellectual's mind, allowing her to explore Brooks's themes in her narrative. Michael Mompellion has flaws and secrets not recorded in Eyam's historical records, allowing him to address the question of lost faith. Faith is the ultimate casualty of the plague; in the end, Anna accepts that she has none. The novel suggests that faith is not necessary for survival, or for contentment.

Laura D. Shumar

Further Reading

Brooks, Geraldine. "Timeless Tact Helps Sustain a Literary Time Traveler." *The New York Times*, July 2, 2001. Brooks's description of her inspiration for *Year of Wonders*. Also discusses life in small communities and emotional issues that remain constant through time.

Lee, Virginia. *Geraldine Brooks' "Year of Wonders": Insight Text Guide*. Elsternwick, Vic.: Insight, 2009. An introductory guide to Brooks's novel *Year of Wonders*, written especially for high school students. Part of a series of literary guides to contemporary texts.

Lynch, Tim, "New Hope From the Plague Village." *British Heritage* 27, no. 2 (May, 2006): 16-17. A historical account of Eyam, England, which was known as the plague village for its self-isolation during the bubonic plague in the mid-seventeenth century. Also mentions a modern genetic study of the descendants of Eyam's survivors.

Steinberg, Sybil, "Geraldine Brooks: Life and Death in Eyam." *Publishers Weekly*, August 15, 2001, pp. 278-279. An interview with Brooks that covers her career and the research for and writing of *Year of Wonders*.

The Yearling

Author: Marjorie Kinnan Rawlings (1896-1953)
First published: 1938
Type of work: Novel
Type of plot: Regional
Time of plot: Late nineteenth century
Locale: Florida scrub country

Principal characters:
JODY BAXTER, a young boy
PENNY BAXTER, his father
ORA BAXTER, his mother
FODDER-WING FORRESTER, Jody's disabled friend
OLIVER HUTTO, Penny's friend
GRANDMA HUTTO, his mother
TWINK WEATHERBY, Oliver's sweetheart

The Story:

The Baxter family consists of Penny Baxter, his plump wife, Ora, and their son, Jody. They live in a simple cabin in the Florida scrub country, where patient, hardworking Penny ekes out a meager living by farming and hunting. Young Jody still sees life through the eyes of a child and finds a boy's pleasure in building a flutter mill (a water wheel) at the spring when he should have been hoeing the garden patch.

One spring morning, the family discovers that Betsy, their black brood sow, has been killed by a bear. Penny recognizes the tracks as those of Old Slewfoot, a giant black bear with one toe missing. Determined to be rid of this offender, he corners the animal in the scrub, but his old gun will not fire, and the bear escapes.

Unable to afford a new gun, Penny trades a worthless dog to his neighbors, the Forresters, for a new double-barreled shotgun of fine make. The Forrester family consists of the old parents, six gigantic, lawless boys, and Fodder-Wing, a deformed and disabled boy who is Jody's best friend. Penny is reluctant to dupe his neighbors, but his very living depends on the destruction of Old Slewfoot. He eases his conscience by telling the Forrester boys truthfully that the dog cannot be trained for hunting. His words convince the suspicious Forresters that the dog is even more valuable than they had thought, and they insist on the trade.

After his father's old gun is repaired, it becomes Jody's great pride. One day, while hunting with his father, he shoots a buck, and Penny sells the venison at the store in Volusia. Afterward, Penny and Jody go to see Grandma Hutto, at whose house they spend the night. In the morning, everyone is made glad by the unexpected arrival of Oliver Hutto, Grandma's son, just home from the sea. Later that day, Oliver goes downtown, where he meets Lem Forrester. Both of the men have been courting the same girl, Twink Weatherby. When the two start to fight, all of Lem's brothers join in against Oliver. Wiry Penny and small Jody also enter the fight with Oliver, because the odds against him are so heavy. Jody is knocked unconscious, and Oliver leaves the fight

badly battered. To keep people from talking, Twink leaves town on the riverboat the next morning.

A short time later, Penny discovers that his hogs have disappeared. He suspects the Forresters of having trapped them to get revenge for the shotgun deal, and he and Jody start to track the hogs. During the search, a rattlesnake bites Penny on the arm. He saves himself by shooting a doe and applying the animal's liver to the bite to draw out the poison. Even in the excitement, Jody notices that the doe has a fawn. While Penny staggers homeward, Jody goes to the Forresters to ask them to ride and fetch Doc Wilson.

The Forresters, with the exception of Lem, evidently hold no grudge over the trading of the dog and the fight in town, and they do all they can for the Baxters. One of the boys brings Doc Wilson to the Baxters' cabin, and later the Forresters round up the hogs and return them. Buck Forrester then stays on at the Baxter cabin to help with the work.

While Penny is still desperately ill, Jody returns to the place where his father had been bitten, and there he finds the helpless young fawn. He is so eager to have it for his own that his parents allow him to bring it home as a pet. Rations are scarcer than ever at the Baxters' home during Penny's illness, but Jody is willing to share his own food and milk with the fawn. Fodder-Wing gives the fawn its name: Flag.

In September a great storm comes, destroying most of the Baxter crops. About a month later, Old Slewfoot visits the Baxter land again and kills a fat hog. Penny, who is in bed with chills and fever, is not able to follow the great black bear. Later, wolves kill one of the Baxters' calves, and, with the Forresters, the Baxters hunt down the whole pack. During the hunt, they find ten bear cubs that have been left motherless by the plague and by hunters. Two of the Forresters take the cubs to Jacksonville and sell them, and Penny and Jody's share of the profits allows them to buy necessities that will tide the Baxters over for the coming winter.

The Baxters plan to spend Christmas in Volusia with Grandma Hutto and to attend the town's festivities on Christmas Eve, but a few days before Christmas, Old Slewfoot again appears and kills a calf. Penny swears that he will kill the raider, and, after several days of determined hunting, he finds and shoots the huge bear.

The Baxters join Grandma Hutto at the Christmas party, and during the evening, Oliver Hutto arrives in town with his wife, Twink. To get revenge, Lem Forrester and his brothers set Grandma Hutto's house on fire and burn it to the ground. Without Oliver's knowing that the house was destroyed by the Forresters, Grandma Hutto, Oliver, and Twink leave town the next morning on the riverboat, having decided to go to Boston to live.

Back in their cabin, the Baxters settle down to a quiet winter of fishing and hunting. Flag, the fawn, has grown and is now a yearling. The fawn has never been a favorite of Ma Baxter because she begrudges him the food and milk that Jody feeds him and because he is a nuisance around the cabin.

In the spring, while Jody is helping his father plant corn, Flag gets into the tobacco field and destroys about half of the young plants. One day, while trying to pull a tree stump out of the ground, Penny suffers a hemorrhage that forces him to spend many days in bed. While he is recovering, Jody has to do all of the farmwork. He watches as the corn they have planted sprouts through the ground. One morning, he finds that Flag has eaten most of the tender green shoots of the corn plants. Mrs. Baxter wants to kill the fawn at once, but Penny suggests that Jody build a fence around the corn to keep Flag out. Jody spends many days replanting the corn and building a high fence around the field, but when the new planting of corn comes up, Flag leaps the high fence with ease and again destroys the green shoots.

Her patience exhausted, Mrs. Baxter takes Penny's gun and shoots the fawn. Her aim is poor, however, and she fails to kill the animal. The unhappy Jody has to shoot his pet again. Jody feels that his parents have betrayed him, and he hates them for it. He leaves the clearing and wanders into the scrub. With the vague idea of running away from home to join the Huttos in Boston, he heads for the river and sets out in Nellie Ginright's dugout canoe. After several days without food, he is picked up by the river mail-boat. He returns home, ashamed and penitent, no longer interested in the flutter mill, which he now considers only a plaything for children.

Critical Evaluation:

"There is of course an affinity between people and places," Marjorie Kinnan Rawlings writes in *Cross Creek* (1942). When she first arrived at Cross Creek, deep in Florida's Ocala National Forest, in 1928, Rawlings seemed an unlikely candidate to fit into the frontier landscape that existed in Florida at the time. She was a sophisticated career woman, an educated and accomplished journalist from Rochester, New York, with little knowledge of the outdoors. The inhabitants of her new home, on the other hand, were rural natives who lived close to the earth and close to natural disasters. Rawlings discovered in their hard lives elements of beauty and meaning that she incorporated into her greatest work, *The Yearling*. The publication of this book in 1938 brought Rawlings the Pulitzer Prize and worldwide recognition as a great original talent.

The affinity between people and places in *The Yearling* is most clearly seen in Penny Baxter, who has chosen to live on Baxter's Island because of its isolation. Shunning city life, which makes "intrusions on the individual spirit," Penny moves to the Florida scrub because the "wild animals seemed less predatory to him than the people he had known." He learns to live in harmony with nature and to subsist on what his land has to offer. The challenge is great because Baxter's Island is "ringed with hunger." Penny's struggles to survive made him Rawlings's favorite character. In an interview that appeared in the *Christian Science Monitor* in 1940, Rawlings explained:

Penny expresses my own philosophy—that life knocks a person down; and he gets up, and it knocks him down again. And that the only strong, manly thing for a man to do when he's down is to take the experience calmly and go on—that is, get up and go at it again.

Penny tries to pass on this philosophy to Jody, who, as a child at the beginning of the story, is interested only in the flutter mill. Jody's desperate desire to domesticate Flag shows how immature and out of harmony with nature he is. By attempting to make a pet out of an animal that is an important part of the Baxters' food supply, Jody is bound for disaster. Second, Jody's passionate love for Flag highlights how lonely he is after Fodder-Wing's death: "Flag had eased a loneliness that had harassed him in the very heart of his family." Penny's offhand remark to Jody regarding Flag, "You're a pair o' yearlin's," illustrates how Flag and Jody have merged by the end of the narrative. Jody's childish—though human—attachment to Flag must end so that Jody may move on to the next stage of his development toward independent, strong adulthood. Both boy and fawn engage in prankish behavior that threatens the precarious survival of the family. Therefore, Flag's death is a grim necessity.

When Jody runs away from home after Flag has been shot, he experiences for himself the "terrifying" power of hunger: "It had a great maw to envelop him and claws that raked across his vitals." Suddenly, he understands his father's lessons in survival. Even though he knows that he will be "lonely all his life," he realizes that this truth is a "man's share," and he can continue.

Jody's evolution toward adulthood is accomplished in great circular journeys that take him away from the security and warmth of his center, Baxter's Island, and into the fierce outer world. His quest is mythic in nature, reinforced by the structure of the book, which encompasses the passing of one year. The book begins and ends in April, the time of renewal. Jody is accompanied by spirits in his journey through the dark woods: the memories of Spaniards who had once roamed afield, Fodder-Wing and his love for all living things, and, finally, the dream of Flag—"a boy and a yearling ran side by side, and were gone forever."

Rawlings related that the inspiration for the novel came from her poignant awareness of the passing of innocent youth into adulthood. She conceived of the work as a "tragic idyll of boyhood" and recalled an experience that she had at the age of ten. She had been standing under a tree on a beautiful April morning when she had a "premonition of maturity": "And at the height of my delight, a sadness came over me, and I understood suddenly that I should not always be a child, and that beyond this carefree moment life was waiting with its responsibilities."

Transmuting real-life experiences and people into art was a struggle that Rawlings faced throughout her writing career. Living in the exotic, semitropical locale of rural, frontier Florida among colorful, eccentric, and strong-minded individualists, she was continually tempted, as a trained journalist, simply to record facts. To do so, however, would have been artistic suicide, because "facts are unreliable and treacherous." She recognized that she must learn a harder task—that is, to give facts "the breath of life." A fact is an empty cup that must be filled with "the prismatic fluid of the creative imagination," as Rawlings told University of Florida students in 1938. Her literary editor, Maxwell Perkins, urged her in this direction in order to make her characters more fictional.

Rawlings achieved the perfect balance between fact and fiction in *The Yearling*. By placing the story's events in the past, in the 1870's, she allowed herself a measure of distance. She also chose uncomplicated characters for her story. In a letter to F. Scott Fitzgerald in 1936, she said that she preferred to write about "the very simple people" because their problems "are only the most fundamental and primitive ones." Finally, she simplified her writing style, perhaps under the influence of her fellow Floridian, Ernest Hemingway,

who was living in Key West in the 1930's and whom Rawlings knew. Although she never publicly acknowledged a debt to Hemingway, critic Gordon Bigelow has noted that she learned how to write a simple declarative sentence from him. The big risk that Rawlings took by moving to Florida and giving all to literature culminated in her production of *The Yearling*, a book that transcends the reality of its place to appeal to children and adults throughout the world.

"Critical Evaluation" by Anna Lillios

Further Reading

Bellman, Samuel. *Marjorie Kinnan Rawlings*. New York: Twayne, 1974. Provides an introductory overview of Rawlings's life and artistic output. The section on *The Yearling* provides background information regarding the novel's composition and the people who inspired Rawlings.

Bigelow, Gordon. *Frontier Eden: The Literary Career of Marjorie Kinnan Rawlings*. Gainesville: University Press of Florida, 1966. An important study of Rawlings's complete works and a source of interviews and eyewitness accounts of Rawlings's life in Cross Creek. The last chapter, "The Literary Artist," focuses on Rawlings's philosophy of composition.

Bloom, Harold, ed. *American Women Fiction Writers, 1900-1960*. Philadelphia: Chelsea House, 1997. Volume 3 includes brief biographies of Rawlings and ten other authors as well as critical essays about their work. Includes analyses of individual books and broader discussion of each author's place in literary history.

Howard, Hugh. *Writers of the American South: Their Literary Landscapes*. Photographs by Roger Straus III. New York: Rizzoli, 2005. Collection of essays discusses the relationship between southern geography and the work of southern writers, illustrated with photographs of the writers' homes and environs. The essay on Rawlings describes how she drew inspiration from the landscape of central Florida.

Parker, Idella, and Mary Keating. *Idella: Marjorie Rawlings' "Perfect Maid."* Gainesville: University Press of Florida, 1992. Presents an entertaining, fascinating look behind the scenes of Rawlings's household in Cross Creek from the perspective of Rawlings's maid, who worked for her from 1940 to 1950.

Silverthorne, Elizabeth. *Marjorie Kinnan Rawlings: Sojourner at Cross Creek*. Woodstock, N.Y.: Overlook Press, 1988. A readable biography that is not too academic. Includes interviews with Norton Baskin, Rawlings's second husband.

The Years

Author: Virginia Woolf (1882-1941)
First published: 1937
Type of work: Novel
Type of plot: Domestic realism
Time of plot: 1880-1937
Locale: London

Principal characters:
COLONEL ABEL PARGITER
ELEANOR,
EDWARD,
MORRIS,
DELIA,
MILLY,
MARTIN, and
ROSE, his children
CELIA, Morris's wife
NORTH and PEGGY, the children of Morris and Celia
PATRICK, Delia's husband
SIR DIGBY PARGITER, the colonel's brother
EUGENIE, his wife
MAGGIE and SARA, their daughters
RENÉ (RENNY), Maggie's husband
KITTY MALONE, later LADY LASSWADE, the Pargiters'
   cousin
NICHOLAS POMJALOVSKY, Eleanor's friend
CROSBY, a servant

The Story:

On a blustery April afternoon in 1880, Colonel Abel Pargiter sits at the window of his club looking out over Piccadilly. Everyone in the street seems to have somewhere to go, some end in view. The colonel feels that there is nothing for him. At home, in their shabbily genteel house on Abercorn Terrace, his wife is dying of cancer; he has a family of three sons and four daughters to provide for, he is retired, and he is not rich. He decides to visit his mistress, Mira, who lives in a side street near Westminster Abbey. When he arrives, dusk is already falling; it fills the dingy rooms with the secret, furtive atmosphere of lust.

In the same dusk, in the house on Abercorn Terrace, Milly and Delia Pargiter are boiling water for tea. Their younger sister Rose is wearing a green-smudged pinafore, and Milly tries to be severe with her in a grown-up fashion. Twelve-year-old, red-haired Martin comes home from school. When the colonel arrives and asks for Eleanor, his oldest daughter, Milly reminds him that it is Eleanor's day for social service. Eleanor soon appears, dropping her books on the table. During their mother's illness she has become the family's mainstay, the keeper of accounts, the soother of hurts, and the arbiter of quarrels. Delia goes to sit with their mother. She resents Mrs. Pargiter's illness and the ties of sickness and home; in her imagination, she sees herself on the platform at a political

meeting with Charles Stewart Parnell, the great Irish leader, beside her. Morris Pargiter, a young barrister, comes home for dinner. The family members are gathered at the table when Crosby, a servant, brings word that Mrs. Pargiter has suffered a relapse. She dies later that same rainy night.

Rain also falls in Oxford, where Edward Pargiter, a student, puts aside his work and daydreams of his cousin, Kitty Malone, a don's daughter with whom he is in love. His friend Hugh Gibbs comes in with talk of horses and women. Another friend, Ashley, appears, but Ashley is jealous of Gibbs, and Edward, unhappy and bored, goes off to bed. Kitty Malone, reading history with eccentric Miss Craddock, admires Jo Robson; he reminds her of a young farmhand who had once kissed her under a rick. Mrs. Malone reads the letter that tells of Mrs. Pargiter's death and thinks of her cousin as a young girl. She decides that Edward will not do; young Lord Lasswade will make a more suitable match. Mrs. Pargiter is buried on a day of shadows and sunshine.

It is cool in England in the autumn of 1891. In the north, Kitty, now Lady Lasswade, shivers as she sits on the terrace with her husband. In Devonshire, Hugh Gibbs tells his wife, Milly, who had been a Pargiter, that the leaves on the trees are still too thick for good hunting. At Oxford, Edward Pargiter, now a don, walks in the crisp air and thinks of poetry. Morris, the lawyer, recalls his childhood as leaves crunch under his feet on the flagstones of the Law Courts. Martin is a soldier in India, and Delia and Rose have left home to lead lives of their own. Only Eleanor remains, tied to her aging father and the house on Abercorn Terrace, keeping accounts, doing social service work, going to the Law Courts with Celia, Morris's wife, and buying presents for the colonel to give to his nieces Maggie and Sara when he goes to dine with his brother, Sir Digby Pargiter. Sir Digby is in politics; his wife, Eugenie, is pretty and frivolous. The colonel has dinner with Digby and Eugenie on the day that Parnell dies.

By midsummer, 1907, Martin is back from India; he is still Captain Pargiter but no longer in the army. Sara Pargiter thinks of her cousins as she lies in bed reading Edward's translation of Sophocles' *Antigone*. Her mother and father have gone out to dinner and have taken Maggie with them; it is Maggie's first grown-up party. Sara has a crooked back, the result of her having been dropped as a child. She reads Edward's book and listens to the music coming from a dance down the street. Finally, she falls asleep.

A year later, Sir Digby and Eugenie are both dead, and their house has been sold. Colonel Pargiter has suffered a stroke. Sometimes Eleanor, who still looks after him, reflects on what a terrible thing old age is. Sir Digby and his wife were fortunate, she thinks, dying in their prime. Rose is now forty years old and mannish in appearance and behavior. She returns from the north, where she has been attending suffragist meetings. Meeting at the Abercorn Terrace house, she and Martin recall the time they quarreled and Rose cut her wrist with a knife.

After their parents' death, Maggie and Sara go to live in Hymas Place, a crescent of shabby old houses. Maggie and Rose meet in a shop, and Rose joins her cousins for lunch on a day in 1910. Delia has married an Irishman. For a brief time, some of the family—Eleanor, Martin, Kitty, Rose, and Sara—come together at a suffragist meeting. That night, while Sara is telling Maggie about the meeting, they hear shouting in the street outside: The king is dead.

After her father's death, Eleanor goes on a holiday in Spain and Greece. She is fifty-five years old, too old to begin a new life. She visits Morris and his wife, Celia, who have two children, North and Peggy. Maggie is married to a Frenchman. The Abercorn Terrace house is sold in 1913, and Crosby goes to live in lodgings in Richmond. She is still loyal to the Pargiters, looking after Martin's laundry and socks.

While returning from his stockbroker's on a spring day in 1914, Martin runs into Sara at St. Paul's and takes her out to lunch. They talk about Rose, who has been jailed after breaking windows during a suffragist demonstration. Later, they

meet Maggie and her baby in Kensington Gardens. That night, Martin dines with the Lasswades. Sitting beside a young girl at dinner, he suddenly feels that he is old and that his life is empty.

The war comes. One night in the winter of 1917, Eleanor goes to dinner with Maggie and her husband, Renny, as well as Nicholas Pomjalovsky, a Pole, and Sara. In the middle of dinner, a German air raid begins. Later, Nicholas tries to explain his hopes for the new world to come after the war. Eleanor feels that here is the man whom she might have married, but Maggie confides that Nicholas loves only other men. Eleanor, Sara, and Nicholas walk across London in the cold darkness. Eleanor has forgotten the air raid and the wail of the sirens.

They sirens wail again, and guns boom, on a November day in 1918. As Crosby is waiting in the queue at a grocer's shop, she hears someone say that the war is over.

In 1937, Eleanor, now more than seventy years old and just back from a trip to India, goes to a party given by Delia, a gathering of the Pargiter clan, with her niece Peggy, who is a doctor in a London hospital. Peggy's brother, North, has sold his farm in Africa; he brings Sara, who had invited him to dinner at her shabby flat. On their way from the theater, Maggie and Renny go with them. Delia is old; Patrick, her Irish husband, is handsome but hard of hearing. Peggy, looking at Delia and Patrick, wonders how people marry and have children. She talks to Martin, who has never been at ease with her; she is his doctor and knows his dread of cancer. Rose comes in; she has grown stout and deaf. Milly waddles beside big, jovial Hugh Gibbs, and North thinks of animals munching in their stalls. Morris, the barrister, is there, as is Edward, the distinguished bachelor-scholar. Kitty Lasswade, now the widow of a governor general, appears in time for supper. Nicholas tries to make a speech, and everyone's health is drunk. The young look at the old, and the old look at the young. Eleanor wonders if there has been a pattern behind these lives, like a theme or motif in music. Then it is time to go. Eleanor stands at the window and watches a taxi drive up to a nearby house. A young man and young woman get out of the cab, and the young man fits his latchkey to the house's front door. The sun is shining; it is a bright new day.

Critical Evaluation:

The entry in Virginia Woolf's diary for November 2, 1932, contains a reference to the novel that was eventually published as *The Years*. In the beginning, it was to be called "The Pargiters," an essay-novel into which she planned to pour the total sum of her experience in the narrative of the experiences of a single family through several generations. The pattern was not to follow that of family chronicles such as John Galsworthy and Hugh Walpole had written; instead, it was to jump chamoislike across gaps in time between 1880 and 1937. A domestic story, *The Years* lacks the bold technical brilliance of *To the Lighthouse* (1927) and *The Waves* (1931). The work may appear at first reading like a reversion to the style of Woolf's earlier books such as *Night and Day* (1919), but nothing could be further from the truth. *The Years* is more than the story of the frustrations, ambitions, triumphs, joys, tragedies, and defeats of a middle-class family. In its episodic pattern, the novel represents an effort to record the process of time passing and to capture in fiction that sudden flash of recognition, the moment of perception, that in earlier periods was the function of poetry alone. In the separate divisions of the novel, descriptions of the seasons and the flowing movement of the prose convey the sense of change and recurrence that Woolf in her later novels tried to dredge from the depths of human consciousness.

In her essay "A Room of One's Own," Woolf describes a young man and woman getting into a taxi together to exemplify her artistic ideal: the "androgynous mind" that unites both male and female principles. The same symbol—here the two are alighting from a taxi—is found at the end of *The Years* and strikes one of the few hopeful notes in the book.

The novel covers roughly the time period of Woolf's own life, a sixty-year span that witnessed massive historical changes. It is this period—the period of late nineteenth century colonial expansion, World War I and the ensuing disillusionment, and the depression and cynicism of the 1930's— that is narrated through the lives of three generations of Pargiters. Although social milieu is more important here than in any previous novel, Woolf does not merely provide a historical chronicle but also explores such themes as uniting the one with the many, bringing order to chaos, and seeing with the androgynous vision. The Pargiter family remains a unit despite the infrequent reunions that occur.

Eleanor Pargiter is perhaps the most important character in the novel, a young woman of about twenty years at the beginning, more than seventy years old at the end. As of the mother's terminal illness, Eleanor is the element that holds the family together. Throughout, her thoughts and situations are given more prominence than those of the others, and she is often shown in the contact she has with the other family members. Woolf makes note of Eleanor's jottings, as when she makes an "I" with lines radiating from that center. This image suggests the ego at the center of each person's perceptions; different events become known from different characters' perspectives. Only the reader is able to see the pattern of the whole.

Eleanor typifies the woman who sacrifices her own ambitions and desires for the good of her aging father. Woolf often commented on this kind of woman, remarking that it was a blessing that her own parents died when she was relatively young, leaving her free to pursue her writing. By the time Colonel Pargiter dies, it is too late for Eleanor to begin her own life.

The themes seen in Woolf's earlier books are found in *The Years*, but the imagery has darkened considerably. Characters are often compared to animals or parts of nature that are gross or horrible: Uncle Edward looks like the shell of an insect; Patrick's face looks like a red gooseberry with a few hairs, and his hands are like bear paws; Milly's fat arms draped with beads remind North of pale asparagus. The idea of the animal in human beings is emphasized by observations about people being "nasty creatures" with "uncontrollable lusts." North characterizes marriage as thirty years of "tut-tut-tut and chew-chew-chew." Such radical dehumanization dominates the book but is most prevalent in the last "Present Day" section. It suggests a fundamental pessimism about human possibilities: Because human beings are purely animal, "progress" is an illusion.

The constant association of progress with death and aging emphasizes this pessimistic outlook. Nicholas, for example, who speaks of a New World in 1917, expounds a similar idea in 1937, by which time there is the sense that optimistic words are empty and meaningless: After his attempted speech, Nicholas brings his glass down, and it shatters; two children sing for the party, but their words are incomprehensible; Eleanor realizes that people know nothing, even about themselves. At the end, when the old Pargiter brothers and sisters are grouped together by a window, the next generation regards them as "unreal" as statues. True communication, self-knowledge, and human progress all seem to be lacking.

The book's structure reinforces the theme of decay and entropy: People grow old and die, and little else changes or improves. The first section is divided into ten parts, each treating a day in a particular year from 1880 to 1918. Historical events—the death of Parnell or Edward VII, air raids during World War I, Armistice Day—are used as a means of bringing together different characters; the historical and social situations are always in the background. The second section, titled "Present Day," encompasses the final quarter of the book.

Throughout the novel, such natural phenomena as rain, moon, wind, sun, and snow are used to connect places and people. Sometimes these phenomena recur from one year to another, so that each subsequent mention gains associations from the earlier ones. The way the sunlight shines through the trees, for example, is noted in both 1910 and 1914. The same objects and actions are periodically mentioned, giving a large network of recurrences to the book, where everything has a place in an order and where nothing happens by chance. Flames, sparks, and smoke are mentioned often, evoking memories of previous thoughts in the characters' minds. The fraying of the wick under the slow teakettle, the spotted ink-stained walrus, and the cooing of pigeons are some of the repeated images that provide links between the years.

Eleanor herself finally realizes that some sort of pattern for the whole exists, and this awareness makes her happy, but she wonders, "Who makes it? Who thinks it?" Eleanor's vision of the pattern brings a note of hope to the ending of the book that counteracts the dark, dehumanized quality of foreboding prevalent in the 1937 section. It is questionable, however, whether her final optimistic image of the young couple and the new day overcomes the pessimistic tone that dominates most of the rest of the book.

"Critical Evaluation" by Margaret McFadden-Gerber

Further Reading

Barrett, Eileen, and Patricia Cramer, eds. *Virginia Woolf: Lesbian Readings*. New York: New York University Press, 1997. The second part of this collection of conference papers focuses on the novels, with lesbian interpretations of *The Years* and six other books.

Bell, Quentin. *Virginia Woolf*. New York: Harcourt Brace Jovanovich, 1972. Standard biography provides background on Woolf's life and work as well as photographs of family and friends, indexes, and appendixes. Contains pertinent references to the creation of *The Years*.

Briggs, Julia. *Virginia Woolf: An Inner Life*. Orlando, Fla: Harcourt, 2005. Biography focuses on Woolf's work and her fascination with the workings of the mind. Traces the creation of each of Woolf's books, from *The Voyage Out* through *Between the Acts*, combining literary analysis with details of Woolf's life.

Goldman, Jane. *The Cambridge Introduction to Virginia Woolf*. New York: Cambridge University Press, 2006.

Provides a wealth of information designed to help students and other readers better understand Woolf's work, including biographical details and discussions of the novels and other writings. One section of the book places Woolf's life and work within its historical, political, and cultural context, including information about the Bloomsbury Group; another section features contemporary reviews and explanations of how Woolf's works have been received over the decades since their first publication.

Gorsky, Susan Rubinow. *Virginia Woolf*. Boston: Twayne, 1989. A good starting place for any research on the author and her works. Discusses *The Years* and other works by Woolf and provides a chronology, annotated bibliography, and index.

Guiguet, Jean. *Virginia Woolf and Her Works*. Translated by Jean Stewart. New York: Harcourt Brace Jovanovich, 1965. Exhaustive study of most of Woolf's works examines *The Years* and other novels individually and in comparison with other works. Provides a brief biography, overview of the historical period, bibliography, and indexes.

Majumdar, Robin, and Allen McLaurin, eds. *Virginia Woolf: The Critical Heritage*. Boston: Routledge & Kegan Paul, 1975. The informative introduction provides a brief biography of Woolf. Individual criticisms of her major and minor works include many references to *The Years*. Supplemented with selected bibliography and index.

Marcus, Jane, ed. *New Feminist Essays on Virginia Woolf*. Lincoln: University of Nebraska Press, 1981. Crucial compilation of essays focuses on women's viewpoints on Woolf's work. Supplies an extremely useful political complement to earlier criticism of *The Years*.

Roe, Sue, and Susan Sellers, eds. *The Cambridge Companion to Virginia Woolf*. New York: Cambridge University Press, 2000. Collection of essays by leading scholars addresses Woolf's life and work from a range of intellectual perspectives. Includes analyses of her novels and discussions of Woolf and modernism, feminism, and psychoanalysis.

Yellow Back Radio Broke-Down

Author: Ishmael Reed (1938-   )
First published: 1969
Type of work: Novel
Type of plot: Satire
Time of plot: Early nineteenth century and twentieth century
Locale: Town of Yellow Back Radio in the western United States

Principal characters:
THE LOOP GAROO KID, a black cowboy and a Voodoo *houngan*
DRAG GIBSON, a ruthless and powerful rancher
CHIEF SHOWCASE, a Native American leader
BO SHMO, leader of the posse sent to hang Loop
BIG LIZZIE, a saloon owner in Yellow Back Radio
THEDA BLACKWELL, U.S. Secretary of Defense
PETE THE PEEK, a U.S. congressman
MUSTACHE SAL, Loop's former lover, now Drag's wife
SKINNY MCCULLOUGH, Gibson's ranch foreman
POPE INNOCENT, Roman Catholic leader

The Story:

The Loop Garoo Kid, a trickster god of the Hoodoo religion, appears incarnated as a circus cowboy in the Old West. His circus is about to play in Yellow Back Radio, its last town for the season, when the children of the town—all armed—surround them. The children had run the adults out of Yellow Back Radio and are about to do the same to Loop's troupe, until they realize that these adults are not normal adults; circus performers, they find, still have a bit of child in them.

The circus performs for the children. Meanwhile, the town's adults are holed up at Drag Gibson's ranch outside town. They sign the town over to Gibson in return for his promise to slaughter the children. After the circus performance, Jake the Barker beguiles the children with tales of the fabled Seven Cities of Cibola; they all decide to go off searching for it. Before they can, however, Gibson's men arrive, shooting everyone in sight. Loop rides off to draw their fire.

Stuck in the desert, Loop has to shoot his horse for food. Bo Shmo and his posse of neo-social realists find him and bury him in sand up to his neck. They smear his face with jam so that he will be eaten alive by insects. Loop is rescued by Chief Showcase, a high-tech American Indian who drops from the sky in a homemade helicopter, scares off Bo's gang, and revives the hero with a canteen filled with champagne.

Meanwhile, Gibson's men return to the ranch and report the slaughter of the children. Just when he is most confident, Gibson hears a mysterious voice and sees a pair of giant black hands at the window. He shoots at the reanimated collection of various animal parts—his wife—and calls in the local doctor to make her death legitimate with a certificate. In a desert cave, Loop performs Hoodoo rituals to send curses on Gibson and his men.

The next morning, Mustache Sal, Gibson's soon-to-be wife, arrives by stagecoach and seduces the ranch hand who had been sent by Gibson to meet her. She retires to her room, then Loop, her former lover, appears in her mirror and chides her for abandoning him. He brands her abdomen with the image of a hell bat. Gibson's men, scared by Loop's curse, which is killing their cattle, are about to leave, but Gibson bribes them to stay by offering shares of the ranch.

Explorers Meriwether Lewis and William Clark consult with Gibson about subduing the Indians. Big Lizzie meets the ranch hands, the marshal, and the Reverend Boyd in her saloon, called the Rabid Black Cougar, and warns them about Loop's powers. Suddenly, Loop appears, disarming all the gunslingers with his whip and leaving the men scared and quivering. The marshal concedes defeat and leaves town.

The morning after her wedding to Gibson, Sal announces to the ranch hands that she is now in charge of the ranch because her husband had died in the night. She had put arsenic in his milk the night before. Gibson suddenly appears, alive, and orders Sal thrown into the swine pit. He then calls in a famous racist gunslinger, John Wesley Hardin, to go after Loop, but Loop sends a python after Hardin, who subdues him.

Meanwhile, Field Marshal Theda Blackwell and U.S. congressman Pete the Peek conspire to stop Loop and to thwart President Thomas Jefferson for his sympathy for blacks. Chief Showcase interrupts their deliberations, pretending to befriend them, and gives them cigars. Blackwell and Pete offer Chief Showcase three states if he helps them destroy the town of Yellow Back Radio. Chief Showcase visits the dying Gibson, but Gibson recovers quickly when he receives a letter from Pope Innocent, announcing a papal visit.

The pope's visit to Yellow Back Radio is a grand celebration that quickly turns to a plot to defeat Loop. Pope Innocent explains the nature of Hoodoo to the ranch hands and gunslingers. He tells them that the key to bringing Loop down is removing the talisman, a mad dog's tooth, from around Loop's neck. Ranch foreman Skinny McCullough bribes two of Loop's flunkies to steal his talisman, and Gibson's men find him. They take him to the guillotine, but before they can execute him, two children whom Loop had rescued from the massacre at Yellow Back Radio come to the rescue. The older citizens turn against Gibson, who falls into the swine pit and is devoured.

Critical Evaluation:

Yellow Back Radio Broke-Down is Ishmael Reed's second novel, and the first after the publication of his manifesto on neo-hoodooism, in which he calls for an African American aesthetic based on Voodoo, Egyptian mythology, and improvisational musical forms. Hoodoo is an aesthetic that challenges the Judeo-Christian tradition, rationalism, and technology.

A freewheeling fantasy, *Yellow Back Radio Broke-Down* utilizes various forms of early twentieth century popular culture—the Western adventure as chronicled by pulp magazines (the source of the name Yellow Back, for the yellowed pulpy paper of the Western magazines and paperback novels) and adventure stories on radio in the 1930's and 1940's. The tone, however, is not nostalgic: It is a satiric acknowledgment of the failure of pop culture to include the experiences of African Americans and other minorities. Reed's novel adapts the epic struggle of good guys against bad guys in the American Western to present the struggle of Reed's American Neo-Hoodoo Church against organized religion, land barons, imperialists, and other exclusionist tyrants.

Reed's concept of neo-hoodooism finds its American influences in Voodoo of New Orleans, Louisiana, but traces it to Haiti and, Reed says, ultimately to the vodun, or Voodoo, religion of West Africa. He follows novelist-anthropologist Zora Neale Hurston and other African American writers before him in reading the Old Testament prophet Moses as learning African conjuring secrets in Egypt and bringing them into the Judeo-Christian tradition. Reed presents the Loop Garoo Kid as an exiled son of Jahweh, an African trickster god mistakenly considered by Western religions to be an evil figure. Loop's name comes from the French werewolf figure Loup Garou (ultimately, a cognate of the word "werewolf" through the Frankish word *garulf*). This French werewolf legend was transplanted to Haiti by French settlers and to New Orleans by the Cajuns, where it became a part of Voodoo culture.

As a work of fiction, *Yellow Back Radio Broke-Down* can be appreciated on a number of levels, even if its satiric value and its esoteric knowledge about African American cultural roots is not fully understood. Part of Reed's point, though, is that such knowledge need not be esoteric; that African religious traditions deserve to be as well known as European religious traditions. On the simplest narrative level, the novel is what one character in the novel calls a "horse opera," meaning a "hackneyed" or "clichéd" Western film. The term was coined by the silent-film cowboy actor William S. Hart, who is quoted by Reed in an epigram at the start of the novel. On this level, Loop is the lone, virtuous hero who goes against the greedy monopolists of the Old West, either railroad tycoons or, as with Drag Gibson, cattle barons trying to control everything, even beyond their ranches. Gibson himself is named for a character actor of Hart's era, Edmund Richard "Hoot" Gibson. The name Drag is a pun on a slang term for cross-dressing as well as for the rearmost rider on a cattle drive, the position known as riding drag.

On another level, *Yellow Back Radio Broke-Down* deconstructs the Western as a genre. Many critics have pointed to the "Broke-Down" of the title as a reference to deconstruction, a term coined by literary critic Jacques Derrida two years before the novel appeared. For Reed, the Western as a genre makes visible the flaws of Western civilization. It considers the resources of the American West—and, in particular, its human resources, the Native Americans—as potential sources of wealth to be exploited. By inverting the clichés, Reed shows how those flaws can be corrected.

On a third level, the novel takes on presuppositions of the time about what the African American novel was supposed to be. In the second chapter, Loop is bushwhacked by Bo Shmo's posse, identified as "neo-social realists," Reed's term for the type of critics who did not like his first novel, *The Free-Lance Pallbearers* (1967), which satirized the social realism of such African American novelists as Ralph Ellison and James Baldwin. Some critics, Reed had asserted, insisted that black Americans need to engage the socioeconomic plight of urban blacks, and novels that did not—most pointedly, Reed's novels—should be shunned. Loop's oft-quoted response to Bo Shmo is clearly Reed's own response:

> [W]hat if I write circuses? No one says a novel has to be one thing. It can be anything it wants to be, a vaudeville show, the six o'clock news, the mumblings of wild men saddled by demons.

Exorcising the demons of wild men is precisely the neo-hoo-doo purpose of *Yellow Back Radio Broke-Down.*

John R. Holmes

Further Reading

Boyer, Jay. *Ishmael Reed.* Boise, Idaho: Boise State University Press, 1993. A fine general introduction to Reed's literary themes. A pamphlet-sized booklet of fifty-two pages in the Boise State Western Writers series. Includes a bibliography.

Dick, Bruce Allen, ed., with Pavel Zemliansky. *The Critical Response to Ishmael Reed.* Westport, Conn.: Greenwood Press, 1999. A collection of reviews and articles, including the editor's interview with Reed. Includes four items on *Yellow Back Radio Broke-Down*: three exchanges between Reed and critic Irving Howe and an article by critic Michel Fabre.

Fabre, Michel. "Postmodern Rhetoric in Ishmael Reed's *Yellow Back Radio Broke-Down.*" In *The Afro-American Novel Since 1960,* edited by Peter Bruck and Wolfgang Karrer. Amsterdam: Gruner, 1982. Identifies Reed's rhetorical techniques in the novel. Reprinted in Bruce Allen Dick's *The Critical Response to Ishmael Reed* (1999).

Flota, Brian. *A Survey of Multicultural San Francisco Bay Literature, 1955-1979: Ishmael Reed, Maxine Hong Kingston, Frank Chin, and the Beat Generation.* Lewis-ton, N.Y.: Edwin Mellen Press, 2009. Places Reed in the context of a half-century of San Francisco ethnic and multicultural literature.

McGee, Patrick. *Ishmael Reed and the Ends of Race.* New York: St. Martin's Press, 1997. McGee looks at Reed's refusal to meet expectations associated traditionally with African American writers, and he examines Reed's use of satire and his antagonism toward political correctness.

Martin, Reginald. *Ishmael Reed and the New Black Aesthetic Critics.* New York: St. Martin's Press, 1988. An analysis not only of Reed's literary theories in the context of late twentieth century African American aesthetics but also of how critics in that movement have treated his fiction.

Mvuyekure, Pierre-Damien. *The "Dark Heathenism" of the American Novelist Ishmael Reed: African Voodoo as American Literary Hoodoo.* Lewiston, N.Y.: Edwin Mellen Press, 2007. Defines Reed's novels as postcolonial writings characterized by neo-hoodoism. Demonstrates how Reed transforms the English language and debates about colonialism into discourses about self-empowerment and self-representation, reconnecting African Americans with Africa.

_____, ed. *A Casebook Study of Ishmael Reed's "Yellow Back Radio Broke-Down."* Chicago: Center for Book Culture, 2003. A collection of four essays that analyze Reed's novel from several perspectives, including that of African Voodoo and American jazz.

The Yemassee
A Romance of Carolina

Author: William Gilmore Simms (1806-1870)
First published: 1835
Type of work: Novel
Type of plot: Adventure
Time of plot: Early eighteenth century
Locale: South Carolina

Principal characters:
SANUTEE, a Yemassee chief
MATIWAN, his wife
OCCONESTOGA, his son
GABRIEL HARRISON, a young settler
HECTOR, Gabriel's black slave
PARSON MATTHEWS, a minister
BESS MATTHEWS, his daughter

The Story:

The English settlers, who at first had to accept aid from the Yemassee Indians when they landed on the South Carolina shores, have become quite powerful by 1715. No longer do they have to be careful not to offend the Indians; instead, they continually set up farms on the wrong side of the boundary line between the white and Indian territories. Sanutee, one of the Yemassee chiefs, has become suspicious of the colonists; he is afraid that they will soon take over all the Yemassee land. In order to keep the colonists from occupying Indian territory, he has made treaties with other tribes and with the Spanish, who are willing to help the Indians defeat the English. Sanutee's life is made unhappy by his son, Occonestoga, who has been tempted by liquor to become a close friend of the whites. Sanutee is too proud of his ancestry and his position to call a drunkard his son, and it is only the constant pleading of his wife, Matiwan, that keeps Sanutee from completely disowning Occonestoga.

One of the recent settlers is Gabriel Harrison, a strange young man whose commanding presence and jolly manner make him both admired and disliked. Among those who like him are Bess Matthews, the daughter of old Parson Matthews, and Walter Grayson, an honorable young farmer. Parson Matthews dislikes Harrison because he finds Harrison too lighthearted and worldly in his manner, and Walter's brother, Hugh, dislikes Harrison because Hugh is also an admirer of Bess. Harrison has brought with him a fine African slave named Hector, who is his constant companion, and a strong and faithful dog named Dugdale. With these two companions, Harrison wanders about the district.

One day in the forest, Harrison comes upon Sanutee fighting with a stranger over the carcass of a deer. He arrives in time to save Sanutee's life, but the proud Indian expresses no gratitude. Harrison learns that the man Sanutee was fighting is a sailor named Dick Chorley, who has recently arrived on the coast. Although Chorley claims that he has come to trade, Harrison rightly suspects that he is really a Spanish agent who has come to arm the Yemassee against the English. Harrison sends Hector to spy on Chorley and Sanutee, who have been joined by Ishiagaska, another Yemassee chief.

Hector, hiding in the brush, overhears Chorley's declaration that he has come to South Carolina to arm the Yemassee. Displaying the wampum belt of an Indian treaty, Chorley asks the Yemassee tribe to join the tribes who are willing to fight the English. Before Hector can return to tell Harrison what he has learned, however, the slave is captured and taken aboard Chorley's ship. Harrison guesses what has become of Hector; he finds Chorley in Parson Matthews's cabin and, through threats, forces the seaman to sign an order freeing Hector. His actions anger the parson, who refuses to suspect Chorley of treason, and the parson denies Harrison the right to wed his daughter, Bess.

In the meantime, the Yemassee chiefs are called to a council and asked to sell more land to the English. Most of the chiefs are willing to sell, but Sanutee, who arrives late to the meeting, makes a stirring speech against the sale. Interrupted by his drunken son, the old Yemassee almost kills Occonestoga. When he hears that the other chiefs intend to sell the land over his protests, Sanutee leaves the meeting and goes to arouse the people against their chiefs. With the aid of

an Indian prophet named Enoree Mattee, he so infuriates the Indians in the crowd that they repudiate the other chiefs and punish them by having the tribal mark cut from their skins, so that they became outcasts from the tribe. Only Occonestoga escapes this punishment.

Occonestoga hides in the woods, where, one day, he saves Bess Matthews's life by killing a rattlesnake that is about to strike her. For this deed, Harrison rewards the young Yemassee with his friendship. Soon afterward, he sends Occonestoga back to the Indian stronghold to learn what the Yemassee are planning. Occonestoga secretly makes his way to his mother, Matiwan, who hides him in her tent. By chance, Sanutee discovers the boy and orders that he be killed after having the tribal mark cut from his skin. In desperation, Matiwan kills her son before the sentence can be carried out, for the tribal mark cannot be cut from a dead man.

Harrison, realizing that Sanutee is about to lead the Yemassee against the whites, does his best to get all the settlers to go to the blockhouse for protection. Parson Matthews insists that the Yemassee have never been more friendly, and he refuses to leave his cabin. Harrison, while scouting in the woods, is captured by Yemassee, but with the aid of Matiwan, who knows of Harrison's kindness toward her son, he escapes. When he attempts to save Bess before the Yemassee can seize her, he is almost recaptured, but Hector and his dog, Dugdale, arrive just in time to save him.

Meanwhile, Chorley has led a party of Yemassee and sailors to the Matthews' cabin and has captured both Bess and her father. Harrison is able to rescue them, however, and he leads them to the blockhouse before the Indian attack begins. A furious struggle then takes place, with men and women fighting side by side to hold off the Yemassee. Both the Grayson brothers have become friendly with Harrison because of the bravery he has shown in saving their families, and together they fight valiantly to save their community. At last, the Yemassee are forced to withdraw.

Harrison makes plans to send many of the settlers to Charleston, where they will be safe until troops can be mustered to defeat the Yemassee permanently. After winning the parson's permission to marry Bess—consent freely given after his heroic defense of the colony—Harrison astonishes the group by announcing that he is in reality Charles Craven, the new governor of the province. He had come to the region in disguise so that he could see for himself the true state of affairs on the frontier. He makes Hugh Grayson commander of the garrison forces. When he offers Hector his freedom, the old slave refuses to be parted from his kind master.

In Charleston, Craven raises a considerable fighting force before returning to do battle with the Yemassee on the banks of the Salkehatchie River. When the Yemassee attack the camp of the white people, the governor's troops, firing from ambush, defeat them. Sanutee falls, mortally wounded, and Craven sees Matiwan run onto the field of battle and fall, weeping, by her husband's body. The last of the Yemassee warriors is dead.

Critical Evaluation:

In early American frontier novels, the Indian was inevitably characterized in one of two ways: either as a noble savage, a natural primitive untainted by civilization's corrupting influences, or, more commonly, as a savage barbarian who took pleasure in cruelty and violence toward innocent white settlers. Even America's most famous author of historical romances, James Fenimore Cooper, divided his Indians into absolutely good and bad types and developed his novels accordingly. Perhaps only William Gilmore Simms in *The Yemassee* succeeded in creating believable, human Indians with mixed qualities, natures, and potentials; that is the primary reason *The Yemassee*, in spite of severe artistic flaws, must be acknowledged as one of the best nineteenth century frontier novels.

Through the first one-third of the book, the action is seen primarily from the Indian viewpoint. Simms carefully describes the Yemassee tribal members as they plan and attempt to execute an uprising against the white settlers. Their motives spring not from innate hostility or from cruelty but from a realization that the powers and needs of the white settlers make the conflict—and their own ultimate defeat—inevitable. Simms thus imports to the Yemassee a kind of doomed, almost tragic, grandeur.

It is in his depiction of the intimate lives of the Yemassee that Simms is most impressive. Unlike Cooper, Simms describes the natives in their own environment and shows their daily routines, tribal mores, rituals, and politics in minute, careful detail. This Indian culture is presented with respect, and individual tribe members are presented as fallible but admirable human beings.

The most vivid portraits are those of Chief Sanutee, his wife, and their son. Sanutee is a proud, intelligent, brave but flawed leader who understands and accepts the unavoidable dissolution of his tribe but nevertheless inspires his people to heroic resistance. His wife, Matiwan, shares her husband's courage and insight, but her compassion elevates her above racial identity, so that she becomes a kind of earth mother figure. Their son, Occonestoga, contaminated by contact with the white culture's whiskey and promises, finally finds his courage and nobility in a time of crisis, although too late to salvage his tribal status. Few scenes in nineteenth century

fiction are as powerful as the one in which, during the ritual that is to strip Occonestoga of his tribal identity, Matiwan kills her own son before the assembled Yemassee to save his honor and dignity.

Had Simms been able to sustain the insights and intensity of the first one-third of the book, *The Yemassee* might have been a great novel. Unfortunately, once the focus of the novel shifts to the white culture, the characters, both Indians and whites, become stock figures, and the novel degenerates into a clichéd adventure story.

Simms's sympathetic treatment of the Yemassee, however, does not mean that he considered them the equal of white people. Even Sanutee "well knew that the superior must necessarily be the ruin of the race which is inferior." As a staunch upholder of the southern position in the pre-Civil War American South, Simms firmly believed in racial superiority and what he and others called an "organic society." In Simms's view, the Indians were doomed because theirs was an inferior race and culture, and, unlike blacks, they could not be placed into any useful positions in the white world. However tragic and seemingly unjust it might be, the displacement or destruction of the Indians was, to Simms, a necessary price.

Further Reading

Busick, Sean R. *A Sober Desire for History: William Gilmore Simms as Historian*. Columbia: University of South Carolina Press, 2005. Describes Simms's efforts to record and comprehend American history and to preserve the past, arguing that the author is best understood as a historian. Addresses Simms's ideas about the relationship of fiction to history.

Frye, Steven. "Metahistory and American Progressivism: Cultural Dialogics in Simms's *The Yemassee*." In *Historiography and Narrative Design in the American Romance: A Study of Four Authors*. Lewiston, N.Y.: Edwin Mellen Press, 2001. Part of a larger work that analyzes romances by Simms and three other nineteenth century American writers, describing how these novels employ various techniques and models for writing history.

Guilds, John Caldwell. *Simms: A Literary Life*. Fayetteville: University of Arkansas Press, 1992. Provides an account of Simms's life and writing, and asserts that Simms's historical fiction provides an "epic study" of the United States and should be recognized as the work of a major writer. Guilds has attempted to rescue Simms from obscurity by editing several twentieth century editions of Simms's novels as well as collections of essays about the author.

Guilds, John Caldwell, and Caroline Collins, eds. *William Gilmore Simms and the American Frontier*. Athens: University of Georgia Press, 1997. Collection of essays focuses on the use of the frontier motif in Simms's works.

Rubin, Louis O., Jr. "The Romance of the Colonial Frontier: Simms, Cooper, the Indians, and the Wilderness." In *American Letters and the Historical Consciousness*, edited by J. Gerald Kennedy and Daniel Mark Fogel. Baton Rouge: Louisiana State University Press, 1987. Discusses the genre of frontier romance and evaluates Simms's portrayal of Native Americans.

Watson, Charles S. *From Nationalism to Secessionism: The Changing Fiction of William Gilmore Simms*. Westport, Conn.: Greenwood Press, 1993. Closely analyzes Simms's work to demonstrate his changing political opinions. From 1825 until 1848, Simms was a nationalist, creating patriotic romances; however, as the United States edged closer to civil war, he became an uncompromising secessionist, as evidenced by his later works. Includes bibliographical references and index.

Wimsatt, Mary Ann. *The Major Fiction of William Gilmore Simms: Cultural Traditions and Literary Form*. Baton Rouge: Louisiana State University Press, 1989. Discusses the backgrounds and traditions of the romance genre, influenced by Sir Walter Scott, that Simms used for his long fiction.

Yonnondio
From the Thirties

Author: Tillie Olsen (1912-2007)
First published: 1974
Type of work: Novel
Type of plot: Psychological realism
Time of plot: Early 1930's
Locale: Wyoming, South Dakota, and a midwestern
    city

Principal characters:
ANNA HOLBROOK, a mother of five young children
JIM HOLBROOK, a coal miner, husband, and father
MAZIE and BESS, their daughters
WILL,
JIMMIE, and
BEN, their sons

The Story:

Anna and Jim Holbrook and their four children—Mazie, Will, Jimmie, and baby Ben—live in a rural Wyoming coal-mining community, where Jim toils as an underground miner. They survive somehow in abject poverty, with most of Jim's wages paid in scrip, usable only at the company store. Jim uses much of the rest of his wages on liquor to cope with the physical and mental strain of long hours underground. The townspeople live in dreaded anticipation of the whistle that announces another underground explosion and cave-in and the death of more miners. They all worry because the mine superintendent's nephew, the new fire boss, never makes the trips to detect the possible presence of methane gas, which explodes when built up.

While Anna slaves with the housework and child care and futilely dreams of an education and better life for the children, Jim dreams the same while he labors for coal that should be red, not black, because it is gotten with the blood of miners. Mazie wonders about education and why blackness is so prevalent—the coal, the miners' faces and hands, the

night—and contrasts it with fire and the sun and the redness of Sheen McEvoy's face, which had been blown off in an explosion, making him crazy.

The earth sucks Jim in to haul out coal to make the rich richer, but Jim and Anna plan to leave the mines for farming in the Dakotas. Before they can go, however, McEvoy grabs Mazie and carries her to a mine shaft. In his deranged thought he intends her as a virginal sacrifice to the mine, so that the mine will stop killing miners. The night watchman saves Mazie and knocks the crazed McEvoy down the shaft instead. Soon after, the Holbrooks depart for South Dakota, hoping for a better life there.

Life is indeed better in South Dakota, in some ways, with pure, soft air and a sense of freedom that makes Jim and Anna sing. Still, they are tenant farmers, and as they had been warned, they cannot survive at it because the bank takes everything. Even after slaving for a year at farming, they end up still owing the bank, which takes away the Holbrook farm and animals.

Still, especially for Mazie, the natural beauty, the birds, and the winds of South Dakota uplift her, despite the continued poverty. An educated South Dakotan encourages her toward schooling, and even gives her the needed books. However, Jim sells the books because the family is near starvation. Anna has another baby, Bess, a hungry mouth to feed with insufficient supplies. Fights between Jim and Anna worsen because of the poverty, and the horribly cold winters and forced indoor life with the children, who are always hungrier and thinner, lead them to move again, this time to a midwestern city—probably Chicago. Jim thinks he can find work in the thriving stockyards and slaughterhouses. Before leaving for the city, Mazie sleeps all night in the hay. Anna, too, breathes in the hay's good smell so she will never forget it.

In sharp contrast to the farm, the city stinks horribly; so, too, does the old house in which the family has to live. Jim cannot find work in a slaughterhouse and must work as a sewer repairmen, bringing home even more stink. Anna becomes pregnant again, but miscarries and nearly dies after Jim forces her to have sex. Jim then retreats into a fantasy world and neglects the children.

Will and Mazie, virtually unsupervised, fail in school, and the entire family nearly starves. Illness necessitates a doctor visit, during which they are told everything they need to make the children well; they are not told how to get the money to pay for the needed care. The powerlessness, helplessness, and sickness of the family continues. A stifling hot summer, in which the temperature stays above 100 degrees, is worsened by a lack of air-conditioning; there is no money even for fans. The impoverished neighborhood worsens, and the elderly and young are dying from the heat. A man has a heart attack at work; his pay is docked and he is charged for use of the company ambulance.

Almost miraculously, though, baby Bess brings hope by energetically and defiantly, and with great satisfaction repeatedly, banging a fruit-jar lid on the table, making the family laugh and giving them relief, hope, and some sort of transcendence from their misery. Will brings a radio home, marking the first time the family has experienced its magic and bringing further relief. Anna tells Jim that the air is changing, that the oppressive heat is ending, and that tomorrow will be better.

Critical Evaluation:

Yonnondio is a compelling, disturbingly real depiction of the lives of an impoverished American family during the early 1930's. Written by Tillie Olsen, who also had survived such poverty growing up, the novel avoids didacticism yet still clearly conveys its message of the virtually endless injustices suffered by the poor under capitalism and the mechanization of work. These systems make "a few fat bellies fatter" while brutalizing workers, most compellingly miner Sheen McEvoy, whose face is blown off in a mine explosion that makes him so crazy he tries to sacrifice Mazie to the mine to stop the killing. The fire boss neglects to inspect the mines to avoid an explosion, and the mine owners disavow such a disaster as an "unavoidable catastrophe" (or, as in the Buffalo Creek mining disaster in West Virginia in the early 1970's, in which fifty-five people died, as an "act of God").

In the slaughterhouse business, the mechanistic system is described by Olsen as "choreographed by Beedo, the B system, speed-up, stopwatch, convey," which dehumanizes the worker and makes him a "component part, geared, meshed, timed, controlled." Dehumanized thus, Jim is brutal to his family, despite his love for them; "there is a need for someone to beat," the same way Mazie also hits Will because of her frustrations lacking a place, a space, of her own.

Intertwined with Olsen's anticapitalist theme is the contrast that she draws between country life and city life, or the natural versus the unnatural. Although farming in South Dakota is not heaven, still, its natural beauty and its fresh and clean breeze, coupled with the songs of the birds, all contribute to sustain the Holbrook family. Despite the abusive bankers who take their farm (the bankers a key element in the capitalistic system), farm life is presented as preferable to the stench, the mechanical dehumanization, the violence, and the deprivation of the inner city to which the Holbrooks move. Mazie survives mentally on her "full soft dream of the farm," where she had been "secure," and tries to avoid looking at the city streets and the city people. When she does really look at them for the first time, they "enter" her "like death."

Anna, Mazie's mother, only recovers from her mental illness after her miscarriage. She goes with her children to an empty section of the city along the river, a place that is "yellow and green and white with flowers and grass and dandelion glory" and with attendant fragrance. Here, Anna picks familiar flowers, reminisces about living among trees, and achieves peace, contentment, and a strange happiness. All these feelings seem to come "up from the grasses, from the earth, from the broad tree trunk at their back," making "the air and self" shine boundless. Thus, Olsen conveys that human sanity is inextricably tied to the world of nature, the antithesis of life in the industrial city.

Probably most compelling about *Yonnondio*, though, is its sheer, powerful accuracy in depicting the psychological realities of Anna and Mazie, especially, as they struggle against overwhelmingly negative circumstances. Through it all they try to retain their human dignity, sense of direction, and hope for the future. Although bordering on overwhelming naturalism, like Theodore Dreiser's novel, *An American Tragedy* (1925), Olsen eschews such cynicism in her characters, giving them a fundamental inner strength, a drive to achieve, and a renewable spirit. Not coincidentally, another female character, the baby Bess, most succinctly epitomizes this view against cynicism and fate as she bangs a fruit-jar lid against the kitchen table, an act that so pleases and relieves the family.

In Olsen's feminist vision, Mazie and Anna share a special strength, the strength to suffer through oppression and deprivation, as women have for thousands of years, but also the strength to continue to struggle and achieve, to overcome all adversity in the end. Thus, Mazie narrowly escapes death and Anna narrowly escapes insanity, but they do escape and overcome. It is the depth and sensitivity of Olsen's female characters that are especially praiseworthy elements of the novel.

Much of the psychological power of the novel's presentation of female characters comes from the poetry of Olsen's fictional technique, influenced greatly by poet Walt Whitman. Indeed, the novel's title and certain lines come from his poems. With oxymorons like "pleasant hurt," poetic metaphors like "the days were bright with the colored balls of song, birds tossed back and forth," and the rhyming beauty of Mazie looking in the garbage dump for "anything that dangles, jangles, bangles, spangles," the novel is abundant in poetry. Mazie, too, feels "sick and mean and screamy, and sad and mad and bad." There is also the poetically and thematically powerful irony, worthy of the formalist poets, of the description of "the younguns pulpy with charity starches" (extremely impoverished children) who "chant the lesson after the teacher: we-are-the-rich-est-country-in-the-worr-uld."

Yonnondio has a unique history. Olsen had begun to write the novel in 1932 at the age of nineteen and at the height of the Great Depression. She worked on the manuscript intermittently into 1936. Decades later, still unpublished, some manuscript pages had been found accidentally. The first four chapters were in almost final form; the last four required considerable editing, but no new writing was added. The novel had been published unfinished.

Overall, given the profoundly realistic depiction of the lives of the poor in 1930's America, the important themes concerning the causes of the poverty and degradation of these human beings, and the poetic creativity and experimentation of Olsen's fictional technique, *Yonnondio* deserves to rank with John Steinbeck's *The Grapes of Wrath* (1939) as one of the two most important novels about the Great Depression. It is also an important novel in the advancement of

modern fictional style. Furthermore, the truism that the sooner Americans forget about the Great Depression, the sooner they will relive it is indicative of the significance of *Yonnondio*, particularly after the stock-market crash of 2008. Indeed, this novel should have a permanent, esteemed place in American literature.

John L. Grigsby

Further Reading

Cardoni, Agnes Toloczko. *Women's Ethical Coming-of-Age: Adolescent Female Characters in the Prose Fiction of Tillie Olsen*. Lanham, Md.: University Press of America, 1998. A survey of Olsen's adolescent female characters, comparing and contrasting their milieux. Includes a bibliography and an index.

Coiner, Constance. *Better Red: The Writing and Resistance of Tillie Olsen and Meridel Le Sueur*. New York: Oxford University Press, 1995. A detailed discussion of the leftist political vision of Olsen as reflected in her personal life, her public activities, in *Yonnondio*, and in her other writings.

Faulkner, Mara. *Protest and Possibility in the Writing of Tillie Olsen*. Charlottesville: University Press of Virginia, 1993. A technical, sophisticated analysis of Olsen's compressed, poetic writing style and of the historical and literary context of her works.

Martin, Abigail. *Tillie Olsen*. Boise, Idaho: Boise State University Press, 1984. A good, brief introduction to Olsen's *Yonnondio* and short-story collection *Tell Me A Riddle* (1961), with effective comparison to other writers' works.

Nelson, Kay Hoyle, and Nancy Huse, eds. *The Critical Response to Tillie Olsen*. Westport, Conn.: Greenwood Press, 1994. A comprehensive collection of essays responding to and analyzing Olsen's major writings, including *Yonnondio*.

Orr, Elaine Neil. *Tillie Olsen and a Feminist Spiritual Vision*. Oxford: University Press of Mississippi, 1987. A thorough, effective analysis of the feminism that is fundamental to all of Olsen's writings.

Pearlman, Mickey, and Abby H. P. Werlock. *Tillie Olsen*. Boston: Twayne, 1991. A good general introduction to all of Olsen's writings, with a chapter on *Yonnondio*.

Reid, Panthea. *Tillie Olsen: One Woman, Many Riddles*. New Brunswick, N.J.: Rutgers University Press, 2010. A comprehensive biographical account of Olsen's life and work based on diaries, letters, manuscripts, private documents, resurrected public records, and interviews. Also corrects fabrications and myths about Olsen.

You Can't Go Home Again

Author: Thomas Wolfe (1900-1938)
First published: 1940
Type of work: Novel
Type of plot: Autobiographical
Time of plot: 1929-1936
Locale: New York, England, and Germany

Principal characters:
GEORGE WEBBER, a writer
ESTHER JACK, the woman he loves
FOXHALL EDWARDS, his editor and best friend
LLOYD MCHARG, a famous novelist
ELSE VON KOHLER, a woman also loved by Webber

The Story:

As George Webber looks out the window of his New York apartment on a spring day in 1929, he is filled with happiness. The bitter despair of the previous year has been lost somewhere in the riotous time he has spent in Europe, and now it is good to be back in New York with the feeling that he knows where he is going. His book has been accepted by a great publishing firm, and Foxhall Edwards, the best editor of the house, has been assigned to help him with the corrections and revisions. George has also resumed his old love affair with Esther Jack, who, married and the mother of a grown daughter, nevertheless returns his love with tenderness and passion. This love, however, is a flaw in George's otherwise great content, for he and Esther seem to be pulling in different directions. She is a famous stage designer who mingles with a sophisticated artistic set, whereas George thinks that he can find himself completely only if he lives among and understands the little people of the world.

Before George's book is published, he tries for the first time to go home again. Home is Libya Hill, a small city in the mountains of Old Catawba. When the aunt who reared George dies, he goes back to Libya Hill for her funeral. There he learns that he can never really go home again, for home is no longer the quiet town of his boyhood; rather, it is a growing city of money-crazy speculators who are concerned only with making huge fortunes out of real estate.

George finds some satisfaction in the small excitement he creates in Libya Hill because he has written a book that is soon to be published. Even that pleasure is not to last long, however, for when he returns to New York and his book—which is about Libya Hill and the people he knew there—is published, almost all the citizens of Libya Hill write him letters filled with threats and curses. George's only motive had been to tell the truth as he sees it, but his old friends and relatives in Libya Hill seem to think that he spied on them throughout his boyhood in order to gossip about them in later years. Even the small fame he receives in New York, where his book is favorably reviewed by the critics, cannot make up for the abusive letters from Libya Hill.

George feels he can redeem himself only by working feverishly on his new book. He moves to Brooklyn, first breaking off his relationship with Esther. This severance from Esther is difficult, but George cannot live a lie himself and attempts to write the truth. In Brooklyn, he does learn to know and love the little people—the derelicts, the prostitutes, the petty criminals—and he learns that they, like so-called good men and women, are all representative of America. George's only real friend is Foxhall Edwards, who has become like a father to him. Edwards is a great man, a gifted editor and a genius at understanding and encouraging those who, like George, find it difficult to believe in anything during the years of the Great Depression. Edwards, too, knows that only through truth can America and the world be saved from destruction, but, unlike George, he believes that the truth cannot be thrust suddenly upon people. He calmly accepts conditions as they exist. George rages at his friend's skepticism.

After four years in Brooklyn, George finishes the first draft of his new book. Tired of New York, he thinks that he might find the atmosphere he needs to complete his manuscript in Europe. In London, he meets Lloyd McHarg, the embodiment of all that George wants to be. George yearns for fame in this period of his life. Because his first book brought him temporary fame, quickly extinguished, he envies McHarg's world reputation as a novelist. George is disillusioned when he learns that McHarg finds fame meaningless. He has held the world in his hand for a time, but nothing has happened. Now he is living feverishly, looking for something he cannot name.

When George decides his manuscript is ready for publication, he returns to New York, makes the corrections Edwards suggests, and then sails again for Europe. He goes to Germany, a country he has not visited since 1928. In 1936, he is more saddened by the change in the German people than he has been by anything else in his life. He had always felt a kinship with the Germans, but they are no longer the people he knew. Persecution and fear tinge every life in that once-proud country, and George, sickened, wonders if there is anyplace in the world where truth and freedom still live.

There are, however, two bright spots in his visit to Germany. The first is the fame that greets him on his arrival. His first book had been well received, and his second, now published, is a great success. For a time, he basks in that glory, but soon he, like McHarg, finds fame an elusive thing that brings no real reward. His other great experience is his love for Else von Kohler. That is also an elusive joy, however, for her roots are deep in Germany, and George knows he must return to the United States to cry out to his own people that they must live the truth and so save the nation from the world's ruin. Before he leaves Germany, he sees more examples of the horror and tyranny under which the people exist, and he leaves with a heavy heart. He realizes once more that one can never go home again.

Back in New York, George knows that he must break at last his ties with Foxhall Edwards. He writes to Edwards, telling him why they can no longer travel the same path. First, he reviews the story of his own life, through which he weaves the story of his desire to make the American people awake to the great need for truth so that they might keep their freedom. He tells Edwards, too, that in his youth he wanted fame and love above all else. Now, having had both, he has learned that they are not enough. Slowly he has learned humility, and he knows that he wants to speak the truth to the downtrodden, to all humanity. Because George knows that he has to try to awaken the slumbering conscience of America, he is saying farewell to his friend, for Edwards believes that if the end of freedom is to be the lot of humanity, fighting against that end is useless.

Sometimes George fears that the battle is lost, but he will never stop fighting as long as there is hope that America will awaken to the truth. He eventually discovers that the real enemy of America is selfishness and greed, disguised as a friend of humankind. He feels that, if he can only get help from the less fortunate people of the nation, he can defeat the enemy. Through George, America might go home again.

Critical Evaluation:

In May, 1938, having broken with his first editor and mentor Maxwell Perkins ("Foxhall Edwards" in the novel), Thomas Wolfe deposited an unfinished manuscript of perhaps a million words on the desk of his new editor, Edward C. Aswell of Harper and Brothers, and left for a tour of the West. In Vancouver, he contracted pneumonia, in Seattle it worsened, and finally, after he had been moved to Johns Hopkins Hospital in Baltimore, it was found that the illness had trig-

gered the release in his lungs of previously latent tuberculosis bacteria, which had gone to the brain; he died on September 15, 1938.

It was thus left to Aswell to assemble, organize, and edit Wolfe's admittedly unfinished material into publishable works. The major results of Aswell's efforts were the two massive novels that chronicle the life and artistic development of George Webber, *The Web and the Rock* (1939) and *You Can't Go Home Again*. Consequently, the episodic, fragmentary, sometimes even arbitrary structure of these books and the unevenness and occasional excessiveness of the writing must in part be the result of the compositional problems—though these flaws also exist in Wolfe's two prior works. There is no way of knowing what the final forms of the novels would have been had Wolfe lived to complete them to his own satisfaction.

It has been said that Wolfe wrote only one book during his career, a thinly disguised autobiography. In a sense this is true, but, like Walt Whitman, the American author who seems most like Wolfe in artistic intention and attitude, Wolfe saw his own experience as the focal point for the experience of a nation still in the process of becoming. Thus, as the major character in Wolfe's novels strives for experience, personal meaning, and a means of artistic expression, he is also trying to seize and formalize the nature and direction of nothing less than American society itself.

You Can't Go Home Again is the most external and social of Wolfe's four major novels. The title sets the theme and action line of the novel. George cannot go "home" to any of the old places, experiences, or ideas that have formed him because every time he attempts to do so, he finds a corruption that has destroyed the thing to which he would return or he finds that he has gone beyond that particular experience and has neither the need nor the desire to repeat it. Metaphorically, "home" is the naïve, idealized vision of America and of George's potential place in it that he had held as a young man but now learns no longer exists and perhaps never did. When George returns to his hometown of Libya Hill to attend his aunt's funeral, he finds the old rural values gone and a new corrupt speculative fever running rampant. Then he sees the collapse of this greedy dream in the beginnings of the Depression. He cannot go back to his physical home because it no longer exists, and he is repelled by what has replaced it. Libya Hill, however, is only a microcosm, a foreshadowing of what he is to encounter. As America enters into the Depression, George comes into painful contact with the results of the American economic and social system as he intimately observes both its victims and its victimizers—and he seeks to disassociate himself from both.

It is Europe and especially Germany, however, that brings George to his final understanding. The notion that artistic success and fame will bring him satisfaction is destroyed by his meeting with the famous novelist Lloyd McHarg (a fictionalized Sinclair Lewis), who finds that only bitterness, loneliness, and alcoholism come from his success. George then completes his education in Germany when he is exposed to the horror of the newly powerful Nazi regime. The Nazi horror, thus, is the logical extension and end result of the greed and corruption George has observed in America, perhaps even the America of the not-too-distant future.

You Can't Go Home Again is not a despairing book, however. It ends with an exhortation. For all the evil and pessimism he has encountered in his education, George continues to feel that humanity in general and America in particular still have the potential to assert their positive capacities and realize the ideals they once possessed. That is what, as an artist in Whitman's bardic tradition, George sees his place in America to be—as a spokesman for that vision.

Further Reading

Bloom, Harold, ed. *Thomas Wolfe.* New York: Chelsea House, 1987. Collection of eight essays by seven writers includes a general overview of Wolfe's fiction and an examination of his treatment of the South. In "Symbolic Patterns in *You Can't Go Home Again,*" Clyde C. Clements discusses the symbolic patterns of reminiscence (family and hometown), progression (business ethic, love, and art), and projection (fame in exile and the father) in this novel.

Ensign, Robert Taylor. *Lean Down Your Ear upon the Earth, and Listen: Thomas Wolfe's Greener Modernism.* Columbia: University of South Carolina Press, 2003. Presents an ecocritical interpretation of Wolfe's work, examining his depiction of the natural world and his characters' connection with it. Includes discussion of *You Can't Go Home Again.*

Holliday, Shawn. *Thomas Wolfe and the Politics of Modernism.* New York: Peter Lang, 2001. Offers a reevaluation of Wolfe's writings, describing how the experimental nature of his fiction and other aspects of his work and life define him as a modernist writer.

Holman, C. Hugh. *The Loneliness at the Core: Studies in Thomas Wolfe.* Baton Rouge: Louisiana State University Press, 1975. Analyzes the ambivalent attitudes of Wolfe, via his hero George Webber, toward the South and its place in modern America.

Idol, John Lane, Jr. *A Thomas Wolfe Companion.* New York: Greenwood Press, 1987. Explains Wolfe's avowed purpose in writing *You Can't Go Home Again* and describes how the work was pieced together and published after Wolfe's death. Identifies the novel's main themes—discovery, growth, illusion and reality, hope, sorrow, dreams and their loss, ambition, freedom, honesty, and loneliness—and discusses its structure.

Johnston, Carol Ingalls. *Of Time and the Artist: Thomas Wolfe, His Novels, and the Critics.* Columbia, S.C.: Camden House, 1996. Examines the bitter relationship between Wolfe and the literary critics and discusses how the author responded to criticism in his fiction and letters. A section on *You Can't Go Home Again* and *The Web and the Rock* provides information about the initial American and German reviews and later reviews from the 1940's until after the 1960's.

McElderry, Bruce R. *Thomas Wolfe.* New York: Twayne, 1964. Explains how closely *You Can't Go Home Again* follows *The Web and the Rock,* summarizes its continuing action and the maturing thoughts of the hero, and shows how significantly the work differs from Wolfe's earlier, more autobiographical novels. Praises the novel's satiric, demonic, and comic episodes.

Snyder, William U. *Thomas Wolfe: Ulysses and Narcissus.* Athens: Ohio University Press, 1971. Demonstrates how events in Wolfe's life, chronologically charted, caused his swings between depression and elation. Draws parallels between these events and elements in *You Can't Go Home Again.*

You Know Me Al
A Busher's Letters

Author: Ring Lardner (1885-1933)
First published: 1915, serial; 1916, book
Type of work: Novel
Type of plot: Satire
Time of plot: c. 1915
Locale: Chicago

Principal characters:
JACK KEEFE, a ballplayer
AL BLANCHARD, his correspondent
FLORRIE, Jack's wife
ALLEN, Jack's brother-in-law, also a ballplayer
MARIE, his wife

The Story:

When Jack Keefe, a baseball pitcher, is brought up from the minor leagues by the Chicago White Sox, he begins writing a series of letters to his hometown friend, Al Blanchard. It is a peculiar friendship, however, for Jack is basically incapable of any of the emotions that real friendship requires. He patronizes Al and uses him. Jack is a braggart and a chronic self-excuser, and the letters give him a chance to exercise his ego. Al apparently never sees through Jack.

So sublimely self-confident that he feels every trifling detail of his life is important, Jack writes full accounts of his adventures. Having neither modesty nor shame, he even includes episodes in which he appears foolish. When Jack reports to training camp on the West Coast, he immediately annoys the team's manager with his overeating, his refusal to take orders, and his laziness. Although he is a powerful right-handed pitcher, he is an indifferent fielder and careless about base runners. The manager tries to handle Jack with irony, but it is lost on him. Whenever Jack has a bad day pitching, he claims that his arm is sore. Any hits made against him are the fault of the fielders, the umpires, or the scorers. Jack also believes that he is irresistible to women. In training camp, he meets a girl from Detroit named Violet, and he plans to romance her when the White Sox are playing in Detroit.

Jack does well enough in spring training to be included on the White Sox roster, but in his first starting assignment against the Tigers, he pitches miserably. The manager leaves him in the game as punishment, and sixteen runs are scored against him. In addition, Ty Cobb steals four bases. As usual, Jack blames his poor performance on a sore arm. By now, the manager is thoroughly disgusted with him, and Jack is sold to a minor-league San Francisco baseball team. He sulks and says he will quit baseball, but he goes. Violet calls him a "busher"—a bush-league player.

In San Francisco, he wins eleven straight games and becomes engaged to a girl named Hazel. Recalled by the White Sox at the end of the season, he pitches well enough to be used in the City Series between the White Sox and the Cubs. Hazel asks him for one hundred dollars to pay her fare to Chicago for their wedding. He sends her only thirty dollars, and she marries a boxer instead. Jack then attempts to marry Violet, but she marries another ballplayer. Jack finally marries Florrie, the sister-in-law of a left-handed White Sox player named Allen.

When Florrie refuses to spend the winter in Bedford, Jack's hometown, they rent an apartment across the hall from Allen and Marie, Allen's wife. There are many quarrels between the two families, most of them occasioned by Jack's stinginess. Jack has always been convinced that all left-handers are crazy, and his trouble with Allen only serves to strengthen his conviction. Allen is planning to take Marie along to spring training. Florrie wants to go too, but Jack says that he cannot afford to take her. Since he feels that he is underpaid, he tries to get a raise from the ball club, even though he has already signed a contract. Charles Comiskey, the owner of the White Sox, has already had contract trouble with Jack and refuses to grant him any concessions.

Jack then tries to join the Federal League, a third major league that is hiring players away from the American and National leagues; however, the Federal League will have nothing to do with him because he has signed a contract with the White Sox. Then his team learns about his attempted defection, and he is sold to a Milwaukee minor-league team as a disciplinary measure. Florrie leaves him, and Jack, protesting that he will not go to the minors again, borrows money from Al to return to Bedford. The White Sox are finally forced to keep Jack because of a technicality in the waiver rule. After gorging himself on food and liquor all winter, Jack is fat when spring training begins, but the manager limits his diet and he gets into good enough shape to be given another chance with the White Sox.

Florrie and Jack reconcile because she is pregnant, and she soon presents him with a son. At first, Jack worries because the baby appears to be left-handed. Florrie names the baby Allen, for her brother-in-law, but Jack insists that the baby is named for Al. Although he continues to display the same old patterns of bragging and complacency, Jack turns out to be a doting father in his own fashion. After a successful season, he is selected to pitch in the City Series, a cause of fresh strife with Florrie because she wants to attend the games and he wants her to stay home with the baby. Jack is not concerned about the money for a babysitter as much as he is worried about the welfare of his son. When the team bribes Florrie to stay home, she uses the money to hire a babysitter. Jack then decides to leave her, but he changes his mind when he learns that Florrie will have custody of the child if he does. After another argument with Allen and Marie, Jack moves his family out of the apartment they all share and for which Allen pays the rent.

The White Sox want Jack to join the world tour the team is making with the Giants, but he does not want to be away from the baby. The real reason the manager wants Jack to be on the tour is to keep him in shape, but Jack believes that baseball fans in other countries want to see him play. The team coaxes him to go as far as Canada by telling him that Christy Mathewson, the famous Giants pitcher, is going that far. Jack is also told that President Woodrow Wilson is afraid Japan will declare war if Jack does not go there to play. Convinced at first, he later begins to worry about the dangers of the ocean voyage and backs down, but when he is told that Allen will be taken in his place, his vindictiveness triumphs over his fear. He sails away with the team, boasting of victories to come.

Critical Evaluation:

Ring Lardner first gained a reputation as a sportswriter. From the beginning, however, he often treated sports with irony and humor. Lardner admired thinking, hardworking athletes and made fun of those players whose talents were paired with flawed thinking. Later, Lardner left sportswriting to satirize wrongheadedness in other aspects of American culture in highly popular newspaper columns, essays, and works of fiction. During the 1920's and early 1930's, Lardner was one of the highest-paid and best-known writers in the United States. A master of irony and the precise use of language, Lardner produced works that continue to impress readers with their insights into the ambiguities and contradictions of American society.

You Know Me Al is generally recognized as Lardner's best attempt at long fiction. Lardner used the device of letters from a would-be big-league pitcher, Jack Keefe, to his hometown Indiana friend, Al Blanchard, to expose the narrator's character flaws and the shortcomings of the popular associa-

tion of the American Dream with material, romantic, and athletic success.

The phrase "you know me" was a common expression among friends in the early twentieth century, usually intended to elicit respect or support for the speaker's accomplishments, personality, or behavior. In Lardner's novel, however, the phrase becomes an ironic refrain that underscores the ineptness of the narrator, generally included after a particularly foolish outburst or confrontation. Such dramatic irony (that is, discrepancy between what characters think they are saying and what they are actually revealing) is a main tool used by Lardner to achieve humorous and satirical effects.

An important motive for Jack's writing of letters is his desire to impress his hometown friend with his skills as a ballplayer, his income, and his success with women. Jack's building up of himself is often undercut by his inclusion of details that suggest a different or opposite picture. For example, Jack boasts of his natural pitching talents, his gifted right arm, and his athletic physique, but he also notes that the manager and coach badger him into learning more about pitching, fielding, and especially thinking. Although his natural talent often results in wins, his other weaknesses lead to nearly as many losses. For example, Jack's hatred of a romantic rival causes Jack to hit the man with a pitched ball when the bases are loaded. Although by the end of the novel he has had a somewhat successful season with the White Sox, earlier he had been sent down to San Francisco to learn more about the game and, for a time, he had been traded to another team because of his shortcomings.

In the same way, Jack's boasts of financial acumen and increased income often prove empty. Like many others caught up in the material aspects of the American Dream, Jack measures success by the money he earns and the things he can afford to buy. He hopes to get rich through sports. In truth, however, he always fails to win the salary demands he places on the team's owner, settling for figures that in earlier letters to Al he has insisted he would never accept. Although he tries to control his spending and his family budget, Florrie, his wife, clearly takes advantage of him repeatedly. Other women in his life do too, so that his relatively comfortable salary is squandered on entertainment, clothes, and overpriced furniture. Once, after overspending, he even has to ask Al for some financial help.

Another part of Jack's dream is to marry a pretty girl and raise an ideal family. Jack sees himself as a great ladies' man. All three sweethearts he romances in the novel, however, take advantage of him and ridicule him. Violet and Hazel eventually reject Jack's romantic advances and marry other, more promising athletes. The rapidity of the changes in

Jack's romantic fortunes ironically underscores his naïve notions of romance. On October 7, he finds out Hazel is married. By October 9, his attempt to renew a relationship with Violet has ended in disaster. He meets Florrie on October 12 and writes on October 14 that they will be getting married, this in spite of his admission that Florrie is not as pretty as Violet or Hazel. By October 17, he is married and claiming to be "the happiest man in the world," even though he goes to great lengths to list in detail every expense of the wedding and honeymoon. The reader understands that Jack's romantic success off the field is as mixed as his athletic success on the pitcher's mound.

Lardner's ironic portrait of Jack is not bitter or hateful. Jack's foolishness is partially redeemed by his devotion to his child and his wrongheaded attempts to do the right thing. Although a braggart, he is not malicious. His mistakes are the mistakes of his American society—ignorance, thoughtlessness, prejudice, laziness, inconsistency, and a tendency to be too impressed with material success.

Aside from its reliance on dramatic irony, Lardner's novel is rich in the skillful use of language. The narrator's voice in the letters is highly conversational, full of idiomatic and slang expressions, often ungrammatical, and showing little acquaintance with the conventions of punctuation. Lardner demonstrates his concern for realism, however, by having Jack spell correctly the long words in his vocabulary, those an up-and-coming athlete like Jack might look up in order to impress his friend. In contrast, misspellings often occur with common words, which a narrator like Jack might have the confidence to think he knows. The language and writing style of the letters realistically and humorously show Jack's relative lack of education and his roots in the rural lower classes of early twentieth century America. The letters are always easy to read and clearly express the narrator's emotional confusion and personality. So effective was Lardner in accurately catching the voice of his fictional characters' semiliteracy in this and other books that the voice has been dubbed "Ringlish."

"Critical Evaluation" by Delmer Davis

Further Reading

Elder, Donald. *Ring Lardner.* Garden City, N.Y.: Doubleday, 1956. First full-length biography of Lardner includes extensive details about the writing, contents, and publication of his Jack Keefe stories. Offers excellent analysis of Lardner's use of language.

Evans, Elizabeth. *Ring Lardner.* New York: Frederick Ungar, 1979. Provides a good critical introduction to Lardner's writings, themes, strengths, and weaknesses. Includes an evaluation of Lardner's fiction.

Fitzgerald, F. Scott. "Ring Lardner, 1885-1933." In *Published and Perished: Memoria, Eulogies, and Remembrances of American Writers*, selected and edited by Steven Gilbar and Dean Stewart. Boston: David R. Godine, 2002. Novelist Fitzgerald's critical remembrance of Lardner describes both his talents and his limitations as a writer and laments that "Ring got less percentage of himself on paper than any other American author of the first flight."

Gale, Robert L. *Characters and Plots in the Fiction of Ring Lardner.* Jefferson, N.C.: McFarland, 2008. Encyclopedia-style resource features entries on the characters and plots in Lardner's short stories, including his baseball stories and stories about Jack Keefe.

Patrick, Walton R. *Ring Lardner.* Boston: Twayne, 1963. Brief volume offers informative critical interpretation of Lardner's literary contributions, with meaningful analysis of the Jack Keefe stories and novels.

Robinson, Douglas. *Ring Lardner and the Other.* New York: Oxford University Press, 1992. Probes Lardner's psychological reactions to his upbringing and emphasizes that his status as a minor writer resulted from his conflicted childhood and adulthood. Asserts that *You Know Me Al* is a pivotal work revealing Lardner's interest in characters whose faults inhibit success in sports and in life.

Yardley, Jonathan. *Ring: A Biography of Ring Lardner.* 1977. Reprint. Lanham, Md.: Rowman & Littlefield, 2001. One of the most complete biographical accounts of Lardner available also presents critical analysis of all his writings, including *You Know Me Al.*

Youma
The Story of a West-Indian Slave

Author: Lafcadio Hearn (1850-1904)
First published: 1890
Type of work: Novel
Type of plot: Psychological realism
Time of plot: 1840's
Locale: Martinique

Principal characters:
YOUMA, a young slave
GABRIEL, another slave, in love with Youma
MAYOTTE, a white child entrusted to Youma's care
MONSIEUR DESRIVIÈRES, Gabriel's master
AIMÉE, wife of M. Desrivières and Mayotte's mother
MADAME PEYRONETTE, Youma's owner and Mayotte's grandmother

The Story:

Youma is a slave and the godchild of Madame Peyronette, who lives in the city of Saint Pierre. Youma's mother had been the nurse of Madame Peyronette's only daughter, Aimée, and the two children, white and black, have grown up together almost as sisters. Even when Aimée, in accord with Creole custom, is sent to a convent to have her manners polished, during the vacations she spends at home she is always in the company of the young black slave.

As the girls grow to womanhood, Aimée begs her mother on several occasions to give Youma her freedom, but Madame Peyronette feels that she is safeguarding Youma by keeping her in slavery. Privately, Madame Peyronette has decided first to find Youma a good husband and then, after she is safely married, to grant her freedom. Before Madame Peyronette can carry out her plan, Aimée marries Monsieur Desrivières, son of a wealthy old Creole family. Upon her marriage, Aimée asks that Youma be permitted to serve her in her new household, a request speedily granted by her mother.

Thirteen months after her wedding, Aimée gives birth to a baby girl. The child is named Marie; the blacks call her by a diminutive, Mayotte. Tragedy strikes the household a year later when Aimée, who had been caught in a chilling rain while riding in an open carriage, falls ill and dies within twenty-four hours. Before she dies, Aimée begs Youma to assume the duties of nurse to little Mayotte. Youma, recalling the kindnesses she has received at the hands of Aimée, vows to do the best she can for the motherless child.

Monsieur Desrivières goes to live on his sugar plantation at Anse-Marine, in another section of the island, for he cannot bear to remain in the same house after his wife's death. Not long after, Madame Peyronette sends little Mayotte, who is in delicate health, to the plantation in Youma's care. The grandmother believes that the climate at the plantation will be better for Mayotte.

The little girl and Youma love the life at the plantation; for both, it is an experience in people. Little Mayotte is irked at times because she is not permitted to mingle freely with the little black children—not because of issues of race but because of fear that the child will be in danger of sunstroke while participating in their games. To pass the time, Mayotte and Youma go for walks in shaded places or sit on the veranda while Youma tells folktales of her race.

One afternoon, Youma warns Mayotte that if she hears too many such tales during the day she will see zombies at night. Mayotte laughs and asks for another story, but that night, she screams to Youma that something is in her room. As Youma steps into the room to calm the child, she feels a tremendous snake under her foot. Keeping the snake imprisoned beneath her foot, Youma calls for help as the serpent wraps itself around her legs and body. When Monsieur Desrivières and the servants arrive with a light, they find Youma holding down a large and poisonous reptile. One of the slaves, Gabriel, swings a cutlass and lops off the snake's head. Fortunately for Youma and the child, Youma had stepped on the snake immediately behind its head, so it had not been able to strike at her with its fangs.

This incident earns for Youma the respect of everyone at the plantation. Gabriel, in particular, shows his admiration by bringing gifts of fruit and spending the hours of early evening listening to her tell stories or sing to little Mayotte. He even makes a rustic bench that he places beside the little pool where Youma takes Mayotte to play in the water. Finally, Gabriel gives Youma a pair of earrings; when she puts them on, he knows that she is willing to marry him. Gabriel, wishing to marry Youma, is told that Madame Peyronette's permission is necessary, as Youma belongs to her. When asked, Madame Peyronette refuses to give permission; she feels that it would be wrong to permit Youma, who has been brought up almost as a white girl, to marry Gabriel, who, although a fine man, is only a field hand.

Gabriel and Youma are grievously disappointed at the denial of their request. When Gabriel, a resourceful fellow, proposes that he and Youma elope and cross the channel to a British-held island where slavery has been abolished, Youma is ready to join him in the plan until she remembers her promise to care for Mayotte. With that promise in mind, she refuses to desert her charge.

Within a few days of the refusal, Youma and Mayotte are sent back to the city. Not long after (the year being 1848), word spreads through the West Indies that a republic has been proclaimed in France and that slavery will soon be abolished in Martinique. There are only 12,000 whites on the island and more than 150,000 blacks. The whites, knowing full well of the troubles in Haiti years before, become extremely cautious in dealing with the black people. Even so, rumors begin to spread that the whites are conspiring to retain slavery. An outbreak of violence begins over the imprudent whipping of a slave on the very eve of emancipation. Thousands of slaves pour into the city from the countryside.

Madame Peyronette, Youma, and Mayotte, after taking refuge with another family in a large, well-built stone house near the army barracks, believe that they will be safe from the mob. When the hordes of slaves pours into the city, however, a crowd gathers in front of the house and finally breaks in. As the whites on the second floor are temporarily out of their reach, the slaves set fire to the house. When some of the whites try to escape by leaping out of windows, the mob kills them immediately.

Youma, in an effort to save Mayotte and herself, goes out on a balcony and identifies herself as a slave. Gabriel, who happens to be in the crowd, tries to save them, but the bloodthirsty mob refuses to let the white child be spared. Youma, rather than leave Mayotte to die alone, stands on the balcony with the child until the walls of the house collapse and kill them both.

Critical Evaluation:

Youma is an ambivalent narrative centering on the dilemma of a young Creole nurse torn between her ingrained sense of selfless loyalty and duty on the one hand and, on the other, a suddenly emerging, contrary impulse toward love and personal happiness. Lafcadio Hearn begins his account with a long and careful expository introduction in which he defines the traditional role of the *da*, the slave nanny of a white child. He so strongly describes the typical black *da*'s devotion to her white charge that he virtually gives away the novel's climax. Then follow fourteen numbered, untitled chapters. In chapter 4, Youma's love interest, stalwart Gabriel, is first mentioned. His attraction to sweet little

Mayotte's beautiful *da* develops in chapters 5 and 6. In the pivotal chapter 7, which ends the first half of the novel, Youma's and Gabriel's owners deny the couple permission to marry. This subtly rationalized but arbitrary cruelty precipitates the personal part of the tragedy. Paralleling Gabriel's no longer quiescent hatred of slavery in general and the heartless behavior of two slave masters in particular is the mounting discontent of the field and town blacks, who are fanned into riotous action by the winds of emancipation blowing through the islands.

Of central thematic importance is the nursery story that Youma tells Mayotte one afternoon. It is about a witch named Dame Kélément and seems, voodoolike, to evoke, once articulated, the appearance of the serpent that night. Youma's bravery in steadfastly holding the serpent down with her bare foot is in turn what fatally impresses the cutlass-wielding Gabriel. That same courage enables Youma to stand immobile with helpless Mayotte in the fire, refuse to escape despite the fact that Mayotte will die in either case, and immolate herself in the flames. When Gabriel sees how calm she is, he is reminded of her identical courage when threatened by the serpent.

Helping to unify the narrative is Hearn's skillful sprinkling in of local-color details. Hearn spent two years on the island of Martinique, freely observed the inhabitants of all classes there and made friends with many, admired their way of life, quickly added a considerable understanding of their Creole dialect to his already thorough knowledge of French, and even climbed Mount Pelée. In 1890, he published *Two Years in the French West Indies*, containing many sketches of island life.

A curious feature of dialogue in *Youma* is its tantalizing mixture of standard French and native patois, sometimes but not always translated. For example, Gabriel praises Youma thus: "*Quaill! ou brave, mafi!—foute! ou sévè!*" Hearn translates only *sévè*, as "severe," meaning "courageous" in context. Hearn's own prose is often similarly quaint. It sometimes reads like a deliberately archaic translation of a foreign text. For example, "'Gabou'... realized for her some figure of the *contes*." Employing a palette of diverse colors in his descriptions, Hearn combines the vividness of African primary colors—especially in the complexions, dress, and jewelry of the slaves—with the West Indian pastels of flowers, houses and fields, beaches and water, and vaporous mountain slopes. Notable is Hearn's startling, if infrequent, use of similes and metaphors. Two examples: "those strange Creole words which, like tropic lizards, change color with position" and "spidery shadows of palm-heads on the floor."

A key element in *Youma* is the heroine's scary story, reluctantly told to the child. Hearn devotes fully eight pages to it and even annotates two native words in it, although he leaves many others unexplained, for example, in the serpent's song, which ends thus: "Bennepè, bennemè—tambou belai!/ Yche p'accoutoumé tambou belai!" Significantly, in the story the serpent does not offer the slightest harm to the little girl, whereas the real serpent attacks Youma. In the folktale, the serpent is transformed back into a man, who then returns the girl safely to her mother. The real serpent, however, goes so far as to wrap its flesh around Youma's thigh. It must be concluded that the episode's symbolism is ambivalent. Is the evil snake under Youma's foot intended to symbolize fatal rebellion? Or perhaps fatal sexual love? Hearn does not say.

The pervasive tone of *Youma* is ironic. The island could be a latter-day Eden, with its slumberous climate, creamy seas, fertile soil, gentle rains, and exotic fruits and flowers—and serpents. The white rulers combine a fancy, indolent lifestyle, austerely aristocratic manners, a brave love of family, and a fierce determination to keep their slaves in their place. The slaves are muscular and lissome, intelligent and highly articulate, but also dominated by voodooism. A curious touch is the fact that the French army, garrisoned in Saint Pierre, is mysteriously ordered not to interfere when the slaves go on their murderous rampage. The dominant religion of the island is Christianity, but one entwined in native superstitions. During the climactic fire, one "négresse" gesticulates like a cannibal at a helpless white mother and her baby. Yet Gabriel's last sight of Youma, with Mayotte in her arms and the fire "serpentined" behind her, reminds him of a statue of the Virgin Mary seen at the anchorage chapel. A final irony comes in the last paragraph of *Youma*, in which Hearn tersely explains that at the very hour of the fire a ship was bearing news to the island of emancipation and universal suffrage for the slave population.

"Critical Evaluation" by Robert L. Gale

Further Reading

Colt, Jonathan. *Wandering Ghost: The Odyssey of Lafcadio Hearn.* New York: Alfred A. Knopf, 1991. Defines *Youma* as a prosaic and sentimental story and then, curiously, links the heroine's memory of her deceased mother to Hearn's yearning for his lost mother.

Gale, Robert L. *A Lafcadio Hearn Companion.* Westport, Conn.: Greenwood Press, 2002. Contains several hundred alphabetically arranged entries providing information on Hearn's works, family members, colleagues, and other aspects of his life and career. Includes bibliography.

Hirakawa, Sukehiro, ed. *Lafcadio Hearn in International Perspectives.* Folkestone, England: Global Oriental, 2007. Collection of essays provides a multicultural look at Hearn's life and writings, including discussions of Hearn as an American writer and the influence of Greece and Japan on his work. One essay examines the image of the Creole mother in *Youma.*

_____. *Rediscovering Lafcadio Hearn: Japanese Legends, Life, and Culture.* Folkestone, England: Global Oriental, 1997. Collection of essays focuses on the reevaluation of Hearn's writing, with contributors refuting critics who dismiss him as a "Victorian Romantic." Naoko Sugiyama discusses *Youma* in "Lafcadio Hearn's *Youma:* Self as Outsider."

Kunst, Arthur E. *Lafcadio Hearn.* New York: Twayne, 1969. Praises *Youma* as admirable in conception, balanced in development, and restrained in effect. Comments on such distractions as sex symbolism, dreams, historical notes, and folktale elements.

Murray, Paul. *A Fantastic Journey: The Life and Literature of Lafcadio Hearn.* Folkestone, England: Japan Library, 1993. Recounts the events of Hearn's life, including his writing and publication of *Youma.* This novel, according to Murray, shares the same faults as Hearn's earlier novel, *Chita:* "weakness of structure, imaginative inadequacy and a cloying sentimentality at the heart of his romanticism."

Stevenson, Elizabeth. *The Grass Lark: A Study of Lafcadio Hearn.* New Brunswick, N.J.: Transaction, 1999. Criticizes *Youma,* despite the novel's early respectful reviews, for its slow start and digressions, insufficient passion, and lack of plot development. Originally published in 1961 as *Lafcadio Hearn,* this updated edition includes a new introduction.

Yu, Beongcheon. *An Ape of Gods: The Art and Thought of Lafcadio Hearn.* Detroit, Mich.: Wayne State University Press, 1964. Summarizes the plot of *Youma* and analyzes the two main characters as idealistically treated but, fortunately, not made into noble savages.

Young Goodman Brown

Author: Nathaniel Hawthorne (1804-1864)
First published: 1835
Type of work: Short fiction
Type of plot: Allegory
Time of plot: Early 1690's
Locale: Salem, colony of Massachusetts

Principal characters:
GOODMAN BROWN, a villager
FAITH, his wife
AN APPARENT DEVIL
A MINISTER
DEACON GOOKIN
GOODY CLOYSE, a catechism teacher

The Story:

Newlywed Goodman Brown sets forth at sunset for the nearby forest, where he apparently has an appointment. Leaving Salem village, he promises his wife, Faith, that he will return after this single night. Confused by Brown's odd behavior and mysterious errand, Faith fails to convince him to remain at home, or at least to delay his journey until the following morning. Criticizing her for doubting his purposes, Brown nevertheless seems conscience-stricken about his own motivations. He vows to be true to Faith and to their religious faith—after this one night. His wife can only hope that this experience, whatever it is, will not change their lives for the worse.

Soon after he walks into the darkening forest, Brown expresses fear that in the gloomy wilderness he could easily be ambushed by the devil himself. He then sees a man (actually, the text suggests that he looks "like" a man) who bears an uncanny resemblance to Brown's own venerated grandfather. This man uses a crooked walking stick that resembles a serpent—from a distance and in the dim light it even seems to wiggle. Asked by the man why he is late for his appointment, Brown responds that Faith had delayed him. As the two walk and talk, Brown periodically voices his apprehension and says he must return to Salem and Faith.

Asserting his family's virtue, Brown disbelieves his companion's account of being well acquainted with the people of New England, including Brown's father and grandfather. Brown then observes the man meeting with his pious catechism teacher, Goody Cloyse, who exclaims the devil's name when the man startles her with a touch of the serpent-staff. She reveals her diabolical deeds as the two chat.

Brown congratulates himself with the thought that, however evil Goody Cloyse proves to be, he will return to Salem with a clear conscience to talk of religious truths with the minister and Deacon Gookin. Brown then overhears the minister and the deacon discuss an unholy congregation and new converts. Apparent evidence mounts that, indeed, the devil is intimate with even moral and religious New Englanders.

Brown is especially troubled by the indiscriminate mingling of the godly and the ungodly. However, he remains defiant and maintains that he still has Faith, whereupon the pink ribbons of his wife flutter down from the sky.

As if struck by a blow, at this instant Brown is overwhelmed by disillusionment: Even his Faith has gone the way of Satan. Despairing and hysterical, he now believes that there is no goodness and the world is wholly evil.

Brown is led to a clearing in the forest where pine trees blaze like gigantic candles above an altar made of stone. The satanic congregation's holy hymns have unholy lyrics. Brown and Faith stand as converts, soon to be initiated into this bizarre congregation and the belief that evil is the sole and essential nature of humankind. They will soon even gaze upon each other's disgusting sinfulness. The devil dips his hand into water that looks like blood, reaching forth to initiate the young couple with the mark of this perverse baptism. In a final impulse of virtue Brown tells Faith to resist Satan. Then there is nothing—no blazing trees, no baptismal blood, no ominously chanting congregation. Brown finds himself alone in the dark, damp, and cool forest. Disoriented, he slowly wanders back to Salem at sunrise.

Was this episode in the woods real, or was it merely a dream? In either case, the experience destroys Brown's ability to accept and enjoy life. Back in Salem, he is ever after a moody and depressed man, distrustful and incapable of joy. All he sees is the evil that has been revealed to him; all he perceives, therefore, is human hypocrisy. He cannot endure listening to preaching and prayers and hymn singing; he snatches a child away from Goody Cloyse as she instructs the girl about religious truths. Villagers cannot understand Brown and his strange and inexplicable transformation. After a long and lonely life, he dies despairing and joyless.

Critical Evaluation:

One of Nathaniel Hawthorne's most anthologized tales, "Young Goodman Brown" shares themes and techniques with much of his other work. Hawthorne's probing of what might be called the psychology of sin (however secular are modern readings), expressed through his characteristic manipulations of symbolism, merge the tale with his other short stories, such as "The Birth-Mark" (1843) and "Ethan Brand: A Chapter from an Abortive Romance" (1850), as well as his novels *The Scarlet Letter* (1850) and *The Blithedale Romance*, published in 1852. (Hawthorne's short stories were written mostly before 1850, and his novels were written after that date.) Hawthorne's ideas, moral vision, and artistry have established him as one of the nation's greatest writers. The suggestive ambiguities in his fiction have made his work particularly amenable to treatment by the full range of modern critical perspectives.

The symbolic significance of places, times, names, and objects seems obvious in "Young Goodman Brown." Salem is the dwelling place of family and community, religion and faith ("faith" the belief and "Faith" the woman). The name Goodman suggests "good man" (although it also had been an equivalent of "mister"). The surrounding wilderness is unknown, a place where one can easily wander from the straight and narrow path. In addition, the scenes in Salem occur during daylight, the scenes in the forest at night. In that dark forest, Brown discovers a prince of darkness (an apparent devil who looks like a man) who appears with his serpent cane as if he has been conjured into being by the word "devil." Has Brown found in that darkness the light or the truth or an acceptable moral standard in that heathen wilderness? Does he remain a naive yet good man?

"Young Goodman Brown" is not, in fact, a simple religious parable about the undeniable evils of life. The statement that "evil is the nature of mankind," after all, is spoken by the Devil (the prince of lies as well as the prince of darkness) in what may have been only Brown's dream. "Young Goodman Brown" is a psychological tale about the impact of this partial truth upon a particularly susceptible mind. If this were not the case, Hawthorne need not have written the final page of the story nor have portrayed Brown in such a negative fashion. Should not the discoverer of truth be rewarded with a positive outcome? Hawthorne does not focus on universal evil or human hypocrisy. Rather, he criticizes Brown as an either/or thinker who never acknowledges the evil in himself. His own diabolical curiosity initially leads him to his appointment in the forest. The devil looks like Brown. After Brown exclaims "my Faith is gone!" he himself becomes "the chief horror of the scene."

Initially, Brown seems aware that his mission is sinful, but eventually he perceives sin only in others. He becomes blind to goodness and avoids human contact. Like so many Hawthorne characters, he becomes a cold observer of life rather than a life-affirming participant. His sin is pride. As the story opens, he is innocent, young, and sheltered. He knows only good. When he sees Faith in the forest, however, he abruptly converts to a belief that only evil exists. Either attitude is simpleminded. He never envisions a complex life that is a mix of good and evil and which in any case must be lived.

What troubles Brown most in the nocturnal forest is "that the good shrank not from the wicked." Even the pink of Faith's ribbons is a mixture of white (purity) and red (associated with guilt and sin in the story). Brown's propensity to think in terms of God or Satan, the flesh or the spirit, and good or evil has been described as typical of early Puritan New England. In this sense, Hawthorne has written a criticism of society like that of *The Scarlet Letter*.

Modern critics have interpreted "Young Goodman Brown" in many ways. The story as a critique of society stands out to some. To psychologically inclined readers, Brown journeys into the psyche. The village represents the superego, whereas the forest and darkness become equivalents of the Freudian id. The entire story becomes a portrait of one human mind that discovers the usually suppressed and disquieting reality of animal instinct.

Gender-conscious readers might see Brown's problem as an inability to accommodate to women as complex individuals. He cannot reconcile the "red" fact of menstrual cycles with the "white" of hallowed motherhood. Faith's own reality is "pink," a color that for Brown can only mean a tainting of purity. Brown either "shrank from the bosom of Faith" for her supposedly evil nature or indulged his sexual appetites—since they do have a number of children. Readers may view "Young Goodman Brown" as literary self-revelation, because to write the story, Hawthorne had to distance himself, to observe the human lot just as Brown did. All these perspectives testify to the richness of the story.

Benjamin S. Lawson

Further Reading

Bell, Millicent, ed. *New Essays on Hawthorne's Major Tales.* New York: Cambridge University Press, 1993. The editor's introduction is a comprehensive survey of Hawthorne's career as a short-story writer. The essays by Michael Colacurio and David Leverenz include analyses of "Young Goodman Brown."

Bloom, Harold, ed. *"Young Goodman Brown": Bloom's Modern Critical Interpretations.* New York: Chelsea House, 2005. A number of notable essays, including the editor's critique of the story as a response to contemporary Transcendentalist ideas about the relationship of self to society. Brown himself is seen as pathetic and too impressionable.

Fogle, Richard Harter. *Hawthorne's Fiction: The Light and the Dark*. Rev. ed. Norman: University of Oklahoma Press, 1964. A classic analysis of the antitheses in Hawthorne, such as light and darkness, clarity and ambiguity, and appearance and reality. Discusses his complexity and the need to reconcile opposites for unity and understanding.

Idol, John L., and Melinda M. Ponder, eds. *Hawthorne and Women: Engendering and Expanding the Hawthorne Tradition*. Amherst: University of Massachusetts Press, 1999. Thorough and informative, this work examines the influence of women on Hawthorne, his frequent inclusion of the female perspective, the contemporary women who reviewed his works, and Hawthorne's continuing influence on women authors, past and present.

Loving, Jerome. "Pretty in Pink: 'Young Goodman Brown' and New-World Dreams." In *Critical Essays on Hawthorne's Short Stories*, edited by Albert J. von Frank. Boston: G. K. Hall, 1991. Loving posits that Faith's pink ribbons are symbols of sensuality, therefore a contrast to the myth of New World innocence. The editor presents samples of commentary on Hawthorne from his own time to the late twentieth century.

Magee, Bruce R. "Faith and Fantasy in 'Young Goodman Brown.'" *Nathaniel Hawthorne Review* 29 (2003): 1-24. Argues that because Brown sees Faith more as an allegorical personification of virtue than as a person, he is already bitterly disillusioned before he enters the forest. The story warns of the dangers inherent in the nineteenth century ideal of women as domestic angels.

Millington, Richard H. *The Cambridge Companion to Nathaniel Hawthorne*. New York: Cambridge University Press, 2004. Essays analyze various aspects of Hawthorne's work, including Hawthorne and American masculinity, and the question of women. Discusses his major novels.

Moore, Margaret B. *The Salem World of Nathaniel Hawthorne*. Columbia: University of Missouri Press, 1998. Moore explores the relationship between Salem, Massachusetts, and its most famous resident, demonstrating how Hawthorne's association with the city influenced his fiction. She discusses the role of Hawthorne's ancestors in the city's colonial history and examines how the author was affected by Salem's religion and politics.

Person, Leland S. *The Cambridge Introduction to Nathaniel Hawthorne*. New York: Cambridge University Press, 2007. An accessible introduction to the author's life and works designed for students and general readers. Includes analysis of Hawthorne's fiction, a brief survey of Hawthorne scholarship, and a bibliography.

Turner, Arlin. *Nathaniel Hawthorne: A Biography*. New York: Oxford University Press, 1980. This standard scholarly biography focuses primarily on Hawthorne the man rather than the artist. The author is considered to be more an involved man of his times rather than the reclusive writer highlighted by many earlier biographers.

Wineapple, Brenda. *Hawthorne: A Life*. New York: Alfred A. Knopf, 2003. The most reliable and thoroughgoing biography since 1980. Clearly written and perceptive comments on Hawthorne's writings. Connects the author's life with the content of many of his short stories, including "Young Goodman Brown," and his novels

Yvain
Or, The Knight with the Lion

Author: Chrétien de Troyes (c. 1150-c. 1190)
First transcribed: Yvain: Ou, Le Chevalier au lion, c. 1170 (English translation, c. 1300)
Type of work: Short fiction
Type of plot: Arthurian romance
Time of plot: Sixth century
Locale: Britain

Principal characters:
YVAIN, a knight of King Arthur's Round Table
LAUDINE DE LANDUC, the lady he marries
LUNETE, a damsel in Laudine de Landuc's service
KING ARTHUR, ruler of the Britons
QUEEN GUINEVERE, his wife
SIR GAWAIN, Yvain's friend and King Arthur's nephew
SIR KAY, the cynical seneschal
HARPIN OF THE MOUNTAIN, a giant slain by Yvain

The Story:

At the season of Pentecost, King Arthur holds his court at Carduel in Wales. After dinner on that feast day, a knight named Calogrenant tells a tale of adventure that is not altogether to his credit, and for which he is mocked by Sir Kay the seneschal. Calogrenant reveals that seven years before he had journeyed beyond the forest of Broceliande. After a night's lodging in the tower of a courteous vavasor he continued on his way until he encountered a giant seventeen feet tall who was guarding some wild bulls in a clearing. The giant told the knight that if he sought some marvel he was to look for a spring in a mysterious wood, for water from the spring poured on a nearby stone would bring down upon him a storm such as few men had ever seen, with bolts of lightning that would blind him and thunder that would shake the earth. All happened as the giant had foretold, and after the storm had ceased, a knight appeared and challenged Calogrenant to a duel because of the great damage that had been caused by the wind and rain Calogrenant had brought about. The two fought and Calogrenant was overthrown. He tells his companions that he had been so shamed in that encounter that he had never told the story before.

One of those who listens to his tale is Yvain, a valiant knight, who swears to avenge the shame of Calogrenant, his German cousin. Yvain is then also mocked by Sir Kay. While they speak, King Arthur comes from his chamber, and Queen Guinevere tells him the tale as she has heard it. The king thereupon swears an oath that he must see these wonders for himself; he says that any of his knights who wishes to come may accompany him on the venture. Yvain, thinking that the quest should be his alone, leaves the court secretly and rides on horseback over mountains and through valleys until he comes to the forest of the magic spring. When he pours a basin of water on the stone, a great storm arises. After the storm the strange knight appears, and he and Yvain battle until their lances splinter and their armor has been pierced in many places. At last Yvain deals the enemy a blow that shatters his helmet and splits his skull, but even then the knight does not fall down at once but gallops off on his horse to take refuge in his castle.

Yvain, riding in close pursuit of his foe, is trapped when a portcullis falls before him as well as another behind him after he has ridden through the castle gate. There the maid Lunete finds him and saves his life with the gift of a magic ring, which makes him invisible while the nobleman's vassals search for the knight who gave their lord his mortal wound. While he is thus protected, Yvain sees the Lady Laudine de Landuc, the mistress of the castle, a lady so fair that he falls in love with her on the spot. The maid Lunete, seeing how mat-

ters stand, conceals Yvain and ministers to his wounds. Between visits to Yvain, she speaks to her lady, urging her to put aside her anger and grief and to take a new husband who will be master of her domain and defender of the magic spring. Lunete is so cunning in her speech that her lady finally agrees to do as the damsel suggests. Then Yvain is brought from the chamber where he has been hidden. Falling on his knees before the Lady Laudine, he begs forgiveness for killing her lord in fair fight. The lady, impressed by Yvain's comeliness and bravery, is soon reconciled, and the two are wed with great rejoicing.

As he had sworn, King Arthur comes with his knights to see the magic spring, and Sir Kay mocks the absent Yvain, who had sworn to avenge his cousin's name. Then the king pours a basin of water on the stone, and immediately the rain begins to fall and the wind to blow. When the storm has subsided, Yvain appears, his armor and helmet concealing his identity, to challenge King Arthur's knights, and Sir Kay begs to be allowed the first encounter. Yvain quickly unhorses the braggart seneschal and then reveals himself to King Arthur and the other knights. All are delighted to find Yvain safe and well. For a week thereafter, Yvain and his lady entertain the royal party with feasting and entertainment of all kinds.

At the end of that time, as the king is preparing to depart, Sir Gawain urges Yvain to return to Britain with them and to take part in all tournaments, so that none can say that so brave a knight has grown weak and slothful in marriage. The Lady Laudine agrees, but on the promise that Yvain will return to her in one year. Before he leaves, she gives him a ring set with a stone that will keep its wearer from all harm as long as he keeps his sweetheart in mind.

So successful is Yvain in all the tournaments that are held throughout the land that he forgets his promise until the Lady Laudine sends a damsel to denounce him as a hypocrite and liar and to demand the return of the ring. Yvain, overcome by remorse at the thought of losing his lady's love, goes mad; he begins living like a wild beast in the forest. A hermit living there finds him, naked and distracted, and gives him bread and water; the hermit takes care of Yvain until one day the noble lady of Noroison and her two damsels find the naked man asleep under a tree. The lady and her maids attend the knight and anoint him with a soothing, magic ointment to restore his wits. When he has recovered, Yvain pledges himself to the lady's support and vows to champion her against Count Alier, who is plundering her lands. So fierce is Yvain's attack on the marauders that the count yields and gives his oath that he will live in peace from that time on. Afterward, having refused to accept the lady's hand in marriage or to take her as his mistress, Yvain rides away in search of new adventures.

One day, as he is wandering through the wood, he comes upon a lion and a fire-breathing serpent that holds the beast by the tail. Yvain draws his sword and slays the scaly monster, and from that time on the grateful lion becomes the knight's inseparable companion. At last, Yvain returns to the magic spring where all his adventures began. There he finds the maid Lunete held prisoner in a nearby chapel by order of the Lady Laudine. The damsel is to be burned the next day, and she weeps that she has no one to defend her against charges brought by a wicked seneschal who has persuaded her mistress that the maid acted falsely in the sad affair of the Lady Laudine's marriage to Yvain. The knight, without revealing himself, promises to act as her champion before he rides away to find lodgings for the night.

At last he comes to the castle of Sir Gawain's brother-in-law, only to learn that the baron is threatened with the death of his four sons, prisoners of a dreaded giant, Harpin of the Mountain, unless the father will give his daughter over to the lewd embraces of the ogre's lackeys. In spite of the fact that he does not have much time, Yvain rides out and slays the giant, with the help of the lion, because of his friendship with the baron's kinsman, Sir Gawain. Refusing to give his name, he says that he wishes to be known only as the Knight with the Lion. Then he rides as fast as his horse can carry him to the chapel in the forest, where the pyre on which Lunete is to be burned has already been prepared. Although he has been wounded in his encounter with the giant, Yvain fights the seneschal and his two brothers. Again, with the lion's help, he is victorious, and the false knights he has slain are burned on the funeral pyre prepared for Lunete. When confronted by the Lady Laudine he again refuses to reveal his identity, so ashamed is he of his inconstancy; he calls himself only the Knight with the Lion. Lunete has recognized him, however, and she accompanies him for some distance when he rides away. She promises to keep his secret, but she declares that she will bring about a reconciliation between him and his lady if it is ever in her power to do so.

The disconsolate Yvain departs to seek other adventures, but he is unable to travel far because of the wounds that he and the lion have suffered in their battles with Harpin of the Mountain and the three false knights. At length he comes to a fair castle where the lord's retainers help him from his horse and attend gently to the lion, which Yvain has been carrying on his shield. There Yvain and the lion stay, attended by maidens skilled in surgery, until both the man and the beast are completely healed. Then they continue on their way.

About that same time, the lord of Noire Espine dies, and his older daughter claims the whole of his estates, saying that she will give no share to her sister. When the younger daughter goes to King Arthur's court to plead her case, she learns that her older sister has been there before her and that Sir Gawain has promised to act as the sister's champion. Granted forty days in which to find a champion of her own, the maid sets out in search of the famed Knight with the Lion.

Along the way she falls ill, but the quest is taken up by a friend whose search brings her at last to the magic spring. When the friend arrives at the spring, Lunete is saying her prayers in the chapel close by; Lunete is able to point out to the traveler the road Yvain had traveled many days before. The maid comes finally to the castle where the knight and the lion were nursed back to health, and, told that they had departed only a short time before, she rides after them as fast as she can. She overtakes the knight and his beast companion, and after she has told her story, Yvain promises to help the younger sister in her need.

Before he can act for the maid, however, he is to engage in still another desperate adventure. Toward nightfall, he and the damsel come to the town of Pesme Avanture, where, as they approach the castle, all the people call out to them to turn back. Yvain pays no heed to their warnings. Entering the castle, the knight finds three hundred maidens working at all kinds of embroidery; they are, they tell him, hostages for the king of the Isle of Damsels, the ransom he has paid to escape doing battle with two half-devils born to a mortal woman and an imp. Yvain and the damsel are courteously received by the lord of the castle, however, and that night everything is done in their honor.

When Yvain prepares to depart the next morning, the owner of the castle tells him that he cannot go without first fighting the sons of evil. The prize, if he wins, will be the hand of the baron's beautiful daughter and dominion over all of her father's lands. Although Yvain tries to refuse the terms of the offer, the lord assures him that no knight who has lodged in the castle can avoid or renounce the battle. The lion is taken away from Yvain and confined, but the beast manages to scratch his way out of the room where he is being held, and he arrives on the scene of the conflict in time to save the sorely wounded Yvain by killing one devil outright and so disconcerting the other that the knight is able to lop off the evil creature's head.

With this victory, Yvain releases the wretched hostages from their imprisonment. Over the protests of the lord of the castle, he renounces the hand of the daughter and rides away with the damsel to the court of King Arthur. The younger sister rejoices when the Knight with the Lion arrives in time to champion her cause against her avaricious sister, who is defended by Sir Gawain. The struggle between the knights lasts all day and into the dusk. By that time both are exhausted, but neither knows the identity of the other until Yvain at last proposes postponement of the contest until the next day. Then Sir Gawain, recognizing his friend's voice, grants him the victory, while Yvain, in turn, refuses this boon and reverses the decision. King Arthur finally solves the problem by granting them equal prowess in arms and conferring upon the younger sister her rights after the older one incautiously admits her attempt to dispossess her sister.

As soon as Yvain is cured of his wounds, he sets out once more for the magic spring, accompanied only by his faithful lion. Again he pours water on the stone and brings down such a storm that the Lady Laudine fears her castle and the town will be washed away. Meanwhile, the damsel Lunete speaks to her mistress in such winning fashion that the lady, losing all the resentment she has held against her husband, promises to restore him to her favor and love. So Yvain and his lady are reconciled after many troubles and trials, to the great happiness of Lunete and all their vassals.

Critical Evaluation:

Yvain is the most elegant and sophisticated of Chrétien de Troyes's romances, exploring the very nature of courtliness through the adventures of its hero, Sir Yvain of King Arthur's Round Table. An important part of his twelfth century romance is chivalric discourse, whereby the characters discover the principles of courtly behavior as much through conversation as through deeds of arms. This code was essentially a set of ethics to which wellborn knights and ladies adhered. It was grounded, above all, in social responsibility. Courtly behavior allowed one to achieve perfect balance in reconciling one's own desires with the necessities demanded by one's social position.

When Yvain fails to keep the one-year deadline imposed on him by his wife, Laudine de Landuc, he is guilty of sacrificing his personal commitment to Laudine to his social duty as a knight. In this respect, he is the counterpart of another of Chrétien's heroes, Sir Erec, who neglects his knightly renown to languish in the arms of his wife, Enide. When Yvain, overcome by grief for having failed to keep his promise, neglects his own knightly responsibilities, he is rightly termed mad. His stripping of his knightly armor is an outward sign of his inward rejection of courtly standards. Yvain ceases to be a knight, and it is appropriate that he is nourished by a hermit during this period of penitence and renunciation. The episode with the lion marks his reentry into the world of knighthood.

Yvain's rescue of the lion shows his new maturity and understanding of proper behavior, since it shows a heart that can pity as well as be brave. It also shows that Yvain is once again capable of right thinking, as he reasons out that it would be better to save the lion rather than the serpent when he finds them in combat. Chrétien's general pragmatism does not desert him here; he adds that, if need be, Yvain is prepared to do battle with the lion as well. The lion, one of the most delightful beasts of medieval romances, is the model of a true knight, bowing in homage to Yvain and continuing along with him as a faithful retainer. It is precisely through the lion's perfect courtly behavior that readers understand that Yvain is now worthy of such loyalty: He has matured in courtliness and is now ready to be finally reconciled with Laudine.

The similarities between the lion incident and the classical Greek fable of Androcles and the lion suggest a possible source; what is interesting is the way Chrétien uses the story of a man helping a wounded lion that later repays him in time of need. The battle with the snake—traditionally a symbol of evil—becomes a struggle between villainy and nobility. It is, in essence, the chivalric battle. Greek fable is translated to medieval Christian iconography.

Yvain is separated from other chivalric romances by the attention paid to the psychological states of the characters and by the way these states are probed through conversation. This is most notable in the exchange between Yvain and Laudine in which Yvain persuades her to marry him even though he has just slain her husband. The way has been prepared for Yvain, however, in a remarkable internal dialogue Laudine has already had with herself, in which she takes both her own part and the part of her husband's slayer. By demonstrating to herself that the unknown knight who has killed her husband meant her no malice or harm, Laudine has readied herself to be won later by Yvain's actual plea on his own behalf.

This kind of psychological resolution of a difficult problem is relatively rare in medieval literature. Typically, psychological issues were explored through allegory, in which allegorical figures such as Mercy or Good Deeds reveal the internal pressures brought to bear on the characters. Romances, on the other hand, are primarily adventure tales, filled with enchantments and acts of prowess. They are stories of action in which the cause of the action is a given, much as a gunshot signals the start of a race. The classic example of this in the Arthurian legends is the love potion that seals the fate of Sir Tristam of Lyonesse and the Belle Yseult. Ignorant of its powers, Tristam and Yseult drink a potion prepared for the wedding night of Yseult and King Mark of Cornwall. Their love is therefore determined, and they follow this fated passion unquestioningly to their deaths. *Yvain* has all the adventures and wonderments common to romance, but it also incorporates the characters' own discussion of their feelings and motives in a way that became increasingly pronounced in later literatures.

While Laudine's easy acquiescence may strike present-day readers as little more than opportunism, Chrétien's language allows us to see the very real problems confronting Laudine. She can no more act independently than can Yvain. If she refuses Yvain, her self, her dependents, and her possessions—in short, everything that makes up her honor—are in jeopardy. It would be improper, as the clever Lunete points out, for her to indulge in a purely private sorrow at the risk of all else and all others. Appropriate courtly behavior demanded that one take responsibility not only for oneself but also for one's retainers. The adultery between Queen Guinevere and Sir Lancelot was mischievous not so much because it was a personal betrayal of King Arthur but because it unsettled and ultimately destroyed the court. In addition, Lunete reminds Laudine that none of her other retainers is brave or competent enough to withstand attack. Chrétien demonstrates the rightness of Laudine's behavior by giving readers the example of a happy and faithful marriage. Courtly to the finish, *Yvain* remains a jewel among medieval romances.

"Critical Evaluation" by Linda J. Turzynski

Further Reading

Duggan, Joseph J. *The Romances of Chrétien de Troyes*. New Haven, Conn.: Yale University Press, 2001. Presents analysis that focuses on the common characteristics of Chrétien's romances, such as the importance of kinship and genealogy, the artful narration, and the depiction of knighthood. Includes discussion of *Yvain*.

Lacy, Norris J. *The Craft of Chrétien de Troyes*. New York: Brill, 1980. Describes all of Chrétien's romances and argues that their meanings can be determined through the comparison of similar episodes. Chapter 3, which covers characterization and symbolism, suggests that the lion in *Yvain* is a symbol of Christ.

Lacy, Norris J., and Joan Tasker Grimbert, eds. *A Companion to Chrétien de Troyes*. New York: D. S. Brewer, 2005.

Collection of essays addresses such topics as Chrétien in history, his patrons, his literary background, the Arthurian legend before him, and the medieval reception and influence of his work. Includes an analysis of *Yvain* in the essay *"Le Chevalier au Lion*: Yvain Lionheart," by Tony Hunt.

Loomis, Roger Sherman. *Arthurian Tradition and Chrétien de Troyes*. 1949. Reprint. New York: Octagon Books, 1982. Shows how Chrétien's romances were influenced by Irish and Welsh mythology. Although Loomis's conclusions have been challenged by later scholars, this classic source remains interesting.

Murray, K. Sarah-Jane. *From Plato to Lancelot: A Preface to Chrétien de Troyes*. Syracuse, N.Y.: Syracuse University Press, 2008. Argues that there were two intersecting sources for Chrétien's romances: the works of Plato, Ovid, and other Greco-Roman writers and the Celtic myths and legends found in Irish monastic scholarship.

Noble, Peter S. *Love and Marriage in Chrétien de Troyes*. Cardiff: University of Wales Press, 1982. Examines the theme of love and marriage in all of Chrétien's romances, concluding that Yvain's situation is different from that of Erec in Chrétien's earlier romance. Laudine is not at fault; rather, Yvain is entirely blameworthy, and he must undergo his trials alone—he, not the marriage, needs testing.

Reichert, Michelle. *Between Courtly Literature and al-Andalus: Matière d'Orient and the Importance of Spain in the Romances of the Twelfth-Century Writer Chrétien de Troyes*. New York: Routledge, 2006. Examines the references to Spain in Chrétien's romances, maintaining that these allusions occur at key moments and are often combined with linguistic "riddles" that suggest how the romances are to be read. Chapter 4 focuses on *Yvain*.

Topsfield, L. T. *Chrétien de Troyes: A Study of the Arthurian Romances*. New York: Cambridge University Press, 1981. Presents an allegorical or symbolic interpretation of Chrétien's work, showing how Yvain's first quest is successfully accomplished when love makes him whole. Notes that the tension in the work is not between knighthood and love but between the rival worlds of Laudine and Arthur.

Z

Zadig
Or, The Book of Fate

Author: Voltaire (1694-1778)
First published: Zadig: Ou, La Destinée, histoire orientale, 1748 (English translation, 1749)
Type of work: Novel
Type of plot: Social satire
Time of plot: Antiquity
Locale: Babylon

Principal characters:
ZADIG, a wealthy young man
MOABDAR, king of Babylon
ASTARTÉ, his queen
SÉMIRE, Zadig's first betrothed
AZORA, Zadig's first wife
CADOR, Zadig's best friend
ARIMAZE "THE ENVIOUS," Zadig's enemy
MISSOUF, an Egyptian woman
SÉTOC, an Arab merchant
ALMONA, Sétoc's wife
NABUSSAN, king of Serendib
ARBOGAD, a happy brigand
ITOBAD, a rich lord
OGUL, another lord and a voluptuary

The Story:

Zadig, a charming young man with a good education and great wealth, lives in the time of King Moabdar in Babylon. Despite the fact that he is a very sensible young man, or perhaps because of it, he never boasts of his own abilities or tries to find fault in others. He expects that with the advantages he modestly enjoys he will have no difficulty in being happy, but he is mistaken in this belief.

In rescuing the beautiful Sémire from kidnappers, Zadig is injured by an arrow in his left eye. The great doctor Hermes predicts that he will lose the eye because wounds in the left eye never heal. When Zadig's eye does heal, the doctor writes a book proving that it could not have happened. Unfortunately, Sémire, to whom Zadig has been betrothed, decides that she does not like one-eyed men. In her ignorance of Zadig's recovery, she marries Orcan, the young nobleman who sent the kidnappers to seize her.

Zadig marries Azora, the wisest girl in the city, who takes a frivolous interest in handsome young men. When she scolds a widow for changing the course of a stream in order to escape from her vow to stay by her husband's tomb as long as the stream flows there, Zadig arranges to have Azora told

that he has died. He then has his friend Cador make friendly overtures to Azora and, having done so, complain of a pain in the spleen for which there is but one cure: rubbing the place with the nose of a man who has been dead no more than twenty-four hours. When Azora then goes to the place where Zadig is supposedly buried, he leaps up to keep her from cutting off his nose with a razor. He says that her act proves she is no better than the widow she had criticized. Finally, when living with Azora becomes too difficult, Zadig leaves her.

One day the queen's dog and the king's horse are lost. Zadig is able to describe the missing animals and their location, but when he then says that he has never seen them, he is imprisoned. He is released after he explains that he was able to tell from marks on the ground what the animals were like, but he has learned a lesson, and when he sees an escaping prisoner, he keeps quiet. Nevertheless, he is fined for looking out his window.

A rich and jealous neighbor named Arimaze, who is called "The Envious," finds a tablet on which Zadig has written a poem. The tablet is broken in half, and the part of the poem on one piece of the tablet could be read as criticism of the king. Arimaze shows that part of the tablet to the king, but just as Zadig is about to be condemned for insulting the monarch, a parrot drops the other half of the tablet in the king's lap. Both the king and the queen—especially the queen—begin to hold Zadig in high esteem. He is awarded a goblet for having been generous enough to speak well of a minister who had incurred the king's wrath; such an act is new in the king's experience, and he values Zadig for it.

Zadig becomes prime minister of Babylon and, through his sensible decisions, wins the hearts of the people. He cures a great lord who is too conceited for his own good by having an orchestra and a choir sing his praises all day long, until the lord in desperation calls a halt to the chorus of praise. Zadig also settles a religious dispute that had gone on for fifteen hundred years, concerning the question of whether one should enter the temple of Mithra with the right foot or the left foot; Zadig jumps in with both feet.

Zadig is popular with the ladies of Babylon, but he succumbs to a woman's advances only once and does so without pleasure, for he is too much in love with Queen Astarté. The wife of Arimaze, enraged because Zadig has rebuffed her, allows her husband to send her garter to the king so that he might be deceived into believing that Zadig and the queen are already lovers. The queen warns Zadig that the king means to kill him, and Zadig escapes to Egypt.

After arriving in Egypt, Zadig comes upon an Egyptian beating a woman. When Zadig intervenes, the jealous Egyptian assumes that Zadig is a rival lover, and a fight ensues that ends in the Egyptian's death. The woman, Missouf, far from being grateful, screams that she wishes Zadig had been killed instead. When four men seize her, Zadig allows her to be taken, not realizing that the four men are couriers from Babylon who have mistaken Missouf for Queen Astarté, who has also disappeared.

Because Zadig has killed a man, the Egyptians condemn him to be a slave, and he is purchased by an Arab merchant named Sétoc. At first the merchant values Zadig's service more than he does Zadig himself, but he finally comes to see the value of Zadig's intelligence and common sense. The incident that reveals Zadig's abilities is one in which Zadig proves a Hebrew guilty of not returning a loan made to him by Sétoc; Zadig pretends that he will bring into court the stone on which the loan had been transacted, whereby he traps the Hebrew into describing the stone, proving that he really is the man to whom the loan had been made.

Zadig next convinces an Arabian widow that she should not leap upon the burning funeral pyre of her husband; he does this by making her realize that there are still attractive young men in the world. He settles a dispute among an Egyp-

tian, an Indian, a Chaldean, a Celt, and others concerning the nature of the universe and its operation by pointing out that all the parties admit the existence of a superior being. He is saved from execution by the priests when Almona, the young widow, pretends that she will allow the priests to make love to her if they sign a pardon; they sign the pardon, but when they come to her, they are greeted by judges who condemn them. Sétoc is so impressed by Almona's cleverness that he marries her.

Zadig shows that one can judge an honest man by making candidates for the comptroller's position engage in a dancing contest. Only one candidate resists the money Zadig has placed in a passageway, and only he dances lightly and with grace, the others being fearful of jostling the money from their pockets. Having performed this service for King Nabussan of Serendib, to whose kingdom Zadig has been sent by Sétoc, Zadig then undertakes to show which of the king's hundred wives are faithful. Only one resists the temptations of money, youth, and power to which Zadig exposes the women.

After settling a revolt of the priests against Nabussan, Zadig, guided as always by the sayings of Zarathustra, sets forth to find news of Queen Astarté. He meets a happy brigand, Arbogad, who reports that King Moabdar has been killed in an uprising, but the robber has no news of the queen. Zadig also meets an unhappy fisherman who lost his money, his wife, and his house during the revolt in Babylon. Since some of the money owed the fisherman was for cream cheese he had sold to Zadig and Queen Astarté, Zadig, without revealing his identity, gives the fisherman half the money he has.

Next, Zadig meets several women who are hunting for a basilisk that is to be used to cure Ogul, their lord and master. Zadig is overjoyed to find Queen Astarté among the women. She informs him that his friend Cador helped her escape from the king, that the king had married Missouf, and that she had frightened the king out of his wits by speaking to him from within a statue in the temple in which she was hidden. The revolt in Babylon resulted from the king's madness, and he had been killed. Queen Astarté was then captured by the prince of Hyrcania and escaped from him only to be captured by the brigand Arbogad, who sold her to Ogul. Zadig cures Ogul by presenting him with a bag and telling him that it contains medicine that will go through his pores only if he punches the bag hard enough—the resultant exercise cures the lord. Zadig thus manages to free Queen Astarté and to win more honor for himself.

Returning to Babylon, Zadig enters a jousting tournament and a battle of wits in order to win Queen Astarté as his wife.

Despite the trickery of Itobad, who steals Zadig's armor and pretends to be the victor after Zadig has won the tournament, Zadig manages to win both contests—partly through the encouragement of the angel Jesrad, who is disguised as a hermit—and he marries Queen Astarté. As king, Zadig is a just and compassionate ruler under whom Babylon becomes a prosperous and happy empire.

Critical Evaluation:

François-Marie Arouet, known to his contemporaries and to posterity as Voltaire, represented classicism in the age of the Enlightenment. He was true to the ideas of logic and nature and presented works of philosophical optimism. The core of meaning in *Zadig* is similar to that of Voltaire's more popular novel *Candide: Ou, L'Optimisme* (1759; *Candide: Or, All for the Best*, 1759). *Zadig* is aptly subtitled *The Book of Fate*. The reader is shown many chance occurrences and their results. Voltaire's theory is that coincidence is really a trial, reward, punishment, or foresight—there are no chance happenings in the larger picture of life. His philosophy implies that people should consider the possible meanings of seemingly random events instead of dismissing them as accidental and therefore unimportant.

Zadig is a testament, as is the rest of Voltaire's writing, to his belief in a system of universal justice and morality that applies to all people of any year or century. His philosophy, cloaked in wit, sarcasm, and satire that was relevant to his own time, still sparkles with truth more than 250 years after it was written.

The question posed in *Zadig* is, Why do bad things happen to good people? The plot takes Zadig through his troubles as he constantly asks himself why the bad things keep happening, forcing the reader to consider the same quandary. Zadig himself is reinforced as a wonderful specimen of maleness and humanity, a person pure of heart, a competent and clever judge, and a brave and winning fighter. Zadig is repeatedly punished for his good and honest nature, but evil is rewarded only in the short term. Just when Zadig is in trouble because his poem has been haphazardly broken in half in such a way that it appears insulting to the king, he is relieved from trouble by a parrot that transports the other half to the king—an even greater unlikelihood. The miracle of chance elevates his status. Had it not been for the earlier unjust and unlikely charge, he would not have been in the circle of the king at all. Although he is introduced to the palace by this unexpected occurrence, he ends up as the court prime minister. He also meets the queen, Astarté, with whom he will eventually live happily ever after. First, however, there are more chance incidents, many of them bad things happening for no

particular reason. Bad events are just as necessary as good events in propelling Zadig toward his eventual destiny.

Zadig's second subtitle translates from the French as "an oriental tale," and indeed, Zadig's ability to go where fate directs and to accept whatever happens without question or offense is based in a philosophy more Eastern than Western. Zadig embodies the nature of Chinese Daoism, which is to take the path of least resistance, as a leaf floats down a stream, going around rocks instead of attempting to go through them. This was a fairly unusual mode of thinking in eighteenth century Europe.

Near the end of *Zadig*, the hero happens upon a hermit who is a disguised angel. The hermit is reading from "the book of fate." The tale that follows is ancient and dates back to the Qur'ān, which was popular in Europe from the thirteenth century on. The hermit does bad things to people who treat him very well and is kind to one who treats him badly. How and why this is possible is the root of Voltaire's book and, incidentally, of Zadig's problems. When questioned by Zadig, the hermit explains that the people he has hurt will learn from their trials and will profit spiritually or monetarily from them. The hermit's conclusive statement is that "there is no evil out of which some good is not born." Zadig attempts to argue, modestly fending off the inevitable moral of this story, but the hermit disappears and leaves Zadig not completely understanding and accepting but unable to disagree.

Zadig becomes a parable, or a parody of a proper story. It is more a didactic argument for living morally and well than it is a plot- and character-oriented novel. All the scenes and people are designed for the purpose of expressing philosophical optimism. The story line is a vehicle in the vein of the classic "hero's quest." Here the holy grail turns out to be that Zadig marries Astarté and becomes king of Babylon. Zadig's greatest assets—wit and the ability to solve problems—keep him constantly moving in the direction of a pleasant resolution, although he must necessarily encounter certain difficulties before fate grants him the big payoff. His troubles are punctual and specific, traditional and random. These occurrences in the life of Zadig are Voltaire's reconfigurations of authentic oriental stories, strung together and sensibly made to order by a single hero character.

Over time, debate has arisen over whether Voltaire should be regarded as a creator and originator of ideas or whether he had the extreme competence to realign and reassert classical philosophies that he respected and that fit into his own scheme of life. Either way, he promises in the opening section of *Zadig* that it will be "a work that says more than it seems to say," and this is accomplished almost as a joke on the reader. Voltaire originally wrote *Zadig* to entertain his aristocratic friends. It was only at their insistence and because of their enthusiasm that he had it published, though he thought of it as a trifle. Nevertheless, this trifle has come to be known as one of Voltaire's best-loved and most accessible and humorous tales. The unlikely event that this "throwaway" piece would become so popular was not accidental or unlikely at all; rather, it was the actualization of its contents. The longevity and acclaim of *Zadig* are testimony to the philosophical optimism that the work slyly and diligently expresses.

"Critical Evaluation" by Beaird Glover

Further Reading

Aldridge, A. Owen. *Voltaire and the Century of Light.* Princeton, N.J.: Princeton University Press, 1975. Biography includes extended discussion of Voltaire's writings, including *Zadig.* Seeks to combine an examination of Voltaire's literature with the history of ideas and to present Voltaire's personality along with his philosophy.

Cronk, Nicholas, ed. *The Cambridge Companion to Voltaire.* New York: Cambridge University Press, 2009. Collection of essays examines Voltaire's life, philosophy, and works, including *Zadig.* Addresses such topics as Voltaire as a storyteller, Voltaire and authorship, and Voltaire and the myth of England.

Davidson, Ian. *Voltaire in Exile: The Last Years.* New York: Grove Press, 2004. Chronicles Voltaire's life during his exile from France, when he actively campaigned against censorship, war, torture, capital punishment, the alliance between church and state, and other perceived injustices. Includes an analysis of much of Voltaire's personal correspondence.

Knapp, Bettina Liebowitz. *Voltaire Revisited.* New York: Twayne, 2000. Good introductory study describes Voltaire's life and devotes separate chapters to all of the genres of his works, including *Zadig* and other philosophical tales.

Sherman, Carol. *Reading Voltaire's Contes: A Semiotics of Philosophical Narration.* Chapel Hill: Studies in the Romance Languages and Literatures, University of North Carolina, 1985. Scholarly work undertakes line-by-line scrutiny of *Zadig*, *Candide*, *Le Micromégas* (1752; *Micromegas*, 1753), and *L'Ingénu* (1767; *The Pupil of Nature*, 1771). Includes charts and graphs that dissect the stories.

Topazio, Virgil W. *Voltaire: A Critical Study of His Major Works.* New York: Random House, 1967. Excellent, eminently readable study is an essential resource on Voltaire's writings, covering his poetry, dramas, and novels. Provides insight into the author's life and the mood of the century in which he was working.

Vartanian, Aram. "*Zadig*: Theme and Counter-Theme." In *Dilemmas du roman*, edited by Catherine Lafarge. Saratoga, Calif.: Anima Libri, 1990. Discusses the philosophical theme of impersonal fate in *Zadig* and notes that the story is told in such a way that its overall meaning emerges from a network of tensions among its various elements.

Zaïre

Author: Voltaire (1694-1778)
First produced: 1732; first published, 1733 (English translation, 1736)
Type of work: Drama
Type of plot: Tragedy
Time of plot: During the reign of Osman, sultan of Jerusalem
Locale: Jerusalem

Principal characters:
OROSMANE (OSMAN), sultan of Jerusalem
LUSIGNAN, a prince in the line of the kings of Jerusalem
ZAÏRE and FATIMA, slaves of the sultan
NERESTAN and CHATILLON, French gentlemen
CORASMIN and MELEDOR, officers of the sultan

The Story:

Fatima and Zaïre are slaves of Orosmane, sultan of Jerusalem, but their lot is not an unpleasant one. Although Orosmane has the power to treat them as mere chattel and to use them for his pleasure, he treats them with respect and consideration. Nevertheless, Fatima is disturbed to find that Zaïre not only is resigned to her fate but also appears actually to enjoy it. When she asks Zaïre to explain why she no longer weeps or looks forward to the return of Nerestan, who has gone to France to seek ransom for them, Zaïre replies that she finds it difficult to yearn for a mode of life she has never known. Since childhood she has been confined to the sultan's seraglio under the care of Orosmane, and she has grown fond of her life and even of her master.

Fatima then reminds Zaïre that Nerestan, who conducted himself nobly in the battle of Damas as part of the Christian army fighting against the Turks, had been captured by Orosmane but, because of his courage, was later released on his word to return with ransom for the Christian prisoners, including Fatima and Zaïre. Zaïre replies that two years have passed since Nerestan's departure and that perhaps Nerestan made the promise to return with ransom for ten slaves only because there was no other way for him to escape a similar servitude. She admits that she admired Nerestan at the time of his promise, but she has decided to think of the matter no longer. Zaïre then confesses to Fatima that Orosmane is her slave—that he loves her and she loves him. She quickly adds that this love does not mean that she has consented to become his mistress. The truth is that Orosmane's love for her is so strong and pure that he plans to wed her.

Fatima, delighted to hear that Zaïre will be elevated from the place of a slave to that of sultana, has but one misgiving—Zaïre is forgetting that she is a Christian. Zaïre replies that she does not even know who her parents were; she has only Nerestan's surmise, because of the cross she has worn since childhood, that she is a Christian. Since she has been a slave from her childhood, it is only natural that her faith reflects the customs of the place where she was reared. With Fatima, Zaïre admits, the situation is different; Fatima was captured in adulthood, and she had deliberately embraced Christianity before becoming a slave. Although Zaïre regards herself as Muslim, she admits that she is impressed by the Christian faith, but she assures Fatima that her love for Orosmane is so strong that she no longer considers becoming a Christian.

Orosmane then enters and expresses his love for Zaïre and his intention to marry her. As he professes his love, a servant comes in and announces the arrival of Nerestan, who enters and tells the sultan that he has come with ransom for the prisoners and that he is willing to remain as Orosmane's slave. The sultan, impressed by Nerestan's honor, replies that he will release not ten but one hundred prisoners. The only ones who will have to remain are Lusignan, a French nobleman who claims the hereditary right to rule in Jerusalem, and Zaïre.

Nerestan protests that Orosmane had promised to release the prisoners, and Zaïre in particular, if the ransom money were brought from France. Orosmane, however, permits no discussion of his decision. He dismisses Nerestan and orders Zaïre to prepare to assume her place as his sultana.

After the others have gone, Orosmane remarks to Corasmin, one of his officers, that Nerestan had sighed and fixed his eyes on Zaïre. When Corasmin warns his master against jealousy, the sultan replies that he cannot be jealous on Zaïre's account because she is truth itself.

Chatillon, a French gentleman released at Orosmane's command, praises Nerestan for having arranged to free the prisoners, but Nerestan is not gratified by Chatillon's praise because of Orosmane's refusal to release Zaïre and Lusignan. Chatillon agrees that without Lusignan, the great Christian leader and soldier who fought so valiantly in defense of Caesarea, there is no joy in his own freedom.

Nerestan then relates how, as an infant, he had been carried from the smoking ruins of the city of Caesarea to the sultan's seraglio. Zaïre had been a fellow captive. Chatillon tries to encourage Nerestan by suggesting that Zaïre might charm Orosmane into releasing Lusignan, but Nerestan knows that Lusignan will not accept liberty under such circumstances.

Zaïre then enters and tells Nerestan that she regrets not being able to return to France with him, but her love for Orosmane makes that impossible. She assures him that she will use her new status to protect the Christians and to relieve the wretched. As evidence of her intentions, she offers Lusignan's freedom, granted at her request by the sultan.

After Lusignan is released, Nerestan tells him how he had been a slave in Solyma almost from his birth and how he had been able to escape to fight with Louis against the Turks. Lusignan, greeting Chatillon, an old friend who was captured with him at Caesarea, reminds the Christian knight that he, Lusignan, had seen his own wife and two sons die there, and that another son and a daughter had been taken from him. Chatillon remembers that he had baptized the daughter just before the Saracens swept her and her brother away.

When Nerestan remarks that he was captured at the age of four, the age of Lusignan's son when he was taken, and when Lusignan notices that Zaïre wears a cross that he had given to his wife as a present, it is revealed that Nerestan and Zaïre are Lusignan's long-lost children. Zaïre, deeply moved by the discovery, vows to be a Christian from this moment onward.

Believing them to be friends from the time they were slaves together, Orosmane permits Zaïre to meet with Nerestan. Unknown to the sultan, however, Zaïre's declaration as a Christian has inspired Nerestan to urge her to give up Orosmane altogether, even after Nerestan learns that Zaïre had hoped to wed the Turk. Zaïre is torn by emotional conflict; she knows Orosmane's virtues and loves him as a person, but she cannot tolerate disappointing the hopes and faith of her brother and father, particularly after learning from Nerestan that their father is near death.

When Zaïre asks Orosmane to defer their nuptials, the sultan is amazed; her excuse, that Lusignan is dying, seems to him insufficient. After Zaïre leaves him in tears, Orosmane rages to Corasmin and reveals his fear that he has cause to be jealous of Nerestan. He resolves not to allow himself to be governed and deceived by Zaïre.

Orosmane confronts Zaïre again and tells her that he no longer loves her, but when she weeps and protests her love, he repents. When she leaves him, however, he wonders again about her virtue. When guards intercept a letter sent to Zaïre by Nerestan, Orosmane interprets the references to secrecy and to faithfulness as signs of a lover's passion, and he accepts Corasmin's suggestion to send the letter on to Zaïre in order that they might observe her behavior. In suppressed fury and jealousy he once more confronts Zaïre and asks her for the name of his rival. Although she insists that she has no other master, he can no longer believe her.

Orosmane has one last faint hope that the romance he suspects is one-sided, instigated by Nerestan, but his slave's report that Zaïre received the letter with trembling and weeping and that she promised to meet Nerestan that night confirms his fear that she loves another. Zaïre, trying desperately, in the meantime, to reconcile her duty to her family and Christianity with her love for Orosmane, hopes that he will understand and pity her.

Orosmane intercepts Zaïre at the place of her meeting with Nerestan and, calling out that she has betrayed him, stabs her to death. When Nerestan arrives and reveals that Zaïre was his sister, the Turk is overcome with grief and remorse. After ordering Corasmin to free all the Christians, he kills himself with his dagger. Nerestan, understanding the depth of Orosmane's remorse and sensing that his love had become perverted by jealousy, laments the sultan's death.

Critical Evaluation:

Although *Zaïre* was one of the most popular plays of the eighteenth century, it lost a considerable amount of prestige as time continued. François-Marie Arouet, known as Voltaire, remains best known for his novels *Zadig: Ou, La Destinée, histoire orientale* (1748; *Zadig: Or, The Book of Fate*, 1749) and *Candide: Ou, L'Optimisme* (1759; *Candide: Or, All for the Best*, 1759), which were created many years after his greatest theatrical successes. Of the fifty-two plays Voltaire wrote, twenty-seven were tragedies. He considered himself first a poet and dramatist and only second a fiction writer and historian. Of the incredible body of work he produced in his eighty-three years, it would probably surprise and perhaps even sadden him to know that his novels have outlasted his plays in literary esteem.

Zaïre was a daring and creative achievement in 1732. While adhering to the classical theatrical tradition, Voltaire still was the most accomplished innovator of his time. Before *Zaïre*, French characters had never appeared on the tragic stage. Written in twenty-two days, *Zaïre* was popular because it included a strong love interest, an element that had been absent from Voltaire's earlier tragedies. His original hit, *Œdipe* (pr. 1718; *Oedipus*, 1761), had been fourteen years earlier, and Voltaire had been reproached because there was not enough "love" in that play and the succeeding ones. Of *Zaïre* he wrote: "They shall have it this time, I swear to you, and it will not be mere gallantry. I am resolved that there shall be nothing so Turkish, so Christian, so amorous, so tender, so furious, as what I am now putting into verse to please them."

The controversy, and probably the popularity of this play, came essentially from its juxtaposition of romantic love and religion. In the play, Voltaire employs the tenet that religion comes to a person as a result of birth and education. Zaïre, who was born a Christian but was from infancy a slave to the sultan and exposed exclusively to the influence of the Muslim faith, faces the dilemma of either forsaking the religion of her father or continuing with the religion she has been taught. If she chooses to be a Christian, she will have to leave both the only life she knows and Orosmane, the greatest love of her life; her life in France will presumably be humble. If she chooses to be a Muslim, she will wed the loving Orosmane and elevate her status from that of slave to that of the sultan's only wife. Zaïre must consider which is better: religion for the sake of her father and brother, who have only just become known to her, or a romantic love that is everything to her. She does not fully confess a choice but opts toward confidence with her family and against telling the truth of her circumstance to her true love. She is unfaithful to him through a breach of honesty, while Orosmane is guilty of plain jealousy, of supposing that the only thing she would possibly keep from him would be desire for another man. In choosing to consult her brother, Zaïre acts against the sultan's wishes, and in leaning toward her religious birthright, she loses the trust of her lover and, more dramatically, her life.

This plot line created a stir in Voltaire's day because religion was not regarded as something to be tampered with or explored objectively as to its value or liability in particular situations. The love relationship is what made this play accessible and enjoyable to theatergoers, but the ultimate cause of the tragedy is religious dogma. Without making his effort too visible or overbearing, Voltaire questions the merit of keeping the tradition of religion intact at the expense of personal happiness. He does no more than question, however; he refrains from providing an answer one way or the other. The great novelty for the time in which the play was first produced was that he did not present one religion as better or more worthwhile than the other. This sort of religious tolerance was not approved of in eighteenth century France and was difficult for many to accept. Both religions are equal in *Zaïre*, where the emphasis is on the opposing strength and importance of love. The two characters who are in love fail miserably at the act of communication; they deceive each other, and both act in selfishness, showing that romantic love, theirs in particular, is not flawless.

Voltaire withholds a conclusion or resolution to the questions he poses. Neither religion is better, neither lover more unselfish than the other, and it remains undecided whether religion or romantic love is better. Voltaire offers no solution to the tremendous ethical dilemma, a point that critics consider to be perhaps the greatest problem in the play.

In accord with Aristotle's classical structure, the entire action of the play takes place in the period of one day. In accord with Voltaire's later and more acclaimed writings, a chance occurrence changes the mood of that single day. The reunion between Zaïre and her family can only happen on this day, the day of her wedding to Orosmane. Everything hinges on this single contrived event. Voltaire presents a different philosophy here than in his more memorable *Candide* and *Zadig*, in which horrible and unlucky events occur at random but later prove to have occurred for a higher and ultimately beneficial purpose. In *Zaïre*, happenstance destroys the hero and heroine, a much more pessimistic viewpoint than Voltaire's later "philosophical optimism."

"Critical Evaluation" by Beaird Glover

Further Reading

Aldridge, A. Owen. *Voltaire and the Century of Light*. Princeton, N.J.: Princeton University Press, 1975. Biography includes extended discussion of Voltaire's writings, including *Zaïre*. Seeks to combine an examination of Voltaire's literature with the history of ideas and to present Voltaire's personality along with his philosophy.

Carlson, Marvin A. *Voltaire and the Theatre of the Eighteenth Century*. Westport, Conn.: Greenwood Press, 1998. Traces the development of Voltaire's theatrical career, providing summaries and reviews of his plays and describing how the plays relate to his social, political, and philosophical ideas. Discusses his involvement in acting, staging, and other aspects of play production in addition to his playwriting.

Cronk, Nicholas, ed. *The Cambridge Companion to Voltaire*. New York: Cambridge University Press, 2009. Collection of essays examines Voltaire's life, philosophy, and works, including *Zaïre*. Addresses such topics as Voltaire as a storyteller, Voltaire and authorship, and Voltaire and theatricality.

Davidson, Ian. *Voltaire in Exile: The Last Years*. New York: Grove Press, 2004. Chronicles Voltaire's life during his exile from France, when he actively campaigned against censorship, war, torture, capital punishment, the alliance between church and state, and other perceived injustices. Includes an analysis of much of Voltaire's personal correspondence.

Howells, R. J., et al., eds. *Voltaire and His World: Studies Presented to W. H. Barber*. Oxford, England: Voltaire Foundation, 1985. Presents critical analysis of the body of Voltaire's theatrical and poetic work. Compares Voltaire to his contemporaries and gives a perspective on his place within the Age of Enlightenment.

Knapp, Bettina Liebowitz. *Voltaire Revisited*. New York: Twayne, 2000. Good introductory study describes Voltaire's life and devotes separate chapters to all of the genres of his works, including drama.

Topazio, Virgil W. *Voltaire: A Critical Study of His Major Works*. New York: Random House, 1967. Excellent, eminently readable study is an essential resource on Voltaire's writings, covering his poetry, dramas, and novels. Provides insight into the author's life and the mood of the century in which he was working.

The Zoo Story

Author: Edward Albee (1928-   )
First produced: 1959; first published, 1959
Type of work: Drama
Type of plot: Absurdist
Time of plot: Late 1950's
Locale: Central Park, New York City

Principal characters:
PETER, a man in his early forties
JERRY, a man in his late thirties

The Story:

Peter, a successful upper-middle-class man who works in the publishing business, is reading on a bench in Central Park in New York City on a sunny summer afternoon. Another man, Jerry, an aimless, rootless outsider who describes himself as a "permanent transient," declares that he has come from the zoo and insists on talking to Peter. Peter does not want to be bothered. He tries to brush off Jerry and get on with his reading, but Jerry confronts him to examine his life. In the course of their conversation, the audience discovers that Peter is married; has two daughters, two parakeets, and two television sets; lives in a nice neighborhood; and has an executive position in textbook publishing. When Peter questions Jerry about his life, Jerry accuses him of trying to make sense out of things and bring order to a chaotic world. Although these two men are nearly the same age, one in his late thirties and the other in his early forties, they seem to have very little in common, at least on the surface.

Jerry tells Peter that he has had only short-term relationships with women. After discussing the difference between fantasy and reality, Jerry abruptly brings the conversation back to the reason for his trip to the zoo. He proceeds to tell Peter a long, detailed story about his landlady and her dog, who are the gatekeepers of his dwelling. Jerry lives in a rooming house, and the landlady's dog attacks him every time he comes in. He is fascinated with and challenged by the dog's hatred and wants to find a way to make contact with the animal. He tells Peter that he decided that he would first try to kill the dog with kindness, and if that did not work, he would simply kill it. He fed the dog hamburgers, but the dog's hatred did not diminish. He then decided to give the dog a poisoned hamburger, but still nothing happened. The dog did not die, nor did it come to love Jerry. For a brief moment, Jerry and the dog looked at each other, but then the dog withdrew from contact with him. Even its hatred seemed gone forever.

Not able to make contact with people, Jerry had tried to make contact with a dog, but even this had failed and proved nothing. Now, whenever he and the dog meet, Jerry tells Peter, they regard each other "with a mixture of sadness and suspicion, and then we feign indifference." An "understanding" has been reached: The dog no longer rushes Jerry, and Jerry no longer feeds or poisons the dog. Jerry then announces, "The Story of Jerry and the Dog, the end," bringing to an effective and dramatic close the important second part of the play.

Upon hearing this story, Peter shouts that he does not understand and does not want to hear any more. Jerry tells Peter that he will explain what happened to him at the zoo, but first he must explain the reason for his visit. Jerry went to the zoo to find out about the way people exist with animals and the way animals exist with one another and with people. After telling Peter that in the zoo everyone is separated from everyone else, Jerry begins to punch Peter and move him off the park bench.

Jerry tells Peter that he is crazy and wants the bench on which Peter is sitting. Peter screams furiously for the police and yells at Jerry to get away from his bench. Jerry says that he needs the bench, calls Peter a vegetable, and prods him to defend the bench. They begin to fight for the bench. Jerry takes out a knife and throws it at Peter's feet. Peter picks up the knife to defend himself. Jerry then charges Peter and impales himself on the knife. Although Jerry is dying, he thanks Peter for not going away and leaving him, and for giving him comfort. With his dying breath, Jerry tells Peter that he has been dispossessed, as he has lost his bench, but he has defended his honor. Jerry has made contact with another human being, even if it has cost him his life. Jerry says that Peter is really not a vegetable but an animal. The entire human condition for Jerry is a zoo story of people (and animals) forever separated by bars. The play ends with Peter howling, "OH MY GOD!" as he leaves Jerry, who is uttering the exact same words, to die.

Critical Evaluation:

Slightly before his thirtieth birthday, when it began to look as if he would not be successful as a writer, Edward Albee sat down at a wobbly table in the kitchen of his Greenwich Village apartment and typed out *The Zoo Story*. The play was first produced in Berlin on September 28, 1959, along with Samuel Beckett's *Krapp's Last Tape* (pr., pb. 1958). Later, the play appeared in twelve other German cities, and it was finally presented in Greenwich Village at the Off-Broadway Provincetown Playhouse on January 14, 1960. Critics hailed the debut of an extraordinary dramatic talent, and Albee quickly emerged as the leader of the American wing of the Theater of the Absurd. He was singled out by many critics as the crucial American dramatist of his generation. The production of his play *Who's Afraid of Virginia Woolf?* in 1962 won him several national awards and marked the peak of his popularity and fame.

Albee's creative masterpieces are both subtle and complex, and they reflect the tension between realism and the Theater of the Absurd. The action and dialogue of *The Zoo Story* are dislocated, arbitrary, and absurd up to the moment of Jerry's death. Jerry spends his dying breath telling the audience what the play means. Jerry explains to Peter the farce and the agony of human isolation. It is because human isolation is so great, and because the "contact" that would end it is so painful and difficult to obtain, that Jerry went to the zoo. What he discovered is that the entire human condition is a zoo story of people (and animals) forever separated by bars. From his experience with the dog, which symbolizes the vicious aspects of society, Jerry learned "the teaching emotion," that combination of kindness and cruelty that forms, for him at least, life itself.

At the same time, Albee engages his audience in harsh social criticism as he attacks the American way of life, the way in which Americans are assumed and expected to live. In the play, Albee explores the relationship between the observed world and its inner reality. He uses the images of nonreason in his attack on the American way of life without accepting the absurdist vision that generated them. Albee is a defender of society's outcasts who are forced to live in a savage society and who have been victimized by the stupidity and bias of the privileged elite.

Albee's multiple and complex themes deal with deeply philosophical subjects also handled by notable European playwrights Eugène Ionesco, Samuel Beckett, and Jean Genet: the breakdown of language, the attempt to live by illusion, the alienation of the individual from others, and the terrible loneliness of every living human being. Critics have pointed out that Albee is working, at least partly, from an existentialist position. Jerry's life can be seen as a struggle for existence in the jungle of the city against the forces that threaten his highly individualistic, nonconformist character, as well as his protest against the consequent isolation with

which a conformist society punishes him for daring to assert such individualism. The confrontation with Peter as a representative of that society becomes a kind of crisis or climax to his entire life. The park bench is the arena for the conflict of values and the attack on the conformist, middle-class emptiness and complacency of Peter's life. Jerry feels compelled and challenged to combat the isolation in his life and to make contact with Peter in the only way possible. Jerry qualifies as an existentialist hero because he makes his choice freely. His decision at the end of the play to impale himself on the knife is a deliberate act. He knows full well what he is doing.

The Zoo Story is considered to be a modern morality play with the themes of human isolation and salvation through sacrifice. Albee employs traditional Christian symbols that serve as an expanded allusion to Christ's sacrifice. Jerry, in his natural state, is alone, a prisoner of self. He must prove his kinship with all other things and creatures, "with a bed, a cockroach, with a mirror," by defying self, thus being in touch with his humanity and the spark of divinity within him. The only way Jerry can smash the walls of his isolation and reach his fellow creatures is through an act of love, a sacrifice so great that it altogether destroys the self that imprisons him and ultimately kills him.

Jerry's death is a deliberate act of protest against the physical and psychological violence of the city; the injustice and indifference of the system; empty, conformist, materialistic American middle-class values; the feeling of life being lived in a void; and the isolation of humanity. The play suggests an uncomfortable conclusion, that the price of survival under these conditions may be the murder of a fellow human being. For Jerry, all humans are divided into two classes: vegetable and animal. The former comprises those who merely subsist, and the latter those who are willing to fight and kill, as animals do, for survival. At the end of the play, the "teaching emotion" plays itself out in full dramatic focus. Peter leaves his vegetable existence and becomes an animal. Through the courageous and noble act that costs him his life, Jerry momentarily connects with Peter, who now has the possibility to live authentically for the first time and become an apostle who will carry the message of humans' caged animality and isolation in the contemporary world.

Milton S. Katz

Further Reading

Amacher, Richard E. *Edward Albee*. Rev. ed. Boston: Twayne, 1982. Chapter 3, "Ancient Tragedy and Modern Absurdity," analyzes the classical plot of *The Zoo Story* and discusses the problems of biblical language, the face of the television screen, and the existential position found in the play. Includes an interesting and informative discussion of the play as a classical Greek tragedy.

Bailey, Lisa M. Siefker. "Absurdly American: Rediscovering the Representation of Violence in *The Zoo Story*." In *Edward Albee: A Casebook*, edited by Bruce J. Mann. New York: Routledge, 2003. Analysis of *The Zoo Story* is included in a collection of essays that trace Albee's development as a playwright and theatrical innovator.

Hayman, Ronald. *Edward Albee*. New York: Frederick Ungar, 1973. Contains a relatively brief and easy-to-follow analysis of the plot and themes of *The Zoo Story*. Concludes that it is not a homosexual play, an absurd play, or a religious play, as other critics contend; rather, it is an outstanding moral play.

Kolin, Philip C. "Albee's Early One-Act Plays: 'A New American Playwright from Whom Much Is to Be Expected.'" In *The Cambridge Companion to Edward Albee*, edited by Stephen Bottoms. New York: Cambridge University Press, 2005. *The Zoo Story* is one of the plays included in this examination of Albee's early work.

Rutenberg, Michael E. *Edward Albee: Playwright in Protest*. New York: DBS, 1969. Presents discussion of Albee as an astute social critic, deeply moral and committed to the cause of human dignity in an ethically moribund age. Chapter 1, on *The Zoo Story*, analyzes the play as a defense of society's outcasts who have been victimized by the stupidity and bias of the successful elite.

Way, Brian. "Albee and the Absurd: *The American Dream* and *The Zoo Story*." In *Edward Albee*, edited by Harold Bloom. New York: Chelsea House, 1987. Provides perceptive and well-articulated analysis of the tension between the realist and absurd dimensions in the play and of Albee's brilliance, inventiveness, intelligence, and moral courage in writing it.

Zimbardo, Rose A. "Symbolism and Naturalism in Edward Albee's *The Zoo Story*." In *Edward Albee: A Collection of Critical Essays*, edited by C. W. E. Bigsby. Englewood Cliffs, N.J.: Prentice-Hall, 1975. Interesting essay discusses *The Zoo Story* as a modern morality play whose theme is human isolation and salvation through sacrifice. Argues that Albee uses traditional Christian symbols because the sacrifice of Christ is perhaps the most effective way in which the story has been told in the past.

Zinman, Toby. "*The Zoo Story*." In *Edward Albee*. Ann Arbor: University of Michigan Press, 2008. Discusses the themes of the play and the techniques that Albee employs in addressing them.

Zoot Suit

Author: Luis Miguel Valdez (1940-   )
First produced: 1978; first published, 1978
Type of work: Drama
Type of plot: Historical
Time of plot: Early 1940's
Locale: Los Angeles

Principal characters:
EL PACHUCO, the narrator
HENRY REYNA, the protagonist, accused of murder
GEORGE SHEARER, a lawyer to Henry
ALICE BLOOMFIELD, a reporter
DELLA BARRIOS, Henry's girlfriend
THE PRESS

The Story:

A large newspaper hangs in place of a curtain. Its large bold print reads ZOOT SUITER HORDES INVADE LOS ANGELES and US NAVY AND MARINES ARE CALLED IN. The narrator, El Pachuco, dressed in his traditional zoot suit, enters from behind the newspaper, ripping it with his switchblade. Speaking in English and Spanish, he tells the audience how every Chicano fantasizes about putting on a zoot suit. He also cautions the audience that the play is both fact and fantasy.

El Pachuco is next seen singing at a barrio dance. The members of the Thirty-eighth Street Gang are present, including Henry Reyna, a twenty-one-year-old Chicano who is the leader of the gang, and his girlfriend, Della Barrios. A rival group, the Downey Gang, comes into the dance hall. Harsh words are exchanged, and at that moment, the police arrive and detain those at the dance hall. Lieutenant Edwards and Sergeant Smith arrest Henry. It is Monday, August 2, 1942.

Alone in a room at the police station, Henry and El Pachuco have a conversation. El Pachuco comments to Henry about the problems facing zoot-suiters. He tells Henry that the war is not overseas but on his own home turf, and he reminds Henry of Chicano pride. Edwards and Smith want Henry to confess to the murder of Jose Williams at Sleepy Lagoon; they believe that Henry is guilty of the crime. They interrogate him, but Henry does not talk.

Sergeant Smith beats Henry unconscious, and the scene shifts to Henry's home on the Saturday night of the dance. Henry tries to reassure his mother, who fears his wearing the zoot suit because of all the trouble zoot-suiters have been having with the police. Henry pays no attention although the newspaper headlines are reporting a Mexican crime wave.

The scene shifts back to the present. Henry and his friends are angry and worried because they have been accused of murder. They all agree not to squeal on one another. George Shearer, an attorney, is hired to defend the boys. At first Henry does not trust him, but George speaks convincingly of his sincere belief in the justice system. Henry then begins explaining the events of that Saturday night. According to Henry, his brother Rudy, who was quite drunk at the time, got into an argument with Rafas, the leader of the Downey Gang. Henry defended his brother. After a near-fatal fight, Henry and Rafas both claimed that their insult had been revenged.

As George prepares the boys' defense, Henry is introduced to Alice Bloomfield, a reporter. They argue in their first encounter, but she and George reassure Henry of the fairness of the justice system. When the trial begins, however, George realizes the difficulty he faces as the judge denies his motions and overrules his objections.

The first person on the witness stand is Della, who recounts the events after the Saturday-night dance. She testifies that the Downey Gang went to Sleepy Lagoon and beat up Henry. Instead of going home, they then went to the Williams ranch and were attacked. As the gang members headed back to their cars, Della saw a man repeatedly hitting another on the ground with a stick. During cross-examination, the prosecutor succeeds in twisting Della's story. With all his objections being overruled, Shearer is not able to present his case adequately. The boys are found guilty and sent to prison for life, and Della is ordered to a state girls' school. El Pachuco calls for a break.

Henry and his friends are next seen doing time at San Quentin. Henry, feeling hopeless, decides to drop his appeal, but Alice is able to talk him into continuing with it. After a visit from George, Henry argues with a guard and is sent to solitary confinement for ninety days. Alice does not know about the solitary confinement and believes that Henry is

dropping the appeal. While in solitary confinement, Henry again talks to El Pachuco, who tells him not to hang on to false hope. Henry turns against El Pachuco. Alice continues to bring Henry optimistic news. At one point, feeling happy, Henry kisses her. While Henry awaits word on the status of his appeal, his brother Rudy joins the Marines.

More than a year later, Henry and the boys are acquitted on the charges of murder. On his return home, Henry's parents throw him a party to celebrate his freedom, and at the party he makes amends with Della. The party does not last long, however, as the police begin to harass his friend Joey. Henry, filled with rage, tries to intervene, but his father holds him back, not wanting Henry to confront the police. Henry, at first ready to strike his father, instead embraces him, and, one by one, the whole family joins in the embrace. As the play ends, various versions of Henry Reyna's fate are offered.

Critical Evaluation:

Luis Miguel Valdez is one of the most prominent figures in Chicano theater. In 1965, Valdez formed El Teatro Campesino, a theater group founded to help striking farmworkers in Delano, California. The popularity and immediacy of Chicano theater grew as similar groups formed on many college campuses and produced one-act plays. The vital social and political themes addressed by these groups and their plays led Valdez to write his most widely acclaimed play, *Zoot Suit*, in 1978. Soon after, the play made its debut at the Mark Taper Forum in Los Angeles, where it received overwhelmingly positive reviews. In 1979, it traveled to Broadway, and in 1981, Valdez wrote and directed a motion-picture adaptation of *Zoot Suit*. The play is an important part not only of Chicano literature but also of contemporary American drama.

Set in the 1940's, the narrative lies between "fact and fantasy." The narrator, El Pachuco, cautions the audience that the work is only a play. The play has, however, a true historical backdrop: the 1942 Sleepy Lagoon murder trial. Henry Reyna, a twenty-one-year-old member of the Thirty-eighth Street Gang, finds himself accused of murder, and after a blatantly biased court trial, he is sentenced to life imprisonment. With the help of the Sleepy Lagoon Defense Committee and Alice Bloomfield, reporter-turned-advocate, the district court of appeals reverses the decision in 1944. After spending more than a year in prison, including the last three months in solitary confinement, Henry Reyna is released. The trial, however, is what creates the passion within the play. The boys of the Thirty-eighth Street Gang are looked upon as social delinquents, as foreigners, and as criminals. At no point during the proceedings do the boys or their attorney, George Shearer, get a fair opportunity to present their case. The trial is presented in only two scenes of act 1, but it propels much of the conflict of the play. Valdez recounts a period—one that was well documented in the Los Angeles daily newspapers—of police brutality, civil unrest, and violation of basic human rights within the Chicano community. The dramatic action of *Zoot Suit* allows audience members to enter a world that many may find too familiar in present-day American society.

The central figure of *Zoot Suit* is the narrator, El Pachuco, who is dressed in a zoot suit—a suit with a wide-shouldered, long, draped coat, and pegged pants—accessorized with a four-foot watch chain hanging from his waist, a hat, and shoes with metal taps. El Pachuco is the commentator and remains present onstage throughout the play. He reminds the audience of the fantastic element of the play but also of the history that informs the play. El Pachuco interacts with characters and the audience. He sings a song in act 1, scene 7, as the couples dance. El Pachuco speaks directly to the audience in English and in Spanish, even in *caló*, a Chicano dialect. He gives the audience background information and provides commentary as he participates in the dramatic action. He also sometimes stops the action to emphasize statements made by others.

The most poignant role El Pachuco plays is in his relationship with Henry Reyna. In act 1, scene 3, El Pachuco acts as a consoler to Henry after his arrest for the murder of Jose Williams. Then, in act 1, scene 6, El Pachuco becomes the voice of caution to Henry when George Shearer, an Anglo attorney, wants to represent Henry and the rest of the boys. The relationship between El Pachuco and Henry develops more on a psychological level in act 2, scene 5. It appears that El Pachuco acts as Henry's conscience as Henry, in this act, thinks aloud. The frustration and anger built up inside Henry are vocalized by El Pachuco as he antagonizes Henry. In a tense moment, Henry lashes out at El Pachuco, who laughingly reminds him and the audience not to take the play so seriously. El Pachuco, in addition to being a chorus, is something of a trickster figure.

Henry Reyna takes on a symbolic role as well. Henry, the Chicano from the barrio, is part of the generation in the 1940's who faced harassment and persecution related to their mode of dress, the zoot suit. He endures a humiliating court proceeding and is sentenced unjustly. Henry knows he cannot fully participate in a world that does not see him as an equal. His dreams of enlisting in the U.S. Navy are dashed. Still, Henry is representative of young Chicanos who seek justice despite the odds. *Zoot Suit* offers no resolution to Henry's situation. Rather, it points to various possible fates

for Henry, indicating Valdez's view that Chicano youths have many paths from which to choose, both good and bad.

One of the innovative stylistic achievements of this play is the backdrop of newspapers. The Press, personified, heightens the emotional context as it brings to light the events that took place in 1942 at Sleepy Lagoon. The Press continues an antagonistic role as prosecutor in the trial against Henry Reyna and his friends. As indicated in the stage directions, the audience's attention is drawn to the newspapers throughout the play—for example, when Dolores Reyna, Henry's mother, folds newspaper sheets as she would clothes. The influence of the press is shown to be pervasive.

The variety of languages and dialects used provides *Zoot Suit* with a richness in tone. Spanish and English are sometimes mixed, and the use of Spanish reaffirms the cultural affinity in the Chicano community. When the Anglo characters George and Alice speak Spanish, they are seen as more approachable and trustworthy. *Caló* is a direct presentation of the zoot-suiter or the pachuco. Its private usage is indicative of the pachuco. The use of *caló* sets the zoot-suiters apart from others in the Chicano community, the separation in this case being an article of distinction, not of alienation.

Carmen Carrillo

Further Reading

Davis, R. G., and Betty Diamond. "*Zoot Suit*: From the Barrio to Broadway." *Ideologies and Literature* 3, no. 15 (January-March, 1981): 124-132. Analyzes the social and historical influences on the play. Traces *Zoot Suit* from the historical events on which it is based through Valdez's creative interpretation of those events. Notes and explores the differences between history and the drama.

Elam, Harry Justin, Jr. *Taking It to the Streets: The Social Protest Theater of Luis Valdez and Amiri Baraka*. Ann Arbor: University of Michigan Press, 1997. Focuses on Valdez's participation in El Teatro Campesino, comparing that theater group's theories and practices with those of Baraka's Black Revolutionary Theater. Examines how the plays performed by both groups during the 1960's and 1970's promoted cultural pride, self-determination, and community empowerment for their audiences.

Huerta, Jorge A. "Luis Valdez's *Zoot Suit*: A New Direction of Chicano Theatre?" *Latin American Theatre Review* 13, no. 2 (Summer, 1980): 69-76. Explores the influence of *Zoot Suit* on Chicano theater. Traces the history of Chicano theater and analyzes *Zoot Suit* as a turning point at which Chicano concerns were brought to wider public attention.

Isenberg, Barbara. "Luis Valdez." In *State of the Arts: California Artists Talk About Their Work*. New York: William Morrow, 2000. Includes a brief interview in which Valdez discusses his work and how it has been influenced by its cultural and historical setting.

Lubenow, Gerald C. "Putting the Border Onstage." *Newsweek*, May 4, 1987, 79. Explores the influence of *Zoot Suit* on the perception of Hispanics. Includes a short biography of Valdez.

Martin, Laura. "Language Form and Language Function in *Zoot Suit* and *The Border*: A Contribution to the Analysis of the Role of Foreign Language in Film." *Studies in Latin American Popular Culture* 3 (1984): 57-69. Explores the usage, function, and meaning of the language in *Zoot Suit*.

O'Connor, Jacqueline. "Facts on Trial: Documentary Theatre and *Zoot Suit*." In *Interrogating America Through Theatre and Performance*, edited by William W. Demastes and Iris Smith Fischer. New York: Palgrave Macmillan, 2007. Examines the play's depiction of American politics and culture.

Ramirez, Elizabeth. "Chicano Theater Reaches the Professional Stage: Luis Valdez's *Zoot Suit*." In *Teaching American Ethnic Literatures: Nineteen Essays*, edited by John R. Maitino and David R. Peck. Albuquerque: University of New Mexico Press, 1996. Presents an examination of the play and discusses its relation to the evolution of Chicano theater and culture.

Valdez, Luis. "*Zoot Suit* and the Pachuco Phenomenon." Interview by Roberta Oroña-Córdova. In *Mexican American Theatre: Then and Now*, edited by Nicoläs Kanellos. Houston: Arte Público, 1983. Valdez discusses the historical influences on the play, its development, and its social messages.

Xavier, Roy Eric. "Politics and Chicano Culture: Luis Valdez and El Teatro Campesino, 1964-1990." In *Chicano Politics and Society in the Late Twentieth Century*, edited by David Montejano. Austin: University of Texas Press, 1999. Focuses on the plays that Valdez wrote for the theater group and their depictions of Mexican American life. Includes commentary on *Zoot Suit*.

Zorba the Greek

Author: Nikos Kazantzakis (1883-1957)
First published: Vios kai politela tou Alexe Zormpa, 1946 (English translation, 1952)
Type of work: Novel
Type of plot: Psychological realism
Time of plot: Mid-twentieth century
Locale: Crete

Principal characters:
ZORBA, a Greek miner, a man of passion and vigor
THE NARRATOR, called "the boss," Zorba's employer
MADAME HORTENSE, an aging and vibrant harlot
THE WIDOW
PAVLI, a young man in love with the widow

The Story:

The narrator, a bookish man, decides to experience life by going into mining operations on Crete. While the narrator is waiting with his crates of books for the weather to clear so that he can board his ship, Zorba enters the café and starts a conversation with him. Enchanted by Zorba's dynamic personality, "the boss," as Zorba calls the narrator, agrees to hire him as personal cook and foreman at the mine. Although he is in his sixties, Zorba possesses tremendous strength and a boundless appetite for physical pleasures.

They arrive at the village near the site of the narrator's mine, where they were welcomed by an aging woman, Madame Hortense, who reveals to them her colorful past life as a courtesan. She drinks copiously while reminiscing about

pleasures and love affairs, and about being the mistress of French, Italian, and Russian admirals and princes. She is now ready, however, to live a life of reflection and repentance.

Zorba's infectious exuberance revives the broken harlot. As they dance, she regains her old sensuality and flirtatiousness. The night continues with music, dancing, food, wine, and lust. Zorba and Madame Hortense satisfy their sexual desires. The narrator witnesses all with wonder but cannot see himself engaging in such behavior.

He is profoundly moved by Zorba's physicality but continues his meditations on philosophy and psychology, always searching for analytic explanations. The narrator is amused by Madame Hortense's reminiscences but is touched at the same time by the power of experience reflected in her memory. He sees the same attachment and sensibility in Zorba, but in him the narrator can see it in concrete action. As Zorba ages, he grows more passionate, not less. The narrator is experiencing a sensual dimension of life that is absent from his abstract speculations.

As the narrator discovers more about Zorba's past, he realizes that Zorba has had a full life as a lover, husband, father, landlord, and beggar. Zorba, however, has never lost his sense of freedom, which is untouched by conventional or Christian morality. His pure animal pleasure is his guide and his theology.

The narrator and Zorba meet a beautiful young widow in the town's tavern, where she is being harassed by the young men of the town, as she often is. Zorba rescues her from her predicament, and the encounter triggers a long dialogue between Zorba and the narrator. Zorba theorizes that a man will burn in hell for allowing a woman to sleep alone, and he encourages the narrator to visit the widow, who is being courted by other men. There are indications that the widow is attracted to the narrator; for example, when she returns to him an umbrella that he has lent her, she also gives him a bottle of rose water and dainty Christmas cookies. He tries to hide these gifts, but Zorba discovers them and says that they are conclusive evidence of her interest. The image of the widow comes to haunt the narrator. He feels that the mere thought of her is taking away his freedom. If he had to choose between falling in love with a woman and reading a book about love, he would choose the book.

At the mining site, Zorba works diligently to restore the dilapidated mine, often exposing himself to danger as he does so. Progress with the work is slow and discouraging. They need wood for the mine, and in a series of delightful and humorous encounters with the leaders of a monastery, Zorba reaches an agreement to harvest wood from their forest. He persuades the boss to give him time and money to invent a means to carry the timber down the hill. When the boss agrees to finance his project, Zorba begins dancing to express his emotions.

On Christmas Eve, Zorba gives a passionate lecture about the significance of Christmas and maintains that the Virgin Mary and the widow are one and the same in God's eyes. The narrator buries his nose in a Buddhist manuscript, refusing to submit to temptation, although Zorba's tutelage is insidiously affecting his repressed sensuality.

Zorba goes to the city to buy materials for harvesting the trees, and he ends up getting drunk and sleeping with prostitutes. He writes a confession to the boss detailing his experiences, and while the narrator is reading the letter, Madame Hortense arrives and asks if Zorba mentions her in it. Feeling pity for her, the narrator makes up fictitious messages to Hortense from Zorba, messages full of promises of marriage, gifts, and happiness. She leaves full of hope and anticipation.

The narrator, immensely affected by Zorba, Madame Hortense, and the Cretan air, wine, and food, begins to think that Zorba is right, that the young widow is destined for him. Meanwhile, young Pavli presents the widow with a passionate letter, but she spits on it and throws it in his face. That same night the narrator, drunk but resolute, knocks on the widow's door. Word soon gets around that he has spent the night with her, and, upon hearing this, Pavli drowns himself in the ocean. His body is found the next morning by his distraught father and a band of Pavli's friends. They blame the widow's liaison with the narrator for Pavli's death.

As Pavli's funeral procession lumbers toward the church, the crowd is stirred into a frenzy by the sight of the widow and the body of the young man. The townspeople stone the widow and finally decapitate her, as Zorba tries unsuccessfully to stop them. The horror-stricken narrator watches the ghastly proceeding.

The narrator later experiences a kind of epiphany, a realization that life has to be lived and not merely studied. He sees that all his books of poetry, philosophy, and religion are mere shadows compared with one moment of Zorbatic living. He accepts the widow's murder as a new beginning to his life.

When Madame Hortense comes to ask Zorba about all the promises he supposedly made in his letter, Zorba realizes that he will have to go along with her wishes. They get married in the moonlight, with the narrator serving as a witness. Hortense is in ecstasy, but she soon becomes fatally ill and dies in Zorba's arms. The villagers arrive and loot her home, taking all of her belongings.

Both the narrator and Zorba feel that they have had enough of Crete. They separate, but the narrator continues to hear stories about Zorba. He learns that Zorba traveled through the Balkans, leading a life of pleasure with wine, women, food, and dancing. Finally he settled down in Serbia and died there, leaving behind a young wife and child.

Critical Evaluation:

Zorba the Greek is based on Nikos Kazantzakis's own experiences while trying to mine low-grade coal during World War I. He engaged a workman named George Zorba to supervise his operation in Peloponnesus. This experience, as well as an earlier scheme to harvest wood from forests, gave Kazantzakis most of the material for his essentially autobiographical novel, which he wrote between 1941 and 1943. The work, which was dedicated to the memory of George Zorba, established Kazantzakis's reputation in the English-speaking world.

Zorba the Greek is not an action-packed story, though some episodes have great passion and dramatic intensity. The novel is essentially a long debate between two men of opposite dispositions. One is a scholar-ascetic who prefers to read about life rather than to experience it; the other is a naïve, trusting, and biologically sophisticated man who represents paganism. The two men represent the undying conflict between the two philosophical poles, Dionysian and Apollonian.

To some extent, the novel concerns the transformation of the narrator. Although Zorba is the main character, Kazantzakis focuses attention on Zorba's effect on the narrator. Nothing changes in Zorba, but he changes everything he touches.

Kazantzakis assigned great importance to Zorba's character and to his philosophy, which was Kazantzakis's synthesis of his favorite ancient and modern philosophies, from Plato to Carl Jung. He would have placed Zorba alongside such luminaries as Homer and Plato. Zorba is not a simple phenomenon. He has a dynamism and complexity that can be interpreted in such different contexts as Friedrich Nietzsche's Dionysian-Apollonian schema or the Buddhist conception of the nothing. Zorba in Nietzschean terms is the Dionysian man, the exuberant extrovert whose sole epistemological meaning is sensual experience and passion. He abhors abstraction and the sterile asceticism of the intellectual life. When words get in the way, he dances to express himself. He is a brute soul, deeply rooted in the earth, with all the astute physical awareness of a wild animal.

The narrator, by contrast, is pallid and book-bound, and he struggles in Platonic and metaphysical valleys of doubt. He is on earth but does not feel it. He is overwhelmed by the titanlike character of Zorba and watches him with delight and envy. The narrator, who represents Kazantzakis in his youth, can feel the conflict of life and death, whereas Zorba sees only the wonder of life.

When asked what he believes in, Zorba summarizes his philosophy by saying that he does not believe in anything or anyone except himself—not because he is better than others, but because Zorba is the only being he has in his power. A rugged individualist, he needs no one to reaffirm his existence and beliefs. He mingles freely with people and departs with no nostalgic sentimentalism. The narrator also believes in individualism, but he soon realizes that his individualism is hollow compared with Zorba's thrilling dances, delightful

indulgences, and childlike fascination with nature. It is Zorba's primitive joy in living that motivates the narrator to pursue the widow.

Although the plot revolves around the character of Zorba, it is transformed by the narrator's abstract mentality. The novel sings the praises of paganism and animal vitality but is firmly in the grip of Kazantzakis's German-educated, analytical mind. It is this underlying methodical analysis that gives the story its dynamism. The intellectual narrator can never be Zorba, who remains a demigod to be observed and admired.

The narrator discovers that Crete is more primitive than the mainland. Because everyone is affected by the environment, even the monks who live in the hilltop monastery, Crete seems to the narrator to be the last bastion of the ancient Greek gods. Perhaps one of them is personified in the person of Zorba, whose passionate dances, playing of the stringed *santui*, and frenzy of sexual love are all characteristic of a savage god on a savage island.

Chogollah Maroufi

Further Reading

Anapliotes, Giannes. *The Real Zorbas and Nikos Kazant-zakis.* Translated by Lewis A. Richards. Amsterdam: A. M. Hakker, 1978. Presents a comprehensive history of Kazantzakis's friendship and adventures with the "real" Zorba, George Zorba, in 1917, during World War I, when they were engaged in coal-mining and tree-harvesting operations.

Bien, Peter. *Kazantzakis: Politics of Spirit.* 2 vols. Princeton, N.J.: Princeton University Press, 1989-2007. Volume 1 of this definitive biography focuses on the evolution of Kazantzakis's personal philosophy from 1906 up to his publication of *Odysseia* in 1938 (this work appeared in English translation in 1958 as *The Odyssey: A Modern Sequel*). Volume 2 describes the period of Kazantzakis's life in which he wrote *Zorba the Greek* and *Ho teleutaios peirasmos* (1955; *The Last Temptation of Christ*, 1960).

_____. "The Mellowed Nationalism of Kazantzakis' *Zorba the Greek*." *Review of National Literatures* 5, no. 2 (Fall, 1974): 113-136. Discusses Zorba's character as an uncommitted patriot who admires Cretan food, oil, wine, and women but does not want to sacrifice his life for Crete.

Dombrowski, Daniel A. *Kazantzakis and God.* Albany: State University of New York Press, 1997. Analyzes Kazantzakis's novels and other works to describe his religious vision, interpreting his ideas in terms of contemporary "process theology." Explains how Kazantzakis combined his ideas about God with a Darwinian belief in the evolution of all creatures—including God.

Dossor, Howard F. *The Existential Theology of Nikos Kazantzakis*. Wallingford, Pa.: Pendle Hill, 2001. Discusses Kazantzakis's religious ideas, describing how Kazantzakis created a personal theology based on his existential belief that human beings are mortal and must live as if they are heading toward death.

Elsman, Kenneth R., and John V. Knapp. "Life-Span Development in Kazantzakis's *Zorba the Greek*." *International Fiction Review* 11, no. 1 (Winter, 1984): 37-44. Analyzes Kazantzakis's novel within its social and political contexts and examines the different transformations and developments of the novel's characters.

Givelski, Paskal. "From Homer to Kazantzakis." *Macedonian Review* 22, no. 2 (1992): 147-150. Offers a useful review and analysis of the connections among Kazantzakis's tragic figures. Gives background that can aid readers in understanding the characters in *Zorba the Greek*, such as the village widow and Pavli, both of whom meet tragic ends.

Levitt, Morton. "The Companion of Kazantzakis: Nietzsche, Bergson and Zorba." In *The Cretan Glance: The World and Art of Kazantzakis*. Columbus: Ohio State University Press, 1980. Presents an excellent discussion of Zorba's philosophy as encompassing elements from Friedrich Nietzsche, Henri Bergson, Karl Marx, Sigmund Freud, and Carl Jung.

Middleton, Darren J. N., and Peter Bien, eds. *God's Struggler: Religion in the Writings of Nikos Kazantzakis*. Macon, Ga.: Mercer University Press, 1996. Collection of essays explores the theme of religion in Kazantzakis's works, including a Greek Orthodox interpretation of his religious ideas, a discussion of mysticism in his writings, and the writer's "theology of struggle."

Owens, Lewis. *Creative Destruction: Nikos Kazantzakis and the Literature of Responsibility*. Macon, Ga.: Mercer University Press, 2003. Detailed study of Kazantzakis's writings includes discussion of how he was influenced by the philosophy of Henri Bergson. Argues that Kazantzakis believed that destruction is a necessary prerequisite of renewed creative activity.

Zuckerman Bound

Author: Philip Roth (1933-   )
First published: 1985; includes *The Ghost Writer*, 1979; *Zuckerman Unbound*, 1981; *The Anatomy Lesson*, 1983; *The Prague Orgy*, 1985
Type of work: Novel
Type of plot: Comic realism
Time of plot: 1956-1976
Locale: Newark, New Jersey; the Berkshires, Massachusetts; New York City; Miami; Chicago; Prague

Principal characters:
NATHAN ZUCKERMAN, a Jewish American writer
VICTOR "DOCTOR" ZUCKERMAN, his father, a podiatrist
SELMA ZUCKERMAN, his mother
E. I. LONOFF, a Russian Jewish writer living in seclusion in the Berkshires
AMY BELLETTE, a Jewish student staying with Lonoff

The Story:

Nathan Zuckerman has published several short stories that, although critically well received, have caused conflict within his family. His story "Higher Education" is a thinly fictionalized account of a family dispute over the distribution of an inheritance, and it portrays Jews in an unflattering and stereotypical—although to Nathan, realistic and necessary—light.

After corresponding with his literary idol, E. I. Lonoff, an older Russian Jewish writer, Zuckerman leaves for a visit to Lonoff's secluded home in the Berkshires in Massachusetts. Zuckerman seeks validation from Lonoff to counter the criticism he is receiving at home; moreover, he wants to see firsthand the writer's life he so idealizes.

Zuckerman's visit with Lonoff shows a marriage in turmoil, the price that a serious writer pays in devotion to his or her craft. Adding to the family strife is the presence of the young, attractive Jewish student currently staying with Lonoff, Amy Bellette. As Nathan retires to bed, he imagines that Amy is none other than Anne Frank, the renowned diarist and Holocaust chronicler. Zuckerman fantasizes about marrying Frank and taking her home to meet his parents. In the morning, it becomes clear again that Amy is not Frank. Zuckerman returns to New York City, but not before Lonoff's wife sets off on foot, intending to leave Lonoff, and Lonoff follows her.

Zuckerman is in the middle of a third divorce. He is now wealthy and famous following the publication of his first novel, *Carnovsky*, a controversial, amoral, and blatantly sexual account of coming of age as a Jew in Newark, New Jersey.

Zuckerman's life, still, becomes unmanageable as the division between his public persona—the same rash, lustful, provocateur that Zuckerman describes in *Carnovsky*—and his private self—generally considerate, proper, and respectful—becomes increasingly hard to discern. He is receiving anonymous phone calls from someone threatening to kidnap his mother, Selma. As he becomes convinced that the threats against his mother are real and are being perpetrated by someone he knows, his ailing father, Victor, takes a turn for the worse in the Miami Beach rest home where he is living.

In Miami Beach, Zuckerman finds out that his father has read *Carnovsky* in its entirety; Victor, a retired podiatrist, is so chagrined by the contents of the book that his family is convinced that the novel will kill him. At his father's deathbed, Doctor Zuckerman whispers his last word into his son's ear: "bastard." Zuckerman then returns briefly to Newark and finds it much changed. He realizes he is truly unbound from his history, his family, and his religion.

Four years later, Zuckerman is living alone in New York, crippled by a debilitating, inexplicable pain in his neck and shoulders; he is living as a shut in, unable to write and administered to by his "harem" of four mistresses. He has tried everything to alleviate the pain, but to no avail, and he turns to self-medicating with copious amounts of alcohol and prescription painkillers.

As Zuckerman considers switching professions entirely—from writer to doctor—he meditates on his mother's recent death. The pain in his body has forced him to consider more urgently his own mortality. He heads to Chicago, and while en route pretends to be a porn-magazine publisher, shocking and offending anyone who will listen to him.

Zuckerman never makes it to his planned destination in Chicago; instead, nearly out of his mind on painkillers, he visits a cemetery with a childhood friend's father and begins having violent delusions; he blacks out and hits his face on a tombstone, forcing him to stay in the hospital for weeks with

his jaw wired shut, both for physical recovery and for rehabilitation.

Zuckerman writes in diary entries about meeting Jewish Czechoslovakian immigrant Zdenek Sisovsky. Through him, he learns of Sisovsky's father's unpublished short stories, written in Hebrew and currently in the possession of Sisovsky's estranged wife, Olga. Sisovsky convinces Zuckerman that the stories need to be recovered and published in the United States.

Traveling to Prague, Zuckerman meets Olga and finally convinces her to hand over the stories, which she jealously guards because of lingering resentment over Sisovsky's departure. As Zuckerman attempts to leave the country with the stories, he is apprehended by Prague government agents; the stories are confiscated, and Zuckerman is sent back to the United States.

Critical Evaluation:

Zuckerman Bound is an important work in Philip Roth's oeuvre, because it sets up a character—Nathan Zuckerman—and themes to which Roth's later works repeatedly turn. His main interests are the relationship between an author and his (or her) work and the relationship between fiction and reality. *Zuckerman Bound* is also unique in American literature as an extended bildungsroman, a chronicle of an artist's development through different phases of his career—from obscurity, to fame, to infamy, to something resembling a balance between being a writer and being human. These are phases that both Roth and Zuckerman would consider at odds, and which certainly complicate one another.

Zuckerman serves as Roth's alter ego in the Zuckerman series of books and as a device for Roth to explore his concerns with the relationship of art to life. The similarities between novelist and character are undeniable: a Newark childhood; study at the University of Chicago; early published stories concerning Jews that the critics praised and Jews found offensive; publication of several "safe" novels before writing sexually frank accounts of adolescence. Zuckerman furthermore provides a thematic and narrative framework for many of Roth's later novels, including *The Counterlife* (1986), *American Pastoral* (1997), *I Married a Communist* (1998), *The Human Stain* (2000), and *Exit Ghost* (2007).

Probably the most salient thread in *Zuckerman Bound* is the exploration of the relationship between real life and fiction and fiction-writing, the seed of which is planted in *The Ghost Writer*, in which Zuckerman begins to experience the peril of using real life as source material. Zuckerman, too, always attempts to use writing to fix the problems that writing has created—another frustrating endeavor, which emerges first around the figure of student Amy Bellette. Zuckerman imagines—indeed, he writes—her into his own life story as Anne Frank, as his wife and unassailable symbol of virtuous Jewishness to bring home to his parents, to wear like a commendation.

Another thematic thread that begins in *The Ghost Writer* and is fleshed out later in the collection is the idea of reconciling individuality with history and familial expectations. Zuckerman incessantly wrestles with knowing his writing must necessarily offend his family's sensibilities, but at the same time he still wants their approbation.

The effects of writing on self-identity are further explored in *Zuckerman Unbound*, as Zuckerman's public identity becomes conflated with the persona of his protagonist, Gilbert Carnovsky. It can be assumed that Doctor Zuckerman conflates his son's identity with the fiction of *Carnovsky* as well, but Zuckerman lacks the wherewithal to try to disprove this, even at his father's deathbed. There, Zuckerman becomes so preoccupied with the words he must say to his father, rather than how to make his father feel, that he writes a scene for himself in which he forgets to be a son; Zuckerman has become so endlessly analytical that he has lost the ability to be, to exist. His whole identity is tied up in being a writer, with all of his experience merely pasturage for the next book. Zuckerman deals with a similar aftermath following his mother's death in *The Anatomy Lesson*, though whatever judgment she has of her son, she reserves.

Zuckerman in *The Anatomy Lesson*, however, has no choice but to simply be—he is locked into a reality of pain that resists any intellectualizing; he can no longer create lives, either his own or others, through writing. His thoughts rapidly change from trying to make meaning through writing, which he has been doing all his life, to trying to make meaning through bodies as a doctor—as his own body has forced him to deal with its reality, he wants to deal with other lives in their respective bodily realities. In essence, his desire to switch from creating characters through writing to affecting patients through medicine is simply a switch in medium; his aims are the same. When, finally, Zuckerman is silenced by his accident at the end of *The Anatomy Lesson*, he is forced again to reevaluate his identity in terms of the body and of language; he is reduced to only a body because he cannot talk. Writing on the chalkboard that is around his neck becomes less an intellectual activity and more a tangible necessity; that writing has been de-intellectualized.

As *The Anatomy Lesson* ends with Zuckerman's silence, *The Prague Orgy* traffics in silence as well. The stories that Zuckerman tries to liberate will never be free of Prague, and they will never speak as intended. This silencing draws attention to another undercurrent of *Zuckerman Bound* as a whole: the final silencing of the Jews during the Holocaust.

The novel does not allude to particular events of Jewish history, with one exception: the Holocaust. It is mentioned once by name, when Zuckerman's mother writes the word "Holocaust" on a piece of paper as her mind spirals into dementia near the end of her life; it is as if the word had been laying dormant and had surfaced as her conscious defenses waned. The other recurring motif of the Holocaust as an indelible part of Jewish identity comes also with the recurring figure of Anne Frank. A major perception of Jewishness that angers Zuckerman is the one-dimensional Jew brought to life in the historical Anne Frank and her diary: suffering and victimized, optimistic and hopeful, but above all, tragic. The positive stereotype of the Holocaust survivor is embodied in Frank, just as the negative stereotype is embodied in William Shakespeare's Shylock—deceptive, self-serving, greedy. Zuckerman wants out of both stereotypes, and he wants to write about Jews as people, not merely as Jews. Even though he cannot escape some of the same tendencies he reviles, Zuckerman still wants out of the whole system— to be unbound.

Alan C. Haslam

Further Reading

Bloom, Harold, ed. *Philip Roth*. Broomall, Pa.: Chelsea House, 2003. A brief but excellent critical overview of Roth's themes and purpose in *Zuckerman Bound*.

Brauner, David. *Philip Roth*. New York: Manchester University Press, 2007. A study of some of Roth's later novels that discusses the paradoxes and other difficulties the works present as a way of illustrating how rewarding it is to read the works.

Cooper, Alan. *Philip Roth and the Jews*. Albany: State University of New York Press, 1996. Examines at length Roth's work as reflective and representative of Jewish American experience.

Hendley, W. Clark. "Philip Roth's *The Ghost Writer*: A Bildungsroman for Today." In *Design, Pattern, Style: Hallmarks of a Developing American Culture*, edited by Don Harkness. Tampa, Fla.: American Studies Press, 1983. Examines Roth's manipulation of the bildungsroman form in *The Ghost Writer*.

Kartiganer, Donald M. "*Zuckerman Bound*: The Celebrant of Silence." In *The Cambridge Companion to Philip Roth*, edited by Timothy Parrish. New York: Cambridge University Press, 2007. Examines the roles and forms of "silencing," both literally and metaphorically, in *Zuck-

erman Bound. Part of a larger study that critiques all of Roth's fiction, examining the themes of sexuality, cultural identity, and the Holocaust in the works.

Pozorski, Aimee. "How to Tell a True Ghost Story: *The Ghost Writer* and the Case of Anne Frank." In *Philip Roth: New Perspectives on an American Author*, edited by Derek Parker Royal. Westport, Conn.: Praeger, 2005. Explores the relationship between the real Anne Frank and Zuckerman's and the larger social conception of her.

Safer, Elaine B. *Mocking the Age: The Later Novels of Philip Roth.* Albany: State University of New York Press, 2006.

Treats Roth in some of his later works as a creator of humor and comedy with tears just beneath the surface. Focuses on the novels from *The Ghost Writer* to *The Plot Against America* (2004).

Wilson, Alexis Kate. "The Ghosts of Zuckerman's Past: The *Zuckerman Bound* Series." In *Philip Roth: New Perspectives on an American Author*, edited by Derek Parker Royal. Westport, Conn.: Praeger, 2005. Discusses in detail Roth's examination of the relationship between life and art in *Zuckerman Bound.*

Zuleika Dobson
Or, An Oxford Love Story

Author: Max Beerbohm (1872-1956)
First published: 1911
Type of work: Novel
Type of plot: Satire
Time of plot: Early twentieth century
Locale: Oxford, England

The Story:

Left an orphan, lovely Zuleika Dobson becomes a governess. Because the older brothers of her charges always fall in love with her, however, she loses one position after another. She moves unhappily from job to job until one enamored elder son teaches her a few simple magic tricks. She then becomes an entertainer at children's parties, where she interests older men if not the children. Before long, she receives an offer to go on the stage, and during a lengthy European stage tour, she crowns success with success. Paris raves over her. Grand dukes ask her to marry them. The pope issues a bull against her. A Russian prince has some of her magic devices, such as the demon egg cup, cast in pure gold. Later, she travels to the United States and is pursued by a fabulous millionaire. Zuleika, however, ignores her admirers. She wants to find a man who is impervious to her charms, feeling that with someone like that she could be happy.

Between theatrical seasons, Zuleika visits her grandfather, the Warden of Judas College at Oxford, where, as usual, every man who sees her falls in love with her. One night, joining Zuleika and her grandfather at dinner is the wealthy, proud, handsome duke of Dorset. He, too, falls in love with

Principal characters:
ZULEIKA DOBSON, a charmer
THE WARDEN OF JUDAS COLLEGE, her grandfather
THE DUKE OF DORSET, an Edwardian dandy
KATIE BATCH, the daughter of his landlady
NOAKS, a poor student

Zuleika at first sight, but his pride and good manners keep him from showing his true feelings. During dinner, he is only casually attentive and on one occasion actually rude. Zuleika is captivated. Thinking that the duke does not love her, she falls in love for the first time in her life. Later that evening, the duke discovers that his shirt studs have turned the same colors as Zuleika's earrings—one black, the other pink. Abashed, the duke flees.

The next morning, Zuleika pays a visit to his flat, where she is let in by his landlady's daughter, Katie Batch. When the duke, unable to restrain himself, confesses his love, Zuleika is disappointed. On her arrival, she had envied Katie the chance to be near him; now she can never feel the same toward him again. The Duke is astounded by her strange attitude and tries to induce her to marry him by reciting his titles and listing his estates, houses, and servants. He tells her of the ghosts that haunt his ancestral home and of the mysterious birds that always appear the day before one of his family is to die. His recital fails to impress Zuleika; in fact, she calls him a snob. The Duke is chagrined when he realizes that Zuleika does not want him as a husband. He is cheered, however, by the fact that she expects him to take her to the boat races that afternoon.

On their way to the races, the duke and Zuleika meet many people. The men immediately fall in love with Zuleika, and the duke, whose good looks have always attracted attention, passes unnoticed. Piqued by his inability to keep Zuleika to himself, the duke threatens to commit suicide. The idea charms Zuleika; no man has ever killed himself for her. As the duke climbs the railing of the barge, however, she changes her mind. Catching his arm, she begs him to wait until the next day. If he will spend the day with her, she will try to make up her mind and give him an answer to his proposal.

The Duke cannot see her that night, for he is to preside at a dinner held by an ancient Oxford club called the Junta, which is so exclusive that for almost two years the duke has been the only member. Each year, he has faithfully nominated and seconded prospective members, only to find each time a blackball in the ballot box. To keep the club from becoming extinct, he has finally voted in two more members. That night, the club is having guests, and the duke does not feel that he can miss the dinner.

The Junta was founded by a man named Greddon, whose lovely mistress was named Nellie O'Mora. At each meeting, Nellie is toasted as the most bewitching person who ever lived or ever will. Rising to propose the toast at that night's dinner, the duke is overcome by confusion. Unwilling to break with tradition or to slight his opinion of Zuleika, he resigns his position as club president. His resignation is a wasted gesture, as neither the other members nor the guests can offer the toast, for they are also in love with Zuleika. The Duke then confesses that he intends to die for her the next day. Not to be outdone and wishing to imitate the duke in all things, the others decide to die with him.

Later that night, when the duke meets Zuleika on the street, he is overcome by love and catches her in his arms, saying that he wants to live to be with her. She chides him for breaking his promise. Still later, he returns and stands under her window. She empties a pitcher of water on him, and the drenching convinces the duke that he is no longer bound by his promise.

As news of the intended suicides spreads swiftly through the colleges, the other undergraduates also become determined to die for Zuleika. The next morning, the duke tries to dissuade them, particularly his friend Noaks, a rough and unattractive boy whom Zuleika had noticed when she first came to Oxford. To keep his friends from dying, the duke is ready to change his own plans, but then a telegram arrives from his old butler, telling him that the birds had appeared the night

before. The Duke is now convinced that he must die. The moment finally comes that afternoon at the boat races. Calling out Zuleika's name, the duke jumps from the barge into the river. Immediately, hundreds of young men run, jump, fall, and totter into the water, calling her name as they go under.

That night, Oxford is empty except for elderly officials and dons. Zuleika hopes that perhaps there is one man who does not love her, that perhaps one young man is left in Oxford. Noaks is still in his room because he had been afraid to die with the others. Zuleika finds him hiding in his room, ashamed, whereupon he becomes engaged to Katie Batch, who before had loved only the duke. Katie embarrasses Zuleika by telling her that the duke died only to keep his ducal promise and not for love of Zuleika, because it was Katie he had really loved. Noaks, humiliated by Zuleika's charge of cowardice, jumps from the window. The last undergraduate in Oxford has perished.

Discouraged because she can find no man insensible to her charms, Zuleika returns to her grandfather's house. Then, struck by a sudden idea, she orders a special train to take her to Cambridge. Perhaps there will be another chance at another university.

Critical Evaluation:

Sir Max Beerbohm was rivaled only by Oscar Wilde in being one of the wittiest writers of the aesthetic movement, and his popularity continued throughout his lifetime, until his death in 1956. He excelled as a critic, essayist, and caricaturist. Some consider *Zuleika Dobson* his only novel, but Beerbohm himself resisted the term "novel," preferring to call the work a fantasy. Whether a novel or a fantasy, *Zuleika Dobson* is definitely a satire.

Beerbohm, who was educated at Merton College, Oxford, lamented the fact that there was no book-length satire about Oxford. He saw the lack of women at Oxford as a stumbling block to good satire, an omission he corrected when he invented Zuleika Dobson, femme fatale extraordinaire, who extinguishes Oxonians with a single glance. Beerbohm began the work in the 1890's, abandoned it, and then revised it for publication in 1911.

As Beerbohm imagined her, Zuleika Dobson is a force of nature, one of those fictional characters that assume life and become real. She owes something to Becky Sharp, the antiheroine of William Makepeace Thackeray's *Vanity Fair* (1847-1848, serial; 1848, book), and she is certainly the reverse of literary governesses such as Charlotte Brontë's *Jane Eyre*. She is, rather, someone true to herself, a Venus borne into an unsuspecting Oxford on the steam of a locomotive rather than on the foam of the sea. Beerbohm introduces her in a single paragraph that employs negation to describe what she is not, thereby leaving much to the imagination of the reader.

Zuleika's suitor, the duke of Dorset, embodies the idea of noblesse oblige and practices such a perfection of manners that his early attempts to rebuff Zuleika are scarcely noticed by her or anyone else. Like Charles Dickens's Mr. Turveydrop in *Bleak House* (1852-1853), the duke exhibits deportment that is "lustrous" and ever at the alert. Beerbohm goes a step beyond Dickens with the duke, whose nobility affords him added occasions to shine. When he commits suicide for love of Zuleika, he dons the blue mantle of the Order of the Garter before leaping into the Isis. Beerbohm is satirizing not only his duke's snobbery but also the whole aesthetic movement, with its refined sensibilities and exquisite tastes. Indeed, the mass suicide of the whole of Judas College is described by Beerbohm as "sacramental," ordained by the gods and a privilege to witness. The unpleasantness and tragedy of a mass suicide is completely exploded by Beerbohm's mock-aesthetic descriptions and observations.

The canny materialism and opportunism of Zuleika are worthy foils for the aesthetic dandyism of the duke and his college fellows. She has collected jewelry from suitors in America and Europe and much portable property as well. When she decamps for Cambridge at the end of the book, the reader feels her career has just begun and foresees that she will go from strength to strength in the conquest of new suitors and acquisition of fresh wealth.

Beerbohm injects into *Zuleika Dobson* several entr'actes in which he tells the reader the history of Judas College; considers the life of Clio, the muse of history; and ponders on the busts of Roman emperors in front of the Sheldonian Theatre. The beauty of Oxford's "dreaming spires" is legendary and so widely celebrated that Beerbohm takes pains to portray the city as too gorgeous, too historic, and too cultured. The stately Roman emperors are seen to sweat in alarm when Zuleika comes to town; Judas College is celebrated as the namesake of the apostle "most remembered and cited" by Christians. Beerbohm even notes Easter week rituals that commemorate Judas by distributing thirty pieces of silver among poor students of the college.

Beerbohm identifies himself as the servant of Clio, the muse of history, but then proceeds to poke fun at Edward Gibbon's *The History of the Decline and Fall of the Roman Empire* (1776-1788) and the work of a number of other historians, thus puncturing their pedantry while showing off his own knowledge. He accuses Clio of being satiated with pulp fiction and therefore addicted to facts, dry facts, very dry facts. In a few short pages, he reduces truth, history, and facts

to dull fare and elevates fantasy to a higher level of writing. In this he is very like his creation Zuleika when she reduces the scholars and pedants of Judas College to lovesick swains willing to die for her.

Zuleika Dobson is full of classical allusions, literary quotations, odd bits of history, snatches of Greek and Latin, and name-dropping of every sort. Beerbohm casts these gems before the reader in the wittiest possible combinations, then dismisses them as being of no importance, not worth mentioning, really too much. Like Zuleika, he takes Oxford's measure and describes its charms, then lightly casts them away.

Beerbohm appears to convey no serious message in *Zuleika Dobson*, to ask no important reform of society as satirists often do, preferring, rather, to tease and entertain. His delightful wit, however, elevates *Zuleika Dobson* to a tour de force. Stylistically, he flirts with aesthetic excess in his use of archaisms and cultural lore, and he simultaneously mocks aesthetic sensibility and proves to be its most accomplished practitioner.

"The incomparable Max," as George Bernard Shaw dubbed him, always knows just how far to take a joke, how many bizarre words and examples to enumerate to keep his satire at its peak while never letting it lapse into excess. He shares this perfect ear with James Joyce and Mark Twain, although the subject matter and sensibilities of these three writers differ greatly.

Zuleika Dobson is a stunning example of style over substance. When Gibbon's historiography is laid aside by the weary reader, *Zuleika Dobson* will still be read with pleasure. Perhaps Beerbohm was as certain of his own ultimate triumph over worthy pedantry and pretentious snobbery as Zuleika Dobson is of her victory over the duke of Dorset. At the very least, Beerbohm saw humor and style as supreme values and employed them with great élan in *Zuleika Dobson*.

"Critical Evaluation" by Isabel B. Stanley

Further Reading

Behrman, S. N. *Portrait of Max: An Intimate Memoir of Sir Max Beerbohm*. New York: Random House, 1960. Written by an old friend of Beerbohm, this work sheds light on the characters in *Zuleika Dobson* that were modeled on acquaintances.

Felstiner, John. *The Lies of Art: Max Beerbohm's Parody and Caricature*. New York: Alfred A. Knopf, 1972. Examines Beerbohm's extravagance, wit, and style, all of which culminate in *Zuleika Dobson*. Draws comparisons between

Zuleika Dobson and James Joyce's *Ulysses* (1922) in the authors' extravagant use of language. Traces other literary influences on Beerbohm.

Hall, N. John. *Max Beerbohm: A Kind of a Life*. New Haven, Conn.: Yale University Press, 2002. Focuses on Beerbohm's work rather than on his life, providing analyses of his writing and caricatures. Concludes that Beerbohm was an "insignificant" writer who did "certain small things extraordinarily well, or in the case of fiction, he makes but a 'small' contribution."

Lynch, Bohun. *Max Beerbohm in Perspective*. New York: Haskell House, 1974. Presents a critical look at Beerbohm's work and takes issue with the form and execution of *Zuleika Dobson*. Also examines the satirical aspects of Beerbohm's depiction of Oxford.

McElderry, Bruce R. *Max Beerbohm*. New York: Twayne, 1972. One of the best books with which to begin a study of Beerbohm. Gives close scrutiny to the role of Oxford in *Zuleika Dobson* and examines the episodic form of the novel and the interludes that punctuate the action of the story.

Riewald, J. G. *Max Beerbohm's Mischievous Wit: A Literary Entertainment*. Assen, the Netherlands: Van Gorcum, 2000. Presents a generally admiring discussion of Beerbohm, describing him as the "greatest English parodist of his time, a parodic genius." Chapter 6, "The Silver Dagger," discusses *Zuleika Dobson*.

_____. *Sir Max Beerbohm, Man and Writer: A Critical Analysis with a Brief Life and Bibliography*. The Hague, the Netherlands: Martinus Nijhoff, 1953. The first and one of the best longer critical studies of Beerbohm. An extended analysis of *Zuleika Dobson* examines distortions of space and time in the work and makes a case for its being a fantasy rather than a novel.

Masterplots

Fourth Edition

Author Index

Abe, Kōbō
Woman in the Dunes, The, 6358
Achebe, Chinua
Things Fall Apart, 5722
Adams, Henry
Democracy, 1455
Education of Henry Adams, The, 1714
Mont-Saint-Michel and Chartres, 3764
Addison, Joseph
Spectator, The, 5458
Æ
Homeward, 2637
Aeschylus
Oresteia, 4201
Persians, The, 4389
Prometheus Bound, 4731
Seven Against Thebes, 5221
Suppliants, The, 5582
Aesop
Aesop's Fables, 64
Agee, James
Death in the Family, A, 1371
Let Us Now Praise Famous Men, 3198
Agnon, Shmuel Yosef
In the Heart of the Seas, 2844
Aiken, Conrad
Preludes for Memnon, 4675
Ainsworth, William Harrison
Jack Sheppard, 2934
Tower of London, The, 5853
Akhmatova, Anna
Requiem, 4875
Alain-Fournier
Wanderer, The, 6171
Albee, Edward
Delicate Balance, A, 1441
Three Tall Women, 5756
Who's Afraid of Virginia Woolf?, 6288
Zoo Story, The, 6474
Alcott, Louisa May
Little Women, 3265

Aldington, Richard
Death of a Hero, 1377
Alegría, Ciro
Broad and Alien Is the World, 745
Aleichem, Sholom
Tevye the Dairyman, 5682
Aleixandre, Vicente
Longing for the Light, A, 3300
Alexie, Sherman
Business of Fancydancing, The, 792
Lone Ranger and Tonto Fistfight in Heaven, The, 3276
Alfieri, Vittorio
Saul, 5124
Algren, Nelson
Man with the Golden Arm, The, 3495
Walk on the Wild Side, A, 6165
Allen, Paula Gunn
Sacred Hoop, The, 5057
Allende, Isabel
Daughter of Fortune, 1347
House of the Spirits, The, 2697
Altamirano, Ignacio Manuel
El Zarco, the Bandit, 1732
Alther, Lisa
Kinflicks, 3051
Other Women, 4243
Alvarez, Julia
How the García Girls Lost Their Accents, 2714
In the Time of the Butterflies, 2847
Amadi, Elechi
Concubine, The, 1113
Amado, Jorge
Dona Flor and Her Two Husbands, 1623
Gabriela, Clove and Cinnamon, 2199
Violent Land, The, 6121
Amis, Kingsley
Lucky Jim, 3374
Amis, Martin
Money, 3751

Anaya, Rudolfo
Bless Me, Ultima, 617
Heart of Aztlán, 2482
Andersen, Hans Christian
Andersen's Fairy Tales, 222
Anderson, Martin. See Nexø, Martin Andersen
Anderson, Maxwell
Winterset, 6345
Anderson, Sherwood
Dark Laughter, 1339
Poor White, 4610
Winesburg, Ohio, 6332
Andreyev, Leonid
Seven Who Were Hanged, The, 5226
Andrić, Ivo
Bridge on the Drina, The, 734
Angelou, Maya
I Know Why the Caged Bird Sings, 2779
Anouilh, Jean
Antigone, 277
Becket, 483
Apollinaire, Guillaume
Alcools, 103
Appelfeld, Aharon
Badenheim 1939, 429
Apuleius, Lucius
Golden Ass, The, 2304
Aquinas, Thomas. See Thomas Aquinas
Arendt, Hannah
Human Condition, The, 2734
Aretino, Pietro
Courtesan, The, 1214
Argote, Luis de Góngora y. See Góngora y Argote, Luis de
Ariosto, Ludovico
Orlando Furioso, 4211
Pretenders, The, 4677
Aristophanes
Acharnians, The, 22
Birds, The, 587
Clouds, The, 1057

Smith, Adam
Wealth of Nations, The, 6233
Smith, Betty
Tree Grows in Brooklyn, A, 5888
Smith, Zadie
White Teeth, 6282
Smollett, Tobias
Adventures of Peregrine Pickle,
The, 47
Adventures of Roderick Random,
The, 51
Expedition of Humphry Clinker,
The, 1920
Snorri Sturluson
Heimskringla, 2514
Snow, C. P.
Conscience of the Rich, The, 1149
Masters, The, 3577
Strangers and Brothers series, 5537
Solzhenitsyn, Aleksandr
August 1914, 373
Cancer Ward, 829
First Circle, 2071
Gulag Archipelago, 1918-1956,
The, 2420
One Day in the Life of Ivan
Denisovich, 4171
Song, Cathy
Picture Bride, 4457
Sontag, Susan
Illness as Metaphor, 2812
Sophocles
Ajax, 87
Antigone, 280
Electra, 1747
Oedipus at Colonus, 4083
Oedipus Tyrannus, 4086
Philoctetes, 4423
Women of Trachis, The, 6386
Sor Juana. *See* **Cruz, Sor Juana**
Inés de la
Soyinka, Wole
Death and the King's Horseman,
1362
Spark, Muriel
Bachelors, The, 422
Memento Mori, 3627
Prime of Miss Jean Brodie, The,
4685

Spengler, Oswald
Decline of the West, The, 1412
Spenser, Edmund
Amoretti, 196
Epithalamion, 1839
Faerie Queene, The, 1936
Mother Hubberds Tale, 3799
Shepheardes Calender, The,
5254
Spinoza, Baruch
Ethics, 1872
Staël, Madame de
Delphine, 1446
Statius
Thebaid, 5695
Stead, Christina
Man Who Loved Children, The,
3490
Steele, Sir Richard
Conscious Lovers, The, 1151
Spectator, The, 5458
Stegner, Wallace
Angle of Repose, 248
Big Rock Candy Mountain, The,
566
Stein, Gertrude
Autobiography of Alice B. Toklas,
The, 379
Making of Americans, The,
3460
Three Lives, 5743
Steinbeck, John
Cannery Row, 841
Chrysanthemums, The, 1011
East of Eden, 1695
Grapes of Wrath, The, 2358
In Dubious Battle, 2839
Moon Is Down, The, 3772
Of Mice and Men, 4098
Tortilla Flat, 5848
Winter of Our Discontent, The,
6338
Stendhal
Charterhouse of Parma, The,
946
Red and the Black, The, 4836
Stephens, James
Crock of Gold, The, 1255
Deirdre, 1428

Sterne, Laurence
Journal to Eliza, 2988
Sentimental Journey, A,
5212
Tristram Shandy, 5913
Stevens, Wallace
Harmonium, 2455
Idea of Order at Key West, The,
2785
Stevenson, Robert Louis
Black Arrow, The, 595
Kidnapped, 3042
Strange Case of Dr. Jekyll and
Mr. Hyde, The, 5523
Treasure Island, 5884
Stoker, Bram
Dracula, 1638
Stone, Robert
Dog Soldiers, 1583
Flag for Sunrise, A, 2084
Stoppard, Tom
Real Thing, The, 4825
Rosencrantz and Guildenstern
Are Dead, 5025
Travesties, 5881
Storey, David
This Sporting Life, 5730
Storm, Theodor
Immensee, 2822
Stowe, Harriet Beecher
Oldtown Folks, 4131
Uncle Tom's Cabin, 6004
Strachey, Lytton
Eminent Victorians, 1774
Strassburg, Gottfried von
Tristan and Isolde, 5904
Straussler, Tomas. *See* **Stoppard,**
Tom
Strindberg, August
Dance of Death, The, 1311
Father, The, 1991
Ghost Sonata, The, 2239
Miss Julie, 3712
Sturluson, Snorri. *See* **Snorri**
Sturluson
Styron, William
Confessions of Nat Turner, The,
1128
Lie Down in Darkness, 3215

Title Index

Geographical Index

List of Geographical Regions

AFGHANISTAN
Hosseini, Khaled, 3081, 5740

ALGERIA
Augustine, Saint, 1116
Camus, Albert, 1956, 5531
Cixous, Hélène, 3163
Derrida, Jacques, 4092

ANCIENT GREECE. *See* GREECE, ANCIENT

ANCIENT ROME. *See* ROME

ANTIGUA
Kincaid, Jamaica, 272

ARGENTINA
Borges, Jorge Luis, 2037
Cortázar, Julio, 2647
Güiraldes, Ricardo, 1618
Hernández, José, 2221
Hudson, W. H., 2396
Mallea, Eduardo, 469, 2042
Puig, Manuel, 3076
Sánchez, Florencio, 2137

AUSTRALIA
Brooks, Geraldine, 3534, 6433
Carey, Peter, 4231
Clavell, James, 5277
Franklin, Miles, 3852
Jolley, Elizabeth, 6243

Keneally, Thomas, 5136
Stead, Christina, 3490
West, Morris, 5274
White, Patrick, 4925, 5891

AUSTRIA
Baum, Vicki, 2349
Bernhard, Thomas, 6392
Broch, Hermann, 1396
Buber, Martin, 2774
Freud, Sigmund, 1033, 2224, 2876
Grillparzer, Franz, 5095
Hofmannsthal, Hugo von, 1744
Jelinek, Elfriede, 4450
Kafka, Franz, 883, 3653, 5897

VENEZUELA

WALES

WEST INDIES. *See* **CARIBBEAN AND WEST INDIES**

YUGOSLAVIA. *See* **BOSNIA**

ZIMBABWE

Chronological List of Titles

The titles of works in this set are listed in chronological order below based on their earliest known date of publication or production. Works originally published or produced in languages other than English are ordered according to their original foreign dates. Works known to have been written a significant time before publication or production, and works first transcribed, are listed by their earlier dates. Furthermore, date ranges are arranged by earliest date in that range.

Unknown

unknown	Cadmus (Unknown), 800
	Cupid and Psyche (Unknown), 1277
	Hercules and His Twelve Labors (Unknown), 2554
	Jason and the Golden Fleece (Unknown), 2947
	Orpheus and Eurydice (Unknown), 4229
	Prometheus Bound (Aeschylus), 4731
	Proserpine and Ceres (Unknown), 4743

Before the Common Era

4500 B.C.E.-200 C.E.	Book of the Dead, The (Unknown), 668
c. 2000 B.C.E.	Gilgamesh Epic, The (Unknown), 2265
twelfth century B.C.E.	Book of Songs, The (Confucius), 656
c. 750 B.C.E.	Iliad (Homer), 2808
c. 725 B.C.E.	Odyssey (Homer), 4077
c. 700 B.C.E.	Works and Days (Hesiod), 6398
sixth century B.C.E.	Ode to Aphrodite (Sappho), 4070
c. 500 B.C.E.	Ramayana (Vālmīki), 4801
498-446 B.C.E.	Odes (Pindar), 4075
472 B.C.E.	Persians, The (Aeschylus), 4389
467 B.C.E.	Seven Against Thebes (Aeschylus), 5221
463 B.C.E.?	Suppliants, The (Aeschylus), 5582
458 B.C.E.	Oresteia (Aeschylus), 4201
c. 442 B.C.E.	Antigone (Sophocles), 280
c. 440 B.C.E.	Ajax (Sophocles), 87
438 B.C.E.	Alcestis (Euripides), 94
c. 435-429 B.C.E.	Women of Trachis, The (Sophocles), 6386
431 B.C.E.	Medea (Euripides), 3607
431-404 B.C.E.	History of the Peloponnesian War (Thucydides), 2618
c. 430 B.C.E.	Children of Herakles, The (Euripides), 975
c. 429 B.C.E.	Oedipus Tyrannus (Sophocles), 4086
428 B.C.E.	Hippolytus (Euripides), 2585
426 B.C.E.	Andromache (Euripides), 233
425 B.C.E.	Acharnians, The (Aristophanes), 22
	History of Herodotus, The (Herotodus), 2597
424 B.C.E.	Knights, The (Aristophanes), 3087
423 B.C.E.	Clouds, The (Aristophanes), 1057
	Suppliants, The (Euripides), 5585
422 B.C.E.	Wasps, The (Aristophanes), 6205
c. 421 B.C.E.	Cyclops (Euripides), 1288
	Peace (Aristophanes), 4348
418-410 B.C.E.	Electra (Sophocles), 1747
415 B.C.E.	Trojan Women, The (Euripides), 5927
414 B.C.E.	Birds, The (Aristophanes), 587
	Iphigenia in Tauris (Euripides), 2904
413 B.C.E.	Electra (Euripides), 1742
412 B.C.E.	Helen (Euripides), 2520
c. 411 B.C.E.	Ion (Euripides), 2899
	Lysistrata (Aristophanes), 3386
	Thesmophoriazusae (Aristophanes), 5703
409 B.C.E.	Philoctetes (Sophocles), 4423
	Phoenician Women, The (Euripides), 4441
c. 405 B.C.E.	Bacchae, The (Euripides), 419
405 B.C.E.	Frogs, The (Aristophanes), 2190
	Iphigenia in Aulis (Euripides), 2902
401 B.C.E.	Oedipus at Colonus (Sophocles), 4083
c. 400 B.C.E.-200 C.E.	Mahabharata, The (Unknown), 3437
fourth century B.C.E.	Aesop's Fables (Aesop), 64
399-347 B.C.E.	Dialogues of Plato, The (Plato), 1501
394-371 B.C.E.	Anabasis (Xenophon), 209
388 B.C.E.	Plutus (Aristophanes), 4526
388-366 B.C.E.	Republic (Plato), 4872
371 B.C.E.?	Cyropaedia (Xenophon), 1299
351-341 B.C.E.	Philippics, The (Demosthenes), 4421

First Century to Sixth Century (Common Era)

Ninth Century to Thirteenth Century

Seventeenth Century

Genre Index

List of Genre Categories

ADVENTURE WRITING. *See* **TRAVEL WRITING**

ANTHROPOLOGY. *See also* **FOLKLORE;
SCIENCE**
Golden Bough, The (Frazer), 2307
Savage Mind, The (Lévi-Strauss), 5127

ART HISTORY
Philosophy of Art (Taine), 4432
Stones of Venice, The (Ruskin), 5508

AUTOBIOGRAPHY. *See also* **DIARIES; MEMOIR**
Apologia pro Vita Sua (Newman), 288
Autobiography of Benjamin Franklin (Franklin),
    385
Autobiography of Benvenuto Cellini (Cellini), 388
Autobiography of John Stuart Mill (Mill), 391
Autobiography of Malcolm X, The (Malcolm X),
    394
Autobiography of W. E. B. Du Bois, The (Du Bois),
    400
Barrio Boy (Galarza), 456
Black Boy (Wright), 598
Black Elk Speaks (Black Elk and Neihardt), 601
Confessions (Augustine), 1116
Confessions (Rousseau), 1119
Death in the Afternoon (Hemingway), 1368
Diary of a Young Girl, The (Frank), 1512

Dust Tracks on a Road (Hurston), 1677
Education of Henry Adams, The (Adams), 1714
Enormous Room, The (Cummings), 1817
Father and Son (Gosse), 1995
Grace Abounding to the Chief of Sinners (Bunyan),
    2343
Hunger of Memory (Rodriguez), 2751
I Know Why the Caged Bird Sings (Angelou), 2779
Incidents in the Life of a Slave Girl (Jacobs), 2853
Liber Amoris (Hazlitt), 3213
Mein Kampf (Hitler), 3614
Moveable Feast, A (Hemingway), 3811
Narrative of the Life of Frederick Douglass, an
    American Slave (Douglass), 3908
Roughing It (Twain), 5031
Son of the Middle Border, A (Garland), 5388
Souls of Black Folk, The (Du Bois), 5439
Travels of Marco Polo, The (Polo), 5877
Up from Slavery (Washington), 6056

BIOGRAPHY
Abraham Lincoln (Sandburg), 6
Book of the City of Ladies, The (Christine de Pizan),
    661
Eminent Victorians (Strachey), 1774
Life of Samuel Johnson, LL.D., The (Boswell), 3232
Lives of the Poets, The (Johnson), 3268
Parallel Lives (Plutarch), 4310

ECONOMICS

ENVIRONMENTAL WRITING. See NATURE WRITING

EPISTOLARY LITERATURE

ESSAYS. See also AUTOBIOGRAPHY; DIARIES; LITERARY CRITICISM AND THEORY

MEMOIR. See also AUTOBIOGRAPHY; DIARIES

NATURE WRITING. See also TRAVEL WRITING

NEW JOURNALISM. See also JOURNALISM

NOVELLAS. See LONG FICTION

NOVELS. See LONG FICTION

PHILOSOPHY. See also POLITICAL PHILOSOPHY; RELIGIOUS PHILOSOPHY

PLAYS. *See* DRAMA

POETRY

POLITICAL PHILOSOPHY

POLITICS. See also ECONOMICS; POLITICAL PHILOSOPHY

PSYCHOLOGY

RELIGIOUS PHILOSOPHY. See also DIDACTIC LITERATURE

SAGAS. See HISTORICAL SAGA

SCIENCE. See also ANTHROPOLOGY; NATURE WRITING; PSYCHOLOGY

SHORT FICTION

SOCIAL CRITICISM. *See also* **ECONOMICS; POLITICAL PHILOSOPHY; RELIGIOUS PHILOSOPHY**

Vindication of the Rights of Woman, with Strictures on Political and Moral Subjects, A (Wollstonecraft), 6115

SOCIAL SCIENCE. *See* **ANTHROPOLOGY; ECONOMICS; FOLKLORE; PSYCHOLOGY**

THEORY, LITERARY. *See* **LITERARY CRITICISM AND THEORY**

TRAVEL WRITING. *See also* **NATURE WRITING**
Black Lamb and Grey Falcon (West), 604
Hakluyt's Voyages (Hakluyt), 2436

YOUNG ADULT FICTION
Chocolate War, The (Comier), 990
Rumble Fish (Hinton), 5045
Time Quartet, The (L'Engle), 5782

Themes and Issues Index

List of Themes and Issues Categories

List of Themes and Issues Categories *(continued)*

List of Themes and Issues Categories *(continued)*

List of Themes and Issues Categories *(continued)*

List of Themes and Issues Categories *(continued)*

List of Themes and Issues Categories *(continued)*

ADVENTURE. *See also* EXPLORATION; QUEST; VOYAGES

AESTHETICS. *See also* ART OR ARTISTS; CREATIVITY; PHILOSOPHY OR PHILOSOPHERS

AFRICA AND AFRICANS

ANTHROPOLOGY

ANTICHRIST FIGURES

ANTIHEROES

ANTI-SEMITISM

ARIZONA

Border Trilogy, The (McCarthy), 677

Waiting to Exhale (McMillan), 6157

ARMIES

Anabasis (Xenophon), 209

August 1914 (Solzhenitsyn), 373

Cyropaedia (Xenophon), 1299

I, Claudius (Graves), 2776

Penguin Island (France), 4370

Plough and the Stars, The (O'Casey), 4520

Quentin Durward (Scott), 4763

Romance of the Three Kingdoms (Luo Guanzhong), 4996

Salammbô (Flaubert), 5074

Thebaid (Statius), 5695

True History, A (Lucian), 5938

Underdogs, The (Azuela), 6036

ARMS OR WEAPONS

Corsican Brothers, The (Dumas, père), 1177

Dumb Waiter, The (Pinter), 1668

Fail-Safe (Burdick and Wheeler), 1942

Gravity's Rainbow (Pynchon), 2364

Octopus, The (Norris), 4058

Republic (Plato), 4872

Wapshot Scandal, The (Cheever), 6182

William Tell (Schiller), 6318

ARSON

Dame Care (Sudermann), 1305

Firebugs, The (Frisch), 2069

Good Man Is Hard to Find, and Other Stories, A (O'Connor), 2330

Tales of Odessa (Babel), 5620

Temple of the Golden Pavilion, The (Mishima), 5666

Violent Bear It Away, The (O'Connor), 6118

Yearling, The (Rawlings), 6436

ART OR ARTISTS. *See also* AESTHETICS; CREATIVITY; SURREALISM

Against the Grain (Huysmans), 72

All Hallows' Eve (Williams), 126

Amazing Adventures of Kavalier and Clay, The (Chabon), 165

Autobiography of Alice B. Toklas, The (Stein), 379

Autobiography of Benvenuto Cellini (Cellini), 388

Black Swan, The (Mann), 609

Bohemians of the Latin Quarter, The (Murger), 642

Book of Evidence, The (Banville), 648

Collector, The (Fowles), 1076

Cousin Pons (Balzac), 1223

Critique of Judgment, The (Kant), 1247

Crome Yellow (Huxley), 1258

De Profundis (Wilde), 1357

Democratic Vistas (Whitman), 1463

Dialogic Imagination, The (Bakhtin), 1499

Diary of Anaïs Nin, The (Nin), 1514

Dog Years (Grass), 1585

Emigrants, The (Sebald), 1764

Endymion, the Man in the Moon (Lyly), 1804

Essay on Criticism, An (Pope), 1853

Free Fall (Golding), 2174

French Lieutenant's Woman, The (Fowles), 2180

Girl with a Pearl Earring (Chevalier), 2268

Golden Fruits, The (Sarraute), 2315

Green Grow the Lilacs (Riggs), 2385

Green Henry (Keller), 2388

Harmonium (Stevens), 2455

Horse's Mouth, The (Cary), 2653

Howl (Ginsberg), 2719

Hugh Selwyn Mauberley (Pound), 2725

Hymn to Intellectual Beauty (Shelley), 2761

Illness as Metaphor (Sontag), 2812

Laughter (Bergson), 3165

Malone Dies (Beckett), 3466

Manette Salomon (Goncourt and Goncourt), 3503

Manifesto of Surrealism (Breton), 3513

Marble Faun, The (Hawthorne), 3531

Men and Women (Browning), 3637

Meridian (Walker), 3646

Molloy (Beckett), 3746

Moon and Sixpence, The (Maugham), 3769

My Name Is Red (Pamuk), 3863

Newcomes, The (Thackeray), 3956

Nuns and Soldiers (Murdoch), 4042

Ode on a Grecian Urn (Keats), 4067

Odes (Pindar), 4075

Of Human Bondage (Maugham), 4094

On the Genealogy of Morals (Nietzsche), 4154

On the Sublime (Longinus), 4166

Personae (Pound), 4392

Philosophy of Art (Taine), 4432

Picture Bride (Song), 4457

Picture of Dorian Gray, The (Wilde), 4459

Poetics (Aristotle), 4550

Poetry of George (George), 4565

Portrait of the Artist as a Young Man, A (Joyce), 4630

Prophet, The (Gibran), 4739

Real Thing, The (Stoppard), 4825

Renaissance, The (Pater), 4863

Roderick Hudson (James), 4984

Romance of Leonardo da Vinci, The (Merezhkovsky), 4988

Sappho (Daudet), 5092

Satires (Persius), 5115

Set This House on Fire (Styron), 5218

Sign in Sidney Brustein's Window, The (Hansberry), 5295
Slow Homecoming (Handke), 5346
Society and Solitude (Emerson), 5377
Solitudes, The (Góngora y Argote), 5385
Song of the Lark, The (Cather), 5401
Sonnets of Michelangelo (Michelangelo), 5415
Sot-Weed Factor, The (Barth), 5433
Spoils of Poynton, The (James), 5466
Stones of Venice, The (Ruskin), 5508
Tarr (Lewis), 5643
To the Lighthouse (Woolf), 5818
Tragic Muse, The (James), 5866
Travesties (Stoppard), 5881
Unnamable, The (Beckett), 6047
World as Will and Idea, The (Schopenhauer), 6403
Zuckerman Bound (Roth), 6482

ASIAN AMERICANS

Donald Duk (Chin), 1628
Eat a Bowl of Tea (Chu), 1702
Floating World, The (Kadohata), 2098
F.O.B. (Hwang), 2107
Jasmine (Mukherjee), 2944
Joy Luck Club, The (Tan), 2999
No-No Boy (Okada), 4006
Obasan (Kogawa), 4049
Picture Bride (Song), 4457
Typical American (Jen), 5983

ASSASSINS OR ASSASSINATIONS

Abraham Lincoln (Sandburg), 6
All the King's Men (Warren), 141
August 1914 (Solzhenitsyn), 373
Billy Bathgate (Doctorow), 577
Black Lamb and Grey Falcon (West), 604
Cenci, The (Shelley), 920

Crabwalk (Grass), 1227
Henry VI, Part III (Shakespeare), 2545
In the Time of the Butterflies (Alvarez), 2847
Julius Caesar (Shakespeare), 3008
Juneteenth (Ellison), 3014
Man's Fate (Malraux), 3519
Marat/Sade (Weiss), 3528
Murder in the Cathedral (Eliot), 3837
Old Gringo, The (Fuentes), 4113
Pale Fire (Nabokov), 4278
Quiet American, The (Greene), 4778
Topdog/Underdog (Parks), 5843
Violent Land, The (Amado), 6121
William Tell (Schiller), 6318

ASTRONAUTS

Right Stuff, The (Wolfe), 4931
2001 (Clarke), 5962

ASTRONOMY

Brief History of Time, A (Hawking), 736
Galileo (Brecht), 2202
Seasons, The (Thomson), 5171
Wilhelm Meister's Travels (Goethe), 6313

ATHEISM

Age of Reason, The (Paine), 81
Essays (Bacon), 1858
Master and Margarita, The (Bulgakov), 3568
Varieties of Religious Experience, The (James), 6080

ATHLETES

Last of the Wine, The (Renault), 3146
Odes (Pindar), 4075
Seeing Things (Heaney), 5188
Separate Peace, A (Knowles), 5215
Shoeless Joe (Kinsella), 5268
This Sporting Life (Storey), 5730

ATLANTIC OCEAN. See also ADVENTURE; PACIFIC OCEAN; SEA OR SEAFARING LIFE; VOYAGES

Israel Potter (Melville), 2913
Lusiads, The (Camões), 3377
Middle Passage (Johnson), 3669
Nigger of the Narcissus, The (Conrad), 3976
Pincher Martin (Golding), 4489
Redburn (Melville), 4842

ATOMIC BOMB. See also COLD WAR; NUCLEAR WARFARE OR WEAPONS; WORLD WAR II

Cat's Cradle (Vonnegut), 907
Hiroshima (Hersey), 2587
Martian Chronicles, The (Bradbury), 3556
Obasan (Kogawa), 4049
Paterson (Williams), 4336
Stand, The (King), 5488

ATONEMENT

Atonement (McEwan), 368
Betrothed, The (Manzoni),

Everyman (Unknown), 1907
Kite Runner, The (Hosseini), 3081
Les Misérables (Hugo), 3194
Magician of Lublin, The (Singer), 3424
Requiem for a Nun (Faulkner), 4877
Resurrection (Tolstoy), 4880
Rites of Passage (Golding), 4955
Scarlet Letter, The (Hawthorne), 5132
Story of Burnt Njal, The (Unknown), 5514

ATTORNEYS OR LAWYERS

American Tragedy, An (Dreiser), 190
Orley Farm (Trollope), 4218
Pickwick Papers (Dickens), 4453

AUTOBIOGRAPHY

BELIEF OR DOUBT

BEREAVEMENT OR GRIEF

BERLIN

BETRAYAL

BIBLE, BIBLICAL IMAGERY, OR BIBLICAL SYMBOLISM

BIBLICAL TIMES

THEMES AND ISSUES INDEX

CHINESE AMERICANS

CHIVALRY

CITIZENSHIP

CITY LIFE

CLERGY

CRUELTY

CULTS

DANCE

DEATH PENALTY. See **CAPITAL PUNISHMENT; PUNISHMENT**

DEBATING

DEBT OR CREDIT, FINANCIAL

DEMOCRACY

DEMONSTRATIONS. See **PROTESTS OR DEMONSTRATIONS; RIOTS**

DEPRESSION, ECONOMIC

DEPRESSION, EMOTIONAL OR MENTAL

DOMESTIC VIOLENCE

DOMESTIC WORK OR WORKERS

DRAMATISTS

DREAMS OR FANTASY

DRUGS. *See also* **SUBSTANCE ABUSE**

DUELS OR DUELING

DUTY

ELECTIONS

EMOTIONS

ENGLISH LANGUAGE

ENLIGHTENMENT

ENTERTAINMENT OR ENTERTAINERS

ENTREPRENEURSHIP OR ENTREPRENEURS

ENVIRONMENT OR ENVIRONMENTAL HEALTH

EPIDEMICS

EQUALITY

EROTICA

ETHNIC GROUPS

FATHERS

FAUSTIAN BARGAINS

FEMINISM

FOOD

FORESTS OR FORESTRY

FORGERY

FORTUNE-TELLING

FRATRICIDE, PARRICIDE, OR FILICIDE

FRONTIER OR PIONEER LIFE

FUNDAMENTALISM

FUNERAL RITES OR CEREMONIES

FUTURE

GEISHAS

GENDER ROLES

GOLD, GOLD MINING, OR GOLDSMITHING

GOOD AND EVIL

GOSSIP

GOVERNMENT

GOVERNORS. *See* POLITICIANS; POLITICS

GRANDPARENTS OR GRANDCHILDREN. *See also* CHILDREN; FAMILIES OR FAMILY LIFE

GUILT

Shadows on the Rock (Cather), 5234

Shawl, The (Ozick), 5237

Snake Pit, The (Undset), 5356

Snows of Kilimanjaro, and Other Stories, The (Hemingway), 5369

Sophie's Choice (Styron), 5427

Stone Angel, The (Laurence), 5503

Strangers on a Train (Highsmith), 5540

Surfacing (Atwood), 5588

Tell Me a Riddle (Olsen), 5655

Thérèse Raquin (Zola), 5714

Thomas and Beulah (Dove), 5733

Visit, The (Dürrenmatt), 6130

Woman Killed with Kindness, A (Heywood), 6365

Young Goodman Brown (Hawthorne), 6460

GUNS. *See* ARMS OR WEAPONS; MURDER OR HOMICIDE; VIOLENCE

GYPSIES AND ROMA PEOPLES

Carmen (Mérimée), 873

Dog Years (Grass), 1585

For Whom the Bell Tolls (Hemingway), 2132

Guy Mannering (Scott), 2427

Hive, The (Cela), 2620

Hunchback of Notre Dame, The (Hugo), 2745

Lavengro (Borrow), 3167

One Hundred Years of Solitude (García Márquez), 4177

Scholar-Gipsy, The (Arnold), 5138

Ship of Fools (Porter), 5260

Wanderer, The (Alain-Fournier), 6171

HALLUCINATIONS OR ILLUSIONS

Don Quixote de la Mancha (Cervantes), 1613

Ghost Sonata, The (Strindberg), 2239

Iceman Cometh, The (O'Neill), 2782

Legend of Sleepy Hollow, The (Irving), 3188

Lost Weekend, The (Jackson), 3334

Maids, The (Genet), 3444

Manifesto of Surrealism (Breton), 3513

Metamorphosis, The (Kafka), 3653

Naked Lunch (Burroughs), 3890

Pale Horse, Pale Rider (Porter), 4281

Pincher Martin (Golding), 4489

Steppenwolf (Hesse), 5494

Surfacing (Atwood), 5588

Tempest, The (Shakespeare), 5660

Temptation of Saint Anthony, The (Flaubert), 5668

HANDICAPPED PERSONS. *See* DISABILITIES OR DISABLED PERSONS

HARLEM RENAISSANCE

Jazz (Morrison), 2950

Mumbo Jumbo (Reed), 3834

Quicksand (Larsen), 4775

HATRED

Baal (Brecht), 413

Desire Under the Elms (O'Neill), 1484

Light in August (Faulkner), 3240

Medea (Euripides), 3607

Paradise (Morrison), 4298

Passing (Larsen), 4322

Thousand Splendid Suns, A (Hosseini), 5740

Timon of Athens (Shakespeare), 5786

War Trash (Jin), 6196

HAWAII

Roughing It (Twain), 5031

HEADS OF STATE. *See also* POLITICIANS; POLITICS

Abraham Lincoln (Sandburg), 6

Absalom and Achitophel (Dryden), 12

Anabasis (Perse), 207

Anabasis (Xenophon), 209

Annals (Tacitus), 266

Antigone (Sophocles), 280

Antony and Cleopatra (Shakespeare), 284

August 1914 (Solzhenitsyn), 373

Bérénice (Racine), 540

Boris Godunov (Pushkin), 681

Caesar and Cleopatra (Shaw), 803

Commentaries (Caesar), 1089

Gorboduc (Norton and Sackville), 2340

Henry IV, Part I (Shakespeare), 2528

Henry IV, Part II (Shakespeare), 2531

Henry V (Shakespeare), 2534

Henry VI, Part I (Shakespeare), 2538

Henry VI, Part II (Shakespeare), 2541

Henry VI, Part III (Shakespeare), 2545

History of Herodotus, The (Herotodus), 2597

History of the Decline and Fall of the Roman Empire, The (Gibbon), 2610

History of the Peloponnesian War (Thucydides), 2618

Julius Caesar (Shakespeare), 3008

Knights, The (Aristophanes), 3087

Lalla Rookh (Moore), 3125

Leviathan (Hobbes), 3207

Mahabharata, The (Unknown), 3437

Memoirs of Hadrian (Yourcenar), 3634

On Heroes, Hero-Worship, and the Heroic in History (Carlyle), 4147

Parallel Lives (Plutarch), 4310

HINDUS OR HINDUISM

HISTORIANS

HISTORY

Fair Maid of Perth, The (Scott), 1945

Finnegans Wake (Joyce), 2063

Foundation Trilogy, The (Asimov), 2157

Four Quartets (Eliot), 2166

Heidi Chronicles, The (Wasserstein), 2508

Heimskringla (Snorri Sturluson), 2514

Hereward the Wake (Kingsley), 2557

History of England, The (Macaulay), 2591

History of the English-Speaking Peoples, A (Churchill), 2612

History of the Kings of Britain (Geoffrey of Monmouth), 2615

Israel Potter (Melville), 2913

John Brown's Body (Benét), 2968

Jurgen (Cabell), 3027

Laugh of the Medusa, The (Cixous), 3163

Long Journey, The (Jensen), 3293

Lusiads, The (Camões), 3377

Magnalia Christi Americana (Mather), 3427

Main Currents in American Thought (Parrington), 3450

Mithridates (Racine), 3727

Mölna Elegy, A (Ekelöf), 3749

Mont-Saint-Michel and Chartres (Adams), 3764

Mumbo Jumbo (Reed), 3834

Narrow Road to the Deep North, The (Matsuo Bashō), 3911

Old Mortality (Scott), 4121

Omeros (Walcott), 4142

Orlando (Woolf), 4207

Past and Present (Carlyle), 4333

Penguin Island (France), 4370

Pharsalia (Lucan), 4409

Phenomenology of Spirit, The (Hegel), 4412

Quest for Certainty, The (Dewey), 4767

Reflections on the Revolution in France (Burke), 4848

Room of One's Own, A (Woolf), 5011

Sartor Resartus (Carlyle), 5098

Second Sex, The (Beauvoir), 5179

Significance of the Frontier in American History, The (Turner), 5302

Storyteller (Silko), 5521

Study of History, A (Toynbee), 5559

Tower, The (Yeats), 5851

White Goddess, The (Graves), 6277

HIV/AIDS. *See* ACQUIRED IMMUNODEFICIENCY SYNDROME

HOLIDAYS

Christmas Carol, A (Dickens), 999

Complete Tales of Uncle Remus, The (Harris), 1107

Independence Day (Ford), 2855

Maud Martha (Brooks), 3583

Raintree County (Lockridge), 4792

Winter of Our Discontent, The (Steinbeck), 6338

HOLLYWOOD, CALIFORNIA. *See also* LOS ANGELES

Blonde (Oates), 633

Day of the Locust, The (West), 1354

Last Tycoon, The (Fitzgerald), 3157

Lost World, The (Jarrell), 3337

Myra Breckinridge (Vidal), 3865

HOLOCAUST, JEWISH

Amazing Adventures of Kavalier and Clay, The (Chabon), 165

Ariel (Plath), 313

Badenheim 1939 (Appelfeld), 429

Diary of a Young Girl, The (Frank), 1512

Emigrants, The (Sebald), 1764

Enemies (Singer), 1806

Everything Is Illuminated (Foer), 1910

Fateless (Kertész), 1988

Kaddish for a Child Not Born (Kertész), 3031

Mr. Cogito (Herbert), 3816

Mr. Sammler's Planet (Bellow), 3819

Night (Wiesel), 3979

Schindler's List (Keneally), 5136

Shawl, The (Ozick), 5237

Sophie's Choice (Styron), 5427

Winds of War, The (Wouk), 6329

HOLY GRAIL OR GRAIL QUEST

Morte d'Arthur, Le (Malory), 3779

Once and Future King, The (White), 4168

Parzival (Wolfram von Eschenbach), 4315

Quest of the Holy Grail, The (Unknown), 4772

HOLY ROMAN EMPIRE

History of the English-Speaking Peoples, A (Churchill), 2612

Song of Roland, The (Unknown), 5394

Wallenstein (Schiller), 6168

HOME. *See also* HOUSES, MANSIONS, OR MANORS

Carmina (Catullus), 875

Cold Mountain (Frazier), 1071

Fifth Child, The (Lessing), 2045

Let Us Now Praise Famous Men (Agee), 3198

Maud Martha (Brooks), 3583

Of Time and the River (Wolfe), 4101

Peer Gynt (Ibsen), 4362

Professor's House, The (Cather), 4728

Purple Dust (O'Casey), 4752

Society and Solitude (Emerson), 5377

Swiss Family Robinson, The (Wyss and Wyss), 5596

Tell Me a Riddle (Olsen), 5655

To Urania (Brodsky), 5822

Typical American (Jen), 5983

HUMAN RIGHTS. *See also* CIVIL RIGHTS

HUMANISM

HUNGER. *See also* FAMINES; POVERTY OR POOR PEOPLE; STARVATION

HUNTING OR HUNTERS

HUSBANDS. *See also* ADULTERY; FATHERS; MARRIAGE; WIVES

IMAGINATION

IMMIGRATION OR EMIGRATION

INTERMARRIAGE

INTERRACIAL RELATIONSHIPS

INVENTIONS OR INVENTORS

IOWA

ISLAM. *See also* MUSLIMS

ISLANDS

JOURNALISM

JOY OR SORROW

JUDGES

LESBIANS. See GAYS AND LESBIANS

LETTERS

LIBEL OR SLANDER

LIBERALISM

LIBRARIES OR LIBRARIANS

Wapshot Chronicle, The
(Cheever), 6179
Wilhelm Meister's Travels
(Goethe), 6313
World as Will and Idea, The
(Schopenhauer), 6403
Zorba the Greek (Kazantzakis),
6479

LIFE AND DEATH

Aeneid (Vergil), 60
All Hallows' Eve (Williams), 126
Andersonville (Kantor), 227
As I Lay Dying (Faulkner), 337
Bells in Winter (Miłosz), 521
Chimeras, The (Nerval), 984
Colossus, and Other Poems, The
(Plath), 1084
Coplas on the Death of His Father
(Manrique), 1168
Crow (Hughes), 1263
Cuttlefish Bones (Montale), 1286
Death in the Afternoon
(Hemingway), 1368
Death of Empedocles, The
(Hölderlin), 1386
District and Circle (Heaney), 1542
Elegy Written in a Country
Churchyard (Gray), 1753
Empire of the Sun (Ballard), 1788
Floating Opera, The (Barth), 2095
Frankenstein (Shelley), 2169
Gilead (Robinson), 2260
House of Life, The (Rossetti),
2688
Idylls (Theocritus), 2790
Left Hand of Darkness, The
(Le Guin), 3182
Long and Happy Life, A (Price),
3284
Lost World, The (Jarrell), 3337
Masque of the Red Death, The
(Poe), 3565
Moon Is Down, The (Steinbeck),
3772
Myth of Sisyphus, The (Camus),
3884
'night, Mother (Norman), 3985
Odyssey (Homer), 4077

On Sepulchres (Foscolo), 4152
Out of Africa (Dinesen), 4258
Pale Horse, Pale Rider (Porter),
4281
Pilgrim at Tinker Creek (Dillard),
4469
Rubáiyát of Omar Khayyám
(FitzGerald), 5039
Sappho (Grillparzer), 5095
Stone Diaries, The (Shields),
5506
Tell-Tale Heart, The (Poe), 5657
Year of Wonders (Brooks), 6433

LIFESTYLES

Accidental Tourist, The (Tyler), 19
Chéri (Colette), 949
Democracy (Didion), 1458
Edible Woman, The (Atwood),
1712
Evelina (Burney), 1896
Final Payments (Gordon), 2054
Giant (Ferber), 2245
Golden Notebook, The (Lessing),
2317
Heidi Chronicles, The
(Wasserstein), 2508
Housekeeping (Robinson), 2705
Joy Luck Club, The (Tan), 2999
Love Medicine (Erdrich), 3351
Maud Martha (Brooks), 3583
Notes of a Native Son (Baldwin),
4033
Passing (Larsen), 4322
Prime of Miss Jean Brodie, The
(Spark), 4685
Purple Dust (O'Casey), 4752
Rameau's Nephew (Diderot),
4804
Roots (Haley), 5017
Slouching Towards Bethlehem
(Didion), 5344
So Big (Ferber), 5371
Song of the Lark, The (Cather),
5401
Storyteller (Silko), 5521
Sula (Morrison), 5567
Tom Brown's School Days
(Hughes), 5830

Two Years Before the Mast
(Dana), 5977
Wuthering Heights (Brontë, E.),
6426

LITERARY CRITICISM

American Notebooks, The
(Hawthorne), 183
Art of Poetry, The (Horace), 332
Autocrat of the Breakfast-Table,
The (Holmes), 403
Biographia Literaria (Coleridge),
584
Dunciad, The (Pope), 1670
Flaubert's Parrot (Barnes), 2087
Golden Fruits, The (Sarraute),
2315
Laugh of the Medusa, The
(Cixous), 3163
Of Grammatology (Derrida),
4092
Poetics (Aristotle), 4550
Room of One's Own, A (Woolf),
5011

LITERATURE

American Scholar, The (Emerson),
188
Anatomy of Criticism (Frye), 212
Art of Fiction, The (James), 327
Art of Poetry, The (Horace), 332
Aspern Papers, The (James), 348
August 1914 (Solzhenitsyn), 373
Biographia Literaria (Coleridge),
584
Blindness and Insight (de Man),
625
Book of Songs (Heine), 658
Boswell's London Journal, 1762-
1763 (Boswell), 690
Cakes and Ale (Maugham), 812
Complete Poems of Emily
Dickinson, The (Dickinson),
1101
Critic, The (Sheridan), 1244
Dance to the Music of Time, A
(Powell), 1314
De Profundis (Wilde), 1357
Defence of Poesie (Sidney), 1420

LOGIC

LONDON

School for Scandal, The (Sheridan), 5143

Second Mrs. Tanqueray, The (Pinero), 5176

Secret Agent, The (Conrad), 5185

Shoemaker's Holiday, The (Dekker), 5271

Sign of Four, The (Doyle), 5298

Small House at Allington, The (Trollope), 5349

Songs of Innocence and of Experience (Blake), 5407

Spectator, The (Addison and Steele), 5458

Spy Who Came in from the Cold, The (le Carré), 5485

Strange Case of Dr. Jekyll and Mr. Hyde, The (Stevenson), 5523

Study in Scarlet, A (Doyle), 5556

Sybil (Disraeli), 5599

Tale of Two Cities, A (Dickens), 5611

Threepenny Opera, The (Brecht), 5759

Time Machine, The (Wells), 5776

Unbearable Bassington, The (Saki), 5995

Under Two Flags (Ouida), 6029

Unsuitable Job for a Woman, An (James), 6050

Voyage Out, The (Woolf), 6142

War of the Worlds, The (Wells), 6193

Water Music (Boyle), 6214

Way of the World, The (Congreve), 6227

Way We Live Now, The (Trollope), 6230

What Maisie Knew (James), 6253

White Teeth (Smith), 6282

Wings of the Dove, The (James), 6335

Years, The (Woolf), 6439

LONELINESS. *See also* **ALIENATION; BOREDOM**

Accidental Tourist, The (Tyler), 19

Breakfast at Tiffany's (Capote), 707

Bus Stop (Inge), 789

Chita (Hearn), 987

Chrysanthemums, The (Steinbeck), 1011

Closed Garden, The (Green), 1053

Color of Darkness (Purdy), 1079

Country Girls Trilogy and Epilogue, The (O'Brien), 1200

Country of the Pointed Firs, The (Jewett), 1204

Courtship of Miles Standish, The (Longfellow), 1217

Cousin Pons (Balzac), 1223

Death of the Heart, The (Bowen), 1393

Demon, The (Lermontov), 1466

Emigrants, The (Sebald), 1764

Esther Waters (Moore), 1866

Eugénie Grandet (Balzac), 1878

Frankenstein (Shelley), 2169

Gilead (Robinson), 2260

Golden Apples, The (Welty), 2302

Green Mansions (Hudson), 2396

Harp-Weaver, and Other Poems, The (Millay), 2458

Haunting of Hill House, The (Jackson), 2466

Heart Is a Lonely Hunter, The (McCullers), 2478

Hotel du Lac (Brookner), 2656

House in Paris, The (Bowen), 2676

Jennie Gerhardt (Dreiser), 2955

Jude the Obscure (Hardy), 3005

Labyrinth of Solitude, The (Paz), 3103

Life of Pi (Martel), 3229

Lonely Passion of Judith Hearne, The (Moore), 3278

Look Homeward, Angel (Wolfe), 3306

Lord of the Flies (Golding), 3316

Man of Feeling, The (Mackenzie), 3480

Man Without a Country, The (Hale), 3498

Member of the Wedding, The (McCullers), 3621

Minister's Black Veil, The (Hawthorne), 3696

Miss Lonelyhearts (West), 3715

Narrow Road to the Deep North, The (Matsuo Bashō), 3911

Nausea (Sartre), 3922

Necklace, The (Maupassant), 3925

'night, Mother (Norman), 3985

Of Human Bondage (Maugham), 4094

Old Maid, The (Wharton), 4115

Other Voices, Other Rooms (Capote), 4240

Poetry of du Bellay (du Bellay), 4563

Ponder Heart, The (Welty), 4603

Quartet in Autumn (Pym), 4758

Reflections in a Golden Eye (McCullers), 4845

Rhinoceros (Ionesco), 4908

Robinson Crusoe (Defoe), 4978

Rose for Emily, A (Faulkner), 5023

Silas Marner (Eliot), 5304

Snows of Kilimanjaro, and Other Stories, The (Hemingway), 5369

Society and Solitude (Emerson), 5377

Swiss Family Robinson, The (Wyss and Wyss), 5596

Taste of Honey, A (Delaney), 5652

To Urania (Brodsky), 5822

Top Girls (Churchill), 5840

Tree of Man, The (White), 5891

Turn of the Screw, The (James), 5943

Under Western Eyes (Conrad), 6033

Vagabond, The (Colette), 6074

Villette (Brontë, C.), 6111

Washington Square (James), 6202

Weary Blues, The (Hughes), 6236

Well, The (Jolley), 6243

LOS ANGELES. *See also* **HOLLYWOOD, CALIFORNIA**

Big Sleep, The (Chandler), 572

Faultline (Taylor), 2005

House Made of Dawn (Momaday), 2679

LOYALTY

LYNCHING

MACHISMO. *See* SEXISM

MAD SCIENTISTS

MADRID

MAGIC OR MAGICIANS

Henry VI, Part III (Shakespeare),
2545
Hobbit, The (Tolkien), 2627
Huon of Bordeaux (Unknown),
2753
Idylls of the King (Tennyson),
2793
Jason and the Golden Fleece
(Unknown), 2947
Jerusalem Delivered (Tasso), 2959
Joe Turner's Come and Gone
(Wilson), 2965
Journey to the West, The (Wu
Chengen), 2996
Jurgen (Cabell), 3027
Kalevala (Lönnrot), 3033
Lancelot (Chrétien de Troyes),
3128
Lay of the Last Minstrel, The
(Scott), 3173
Mabinogion, The (Unknown),
3395
Magician of Lublin, The (Singer),
3424
Manfred (Byron), 3507
Memoirs of a Physician (Dumas,
père, and Maquet), 3630
Midnight's Children (Rushdie),
3676
Old Wives' Tale, The (Peele), 4128
Once and Future King, The
(White), 4168
Palm-Wine Drinkard, The
(Tutuola), 4285
Quest of the Holy Grail, The
(Unknown), 4772
Return of the King, The (Tolkien),
4887
Rip Van Winkle (Irving), 4945
Ruslan and Lyudmila (Pushkin),
5050
Savage Mind, The (Lévi-Strauss),
5127
Song of Hiawatha, The
(Longfellow), 5391
Song of Roland, The (Unknown),
5394
Strange Stories from a Chinese
Studio (Pu Songling), 5529

Tempest, The (Shakespeare),
5660
Tragedy of Tragedies, The
(Fielding), 5863
Two Towers, The (Tolkien), 5965
Undine (La Motte-Fouqué), 6041
Vathek (Beckford), 6083
Wild Ass's Skin, The (Balzac),
6297
Witches of Eastwick, The
(Updike), 6350
Women of Trachis, The
(Sophocles), 6386
Yellow Back Radio Broke-Down
(Reed), 6443
Yvain (Chrétien de Troyes), 6462

MAINE
Carrie (King), 877
Empire Falls (Russo), 1785
'Salem's Lot (King), 5077

MANNERS OR CUSTOMS
Adventures of Peregrine Pickle,
The (Smollett), 47
Art of Love (Ovid), 329
Batouala (Maran), 466
Black Boy (Wright), 598
Book of the Courtier, The
(Castiglione), 664
Bride Price, The (Emecheta), 719
Death in the Afternoon
(Hemingway), 1368
Emma (Austen), 1777
Euphues, the Anatomy of Wit
(Lyly), 1885
Evelina (Burney), 1896
Every Man out of His Humour
(Jonson), 1903
Female Quixote, The (Lennox),
2026
Feminine Mystique, The (Friedan),
2029
Guy Mannering (Scott), 2427
Headlong Hall (Peacock), 2475
Hero with a Thousand Faces, The
(Campbell), 2567
History of Henry Esmond,
Esquire, The (Thackeray), 2594

House of Mirth, The (Wharton),
2691
I Know Why the Caged Bird Sings
(Angelou), 2779
Joseph Andrews (Fielding), 2980
Kenilworth (Scott), 3040
Lady Chatterley's Lover
(Lawrence), 3105
Lais of Marie de France, The
(Marie de France), 3120
Little Women (Alcott), 3265
Lottery, The (Jackson), 3340
Main Street (Lewis), 3452
Man of Feeling, The (Mackenzie),
3480
Man of Mode, The (Etherege),
3484
Manon Lescaut (Prévost), 3516
Mansfield Park (Austen), 3522
Middlemarch (Eliot), 3672
Misanthrope, The (Molière), 3704
My Ántonia (Cather), 3849
Pamela (Richardson), 4288
Parade's End (Ford), 4295
Pelle the Conqueror (Nexø), 4364
Penguin Island (France), 4370
Penrod (Tarkington), 4373
Persuasion (Austen), 4395
Picture Bride (Song), 4457
Pride and Prejudice (Austen),
4680
Rabbit Boss (Sanchez), 4787
Rainbow, The (Lawrence), 4789
Rameau's Nephew (Diderot), 4804
Reivers, The (Faulkner), 4851
Roots (Haley), 5017
Second Sex, The (Beauvoir), 5179
Sense and Sensibility (Austen),
5205
Seventeen (Tarkington), 5229
Shoemaker's Holiday, The
(Dekker), 5271
Shōgun (Clavell), 5277
Subjection of Women, The (Mill),
5561
Sula (Morrison), 5567
Two Years Before the Mast
(Dana), 5977
Waiting (Jin), 6145

MARTYRS OR MARTYRDOM

MASS MEDIA. See also COMMUNICATION; JOURNALISM

MASSACHUSETTS

MASSACRES

MATERIALISM, CULTURAL

MEDICINE

MEMORY. *See also* NOSTALGIA

MEN

MENTAL OR EMOTIONAL ILLNESS

MERCHANTS

METAMORPHOSIS OR TRANSMOGRIFICATION

METAPHYSICS

MEXICAN AMERICANS. See also LATINOS AND LATINAS

MIGRANT LABOR

MILITARY LIFE OR SERVICE

MILLS OR MILLWORK

MIND AND BODY

MINES, MINERS, OR MINING

MIXED-RACE PEOPLE. *See* **BIRACIAL OR MIXED-RACE PEOPLE**

MOUNTAINS

MULTICULTURALISM OR DIVERSITY

MURDER OR HOMICIDE. See also ARMS OR WEAPONS

MUSIC OR MUSICIANS. *See also* SINGING OR SINGERS

MUSLIMS. *See also* ISLAM

MUTINY

MYSTERIES

MYSTICISM

MYTHICAL ANIMALS

MYTHOLOGY OR MYTHS

NATIONALISM

NATIVE AMERICANS OR AMERICAN INDIANS

NATURAL HISTORY

NATURALISTS

NATURE

NEW YORK CITY

NORTH CAROLINA

NORTHEAST, U.S.

OCCULTISM OR THE OCCULT

OHIO

OKLAHOMA

OLD AGE OR ELDERLY PEOPLE.
See also AGING

OMENS

OTHER WORLDS

OUTLAWS

PACIFIC NORTHWEST, U.S.

PACIFIC OCEAN. *See also* ADVENTURE; ATLANTIC OCEAN; SEA OR SEAFARING LIFE

PARENTS AND CHILDREN

POISON

POLICE AND POLICE OFFICERS. See also DETECTIVES; PRIVATE INVESTIGATORS

POLITICAL SCIENCE

POLITICIANS. See also GOVERNMENT; PRESIDENTS

POLITICS

POLYGAMY OR BIGAMY

POPES, ROMAN CATHOLIC

POPULAR CULTURE

POVERTY OR POOR PEOPLE.
See also HUNGER; WORK OR WORKERS; WORKING CLASSES

POWER, PERSONAL OR SOCIAL

PRAGMATISM

PRAYER

PREACHING

RENAISSANCE

RESTAURANTS, BARS, TAVERNS, OR PUBS

RETIREMENT. See also AGING; OLD AGE OR ELDERLY PEOPLE

REVENGE

REVOLUTIONARIES

RUSSIAN REVOLUTION

SACRIFICE, HUMAN

SAILING OR SAILORS. *See also* BOATS OR BOATING; SEA OR SEAFARING LIFE

SELF-CONFIDENCE

SELF-DISCOVERY

SEXISM

SHEPHERDS

SHIPWRECKS

SIBLINGS

SICK PERSONS

SIGNS OR SYMBOLS

SIN OR ORIGINAL SIN. *See also* **BLASPHEMY; GREED; GUILT**

SINGING OR SINGERS. *See also* MUSIC OR MUSICIANS; SONGS OR SONGWRITERS

SINGLE PARENTS OR SINGLE-PARENT FAMILIES

SINGLE PEOPLE

SLAVERY OR SLAVES

SLEEP

SMALL-TOWN LIFE. *See also* RURAL OR COUNTRY LIFE

SOLDIERS

SONGS OR SONGWRITERS. *See also* SINGING OR SINGERS

SOUL

SOUTH DAKOTA

SOUTH OR SOUTHERNERS, U.S.

SOUTH PACIFIC

SOUTHWEST, U.S.

SPACE FLIGHT OR TRAVEL

SPANISH CIVIL WAR

SPIRITUAL LIFE OR SPIRITUALITY

SPORTS

STARVATION. See also HUNGER

STEPFAMILIES. See also DIVORCE; FAMILIES OR FAMILY LIFE

STEREOTYPES

STORMS. See also BLIZZARDS

STORYTELLING

STRIKES OR LOCKOUTS

STUDENTS OR STUDENT LIFE.
See also COLLEGES OR UNIVERSITIES

SUFFRAGE OR VOTING RIGHTS

SUICIDE

SUPERNATURAL

SUPERSTITION

SURREALISM

SURVIVAL OR SURVIVALISM

SWINDLING

TRUTHFULNESS AND FALSEHOOD

TUTORING

TWINS OR MULTIPLE-BIRTH SIBLINGS

TYRANTS OR TYRANNY. See also DICTATORS; POLITICIANS; POWER, PERSONAL OR SOCIAL; PRESIDENTS

UNDERGROUND RAILROAD, U.S.

UNIONS OR UNIONISM. See also LABOR UNIONS

UNIVERSE

UPPER CLASSES

UTAH

UTOPIAS

VALUES. *See also* **ETHICS; MORALITY OR MORALS**

VIRGINIA

VIRGINITY

VISIONS, EPIPHANIES, OR REVELATIONS

VOYAGES. See also ADVENTURE; QUEST; SAILING AND SAILORS; SEA OR SEAFARING LIFE

WASHINGTON, D.C.

WATER. See also RIVERS OR WATERWAYS

WEALTH. See also BANKRUPTCY OR FINANCIAL CRISIS; CORRUPTION; ECONOMICS; GREED

WEAPONS. *See* **ARMS OR WEAPONS; ATOMIC BOMB; MURDER OR HOMICIDE; NUCLEAR WARFARE OR WEAPONS**

WEATHER. *See also* **SEASONS**

WEST, U.S.

Myra Breckinridge (Vidal), 3865

Naked Lunch (Burroughs), 3890

Octopus, The (Norris), 4058

Of Mice and Men (Steinbeck), 4098

Pale Horse, Pale Rider (Porter), 4281

Postman Always Rings Twice, The (Cain), 4640

Rabbit Boss (Sanchez), 4787

Roan Stallion (Jeffers), 4963

Rumble Fish (Hinton), 5045

Shining, The (King), 5257

Significance of the Frontier in American History, The (Turner), 5302

Slouching Towards Bethlehem (Didion), 5344

Song of the Lark, The (Cather), 5401

Stand, The (King), 5488

Tamar (Jeffers), 5634

Time of Your Life, The (Saroyan), 5780

Tortilla Flat (Steinbeck), 5848

Two Years Before the Mast (Dana), 5977

Waiting to Exhale (McMillan), 6157

Walk on the Wild Side, A (Algren), 6165

White Album, The (Didion), 6271

Woman Warrior, The (Kingston), 6371

Yellow Back Radio Broke-Down (Reed), 6443

WESTERNS

Big Sky, The (Guthrie), 569

Border Trilogy, The (McCarthy), 677

Fifth Horseman, The (Villarreal), 2048

Green Grow the Lilacs (Riggs), 2385

Little Big Man (Berger), 3252

Ox-Bow Incident, The (Clark), 4270

Prairie, The (Cooper), 4656

Surrounded, The (McNickle), 5591

Virginian, The (Wister), 6124

Yellow Back Radio Broke-Down (Reed), 6443

WHALES OR WHALING

Moby Dick (Melville), 3730

Omoo (Melville), 4144

True History, A (Lucian), 5938

Twenty Thousand Leagues Under the Sea (Verne), 5952

WIDOWS AND WIDOWERS

Annie Allen (Brooks), 269

Barren Ground (Glasgow), 453

Black Swan, The (Mann), 609

Cakes and Ale (Maugham), 812

Delphine (Staël), 1446

Dona Flor and Her Two Husbands (Amado), 1623

Duchess of Malfi, The (Webster), 1659

Eustace Diamonds, The (Trollope), 1888

Heat of the Day, The (Bowen), 2502

House of Gentlefolk, A (Turgenev), 2685

Human Comedy, The (Saroyan), 2731

In the Wilderness (Undset), 2850

Marquise of O——, The (Kleist), 3548

Mighty and Their Fall, The (Compton-Burnett), 3682

Mrs. Ted Bliss (Elkin), 3828

Myra Breckinridge (Vidal), 3865

Pepita Jiménez (Valera), 4380

Piano Lesson, The (Wilson), 4447

Praisesong for the Widow (Marshall), 4662

Princess of Clèves, The (La Fayette), 4703

Quartet in Autumn (Pym), 4758

Ralph Roister Doister (Udall), 4798

Romantic Comedians, The (Glasgow), 4998

Satiromastix (Dekker), 5118

Thomas and Beulah (Dove), 5733

Thousand Cranes (Kawabata), 5737

Torch Song Trilogy (Fierstein), 5845

Tristram Shandy (Sterne), 5913

Where Angels Fear to Tread (Forster), 6263

Wives and Daughters (Gaskell), 6354

Zorba the Greek (Kazantzakis), 6479

WILDERNESS

Deliverance (Dickey), 1444

My Brilliant Career (Franklin), 3852

Pioneers, The (Cooper), 4492

Prairie, The (Cooper), 4656

Roughing It (Twain), 5031

WILDLIFE

Call of the Wild, The (London), 821

Compleat Angler, The (Walton), 1099

Green Hills of Africa (Hemingway), 2391

Pilgrim at Tinker Creek (Dillard), 4469

Where I'm Calling From (Carver), 6266

WILLS

Cousin Pons (Balzac), 1223

Crying of Lot 49, The (Pynchon), 1272

Dead Souls (Gogol), 1359

Eustace Diamonds, The (Trollope), 1888

Felix Holt, the Radical (Eliot), 2019

Floating Opera, The (Barth), 2095

Forsyte Saga, The (Galsworthy), 2140

Great Testament, The (Villon), 2379

Howards End (Forster), 2716

Jennie Gerhardt (Dreiser), 2955

Memento Mori (Spark), 3627

Nicholas Nickleby (Dickens), 3966

Orley Farm (Trollope), 4218

Our Mutual Friend (Dickens), 4252

Philosopher or Dog? (Machado de Assis), 4426

Rob Roy (Scott), 4966

St. Peter's Umbrella (Mikszáth), 5069

School for Husbands, The (Molière), 5140

Thousand Acres, A (Smiley), 5735

Uncle Silas (Le Fanu), 6000

Volpone (Jonson), 6132

Wandering Jew, The (Sue), 6174

WIT OR HUMOR

Ada or Ardor (Nabokov), 25

Adventures of Peregrine Pickle, The (Smollett), 47

Cat's Cradle (Vonnegut), 907

Clayhanger Trilogy, The (Bennett), 1039

Cold Comfort Farm (Gibbons), 1068

Crying of Lot 49, The (Pynchon), 1272

Egoist, The (Meredith), 1729

Foreign Affairs (Lurie), 2135

Giles Goat-Boy (Barth), 2262

Headlong Hall (Peacock), 2475

Heidi Chronicles, The (Wasserstein), 2508

Heroes of Romances, The (Boileau-Despréaux), 2569

Laughter (Bergson), 3165

Life of Samuel Johnson, LL.D., The (Boswell), 3232

Life on the Mississippi (Twain), 3234

Lucky Jim (Amis), 3374

Maxims, The (La Rochefoucauld), 3592

Misanthrope, The (Molière), 3704

My Life and Hard Times (Thurber), 3858

Napoleon of Notting Hill, The (Chesterton), 3902

Northanger Abbey (Austen), 4023

Orlando (Woolf), 4207

Our Ancestors (Calvino), 4246

Pickwick Papers (Dickens), 4453

Poor Richard's Almanack (Franklin), 4608

Riceyman Steps (Bennett), 4915

Sentimental Journey, A (Sterne), 5212

Sirens of Titan, The (Vonnegut), 5319

Tale of a Tub, A (Swift), 5605

Tristram Shandy (Sterne), 5913

Unbearable Bassington, The (Saki), 5995

Under the Greenwood Tree (Hardy), 6017

Vile Bodies (Waugh), 6102

World According to Garp, The (Irving), 6400

Zuleika Dobson (Beerbohm), 6485

WITCHES OR WITCHCRAFT

Almanac of the Dead (Silko), 148

Andersen's Fairy Tales (Andersen), 222

Bless Me, Ultima (Anaya), 617

Chronicles of Narnia, The (Lewis), 1005

Conjure Woman, The (Chesnutt), 1142

Crucible, The (Miller), 1266

Golden Ass, The (Apuleius), 2304

Grimm's Fairy Tales (Grimm and Grimm), 2404

Harry Potter novels (Rowling), 2461

Henry VI, Part I (Shakespeare), 2538

Henry VI, Part II (Shakespeare), 2541

Henry VI, Part III (Shakespeare), 2545

Kalevala (Lönnrot), 3033

Lady's Not for Burning, The (Fry), 3117

Macbeth (Shakespeare), 3402

Magnalia Christi Americana (Mather), 3427

Obscene Bird of Night, The (Donoso), 4055

Once and Future King, The (White), 4168

Paterson (Williams), 4336

Romance of Leonardo da Vinci, The (Merezhkovsky), 4988

Saga of Grettir the Strong, The (Unknown), 5059

Saint Joan (Shaw), 5066

Sunken Bell, The (Hauptmann), 5576

Witches of Eastwick, The (Updike), 6350

Xala (Sembène), 6430

WIVES. See also ADULTERY; HUSBANDS; MARRIAGE; MOTHERS

Adolphe (Constant), 34

Amores (Ovid), 193

Andromache (Euripides), 233

Candida (Shaw), 832

Canterbury Tales, The (Chaucer), 847

Cass Timberlane (Lewis), 880

Cat on a Hot Tin Roof (Williams), 895

Dance of Death, The (Strindberg), 1311

Double-Dealer, The (Congreve), 1631

Dramatis Personae (Browning), 1644

Father, The (Strindberg), 1991

Feminine Mystique, The (Friedan), 2029

Giant (Ferber), 2245

Handmaid's Tale, The (Atwood), 2449

Hours, The (Cunningham), 2664

House of Life, The (Rossetti), 2688

Joe Turner's Come and Gone (Wilson), 2965

Jurgen (Cabell), 3027